D0065067

WITHDRAWN

THE COMPLETE BOOK OF BIBLE QUOTATIONS

THE COMPLETE BOOK OF BIBLE QUOTATIONS

Edited by Mark L. Levine and Eugene Rachlis

PUBLISHED BY POCKET BOOKS NEW YORK

An *Original* publication of POCKET BOOKS

POCKET BOOKS, a division of Simon & Schuster, Inc.,
1230 Avenue of the Americas, New York, N.Y. 10020

ISBN: 0-671-49864-9

First Pocket Books trade paperback printing November, 1986

10 9 8 7 6 5 4 3 2

POCKET and colophon are registered trademarks
of Simon & Schuster, Inc.

Printed in the U.S.A.

INTRODUCTION

Most books of quotations—Bartlett's and H. L. Mencken's come immediately to mind—contain only the most familiar quotations from the Bible, the popular phrases and verses that virtually everyone knows and is fond of. The Bible, however, contains thousands of additional phrases and verses that are just as beautiful and just as significant, yet are not as well known or used as often because they haven't been identified as "quotations."

The Complete Book of Bible Quotations contains not only the Bible's famous lines and phrases, but also those phrases that *should be* famous—by virtue of what is said or the way it is said. It is the definitive source book of quotations from the Bible, truly a "Bartlett's of the Bible."

"Quotability"—how the phrase sounds, in speech and on paper—was an essential element in every selection. We carefully re-read the entire Bible and chose only those verses and phrases that we believed to be of such style, beauty and brevity that individuals would readily repeat them to make a point or illustrate an image in conversation, sermons, speeches, and in writing.

We selected over 6,000 different quotations and classified them into more than 800 categories. There are quotations from every one of the Bible's sixty-six books. Each quotation has been placed into an average of two categories (though some may only be in one and a handful in as many as five). Cross-references to related categories with pertinent quotations are indicated where applicable.

Categorizing the quotations was difficult. We took particular care to make sure that each quotation was properly categorized and in context. We not only used our own judgment but consulted with clergy and Biblical scholars and availed ourselves of numerous translations and Biblical commentaries.

If not limited by space, we could have put each quotation into far more categories than we did. But of necessity, we made choices and selected only those that we considered most appropriate and most likely to be helpful to you; we also included in certain categories quotations about both the topic and its antonym. Please keep in mind that, because of the criteria used in selecting these quotations, the book is not intended to be a compilation of everything the Bible says on each subject.

We have given the chapter and verse citation for every quotation in the book and urge you to refer to the Bible for the full context in which each phrase appears. In the chapter and verse references, we have used *"e.g."* to indicate that the phrase appears several times in the Bible even though we have generally listed only one reference. We have used *"see also"* to indicate a verse similar but not identical to the one quoted where we thought you might want to consult that verse too.

We also compiled an extensive Index which gives the key words in every quotation in the book, together with a few adjacent words to provide the context. This serves both as a supplement to the main categories in the book and to help readers find a quotation when they remember a word or two but not the entire quotation.

In addition, we have provided in an Appendix the full text of six lengthier passages from the Bible that we consider particularly beautiful, meaningful and quotable in their entirety. Many more could, of course, have been included.

The translation used is the King James Version, universally renowned for its poetic and beautiful language. The only changes made from the King James Version were to capitalize second- and third-person pronouns in the New Testament which refer to Jesus, and first-, second- and third-person pronouns in the Old and New Testaments which refer to God.

Mark L. Levine
Eugene Rachlis

ACKNOWLEDGMENTS

No book of this size can be prepared without the assistance of a great many people.

In particular, we wish to thank Diana Bryant, Howard Cutler, Nick Egleson, Diana Finch, Sophie Greenblatt, Sheila Heyman, Sydny Miner, Katherine Romaine, Charles Salzberg, Jan Stone, Anna Van and Stephanie von Hirschberg.

We are also deeply indebted to Professor Douglas Stuart, chairman of the Biblical Studies Department and Professor of Old Testament at Gordon-Conwell Theological Seminary in South Hamilton, Massachusetts, and to Dr. Gregory K. Beale, Professor of New Testament at Gordon-Conwell, for reviewing the categorization of the quotations. Any errors in final placement, however, are not their fault but ours.

Finally, we wish to thank those who have been so supportive and encouraging while we were working on the book: John Bender, George Blumenthal, Chuck Dubroff, Danny Greenberg, Loretta McCarthy, Katherine Rachlis, Don Resnicoff, Paul Rooney, Matt Ropiecki and Rebecca Rozen.

CONTENTS

Blessing
Blindness
Blood
Boasting
Body
Books
Boredom—*See* Pleasure
Born Again
Borrowing
Bravery—*See* Courage
Bread of Life
Bribery
Brotherhood
Brothers—*See* Siblings
Building
Burdens
Burial
Business

Calling—*See* Mission
Candor
Capacity
Capital Punishment
Captivity
Care—*See* Devotion, Comfort
Carnage
Carnality
Caution—*See* Vigilance, Warning,
   Prudence
Celebration
Celibacy
Census
Certainty
Challenges
Chance
Change
Chaos
Character
Charity
Chastisement
Cheating—*See* Honesty, Lies
Child-Rearing
Childbirth—*See* Birth
Childlessness
Children
Choice
Chosen People
Christ—*See* Messiah, Messianic
   Hopes and Prophecies, Jesus
Christ Eternal

Christianity
Christians
Christmas
Church and State
Church Governance—*See*
   Leadership, Clergy
Churches
Circumcision
Clarity
Clergy
Comfort
Commandments
Commitment
Common Sense—*See* Wisdom
Communication
Communion
Companions
Compassion
Competition
Complacency
Complaints
Compromise
Conceit
Conduct—*See* Behavior
Conduct toward God
Confession
Confidence
Conflict of Interest—*See* Loyalty,
   Allegiance
Conformity
Confusion
Conquest
Conscience
Consecration
Consequences
Consistency
Conspiracy—*See* Crime, Betrayal
Contamination
Contemplation
Contempt
Contentment
Continuity
Contrition
Controversy
Conversion
Cooperation
Corruption
Courage
Courtesy
Covenant

Cowardice
Creation
Creativity—*See* Building,
    Achievement, Planning
Credibility
Crime
Criminals
Criticism
Crucifixion
Cruelty
Cultivation
Curses
Cynicism

Damnation
Dance
Danger
Darkness—*See* Light and Darkness,
    Enlightenment
Death
Debt—*See* Borrowing
Decadence
Deception
Decisions
Deeds
Defeat
Defiance—*See* Arrogance, Audacity
Delay—*See* Laziness, Patience,
    Procrastination
Deliverance
Denial
Dependence—*See* Reliance, God's
    Protection
Depravity
Depression
Deprivation
Desecration—*See* Sacrilege, Holiness
Desire
Desolation
Despair
Destiny
Destruction
Determination
Devil—*See* Satan, Evil
Devotion
Diligence
Diplomacy—*See* Tact
Disappointment
Disarmament—*See* Weapons, War
    and Peace

Disbelief—*See* Godlessness,
    Skepticism, Doubt
Discernment
Disciples
Discipline
Discontent—*See* Contentment,
    Satisfaction
Discretion—*See* Prudence, Silence,
    Understanding
Dishonesty
Disobedience
Distance
Diversity
Divinity
Divorce
Doctrine
Doom
Doubt
Dreams
Drunkenness
Duty
Duty, Neglect of

Earth
Education
Effort
Ego—*See* Conceit, Arrogance,
    Humility
Eloquence
Embarrassment—*See* Shame
Emotions—*See* Love, Hatred,
    Happiness, Fear, Sorrow
Empathy
Employees
Employers—*See* Business, Work
Encouragement
End Days
Endings
Endurance—*See* Strength, Fortitude,
    Perseverance, Diligence
Enemies
Enlightenment
Enthusiasm
Environment—*See* Nature
Envy
Ephemera
Equality
Escape
Estrangement
Eternal Life

Eternity
Ethics—*See* Behavior, Honesty, Law
Evangelism
Evidence—*See* Capital Punishment,
  Judging, Perjury, Proof
Evil
Exaltation
Exasperation
Excess
Excuses
Exercise—*See* Physical Fitness
Exile
Exorcism
Expectation
Experience
Exposure

Failure
Fairness
Faith
Faithfulness
Faithlessness
False Gods
False Prophets
Fame
Family
Famine
Farming—*See* Animals, Cultivation,
  Growth
Fashion—*See* Appearance,
  Materialism, Beauty, Change
Fasting
Favoritism
Fear
Fear of God
Fellowship
Fertility
Fidelity—*See* Faithfulness, Loyalty,
  Commitment
Finance—*See* Borrowing
Firstborn
Flattery
Flavor
Floods
Folly
Food
Fools
Foreigners
Forgiveness

Fornication
Fortitude
Frailty
Freedom
Friendship
Frustration
Fulfillment
Futility
Future

Generosity
Gifts
Gloating
Glory
Gluttony
Goals
God
God's Anger
God's Glory
God's Goodness—*See* Goodness
God's Greatness
God's Knowledge
God's Love
God's Mercy
God's People
God's Power
God's Presence
God's Protection
God's Support
God's Temple
God's Uniqueness
God's Will
God's Word
God, Names of
God, Traits of
Godlessness
Godliness
Good and Evil
Goodness
Gospel
Gossip
Government
Grace
Grandchildren
Gratitude
Greatness
Greed
Greetings—*See* Salutations
Grief

Joy—*See* Happiness, Laughter, Tears
Judas
Judging
Judgment
Judgment Day
Justice
Justification

Kindness
Kingdom of God
Kingdom of Heavan
Kings—*See* Monarchy
Knowledge
Knowledge of God

Labor—*See* Work, Business
Lament
Language—*See* Speech, Eloquence,
 Communication
Last Judgment—*See* Judgment Day,
 Apocalypse
Laughter
Law
Lawlessness
Laziness
Leadership
Leniency—*See* Compassion,
 Forgiveness, Punishment
Lies
Life
Life and Death
Light and Darkness
Liquor
Listening—*See* Heedfulness
Loneliness
Longevity—*See* Age, Mortality
Loss
Love
Love of God
Loyalty
Luck—*See* Chance
Lust

Madness
Man and Woman
Management—*See* Leadership,
 Business
Mankind
Manners—*See* Courtesy
Marriage

Martyrdom
Materialism
Maturity
Mediation
Medicine—*See* Healing
Meekness
Memorials—*See* Burial,
 Remembrance
Memory—*See* Remembrance
Menstruation
Mercy
Merit—*See* Worthiness, Success,
 Justice, Reward
Messengers—*See* News, Reliability
Messiah
Messianic Hopes and Prophecies
Ministry
Miracles
Misery—*See* Anguish
Misjudgment
Mission
Missionaries—*See* Evangelism
Mobs
Mockery
Models
Modesty
Monarchy
Money
Monotheism
Morality—*See* Decadence,
 Depravity, Immorality,
 Righteousness
Mortality
Motherhood—*See* Birth,
 Childlessness, Children, Fertility,
 Jesus (Birth of), Parents
Motivation
Mourning
Murder
Music
Mystery
Myth

Nagging
Naivete
Nakedness
Names
Nature
Need
Negotiation

Quantity
Questioning—*See* Authority,
    Doctrine, Skepticism
Quotations

Rain
Rainbow
Rashness
Readiness
Rebellion
Rebirth—*See* Born Again, Jesus
    (Acceptance Of)
Reciprocity
Redemption
Refuge—*See* Safety
Regret
Rehabilitation
Rejection
Reliability
Reliance
Remembrance
Renewal
Repentance
Representatives—*See* Status,
    Spokesmen, Reliability
Reputation
Rescue—*See* Danger, Assistance,
    Deliverance
Respect
Responsibility
Restitution
Restoration
Restraint
Resurrection
Retribution
Revelation
Revenge
Reverence
Reversal
Revolution—*See* Strife, Rebellion
Reward
Riddles
Righteousness
Risk
Rituals
Robbery
Romance

Sabbath
Sacrifice
Sacrifices

Sacrilege
Safety
Salutations
Salvation
Sanctuary
Sarcasm—*See* Mockery
Satan
Satisfaction
Scapegoat
Scheming
Scorn
Scripture
Searching
Seas—*See* Oceans
Seasons
Second Coming
Secrecy
Security
Seduction—*See* Temptation
Self-Awareness
Self-Confidence—*See* Confidence
Self-Control
Self-Deception
Self-Denial
Self-Hatred
Self-Incrimination
Self-Interest
Self-Pity
Self-Righteousness
Self-Sufficiency—*See* Cooperation
Selfishness
Selflessness
Separation
Serenity
Servants—*See* Employees, Freedom,
    Slavery, Work
Service—*See* Ministry, Charity,
    Altruism
Service to God
Severity
Sex—*See* Adultery, Carnality,
    Celibacy, Homosexuality,
    Immorality, Fornication, Incest,
    Lust
Shame
Shamelessness—*See* Audacity
Sharing
Sharpness
Siblings
Sickness—*See* Healing, Miracles

THE BOOKS OF THE BIBLE

The Old Testament

Genesis
Exodus
Leviticus
Numbers
Deuteronomy
Joshua
Judges
Ruth
I Samuel
II Samuel
I Kings
II Kings
I Chronicles
II Chronicles
Ezra
Nehemiah
Esther
Job
Psalms
Proverbs

Ecclesiastes
Song of Solomon
Isaiah
Jeremiah
Lamentations
Ezekiel
Daniel
Hosea
Joel
Amos
Obadiah
Jonah
Micah
Nahum
Habakkuk
Zephaniah
Haggai
Zechariah
Malachi

The New Testament

Matthew
Mark
Luke
John
The Acts
Romans
I Corinthians
II Corinthians
Galatians
Ephesians
Philippians
Colossians
I Thessalonians
II Thessalonians

I Timothy
II Timothy
Titus
Philemon
Hebrews
James
I Peter
II Peter
I John
II John
III John
Jude
Revelation

THE BOOKS OF THE BIBLE

Abbreviations

Acts	The Acts
Amos	Amos
1 Chron.	I Chronicles
2 Chron.	II Chronicles
Col.	Colossians
1 Cor.	I Corinthians
2 Cor.	II Corinthians
Dan.	Daniel
Deut.	Deuteronomy
Eccl.	Ecclesiastes
Eph.	Ephesians
Esther	Esther
Ex.	Exodus
Ezek.	Ezekiel
Ezra	Ezra
Gal.	Galatians
Gen.	Genesis
Hab.	Habakkuk
Hag.	Haggai
Heb.	Hebrews
Hos.	Hosea
Isa.	Isaiah
James	James
Jer.	Jeremiah
Job	Job
Joel	Joel
John	John
1 John	I John
2 John	II John
3 John	III John
Jonah	Jonah
Josh.	Joshua

Jude	Jude
Judg.	Judges
1 Kings	I Kings
2 Kings	II Kings
Lam.	Lamentations
Lev.	Leviticus
Luke	Luke
Mal.	Malachi
Mark	Mark
Matt.	Matthew
Mic.	Micah
Nah.	Nahum
Neh.	Nehemiah
Num.	Numbers
Obad.	Obadiah
1 Pet.	I Peter
2 Pet.	II Peter
Philem.	Philemon
Phil.	Philippians
Prov.	Proverbs
Ps.	Psalms
Rev.	Revelation
Rom.	Romans
Ruth	Ruth
1 Sam.	I Samuel
2 Sam.	II Samuel
Song	Song of Solomon
1 Thess.	I Thessalonians
2 Thess.	II Thessalonians
1 Tim.	I Timothy
2 Tim.	II Timothy
Titus	Titus
Zech.	Zechariah
Zeph.	Zephaniah

A

ABANDONMENT

He will not forsake thee, neither destroy thee, nor forget the covenant of thy fathers which He sware unto them.
Deut. 4:31

How should one chase a thousand, and two put ten thousand to flight, except their Rock had sold them, and the Lord had shut them up?
Deut. 32:30

The Lord will not forsake His people for His great name's sake.
1 Sam. 12:22

And when Saul enquired of the Lord, the Lord answered him not.
1 Sam. 28:6

God is departed from me, and answereth me no more, neither by prophets, nor by dreams.
Saul to Samuel
1 Sam. 28:15

Let Him not leave us, nor forsake us.
1 Kings 8:57

I will forsake the remnant of Mine inheritance, and deliver them into the hand of their enemies.
2 Kings 21:14

Thus saith the Lord, Ye have forsaken Me, and therefore have I also left you.
2 Chron. 12:5

If ye forsake Him, He will forsake you.
2 Chron. 15:2

God will not cast away a perfect man, neither will He help the evil doers.
Job 8:20

Wherefore hidest Thou Thy face, and holdest me for Thine enemy?
Job 13:24

How long wilt Thou forget me, O Lord? for ever? how long wilt Thou hide Thy face from me?
Ps. 13:1

My God, my God, why hast Thou forsaken me?
Ps. 22:1, Matt. 27:46,
Mark 15:34

When my father and my mother forsake me, then the Lord will take me up.
Ps. 27:10

I have been young, and now am old; yet have I not seen the righteous forsaken.
Ps. 37:25

Forsake me not, O Lord: O my God, be not far from me.
Ps. 38:21
See also Ps. 71:12

God my rock, Why hast Thou forgotten me?
Ps. 42:9

Wilt Thou hide Thyself for ever?
Ps. 89:46

Wherefore should the heathen say, Where is now their God?
Ps. 115:2
See also Ps. 79:10

I have done judgment and justice: leave me not to mine oppressors.
Ps. 119:121

If I forget thee, O Jerusalem, let my right hand forget her cunning.
Ps. 137:5

When ye spread forth your hands, I will hide Mine eyes from you.
Isa. 1:15

For a small moment have I forsaken thee; but with great mercies will I gather thee.
Isa. 54:7

I have forsaken Mine house, I have left Mine heritage; I have given the dearly beloved of My soul into the hand of her enemies.
Jer. 12:7

Among all her lovers she hath none to comfort her.
(her: Jerusalem)
Lam. 1:2

Wherefore dost Thou forget us for ever, and forsake us so long time?
Lam. 5:20

I will not leave you comfortless: I will come to you.
> Jesus
> *John 14:18*

I will never leave thee, nor forsake thee.
> (I: God)
> *Heb. 13:5*
> *See also Deut. 31:6, Josh. 1:5*

[*See also* Rejection]

ABILITY

Seest thou a man diligent in his business? he shall stand before kings.
> *Prov. 22:29*

Nothing shall be impossible unto you.
> Jesus
> *Matt. 17:20*

All things are possible to him that believeth.
> Jesus
> *Mark 9:23*

Every one that is perfect shall be as his master.
> Jesus
> *Luke 6:40*

The Son can do nothing of Himself, but what He seeth the Father do.
> Jesus
> *John 5:19*

I can of mine own self do nothing.
> Jesus
> *John 5:30*

There are diversities of gifts, but the same Spirit.
> *1 Cor. 12:4*

Our sufficiency is of God.
> *2 Cor. 3:5*

I can do all things through Christ which strengtheneth me.
> *Phil. 4:13*

Neglect not the gift that is in thee.
> *1 Tim. 4:14*

[*See also* Achievement, Character, Competition]

ABSENCE

The Lord watch between me and thee, when we are absent one from another.
> *Gen. 31:49*

Absent in body, but present in spirit.
> *1 Cor. 5:3*

Though I be absent in the flesh, yet am I with you in the spirit.
> *Col. 2:5*

ABUNDANCE

I will make thy seed as the dust of the earth: so that if a man can number the dust of the earth, then shall thy seed also be numbered.
> God to Abram
> *Gen. 13:16*
> *See also Gen. 28:14*

And ye shall eat the fat of the land.
> *Gen. 45:18*

Who can count the dust of Jacob, and the number of the fourth part of Israel?
> *Num. 23:10*

Their camels were without number, as the sand by the sea side for multitude.
> *Judg. 7:12*
> *See also 1 Sam. 13:5, 2 Sam. 17:11*

My cup runneth over.
> *Ps. 23:5*

They are more than the hairs of mine head.
> (they: iniquities)
> *Ps. 40:12*

[*See also* Excess, Infinity, Quantity]

ACCEPTANCE

But I must die in this land, I must not go over Jordan.
> Moses
> *Deut. 4:22*

Do to me according to that which hath proceeded out of thy mouth.
> *Judg. 11:36*

It is the Lord: let Him do what seemeth Him good.
> *1 Sam. 3:18*
> *See also 2 Sam. 15:26*

Hearken unto their voice, and make them a king.
> God to Samuel
> *1 Sam. 8:22*

Now he is dead, wherefore should I fast? can I bring him back again?
> David, about his son
> *2 Sam. 12:23*

Let him alone, and let him curse; for the Lord hath bidden him.
> *2 Sam. 16:11*

Fear not to be the servants of the Chaldees.
> *2 Kings 25:24*

Naked came I out of my mother's womb, and naked shall I return hither.
> *Job 1:21*

The Lord gave, and the Lord hath taken away; blessed be the name of the Lord.
> *Job 1:21*

Shall we receive good at the hand of God, and shall we not receive evil?
> *Job 2:10*

If I be wicked, woe unto me.
> *Job 10:15*

If I hold my tongue, I shall give up the ghost.
> *Job 13:19*

Acquaint now thyself with Him, and be at peace: thereby good shall come unto thee.
> *Job 22:21*

The hypocrites in heart heap up wrath: they cry not when He bindeth them.
> *Job 36:13*

Let the righteous smite me; it shall be a kindness.
> *Ps. 141:5*

That which is crooked cannot be made straight: and that which is wanting cannot be numbered.
> *Eccl. 1:15*

A time to get, and a time to lose.
> *Eccl. 3:6*

Who can make that straight, which He hath made crooked?
> *Eccl. 7:13*

Serve the king of Babylon, and live.
> *Jer. 27:17*

Whether it be good, or whether it be evil, we will obey the voice of the Lord.
> *Jer. 42:6*

Not what I will, but what Thou wilt.
> Jesus
> *Mark 14:36*
> *See also Matt. 26:39, Luke 22:42*

Father, into Thy hands I commend my spirit.
> Jesus
> *Luke 23:46*

The cup which my Father hath given me, shall I not drink it?
> Jesus
> *John 18:11*

He bearing His cross went forth. (He: Jesus)
> *John 19:17*

What was I, that I could withstand God?
> Peter
> *Acts 11:17*

The will of the Lord be done.
> *Acts 21:14*

If a spirit or an angel hath spoken to him, let us not fight against God.
> Pharisees, about Paul
> *Acts 23:9*

Being reviled, we bless; being persecuted, we suffer it.
> *1 Cor. 4:12*

Do all things without murmurings and disputings.
> *Phil. 2:14*

Despise not thou the chastening of the Lord.
> *Heb. 12:5*

Servants, be subject to your masters with all fear; not only to the good and gentle.
> *1 Pet. 2:18*
> *See also Eph. 6:5*

If, when ye do well, and suffer for it, ye take it patiently, this is acceptable with God.
> *1 Pet. 2:20*

It is better, if the will of God be so, that ye suffer for well doing, than for evil doing.
> *1 Pet. 3:17*

Here is the patience and the faith of the saints.
Rev. 13:10

[*See also* Contentment, Restraint]

ACCOUNTABILITY

See Obligation, Responsibility.

ACCURACY

Every one could sling stones at an hair breadth, and not miss.
Judg. 20:16

Their arrows shall be as of a mighty expert man; none shall return in vain.
Jer. 50:9

ACCUSATIONS

Ye are spies; to see the nakedness of the land ye are come.
Joseph to his brothers
Gen. 42:9

Wherefore have ye rewarded evil for good?
Gen. 44:4

How long wilt thou be drunken? put away thy wine from thee.
Eli to Hannah
1 Sam. 1:14

And Nathan said to David, Thou art the man.
2 Sam. 12:7

My desire is, that the Almighty would answer me, and that mine adversary had written a book.
Job 31:35

The stone shall cry out of the wall, and the beam out of the timber shall answer it.
Hab. 2:11

Doth our law judge any man, before it hear him, and know what he doeth?
Nicodemus
John 7:51

He that is without sin among you, let him first cast a stone.
Jesus
John 8:7

Woman, where are those thine accusers?
Jesus
John 8:10

If I have spoken evil, bear witness of the evil.
Jesus
John 18:23

If He were not a malefactor, we would not have delivered Him up unto thee.
John 18:30

Behold the man!
Pilate
John 19:5

[*See also* Criticism]

ACHIEVEMENT

If thou doest well, shalt thou not be accepted?
God to Cain
Gen. 4:7

The dead which he slew at his death were more than they which he slew in his life.
(he: Samson)
Judg. 16:30

Except the Lord build the house, they labour in vain that build it.
Ps. 127:1

The desire accomplished is sweet to the soul.
Prov. 13:19

Through wisdom is an house builded; and by understanding it is established.
Prov. 24:3

There is nothing better, than that a man should rejoice in his own works.
Eccl. 3:22

A good name is better than precious ointment; and the day of death than the day of one's birth.
Eccl. 7:1

By their fruits ye shall know them.
Jesus
Matt. 7:20
See also Matt. 7:16, Luke 6:44

■ 4 ■

All things are delivered to me of my Father.
Jesus
Luke 10:22
See also Matt. 11:27

Can a devil open the eyes of the blind?
John 10:21

The works that I do in my Father's name, they bear witness of me.
Jesus
John 10:25

For which of those works do ye stone me?
Jesus
John 10:32

Without me ye can do nothing.
Jesus
John 15:5

Do all to the glory of God.
1 Cor. 10:31

I have fought a good fight, I have finished my course, I have kept the faith.
2 Tim. 4:7

He who hath builded the house hath more honour than the house.
Heb. 3:3

Every house is builded by some man; but He that built all things is God.
Heb. 3:4

Look to yourselves, that we lose not those things which we have wrought.
2 John 8

It is done.
Rev. 16:17

[*See also* Deeds, Success, Victory]

ACKNOWLEDGMENT

In all thy ways acknowledge Him.
Prov. 3:6

Hear, ye that are far off, what I have done; and, ye that are near, acknowledge My might.
Isa. 33:13

I will say, It is My people: and they shall say, The Lord is my God.
Zech. 13:9

Elias is come already, and they knew him not.
Jesus
Matt. 17:12

Truly this was the Son of God.
Matt. 27:54
See also Mark 15:39

Whosoever shall confess me before men, him shall the Son of man also confess before the angels of God.
Jesus
Luke 12:8
See also Matt. 10:32

Sir, I perceive that Thou art a prophet.
John 4:19

He that honoureth not the Son honoureth not the Father which hath sent Him.
Jesus
John 5:23

Every tongue should confess that Jesus Christ is Lord.
Phil. 2:11

All shall know Me, from the least to the greatest.
Heb. 8:11
See also Jer. 31:34

[*See also* Jesus (Acceptance of), Knowledge of God]

ACTION

See Deeds.

ADAPTABILITY

Unto the Jews I became as a Jew, that I might gain the Jews.
1 Cor. 9:20

To the weak became I as weak, that I might gain the weak.
1 Cor. 9:22

I am made all things to all men, that I might by all means save some.
1 Cor. 9:22

[*See also* Behavior, Conformity]

Thou shalt not commit adultery.
Seventh Commandment
Ex. 20:14, Matt. 5:27
See also, e.g., Deut. 5:18, Mark 10:19

Thou shalt not covet thy neighbour's wife.
Ex. 20:17

The adulterer and the adulteress shall surely be put to death.
Lev. 20:10

Her belly shall swell, and her thigh shall rot: and the woman shall be a curse among her people.
Num. 5:27

Wherefore hast thou despised the commandment of the Lord, to do evil in His sight?
(thou: David)
2 Sam. 12:9

It is a fire that consumeth to destruction.
Job 31:12

The lips of a strange woman drop as an honeycomb, and her mouth is smoother than oil.
Prov. 5:3

Drink waters out of thine own cistern, and running waters out of thine own well.
Prov. 5:15

Lust not after her beauty in thine heart; neither let her take thee with her eyelids.
Prov. 6:25

Can a man take fire in his bosom, and his clothes not be burned?
Prov. 6:27

Can one go upon hot coals, and his feet not be burned?
Prov. 6:28

Whoso committeth adultery with a woman lacketh understanding: he that doeth it destroyeth his own soul.
Prov. 6:32

His reproach shall not be wiped away.
Prov. 6:33

He goeth after her straightway, as an ox goeth to the slaughter.
Prov. 7:22

Let not thine heart decline to her ways, go not astray in her paths.
Prov. 7:25

She hath cast down many wounded: yea, many strong men have been slain by her.
Prov. 7:26

Her house is the way to hell.
Prov. 7:27

She eateth, and wipeth her mouth, and saith, I have done no wickedness.
(She: adulteress)
Prov. 30:20

I will be a swift witness against the sorcerers, and against the adulterers, and against false swearers, and against those that oppress the hireling in his wages.
Mal. 3:5

Whosoever looketh on a woman to lust after her hath committed adultery with her already in his heart.
Jesus
Matt. 5:28

Whosoever shall put away his wife, saving for the cause of fornication, causeth her to commit adultery.
Jesus
Matt. 5:32
See also Luke 16:18

Whosoever shall marry her that is divorced committeth adultery.
Jesus
Matt. 5:32
See also Matt. 19:9, Luke 16:18

It is not lawful for thee to have thy brother's wife.
John the Baptist to Herod
Mark 6:18

If a woman shall put away her husband, and be married to another, she committeth adultery.
Jesus
Mark 10:12

Thou that sayest a man should not commit adultery, dost thou commit adultery?
Rom. 2:22

Whoremongers and adulterers God will judge.
Heb. 13:4

He that said, Do not commit adultery, said also, Do not kill.
James 2:11

[*See also* Divorce]

ADVERSITY

The more they afflicted them, the more they multiplied and grew.
(them: Hebrews in Egypt)
Ex. 1:12

God hath delivered me to the ungodly, and turned me over into the hands of the wicked.
Job 16:11

Princes have persecuted me without a cause: but my heart standeth in awe of Thy word.
Ps. 119:161

We are perplexed, but not in despair; Persecuted, but not forsaken; cast down, but not destroyed.
2 Cor. 4:8–9

Behold, the devil shall cast some of you into prison, that ye may be tried.
Jesus
Rev. 2:10

[*See also* Prosperity]

ADVICE

Consider of it, take advice, and speak your minds.
Judg. 19:30

Blessed be thy advice, and blessed be thou, which hast kept me this day from coming to shed blood.
1 Sam. 25:33

I hate him; for he doth not prophesy good concerning me, but evil.
1 Kings 22:8

Speak that which is good.
1 Kings 22:13

Tell me nothing but that which is true in the name of the Lord.
1 Kings 22:16

If the prophet had bid thee do some great thing, wouldest thou not have done it?
2 Kings 5:13

But he forsook the counsel which the old men gave him.
2 Chron. 10:8

Your remembrances are like unto ashes.
Job 13:12

Receive my sayings; and the years of thy life shall be many.
(thy: children)
Prov. 4:10

Hear instruction, and be wise, and refuse it not.
Prov. 8:33

Give instruction to a wise man, and he will be yet wiser: teach a just man, and he will increase in learning.
Prov. 9:9

The lips of the righteous feed many.
Prov. 10:21

In the multitude of counsellors there is safety.
Prov. 11:14, Prov. 24:6

The thoughts of the righteous are right: but the counsels of the wicked are deceit.
Prov. 12:5

The way of a fool is right in his own eyes: but he that hearkeneth unto counsel is wise.
Prov. 12:15

A word spoken in due season, how good is it!
Prov. 15:23

Hear counsel, and receive instruction, that thou mayest be wise in thy latter end.
Prov. 19:20

With good advice make war.
Prov. 20:18

Speak not in the ears of a fool: for he will despise the wisdom of thy words.
Prov. 23:9

A flattering mouth worketh ruin.
Prov. 26:28

Better is a poor and a wise child than an old and foolish king, who will no more be admonished.
Eccl. 4:13

The poor man's wisdom is despised, and his words are not heard.
Eccl. 9:16

Thou art wearied in the multitude of thy counsels.
Isa. 47:13

They shall be as stubble; the fire shall burn them.
(They: false advisers)
Isa. 47:14

Hearken not ye to your prophets, nor to your diviners, nor to your dreamers, nor to your enchanters.
Jer. 27:9

Where are now your prophets which prophesied unto you, saying, The king of Babylon shall not come?
Jer. 37:19

If I declare it unto thee, wilt thou not surely put me to death?
Jer. 38:15

Is counsel perished from the prudent? is their wisdom vanished?
Jer. 49:7

He that heareth, and doeth not, is like a man that without a foundation built an house upon the earth.
Jesus
Luke 6:49
See also Matt. 7:26

These things I say, that ye might be saved.
Jesus
John 5:34

Thou therefore which teachest another, teachest thou not thyself?
Rom. 2:21

I have not written unto you because ye know not the truth, but because ye know it.
1 John 2:21

[*See also* Candor, Criticism, Guidance]

AGE

And all the days of Methuselah were nine hundred sixty and nine years.
Gen. 5:27

Thou shalt be buried in a good old age.
Gen. 15:15

Behold now, I am old, I know not the day of my death.
Abraham
Gen. 27:2

Honour the face of the old man.
Lev. 19:32

Thou art old and stricken in years, and there remaineth yet very much land to be possessed.
God to Joshua
Josh. 13:1

Can I hear any more the voice of singing men and singing women?
2 Sam. 19:35

With the ancient is wisdom; and in length of days understanding.
Job 12:12

Art thou the first man that was born? or wast thou made before the hills?
Job 15:7

They that are younger than I have me in derision, whose fathers I would have disdained to have set with the dogs of my flock.
Job 30:1

Great men are not always wise: neither do the aged understand judgment.
Job 32:9

I have been young, and now am old; yet have I not seen the righteous forsaken.
Ps. 37:25

Cast me not off in the time of old age; forsake me not when my strength faileth.
Ps. 71:9

When I am old and greyheaded, O God, forsake me not.
Ps. 71:18

My soul is full of troubles: and my life draweth nigh unto the grave.
Ps. 88:3

The hoary head is a crown of glory, if it be found in the way of righteousness.
Prov. 16:31

Despise not thy mother when she is old.
Prov. 23:22

All things have I seen in the days of my vanity.
Eccl. 7:15

Even to your old age I am He; and even to hoar hairs will I carry you.
Isa. 46:4

Rebuke not an elder, but intreat him as a father.
1 Tim. 5:1

Submit yourselves unto the elder.
1 Pet. 5:5

[*See also* Life, Maturity, Mortality, Youth]

AGGRESSIVENESS

The young lions roar after their prey, and seek their meat from God.
Ps. 104:21

They shall roar like young lions: yea, they shall roar, and lay hold of the prey.
Isa. 5:29

AGREEMENT

Did not I serve with thee for Rachel?
Jacob to Laban
Gen. 29:25

If thou utter this our business, then we will be quit of thine oath.
Josh. 2:20

The Lord be witness between us, if we do not so according to thy words.
Judg. 11:10

They shall see eye to eye.
Isa. 52:8

[*See also* Arguments, Negotiation]

ALCOHOL

See Drunkenness, Liquor.

ALIENATION

See Abandonment, Betrayal.

ALLEGIANCE

Who is on the Lord's side? let him come unto me.
Moses
Ex. 32:26

Him shalt thou serve, and to Him shalt thou cleave, and swear by His name.
Deut. 10:20

As I was with Moses, so I will be with thee.
God to Joshua
Josh. 1:5, Josh. 3:7

Swear unto me by the Lord.
Josh. 2:12

Art thou for us, or for our adversaries?
Josh. 5:13

I am with thee according to thy heart.
Armor-bearer to Jonathan
1 Sam. 14:7

Is this thy kindness to thy friend?
Absalom to Hushai
2 Sam. 16:17

If I do not remember thee, let my tongue cleave to the roof of my mouth.
Ps. 137:6

Unto Me every knee shall bow, every tongue shall swear.
Isa. 45:23
See also Rom. 14:11

Circumcise yourselves to the Lord.
Jer. 4:4

They shall be My people, and I will be their God.
E.g., Jer. 24:7

The Lord is good unto them that wait for Him, to the soul that seeketh Him.
Lam. 3:25

Ye shall be My people, and I will be your God.
E.g., Ezek. 36:28

He that taketh not his cross, and followeth after me, is not worthy of me.
Jesus
Matt. 10:38
See also Luke 14:27

This people honoureth me with their lips, but their heart is far from me.
Jesus
Mark 7:6
See also Matt. 15:8

Whosoever will come after me, let him deny himself, and take up his cross, and follow me.
Jesus
Mark 8:34
See also Matt. 16:24, Luke 9:23

Come, take up the cross, and follow me.
Jesus
Mark 10:21
See also Matt. 19:21, Luke 18:22

My sheep hear my voice, and I know them, and they follow me.
Jesus
John 10:27

Ye cannot drink the cup of the Lord, and the cup of devils.
1 Cor. 10:21

[*See also* Betrayal, Faithfulness, Loyalty]

ALLIES

The Lord shall fight for you, and ye shall hold your peace.
Ex. 14:14

I will be an enemy unto thine enemies, and an adversary unto thine adversaries.
God
Ex. 23:22

Slack not thy hand from thy servants; come up to us quickly, and save us.
Josh. 10:6

I am as thou art, my people as thy people, my horses as thy horses.
1 Kings 22:4, 2 Kings 3:7
See also 2 Chron. 18:3

Shouldest thou help the ungodly, and love them that hate the Lord?
2 Chron. 19:2

The battle is not your's, but God's.
2 Chron. 20:15
See also 1 Sam. 17:47

Our help is in the name of the Lord.
Ps. 124:8

I have trodden the winepress alone; and of the people there was none with me.
Isa. 63:3

He that is not against us is for us.
Jesus
Luke 9:50
See also Matt. 12:30, Mark 9:40

[*See also* Allegiance, Enemies, Loyalty]

ALTERNATIVES

See Choice, Compromise.

ALTRUISM

I was eyes to the blind, and feet was I to the lame.
Job 29:15

The cause which I knew not I searched out.
Job 29:16

He that hath pity upon the poor lendeth unto the Lord; and that which he hath given will He pay him again.
Prov. 19:17

Cast thy bread upon the waters: for thou shalt find it after many days.
Eccl. 11:1

Whosoever will be great among you, let him be your minister.
Jesus
Matt. 20:26
See also Mark 10:43

The Son of man came not to be ministered unto, but to minister, and to give His life a ransom for many.
Jesus
Matt. 20:28, Mark 10:45

If ye lend to them of whom ye hope to receive, what thank have ye? for sinners also lend to sinners, to receive as much again.
Jesus
Luke 6:34

Give, and it shall be given unto you.
Jesus
Luke 6:38

Thou shalt be recompensed at the resurrection of the just.
Jesus
Luke 14:14

He that was healed wist not who it was.
John 5:13

It is more blessed to give than to receive.
Jesus
Acts 20:35

Even Christ pleased not Himself.
Rom. 15:3

Let no man seek his own, but every man another's wealth.
1 Cor. 10:24

By love serve one another.
Gal. 5:13

As we have therefore opportunity, let us do good unto all men.
Gal. 6:10

[*See also* Charity, Generosity, Selfishness, Selflessness]

AMBITION

Now nothing will be restrained from them, which they have imagined to do.
Gen. 11:6

Seek ye the priesthood also?
Moses to Korah the Levite
Num. 16:10

Should I forsake my sweetness, and my good fruit, and go to be promoted over the trees?
Fig tree to other trees
Judg. 9:11

Should I leave my wine, which cheereth God and man, and go to be promoted over the trees?
Vine to trees
Judg. 9:13

What can he have more but the kingdom?
Saul about David
1 Sam. 18:8

The desire of the wicked shall perish.
Ps. 112:10

His breath goeth forth, he returneth to his earth; in that very day his thoughts perish.
Ps. 146:4

The desire accomplished is sweet to the soul.
Prov. 13:19

The foolishness of man perverteth his way.
Prov. 19:3

Labour not to be rich.
Prov. 23:4

Hell and destruction are never full; so the eyes of man are never satisfied.
Prov. 27:20

He that maketh haste to be rich shall not be innocent.
Prov. 28:20

The eye is not satisfied with seeing, nor the ear filled with hearing.
Eccl. 1:8

Better is an handful with quietness, than both the hands full with travail and vexation of spirit.
Eccl. 4:6

All the labour of man is for his mouth, and yet the appetite is not filled.
Eccl. 6:7

Seekest thou great things for thyself? seek them not.
Jer. 45:5

He that seeketh findeth.
Jesus
Matt. 7:8, Luke 11:10

It is enough for the disciple that he be as his master, and the servant as his lord.
Jesus
Matt. 10:25

Whosoever will be great among you, let him be your minister.
Jesus
Matt. 20:26
See also Mark 10:43

If any man desire to be first, the same shall be last of all, and servant of all.
Jesus
Mark 9:35

Whosoever exalteth himself shall be abased; and he that humbleth himself shall be exalted.
Jesus
Luke 14:11
See also Matt. 23:12

Let us not be desirous of vain glory.
Gal. 5:26

Let nothing be done through strife or vainglory.
Phil. 2:3

I have learned, in whatsoever state I am, therewith to be content.
Phil. 4:11

Set your affection on things above, not on things on the earth.
Col. 3:2

If a man desire the office of a bishop, he desireth a good work.
1 Tim. 3:1

They that will be rich fall into temptation and a snare.
1 Tim. 6:9

The fruits that thy soul lusted after are departed from thee.
Rev. 18:14

[*See also* Goals, Leadership, Satisfaction]

ANARCHY

See Chaos, Lawlessness.

ANCESTRY

See Heritage.

ANGELS

They are equal unto the angels; and are the children of God.
Jesus
Luke 20:36

A vision of angels, which said that He was alive.
Luke 24:23

Know ye not that we shall judge angels?
1 Cor. 6:3

Be not forgetful to entertain strangers: for thereby some have entertained angels unawares.
Heb. 13:2

God spared not the angels that sinned, but cast them down to hell.
2 Pet. 2:4

ANGER

They be chafed in their minds, as a bear robbed of her whelps in the field.
2 Sam. 17:8

Wrath killeth the foolish man, and envy slayeth the silly one.
Job 5:2

Cease from anger, and forsake wrath.
Ps. 37:8

The king's favour is toward a wise servant: but his wrath is against him that causeth shame.
Prov. 14:35

A soft answer turneth away wrath.
Prov. 15:1

He that is slow to anger appeaseth strife.
Prov. 15:18

The wrath of a king is as messengers of death.
Prov. 16:14

He that is slow to anger is better than the mighty.
Prov. 16:32

The king's wrath is as the roaring of a lion; but his favour is as dew upon the grass.
Prov. 19:12

A gift in secret pacifieth anger.
Prov. 21:14

Make no friendship with an angry man.
Prov. 22:24

Wrath is cruel, and anger is outrageous; but who is able to stand before envy?
Prov. 27:4

Wise men turn away wrath.
Prov. 29:8

An angry man stirreth up strife.
Prov. 29:22

Anger resteth in the bosom of fools.
Eccl. 7:9

In wrath remember mercy.
Hab. 3:2

Whosoever is angry with his brother without a cause shall be in danger of the judgment.
Jesus
Matt. 5:22

Let not the sun go down upon your wrath.
    Eph. 4:26

Provoke not your children to wrath.
    Eph. 6:4

Let every man be swift to hear, slow to speak, slow to wrath.
    James 1:19

The wrath of man worketh not the righteousness of God.
    James 1:20

[*See also* Arguments, Exasperation, God's Anger, Provocation, Restraint, Temper]

ANGUISH

Hast thou not reserved a blessing for me?
    Esau to Isaac
    Gen. 27:36

Hast thou but one blessing, my father?
    Esau to Isaac
    Gen. 27:38

Are there yet any more sons in my womb, that they may be your husbands?
    Naomi to Ruth and Orpah
    Ruth 1:11

The hand of the Lord is gone out against me.
    Ruth 1:13

Call me Mara: for the Almighty hath dealt very bitterly with me.
    Ruth 1:20

Anguish is come upon me, because my life is yet whole in me.
    2 Sam. 1:9

I rent my garment and my mantle, and plucked off the hair of my head and of my beard.
    Ezra 9:3

How can I endure to see the evil that shall come unto my people?
    Esther 8:6

Wherefore is light given to him that is in misery, and life unto the bitter in soul?
    Job 3:20

My sighing cometh before I eat, and my roarings are poured out like the waters.
    Job 3:24

The arrows of the Almighty are within me, the poison whereof drinketh up my spirit.
    Job 6:4

When I looked for good, then evil came unto me: and when I waited for light, there came darkness.
    Job 30:26

Be not far from me; for trouble is near; for there is none to help.
    Ps. 22:11

The plowers plowed upon my back: they made long their furrows.
    Ps. 129:3

The heart knoweth his own bitterness.
    Prov. 14:10

We roar all like bears, and mourn sore like doves.
    Isa. 59:11

How is the gold become dim!
    Lam. 4:1

Woe is me!
    E.g., Mic. 7:1

There shall be weeping and gnashing of teeth.
    Jesus
    E.g., Matt. 8:12

My soul is exceeding sorrowful, even unto death.
    Jesus
    Matt. 26:38
    See also Mark 14:34

Eli, Eli, lama sabachthani?
    Jesus
    Matt. 27:46
    See also Mark 15:34

My God, my God, why hast Thou forsaken me?
    Jesus
    Matt. 27:46, Mark 15:34
    See also Ps. 22:1

O wretched man that I am! who shall deliver me from the body of this death?
    Rom. 7:24

The merchants of the earth shall weep and mourn over her; for no man buyeth their merchandise any more.
    (her: Babylon)
    Rev. 18:11

[See also Depression, Despair, Grief, Mourning, Sorrow, Suffering, Torment]

ANIMALS

Let them have dominion over the fish of the sea, and over the fowl of the air, and over the cattle, and over all the earth, and over every creeping thing that creepeth.
(them: mankind)
Gen. 1:26

Of every living thing of all flesh, two of every sort shalt thou bring into the ark, to keep them alive with thee.
Gen. 6:19

Every moving thing that liveth shall be meat for you.
Gen. 9:3

Be ye not as the horse, or as the mule, which have no understanding.
Ps. 32:9

Thou takest away their breath, they die, and return to their dust.
(they: animals)
Ps. 104:29

A righteous man regardeth the life of his beast.
Prov. 12:10

The wolf also shall dwell with the lamb, and the leopard shall lie down with the kid; and the calf and the young lion and the fatling together.
Isa. 11:6

[See also Snakes]

ANNIHILATION

I would make the remembrance of them to cease from among men.
Deut. 32:26

Slay both man and woman, infant and suckling, ox and sheep, camel and ass.
Samuel to Saul
1 Sam. 15:3

I beat them as small as the dust of the earth, I did stamp them as the mire of the street.
2 Sam. 22:43

I will bring evil upon thee, and will take away thy posterity.
1 Kings 21:21

Their memorial is perished with them.
Ps. 9:6

They shall have no pity on the fruit of the womb; their eye shall not spare children.
Isa. 13:18

Spare ye not her young men; destroy ye utterly all her host.
Jer. 51:3

They shall not take of thee a stone for a corner, nor a stone for foundations; but thou shalt be desolate for ever, saith the Lord.
Jer. 51:26

He that is far off shall die of the pestilence; and he that is near shall fall by the sword; and he that remaineth and is besieged shall die by the famine.
Ezek. 6:12

Though thou be sought for, yet shalt thou never be found again.
Ezek. 26:21

[See also Carnage, Desolation, Destruction]

ANNUNCIATION

See Jesus (Birth of).

ANTICHRIST

Antichrist shall come.
1 John 2:18

Even now are there many antichrists.
1 John 2:18

He is antichrist, that denieth the Father and the Son.
1 John 2:22

Even now already is it in the world.
1 John 4:3

ANXIETY

See Worry.

APOCALYPSE

At the time appointed the end shall be.
Dan. 8:19
See also Dan. 11:27

Such things must needs be.
Jesus
Mark 13:7

When ye shall hear of wars and commotions, be not terrified: for these things must first come to pass.
Jesus
Luke 21:9
See also Matt. 24:6, Mark 13:7

Nation shall rise against nation, and kingdom against kingdom: And great earthquakes shall be in divers places, and famines, and pestilences; and fearful sights and great signs shall there be from heaven.
Jesus
Luke 21:10–11
See also Matt. 24:6, Mark 13:8

Watch ye therefore, and pray always, that ye may be accounted worthy to escape all these things.
Jesus
Luke 21:36

The end of all things is at hand: be ye therefore sober, and watch unto prayer.
1 Pet. 4:7

I looked, and behold a pale horse: and his name that sat on him was Death, and Hell followed with him.
Rev. 6:8

[*See also* End Days, Judgment Day, Second Coming]

APPEARANCE

The Lord seeth not as man seeth, for man looketh on the outward appearance, but the Lord looketh on the heart.
1 Sam. 16:7

Thou art but a youth, and he a man of war.
Saul to David about Goliath
1 Sam. 17:33

Why take ye thought for raiment?
Jesus
Matt. 6:28

Consider the lilies of the field, how they grow; they toil not, neither do they spin: And yet I say unto you, That even Solomon in all his glory was not arrayed like one of these.
Jesus
Matt. 6:28–29
See also Luke 12:27

Ye are like unto whited sepulchres, which indeed appear beautiful outward.
Jesus
Matt. 23:27

Ye also outwardly appear righteous unto men, but within ye are full of hypocrisy and iniquity.
Jesus
Matt. 23:28

Judge not according to the appearance, but judge righteous judgment.
Jesus
John 7:24

Ye judge after the flesh; I judge no man.
Jesus
John 8:15

He is not a Jew, which is one outwardly.
Rom. 2:28

Neither is that circumcision, which is outward in the flesh.
Rom. 2:28

If a man have long hair, it is a shame unto him.
1 Cor. 11:14

If a woman have long hair, it is a glory to her.
1 Cor. 11:15

Let no man think me a fool; if otherwise, yet as a fool receive me.
2 Cor. 11:16

God accepteth no man's person.
Gal. 2:6

[*See also* Deception, Materialism, Ostentation, Status]

APPRECIATION

And they shall know that I am the Lord their God, that brought them forth out of the land of Egypt.
Ex. 29:46

Thou art good in my sight, as an angel of God.
1 Sam. 29:9

He was in the world, and the world was made by Him, and the world knew Him not.
John 1:10

He came unto His own, and His own received Him not.
John 1:11

[*See also* Contentment, Gratitude, Satisfaction]

APPROVAL

And God saw the light, that it was good.
Gen. 1:4

And God saw every thing that He had made, and, behold, it was very good.
Gen. 1:31

Well done, thou good and faithful servant. (parable of the talents)
Matt. 25:21

I receive not honour from men.
Jesus
John 5:41

If I yet pleased men, I should not be the servant of Christ.
Gal. 1:10

[*See also* God's Support]

ARCHITECTURE

See Building.

ARGUMENTS

Strive not with a man without cause, if he have done thee no harm.
Prov. 3:30

Hatred stirreth up strifes: but love covereth all sins.
Prov. 10:12

It is an honour for a man to cease from strife.
Prov. 20:3

Debate thy cause with thy neighbour himself; and discover not a secret to another.
Prov. 25:9

A soft tongue breaketh the bone.
Prov. 25:15

Wise men turn away wrath.
Prov. 29:8

An angry man stirreth up strife.
Prov. 29:22

Produce your cause, saith the Lord; bring forth your strong reasons.
Isa. 41:21

Agree with thine adversary quickly, whiles thou art in the way with him.
Jesus
Matt. 5:25

Sirs, ye are brethren; why do ye wrong one to another?
Acts 7:26

Strive not about words to no profit.
2 Tim. 2:14

Follow peace with all men, and holiness, without which no man shall see the Lord.
Heb. 12:14

[*See also* Anger, Controversy, Peace, Strife, Temper]

ARMIES

See Peace, War, War and Peace.

ARROGANCE

Who is the Lord, that I should obey His voice to let Israel go?
Pharaoh
Ex. 5:2

How long wilt thou refuse to humble thyself before Me? let My people go.
God to Pharaoh
Ex. 10:3

Let not arrogancy come out of your mouth: for the Lord is a God of knowledge, and by Him actions are weighed.
1 Sam. 2:3

Thine eyes are upon the haughty, that Thou mayest bring them down.
2 Sam. 22:28

Which way went the Spirit of the Lord from me to speak unto thee?
1 Kings 22:24

On whom dost thou trust, that thou rebellest against me?
King of Assyria to King of Judah
2 Kings 18:20, Isa. 36:5

Have the gods of the nations delivered them which my fathers have destroyed?
Sennacherib to Hezekiah
2 Kings 19:12, Isa. 37:12

Thy rage against Me and thy tumult is come up into Mine ears.
2 Kings 19:28
See also Isa. 37:29

Canst thou by searching find out God?
Job 11:7

What knowest thou, that we know not? what understandest thou, which is not in us?
Eliphaz to Job
Job 15:9

Is it any pleasure to the Almighty, that thou art righteous?
Job 22:3

Have the gates of death been opened unto thee? or hast thou seen the doors of the shadow of death?
God to Job
Job 38:17

Hast thou perceived the breadth of the earth? declare if thou knowest it all.
God to Job
Job 38:18

Gavest thou the goodly wings unto the peacocks?
God to Job
Job 39:13

Him that hath an high look and a proud heart will not I suffer.
Ps. 101:5

Let not the proud oppress me.
Ps. 119:122

These six things doth the Lord hate: yea, seven are an abomination unto Him: A proud look, a lying tongue, and hands that shed innocent blood, An heart that deviseth wicked imaginations, feet that be swift in running to mischief, A false witness that speaketh lies, and he that soweth discord among brethren.
Prov. 6:16–19

The bricks are fallen down, but we will build with hewn stones.
Isa. 9:10

I will cause the arrogancy of the proud to cease, and will lay low the haughtiness of the terrible.
Isa. 13:11

We have made a covenant with death, and with hell are we at agreement.
Isa. 28:15

According to all that she hath done, do unto her: for she hath been proud against the Lord, against the Holy One of Israel.
Jer. 50:29

I am against thee, O thou most proud, saith the Lord God of hosts.
Jer. 50:31

The most proud shall stumble and fall, and none shall raise him up.
Jer. 50:32

Thou art a man, and not God.
Ezek. 28:2

Wilt thou yet say before him that slayeth thee, I am God?
Ezek. 28:9

Thou shalt be a man, and no God, in the hand of him that slayeth thee.
Ezek. 28:9

Why tempt ye me?
Jesus
Mark 12:15, Luke 20:23,
Matt. 22:18

Dost thou teach us?
John 9:34

Who art thou that judgest another man's servant?
Rom. 14:4
See also James 4:12

[*See also* Audacity, Boasting, Conceit, Gloating, Humility, Pride]

ASCENSION

He was received up into heaven, and sat on the right hand of God.
Mark 16:19

Whither I go, ye cannot come.
Jesus
John 8:21, John 13:33
See also John 7:34

ASSASSINATION

Cursed be he that taketh reward to slay an innocent person.
Deut. 27:25

I have a message from God unto thee.
Ehud to King of Moab
Judg. 3:20

Turn in, my lord, turn in to me; fear not.
Jael to Sisera
Judg. 4:18

Where he bowed, there he fell down dead.
Judg. 5:27

Who can stretch forth his hand against the Lord's anointed, and be guiltless?
David to his servant
1 Sam. 26:9

[*See also* Murder]

ASSISTANCE

I sent the hornet before you.
Josh. 24:12

They fought from heaven; the stars in their courses fought against Sisera.
Judg. 5:20

Wherefore then dost thou ask of me, seeing the Lord is departed from thee, and is become thine enemy?
Samuel to Saul
1 Sam. 28:16

If the Lord do not help thee, whence shall I help thee?
2 Kings 6:27

Call now, if there be any that will answer thee.
Job 5:1

Unto God would I commit my cause.
Job 5:8

Why standest Thou afar off, O Lord? why hidest Thou Thyself in times of trouble?
Ps. 10:1

Lighten mine eyes, lest I sleep the sleep of death.
Ps. 13:3

Lord, be Thou my helper.
Ps. 30:10

Save me for Thy mercies' sake.
E.g., Ps. 31:16

O Lord: keep not silence: O Lord, be not far from me.
Ps. 35:22

O Lord, make haste to help me.
Ps. 40:13

Call upon Me in the day of trouble: I will deliver thee, and thou shalt glorify Me.
Ps. 50:15

As for me, I will call upon God; and the Lord shall save me.
Ps. 55:16

Vain is the help of man.
Ps. 60:11

Save me, O God; for the waters are come in unto my soul.
Ps. 69:1

Hide not Thy face from Thy servant; for I am in trouble.
Ps. 69:17
See also Ps. 102:2

I am poor and needy: make haste unto me, O God.
Ps. 70:5
See also Ps. 40:17

O God, be not far from me.
Ps. 71:12
See also Ps. 22:11

There is none upon earth that I desire beside Thee.
Ps. 73:25

Keep not Thou silence, O God: hold not Thy peace.
Ps. 83:1

Unless the Lord had been my help, my soul had almost dwelt in silence.
Ps. 94:17

Help me, O Lord my God: O save me according to Thy mercy.
Ps. 109:26

I was brought low, and He helped me.
Ps. 116:6

I will lift up mine eyes unto the hills, from whence cometh my help.
Ps. 121:1

My help cometh from the Lord, which made heaven and earth.
Ps. 121:2

The Lord is nigh unto all them that call upon Him, to all that call upon Him in truth.
Ps. 145:18

Better is a neighbour that is near than a brother far off.
Prov. 27:10

Incline Thine ear, O Lord, and hear; open Thine eyes, O Lord, and see.
Isa. 37:17
See also 2 Kings 19:16

In Me is thine help.
Hos. 13:9

He knoweth them that trust in Him.
Nah. 1:7

They shall call on My name, and I will hear them.
Zech. 13:9

They that be whole need not a physician, but they that are sick.
Jesus
Matt. 9:12
See also Mark 2:17, Luke 5:31

He saved others; Himself He cannot save.
Matt. 27:42, Mark 15:31
See also Luke 23:35

Whosoever shall call on the name of the Lord shall be saved.
E.g., Acts 2:21
See also Joel 2:32

[*See also* Deliverance, God's Protection, Prayer, Safety, Trouble]

ASTROLOGY

Let now the astrologers, the stargazers, the monthly prognosticators, stand up, and save thee from these things.
Isa. 47:13

They shall be as stubble; the fire shall burn them.
(They: false advisers)
Isa. 47:14

Be not dismayed at the signs of heaven; for the heathen are dismayed at them.
Jer. 10:2

ASYLUM

See Sanctuary.

ATHEISM

The fool hath said in his heart, There is no God.
Ps. 14:1, Ps. 53:1

[*See also* Godlessness]

ATTITUDE

Thy heart is not right in the sight of God.
Acts 8:21

We should serve in newness of spirit, and not in the oldness of the letter.
Rom. 7:6

To be carnally minded is death; but to be spiritually minded is life and peace.
Rom. 8:6

There is nothing unclean of itself: but to him that esteemeth any thing to be unclean, to him it is unclean.
Rom. 14:14

God loveth a cheerful giver.
2 Cor. 9:7

Be renewed in the spirit of your mind.
Eph. 4:23

Unto the pure all things are pure.
Titus 1:15

Unto them that are defiled and unbelieving is nothing pure; but even their mind and conscience is defiled.
Titus 1:15

[See also Character, Motivation, Perspective]

AUDACITY

Wherefore do ye tempt the Lord?
Moses
Ex. 17:2

Who is this uncircumcised Philistine, that he should defy the armies of the living God?
David, about Goliath
1 Sam. 17:26

What is the Almighty, that we should serve Him?
Job 21:15

What profit should we have, if we pray unto Him?
Job 21:15

Where wast thou when I laid the foundations of the earth?
God to Job
Job 38:4

I will ascend above the heights of the clouds; I will be like the most High.
Isa. 14:14

Shall the clay say to him that fashioneth it, What makest thou?
Isa. 45:9
See also, e.g., Isa. 29:16, Rom. 9:20

Wherefore will ye plead with Me? ye all have transgressed against Me.
Jer. 2:29

As I live, saith the Lord God, I will not be enquired of by you.
Ezek. 20:3, 31

Be ye come out, as against a thief, with swords and staves?
Jesus
Luke 22:52

O man, who art thou that repliest against God?
Rom. 9:20

[See also Arrogance]

What is the chaff to the wheat? saith the Lord.
Jer. 23:28

If they be prophets, and if the word of the Lord be with them, let them now make intercession to the Lord of hosts.
Jer. 27:18

He whom God hath sent speaketh the words of God.
John 3:34

He that is of God heareth God's words.
Jesus
John 8:47

I am the true vine.
Jesus
John 15:1

The body is of Christ.
Col. 2:17

[See also Deception, False Prophets, Proof]

AUTHORITY

And God made two great lights; the greater light to rule the day, and the lesser light to rule the night.
Gen. 1:16

Let them have dominion over the fish of the sea, and over the fowl of the air, and over the cattle, and over all the earth, and over every creeping thing that creepeth.
(them: mankind)
Gen. 1:26

Be fruitful, and multiply, and replenish the earth, and subdue it.
Gen. 1:28

Thy desire shall be to thy husband, and he shall rule over thee.
God to Eve
Gen. 3:16

Thus saith the Lord.
E.g., 2 Chron. 34:24

A people whom I have not known shall serve me.
Ps. 18:43
See also 2 Sam. 22:44

Where the word of a king is, there is power.
Eccl. 8:4

The ox knoweth his owner, and the ass his master's crib: but Israel doth not know, My people doth not consider.
Isa. 1:3

He shall open, and none shall shut; and he shall shut, and none shall open.
Isa. 22:22

Shall the clay say to him that fashioneth it, What makest thou?
Isa. 45:9
See also, e.g., Isa. 29:16, Rom. 9:20

Who is like Me? and who will appoint Me the time? and who is that shepherd that will stand before Me?
Jer. 49:19, Jer. 50:44

And ye shall know that I am the Lord.
E.g., Ezek. 25:5

For I have spoken it, saith the Lord God.
E.g., Ezek. 28:10

To sit on my right hand, and on my left, is not mine to give, but it shall be given to them for whom it is prepared of my Father.
Jesus
Matt. 20:23
See also Mark 10:40

He that cometh from above is above all.
John 3:31

The Father judgeth no man, but hath committed all judgment unto the Son.
Jesus
John 5:22

I am come in my Father's name, and ye receive me not.
Jesus
John 5:43

I have not spoken of myself; but the Father which sent me.
Jesus
John 12:49
See also John 14:10

My Father is greater than I.
Jesus
John 14:28

I am the vine, ye are the branches.
Jesus
John 15:5

My kingdom is not of this world.
Jesus
John 18:36

Thou couldest have no power at all against me, except it were given thee from above.
Jesus
John 19:11

If I will that he tarry till I come, what is that to thee?
Jesus to Peter, about John
John 21:22

Him shall ye hear in all things whatsoever He shall say unto you.
Acts 3:22
See also Deut. 18:15

By what power, or by what name, have ye done this?
(ye: Peter and John)
Acts 4:7

We ought to obey God rather than men.
Acts 5:29

Jesus I know, and Paul I know; but who are ye?
Acts 19:15

I appeal unto Caesar.
Acts 25:11

What things soever the law saith, it saith to them who are under the law.
Rom. 3:19

Let every soul be subject unto the higher powers.
Rom. 13:1

There is no power but of God.
Rom. 13:1

The powers that be are ordained of God.
Rom. 13:1

Pay ye tribute also: for they are God's ministers.
Rom. 13:6

He that judgeth me is the Lord.
1 Cor. 4:4

Shall I come unto you with a rod, or in love?
1 Cor. 4:21

The head of every man is Christ; and the head of the woman is the man; and the head of Christ is God.
1 Cor. 11:3

He is the head of the body, the church.
(He: Jesus)
Col. 1:18

Ye are complete in Him, which is the head
of all principality and power.
(Him: Jesus)
Col. 2:10

I suffer not a woman to teach, nor to usurp
authority over the man, but to be in silence.
1 Tim. 2:12

For Adam was first formed, then Eve.
1 Tim. 2:13

Without all contradiction the less is blessed
of the better.
Heb. 7:7

[*See also* God's Power, Government,
Leadership, Obedience]

AVARICE

See Greed.

AWE

I have seen God face to face, and my life is
preserved.
Jacob
Gen. 32:30

Who is like unto Thee, O Lord, among the
gods? who is like Thee, glorious in holiness, fearful in praises, doing wonders?
Ex. 15:11

Speak thou with us, and we will hear: but
let not God speak with us, lest we die.
Israelites to Moses
Ex. 20:19

What hath God wrought!
Num. 23:23

Did ever people hear the voice of God
speaking out of the midst of the fire, as
thou hast heard, and live?
Deut. 4:33

We shall surely die, because we have seen
God.
Judg. 13:22

The mountains skipped like rams, and the
little hills like lambs.
Ps. 114:4

Mine eyes have seen the King, the Lord of
hosts.
Isa. 6:5

Fear ye not Me? saith the Lord: will ye not
tremble at My presence?
Jer. 5:22

Let all the inhabitants of the land tremble:
for the day of the Lord cometh, for it is
nigh at hand.
Joel 2:1

Who may abide the day of his coming? and
who shall stand when he appeareth?
Mal. 3:2

Unto you that fear My name shall the Sun
of righteousness arise with healing in his
wings.
Mal. 4:2

What manner of man is this, that even the
winds and the sea obey Him!
Matt. 8:27
See also Mark 4:41, Luke 8:25

A great prophet is risen up among us.
Luke 7:16

Sir, I perceive that Thou art a prophet.
John 4:19

Why marvel ye at this?
Acts 3:12

When He had opened the seventh seal,
there was silence in heaven about the space
of half an hour.
Rev. 8:1

[*See also* Fear of God, Reverence, Won-
ders]

BACKSLIDING

If ye forsake the Lord, and serve strange
gods, then He will turn and do you hurt.
Josh. 24:20

They turned quickly out of the way which their fathers walked in.
Judg. 2:17

And the children of Israel remembered not the Lord their God.
Judg. 8:34

And the children of Israel did evil again in the sight of the Lord.
E.g., Judg. 13:1

His heart was not perfect with the Lord his God.
E.g., 1 Kings 11:4

He forsook the Lord God of his fathers, and walked not in the way of the Lord.
2 Kings 21:22

If thou forsake Him, He will cast thee off for ever.
1 Chron. 28:9

If ye forsake Him, He will forsake you.
2 Chron. 15:2

His power and His wrath is against all them that forsake Him.
Ezra 8:22

They that are far from Thee shall perish.
Ps. 73:27

Correction is grievous unto him that forsaketh the way.
Prov. 15:10

The ox knoweth his owner, and the ass his master's crib: but Israel doth not know, My people doth not consider.
Isa. 1:3

They that forsake the Lord shall be consumed.
Isa. 1:28

Woe to the rebellious children, saith the Lord, that take counsel, but not of Me.
Isa. 30:1

All we like sheep have gone astray.
Isa. 53:6

It is an evil thing and bitter, that thou hast forsaken the Lord thy God.
Jer. 2:19

Can a maid forget her ornaments, or a bride her attire? yet My people have forgotten Me days without number.
Jer. 2:32

Thou hast played the harlot with many lovers; yet return again to Me, saith the Lord.
Jer. 3:1

All that forsake Thee shall be ashamed.
Jer. 17:13

Go not after other gods to serve them.
Jer. 25:6, Jer. 35:15

How long wilt thou go about, O thou backsliding daughter?
Jer. 31:22

They have turned unto Me the back, and not the face.
Jer. 32:33

My people hath been lost sheep: their shepherds have caused them to go astray.
Jer. 50:6

The righteousness of the righteous shall not deliver him in the day of his transgression.
Ezek. 33:12

When the righteous turneth from his righteousness, and committeth iniquity, he shall even die thereby.
Ezek. 33:18

Woe unto them! for they have fled from Me: destruction unto them! because they have transgressed against Me.
Hos. 7:13

Thou hast gone a whoring from thy God.
Hos. 9:1

Having begun in the Spirit, are ye now made perfect by the flesh?
Gal. 3:3

Count him not as an enemy, but admonish him as a brother.
2 Thess. 3:15

If any man draw back, My soul shall have no pleasure in him.
Heb. 10:38

The dog is turned to his own vomit again.
2 Pet. 2:22
See also Prov. 26:11

Remember therefore from whence thou art fallen, and repent.
Jesus
Rev. 2:5

[*See also* Disobedience, Estrangement, Godlessness, Idolatry, Obedience]

BAPTISM

I indeed have baptized you with water: but He shall baptize you with the Holy Ghost.
> John the Baptist
> *Mark 1:8*
> See also *Matt. 3:11, Luke 3:16*

He that believeth and is baptized shall be saved; but he that believeth not shall be damned.
> Jesus
> *Mark 16:16*

Except a man be born of water and of the Spirit, he cannot enter into the kingdom of God.
> Jesus
> *John 3:5*

Repent, and be baptized every one of you in the name of Jesus Christ.
> *Acts 2:38*

Here is water; what doth hinder me to be baptized?
> *Acts 8:36*

Can any man forbid water?
> *Acts 10:47*

The baptism of repentance.
> *Acts 13:24*

Arise, and be baptized, and wash away thy sins.
> *Acts 22:16*

One Lord, one faith, one baptism.
> *Eph. 4:5*

Not by water only, but by water and blood.
> *1 John 5:6*

BARGAINING

See Agreement, Negotiation, Reciprocity.

BATTLE CALLS

Who is on the Lord's side? let him come unto me.
> Moses
> *Ex. 32:26*

Shout; for the Lord hath given you the city.
> Joshua, at Jericho
> *Josh. 6:16*

The Spirit of the Lord came upon Gideon, and he blew a trumpet.
> *Judg. 6:34*

The sword of the Lord, and of Gideon.
> *Judg. 7:18, 20*

Remember the Lord, which is great and terrible, and fight for your brethren, your sons, and your daughters.
> *Neh. 4:14*

Set ye up a standard in the land, blow the trumpet among the nations, prepare the nations against her.
> *Jer. 51:27*

If the trumpet give an uncertain sound, who shall prepare himself to the battle?
> *1 Cor. 14:8*

BATTLES

See War.

BEATITUDES

See the Appendix at p. 422.

BEAUTY

The sons of God saw the daughters of men that they were fair.
> *Gen. 6:2*

How goodly are thy tents, O Jacob, and thy tabernacles, O Israel!
> *Num. 24:5*

As thou art, so were they; each one resembled the children of a king.
> *Judg. 8:18*

From the sole of his foot even to the crown of his head there was no blemish in him.
> (him: Absalom)
> *2 Sam. 14:25*

As a jewel of gold in a swine's snout, so is a fair woman which is without discretion.
> *Prov. 11:22*

Favour is deceitful, and beauty is vain: but

a woman that feareth the Lord, she shall be praised.
> *Prov. 31:30*

I am black, but comely, O ye daughters of Jerusalem.
> *Song 1:5*

I am the rose of Sharon, and the lily of the valleys.
> *Song 2:1*

As the lily among thorns, so is my love among the daughters.
> *Song 2:2*

Thy two breasts are like two young roes that are twins, which feed among the lilies.
> *Song 4:5*
> *See also Song 7:3*

Fair as the moon, clear as the sun.
> *Song 6:10*

The joints of thy thighs are like jewels, the work of the hands of a cunning workman.
> *Song 7:1*

Thy navel is like a round goblet, which wanteth not liquor.
> *Song 7:2*

Though thou deckest thee with ornaments of gold, though thou rentest thy face with painting, in vain shalt thou make thyself fair.
> *Jer. 4:30*

But thou didst trust in thine own beauty.
> *Ezek. 16:15*

Consider the lilies of the field, how they grow; they toil not, neither do they spin: And yet I say unto you, That even Solomon in all his glory was not arrayed like one of these.
> Jesus
> *Matt. 6:28–29*
> *See also Luke 12:27*

[*See also* Appearance, Body]

BEGINNINGS

In the beginning God created the heaven and the earth.
> *Gen. 1:1*

When I begin, I will also make an end.
> God to Samuel
> *1 Sam. 3:12*

The wicked are estranged from the womb: they go astray as soon as they be born, speaking lies.
> *Ps. 58:3*

A time to be born, and a time to die; a time to plant, and a time to pluck up that which is planted.
> *Eccl. 3:2*

A time to break down, and a time to build up.
> *Eccl. 3:3*

New wine must be put into new bottles.
> Jesus
> *Mark 2:22, Luke 5:38*
> *See also Matt. 9:17*

In the beginning was the Word, and the Word was with God, and the Word was God.
> *John 1:1*

He is before all things, and by Him all things consist.
> (Him: Jesus)
> *Col. 1:17*

Behold, how great a matter a little fire kindleth!
> *James 3:5*

I am Alpha and Omega, the beginning and the end, the first and the last.
> Jesus
> *Rev. 22:13*
> *See also Rev. 1:8, 11, Rev. 21:6*

[*See also* Creation, Endings]

BEHAVIOR

Ye shall not steal, neither deal falsely, neither lie one to another.
> *Lev. 19:11*

Be ye holy.
> *Lev. 20:7*

Take heed to thyself, and keep thy soul diligently, lest thou forget the things which thine eyes have seen.
> *Deut. 4:9*

Ye shall walk in all the ways which the

Lord your God hath commanded you, that ye may live, and that it may be well with you.
Deut. 5:33

Ye shall not tempt the Lord your God.
Deut. 6:16

Do that which is right and good in the sight of the Lord.
Deut. 6:18

Walk in all His ways.
E.g., Deut. 10:12

I have set before thee this day life and good, and death and evil.
Deut. 30:15

Take good heed therefore unto yourselves, that ye love the Lord your God.
Josh. 23:11
See also Deut. 4:15

Turn ye from your evil ways, and keep My commandments and My statutes.
2 Kings 17:13

Stand up and bless the Lord your God for ever and ever.
Neh. 9:5

Shall mortal man be more just than God? shall a man be more pure than his maker?
Job 4:17

If iniquity be in thine hand, put it far away.
Job 11:14

Trust in the Lord, and do good.
Ps. 37:3

The steps of a good man are ordered by the Lord: and He delighteth in his way.
Ps. 37:23

Teach me Thy way, O Lord; I will walk in Thy truth.
Ps. 86:11

Fear the Lord, and depart from evil.
Prov. 3:7
See also Ps. 34:14, Ps. 37:27

Enter not into the path of the wicked, and go not in the way of evil men.
Prov. 4:14

These six things doth the Lord hate: yea, seven are an abomination unto Him: A proud look, a lying tongue, and hands that shed innocent blood, An heart that deviseth wicked imaginations, feet that be swift in running to mischief, A false witness that speaketh lies, and he that soweth discord among brethren.
Prov. 6:16–19

When a man's ways please the Lord, he maketh even his enemies to be at peace with him.
Prov. 16:7

A man's heart deviseth his way: but the Lord directeth his steps.
Prov. 16:9

Be not over much wicked, neither be thou foolish: why shouldest thou die before thy time?
Eccl. 7:17

Learn to do well.
Isa. 1:17

He will teach us of His ways, and we will walk in His paths.
Isa. 2:3, Mic. 4:2

Come ye, and let us walk in the light of the Lord.
Isa. 2:5

This is the way, walk ye in it.
Isa. 30:21

My thoughts are not your thoughts, neither are your ways My ways, saith the Lord.
Isa. 55:8

Keep ye judgment, and do justice.
Isa. 56:1

Learn not the way of the heathen.
Jer. 10:2

Break off thy sins by righteousness, and thine iniquities by showing mercy to the poor.
Dan. 4:27

Sow to yourselves in righteousness, reap in mercy.
Hos. 10:12

The ways of the Lord are right, and the just shall walk in them: but the transgressors shall fall therein.
Hos. 14:9

Hate the evil, and love the good, and establish judgment in the gate.
Amos 5:15

What doth the Lord require of thee, but to

do justly, and to love mercy, and to walk humbly with thy God?
Mic. 6:8

Consider your ways.
Hag. 1:5, 7

Execute true judgment, and show mercy and compassions every man to his brother.
Zech. 7:9

Bless them that curse you, do good to them that hate you.
Jesus
Matt. 5:44

All things whatsoever ye would that men should do to you, do ye even so to them.
Jesus
Matt. 7:12

Strait is the gate, and narrow is the way, which leadeth unto life, and few there be that find it.
Jesus
Matt. 7:14

As ye would that men should do to you, do ye also to them likewise.
Jesus
Luke 6:31

If ye do good to them which do good to you, what thank have ye? for sinners also do even the same.
Jesus
Luke 6:33
See also Matt. 5:46

Do as I have done to you.
Jesus
John 13:15

Love one another.
Jesus
E.g., John 13:34

Abhor that which is evil; cleave to that which is good.
Rom. 12:9

All things are lawful unto me, but all things are not expedient.
1 Cor. 6:12
See also 1 Cor. 10:23

They which preach the gospel should live of the gospel.
1 Cor. 9:14

Be ye followers of me, even as I also am of Christ.
1 Cor. 11:1

Let all things be done decently and in order.
1 Cor. 14:40

Awake to righteousness, and sin not.
1 Cor. 15:34

We walk by faith, not by sight.
2 Cor. 5:7

Walk in the Spirit, and ye shall not fulfil the lust of the flesh.
Gal. 5:16

If we live in the Spirit, let us also walk in the Spirit.
Gal. 5:25

Be ye kind one to another.
Eph. 4:32

Be ye therefore followers of God, as dear children.
Eph. 5:1

Walk in love, as Christ also hath loved us.
Eph. 5:2

Walk as children of light.
Eph. 5:8

Walk circumspectly, not as fools, but as wise.
Eph. 5:15

Walk worthy of the Lord.
Col. 1:10
See also 1 Thess. 2:12

As ye have therefore received Christ Jesus the Lord, so walk ye in Him.
Col. 2:6

Put off all these; anger, wrath, malice, blasphemy, filthy communication out of your mouth.
Col. 3:8

Study to be quiet, and to do your own business.
1 Thess. 4:11

Let us, who are of the day, be sober, putting on the breastplate of faith and love; and for an helmet, the hope of salvation.
1 Thess. 5:8

Abstain from all appearance of evil.
1 Thess. 5:22

Do good.
1 Tim. 6:18

Flee also youthful lusts: but follow righteousness, faith, charity, peace.
2 Tim. 2:22

Be sober, grave, temperate, sound in faith, in charity, in patience.
Titus 2:2

Be in behaviour as becometh holiness.
Titus 2:3

Make straight paths for your feet, lest that which is lame be turned out of the way.
Heb. 12:13

Love as brethren, be pitiful, be courteous.
1 Pet. 3:8

If we walk in the light, as He is in the light, we have fellowship one with another.
1 John 1:7

Keep yourselves in the love of God, looking for the mercy of our Lord Jesus Christ.
Jude 21

[*See also* Attitude, Conduct toward God, Conformity, Deeds, Good and Evil, Love, Sin, and the Appendix at p. 419.]

BELIEF

Thou shalt find Him, if thou seek Him with all thy heart and with all thy soul.
Deut. 4:29

If ye will hear His voice, Harden not your heart.
Ps. 95:7–8
See also, e.g., Heb. 3:15

If ye will not believe, surely ye shall not be established.
Isa. 7:9

He that believeth shall not make haste.
Isa. 28:16

Come, and let us join ourselves to the Lord.
Jer. 50:5

Believe ye that I am able to do this?
Jesus
Matt. 9:28

Whosoever therefore shall confess me before men, him will I confess also before my Father which is in heaven. But whosoever shall deny me before men, him will I also deny before my Father which is in heaven.
Jesus
Matt. 10:32–33

Because they had no root, they withered away.
Jesus
Matt. 13:6
See also Mark 4:6

With God all things are possible.
Jesus
Matt. 19:26, Mark 10:27
See also Luke 18:27

Whatsoever ye shall ask in prayer, believing, ye shall receive.
Jesus
Matt. 21:22
See also Mark 11:24

He that believeth and is baptized shall be saved; but he that believeth not shall be damned.
Jesus
Mark 16:16

As many as received Him, to them gave He power to become the sons of God.
John 1:12

Ye receive not our witness.
Jesus
John 3:11

If I have told you earthly things, and ye believe not, how shall ye believe, if I tell you of heavenly things?
Jesus
John 3:12

He that believeth not is condemned already, because he hath not believed in the name of the only begotten Son of God.
Jesus
John 3:18

He that believeth not the Son shall not see life; but the wrath of God abideth on him.
John 3:36

Know that this is indeed the Christ, the Saviour of the world.
John 4:42

Except ye see signs and wonders, ye will not believe.
Jesus
John 4:48

He that heareth my word, and believeth on Him that sent me, hath everlasting life.
> Jesus
> *John 5:24*

Had ye believed Moses, ye would have believed me: for he wrote of me.
> Jesus
> *John 5:46*

No man can come to me, except the Father which hath sent me draw him.
> Jesus
> *John 6:44*
> *See also John 6:65*

He that followeth me shall not walk in darkness.
> Jesus
> *John 8:12*

Lord, I believe.
> *John 9:38*

Though ye believe not me, believe the works.
> Jesus
> *John 10:38*

He that believeth in me, though he were dead, yet shall he live.
> Jesus
> *John 11:25*

Whosoever liveth and believeth in me shall never die.
> Jesus
> *John 11:26*

He that believeth on me, believeth not on me, but on Him that sent me.
> Jesus
> *John 12:44*

Ye believe in God, believe also in me.
> Jesus
> *John 14:1*

Blessed are they that have not seen, and yet have believed.
> Jesus
> *John 20:29*

I believe that Jesus Christ is the Son of God.
> *Acts 8:37*

By Him all that believe are justified.
> *Acts 13:39*

Believe on the Lord Jesus Christ, and thou shalt be saved.
> *Acts 16:31*

Whosoever believeth on Him shall not be ashamed.
> *Rom. 9:33, Rom. 10:11*

With the heart man believeth unto righteousness.
> *Rom. 10:10*

How shall they believe in Him of whom they have not heard?
> *Rom. 10:14*

The woman which hath an husband that believeth not, and if he be pleased to dwell with her, let her not leave him.
> *1 Cor. 7:13*

The unbelieving husband is sanctified by the wife, and the unbelieving wife is sanctified by the husband.
> *1 Cor. 7:14*

If we believe not, yet He abideth faithful: He cannot deny Himself.
> *2 Tim. 2:13*

He that cometh to God must believe that He is, and that He is a rewarder of them that diligently seek Him.
> *Heb. 11:6*

Believe not every spirit.
> *1 John 4:1*

He that believeth not God hath made Him a liar.
> (Him: Jesus)
> *1 John 5:10*

[*See also* Doubt, Faith, Jesus, Jesus (Acceptance of), Prayer, Sincerity, Skepticism]

BELIEVERS

They that trust in the Lord shall be as mount Zion, which cannot be removed.
> *Ps. 125:1*

They that wait upon the Lord shall renew their strength; they shall mount up with wings as eagles; they shall run, and not be weary.
> *Isa. 40:31*

Ye are the temple of God.
1 Cor. 3:16

The temple of God is holy, which temple ye are.
1 Cor. 3:17

Ye are Christ's; and Christ is God's.
1 Cor. 3:23

The saints shall judge the world.
1 Cor. 6:2

He that is called in the Lord, being a servant, is the Lord's freeman.
1 Cor. 7:22

Are not ye my work in the Lord?
1 Cor. 9:1

Ye are all one in Christ Jesus.
Gal. 3:28

We are the circumcision, which worship God in the spirit, and rejoice in Christ Jesus.
Phil. 3:3

Let us, who are of the day, be sober, putting on the breastplate of faith and love; and for an helmet, the hope of salvation.
1 Thess. 5:8

The Lord knoweth them that are His.
2 Tim. 2:19

[*See also* Chosen People, Christians, God's People]

BENEVOLENCE

See Altruism, Charity, Deeds.

BESTIALITY

See Sodomy.

BETRAYAL

Entice thy husband, that he may declare unto us the riddle.
(he: Samson)
Judg. 14:15
See also Judg. 16:5

If ye had not plowed with my heifer, ye had not found out my riddle.
Samson to Philistines
Judg. 14:18

Tell me, I pray thee, wherein thy great strength lieth.
Delilah
Judg. 16:6

The Philistines be upon thee, Samson.
Delilah
E.g., Judg. 16:20

Set ye Uriah in the forefront of the hottest battle.
David, about Bathsheba's husband
2 Sam. 11:15

He that speaketh flattery to his friends, even the eyes of his children shall fail.
Job 17:5

They whom I loved are turned against me.
Job 19:19

Thy tongue deviseth mischiefs; like a sharp razor, working deceitfully.
Ps. 52:2

It was not an enemy that reproached me; then I could have borne it.
Ps. 55:12

Devise not evil against thy neighbour.
Prov. 3:29

Discover not a secret to another.
Prov. 25:9

Confidence in an unfaithful man in time of trouble is like a broken tooth, and a foot out of joint.
Prov. 25:19

Mine heritage is unto Me as a lion in the forest; it crieth out against Me: therefore have I hated it.
Jer. 12:8

Her friends have dealt treacherously with her, they are become her enemies.
Lam. 1:2

To subvert a man in his cause, the Lord approveth not.
Lam. 3:36

Keep the doors of thy mouth from her that lieth in thy bosom.
Mic. 7:5

Why do we deal treacherously every man against his brother?
Mal. 2:10

Judas Iscariot.
E.g., Matt. 26:14

Thirty pieces of silver.
Matt. 26:15

Woe unto that man by whom the Son of man is betrayed! it had been good for that man if he had not been born.
Jesus
Matt. 26:24
See also Mark 14:21, Luke 22:22

Behold, the hour is at hand, and the Son of man is betrayed into the hands of sinners.
Jesus
Matt. 26:45
See also Mark 14:41

Whomsoever I shall kiss, that same is He: hold Him fast.
Matt. 26:48
See also Mark 14:44

One of you which eateth with me shall betray me.
Jesus
Mark 14:18
See also Matt. 26:21

He that betrayeth me is at hand.
Jesus
Mark 14:42
See also Matt. 26:46

The hand of him that betrayeth me is with me on the table.
Jesus
Luke 22:21
See also Matt. 26:21

Betrayest thou the Son of man with a kiss?
Jesus
Luke 22:48

Have not I chosen you twelve, and one of you is a devil?
Jesus
John 6:70

Ye are not all clean.
Jesus
John 13:11

He that eateth bread with me hath lifted up his heel against me.
Jesus
John 13:18

Verily, verily, I say unto you, that one of you shall betray me.
Jesus
John 13:21
See also Matt. 26:21

That thou doest, do quickly.
Jesus
John 13:27

Of your own selves shall men arise, speaking perverse things.
Acts 20:30

[*See also* Allegiance, Deception, Loyalty, Treachery]

BIRTH

In sorrow thou shalt bring forth children.
God to Eve
Gen. 3:16

For this child I prayed; and the Lord hath given me my petition.
Hannah
1 Sam 1:27

In sin did my mother conceive me.
Ps. 51:5

A time to be born, and a time to die.
Eccl. 3:2

Before I formed thee in the belly I knew thee.
Jer. 1:5

Before thou camest forth out of the womb I sanctified thee.
God to Jeremiah
Jer. 1:5

The anguish as of her that bringeth forth her first child.
Jer. 4:31

Cursed be the day wherein I was born: let not the day wherein my mother bare me be blessed.
Jer. 20:14

That which is born of the flesh is flesh; and that which is born of the Spirit is spirit.
Jesus
John 3:6

As soon as she is delivered of the child, she remembereth no more the anguish.
Jesus
John 16:21

[*See also* Fertility, Jesus (Birth of)]

BITTERNESS

Their grapes are grapes of gall, their clusters are bitter.
Deut. 32:32

Call me Mara: for the Almighty hath dealt very bitterly with me.
Ruth 1:20

Knowest thou not that it will be bitterness in the latter end?
2 Sam. 2:26

The heart knoweth his own bitterness.
Prov. 14:10

He hath filled me with bitterness, He hath made me drunken with wormwood.
Lam. 3:15

It shall make thy belly bitter, but it shall be in thy mouth sweet as honey.
Rev. 10:9

[*See also* Anguish]

BLAME

The woman whom Thou gavest to be with me, she gave me of the tree, and I did eat.
Adam
Gen. 3:12

The serpent beguiled me, and I did eat.
Eve
Gen. 3:13

Upon me be thy curse, my son: only obey my voice.
Rebekah to Jacob
Gen. 27:13

His blood shall be upon him.
Lev. 20:9

Let not mine hand be upon him, but let the hand of the Philistines be upon him.
Saul about David
1 Sam. 18:17

Art thou he that troubleth Israel?
Ahab to Elijah
1 Kings 18:17

If thou wert pure and upright; surely now He would awake for thee.
Job 8:6

He hath borne our griefs, and carried our sorrows: yet we did esteem him stricken, smitten of God, and afflicted.
Isa. 53:4

Hast thou not procured this unto thyself, in that thou hast forsaken the Lord thy God?
God to Jews
Jer. 2:17

The fathers have eaten sour grapes, and the children's teeth are set on edge.
Ezek. 18:2
See also Jer. 31:29

What shall we do unto thee, that the sea may be calm unto us?
Sailors to Jonah
Jonah 1:11

Lay not upon us innocent blood: for thou, O Lord, hast done as it pleased Thee.
Sailors to God
Jonah 1:14

Mine anger was kindled against the shepherds, and I punished the goats.
Zech. 10:3

If thy right hand offend thee, cut it off, and cast it from thee.
Jesus
Matt. 5:30
See also Matt. 18:8, Mark 9:43

Judge not, that ye be not judged.
Jesus
Matt. 7:1
See also Luke 6:37

Why beholdest thou the mote that is in thy brother's eye, but considerest not the beam that is in thine own eye?
Jesus
Matt. 7:3
See also Luke 6:41

Ye shall be hated of all men for my name's sake: but he that endureth to the end shall be saved.
Jesus
Matt. 10:22
See also Mark 13:13, Luke 21:17

If thine eye offend thee, pluck it out, and cast it from thee.
Jesus
Matt. 18:9
See also Matt. 5:29, Mark 9:47

I am innocent of the blood of this just
person.
> Pilate
> *Matt. 27:24*

He that is without sin among you, let him
first cast a stone.
> Jesus
> *John 8:7*

If I do that I would not, it is no more I that
do it, but sin that dwelleth in me.
> *Rom. 7:20*
> *See also Rom. 7:17*

[*See also* Guilt, Responsibility, Scapegoat]

BLASPHEMY

Who is the Lord, that I should obey His
voice to let Israel go?
> Pharaoh
> *Ex. 5:2*

Thou shalt not take the name of the Lord
thy God in vain.
> Third Commandment
> *Ex. 20:7, Deut. 5:11*

Whosoever curseth his God shall bear his
sin.
> *Lev. 24:15*

The Lord will not hold him guiltless that
taketh His name in vain.
> *Deut. 5:11, Ex. 20:7*

Let not thy God in whom thou trustest
deceive thee.
> *2 Kings 19:10, Isa. 37:10*

What is the Almighty, that we should serve
Him?
> *Job 21:15*

It profiteth a man nothing that he should
delight himself with God.
> *Job 34:9*

How long shall the adversary reproach?
shall the enemy blaspheme Thy name for
ever?
> *Ps. 74:10*

Whoso mocketh the poor reproacheth his
Maker.
> *Prov. 17:5*

Jerusalem is ruined, and Judah is fallen:
because their tongue and their doings are
against the Lord.
> *Isa. 3:8*

I will ascend above the heights of the
clouds; I will be like the most High.
> *Isa. 14:14*

My name continually every day is blasphemed.
> *Isa. 52:5*
> *See also Rom. 2:24*

Pollute ye My holy name no more with
your gifts, and with your idols.
> *Ezek. 20:39*

And who is that God that shall deliver you
out of my hands?
> Nebuchadnezzar
> *Dan. 3:15*

It is vain to serve God: and what profit is it
that we have kept His ordinance?
> *Mal. 3:14*

All manner of sin and blasphemy shall be
forgiven unto men: but the blasphemy
against the Holy Ghost shall not be forgiv-
en unto men.
> Jesus
> *Matt. 12:31*
> *See also Matt. 12:32, Mark 3:29*

Whosoever shall speak a word against the
Son of man, it shall be forgiven him: but
unto him that blasphemeth against the
Holy Ghost it shall not be forgiven.
> Jesus
> *Luke 12:10*
> *See also Matt. 12:32*

[*See also* Heresy, Profanity]

BLESSING

In thee shall all families of the earth be
blessed.
> God to Abram
> *Gen. 12:3*
> *See also Gen. 28:14*

Cursed be every one that curseth thee, and
blessed be he that blesseth thee.
> Isaac to Jacob
> *Gen. 27:29*
> *See also Num. 24:9*

Hast thou not reserved a blessing for me?
Esau to Isaac
Gen. 27:36

I will not let thee go, except thou bless me.
Jacob to Angel
Gen. 32:26

A nation and a company of nations shall be of thee, and kings shall come out of thy loins.
Gen. 35:11

And God Almighty give you mercy before the man.
Jacob to his sons
Gen. 43:14

Go in peace.
E.g., Ex. 4:18

The Lord bless thee, and keep thee: The Lord make His face shine upon thee, and be gracious unto thee: The Lord lift up His countenance upon thee, and give thee peace.
Num. 6:24–26

Behold, I set before you this day a blessing and a curse; A blessing, if ye obey the commandments of the Lord your God, which I command you this day: And a curse, if ye will not obey.
Deut. 11:26–28

Blessed shalt thou be in the city, and blessed shalt thou be in the field.
Deut. 28:3

As thy days, so shall thy strength be.
Deut. 33:25

The Lord thy God be with thee, as He was with Moses.
Josh. 1:17

The Lord deal kindly with you, as ye have dealt with the dead, and with me.
Naomi
Ruth 1:8

The Lord be with you.
Ruth 2:4
See also 1 Sam. 17:37

The Lord bless thee.
Ruth 2:4

The Lord our God be with us, as He was with our fathers.
1 Kings 8:57

Peace be unto thee, and peace be to thine helpers; for thy God helpeth thee.
1 Chron. 12:18

Think upon me, my God, for good.
Neh. 5:19
See also Neh. 12:31

Thou preparest a table before me in the presence of mine enemies: Thou anointest my head with oil; my cup runneth over.
Ps. 23:5

Surely goodness and mercy shall follow me all the days of my life: and I will dwell in the house of the Lord for ever.
Ps. 23:6

God be merciful unto us, and bless us; and cause His face to shine upon us.
Ps. 67:1

The curse of the Lord is in the house of the wicked: but He blesseth the habitation of the just.
Prov. 3:33

God giveth to a man that is good in His sight wisdom, and knowledge, and joy.
Eccl. 2:26

Blessed be the name of God for ever and ever.
Dan. 2:20
See also Ps. 145:1

If the house be worthy, let your peace come upon it: but if it be not worthy, let your peace return to you.
Jesus
Matt. 10:13

He that is mighty hath done to me great things; and holy is His name.
Mary
Luke 1:49

To day shalt thou be with me in paradise.
Jesus to malefactor on cross
Luke 23:43

Receive ye the Holy Ghost.
Jesus
John 20:22

I will give you the sure mercies of David.
Acts 13:34
See also Isa. 55:3

I commend you to God, and to the word of His grace.
Paul
Acts 20:32

The gifts and calling of God are without repentance.
Rom. 11:29

The God of peace be with you all.
Rom. 15:33

Eye hath not seen, nor ear heard, neither have entered into the heart of man, the things which God hath prepared for them that love Him.
1 Cor. 2:9
See also Isa. 64:4

Grace be with all them that love our Lord Jesus Christ in sincerity.
Eph. 6:24

The grace of our Lord Jesus Christ be with you all.
Phil. 4:23

The Lord be with you all.
2 Thess. 3:16

Out of the same mouth proceedeth blessing and cursing.
James 3:10

Peace be with you all that are in Christ Jesus.
1 Pet. 5:14

Grace be with you, mercy, and peace.
2 John 3

Mercy unto you, and peace, and love.
Jude 2

[*See also* Curses, Reward, and the Appendix at p. 422]

BLINDNESS

Cursed be he that maketh the blind to wander out of the way.
Deut. 27:18

I was eyes to the blind, and feet was I to the lame.
Job 29:15

The Lord openeth the eyes of the blind.
Ps. 146:8

The eyes of the blind shall be opened, and the ears of the deaf shall be unstopped.
Isa. 35:5

If the blind lead the blind, both shall fall into the ditch.
Jesus
Matt. 15:14
See also Luke 6:39

[*See also* Enlightenment, Handicapped, Miracles, Sight, Stubbornness]

BLOOD

It is the blood that maketh an atonement for the soul.
Lev. 17:11

The life of all flesh is the blood thereof.
Lev. 17:14

This is my blood of the new testament, which is shed for many for the remission of sins.
Jesus
Matt. 26:28
See also Mark 14:24, Luke 22:20

Without shedding of blood is no remission.
Heb. 9:22

The blood of Jesus Christ His Son cleanseth us from all sin.
1 John 1:7

[*See also* Guilt, Murder, Punishment]

BOASTING

Where is now thy mouth?
Judg. 9:38

I will give thy flesh unto the fowls of the air, and to the beasts of the field.
Goliath to David
1 Sam. 17:44

Let not him that girdeth on his harness boast himself as he that putteth it off.
1 Kings 20:11

A prudent man concealeth knowledge: but the heart of fools proclaimeth foolishness.
Prov. 12:23

For men to search their own glory is not glory.
Prov. 25:27

Boast not thyself of to morrow; for thou knowest not what a day may bring forth.
Prov. 27:1

Let not the wise man glory in his wisdom, neither let the mighty man glory in his might, let not the rich man glory in his riches.
Jer. 9:23

Rejoice not against me, O mine enemy: when I fall, I shall arise.
Mic. 7:8

He that speaketh of himself seeketh his own glory.
Jesus
John 7:18

If I honour myself, my honour is nothing.
Jesus
John 8:54

If thou boast, thou bearest not the root, but the root thee.
Rom. 11:18

He that glorieth, let him glory in the Lord.
E.g., 1 Cor. 1:31
See also Jer. 9:24

Though I would desire to glory, I shall not be a fool; for I will say the truth.
2 Cor. 12:6

God forbid that I should glory, save in the cross of our Lord Jesus Christ.
Gal. 6:14

How much she hath glorified herself, and lived deliciously, so much torment and sorrow give her.
(she: Babylon)
Rev. 18:7

[*See also* Arrogance, Gloating]

BODY

Dust thou art, and unto dust shalt thou return.
Gen. 3:19

Thy two breasts are like two young roes that are twins, which feed among the lilies.
Song 4:5
See also Song 7:3

His legs are as pillars of marble, set upon sockets of fine gold.
Song 5:15

Thy navel is like a round goblet, which wanteth not liquor.
Song 7:2

Thy neck is as a tower of ivory; thine eyes like the fishpools in Heshbon.
Song 7:4

Thy nose is as the tower of Lebanon which looketh toward Damascus.
Song 7:4

Thy stature is like to a palm tree, and thy breasts to clusters of grapes.
Song 7:7

The light of the body is the eye.
Jesus
Matt. 6:22, Luke 11:34

Fear not them which kill the body, but are not able to kill the soul.
Jesus
Matt. 10:28
See also Luke 12:4

The body is not for fornication, but for the Lord.
1 Cor. 6:13

Your bodies are the members of Christ.
1 Cor. 6:15

Your body is the temple of the Holy Ghost.
1 Cor. 6:19

Glorify God in your body, and in your spirit.
1 Cor. 6:20

It is sown in corruption; it is raised in incorruption.
1 Cor. 15:42

[*See also* Appearance, Beauty, Carnality, Physical Fitness, Speech]

BOOKS

Oh that my words were now written! oh that they were printed in a book!
Job 19:23

My desire is, that the Almighty would answer me, and that mine adversary had written a book.
Job 31:35

Of making many books there is no end.
Eccl. 12:12

If they should be written every one, I suppose that even the world itself could not contain the books that should be written.
John 21:25

What thou seest, write in a book, and send it unto the seven churches.
Jesus
Rev. 1:11

[*See also* History]

BOREDOM

See Pleasure.

BORN AGAIN

Except a man be born again, he cannot see the kingdom of God.
Jesus
John 3:3

Except a man be born of water and of the Spirit, he cannot enter into the kingdom of God.
Jesus
John 3:5

Ye must be born again.
Jesus
John 3:7

Though ye have ten thousand instructors in Christ, yet have ye not many fathers.
1 Cor. 4:15

If any man be in Christ, he is a new creature.
2 Cor. 5:17

Whosoever is born of God doth not commit sin.
1 John 3:9

[*See also* Jesus (Acceptance of)]

BORROWING

Thou shalt lend unto many nations, but thou shalt not borrow.
Deut. 15:6
See also Deut. 28:12

The wicked borroweth, and payeth not again: but the righteous showeth mercy, and giveth.
Ps. 37:21

He that is surety for a stranger shall smart for it.
Prov. 11:15

The borrower is servant to the lender.
Prov. 22:7

Better is it that thou shouldest not vow, than that thou shouldest vow and not pay.
Eccl. 5:5

As with the buyer, so with the seller; as with the lender, so with the borrower; as with the taker of usury, so with the giver of usury to him.
Isa. 24:2

Give to him that asketh thee, and from him that would borrow of thee turn not thou away.
Jesus
Matt. 5:42
See also Luke 6:30

[*See also* Generosity, Usury]

BRAVERY

See Courage.

BREAD OF LIFE

Labour not for the meat which perisheth, but for that meat which endureth unto everlasting life.
Jesus
John 6:27

The bread of God is He which cometh down from heaven, and giveth life unto the world.
Jesus
John 6:33

I am the bread of life: he that cometh to me

shall never hunger; and he that believeth on me shall never thirst.
Jesus
John 6:35

I am the living bread which came down from heaven: if any man eat of this bread, he shall live for ever.
Jesus
John 6:51
See also John 6:58

[*See also* Eternal Life, Food]

BRIBERY

Thou shalt not respect persons, neither take a gift.
Deut. 16:19
See also Deut. 1:17

A gift doth blind the eyes of the wise, and pervert the words of the righteous.
Deut. 16:19
See also Ex. 23:8

Fire shall consume the tabernacles of bribery.
Job 15:34

A gift in secret pacifieth anger.
Prov. 21:14

A gift destroyeth the heart.
Eccl. 7:7

[*See also* Corruption, Gifts, Greed, Money]

BROTHERHOOD

Am I my brother's keeper?
Cain
Gen. 4:9

Thou shalt love thy neighbour as thyself.
E.g., Lev. 19:18, Matt. 19:19

Love ye therefore the stranger: for ye were strangers in the land of Egypt.
Deut. 10:19

Did not He that made me in the womb make him?
Job 31:15

Behold, how good and how pleasant it is for brethren to dwell together in unity!
Ps. 133:1

If two lie together, then they have heat: but how can one be warm alone?
Eccl. 4:11

The wolf and the lamb shall feed together, and the lion shall eat straw like the bullock.
Isa. 65:25

Execute true judgment, and show mercy and compassions every man to his brother.
Zech. 7:9

Let none of you imagine evil against his brother in your heart.
Zech. 7:10
See also Zech. 8:17

Have we not all one father? hath not one God created us?
Mal. 2:10

Why do we deal treacherously every man against his brother?
Mal. 2:10

Whosoever is angry with his brother without a cause shall be in danger of the judgment.
Jesus
Matt. 5:22

On earth peace, good will toward men.
Luke 2:14

As ye would that men should do to you, do ye also to them likewise.
Jesus
Luke 6:31
See also Matt. 7:12

Love one another.
Jesus
E.g., John 13:34

Sirs, ye are brethren; why do ye wrong one to another?
Acts 7:26

Follow peace with all men, and holiness without which no man shall see the Lord.
Heb. 12:14

Let brotherly love continue.
Heb. 13:1

He that saith he is in the light, and hateth his brother, is in darkness even until now.
1 John 2:9

He that loveth not his brother abideth in death.
1 John 3:14

He that loveth not his brother whom he hath seen, how can he love God whom he hath not seen?
1 John 4:20

He who loveth God love his brother also.
1 John 4:21

[*See also* Enemies, Equality, Fellowship, Friendship, Hatred, Love, Peace, Universality]

BROTHERS

See Siblings.

BUILDING

Let the foundations thereof be strongly laid.
Ezra 6:3

Except the Lord build the house, they labour in vain that build it.
Ps. 127:1

Through wisdom is an house builded; and by understanding it is established.
Prov. 24:3

By much slothfulness the building decayeth.
Eccl. 10:18

He who hath builded the house hath more honour than the house.
Heb. 3:3

Every house is builded by some man; but He that built all things is God.
Heb. 3:4

[*See also* Planning]

BURDENS

Come unto me, all ye that labour and are heavy laden, and I will give you rest.
Jesus
Matt. 11:28

Him they compelled to bear His cross.
(Him: Simon)
Matt. 27:32
See also John 19:17

Ye lade men with burdens grievous to be borne, and ye yourselves touch not the burdens with one of your fingers.
Jesus
Luke 11:46
See also Matt. 23:4

Bear ye one another's burdens.
Gal. 6:2

[*See also* Acceptance, Comfort, Oppression, Responsibility, Worry]

BURIAL

Bury me not, I pray thee, in Egypt.
Jacob to Joseph
Gen. 47:29

The carcase of Jezebel shall be as dung upon the face of the field.
2 Kings 9:37

They shall not say, This is Jezebel.
2 Kings 9:37

The potter's field, to bury strangers in.
Matt. 27:7

[*See also* Death, Remembrance]

BUSINESS

Because thou art my brother, shouldest thou therefore serve me for nought? tell me, what shall thy wages be?
Laban to Jacob
Gen. 29:15

Ye shall do no unrighteousness in judgment, in meteyard, in weight, or in measure.
Lev. 19:35

Thou shalt not oppress an hired servant that is poor and needy.
Deut. 24:14

Thou shalt not have in thy bag divers weights, a great and a small.
Deut. 25:13

All that do unrighteously, are an abomination unto the Lord thy God.
Deut. 25:16

A false balance is abomination to the Lord: but a just weight is His delight.
Prov. 11:1

He that withholdeth corn, the people shall curse him: but blessing shall be upon the head of him that selleth it.
Prov. 11:26

Divers weights, and divers measures, both of them are alike abomination to the Lord.
Prov. 20:10
See also Prov. 20:23

It is naught, it is naught, saith the buyer: but when he is gone his way, then he boasteth.
Prov. 20:14

Seest thou a man diligent in his business? he shall stand before kings.
Prov. 22:29

Ye shall have just balances.
Ezek. 45:10

He is a merchant, the balances of deceit are in his hand: he loveth to oppress.
Hos. 12:7

The kingdom of heaven is like unto a merchant man, seeking goodly pearls.
Jesus
Matt. 13:45

The merchants of the earth shall weep and mourn over her; for no man buyeth their merchandise any more.
(her: Babylon)
Rev. 18:11

[*See also* Employees, Honesty, Leadership, Work]

CALLING

See Mission.

CANDOR

How long shall this man be a snare unto us? let the men go.
Advisers to Pharaoh
Ex. 10:7

Knowest thou not yet that Egypt is destroyed?
Pharaoh's servants to Pharaoh
Ex. 10:7

I will speak in the anguish of my spirit; I will complain in the bitterness of my soul.
Job 7:11

Let me alone, that I may speak, and let come on me what will.
Job 13:13

He that hideth hatred with lying lips, and he that uttereth a slander, is a fool.
Prov. 10:18

Open rebuke is better than secret love.
Prov. 27:5

A time to keep silence, and a time to speak.
Eccl. 3:7

This man seeketh not the welfare of this people, but the hurt.
(man: Jeremiah)
Jer. 38:4

If I declare it unto thee, wilt thou not surely put me to death?
Jer. 38:15

Whatsoever thing the Lord shall answer you, I will declare it unto you; I will keep nothing back.
Jer. 42:4

Though I would desire to glory, I shall not be a fool; for I will say the truth.
2 Cor. 12:6

If I yet pleased men, I should not be the servant of Christ.
Gal. 1:10

[*See also* Advice, Honesty, Prudence, Truth]

CAPACITY

All the rivers run into the sea; yet the sea is not full.
Eccl. 1:7

[*See also* Ability]

CAPITAL PUNISHMENT

He that smiteth a man, so that he die, shall be surely put to death.
Ex. 21:12

He that smiteth his father, or his mother, shall be surely put to death.
Ex. 21:15

He that killeth a man, he shall be put to death.
Lev. 24:21
See also Lev. 24:17

One witness shall not testify against any person to cause him to die.
Num. 35:30

Ye shall take no satisfaction for the life of a murderer, which is guilty of death: but he shall be surely put to death.
Num. 35:31

At the mouth of two witnesses, or three witnesses, shall he that is worthy of death be put to death; but at the mouth of one witness he shall not be put to death.
Deut. 17:6

[*See also* Murder, Punishment]

CAPTIVITY

Behold, I am in your hand: do with me as seemeth good and meet unto you.
Jer. 26:14

Thou hast broken the yokes of wood; but thou shalt make for them yokes of iron.
Jer. 28:13

[*See also* Exile, Freedom, Imprisonment, Outcast, Slavery]

CARE

See Comfort, Devotion.

CARNAGE

In the place where dogs licked the blood of Naboth shall dogs lick thy blood, even thine.
(thy: Ahab)
1 Kings 21:19

The dogs shall eat Jezebel by the wall of Jezreel.
1 Kings 21:23

When they arose early in the morning, behold, they were all dead corpses.
2 Kings 19:35, Isa. 37:36

The sword shall devour, and it shall be satiate and made drunk with their blood.
Jer. 46:10

[*See also* Violence, War]

CARNALITY

The law is spiritual: but I am carnal.
Rom. 7:14

In me (that is, in my flesh,) dwelleth no good thing.
Rom. 7:18

With the mind I myself serve the law of God; but with the flesh the law of sin.
Rom. 7:25

They that are after the flesh do mind the things of the flesh; but they that are after the Spirit the things of the Spirit.
Rom. 8:5

The carnal mind is enmity against God.
Rom. 8:7

They that are in the flesh cannot please God.
Rom. 8:8

If ye live after the flesh, ye shall die.
Rom. 8:13

[*See also* Fornication, Lust, Spirituality]

CAUTION

See Prudence, Vigilance, Warning.

CELEBRATION

To every one a loaf of bread, and a good piece of flesh, and a flagon of wine.
1 Chron. 16:3

Go your way, eat the fat, and drink the sweet.
Neh. 8:10

The joy of Jerusalem was heard even afar off.
Neh. 12:43

Let the heavens rejoice, and let the earth be glad; let the sea roar, and the fulness thereof.
Ps. 96:11
See also 1 Chron. 16:31–32

Make a joyful noise unto the Lord, all the earth: make a loud noise, and rejoice, and sing praise.
Ps. 98:4
See also Ps. 100:1

This is the day which the Lord hath made; we will rejoice and be glad in it.
Ps. 118:24

Let us eat and drink; for to morrow we shall die.
Isa. 22:13, 1 Cor. 15:32

When thou makest a feast, call the poor, the maimed, the lame, the blind: And thou shalt be blessed; for they cannot recompense thee.
Jesus
Luke 14:13–14

Bring hither the fatted calf.
Luke 15:23

Rejoice in the Lord always.
E.g., Phil. 4:4

Rejoice evermore.
1 Thess. 5:16

[*See also* Happiness, Pleasure]

CELIBACY

He that is able to receive it, let him receive it.
Jesus
Matt. 19:12

It is good for a man not to touch a woman.
1 Cor. 7:1

It is better to marry than to burn.
1 Cor. 7:9

He that giveth her in marriage doeth well; but he that giveth her not in marriage doeth better.
1 Cor. 7:38

[*See also* Marriage]

CENSUS

Number ye the people, that I may know the number of the people.
2 Sam. 24:2

CERTAINTY

When I begin, I will also make an end.
God to Samuel
1 Sam. 3:12

He is not a man, that He should repent.
1 Sam. 15:29

As the Lord liveth, the Lord shall smite him.
1 Sam. 26:10

How long halt ye between two opinions?
1 Kings 18:21

Boast not thyself of to morrow; for thou knowest not what a day may bring forth.
Prov. 27:1

I have spoken it, I will also bring it to pass.
Isa. 46:11

I the Lord have spoken it.
Ezek. 5:13, 17

Wheresoever the carcase is, there will the eagles be gathered together.
Jesus
Matt. 24:28
See also Luke 17:37

Though I should die with Thee, yet will I not deny Thee.
Peter to Jesus
Matt. 26:35
See also Mark 14:31

If the goodman of the house had known what hour the thief would come, he would have watched.
Jesus
Luke 12:39
See also Matt. 24:43

What I have written I have written.
Pilate
John 19:22

One man esteemeth one day above another: another esteemeth every day alike. Let every man be fully persuaded in his own mind.
Rom. 14:5

If the trumpet give an uncertain sound, who shall prepare himself to the battle?
1 Cor. 14:8

The word of God is quick, and powerful, and sharper than any twoedged sword.
Heb. 4:12

Ye ought to say, If the Lord will, we shall live, and do this, or that.
James 4:15

[*See also* Chance, Decisions, Indecision]

CHALLENGES

Give me a man, that we may fight together.
Goliath
1 Sam. 17:10

Call ye on the name of your gods, and I will call on the name of the Lord.
Elijah
1 Kings 18:24

Come, let us see one another in the face.
2 Chron. 25:17

Touch all that he hath, and he will curse Thee to Thy face.
Satan to God, about Job
Job 1:11

All that he hath is in thy power; only upon himself put not forth thine hand.
God to Satan, about Job
Job 1:12

If Thou be the Son of God, command that these stones be made bread.
Devil to Jesus
Matt. 4:3
See also Luke 4:3

Thou shalt not tempt the Lord thy God.
Jesus
Matt. 4:7, Luke 4:12
See also Deut. 6:16

Ye say that I am.
Jesus
Luke 22:70

Why tempt ye God?
Acts 15:10

[*See also* Competition, Testing]

CHANCE

The lot is cast into the lap; but the whole disposing thereof is of the Lord.
Prov. 16:33

The race is not to the swift, nor the battle to the strong, neither yet bread to the wise, nor yet riches to men of understanding, nor yet favour to men of skill; but time and chance happeneth to them all.
Eccl. 9:11

CHANGE

Can the Ethiopian change his skin, or the leopard his spots? then may ye also do good, that are accustomed to do evil.
Jer. 13:23

New wine must be put into new bottles.
Jesus
Mark 2:22, Luke 5:38
See also Matt. 9:17

The fashion of this world passeth away.
1 Cor. 7:31

Old things are passed away; behold, all things are become new.
2 Cor. 5:17

He which persecuted us in times past now preacheth the faith which once he destroyed.
(He: Paul)
Gal. 1:23

Jesus Christ the same yesterday, and to day, and for ever.
Heb. 13:8

[*See also* Adaptability, Conversion, Habit]

CHAOS

The earth was without form, and void; and darkness was upon the face of the deep.
Gen. 1:2

They shall fight every one against his brother, and every one against his neighbour; city against city, and kingdom against kingdom.
Isa. 19:2

The fathers shall eat the sons in the midst of thee, and the sons shall eat their fathers.
Ezek. 5:10

God is not the author of confusion, but of peace.
1 Cor. 14:33

[*See also* Confusion]

CHARACTER

The excellency of dignity.
Gen. 49:3

Unstable as water, thou shalt not excel.
Gen. 49:4

What doth the Lord thy God require of thee, but to fear the Lord thy God, to walk in all His ways, and to love Him, and to serve the Lord thy God with all thy heart and with all thy soul.
Deut. 10:12

As the man is, so is his strength.
Judg. 8:21

As his name is, so is he.
1 Sam. 25:25

Be thou strong therefore, and show thyself a man.
David to Solomon
1 Kings 2:2

What, is thy servant a dog, that he should do this great thing?
2 Kings 8:13

Dost thou still retain thine integrity? curse God, and die.
Job's wife to Job
Job 2:9

Surely men of low degree are vanity, and men of high degree are a lie.
Ps. 62:9

Let not mercy and truth forsake thee: bind them about thy neck.
Prov. 3:3

He that walketh uprightly walketh surely.
Prov. 10:9

A false witness will utter lies.
Prov. 14:5

Even a child is known by his doings.
Prov. 20:11

Iron sharpeneth iron; so a man sharpeneth the countenance of his friend.
Prov. 27:17

Better is the poor that walketh in his uprightness, than he that is perverse in his ways, though he be rich.
Prov. 28:6

Ye are the salt of the earth.
Jesus
Matt. 5:13

If thine eye be evil, thy whole body shall be full of darkness.
Jesus
Matt. 6:23
See also Luke 11:34

Every good tree bringeth forth good fruit; but a corrupt tree bringeth forth evil fruit.
Jesus
Matt. 7:17
See also Luke 6:43

The tree is known by his fruit.
Jesus
Matt. 12:33
See also Luke 6:44

Out of the abundance of the heart the mouth speaketh.
Jesus
Matt. 12:34

A good man out of the good treasure of the heart bringeth forth good things: and an

evil man out of the evil treasure bringeth forth evil things.
Jesus
Matt. 12:35

Because they had no root, they withered away.
Jesus
Matt. 13:6
See also Mark 4:6

Take heed therefore that the light which is in thee be not darkness.
Jesus
Luke 11:35

How can a man that is a sinner do such miracles?
Pharisees, about Jesus
John 9:16

They that are after the flesh do mind the things of the flesh; but they that are after the Spirit the things of the Spirit.
Rom. 8:5

We then that are strong ought to bear the infirmities of the weak.
Rom. 15:1

By the grace of God I am what I am: and His grace which was bestowed upon me was not in vain.
1 Cor. 15:10

Evil communications corrupt good manners.
1 Cor. 15:33

These are wells without water, clouds that are carried with a tempest.
2 Pet. 2:17

Clouds they are without water, carried about of winds; trees whose fruit withereth.
Jude 12

[*See also* Ability, Attitude, Behavior, Honesty, Integrity]

CHARITY

Thou shalt not harden thine heart, nor shut thine hand from thy poor brother.
Deut. 15:7

Thou shalt open thine hand wide unto thy brother, to thy poor, and to thy needy, in thy land.
Deut. 15:11

Every man shall give as he is able, according to the blessing of the Lord thy God which He hath given thee.
Deut. 16:17

Thou shalt not bring the hire of a whore, or the price of a dog, into the house of the Lord.
Deut. 23:18

Send portions unto them for whom nothing is prepared.
Neh. 8:10

The cause which I knew not I searched out.
Job 29:16

Blessed is he that considereth the poor: the Lord will deliver him in time of trouble.
Ps. 41:1

The sacrifice of the wicked is an abomination to the Lord: but the prayer of the upright is His delight.
Prov. 15:8

Whoso stoppeth his ears at the cry of the poor, he also shall cry himself, but shall not be heard.
Prov. 21:13

He that giveth unto the poor shall not lack: but he that hideth his eyes shall have many a curse.
Prov. 28:27

Will a man rob God? Yet ye have robbed Me.
Mal. 3:8

Wherein have we robbed Thee? In tithes and offerings.
Mal. 3:8

First be reconciled to thy brother, and then come and offer thy gift.
Jesus
Matt. 5:24

Do not your alms before men, to be seen of them: otherwise ye have no reward of your Father which is in heaven.
Jesus
Matt. 6:1

When thou doest thine alms, do not sound

a trumpet before thee, as the hypocrites do.
Jesus
Matt. 6:2

When thou doest alms, let not thy left hand know what thy right hand doeth.
Jesus
Matt. 6:3

If thou wilt be perfect, go and sell that thou hast, and give to the poor, and thou shalt have treasure in heaven: and come and follow me.
Jesus
Matt. 19:21
See also Mark 10:21, Luke 18:22

Inasmuch as ye have done it unto one of the least of these my brethren, ye have done it unto me.
Jesus
Matt. 25:40
See also Matt. 25:45

Sell that ye have, and give alms.
Jesus
Luke 12:33

When thou makest a feast, call the poor, the maimed, the lame, the blind: And thou shalt be blessed; for they cannot recompense thee.
Jesus
Luke 14:13–14

Silver and gold have I none; but such as I have give I thee.
Acts 3:6

Thy money perish with thee, because thou hast thought that the gift of God may be purchased with money.
Acts 8:20

He that giveth, let him do it with simplicity.
Rom. 12:8

And though I bestow all my goods to feed the poor, and though I give my body to be burned, and have not charity, it profiteth me nothing.
(charity: love)
1 Cor. 13:3

Every man according as he purposeth in his heart, so let him give.
2 Cor. 9:7

God loveth a cheerful giver.
2 Cor. 9:7

Remember the poor.
Gal. 2:10

[*See also* Altruism, Generosity, Love, Poverty, Sharing, Tithe, Underprivileged]

CHASTISEMENT

Art thou come unto me to call my sin to remembrance?
1 Kings 17:18

Hast thou killed, and also taken possession?
(thou: Ahab)
1 Kings 21:19

Happy is the man whom God correcteth.
Job 5:17

Rebuke me not in Thine anger, neither chasten me in Thy hot displeasure.
Ps. 6:1
See also Ps. 38:1

Despise not the chastening of the Lord: neither be weary of His correction.
Prov. 3:11

Whom the Lord loveth He correcteth.
Prov. 3:12

Lift up thy voice like a trumpet, and show My people their transgression.
Isa. 58:1

Prophesy against them, prophesy, O son of man.
Ezek. 11:4

Neither do I condemn thee: go, and sin no more.
Jesus
John 8:11

Them that sin rebuke before all, that others also may fear.
(Them: church leaders)
1 Tim. 5:20

Despise not thou the chastening of the Lord.
Heb. 12:5

Whom the Lord loveth He chasteneth.
Heb. 12:6

[*See also* Discipline, Guidance, Punishment]

CHEATING

See Honesty, Lies.

CHILD-REARING

He that spareth his rod hateth his son: but he that loveth him chasteneth him betimes.
Prov. 13:24

Chasten thy son while there is hope, and let not thy soul spare for his crying.
Prov. 19:18

Train up a child in the way he should go: and when he is old, he will not depart from it.
Prov. 22:6

Foolishness is bound in the heart of a child; but the rod of correction shall drive it far from him.
Prov. 22:15

Withhold not correction from the child: for if thou beatest him with the rod, he shall not die.
Prov. 23:13

Thou shalt beat him with the rod, and shalt deliver his soul from hell.
Prov. 23:14

A child left to himself bringeth his mother to shame.
Prov. 29:15

Even the sea monsters draw out the breast, they give suck to their young ones.
Lam. 4:3

Provoke not your children to wrath.
Eph. 6:4

Fathers, provoke not your children to anger, lest they be discouraged.
Col. 3:21

[*See also* Children, Parents]

CHILDBIRTH

See Birth.

CHILDLESSNESS

Give me children, or else I die.
Rachel to Jacob
Gen. 30:1

The Lord had shut up her womb.
(her: Hannah)
1 Sam. 1:5

Am not I better to thee than ten sons?
(I: Hannah's husband)
1 Sam. 1:8

I am a woman of a sorrowful spirit.
Hannah
1 Sam. 1:15

Sing, O barren, thou that didst not bear; break forth into singing, and cry aloud, thou that didst not travail with child: for more are the children of the desolate than the children of the married wife, saith the Lord.
Isa. 54:1
See also Gal. 4:27

[*See also* Fertility]

CHILDREN

Be fruitful, and multiply.
E.g., Gen. 1:28

Be fruitful, and multiply, and replenish the earth.
God to Noah, after the flood
Gen. 9:1

The smell of my son is as the smell of a field which the Lord hath blessed.
Gen. 27:27

Thy seed shall be as the dust of the earth.
God to Jacob
Gen. 28:14
See also Gen. 13:16

Israel loved Joseph more than all his children, because he was the son of his old age.
Gen. 37:3

If I be bereaved of my children, I am bereaved.
Gen. 43:14

The males shall be the Lord's.
Ex. 13:12

Do not prostitute thy daughter, to cause her to be a whore; lest the land fall to

whoredom, and the land become full of wickedness.
Lev. 19:29

Ye are the children of the Lord your God.
Deut. 14:1

He walked in all the sins of his father.
E.g., 1 Kings 15:3

Children are an heritage of the Lord: and the fruit of the womb is His reward.
Ps. 127:3

As arrows are in the hand of a mighty man; so are children of the youth. Happy is the man that hath his quiver full of them.
Ps. 127:4–5

A wise son maketh a glad father: but a foolish son is the heaviness of his mother.
Prov. 10:1

A fool despiseth his father's instruction.
Prov. 15:5

A wise son maketh a glad father: but a foolish man despiseth his mother.
Prov. 15:20

A foolish son is a grief to his father, and bitterness to her that bare him.
Prov. 17:25

A foolish son is the calamity of his father.
Prov. 19:13

He that begetteth a wise child shall have joy of him.
Prov. 23:24

A little child shall lead them.
Isa. 11:6

The seed of evildoers shall never be renowned.
Isa. 14:20

More are the children of the desolate than the children of the married wife, saith the Lord.
Isa. 54:1

Whoso shall receive one such little child in my name receiveth me.
Jesus
Matt. 18:5
See also Mark 9:37, Luke 9:48

Out of the mouth of babes and sucklings Thou hast perfected praise.
Jesus
Matt. 21:16
See also Ps. 8:2

Whosoever shall offend one of these little ones that believe in me, it is better for him that a millstone were hanged about his neck, and he were cast into the sea.
Jesus
Mark 9:42
See also Matt. 18:6, Luke 17:2

Suffer the little children to come unto me, and forbid them not: for of such is the kingdom of God.
Jesus
Mark 10:14
See also Matt. 19:14, Luke 18:16

Whosoever shall not receive the kingdom of God as a little child, he shall not enter therein.
Jesus
Mark 10:15
See also Luke 18:17

We are the children of God.
Rom. 8:16

When I was a child, I spake as a child, I understood as a child, I thought as a child: but when I became a man, I put away childish things.
1 Cor. 13:11

Children, obey your parents in the Lord.
Eph. 6:1

What son is he whom the father chasteneth not?
Heb. 12:7

I have no greater joy than to hear that my children walk in truth.
3 John 4

[*See also* Birth, Child-Rearing, Fertility, Firstborn, Grandchildren, Maturity, Parents, Youth]

CHOICE

If thou wilt take the left hand, then I will go to the right; or if thou depart to the right hand, then I will go to the left.
Gen. 13:9

Behold, I set before you this day a blessing and a curse; A blessing, if ye obey the commandments of the Lord your God, which I command you this day: And a curse, if ye will not obey.
> *Deut. 11:26–28*

I have set before thee this day life and good, and death and evil.
> *Deut. 30:15*

Choose life, that both thou and thy seed may live.
> *Deut. 30:19*

Choose you this day whom ye will serve.
> *Josh. 24:15*

But as for me and my house, we will serve the Lord.
> *Josh. 24:15*

Ye are witnesses against yourselves that ye have chosen you the Lord, to serve Him.
> *Josh. 24:22*

I offer thee three things; choose thee one of them, that I may do it unto thee.
> God to David
> *2 Sam. 24:12, 1 Chron. 21:10*

How long halt ye between two opinions? if the Lord be God, follow Him: but if Baal, then follow him.
> Elijah to Israelites
> *1 Kings 18:21*

Serve the king of Babylon, and live.
> *Jer. 27:17*

Seek good, and not evil, that ye may live.
> *Amos 5:14*

He shall separate them one from another, as a shepherd divideth his sheep from the goats.
> Jesus
> *Matt. 25:32*

Ye have not chosen me, but I have chosen you.
> Jesus
> *John 15:16*

Not this man, but Barabbas.
> *John 18:40*
> *See also Luke 23:18*

Seeing ye put it from you, and judge yourselves unworthy of everlasting life, lo, we turn to the Gentiles.
> Paul to Jews
> *Acts 13:46*

All things are lawful unto me, but all things are not expedient.
> *1 Cor. 6:12*
> *See also 1 Cor. 10:23*

Eschew evil, and do good.
> *1 Pet. 3:11*

Follow not that which is evil, but that which is good.
> *3 John 11*

[*See also* Battle Calls, Good and Evil, Indecision, Loyalty]

CHOSEN PEOPLE

I will make of thee a great nation.
> God to Abram
> *Gen. 12:2*

In thy seed shall all the nations of the earth be blessed; because thou hast obeyed My voice.
> God to Abraham
> *Gen. 22:18*

Thus saith the Lord, Israel is My son, even My firstborn.
> *Ex. 4:22*

I will take you to Me for a people, and I will be to you a God.
> *Ex. 6:7*

Ye shall be a peculiar treasure unto Me above all people: for all the earth is Mine.
> *Ex. 19:5*

And they shall know that I am the Lord their God, that brought them forth out of the land of Egypt.
> *Ex. 29:46*

I will walk among you, and will be your God, and ye shall be My people.
> *Lev. 26:12*
> *See also 2 Cor. 6:16*

Who can count the dust of Jacob, and the number of the fourth part of Israel?
> *Num. 23:10*

He lay down as a lion, and as a great lion: who shall stir him up?
Num. 24:9

Blessed is he that blesseth thee, and cursed is he that curseth thee.
Num. 24:9

Surely this great nation is a wise and understanding people.
Deut. 4:6

Did ever people hear the voice of God speaking out of the midst of the fire, as thou hast heard, and live?
Deut. 4:33

The Lord made not this covenant with our fathers, but with us, even us, who are all of us here alive this day.
Deut. 5:3

Thou art an holy people unto the Lord thy God.
E.g., Deut. 7:6

The Lord thy God hath chosen thee to be a special people unto Himself.
Deut. 7:6

The Lord did not set His love upon you, nor choose you, because ye were more in number than any people; for ye were the fewest of all people: But because the Lord loved you.
Deut. 7:7–8

All people of the earth shall see that thou art called by the name of the Lord; and they shall be afraid of thee.
Deut. 28:10

The Lord's portion is His people.
Deut. 32:9

The apple of His eye.
Deut. 32:10

They are a nation void of counsel, neither is there any understanding in them.
Deut. 32:28

It hath pleased the Lord to make you His people.
1 Sam. 12:22

They shall dwell in their place, and shall be moved no more.
1 Chron. 17:9

He reproved kings for their sakes.
Ps. 105:14, 1 Chron. 16:21

Touch not Mine anointed, and do My prophets no harm.
Ps. 105:15, 1 Chron. 16:22

He that keepeth Israel shall neither slumber nor sleep.
Ps. 121:4

The Lord hath chosen Jacob unto Himself, and Israel for His peculiar treasure.
Ps. 135:4

The ox knoweth his owner, and the ass his master's crib: but Israel doth not know, My people doth not consider.
Isa. 1:3

The vineyard of the Lord of hosts is the house of Israel.
Isa. 5:7

They shall be My people, and I will be their God.
E.g., Jer. 24:7

Again I will build thee, and thou shalt be built, O virgin of Israel.
Jer. 31:4

He that scattered Israel will gather him, and keep him, as a shepherd doth his flock.
Jer. 31:10

The number of the children of Israel shall be as the sand of the sea, which cannot be measured nor numbered.
Hos. 1:10

[*See also* Believers, Circumcision, Covenant, God's People]

CHRIST

See Jesus, Messiah, Messianic Hopes and Prophecies.

CHRIST ETERNAL

Heaven and earth shall pass away, but my words shall not pass away.
Jesus
Matt. 24:35, Mark 13:31, Luke 21:33

Lo, I am with you alway, even unto the end of the world.
Jesus
Matt. 28:20

Of His kingdom there shall be no end.
(His: Jesus)
Luke 1:33

Before Abraham was, I am.
Jesus
John 8:58

Christ being raised from the dead dieth no more.
Rom. 6:9

Thy throne, O God, is for ever and ever.
Heb. 1:8

They shall perish; but Thou remainest.
Heb. 1:11

Jesus Christ the same yesterday, and to day, and for ever.
Heb. 13:8

I am alive for evermore.
Jesus
Rev. 1:18

I am Alpha and Omega, the beginning and the end, the first and the last.
Jesus
Rev. 22:13
See also Rev. 1:8, 11, Rev. 21:6

[*See also* Eternal Life, Eternity, Jesus, Resurrection]

CHRISTIANITY

Thou art Peter, and upon this rock I will build my church; and the gates of hell shall not prevail against it.
Jesus
Matt. 16:18

There shall be one fold, and one shepherd.
Jesus
John 10:16

CHRISTIANS

By this shall all men know that ye are my disciples, if ye have love one to another.
Jesus
John 13:35

The disciples were called Christians first in Antioch.
Acts 11:26

We are the children of God.
Rom. 8:16

Ye are the body of Christ.
1 Cor. 12:27

We are unto God a sweet savour of Christ.
2 Cor. 2:15

Thou art no more a servant, but a son.
Gal. 4:7

Ye who sometimes were far off are made nigh by the blood of Christ.
Eph. 2:13

Ye are no more strangers and foreigners, but fellowcitizens with the saints.
Eph. 2:19

Walk worthy of the vocation wherewith ye are called.
Eph. 4:1

Be ye therefore followers of God, as dear children.
Eph. 5:1

The dead in Christ shall rise first.
1 Thess. 4:16

Ye are all the children of light, and the children of the day.
1 Thess. 5:5

If any man suffer as a Christian, let him not be ashamed.
1 Pet. 4:16

The world knoweth us not, because it knew Him not.
1 John 3:1

[*See also* Believers, Christianity, God's People, Persecution]

CHRISTMAS

Unto you is born this day in the city of David a Saviour, which is Christ the Lord.
Luke 2:11

CHURCH AND STATE

Render therefore unto Caesar the things which are Caesar's; and unto God the things that are God's.
Jesus
Matt. 22:21
See also Mark 12:17, Luke 20:25

My kingdom is not of this world.
Jesus
John 18:36

Look ye to it; for I will be no judge of such matters.
Acts 18:15

I stand at Caesar's judgment seat, where I ought to be judged: to the Jews have I done no wrong.
Paul
Acts 25:10

[*See also* Government]

CHURCH GOVERNANCE

See Clergy, Leadership.

CHURCHES

Let them make Me a sanctuary; that I may dwell among them.
Ex. 25:8

I dwell in an house of cedar, but the ark of God dwelleth within curtains.
David
2 Sam. 7:2

I have surely built Thee an house to dwell in, a settled place for Thee to abide in for ever.
Solomon to God
1 Kings 8:13

Who is able to build Him an house, seeing the heaven and heaven of heavens cannot contain Him?
2 Chron. 2:6

Heaven and the heaven of heavens cannot contain Thee; how much less this house which I have built!
Solomon
2 Chron. 6:18
See also 1 Kings 8:27

I will not give sleep to mine eyes, or slumber to mine eyelids, Until I find out a place for the Lord.
Ps. 132:4–5

Mine house shall be called an house of prayer for all people.
Isa. 56:7

I will be glorified, saith the Lord.
Hag. 1:8

Thou art Peter, and upon this rock I will build my church; and the gates of hell shall not prevail against it.
Jesus
Matt. 16:18

My house is the house of prayer: but ye have made it a den of thieves.
Jesus
Luke 19:46
See also Matt. 21:13, Mark 11:17

Heaven is My throne, and earth is My footstool: what house will ye build Me? saith the Lord.
Acts 7:49
See also Isa. 66:1

God that made the world and all things therein, seeing that He is Lord of heaven and earth, dwelleth not in temples made with hands.
Acts 17:24

We, being many, are one body in Christ, and every one members one of another.
Rom. 12:5

Let your women keep silence in the churches: for it is not permitted unto them to speak.
1 Cor. 14:34

It is a shame for women to speak in the church.
1 Cor. 14:35

He is the head of the body, the church.
(He: Jesus)
Col. 1:18

If a man know not how to rule his own house, how shall he take care of the church of God?
1 Tim. 3:5

[*See also* God's Presence, God's Temple, Prayer, Worship]

CIRCUMCISION

Ye shall circumcise the flesh of your foreskin; and it shall be a token of the covenant betwixt Me and you.
Gen. 17:11

Circumcise therefore the foreskin of your heart, and be no more stiffnecked.
Deut. 10:16

Circumcise yourselves to the Lord.
Jer. 4:4

Neither is that circumcision, which is outward in the flesh.
Rom. 2:28

Circumcision is that of the heart, in the spirit, and not in the letter; whose praise is not of men, but of God.
Rom. 2:29

What advantage then hath the Jew? or what profit is there of circumcision?
Rom. 3:1

Circumcision is nothing, and uncircumcision is nothing, but the keeping of the commandments of God.
1 Cor. 7:19

In Jesus Christ neither circumcision availeth any thing, nor uncircumcision; but faith which worketh by love.
Gal. 5:6

We are the circumcision, which worship God in the spirit, and rejoice in Christ Jesus.
Phil. 3:3

[*See also* Chosen People, Covenant, Rituals]

CLARITY

They are all plain to him that understandeth, and right to them that find knowledge.
Prov. 8:9

Write the vision, and make it plain.
Hab. 2:2

Now we see through a glass, darkly; but then face to face.
1 Cor. 13:12

[*See also* Communication, Eloquence, Speech]

CLERGY

The Lord is their inheritance.
Deut. 18:2

I will raise Me up a faithful priest.
1 Sam. 2:35

Ye are holy unto the Lord.
Ezra 8:28

They shall teach My people the difference between the holy and profane.
Ezek. 44:23

The priest's lips should keep knowledge.
Mal. 2:7

They which preach the gospel should live of the gospel.
1 Cor. 9:14

Woe is unto me, if I preach not the gospel!
1 Cor. 9:16

Know them which labour among you, and are over you in the Lord.
1 Thess. 5:12

Esteem them very highly in love for their work's sake.
1 Thess. 5:13

Let the elders that rule well be counted worthy of double honour.
1 Tim. 5:17

[*See also* Ministry, Preaching, Priesthood]

COMFORT

Fear not, for I am with thee, and will bless thee, and multiply thy seed.
God to Isaac
Gen. 26:24

Peace be unto thee; fear not: thou shalt not die.
Judg. 6:23

Ye are forgers of lies, ye are all physicians of no value.
Job to his friends
Job 13:4

Miserable comforters are ye all.
Job to his friends
Job 16:2

Thou, O Lord, art a shield for me; my glory, and the lifter up of mine head.
Ps. 3:3

He maketh me to lie down in green pastures: He leadeth me beside the still waters. He restoreth my soul.
Ps. 23:2–3

Thy rod and Thy staff they comfort me.
Ps. 23:4

I looked for some to take pity, but there was none; and for comforters, but I found none.
Ps. 69:20

Thy statutes have been my songs in the house of my pilgrimage.
Ps. 119:54

Trouble and anguish have taken hold on me: yet Thy commandments are my delights.
Ps. 119:143

Comfort ye, comfort ye My people, saith your God.
Isa. 40:1

When thou passest through the waters, I will be with thee; and through the rivers, they shall not overflow thee: when thou walkest through the fire, thou shalt not be burned.
Isa. 43:2

I, even I, am He that comforteth you.
Isa. 51:12

As one whom his mother comforteth, so will I comfort you.
Isa. 66:13

Is there no balm in Gilead? is there no physician there?
Jer. 8:22

Mine eye runneth down with water, because the comforter that should relieve my soul is far from me.
Lam. 1:16

Do not My words do good to him that walketh uprightly?
Mic. 2:7

My spirit remaineth among you: fear ye not.
Hag. 2:5

Blessed are they that mourn: for they shall be comforted.
Jesus
Matt. 5:4

Come unto me, all ye that labour and are heavy laden, and I will give you rest.
Jesus
Matt. 11:28

I am meek and lowly in heart: and ye shall find rest unto your souls.
Jesus
Matt. 11:29

Be of good cheer; it is I; be not afraid.
Jesus
Matt. 14:27, Mark 6:50
See also John 6:20

Tarry ye here, and watch with me.
Jesus
Matt. 26:38
See also Mark 14:34

Whosoever shall give you a cup of water to drink in my name, because ye belong to Christ, verily I say unto you, he shall not lose his reward.
Jesus
Mark 9:41

In my Father's house are many mansions.
Jesus
John 14:2

He shall give you another Comforter, that He may abide with you for ever.
Jesus
John 14:16

I will not leave you comfortless: I will come to you.
Jesus
John 14:18

Peace I leave with you, my peace I give unto you.
Jesus
John 14:27

Let not your heart be troubled, neither let it be afraid.
Jesus
John 14:27
See also John 14:1

Be of good cheer; I have overcome the world.
Jesus
John 16:33

Woman, why weepest thou?
Jesus to Mary Magdalene
John 20:15

The Father of mercies, and the God of all comfort.
  2 Cor. 1:3

[*See also* Anguish, Fear, Grief, Mourning, Sympathy]

COMMANDMENTS

If a soul sin, and commit any of these things which are forbidden to be done by the commandments of the Lord; though he wist it not, yet is he guilty.
  Lev. 5:17

Do them, that ye may live.
  Deut. 4:1
  See also Luke 10:28

Keep therefore and do them; for this is your wisdom and your understanding in the sight of the nations.
  Deut. 4:6

And thou shalt teach them diligently unto thy children, and shalt talk of them when thou sittest in thine house, and when thou walkest by the way, and when thou liest down, and when thou risest up.
  Deut. 6:7
  See also Deut. 11:19

Thou shalt keep the commandments of the Lord thy God, to walk in His ways, and to fear Him.
  Deut. 8:6

Behold, I set before you this day a blessing and a curse; A blessing, if ye obey the commandments of the Lord your God, which I command you this day: And a curse, if ye will not obey.
  Deut. 11:26–28

What thing soever I command you, observe to do it: thou shalt not add thereto, nor diminish from it.
  Deut. 12:32

Do them, that ye may prosper in all that ye do.
  Deut. 29:9

The word is very nigh unto thee, in thy mouth, and in thy heart.
  Deut. 30:14
  See also Rom. 10:8

It is not a vain thing for you; because it is your life.
  Deut. 32:47

Turn not from it to the right hand or to the left, that thou mayest prosper whithersoever thou goest.
  Josh. 1:7

Keep His commandments.
  E.g., Josh. 22:5

Let it be done according to the law.
  Ezra 10:3

Lay up His words in thine heart.
  Job 22:22

The testimony of the Lord is sure, making wise the simple.
  Ps. 19:7

More to be desired are they than gold, yea, than much fine gold: sweeter also than honey and the honeycomb.
  Ps. 19:10

Thy word have I hid in mine heart, that I might not sin against Thee.
  Ps. 119:11

Teach me, O Lord, the way of Thy statutes; and I shall keep it unto the end.
  Ps. 119:33

Thy statutes have been my songs in the house of my pilgrimage.
  Ps. 119:54

Give me understanding, that I may learn Thy commandments.
  Ps. 119:73
  See also Ps. 119:34

Thy law is my delight.
  Ps. 119:77, 174
  See also Ps. 119:143

Thy law is the truth.
  Ps. 119:142

Great peace have they which love Thy law.
  Ps. 119:165

He that keepeth the commandment keepeth his own soul; but he that despiseth His ways shall die.
  Prov. 19:16

He that keepeth the law, happy is he.
  Prov. 29:18

He will teach us of His ways, and we will walk in His paths.
Isa. 2:3, Mic. 4:2

Out of Zion shall go forth the law, and the word of the Lord from Jerusalem.
Isa. 2:3

This is the way, walk ye in it.
Isa. 30:21

Remember ye the law of Moses My servant.
Mal. 4:4

Whosoever shall do and teach them, the same shall be called great in the kingdom of heaven.
Jesus
Matt. 5:19

All things whatsoever ye would that men should do to you, do ye even so to them.
Jesus
Matt. 7:12
See also Luke 6:31

If thou wilt enter into life, keep the commandments.
Jesus
Matt. 19:17

Thou shalt love the Lord thy God with all thy heart, and with all thy soul, and with all thy mind. This is the first and great commandment.
Jesus
Matt. 22:37–38
See also Mark 12:29–30, Luke 10:27

Thou knowest the commandments, Do not commit adultery, Do not kill, Do not steal, Do not bear false witness, Defraud not, Honour thy father and mother.
Jesus
Mark 10:19
See also Matt. 19:18–19, Luke 18:20

It is easier for heaven and earth to pass, than one tittle of the law to fail.
Jesus
Luke 16:17
See also Matt. 5:18

The law was given by Moses, but grace and truth came by Jesus Christ.
John 1:17

A new commandment I give unto you, That ye love one another.
Jesus
John 13:34

This is my commandment, That ye love one another, as I have loved you.
Jesus
John 15:12

As many as have sinned without law shall also perish without law.
Rom. 2:12

By the law is the knowledge of sin.
Rom. 3:20
See also Rom. 4:15

Do we then make void the law through faith? God forbid.
Rom. 3:31

I had not known sin, but by the law.
Rom. 7:7

When the commandment came, sin revived.
Rom. 7:9

The law is spiritual: but I am carnal.
Rom. 7:14

He that loveth another hath fulfilled the law.
Rom. 13:8
See also Rom. 13:10

The letter killeth, but the spirit giveth life.
2 Cor. 3:6

A man is not justified by the works of the law, but by the faith of Jesus Christ.
Gal. 2:16

By the works of the law shall no flesh be justified.
Gal. 2:16

I through the law am dead to the law, that I might live unto God.
Gal. 2:19

If righteousness come by the law, then Christ is dead in vain.
Gal. 2:21

No man is justified by the law in the sight of God.
Gal. 3:11

Christ hath redeemed us from the curse of the law.
Gal. 3:13

It was ordained by angels in the hand of a mediator.
Gal. 3:19

Before faith came, we were kept under the law.
Gal. 3:23

The law was our schoolmaster to bring us unto Christ, that we might be justified by faith.
Gal. 3:24

All the law is fulfilled in one word, even in this; Thou shalt love thy neighbour as thyself.
Gal. 5:14

I will put My laws into their hearts, and in their minds will I write them.
Heb. 10:16
See also Jer. 31:33

He that said, Do not commit adultery, said also, Do not kill.
James 2:11

I write no new commandment unto you.
1 John 2:7

This is His commandment, That we should believe on the name of His Son Jesus Christ, and love one another.
1 John 3:23

[*See also* God's Word, Gospel, Law, Obedience, Scripture, Sin, and the Appendix at p. 419].

COMMITMENT

With all thy heart and with all thy soul.
E.g., Deut. 10:12
See also Deut. 11:13

I am my beloved's, and my beloved is mine.
Song 6:3

I am my beloved's, and his desire is toward me.
Song 7:10

Because they had no root, they withered away.
Jesus
Matt. 13:6
See also Mark 4:6

I seek not your's, but you.
2 Cor. 12:14

Let us run with patience the race that is set before us.
Heb. 12:1

Because thou art lukewarm, and neither cold nor hot, I will spue thee out of my mouth.
Jesus
Rev. 3:16
See also Rev. 3:15

[*See also* Devotion, Impartiality, Neutrality, Perseverance, Sincerity]

COMMON SENSE

See Wisdom.

COMMUNICATION

Let us go down, and there confound their language, that they may not understand one another's speech.
Gen. 11:7

Babel; because the Lord did there confound the language.
Gen. 11:9

Come now, and let us reason together, saith the Lord.
Isa. 1:18

He that speaketh in an unknown tongue speaketh not unto men, but unto God: for no man understandeth him.
1 Cor. 14:2

He that speaketh in an unknown tongue edifieth himself; but he that prophesieth edifieth the church.
1 Cor. 14:4

Greater is he that prophesieth than he that speaketh with tongues.
1 Cor. 14:5

Except ye utter by the tongue words easy to be understood, how shall it be known what is spoken? for ye shall speak into the air.
1 Cor. 14:9

If I know not the meaning of the voice, I shall be unto him that speaketh a barbar-

ian, and he that speaketh shall be a barbarian unto me.
1 Cor. 14:11

[*See also* Clarity, Eloquence, News, Speech]

COMMUNION

Take, eat; this is my body.
Jesus
Matt. 26:26, Mark 14:22

This is my blood of the new testament, which is shed for many for the remission of sins.
Jesus
Matt. 26:28
See also Mark 14:24, Luke 22:20

Except ye eat the flesh of the Son of man, and drink His blood, ye have no life in you.
Jesus
John 6:53
See also John 6:54

He that eateth me, even he shall live by me.
Jesus
John 6:57

This is my body, which is broken for you: this do in remembrance of me.
Jesus
1 Cor. 11:24
See also Luke 22:19

This cup is the new testament in my blood: this do ye, as oft as ye drink it, in remembrance of me.
Jesus
1 Cor. 11:25
See also Luke 22:20

[*See also* Bread of Life]

COMPANIONS

Put not thine hand with the wicked to be an unrighteous witness.
Ex. 23:1

Thou shalt not follow a multitude to do evil.
Ex. 23:2

Blessed is the man that walketh not in the counsel of the ungodly, nor standeth in the way of sinners, nor sitteth in the seat of the scornful.
Ps. 1:1

If sinners entice thee, consent thou not.
Prov. 1:10

Forsake the foolish, and live.
Prov. 9:6

He that walketh with wise men shall be wise: but a companion of fools shall be destroyed.
Prov. 13:20

He that is a companion of riotous men shameth his father.
Prov. 28:7

Thou dwellest in the midst of a rebellious house.
Ezek. 12:2

Depart from me, all ye workers of iniquity.
Jesus
Luke 13:27
See also Matt. 7:23

Evil communications corrupt good manners.
1 Cor. 15:33

Withdraw yourselves from every brother that walketh disorderly.
2 Thess. 3:6

[*See also* Cooperation, Fellowship, Friendship]

COMPASSION

Thou shalt not harden thine heart, nor shut thine hand from thy poor brother.
Deut. 15:7

Thou shalt open thine hand wide unto thy brother, to thy poor, and to thy needy, in thy land.
Deut. 15:11

Remember that thou wast a bondman in the land of Egypt, and the Lord thy God redeemed thee.
Deut. 15:15
See also Deut. 5:15, Deut. 24:22

Blessed be ye of the Lord; for ye have compassion on me.
> Saul
> *1 Sam. 23:21*

Deal gently for my sake with the young man, even with Absalom.
> *2 Sam. 18:5*

This day thou shalt bear no tidings, because the king's son is dead.
> *2 Sam. 18:20*

O my Lord, give her the living child, and in no wise slay it.
> *1 Kings 3:26*

Thine eyes shall not see all the evil which I will bring upon this place.
> *2 Kings 22:20*

Have pity upon me, O ye my friends; for the hand of God hath touched me.
> *Job 19:21*

I was eyes to the blind, and feet was I to the lame.
> *Job 29:15*

According to the greatness of Thy power preserve Thou those that are appointed to die.
> *Ps. 79:11*

The Lord is merciful and gracious, slow to anger, and plenteous in mercy.
> *Ps. 103:8*

As a father pitieth his children, so the Lord pitieth them that fear Him.
> *Ps. 103:13*

He knoweth our frame; He remembereth that we are dust.
> *Ps. 103:14*

He raiseth up the poor out of the dust, and lifteth the needy out of the dunghill.
> *Ps. 113:7*
> *See also 1 Sam. 2:8*

Let Thy tender mercies come unto me, that I may live.
> *Ps. 119:77*

Though the Lord be high, yet hath He respect unto the lowly.
> *Ps. 138:6*

The Lord is gracious, and full of compassion; slow to anger, and of great mercy.
> *Ps. 145:8*

He that hath mercy on the poor, happy is he.
> *Prov. 14:21*

He that honoureth Him hath mercy on the poor.
> *Prov. 14:31*

He that hath pity upon the poor lendeth unto the Lord; and that which he hath given will He pay him again.
> *Prov. 19:17*

Relieve the oppressed, judge the fatherless, plead for the widow.
> *Isa. 1:17*

I have heard thy prayer, I have seen thy tears: behold, I will add unto thy days fifteen years.
> God to Hezekiah
> *Isa. 38:5*
> *See also 2 Kings 20:5–6*

Can a woman forget her sucking child, that she should not have compassion on the son of her womb?
> *Isa. 49:15*

Is it not to deal thy bread to the hungry, and that thou bring the poor that are cast out to thy house?
> *Isa. 58:7*

In My wrath I smote thee, but in My favour have I had mercy on thee.
> *Isa. 60:10*

Thou art a gracious God, and merciful, slow to anger, and of great kindness, and repentest Thee of the evil.
> *Jonah 4:2*

Love mercy.
> *Mic. 6:8*

Show mercy and compassions every man to his brother.
> *Zech. 7:9*

Oppress not the widow, nor the fatherless, the stranger, nor the poor.
> *Zech. 7:10*

Pray for them which despitefully use you, and persecute you.
> Jesus
> *Matt. 5:44*
> *See also Luke 6:28*

For I was an hungred, and ye gave me meat: I was thirsty, and ye gave me drink: I

was a stranger, and ye took me in: Naked, and ye clothed me: I was sick, and ye visited me: I was in prison, and ye came unto me.
Jesus
Matt. 25:35–36

Inasmuch as ye have done it unto one of the least of these my brethren, ye have done it unto me.
Jesus
Matt. 25:40
See also Matt. 25:45

He hath filled the hungry with good things; and the rich He hath sent empty away.
Luke 1:53

The law was given by Moses, but grace and truth came by Jesus Christ.
John 1:17

Neither do I condemn thee: go, and sin no more.
Jesus
John 8:11

Comfort the feebleminded, support the weak, be patient toward all men.
1 Thess. 5:14

Remember them that are in bonds, as bound with them; and them which suffer adversity, as being yourselves also in the body.
Heb. 13:3

Love as brethren, be pitiful, be courteous.
1 Pet. 3:8

[*See also* Charity, Comfort, Empathy, God's Mercy, Kindness, Mercy, Suffering, Sympathy, Understanding]

COMPETITION

The race is not to the swift, nor the battle to the strong, neither yet bread to the wise, nor yet riches to men of understanding, nor yet favour to men of skill; but time and chance happeneth to them all.
Eccl. 9:11

If thou hast run with the footmen, and they have wearied thee, then how canst thou contend with horses?
Jer. 12:5

They which run in a race run all, but one receiveth the prize.
1 Cor. 9:24

Run, that ye may obtain.
1 Cor. 9:24

They do it to obtain a corruptible crown; but we an incorruptible.
1 Cor. 9:25

I press toward the mark for the prize of the high calling of God in Christ Jesus.
Phil. 3:14

I have fought a good fight, I have finished my course, I have kept the faith.
2 Tim. 4:7

Let us run with patience the race that is set before us.
Heb. 12:1

[*See also* Loss]

COMPLACENCY

Because thou art lukewarm, and neither cold nor hot, I will spue thee out of my mouth.
Jesus
Rev. 3:16
See also Rev. 3:15

COMPLAINTS

Ye have wept in the ears of the Lord.
Num. 11:18

Doth the wild ass bray when he hath grass?
Job 6:5

I will speak in the anguish of my spirit; I will complain in the bitterness of my soul.
Job 7:11

Should thy lies make men hold their peace?
Job 11:3

As for me, is my complaint to man?
Job 21:4

Why dost thou strive against Him? for He giveth not account of any of His matters.
Job 33:13

Wilt thou condemn Him that is most just?
Job 34:17

Neither murmur ye.
1 Cor. 10:10

Do all things without murmurings and disputings.
Phil. 2:14

Murmurers, complainers, walking after their own lusts.
Jude 16

[*See also* Acceptance, Contentment]

COMPROMISE

If thou wilt take the left hand, then I will go to the right; or if thou depart to the right hand, then I will go to the left.
Gen. 13:9

Peradventure there shall lack five of the fifty righteous: wilt Thou destroy all the city for lack of five?
Gen. 18:28

Do with them what seemeth good unto you: but unto this man do not so vile a thing.
Judg. 19:24

Divide the living child in two, and give half to the one, and half to the other.
1 Kings 3:25

Ye cannot serve God and mammon.
Jesus
Matt. 6:24, Luke 16:13

Ye cannot drink the cup of the Lord, and the cup of devils.
1 Cor. 10:21

[*See also* Arguments, Grudges, Mediation]

CONCEIT

To whom would the king delight to do honour more than to myself?
Haman
Esther 6:6

Art thou the first man that was born? or wast thou made before the hills?
Job 15:7

Hast thou heard the secret of God?
Job 15:8

Seest thou a man wise in his own conceit? there is more hope of a fool than of him.
Prov. 26:12

The sluggard is wiser in his own conceit than seven men that can render a reason.
Prov. 26:16

He that trusteth in his own heart is a fool.
Prov. 28:26

Be not righteous over much; neither make thyself over wise.
Eccl. 7:16

Woe unto them that are wise in their own eyes.
Isa. 5:21
See also Prov. 3:7

Thy wisdom and thy knowledge, it hath perverted thee; and thou hast said in thine heart, I am, and none else beside me.
Isa. 47:10

Thy terribleness hath deceived thee, and the pride of thine heart.
Jer. 49:16

But thou didst trust in thine own beauty.
Ezek. 16:15

Thou hast corrupted thy wisdom by reason of thy brightness.
Ezek. 28:17

The pride of thine heart hath deceived thee.
Obad. 3

Every one that exalteth himself shall be abased; and he that humbleth himself shall be exalted.
Jesus
Luke 18:14
See also Luke 14:11

They loved the praise of men more than the praise of God.
John 12:43

Jesus I know, and Paul I know; but who are ye?
Acts 19:15

Professing themselves to be wise, they became fools.
Rom. 1:22

Be not wise in your own conceits.
Rom. 12:16

I will destroy the wisdom of the wise, and

will bring to nothing the understanding of the prudent.
> 1 Cor. 1:19
> See also Isa. 29:14

Let no man deceive himself.
> 1 Cor. 3:18

Knowledge puffeth up, but charity edifieth.
> (charity: love)
> 1 Cor. 8:1

Let us not be desirous of vain glory.
> Gal. 5:26

If a man think himself to be something, when he is nothing, he deceiveth himself.
> Gal. 6:3

Let nothing be done through strife or vainglory.
> Phil. 2:3

[See also Arrogance, Boasting, Gloating, Humility, Pride, Self-Awareness, Self-Righteousness]

CONDUCT

See Behavior.

CONDUCT TOWARD GOD

Walk before Me, and be thou perfect.
> God to Abram
> Gen. 17:1

What doth the Lord thy God require of thee, but to fear the Lord thy God, to walk in all His ways, and to love Him, and to serve the Lord thy God with all thy heart and with all thy soul.
> Deut. 10:12

Thou shalt fear the Lord thy God; Him shalt thou serve, and to Him shalt thou cleave, and swear by His name.
> Deut. 10:20
> See also Deut. 6:13

Thou shalt be perfect with the Lord thy God.
> Deut. 18:13

How should man be just with God?
> Job 9:2

[See also Behavior, Fear of God, Love of God, Service to God, and the Appendix at p. 419]

CONFESSION

I have sinned against the Lord.
> David
> 2 Sam. 12:13

We have sinned, and have done perversely, we have committed wickedness.
> 1 Kings 8:47

We have sinned, we have done amiss, and have dealt wickedly.
> 2 Chron. 6:37

My sin is ever before me.
> Ps. 51:3

My sins are not hid from Thee.
> Ps. 69:5

We have sinned with our fathers, we have committed iniquity, we have done wickedly.
> Ps. 106:6

Acknowledge thine iniquity, that thou hast transgressed against the Lord.
> Jer. 3:13

We have sinned against the Lord our God, we and our fathers, from our youth even unto this day.
> Jer. 3:25

We have sinned, we have done wickedly.
> Dan. 9:15

Depart from me; for I am a sinful man, O Lord.
> Luke 5:8

Father, I have sinned against heaven, and before thee.
> Luke 15:18
> See also Luke 15:21

Confess your faults one to another.
> James 5:16

If we confess our sins, He is faithful and just to forgive us our sins.
> 1 John 1:9

[See also Acknowledgment, Contrition, Forgiveness, Repentance]

CONFIDENCE

Let us go up at once, and possess it; for we are well able to overcome it.
> (it: Canaan)
> *Num. 13:30*

Is not the Lord gone out before thee?
> *Judg. 4:14*

There is no restraint to the Lord to save by many or by few.
> Jonathan
> *1 Sam. 14:6*

The Lord that delivered me out of the paw of the lion, and out of the paw of the bear, He will deliver me out of the hand of this Philistine.
> David
> *1 Sam. 17:37*

This day will the Lord deliver thee into mine hand.
> David to Goliath
> *1 Sam. 17:46*

The battle is the Lord's.
> *1 Sam. 17:47*

Be strong, and of good courage; dread not, nor be dismayed.
> *E.g., 1 Chron. 22:13*

Our God shall fight for us.
> *Neh. 4:20*

Let me be weighed in an even balance, that God may know mine integrity.
> *Job 31:6*

Yea, though I walk through the valley of the shadow of death, I will fear no evil: for Thou art with me.
> *Ps. 23:4*

Be of good courage, and He shall strengthen your heart, all ye that hope in the Lord.
> *Ps. 31:24*
> *See also Ps. 27:14*

He only is my rock and my salvation: He is my defence; I shall not be moved.
> *Ps. 62:6*

In Thee, O Lord, do I put my trust.
> *Ps. 71:1*
> *See also, e.g., 1 Sam. 22:3*

The Lord is on my side; I will not fear: what can man do unto me?
> *Ps. 118:6*

He that walketh uprightly walketh surely.
> *Prov. 10:9*

Lift up thy voice with strength; lift it up, be not afraid.
> *Isa. 40:9*

Thy God whom thou servest continually, He will deliver thee.
> *Dan. 6:16*

The flight shall perish from the swift, and the strong shall not strengthen his force, neither shall the mighty deliver himself.
> *Amos 2:14*

Rejoice not against me, O mine enemy: when I fall, I shall arise.
> *Mic. 7:8*

With God all things are possible.
> Jesus
> *Matt. 19:26, Mark 10:27*
> *See also Luke 18:27*

All things are possible to him that believeth.
> Jesus
> *Mark 9:23*

If God be for us, who can be against us?
> *Rom. 8:31*

Let him that thinketh he standeth take heed lest he fall.
> *1 Cor. 10:12*

I can do all things through Christ which strengtheneth me.
> *Phil. 4:13*

Fathers, provoke not your children to anger, lest they be discouraged.
> *Col. 3:21*

Be not soon shaken in mind.
> *2 Thess. 2:2*

God hath not given us the spirit of fear; but of power, and of love, and of a sound mind.
> *2 Tim. 1:7*

I am not ashamed: for I know whom I have believed.
> *2 Tim. 1:12*

Cast not away therefore your confidence, which hath great recompence of reward.
> *Heb. 10:35*

Lift up the hands which hang down, and
the feeble knees.
Heb. 12:12

The Lord is my helper, and I will not fear
what man shall do unto me.
Heb. 13:6

[*See also* Courage, Faith, Pride, Reliability, Timidity]

CONFLICT OF INTEREST

See Allegiance, Loyalty.

CONFORMITY

Be not conformed to this world.
Rom. 12:2

For though we walk in the flesh, we do not
war after the flesh.
2 Cor. 10:3

Know ye not that the friendship of the
world is enmity with God?
James 4:4

They think it strange that ye run not with
them to the same excess of riot.
1 Pet. 4:4

Love not the world, neither the things that
are in the world.
1 John 2:15

[*See also* Behavior, Worldliness]

CONFUSION

Let us go down, and there confound their
language, that they may not understand
one another's speech.
Gen. 11:7

Babel; because the Lord did there confound the language.
Gen. 11:9

Where envying and strife is, there is confusion and every evil work.
James 3:16

[*See also* Chaos]

CONQUEST

If the Lord delight in us, then He will bring
us into this land.
Joshua and Caleb
Num. 14:8

There shall not a man of them stand before
thee.
God to Joshua
Josh. 10:8

The hill is not enough for us.
Josh. 17:16

Ye shall possess their land, as the Lord
your God hath promised unto you.
Josh. 23:5

Behold, I have delivered the land into his
hand.
Judg. 1:2

Whomsoever the Lord our God shall drive
out from before us, them will we possess.
Judg. 11:24

We will light upon him as the dew falleth
on the ground.
2 Sam. 17:12

There was none that moved the wing, or
opened the mouth, or peeped.
Isa. 10:14

They are cruel, and have no mercy; their
voice roareth like the sea.
Jer. 6:23

She that was great among the nations, and
princess among the provinces, how is she
become tributary!
Lam. 1:1

Our inheritance is turned to strangers, our
houses to aliens.
Lam. 5:2

[*See also* War]

CONSCIENCE

Thou knowest all the wickedness which
thine heart is privy to.
1 Kings 2:44

My righteousness I hold fast, and will not
let it go: my heart shall not reproach me so
long as I live.
Job 27:6

The wicked flee when no man pursueth.
   Prov. 28:1

Whether it be right in the sight of God to
hearken unto you more than unto God,
judge ye.
   Acts 4:19

I have lived in all good conscience before
God until this day.
   Acts 23:1

Herein do I exercise myself, to have always
a conscience void of offence toward God,
and toward men.
   Acts 24:16

We trust we have a good conscience, in all
things willing to live honestly.
   Heb. 13:18

[*See also* Guilt, Honesty, Integrity, Soul]

CONSECRATION

Sanctify unto Me all the firstborn.
   Ex. 13:2

The males shall be the Lord's.
   Ex. 13:12

The firstborn of thy sons shalt thou give
unto Me.
   Ex. 22:29

The tabernacle shall be sanctified by My
glory.
   Ex. 29:43

Every male that openeth the womb shall
be called holy to the Lord.
   Luke 2:23

[*See also* Holiness]

CONSEQUENCES

His wife looked back from behind him, and
she became a pillar of salt.
   Gen. 19:26

Because ye are turned away from the Lord,
therefore the Lord will not be with you.
   Num. 14:43

Because thou hast rejected the word of the

Lord, He hath also rejected thee from
being king.
   Samuel to Saul
   1 Sam. 15:23

Thus saith the Lord, Ye have forsaken Me,
and therefore have I also left you.
   2 Chron. 12:5

Let me alone, that I may speak, and let
come on me what will.
   Job 13:13

His mischief shall return upon his own
head.
   Ps. 7:16

The labour of the righteous tendeth to life:
the fruit of the wicked to sin.
   Prov. 10:16

With what measure ye mete, it shall be
measured to you.
   Jesus
   Mark 4:24
   See also Luke 6:38

Give, and it shall be given unto you.
   Jesus
   Luke 6:38

By one man's disobedience many were
made sinners.
   Rom. 5:19

He that soweth to his flesh shall of the flesh
reap corruption; but he that soweth to the
Spirit shall of the Spirit reap life everlasting.
   Gal. 6:8

If we deny Him, He also will deny us.
   2 Tim. 2:12

[*See also* Punishment, Reciprocity, Retribution, Revenge, Reward]

CONSISTENCY

Of thorns men do not gather figs, nor of a
bramble bush gather they grapes.
   Jesus
   Luke 6:44

He that is faithful in that which is least is
faithful also in much.
   Jesus
   Luke 16:10

He that is unjust in the least is unjust also in much.
Jesus
Luke 16:10

Doth a fountain send forth at the same place sweet water and bitter?
James 3:11

Can the fig tree, my brethren, bear olive berries?
James 3:12

[*See also* Adaptability, Character]

CONSPIRACY

See Betrayal, Crime.

CONTAMINATION

Shall one man sin, and wilt Thou be wroth with all the congregation?
Num. 16:22

Keep yourselves from the accursed thing, lest ye make yourselves accursed.
Josh. 6:18

A little leaven leaveneth the whole lump.
1 Cor. 5:6, Gal. 5:9

Be not partakers of her sins.
(her: Babylon)
Rev. 18:4

[*See also* Corruption, Purity]

CONTEMPLATION

Whatsoever things are true, whatsoever things are honest, whatsoever things are just, whatsoever things are pure, whatsoever things are lovely, whatsoever things are of good report; if there be any virtue, and if there be any praise, think on these things.
Phil. 4:8

[*See also* Thoughts]

CONTEMPT

Am I a dog, that thou comest to me with staves?
Goliath to David
1 Sam. 17:43

If thou wilt give me half thine house, I will not go in with thee, neither will I eat bread nor drink water in this place.
1 Kings 13:8

They that are younger than I have me in derision, whose fathers I would have disdained to have set with the dogs of my flock.
Job 30:1

Blessed are ye, when men shall revile you, and persecute you, and shall say all manner of evil against you falsely, for my sake.
Jesus
Matt. 5:11

[*See also* Hatred, Scorn]

CONTENTMENT

Would to God we had been content, and dwelt on the other side Jordan!
Josh. 7:7

Should I forsake my sweetness, and my good fruit, and go to be promoted over the trees?
Fig tree to other trees
Judg. 9:11

Should I leave my wine, which cheereth God and man, and go to be promoted over the trees?
Vine to trees
Judg. 9:13

Doth the wild ass bray when he hath grass?
Job 6:5

Better is little with the fear of the Lord than great treasure and trouble therewith.
Prov. 15:16

Give me neither poverty nor riches; feed me with food convenient for me.
Prov. 30:8

The eye is not satisfied with seeing, nor the ear filled with hearing.
Eccl. 1:8

Better is an handful with quietness, than

both the hands full with travail and vexation of spirit.
Eccl. 4:6

Mine eyes have seen Thy salvation, Which Thou hast prepared before the face of all people.
Simeon
Luke 2:30–31

We have peace with God through our Lord Jesus Christ.
Rom. 5:1

As the Lord hath called every one, so let him walk.
1 Cor. 7:17

Let every man abide in the same calling wherein he was called.
1 Cor. 7:20

The peace of God, which passeth all understanding.
Phil. 4:7

I have learned, in whatsoever state I am, therewith to be content.
Phil. 4:11

Godliness with contentment is great gain.
1 Tim. 6:6

Be content with such things as ye have.
Heb. 13:5

They shall hunger no more, neither thirst any more; neither shall the sun light on them, nor any heat.
Rev. 7:16

[*See also* Greed, Happiness, Satisfaction, Serenity]

CONTINUITY

As I was with Moses, so I will be with thee.
God to Joshua
Josh. 1:5, Josh. 3:7

The sun also ariseth.
Eccl. 1:5

Unto the place from whence the rivers come, thither they return again.
Eccl. 1:7

A time to be born, and a time to die; a time to plant, and a time to pluck up that which is planted.
Eccl. 3:2

The morning cometh, and also the night.
Isa. 21:12

CONTRITION

Thou art more righteous than I: for thou hast rewarded me good, whereas I have rewarded thee evil.
Saul to David
1 Sam. 24:17

I have sinned.
Saul to David
1 Sam. 26:21

Behold, I have played the fool, and have erred exceedingly.
1 Sam. 26:21

I beseech Thee, O Lord, take away the iniquity of Thy servant; for I have done very foolishly.
David to God
2 Sam. 24:10

Because he humbleth himself before Me, I will not bring the evil in his days: but in his son's days will I bring the evil.
1 Kings 21:29

Thou hast done right, but we have done wickedly.
Israelites to God
Neh. 9:33

Behold, I am vile; what shall I answer Thee?
Job to God
Job 40:4

A broken and a contrite heart, O God, Thou wilt not despise.
Ps. 51:17

I have gone astray like a lost sheep; seek Thy servant.
Ps. 119:176
See also Isa. 53:6

God be merciful to me a sinner.
Luke 18:13

Lord, remember me when Thou comest into Thy kingdom.
Malefactor, on cross, to Jesus
Luke 23:42

Many of the saints did I shut up in prison.
Paul
Acts 26:10

[See also Confession, Humility, Regret]

CONTROVERSY

Him that is weak in the faith receive ye, but not to doubtful disputations.
Rom. 14:1

Foolish and unlearned questions avoid, knowing that they do gender strifes.
2 Tim. 2:23

The servant of the Lord must not strive.
2 Tim. 2:24

Avoid foolish questions.
Titus 3:9

A man that is an heretick after the first and second admonition reject.
Titus 3:10

[See also Anger, Arguments, Strife]

CONVERSION

Thy people shall be my people, and thy God my God.
Ruth 1:16

I am sought of them that asked not for Me; I am found of them that sought Me not.
Isa. 65:1
See also Rom. 10:20

Except ye be converted, and become as little children, ye shall not enter into the kingdom of heaven.
Jesus
Matt. 18:3

Repent ye therefore, and be converted, that your sins may be blotted out.
Acts 3:19

Lord, what wilt Thou have me to do?
Saul to Jesus
Acts 9:6

There fell from his eyes as it had been scales: and he received sight forthwith, and arose, and was baptized.
(he: Saul)
Acts 9:18

The hand of the Lord was with them: and a great number believed.
Acts 11:21

Seeing ye put it from you, and judge

yourselves unworthy of everlasting life, lo, we turn to the Gentiles.
Paul to Jews
Acts 13:46

I have set thee to be a light of the Gentiles, that thou shouldest be for salvation unto the ends of the earth.
Acts 13:47
See also Isa. 49:6

God, which knoweth the hearts, bare them witness, giving them the Holy Ghost.
Acts 15:8

He which persecuted us in times past now preacheth the faith which once he destroyed.
(He: Paul)
Gal. 1:23

[See also Born Again, Evangelism, Jesus (Acceptance of)]

COOPERATION

Now nothing will be restrained from them, which they have imagined to do.
Gen. 11:6

Is not the hand of Joab with thee in all this?
2 Sam. 14:19

I am as thou art, and my people as thy people.
2 Chron. 18:3
See also 1 Kings 22:4

Shouldest thou help the ungodly, and love them that hate the Lord?
2 Chron. 19:2

Through wisdom is an house builded; and by understanding it is established.
Prov. 24:3

Two are better than one; because they have a good reward for their labour.
Eccl. 4:9

Woe to him that is alone when he falleth; for he hath not another to help him up.
Eccl. 4:10

If two lie together, then they have heat: but how can one be warm alone?
Eccl. 4:11

A threefold cord is not quickly broken.
Eccl. 4:12

Can two walk together, except they be agreed?
Amos 3:3

Whosoever shall compel thee to go a mile, go with him twain.
Jesus
Matt. 5:41

One soweth, and another reapeth.
Jesus
John 4:37

He that planteth and he that watereth are one.
1 Cor. 3:8

Let us walk by the same rule, let us mind the same thing.
Phil. 3:16

He that biddeth him God speed is partaker of his evil deeds.
2 John 11

See also Brotherhood, Planning, Unity, Work]

CORRUPTION

Thou canst not stand before thine enemies, until ye take away the accursed thing from among you.
Josh. 7:13

Wherefore kick ye at My sacrifice and at Mine offering?
1 Sam. 2:29

will raise Me up a faithful priest.
1 Sam. 2:35

His sons walked not in his ways, but turned aside after lucre.
1 Sam. 8:3

Hast thou killed, and also taken possession?
(thou: Ahab)
1 Kings 21:19

Who can bring a clean thing out of an unclean? not one.
Job 14:4

Fire shall consume the tabernacles of bribery.
Job 15:34

There is none that doeth good, no, not one.
Ps. 14:3, Ps. 53:3, Rom. 3:12

Lord, how long shall the wicked, how long shall the wicked triumph?
Ps. 94:3

The profit of the earth is for all: the king himself is served by the field.
Eccl. 5:9

One sinner destroyeth much good.
Eccl. 9:18

From the least of them even unto the greatest of them every one is given to covetousness; and from the prophet even unto the priest every one dealeth falsely.
Jer. 6:13
See also Jer. 8:10

Woe unto him that buildeth his house by unrighteousness, and his chambers by wrong.
Jer. 22:13

All that honoured her despise her, because they have seen her nakedness.
Lam. 1:8

Woe be to the shepherds of Israel that do feed themselves! should not the shepherds feed the flocks?
Ezek. 34:2

They sold the righteous for silver, and the poor for a pair of shoes.
Amos 2:6

Ye have turned judgment into gall, and the fruit of righteousness into hemlock.
Amos 6:12

The best of them is as a brier: the most upright is sharper than a thorn hedge.
Mic. 7:4

Do violence to no man, neither accuse any falsely.
Luke 3:14

Save yourselves from this untoward generation.
Acts 2:40

Keep thyself pure.
1 Tim. 5:22

Unto them that are defiled and unbelieving is nothing pure; but even their mind and conscience is defiled.
Titus 1:15

The law maketh men high priests which have infirmity.
Heb. 7:28

If ye have respect to persons, ye commit sin.
James 2:9

All nations have drunk of the wine of the wrath of her fornication.
(her: Babylon)
Rev. 18:3

The merchants of the earth are waxed rich through the abundance of her delicacies.
(her: Babylon)
Rev. 18:3

[*See also* Bribery, Decadence, Good and Evil, Honesty, Injustice, Lawlessness, Purity, Wickedness]

COURAGE

Be strong, and quit yourselves like men.
1 Sam. 4:9

Let no man's heart fail because of him; thy servant will go and fight with this Philistine.
David, about Goliath
1 Sam. 17:32

They were swifter than eagles, they were stronger than lions.
2 Sam. 1:23

Let us play the men for our people.
2 Sam. 10:12

Is not this the blood of the men that went in jeopardy of their lives?
2 Sam. 23:17

With the jeopardy of their lives they brought it.
1 Chron. 11:19

Be of good courage.
E.g., 1 Chron. 19:13

Should such a man as I flee?
Neh. 6:11

He mocketh at fear, and is not affrighted; neither turneth he back from the sword.
Job 39:22

The Lord is the strength of my life; of whom shall I be afraid?
Ps. 27:1

Be of good courage, and He shall strengthen your heart, all ye that hope in the Lord.
Ps. 31:24
See also Ps. 27:14

I have trodden the winepress alone; and of the people there was none with me.
Isa. 63:3

Be not afraid of them, neither be afraid of their words.
Ezek. 2:6

When my soul fainted within me I remembered the Lord.
Jonah 2:7

Fear not, but let your hands be strong.
Zech. 8:13

The voice of one crying in the wilderness.
Matt. 3:3, Mark 1:3,
Luke 3:4, John 1:23
See also Isa. 40:3

Let them come themselves and fetch us out.
Acts 16:37

As thou hast testified of me in Jerusalem, so must thou bear witness also at Rome.
Jesus
Acts 23:11

Be strong in the Lord, and in the power of His might.
Eph. 6:10

Fear none of those things which thou shalt suffer.
Jesus
Rev. 2:10

[*See also* Confidence, Encouragement, Fear]

COURTESY

The poor useth intreaties; but the rich answereth roughly.
Prov. 18:23

Give none offence.
1 Cor. 10:32

Let your speech be alway with grace, seasoned with salt, that ye may know how ye ought to answer every man.
Col. 4:6

Love as brethren, be pitiful, be courteous.
1 Pet. 3:8

■ 70 ■

[*See also* Behavior, Hospitality]

COVENANT

Neither shall there any more be a flood to destroy the earth.
Gen. 9:11

I do set My bow in the cloud, and it shall be for a token of a covenant between Me and the earth.
God to Noah
Gen. 9:13

I will make of thee a great nation.
God to Abram
Gen. 12:2

In thee shall all families of the earth be blessed.
God to Abram
Gen. 12:3
See also Gen. 28:14

My covenant is with thee, and thou shalt be a father of many nations.
God to Abram
Gen. 17:4

Ye shall circumcise the flesh of your foreskin; and it shall be a token of the covenant betwixt Me and you.
Gen. 17:11

I will multiply thy seed as the stars of the heaven, and as the sand which is upon the sea shore.
God to Abraham
Gen. 22:17

Thy seed shall be as the dust of the earth.
God to Jacob
Gen. 28:14
See also Gen. 13:16

It is a covenant of salt for ever before the Lord.
Num. 18:19

He will not forsake thee, neither destroy thee, nor forget the covenant of thy fathers which He sware unto them.
Deut. 4:31

The Lord made not this covenant with our fathers, but with us, even us, who are all of us here alive this day.
Deut. 5:3

There hath not failed one word of all His good promise.
1 Kings 8:56

The covenant that I have made with you ye shall not forget; neither shall ye fear other gods.
2 Kings 17:38

Unto thee will I give the land of Canaan, the lot of your inheritance.
1 Chron. 16:18, Ps. 105:11

I will ordain a place for My people Israel.
1 Chron. 17:9

He will ever be mindful of His covenant.
Ps. 111:5
See also 1 Chron. 16:15

Cursed be the man that obeyeth not the words of this covenant.
Jer. 11:3

Remember, break not Thy covenant with us.
Jer. 14:21

Ye shall be My people, and I will be your God.
E.g., Jer. 30:22
See also Jer. 24:7

Come, and let us join ourselves to the Lord.
Jer. 50:5

This is my blood of the new testament, which is shed for many for the remission of sins.
Jesus
Matt. 26:28
See also Mark 14:24, Luke 22:20

This cup is the new testament in my blood: this do ye, as oft as ye drink it, in remembrance of me.
Jesus
1 Cor. 11:25
See also Luke 22:20

If that first covenant had been faultless, then should no place have been sought for the second.
Heb. 8:7

In that He saith, A new covenant, He hath made the first old.
Heb. 8:13

[*See also* Chosen People, Circumcision]

COWARDICE

The sound of a shaken leaf shall chase them.
Lev. 26:36

We be not able to go up against the people; for they are stronger than we.
Num. 13:31

The hearts of the people melted, and became as water.
Josh. 7:5

O Lord, what shall I say, when Israel turneth their backs before their enemies!
Josh. 7:8

As people being ashamed steal away when they flee in battle.
2 Sam. 19:3

Should such a man as I flee?
Neh. 6:11

Their might hath failed; they became as women.
Jer. 51:30

[*See also* Defeat, Fear, Timidity]

CREATION

In the beginning God created the heaven and the earth.
Gen. 1:1

The earth was without form, and void; and darkness was upon the face of the deep.
Gen. 1:2

And God said, Let there be light: and there was light.
Gen. 1:3

And God made two great lights; the greater light to rule the day, and the lesser light to rule the night.
Gen. 1:16

God created man in His own image, in the image of God created He him; male and female created He them.
Gen. 1:27
See also Gen. 5:1–2

And God saw every thing that He had made, and, behold, it was very good.
Gen. 1:31

The Lord God formed man of the dust of the ground, and breathed into his nostrils the breath of life.
Gen. 2:7

The rib, which the Lord God had taken from man, made He a woman.
Gen. 2:22

Male and female created He them; and blessed them.
Gen. 5:2

It repented the Lord that He had made man on the earth.
Gen. 6:6

Who hath made man's mouth? or who maketh the dumb, or deaf, or the seeing, or the blind? have not I the Lord?
Ex. 4:11

In six days the Lord made heaven and earth, the sea, and all that in them is.
Ex. 20:11

In six days the Lord made heaven and earth, and on the seventh day He rested, and was refreshed.
Ex. 31:17

Hast Thou not poured me out as milk, and curdled me like cheese?
Job 10:10

He stretcheth out the north over the empty place, and hangeth the earth upon nothing.
Job 26:7

Who laid the corner stone thereof?
Job 38:6

By the word of the Lord were the heavens made.
Ps. 33:6

He spake, and it was done; He commanded, and it stood fast.
Ps. 33:9

It is He that hath made us, and not we ourselves.
Ps. 100:3

I will praise Thee; for I am fearfully and wonderfully made.
Ps. 139:14

The Lord hath made all things for Himself: yea, even the wicked for the day of evil.
Prov. 16:4

I have created him for My glory, I have formed him; yea, I have made him.
Isa. 43:7

He hath established it, He created it not in vain, He formed it to be inhabited.
Isa. 45:18

We are the clay, and Thou our potter.
Isa. 64:8

We all are the work of Thy hand.
Isa. 64:8

I create new heavens and a new earth: and the former shall not be remembered, nor come into mind.
Isa. 65:17

He hath made the earth by His power.
Jer. 10:12

He hath established the world by His wisdom, and hath stretched out the heavens by His discretion.
Jer. 10:12

He hath made the earth by His power, He hath established the world by His wisdom.
Jer. 51:15

Without Him was not any thing made.
John 1:3

Lord, Thou art God, which hast made heaven, and earth, and the sea.
Acts 4:24

Hath not My hand made all these things?
Acts 7:50
See also Isa. 66:2

The man is not of the woman; but the woman of the man.
1 Cor. 11:8

By Him were all things created, that are in heaven, and that are in earth.
(Him: Jesus)
Col. 1:16

Every house is builded by some man; but He that built all things is God.
Heb. 3:4

[*See also* Beginnings]

CREATIVITY

See Achievement, Building, Planning.

CREDIBILITY

Is the Lord's hand waxed short?
Num. 11:23

I have not said in vain that I would do this evil unto them.
Ezek. 6:10

How can ye, being evil, speak good things?
Jesus
Matt. 12:34

If I bear witness of myself, my witness is not true.
Jesus
John 5:31

If we receive the witness of men, the witness of God is greater.
1 John 5:9

[*See also* Belief, Doubt, Skepticism]

CRIME

Thou shalt not steal.
Eighth Commandment
Ex. 20:15
See also Lev. 19:11, Deut. 5:19, Matt. 19:18

Ye shall not pollute the land wherein ye are.
Num. 35:33

Defile not therefore the land which ye shall inhabit.
Num. 35:34

Why hast thou troubled us? the Lord shall trouble thee this day.
Joshua to Achan
Josh. 7:25

Wickedness proceedeth from the wicked: but mine hand shall not be upon thee.
1 Sam. 24:13

Enter not into the path of the wicked, and go not in the way of evil men.
Prov. 4:14

Men do not despise a thief, if he steal to satisfy his soul when he is hungry.
Prov. 6:30

Treasures of wickedness profit nothing.
Prov. 10:2

He that pursueth evil pursueth it to his own death.
Prov. 11:19

Whoso is partner with a thief hateth his own soul.
Prov. 29:24

Woe to the bloody city! it is all full of lies and robbery.
(it: Nineveh)
Nah. 3:1

The thief cometh not, but for to steal, and to kill, and to destroy.
Jesus
John 10:10

[*See also* Depravity, Evil, Lawlessness, Restitution, Scheming, Wicked People, Wickedness]

CRIMINALS

He taketh the wise in their own craftiness.
Job 5:13

They are of those that rebel against the light.
Job 24:13

The morning is to them even as the shadow of death.
Job 24:17

There is no darkness, nor shadow of death, where the workers of iniquity may hide themselves.
Job 34:22

They say, Who shall see them?
Ps. 64:5

As a cage is full of birds, so are their houses full of deceit.
Jer. 5:27

They consider not in their hearts that I remember all their wickedness.
Hos. 7:2

Woe to them that devise iniquity, and work evil upon their beds!
Mic. 2:1

Woe to him that increaseth that which is not his!
Hab. 2:6

Let him that stole steal no more: but rather let him labour, working with his hands.
Eph. 4:28

[*See also* Crime, Depravity, Evil, Lawlessness, Restitution, Scheming, Wicked People, Wickedness]

CRITICISM

Ye are forgers of lies, ye are all physicians of no value.
Job to his friends
Job 13:4

The foolish man reproacheth Thee daily.
Ps. 74:22

Reprove not a scorner, lest he hate thee: rebuke a wise man, and he will love thee.
Prov. 9:8

He that refuseth reproof erreth.
Prov. 10:17

Whoso loveth instruction loveth knowledge: but he that hateth reproof is brutish.
Prov. 12:1

A wise son heareth his father's instruction: but a scorner heareth not rebuke.
Prov. 13:1

A fool despiseth his father's instruction.
Prov. 15:5

He that hateth reproof shall die.
Prov. 15:10

A scorner loveth not one that reproveth him.
Prov. 15:12

A reproof entereth more into a wise man than an hundred stripes into a fool.
Prov. 17:10

Faithful are the wounds of a friend; but the kisses of an enemy are deceitful.
Prov. 27:6

It is better to hear the rebuke of the wise, than for a man to hear the song of fools.
Eccl. 7:5

Take no heed unto all words that are spoken; lest thou hear thy servant curse thee.
Eccl. 7:21

He hath made my mouth like a sharp sword.
Isa. 49:2

Fear ye not the reproach of men, neither be ye afraid of their revilings.
Isa. 51:7

They hate him that rebuketh in the gate, and they abhor him that speaketh uprightly.
Amos 5:10

Judge not, that ye be not judged.
Jesus
Matt. 7:1

With what judgment ye judge, ye shall be judged.
Jesus
Matt. 7:2

First cast out the beam out of thine own eye; and then shalt thou see clearly to cast out the mote out of thy brother's eye.
Jesus
Matt. 7:5
See also Luke 6:42

Physician, heal thyself.
Luke 4:23

Judge not, and ye shall not be judged: condemn not, and ye shall not be condemned.
Jesus
Luke 6:37

If thy brother trespass against thee, rebuke him; and if he repent, forgive him.
Jesus
Luke 17:3

Ye judge after the flesh; I judge no man.
Jesus
John 8:15

Wherein thou judgest another, thou condemnest thyself.
Rom. 2:1

Who art thou that judgest another man's servant?
Rom. 14:4

No chastening for the present seemeth to be joyous.
Heb. 12:11

Who art thou that judgest another?
James 4:12

What glory is it, if, when ye be buffeted for your faults, ye shall take it patiently?
1 Pet. 2:20

If, when ye do well, and suffer for it, ye take it patiently, this is acceptable with God.
1 Pet. 2:20

[*See also* Accusations, Chastisement, Discipline, Guidance, Public Opinion, Scorn, Slander]

CRUCIFIXION

They shall mock Him, and shall scourge Him, and shall spit upon Him, and shall kill Him: and the third day He shall rise again.
Jesus
Mark 10:34
See also Luke 18:33

Father, into Thy hands I commend my spirit.
Jesus
Luke 23:46

Ye shall weep and lament, but the world shall rejoice.
Jesus
John 16:20

They cried out, saying, Crucify Him, crucify Him.
John 19:6, Luke 23:21
See also, e.g., Matt. 27:23, Mark 15:13

He bowed His head, and gave up the ghost.
John 19:30

Through ignorance ye did it.
Acts 3:17

Christ died for the ungodly.
Rom. 5:6

Christ died for us.
Rom. 5:8

In that He died, He died unto sin once: but in that He liveth, He liveth unto God.
Rom. 6:10

We preach Christ crucified, unto the Jews a stumblingblock, and unto the Greeks foolishness.
1 Cor. 1:23

Had they known it, they would not have crucified the Lord.
1 Cor. 2:8

Christ died for our sins.
1 Cor. 15:3

He died for all.
2 Cor. 5:15

I am crucified with Christ: nevertheless I live.
Gal. 2:20

Ye who sometimes were far off are made nigh by the blood of Christ.
Eph. 2:13

If God so loved us, we ought also to love one another.
1 John 4:11

Worthy is the Lamb that was slain.
Rev. 5:12 '

[*See also* Jesus (Last Words on the Cross), Martyrdom, Messianic Hopes and Prophecies, Sacrifice]

CRUELTY

I will harden his heart, that he shall not let the people go.
Ex. 4:21

Let me not fall into the hand of man.
1 Chron. 21:13, 2 Sam. 24:14

In my thirst they gave me vinegar to drink.
Ps. 69:21

The merciful man doeth good to his own soul: but he that is cruel troubleth his own flesh.
Prov. 11:17

The tender mercies of the wicked are cruel.
Prov. 12:10

They shall have no pity on the fruit of the womb; their eye shall not spare children.
Isa. 13:18

They are cruel, and have no mercy; their voice roareth like the sea.
Jer. 6:23

They sold the righteous for silver, and the poor for a pair of shoes.
Amos 2:6

I was an hungred, and ye gave me no meat: I was thirsty, and ye gave me no drink.
Jesus
Matt. 25:42

He shall have judgment without mercy, that hath showed no mercy.
James 2:13

[*See also* Oppression, Persecution, Tyranny]

CULTIVATION

Six years thou shalt sow thy land, and shalt gather in the fruits thereof: But the seventh year thou shalt let it rest and lie still; that the poor of thy people may eat.
Ex. 23:10–11

He causeth the grass to grow for the cattle, and herb for the service of man.
Ps. 104:14

They that sow in tears shall reap in joy.
Ps. 126:5

He that goeth forth and weepeth, bearing precious seed, shall doubtless come again with rejoicing, bringing his sheaves with him.
Ps. 126:6

A time to plant, and a time to pluck up.
Eccl. 3:2

I have planted, Apollos watered; but God gave the increase.
1 Cor. 3:6

He that planteth and he that watereth are one.
1 Cor. 3:8

[*See also* Growth, Nature]

CURSES

Upon thy belly shalt thou go, and dust shalt thou eat all the days of thy life.
God to serpent
Gen. 3:14

A fugitive and a vagabond shalt thou be in the earth.
Gen. 4:12

How shall I curse, whom God hath not

cursed? or how shall I defy, whom the Lord hath not defied?
> Balaam to Balak
> *Num. 23:8*

Cursed be the man before the Lord, that riseth up and buildeth this city Jericho.
> *Josh. 6:26*

The sword shall never depart from thine house.
> (thine: David)
> *2 Sam. 12:10*

Get thee to thine own house: and when thy feet enter into the city, the child shall die.
> *1 Kings 14:12*

Touch all that he hath, and he will curse Thee to Thy face.
> Satan to God, about Job
> *Job 1:11*

Dost thou still retain thine integrity? curse God, and die.
> Job's wife to Job
> *Job 2:9*

Let their way be dark and slippery.
> *Ps. 35:6*

Let his children be fatherless, and his wife a widow.
> *Ps. 109:9*

I will prepare thee unto blood, and blood shall pursue thee.
> *Ezek. 35:6*

Give them, O Lord: what wilt Thou give? give them a miscarrying womb and dry breasts.
> *Hos. 9:14*

Thou shalt eat, but not be satisfied.
> *Mic. 6:14*

I will curse your blessings.
> God to wayward priests
> *Mal. 2:2*

Bless them that curse you.
> Jesus
> *Matt. 5:44, Luke 6:28*

Bless them which persecute you: bless, and curse not.
> *Rom. 12:14*

If any man love not the Lord Jesus Christ, let him be Anathema.
> *1 Cor. 16:22*

[*See also* Blasphemy, Blessing, Disobedience, Profanity, Punishment, Speech]

CYNICISM

The sword devoureth one as well as another.
> David, about Bathsheba's husband
> *2 Sam. 11:25*

Vanity of vanities; all is vanity.
> *Eccl. 1:2*
> See also Eccl. 12:8

Behold, all is vanity and vexation of spirit.
> *Eccl. 1:14*
> See also, e.g., Eccl. 2:17

He that increaseth knowledge increaseth sorrow.
> *Eccl. 1:18*

What hath man of all his labour, and of the vexation of his heart, wherein he hath laboured under the sun?
> *Eccl. 2:22*

What profit hath he that hath laboured for the wind?
> *Eccl. 5:16*

A man hath no better thing under the sun, than to eat, and to drink, and to be merry.
> *Eccl. 8:15*

Money answereth all things.
> *Eccl. 10:19*

Can there any good thing come out of Nazareth?
> *John 1:46*

If ye believe not his writings, how shall ye believe my words?
> Jesus, about Moses
> *John 5:47*

[*See also* Doubt, Skepticism]

D

DAMNATION

If thy right eye offend thee, pluck it out, and cast it from thee: for it is profitable for thee that one of thy members should perish, and not that thy whole body should be cast into hell.
>Jesus
>*Matt. 5:29*
>*See also Matt. 18:9*

Wide is the gate, and broad is the way, that leadeth to destruction.
>Jesus
>*Matt. 7:13*

Ye serpents, ye generation of vipers, how can ye escape the damnation of hell?
>Jesus
>*Matt. 23:33*

If thy foot offend thee, cut it off: it is better for thee to enter halt into life, than having two feet to be cast into hell.
>Jesus
>*Mark 9:45*
>*See also Matt. 18:8*

He that believeth not shall be damned.
>Jesus
>*Mark 16:16*

Fear Him, which after He hath killed hath power to cast into hell; yea, I say unto you, Fear Him.
>Jesus
>*Luke 12:5*
>*See also Matt. 10:28*

He that believeth not is condemned already, because he hath not believed in the name of the only begotten Son of God.
>Jesus
>*John 3:18*

They that have done good, unto the resurrection of life; and they that have done evil, unto the resurrection of damnation.
>Jesus
>*John 5:29*

We are not of them who draw back unto perdition; but of them that believe to the saving of the soul.
>*Heb. 10:39*

God spared not the angels that sinned, but cast them down to hell.
>*2 Pet. 2:4*

Whosoever was not found written in the book of life was cast into the lake of fire.
>*Rev. 20:15*

[*See also* Death, Hell, Salvation]

DANCE

Let them praise His name in the dance: let them sing praises unto Him with the timbrel and harp.
>*Ps. 149:3*
>*See also Ps. 150:4*

A time to mourn, and a time to dance.
>*Eccl. 3:4*

We have piped unto you, and ye have not danced; we have mourned unto you, and ye have not lamented.
>Jesus
>*Matt. 11:17*
>*See also Luke 7:32*

[*See also* Music, Song]

DANGER

Thou shalt fear day and night, and shalt have none assurance of thy life.
>*Deut. 28:66*

The Philistines be upon thee, Samson.
>*E.g., Judges 16:9*

Let all thy wants lie upon me; only lodge not in the street.
>*Judg. 19:20*

There is but a step between me and death.
>*1 Sam. 20:3*

He that seeketh my life seeketh thy life.
>David to Abiathar
>*1 Sam. 22:23*

The wicked watcheth the righteous, and seeketh to slay him.
>*Ps. 37:32*

We are counted as sheep for the slaughter.
Ps. 44:22

We went through fire and through water.
Ps. 66:12

A thousand shall fall at thy side, and ten thousand at thy right hand; but it shall not come nigh thee.
Ps. 91:7

Though I walk in the midst of trouble, Thou wilt revive me.
Ps. 138:7

Sharp as a twoedged sword.
Prov. 5:4

Can a man take fire in his bosom, and his clothes not be burned?
Prov. 6:27

Can one go upon hot coals, and his feet not be burned?
Prov. 6:28

Let a bear robbed of her whelps meet a man, rather than a fool in his folly.
Prov. 17:12

Go not forth into the field, nor walk by the way; for the sword of the enemy and fear is on every side.
Jer. 6:25

The sword is without, and the pestilence and the famine within.
Ezek. 7:15

Our God whom we serve is able to deliver us from the burning fiery furnace.
Dan. 3:17

I send you forth as sheep in the midst of wolves: be ye therefore wise as serpents, and harmless as doves.
Jesus
Matt. 10:16

Behold, I send you forth as lambs among wolves.
Jesus
Luke 10:3

In perils in the city, in perils in the wilderness, in perils in the sea, in perils among false brethren.
2 Cor. 11:26

Behold, how great a matter a little fire kindleth!
James 3:5

The second woe is past; and, behold, the third woe cometh quickly.
Rev. 11:14

[*See also* Safety, Traps, Trouble]

DARKNESS

See Enlightenment, Light and Darkness.

DEATH

Dust thou art, and unto dust shalt thou return.
Gen. 3:19

Then Abraham gave up the ghost, and died in a good old age.
Gen. 25:8

Now let me die, since I have seen thy face, because thou art yet alive.
Jacob to Joseph
Gen. 46:30

Your carcases shall fall in this wilderness.
God to Israelites
Num. 14:29

Let me die the death of the righteous, and let my last end be like his!
Num. 23:10

Alas, who shall live when God doeth this!
Balaam
Num. 24:23

He that is hanged is accursed of God.
Deut. 21:23
See also Gal. 3:13

This day I am going the way of all the earth.
Josh. 23:14

Why tarry the wheels of his chariots?
Judg. 5:28

And Samson said, Let me die with the Philistines.
Judg. 16:30

Where thou diest, will I die, and there will I be buried.
Ruth 1:17

I went out full, and the Lord hath brought me home again empty.
Ruth 1:21

To morrow shalt thou and thy sons be with me.
> Samuel, after his death, to Saul
> *1 Sam. 28:19*

In their death they were not divided.
> (they: Saul and Jonathan)
> *2 Sam. 1:23*

The sword devoureth one as well as another.
> David, about Bathsheba's husband
> *2 Sam. 11:25*

Can I bring him back again?
> David, about his son
> *2 Sam. 12:23*

I shall go to him, but he shall not return to me.
> David, about his son
> *2 Sam. 12:23*

I go the way of all the earth.
> *1 Kings 2:2*

I will not put thee to death with the sword.
> *1 Kings 2:8*

Set thine house in order; for thou shalt die, and not live.
> *2 Kings 20:1, Isa. 38:1*

Thou shalt be gathered into thy grave in peace.
> *2 Kings 22:20*

He died in a good old age, full of days, riches, and honour.
> (He: David)
> *1 Chron. 29:28*

There the wicked cease from troubling; and there the weary be at rest.
> *Job 3:17*

The small and great are there; and the servant is free from his master.
> Job, speaking of death
> *Job 3:19*

He that goeth down to the grave shall come up no more.
> *Job 7:9*

He destroyeth the perfect and the wicked.
> *Job 9:22*

Before I go whence I shall not return, even to the land of darkness and the shadow of death.
> *Job 10:21*

Man dieth, and wasteth away: yea, man giveth up the ghost, and where is he?
> *Job 14:10*

If a man die, shall he live again?
> *Job 14:14*

My breath is corrupt, my days are extinct, the graves are ready for me.
> *Job 17:1*

I have said to corruption, Thou art my father: to the worm, Thou art my mother, and my sister.
> *Job 17:14*

Though after my skin worms destroy this body, yet in my flesh shall I see God.
> *Job 19:26*

They shall lie down alike in the dust, and the worms shall cover them.
> *Job 21:26*

Drought and heat consume the snow waters: so doth the grave those which have sinned.
> *Job 24:19*

The worm shall feed sweetly on him; he shall be no more remembered.
> (him: the wicked)
> *Job 24:20*

Have the gates of death been opened unto thee? or hast thou seen the doors of the shadow of death?
> God to Job
> *Job 38:17*

In death there is no remembrance of Thee: in the grave who shall give Thee thanks?
> *Ps. 6:5*

Lighten mine eyes, lest I sleep the sleep of death.
> *Ps. 13:3*

Yea, though I walk through the valley of the shadow of death, I will fear no evil: for Thou art with me.
> *Ps. 23:4*

Like sheep they are laid in the grave; death shall feed on them.
> *Ps. 49:14*

They that are far from Thee shall perish.
> *Ps. 73:27*

What man is he that liveth, and shall not see death?
> *Ps. 89:48*

Thou takest away their breath, they die, and return to their dust.
(they: animals)
Ps. 104:29

The dead praise not the Lord.
Ps. 115:17

Righteousness delivereth from death.
Prov. 10:2, Prov. 11:4

When the wicked perish, there is shouting.
Prov. 11:10

There are three things that are never satisfied, yea, four things say not, It is enough: The grave; and the barren womb; the earth that is not filled with water; and the fire that saith not, It is enough.
Prov. 30:15–16

How dieth the wise man? as the fool.
Eccl. 2:16

That which befalleth the sons of men befalleth beasts.
Eccl. 3:19

All go unto one place.
Eccl. 3:20
See also Eccl. 6:6

As he came forth of his mother's womb, naked shall he return.
Eccl. 5:15

It is better to go to the house of mourning, than to go to the house of feasting: for that is the end of all men; and the living will lay it to his heart.
Eccl. 7:2

There is no man that hath power over the spirit to retain the spirit.
Eccl. 8:8

All things come alike to all.
Eccl. 9:2

Remember the days of darkness; for they shall be many.
Eccl. 11:8

The spirit shall return unto God who gave it.
Eccl. 12:7

Hell hath enlarged herself, and opened her mouth without measure.
Isa. 5:14

Hell from beneath is moved for thee to meet thee at thy coming.
Isa. 14:9

The worm is spread under thee, and the worms cover thee.
Isa. 14:11

He will swallow up death in victory.
Isa. 25:8

We have made a covenant with death, and with hell are we at agreement.
Isa. 28:15

The grave cannot praise Thee, death cannot celebrate Thee: they that go down into the pit cannot hope for Thy truth.
Isa. 38:18

He is brought as a lamb to the slaughter.
Isa. 53:7
See also Jer. 11:19, Acts 8:32

The righteous is taken away from the evil to come.
Isa. 57:1

They shall sleep a perpetual sleep.
Jer. 51:57

Abroad the sword bereaveth, at home there is as death.
Lam. 1:20

They that be slain with the sword are better than they that be slain with hunger.
Lam. 4:9

I have no pleasure in the death of him that dieth, saith the Lord God.
Ezek. 18:32

I have no pleasure in the death of the wicked.
Ezek. 33:11

Turn ye, turn ye from your evil ways; for why will ye die?
Ezek. 33:11
See also Jonah 3:8

I will prepare thee unto blood, and blood shall pursue thee.
Ezek. 35:6

There be some standing here, which shall not taste of death, till they see the Son of man coming in His kingdom.
Jesus
Matt. 16:28
See also Mark 9:1, Luke 9:27

Wheresoever the carcase is, there will the eagles be gathered together.
Jesus
Matt. 24:28
See also Luke 17:37

Except ye repent, ye shall all likewise perish.
Jesus
Luke 13:3

Whosoever believeth in Him should not perish, but have eternal life.
Jesus
John 3:15
See also John 3:16

If a man keep my saying, he shall never see death.
Jesus
John 8:51

Yet a little while, and the world seeth me no more.
Jesus
John 14:19

I come to Thee.
Jesus
John 17:11

It is finished.
Jesus
John 19:30

Scarcely for a righteous man will one die: yet peradventure for a good man some would even dare to die.
Rom. 5:7

He that is dead is freed from sin.
Rom. 6:7

If ye live after the flesh, ye shall die.
Rom. 8:13

No man dieth to himself.
Rom. 14:7

The last enemy that shall be destroyed is death.
1 Cor. 15:26

Death is swallowed up in victory.
1 Cor. 15:54

O death, where is thy sting? O grave, where is thy victory?
1 Cor. 15:55
See also Hos. 13:14

The sting of death is sin; and the strength of sin is the law.
1 Cor. 15:56

We brought nothing into this world, and it is certain we can carry nothing out.
1 Tim. 6:7

Where a testament is, there must also of necessity be the death of the testator.
Heb. 9:16

Sin, when it is finished, bringeth forth death.
James 1:15

As the body without the spirit is dead, so faith without works is dead also.
James 2:26
See also James 2:24

Shortly I must put off this my tabernacle.
2 Pet. 1:14

I looked, and behold a pale horse: and his name that sat on him was Death, and Hell followed with him.
Rev. 6:8

In those days shall men seek death, and shall not find it; and shall desire to die, and death shall flee from them.
Rev. 9:6

Blessed are the dead which die in the Lord from henceforth.
Rev. 14:13

Blessed and holy is he that hath part in the first resurrection: on such the second death hath no power.
Rev. 20:6

Death and hell were cast into the lake of fire. This is the second death.
Rev. 20:14

There shall be no more death, neither sorrow, nor crying, neither shall there be any more pain: for the former things are passed away.
Rev. 21:4

[*See also* Annihilation, Burial, Crucifixion, Damnation, Despair, Destruction, Eternal Life, Hanging, Life, Life and Death, Martyrdom, Mortality, Mourning, Punishment, Resurrection]

DEBT

See Borrowing.

DECADENCE

Sodom and Gomorrah.
Gen. 18:20, Gen. 19:28

Thou art waxen fat, thou art grown thick, thou art covered with fatness.
Deut. 32:15

Ye are like unto whited sepulchres, which indeed appear beautiful outward.
Jesus
Matt. 23:27

Wasted his substance with riotous living.
(his: the prodigal son)
Luke 15:13

Clouds they are without water, carried about of winds; trees whose fruit withereth.
Jude 12

Babylon the great is fallen, is fallen, and is become the habitation of devils.
Rev. 18:2

All nations have drunk of the wine of the wrath of her fornication.
(her: Babylon)
Rev. 18:3

Be not partakers of her sins.
(her: Babylon)
Rev. 18:4

How much she hath glorified herself, and lived deliciously, so much torment and sorrow give her.
(she: Babylon)
Rev. 18:7

Alas, alas that great city Babylon, that mighty city! for in one hour is thy judgment come.
Rev. 18:10

The fruits that thy soul lusted after are departed from thee.
Rev. 18:14

Without are dogs, and sorcerers, and whoremongers, and murderers, and idolaters, and whosoever loveth and maketh a lie.
Rev. 22:15

[*See also* Corruption, Depravity, Evil, Immorality, Wickedness]

DECEPTION

Why didst thou not tell me that she was thy wife?
Pharaoh to Abram
Gen. 12:18

And Jacob said unto his father, I am Esau thy firstborn.
Gen. 27:19

The voice is Jacob's voice, but the hands are the hands of Esau.
Isaac
Gen. 27:22

Did not I serve with thee for Rachel?
Jacob to Laban
Gen. 29:25

Wherefore have ye beguiled us?
Josh. 9:22

I have a secret errand unto thee, O king.
Ehud to King of Moab
Judg. 3:19

Turn in, my lord, turn in to me; fear not.
Jael to Sisera
Judg. 4:18

He asked water, and she gave him milk.
(she: Jael)
Judg. 5:25

Thou dost but hate me, and lovest me not.
Samson's wife
Judg. 14:16

What meaneth then this bleating of the sheep in mine ears?
1 Sam. 15:14

Wherefore then layest thou a snare for my life, to cause me to die?
1 Sam. 28:9

I am a prophet also as thou art; and an angel spake unto me by the word of the Lord.
1 Kings 13:18

Why feignest thou thyself to be another?
1 Kings 14:6

Ahab served Baal a little; but Jehu shall serve him much.
2 Kings 10:18

Let us build with you: for we seek your God, as ye do.
Ezra 4:2

As one man mocketh another, do ye so mock Him?
Job 13:9

The workers of iniquity, which speak peace to their neighbours, but mischief is in their hearts.
Ps. 28:3

Saying, Peace, peace; when there is no peace.
Jer. 6:14, Jer. 8:11
See also Ezek. 13:10

Let not your prophets and your diviners, that be in the midst of you, deceive you.
Jer. 29:8

Ye say, The Lord saith it; albeit I have not spoken.
Ezek. 13:7

Cursed be the deceiver.
Mal. 1:14

Beware of false prophets, which come to you in sheep's clothing, but inwardly they are ravening wolves.
Jesus
Matt. 7:15

Take heed that ye be not deceived.
Jesus
Luke 21:8
See also Matt. 24:4, Mark 13:5

Let no man deceive himself.
1 Cor. 3:18

Who hath bewitched you, that ye should not obey the truth?
Gal. 3:1

Let no man deceive you with vain words.
Eph. 5:6

Beware lest any man spoil you through philosophy and vain deceit.
Col. 2:8

By thy sorceries were all nations deceived.
Rev. 18:23

[*See also* Appearance, Dishonesty, Hypocrisy, Lies, Self-Deception, Truth]

DECISIONS

Do what seemeth good unto thee.
Israelites to Saul
1 Sam. 14:40

Let us choose to us judgment: let us know among ourselves what is good.
Job 34:4

A time to keep, and a time to cast away.
Eccl. 3:6

A time to keep silence, and a time to speak.
Eccl. 3:7

Not as I will, but as Thou wilt.
Jesus
Matt. 26:39
See also Mark 14:36, Luke 22:42

[*See also* Certainty, Choice, Compromise, Indecision, Procrastination, Time, and the Appendix at p. 421]

DEEDS

The Lord is a God of knowledge, and by Him actions are weighed.
1 Sam. 2:3

Even a child is known by his doings.
Prov. 20:11

God shall bring every work into judgment.
Eccl. 12:14

Let your light so shine before men, that they may see your good works.
Jesus
Matt. 5:16

By their fruits ye shall know them.
Jesus
Matt. 7:20
See also Matt. 7:16

Whosoever heareth these sayings of mine, and doeth them, I will liken him unto a wise man, which built his house upon a rock.
Jesus
Matt. 7:24

He shall reward every man according to his works.
Jesus
Matt. 16:27

Bring forth therefore fruits worthy of repentance.
Luke 3:8

Every tree is known by his own fruit.
Jesus
Luke 6:44
See also Matt. 7:17, Matt. 12:33

Why call ye me, Lord, Lord, and do not the things which I say?
Jesus
Luke 6:46

He that doeth truth cometh to the light, that his deeds may be made manifest.
Jesus
John 3:21

If this counsel or this work be of men, it will come to nought: But if it be of God, ye cannot overthrow it.
Acts 5:38–39

Glory, honour, and peace, to every man that worketh good.
Rom. 2:10

Not the hearers of the law are just before God, but the doers of the law shall be justified.
Rom. 2:13

A man is justified by faith without the deeds of the law.
Rom. 3:28

By the works of the law shall no flesh be justified.
Gal. 2:16

Whatsoever ye do in word or deed, do all in the name of the Lord Jesus.
Col. 3:17

Be rich in good works.
1 Tim. 6:18

They profess that they know God; but in works they deny Him.
Titus 1:16

Not by works of righteousness which we have done, but according to His mercy He saved us.
Titus 3:5

With such sacrifices God is well pleased.
Heb. 13:16

Be ye doers of the word, and not hearers only.
James 1:22

Faith without works is dead.
James 2:20
See also James 2:17

By works was faith made perfect.
James 2:22

By works a man is justified, and not by faith only.
James 2:24
See also James 2:26

So is the will of God, that with well doing ye may put to silence the ignorance of foolish men.
1 Pet. 2:15

It is better, if the will of God be so, that ye suffer for well doing, than for evil doing.
1 Pet. 3:17

Let us not love in word, neither in tongue; but in deed and in truth.
1 John 3:18

I have not found thy works perfect before God.
Jesus
Rev. 3:2

[*See also* Achievement, Benevolence, Ministry]

DEFEAT

Knowest thou not yet that Egypt is destroyed?
Pharaoh's servants to Pharaoh
Ex. 10:7

How should one chase a thousand, and two put ten thousand to flight, except their Rock had sold them, and the Lord had shut them up?
Deut. 32:30

Thus shall the Lord do to all your enemies against whom ye fight.
Josh. 10:25

Whithersoever they went out, the hand of the Lord was against them for evil.
Judg. 2:15

How are the mighty fallen, and the weapons of war perished!
2 Sam. 1:27

Their gods are gods of the hills; therefore they were stronger than we.
1 Kings 20:23

He shall not come into this city, nor shoot an arrow there.
2 Kings 19:32, Isa. 37:33

By the way that he came, by the same shall he return.
2 Kings 19:33, Isa. 37:34

All the men of war fled by night.
2 Kings 25:4

They cried, but there was none to save them: even unto the Lord, but He answered them not.
Ps. 18:41

How art thou fallen from heaven, O Lucifer, son of the morning!
Isa. 14:12

Their might hath failed; they became as women.
Jer. 51:30

Babylon shall become heaps, a dwelling-place for dragons, an astonishment, and an hissing, without an inhabitant.
Jer. 51:37

They shall sleep a perpetual sleep.
Jer. 51:57

How doth the city sit solitary, that was full of people! how is she become as a widow!
Lam. 1:1
See also Lam. 1:2–22

I will deliver thee into the hand of them whom thou hatest.
Ezek. 23:28

Lament like a virgin girded with sackcloth for the husband of her youth.
Joel 1:8

The flight shall perish from the swift, and the strong shall not strengthen his force, neither shall the mighty deliver himself.
Amos 2:14

He that is courageous among the mighty shall flee away naked in that day.
Amos 2:16

The light of a candle shall shine no more at all in thee.
Rev. 18:23

The voice of the bridegroom and of the bride shall be heard no more at all in thee.
Rev. 18:23

[*See also* Desolation, Destruction, Humiliation, Success, Victory]

DEFIANCE

See Arrogance, Audacity.

DELAY

See Laziness, Patience, Procrastination.

DELIVERANCE

I am the Lord thy God, which have brought thee out of the land of Egypt, out of the house of bondage.
Ex. 20:2
See also, e.g., Ex. 29:46, Deut. 5:6

The Lord brought us forth out of Egypt with a mighty hand, and with an outstretched arm.
Deut. 26:8

Slack not thy hand from thy servants; come up to us quickly, and save us.
Josh. 10:6

Ye cried to Me, and I delivered you out of their hand.
Judg. 10:12

He raiseth up the poor out of the dust, and lifteth up the beggar from the dunghill.
1 Sam. 2:8
See also Ps. 113:7

I will call on the Lord, who is worthy to be praised: so shall I be saved from mine enemies.
2 Sam. 22:4
See also Ps. 18:3

He shall deliver you out of the hand of all your enemies.
2 Kings 17:39

He shall hear a rumour, and shall return to his own land.
(He: Sennacherib)
2 Kings 19:7
See also Isa. 37:7

Save Thou us out of his hand, that all the

kingdoms of the earth may know that Thou art the Lord God, even Thou only.
2 Kings 19:19
See also Isa. 37:20

Deliver us from the heathen, that we may give thanks to Thy holy name.
1 Chron. 16:35

He delivereth the poor in his affliction.
Job 36:15

The Lord blessed the latter end of Job more than his beginning.
Job 42:12

I sought the Lord, and He heard me, and delivered me from all my fears.
Ps. 34:4

Unto God the Lord belong the issues from death.
Ps. 68:20

Deliver me because of mine enemies.
Ps. 69:18

Deliver me in Thy righteousness, and cause me to escape.
Ps. 71:2

Incline Thine ear unto me, and save me.
Ps. 71:2

How long, Lord?
Ps. 79:5, Ps. 89:46

He saved them for His name's sake, that He might make His mighty power to be known.
Ps. 106:8

They cry unto the Lord in their trouble, and He saveth them out of their distresses.
Ps. 107:19

Save with Thy right hand, and answer me.
Ps. 108:6
See also Ps. 60:5

I will lift up mine eyes unto the hills, from whence cometh my help.
Ps. 121:1

Bring my soul out of prison, that I may praise Thy name.
Ps. 142:7

The righteousness of the upright shall deliver them.
Prov. 11:6

Through knowledge shall the just be delivered.
Prov. 11:9

They shall cry unto the Lord because of the oppressors, and He shall send them a saviour.
Isa. 19:20

He that scattered Israel will gather him, and keep him, as a shepherd doth his flock.
Jer. 31:10

Their Redeemer is strong; the Lord of hosts is His name.
Jer. 50:34

My God hath sent His angel, and hath shut the lions' mouths.
Dan. 6:22

He delivereth and rescueth, and He worketh signs and wonders in heaven and in earth.
Dan. 6:27

Whosoever shall call on the name of the Lord shall be delivered.
Joel 2:32

The earth with her bars was about me for ever: yet hast Thou brought up my life from corruption.
Jonah 2:6

The Lord shall yet comfort Zion, and shall yet choose Jerusalem.
Zech. 1:17

He hath sent me to heal the brokenhearted, to preach deliverance to the captives.
Jesus
Luke 4:18
See also Isa. 61:1

O wretched man that I am! who shall deliver me from the body of this death?
Rom. 7:24

I was delivered out of the mouth of the lion.
2 Tim. 4:17

The Lord knoweth how to deliver the godly out of temptations.
2 Pet. 2:9

[*See also* Escape, Exile, Freedom, Safety, Salvation]

Shall the work say of him that made it, He made me not?
> E.g., Isa. 29:16
> See also, e.g., Isa. 45:9, Rom. 9:20

Whosoever shall deny me before men, him will I also deny before my Father which is in heaven.
> Jesus
> Matt. 10:33
> See also Luke 12:9

Before the cock crow, thou shalt deny me thrice.
> Jesus
> Matt. 26:34, 75
> See also Mark 14:30, John 13:38, Luke 22:34

Though I should die with Thee, yet will I not deny Thee.
> Peter to Jesus
> Matt. 26:35
> See also Mark 14:31

And immediately the cock crew.
> Matt. 26:74, John 18:27
> See also Luke 22:60

I know not this man of whom ye speak.
> Peter of Jesus
> Mark 14:71
> See also, e.g., Matt. 26:74

If I should say, I know Him not, I shall be a liar like unto you: but I know Him, and keep His saying.
> Jesus
> John 8:55

If we deny Him, He also will deny us.
> 2 Tim. 2:12

If we believe not, yet He abideth faithful: He cannot deny Himself.
> 2 Tim. 2:13

Whosoever denieth the Son, the same hath not the Father.
> 1 John 2:23

[See also Atheism, Blasphemy, Godlessness, Self-Denial]

DEPENDENCE

See God's Protection, Reliance.

Do with them what seemeth good unto you: but unto this man do not so vile a thing.
> Judg. 19:24

There was no such deed done nor seen from the day that the children of Israel came up out of the land of Egypt unto this day.
> Judg. 19:30

He that is of a perverse heart shall be despised.
> Prov. 12:8

The great whore that sitteth upon many waters.
> (Babylon)
> Rev. 17:1

Babylon the Great, the Mother of Harlots and Abominations of the Earth.
> Rev. 17:5

[See also Decadence, Evil, Immorality, Sin, Wickedness]

DEPRESSION

Why is thy countenance sad, seeing thou art not sick?
> Neh. 2:2

My soul is weary of my life.
> Job 10:1

I have said to corruption, Thou art my father: to the worm, Thou art my mother, and my sister.
> Job 17:14

God my rock, Why hast Thou forgotten me?
> Ps. 42:9

Save me, O God; for the waters are come in unto my soul.
> Ps. 69:1

My soul is full of troubles: and my life draweth nigh unto the grave.
> Ps. 88:3

My days are like a shadow that declineth; and I am withered like grass.
> Ps. 102:11

A merry heart doeth good like a medicine: but a broken spirit drieth the bones.
Prov. 17:22

A wounded spirit who can bear?
Prov. 18:14

Behold, all is vanity and vexation of spirit.
Eccl. 1:14
See also, e.g., Eccl. 2:17

Therefore I hated life.
Eccl. 2:17

[*See also* Despair, Sorrow]

DEPRIVATION

He satisfieth the longing soul, and filleth the hungry soul with goodness.
Ps. 107:9

To the hungry soul every bitter thing is sweet.
Prov. 27:7

Every one that thirsteth, come ye to the waters, and he that hath no money; come ye, buy, and eat.
Isa. 55:1

If any man thirst, let him come unto me, and drink.
Jesus
John 7:37

They shall hunger no more, neither thirst any more; neither shall the sun light on them, nor any heat.
Rev. 7:16

I will give unto him that is athirst of the fountain of the water of life freely.
Jesus
Rev. 21:6

[*See also* Bread of Life, Famine, Hunger, Thirst]

DESECRATION

See Holiness, Sacrilege.

DESIRE

Get her for me; for she pleaseth me well.
Samson to his father
Judg. 14:3

The desire accomplished is sweet to the soul.
Prov. 13:19

Better is the sight of the eyes than the wandering of the desire.
Eccl. 6:9

In the broad ways I will seek him whom my soul loveth.
Song 3:2

I am my beloved's, and his desire is toward me.
Song 7:10

We should not lust after evil things.
1 Cor. 10:6

When lust hath conceived, it bringeth forth sin.
James 1:15

Ye lust, and have not.
James 4:2

The world passeth away, and the lust thereof: but he that doeth the will of God abideth for ever.
1 John 2:17

[*See also* Carnality, Jealousy, Lust]

DESOLATION

Jerusalem is ruined, and Judah is fallen: because their tongue and their doings are against the Lord.
Isa. 3:8

The land shall be utterly emptied, and utterly spoiled: for the Lord hath spoken this word.
Isa. 24:3

Babylon shall become heaps, a dwelling-place for dragons, an astonishment, and an hissing, without an inhabitant.
Jer. 51:37

How doth the city sit solitary, that was full of people! how is she become as a widow!
Lam. 1:1
See also Lam. 1:2–22

I shall make thee a desolate city, like the cities that are not inhabited.
Ezek. 26:19

They shall be desolate in the midst of the countries that are desolate.
Ezek. 30:7

When the whole earth rejoiceth, I will make thee desolate.
Ezek. 35:14

All they that look upon thee shall flee from thee.
(thee: Nineveh)
Nah. 3:7

Nineveh is laid waste: who will bemoan her?
Nah. 3:7

[*See also* Annihilation, Destruction, Loneliness]

DESPAIR

Behold, I am at the point to die: and what profit shall this birthright do to me?
Esau to Jacob
Gen. 25:32

Give me children, or else I die.
Rachel to Jacob
Gen. 30:1

Hast thou taken us away to die in the wilderness?
Israelites to Moses
Ex. 14:11
See also Num. 21:5

What shall I do unto this people? they be almost ready to stone me.
Moses
Ex. 17:4

Would God that we had died in the land of Egypt!
Num. 14:2

O that they were wise, that they understood this, that they would consider their latter end!
Deut. 32:29

Would to God we had been content, and dwelt on the other side Jordan!
Josh. 7:7

Now shall I die for thirst, and fall into the hand of the uncircumcised?
Judg. 15:18

I have drunk neither wine nor strong drink, but have poured out my soul before the Lord.
1 Sam. 1:15

God is departed from me, and answereth me no more, neither by prophets, nor by dreams.
Saul to Samuel
1 Sam. 28:15

I, even I only, am left; and they seek my life, to take it away.
1 Kings 19:10, 14
See also Rom. 11:3

This day is a day of trouble, and of rebuke, and blasphemy.
2 Kings 19:3, Isa. 37:3

Let the day perish wherein I was born.
Job 3:3

Why died I not from the womb? why did I not give up the ghost when I came out of the belly?
Job 3:11

What is mine end, that I should prolong my life?
Job 6:11

Is my strength the strength of stones? or is my flesh of brass?
Job 6:12

My days are swifter than a weaver's shuttle, and are spent without hope.
Job 7:6

Where, and who is He?
Job 9:24

If I be wicked, why then labour I in vain?
Job 9:29

My soul is weary of my life.
Job 10:1

Wherefore then hast Thou brought me forth out of the womb? Oh that I had given up the ghost, and no eye had seen me!
Job 10:18

God hath delivered me to the ungodly, and turned me over into the hands of the wicked.
Job 16:11

O that one might plead for a man with God, as a man pleadeth for his neighbour!
Job 16:21

My breath is corrupt, my days are extinct, the graves are ready for me.
Job 17:1

If I wait, the grave is mine house: I have made my bed in the darkness.
Job 17:13

Where is now my hope?
Job 17:15

I cry aloud, but there is no judgment.
Job 19:7

Mine hope hath He removed like a tree.
Job 19:10

I cry unto Thee, and Thou dost not hear me: I stand up, and Thou regardest me not.
Job 30:20

I am a brother to dragons, and a companion to owls.
Job 30:29

It profiteth a man nothing that he should delight himself with God.
Job 34:9

How long wilt Thou forget me, O Lord? for ever? how long wilt Thou hide Thy face from me?
Ps. 13:1

There is none that doeth good, no, not one.
Ps. 14:3, Ps. 53:3, Rom. 3:12

My God, my God, why hast Thou forsaken me?
Ps. 22:1, Matt. 27:46, Mark 15:34

I cry in the daytime, but Thou hearest not; and in the night season, and am not silent.
Ps. 22:2

I am forgotten as a dead man out of mind: I am like a broken vessel.
Ps. 31:12

I am poor and needy: make haste unto me, O God.
Ps. 70:5
See also Ps. 40:17

Wilt Thou hide Thyself for ever?
Ps. 89:46

Out of the depths have I cried unto Thee, O Lord.
Ps. 130:1

Bring my soul out of prison, that I may praise Thy name.
Ps. 142:7

Let him drink, and forget his poverty, and remember his misery no more.
Prov. 31:7

Vanity of vanities; all is vanity.
Eccl. 1:2

This also is vanity.
Eccl. 2:15

All his days are sorrows, and his travail grief; yea, his heart taketh not rest in the night.
Eccl. 2:23

All that cometh is vanity.
Eccl. 11:8

Vanity of vanities, saith the preacher; all is vanity.
Eccl. 12:8

I sought him, but I found him not.
Song 3:1, 2

Let us be called by thy name, to take away our reproach.
Isa. 4:1

Fear, and the pit, and the snare, are upon thee, O inhabitant of the earth.
Isa. 24:17

Mine eyes fail with looking upward: O Lord, I am oppressed.
Isa. 38:14

Is not the Lord in Zion?
Jer. 8:19

The harvest is past, the summer is ended, and we are not saved.
Jer. 8:20

Cursed be the day wherein I was born: let not the day wherein my mother bare me be blessed.
Jer. 20:14

Wherefore came I forth out of the womb to see labour and sorrow?
Jer. 20:18

O earth, earth, earth, hear the word of the Lord.
Jer. 22:29

They have cut off my life in the dungeon, and cast a stone upon me.
Lam. 3:53

I called upon Thy name, O Lord, out of the low dungeon.
Lam. 3:55

It is better for me to die than to live.
Jonah 4:3, 8

Eli, Eli, lama sabachthani?
Jesus
Matt. 27:46
See also Mark 15:34

He that cometh to me shall never hunger; and he that believeth on me shall never thirst.
Jesus
John 6:35

Strangers from the covenants of promise, having no hope, and without God in the world.
Eph. 2:12

Alas, alas that great city Babylon, that mighty city! for in one hour is thy judgment come.
Rev. 18:10

[*See also* Abandonment, Anguish, Death, Depression, Faith, Hope, Self-Pity]

DESTINY

It was not you that sent me hither, but God.
Joseph to his brothers
Gen. 45:8

Such as are for death, to death; and such as are for the sword, to the sword; and such as are for the famine, to the famine; and such as are for the captivity, to the captivity.
Jer. 15:2

As the clay is in the potter's hand, so are ye in Mine hand, O house of Israel.
Jer. 18:6
See also Rom. 9:21

[*See also* Chance]

DESTRUCTION

Neither shall there any more be a flood to destroy the earth.
Gen. 9:11

Wilt Thou also destroy the righteous with the wicked?
Abraham to God
Gen. 18:23

Alas, who shall live when God doeth this!
Balaam
Num. 24:23

As a consuming fire He shall destroy them, and He shall bring them down before thy face.
Deut. 9:3

The sword without, and terror within, shall destroy both the young man and the virgin, the suckling also with the man of gray hairs.
Deut. 32:25

Cursed be the man before the Lord, that riseth up and buildeth this city Jericho.
Josh. 6:26

Joshua drew not his hand back, wherewith he stretched out the spear.
Josh. 8:26

Why wilt thou swallow up the inheritance of the Lord?
2 Sam. 20:19

I will wipe Jerusalem as a man wipeth a dish, wiping it, and turning it upside down.
2 Kings 21:13

The way of the Lord is strength to the upright: but destruction shall be to the workers of iniquity.
Prov. 10:29

A time to break down, and a time to build up.
Eccl. 3:3

A time to rend, and a time to sew.
Eccl. 3:7

Take us the foxes, the little foxes, that spoil the vines: for our vines have tender grapes.
Song 2:15

Howl ye; for the day of the Lord is at hand.
Isa. 13:6

Her time is near to come, and her days shall not be prolonged.
(Her: Babylon)
Isa. 13:22

As with the people, so with the priest; as with the servant, so with his master; as with the maid, so with her mistress; as with the buyer, so with the seller; as with the lender, so with the borrower; as with the taker of usury, so with the giver of usury to him.
Isa. 24:2

The moth shall eat them up like a garment, and the worm shall eat them like wool.
Isa. 51:8

I have created the waster to destroy.
Isa. 54:16

I will not pity, nor spare, nor have mercy, but destroy them.
Jer. 13:14

That which I have built will I break down, and that which I have planted I will pluck up, even this whole land.
Jer. 45:4

Destruction cometh; it cometh out of the north.
Jer. 46:20

I will bring them down like lambs to the slaughter, like rams with he goats.
Jer. 51:40

Abroad the sword bereaveth, at home there is as death.
Lam. 1:20

In the day of the Lord's anger none escaped nor remained.
Lam. 2:22

Your altars shall be desolate, and your images shall be broken: and I will cast down your slain men before your idols.
Ezek. 6:4

He that is in the field shall die with the sword; and he that is in the city, famine and pestilence shall devour him.
Ezek. 7:15

They shall seek peace, and there shall be none.
Ezek. 7:25

Though these three men, Noah, Daniel, and Job, were in it, they should deliver but their own souls by their righteousness.
Ezek. 14:14

The suburbs shall shake at the sound of the cry of thy pilots.
Ezek. 27:28

That which the locust hath left hath the cankerworm eaten; and that which the cankerworm hath left hath the caterpillar eaten.
Joel 1:4

Shall there be evil in a city, and the Lord hath not done it?
Amos 3:6

I will make thy grave; for thou art vile.
(thy: Nineveh)
Nah. 1:14

All the earth shall be devoured with the fire of My jealousy.
Zeph. 3:8

The abomination of desolation.
Jesus
Matt. 24:15, Mark 13:14

Destroy this temple, and in three days I will raise it up.
Jesus
John 2:19

The second woe is past; and, behold, the third woe cometh quickly.
Rev. 11:14

Armageddon.
Rev. 16:16

It is done.
Rev. 16:17

Every island fled away, and the mountains were not found.
Rev. 16:20

Alas, alas that great city Babylon, that mighty city! for in one hour is thy judgment come.
Rev. 18:10

The merchants of the earth shall weep and mourn over her; for no man buyeth their merchandise any more.
(her: Babylon)
Rev. 18:11

[*See also* Annihilation, Carnage, Defeat,

Desolation, Doom, Restoration, Terror, Violence]

DETERMINATION

I will not let thee go, except thou bless me.
> Jacob to Angel
> *Gen. 32:26*

Joshua drew not his hand back, wherewith he stretched out the spear.
> *Josh. 8:26*

Intreat me not to leave thee.
> *Ruth 1:16*

He turned not to the right hand nor to the left.
> *2 Sam. 2:19*

If thou seek Him, He will be found of thee.
> *1 Chron. 28:9*
> *See also 2 Chron. 15:2*

Waters wear the stones.
> *Job 14:19*

I shall not die, but live, and declare the works of the Lord.
> *Ps. 118:17*

Let not your eye spare, neither have ye pity.
> *Ezek. 9:5*

I will do it; I will not go back, neither will I spare, neither will I repent.
> *Ezek. 24:14*

Stand fast in the faith.
> *1 Cor. 16:13*

Lift up the hands which hang down, and the feeble knees.
> *Heb. 12:12*

[*See also* Diligence, Effort, Fortitude, Perseverance, Work]

DEVIL

See Evil, Satan.

DEVOTION

Serve the Lord thy God with all thy heart and with all thy soul.
> *Deut. 10:12*
> *See also, e.g., Josh. 22:5*

Whither thou goest, I will go; and where thou lodgest, I will lodge: thy people shall be my people, and thy God my God.
> *Ruth 1:16*

Where thou diest, will I die, and there will I be buried.
> *Ruth 1:17*

Prepare your hearts unto the Lord, and serve Him only.
> Samuel to Israelites
> *1 Sam. 7:3*

Turn not aside from following the Lord.
> *1 Sam. 12:20*

Fear the Lord, and serve Him in truth with all your heart.
> *1 Sam. 12:24*

As the Lord liveth, and as thy soul liveth, I will not leave thee.
> *E.g., 2 Kings 2:2*

Set your heart and your soul to seek the Lord your God.
> *1 Chron. 22:19*

With a perfect heart and with a willing mind.
> *1 Chron. 28:9*

If ye seek Him, He will be found of you.
> *2 Chron. 15:2*
> *See also 1 Chron. 28:9*

My soul thirsteth for Thee.
> *Ps. 63:1*

Seek the Lord, and His strength: seek His face evermore.
> *Ps. 105:4*
> *See also 1 Chron. 16:11*

I will not give sleep to mine eyes, or slumber to mine eyelids, Until I find out a place for the Lord.
> *Ps. 132:4–5*

With my soul have I desired Thee in the night; yea, with my spirit within me will I seek Thee early.
> *Isa. 26:9*

Circumcise yourselves to the Lord.
> *Jer. 4:4*

Ye shall seek Me, and find Me, when ye shall search for Me with all your heart.
> *Jer. 29:13*

Come, and let us go up to the mountain of

the Lord, and to the house of the God of Jacob.
Mic. 4:2

Seek ye the Lord, all ye meek of the earth.
Zeph. 2:3

They shall be My people, and I will be their God.
E.g., Zech. 8:8

With all thy heart, and with all thy soul, and with all thy mind.
Jesus
Matt. 22:37, Mark 12:29

Whosoever he be of you that forsaketh not all that he hath, he cannot be my disciple.
Jesus
Luke 14:33

The good shepherd giveth his life for the sheep.
Jesus
John 10:11

The hireling fleeth, because he is an hireling, and careth not for the sheep.
Jesus
John 10:13

I am ready not to be bound only, but also to die at Jerusalem for the name of the Lord Jesus.
Acts 21:13

Neither is that circumcision, which is outward in the flesh.
Rom. 2:28

Who shall separate us from the love of Christ? shall tribulation, or distress, or persecution, or famine, or nakedness, or peril, or sword?
Rom. 8:35

He that is unmarried careth for the things that belong to the Lord, how he may please the Lord: But he that is married careth for the things that are of the world, how he may please his wife.
1 Cor. 7:32–33

She that is married careth for the things of the world, how she may please her husband.
1 Cor. 7:34

Ye would have plucked out your own eyes, and have given them to me.
Gal. 4:15

Sanctify the Lord God in your hearts.
1 Pet. 3:15

[*See also* Allegiance, Commitment, Faithfulness, Love, Love of God, Loyalty, Service to God, Sincerity, Worship]

DILIGENCE

He that goeth forth and weepeth, bearing precious seed, shall doubtless come again with rejoicing, bringing his sheaves with him.
Ps. 126:6

Go to the ant, thou sluggard; consider her ways, and be wise.
Prov. 6:6

Seest thou a man diligent in his business? he shall stand before kings.
Prov. 22:29

He that tilleth his land shall have plenty of bread.
Prov. 28:19

The ants are a people not strong, yet they prepare their meat in the summer.
Prov. 30:25

In the morning sow thy seed, and in the evening withhold not thine hand.
Eccl. 11:6

Cursed be he that keepeth back his sword from blood.
Jer. 48:10

They pursued us upon the mountains, they laid wait for us in the wilderness.
Lam. 4:19

By thy great wisdom and by thy traffick hast thou increased thy riches.
Ezek. 28:5

Seek, and ye shall find.
Jesus
Matt. 7:7, Luke 11:9

No man, having put his hand to the plough, and looking back, is fit for the kingdom of God.
Jesus
Luke 9:62

Be ye stedfast, unmoveable, always abounding in the work of the Lord.
1 Cor. 15:58

He which soweth bountifully shall reap also bountifully.
2 Cor. 9:6

Stand fast in the Lord, my dearly beloved.
Phil. 4:1

Study to be quiet, and to do your own business.
1 Thess. 4:11

Study to show thyself approved unto God, a workman that needeth not to be ashamed.
2 Tim. 2:15

[*See also* Effort, Laziness, Perseverance, Steadfastness]

DIPLOMACY

See Tact.

DISAPPOINTMENT

Behold it with thine eyes: for thou shalt not go over this Jordan.
God to Moses
Deut. 3:27

But I must die in this land, I must not go over Jordan.
Moses
Deut. 4:22

Thou shalt see the land before thee; but thou shalt not go thither.
God to Moses
Deut. 32:52

When I looked for good, then evil came unto me: and when I waited for light, there came darkness.
Job 30:26

Or ever the silver cord be loosed, or the golden bowl be broken.
Eccl. 12:6

He looked that it should bring forth grapes, and it brought forth wild grapes.
Isa. 5:2

He looked for judgment, but behold oppression; for righteousness, but behold a cry.
Isa. 5:7

As when an hungry man dreameth, and, behold, he eateth; but he awaketh, and his soul is empty: or as when a thirsty man dreameth, and, behold, he drinketh; but he awaketh, and, behold, he is faint.
Isa. 29:8

They shall not be ashamed that wait for Me.
Isa. 49:23

We wait for light, but behold obscurity; for brightness, but we walk in darkness.
Isa. 59:9

How is the gold become dim!
Lam. 4:1

Ye have built houses of hewn stone, but ye shall not dwell in them; ye have planted pleasant vineyards, but ye shall not drink wine of them.
Amos 5:11
See also Zeph. 1:13

Ye looked for much, and, lo, it came to little.
Hag. 1:9

What, could ye not watch with me one hour?
Jesus
Matt. 26:40
See also Mark 14:37

[*See also* Effort, Expectation, Failure, Frustration, Futility, Hope]

DISARMAMENT

See War and Peace, Weapons.

DISBELIEF

See Doubt, Godlessness, Skepticism.

DISCERNMENT

Give therefore Thy servant an understanding heart to judge Thy people, that I may discern between good and bad.
Solomon
1 Kings 3:9

Let us choose to us judgment: let us know among ourselves what is good.
Job 34:4

As a jewel of gold in a swine's snout, so is a fair woman which is without discretion.
Prov. 11:22

A wise man's heart discerneth both time and judgment.
Eccl. 8:5

Butter and honey shall he eat, that he may know to refuse the evil, and choose the good.
Isa. 7:15

O ye hypocrites, ye can discern the face of the sky; but can ye not discern the signs of the times?
Jesus
Matt. 16:3
See also Luke 12:56

[*See also* Folly, Perception, Understanding]

DISCIPLES

Follow me, and I will make you fishers of men.
Jesus
Matt. 4:19
See also Mark 1:17

I send you forth as sheep in the midst of wolves: be ye therefore wise as serpents, and harmless as doves.
Jesus
Matt. 10:16

The disciple is not above his master, nor the servant above his lord.
Jesus
Matt. 10:24
See also Luke 6:40, John 13:16

He that taketh not his cross, and followeth after me, is not worthy of me.
Jesus
Matt. 10:38
See also Luke 14:27

Whosoever will come after me, let him deny himself, and take up his cross, and follow me.
Jesus
Mark 8:34
See also Matt. 16:24, Luke 9:23

Go ye into all the world, and preach the gospel to every creature.
Jesus
Mark 16:15

He that despiseth you despiseth me; and he that despiseth me despiseth Him that sent me.
Jesus
Luke 10:16

Whosoever he be of you that forsaketh not all that he hath, he cannot be my disciple.
Jesus
Luke 14:33

Have not I chosen you twelve, and one of you is a devil?
Jesus
John 6:70

If ye continue in my word, then are ye my disciples indeed.
Jesus
John 8:31

If any man serve me, him will my Father honour.
Jesus
John 12:26

By this shall all men know that ye are my disciples, if ye have love one to another.
Jesus
John 13:35

I am the vine, ye are the branches.
Jesus
John 15:5

Ye have not chosen me, but I have chosen you.
Jesus
John 15:16

Follow me.
Jesus
John 21:19

[*See also* Evangelism, Leadership]

DISCIPLINE

As a man chasteneth his son, so the Lord thy God chasteneth thee.
Deut. 8:5

Let the righteous smite me; it shall be a kindness.
Ps. 141:5

A rod is for the back of him that is void of understanding.
Prov. 10:13

He that spareth his rod hateth his son: but he that loveth him chasteneth him betimes.
Prov. 13:24

Correction is grievous unto him that forsaketh the way.
Prov. 15:10

He that refuseth instruction despiseth his own soul.
Prov. 15:32

Chasten thy son while there is hope, and let not thy soul spare for his crying.
Prov. 19:18

Foolishness is bound in the heart of a child; but the rod of correction shall drive it far from him.
Prov. 22:15

Withhold not correction from the child: for if thou beatest him with the rod, he shall not die.
Prov. 23:13

A whip for the horse, a bridle for the ass, and a rod for the fool's back.
Prov. 26:3

A child left to himself bringeth his mother to shame.
Prov. 29:15

I was chastised, as a bullock unaccustomed to the yoke.
Jer. 31:18

Shall I come unto you with a rod, or in love?
1 Cor. 4:21

What son is he whom the father chasteneth not?
Heb. 12:7

No chastening for the present seemeth to be joyous.
Heb. 12:11

It yieldeth the peaceable fruit of righteousness unto them which are exercised thereby.
Heb. 12:11

As many as I love, I rebuke and chasten.
Jesus
Rev. 3:19

[*See also* Chastisement, Criticism, Punishment, Self-Control]

DISCONTENT

See Contentment, Satisfaction.

DISCRETION

See Prudence, Silence, Understanding.

DISHONESTY

Put not thine hand with the wicked to be an unrighteous witness.
Ex. 23:1

With flattering lips and with a double heart do they speak.
Ps. 12:2

He that worketh deceit shall not dwell within my house.
Ps. 101:7

He that telleth lies shall not tarry in my sight.
Ps. 101:7

Deceit is in the heart of them that imagine evil.
Prov. 12:20

Better is a little with righteousness than great revenues without right.
Prov. 16:8

He that hath a perverse tongue falleth into mischief.
Prov. 17:20

He that speaketh lies shall perish.
Prov. 19:9

A poor man is better than a liar.
Prov. 19:22

Divers weights, and divers measures, both of them are alike abomination to the Lord.
Prov. 20:10
See also Prov. 20:23

We have made lies our refuge, and under falsehood have we hid ourselves.
Isa. 28:15

Woe unto them that seek deep to hide their counsel from the Lord.
Isa. 29:15

Trust ye not in lying words.
Jer. 7:4

They bend their tongues like their bow for lies.
Jer. 9:3

He that getteth riches, and not by right, shall leave them in the midst of his days.
Jer. 17:11

With lies ye have made the heart of the righteous sad.
Ezek. 13:22

He is a merchant, the balances of deceit are in his hand: he loveth to oppress.
Hos. 12:7

He that is unjust in the least is unjust also in much.
Jesus
Luke 16:10

Thou hast not lied unto men, but unto God.
Acts 5:4

[See also Candor, Honesty, Lies, Truth]

DISOBEDIENCE

She took of the fruit thereof, and did eat.
(She: Eve)
Gen. 3:6

His wife looked back from behind him, and she became a pillar of salt.
Gen. 19:26

How long wilt thou refuse to humble thyself before Me? let My people go.
God to Pharaoh
Ex. 10:3

How long refuse ye to keep My commandments and My laws?
Ex. 16:28

Wherefore do ye tempt the Lord?
Moses
Ex. 17:2

Moses lifted up his hand, and with his rod he smote the rock.
Num. 20:11

Ye have been rebellious against the Lord from the day that I knew you.
Deut. 9:24

Because thou hast rejected the word of the Lord, He hath also rejected thee from being king.
Samuel to Saul
1 Sam. 15:23

Wherefore hast thou despised the commandment of the Lord, to do evil in His sight?
(thou: David)
2 Sam. 12:9

His heart was not perfect with the Lord his God.
E.g., 1 Kings 11:4

Great is the wrath of the Lord that is kindled against us, because our fathers have not hearkened unto the words of this book.
2 Kings 22:13

He did that which was evil in the sight of the Lord his God.
E.g., 2 Chron. 36:12

A stubborn and rebellious generation; a generation that set not their heart aright, and whose spirit was not stedfast with God.
Ps. 78:8

Rivers of waters run down mine eyes, because they keep not Thy law.
Ps. 119:136

Stolen waters are sweet, and bread eaten in secret is pleasant.
Prov. 9:17

This is a rebellious people, lying children, children that will not hear the law of the Lord.
Isa. 30:9

When I called, ye did not answer; when I spake, ye did not hear.
Isa. 65:12

This is a nation that obeyeth not the voice of the Lord.
Jer. 7:28

The stork in the heaven knoweth her appointed times; and the turtle and the crane and the swallow observe the time of their coming; but My people know not the judgment of the Lord.
God to Jews
Jer. 8:7

Cursed be the man that obeyeth not the words of this covenant.
Jer. 11:3

I have spoken unto them, but they have not heard; and I have called unto them, but they have not answered.
Jer. 35:17

Thou dwellest in the midst of a rebellious house.
Ezek. 12:2

They hear thy words, but they do them not.
God to Ezekiel
Ezek. 33:32

We obeyed not His voice.
Dan. 9:14

They made their hearts as an adamant stone, lest they should hear the law.
Zech. 7:12

Every one that heareth these sayings of mine, and doeth them not, shall be likened unto a foolish man, which built his house upon the sand.
Jesus
Matt. 7:26
See also Luke 6:49

Laying aside the commandment of God, ye hold the tradition of men.
Jesus
Mark 7:8

Remember Lot's wife.
Jesus
Luke 17:32

He that loveth me not keepeth not my sayings.
Jesus
John 14:24

By one man's disobedience many were made sinners.
Rom. 5:19

If I do that I would not, it is no more I that do it, but sin that dwelleth in me.
Rom. 7:20
See also Rom. 7:17

Who hath bewitched you, that ye should not obey the truth?
Gal. 3:1

The wrath of God cometh on the children of disobedience.
Col. 3:6

He therefore that despiseth, despiseth not man, but God.
1 Thess. 4:8

Whosoever shall keep the whole law, and yet offend in one point, he is guilty of all.
James 2:10

He that saith, I know Him, and keepeth not His commandments, is a liar.
(Him: Jesus)
1 John 2:4

[*See also* Backsliding, Blame, Curses, Obedience, Punishment, Rebellion, Rejection, Sin]

DISTANCE

From Dan even to Beersheba.
Judg. 20:1

DIVERSITY

All the people, both small and great.
2 Kings 23:2

There are diversities of gifts, but the same Spirit.
1 Cor. 12:4

There are differences of administrations, but the same Lord.
1 Cor. 12:5

In a great house there are not only vessels of gold and of silver, but also of wood and of earth.
2 Tim. 2:20

DIVINITY

Of a truth Thou art the Son of God.
Matt. 14:33

Truly this was the Son of God.
Matt. 27:54
See also Mark 15:39

Ye say that I am.
Jesus
Luke 22:70

I saw, and bare record that this is the Son of God.
John 1:34

He that cometh from above is above all.
John 3:31

I and my Father are one.
Jesus
John 10:30

He was come from God, and went to God.
(He: Jesus)
John 13:3

He that hath seen me hath seen the Father.
Jesus
John 14:9

I am in the Father, and the Father in me.
Jesus
John 14:11

I believe that Jesus Christ is the Son of God.
Acts 8:37

One Lord, one faith, one baptism.
Eph. 4:5

In Him dwelleth all the fulness of the Godhead bodily.
(Him: Jesus)
Col. 2:9

[*See also* Acknowledgment, God, Jesus]

DIVORCE

Whosoever shall put away his wife, saving for the cause of fornication, causeth her to commit adultery.
Jesus
Matt. 5:32

Whosoever shall marry her that is divorced committeth adultery.
Jesus
Matt. 5:32
See also Matt. 19:9, Luke 16:18

What therefore God hath joined together, let not man put asunder.
Jesus
Matt. 19:6, Mark 10:9

Whosoever shall put away his wife, except it be for fornication, and shall marry another, committeth adultery.
Jesus
Matt. 19:9
See also Mark 10:11

If a woman shall put away her husband, and be married to another, she committeth adultery.
Jesus
Mark 10:12

Whosoever putteth away his wife, and marrieth another, committeth adultery.
Jesus
Luke 16:18

Let not the husband put away his wife.
1 Cor. 7:11

Art thou bound unto a wife? seek not to be loosed.
1 Cor. 7:27

[*See also* Marriage]

DOCTRINE

My doctrine shall drop as the rain, my speech shall distil as the dew.
Deut. 32:2

My doctrine is not mine, but His that sent me.
Jesus
John 7:16

We henceforth be no more children, tossed to and fro, and carried about with every wind of doctrine, by the sleight of men, and cunning craftiness, whereby they lie in wait to deceive.
Eph. 4:14

Give attendance to reading, to exhortation, to doctrine.
1 Tim. 4:13

Speak thou the things which become sound doctrine.
Titus 2:1

Avoid foolish questions.
Titus 3:9

[*See also* Controversy]

DOOM

If thou return at all in peace, the Lord hath not spoken by me.
1 Kings 22:28
See also 2 Chron. 18:27

Out of the serpent's root shall come forth a

cockatrice, and his fruit shall be a fiery flying serpent.
Isa. 14:29

Howl, O gate; cry, O city; thou, whole Palestina, art dissolved.
Isa. 14:31

He who fleeth from the noise of the fear shall fall into the pit; and he that cometh up out of the midst of the pit shall be taken in the snare.
Isa. 24:18
See Jer. 48:44

I will bring My words upon this city for evil, and not for good.
Jer. 39:16

In vain shalt thou use many medicines; for thou shalt not be cured.
Jer. 46:11

They hunt our steps, that we cannot go in our streets: our end is near, our days are fulfilled.
Lam. 4:18

The time is come, the day of trouble is near.
Ezek. 7:7
See also Ezek. 7:12

Let not the buyer rejoice, nor the seller mourn: for wrath is upon all the multitude.
Ezek. 7:12

Woe, woe unto thee! saith the Lord God.
Ezek. 16:23

The day of the Lord is near.
Ezek. 30:3

[*See also* Apocalypse, Destruction, Punishment, Terror]

DOUBT

Lord, wherefore hast Thou so evil entreated this people?
Moses
Ex. 5:22

Is the Lord among us, or not?
Ex. 17:7

Moses lifted up his hand, and with his rod he smote the rock.
Num. 20:11

If the Lord be with us, why then is all this befallen us?
Judg. 6:13

Where be all His miracles which our fathers told us of?
Judg. 6:13

Art thou He that should come, or do we look for another?
Matt. 11:3
See also Luke 7:19

We have here but five loaves, and two fishes.
His disciples to Jesus
Matt. 14:17
See also Luke 9:13

O thou of little faith, wherefore didst thou doubt?
Jesus
Matt. 14:31

O ye of little faith.
Jesus
E.g., Matt. 16:8

O faithless and perverse generation, how long shall I be with you? how long shall I suffer you?
Jesus
Matt. 17:17
See also Mark 9:19, Luke 9:41

Help Thou mine unbelief.
Mark 9:24

How shall this be, seeing I know not a man?
Luke 1:34

Except I shall see in His hands the print of the nails, and put my finger into the print of the nails, and thrust my hand into His side, I will not believe.
Thomas
John 20:25

Reach hither thy hand, and thrust it into my side: and be not faithless, but believing.
Jesus
John 20:27

Him that is weak in the faith receive ye, but not to doubtful disputations.
Rom. 14:1

Stand fast, and hold the traditions which ye have been taught.
2 Thess. 2:15

He that wavereth is like a wave of the sea driven with the wind.
James 1:6

[*See also* Belief, Faith, Hope, Skepticism]

DREAMS

They hated him yet the more for his dreams, and for his words.
(They: Joseph's brothers)
Gen. 37:8

Do not interpretations belong to God?
Gen. 40:8

What God is about to do He showeth unto Pharaoh.
Gen. 41:28

Thou scarest me with dreams, and terrifiest me through visions.
Job 7:14

When deep sleep falleth upon men, in slumberings upon the bed; Then He openeth the ears of men, and sealeth their instruction.
Job 33:15–16

I sleep, but my heart waketh: it is the voice of my beloved that knocketh.
Song 5:2

As when an hungry man dreameth, and, behold, he eateth; but he awaketh, and his soul is empty: or as when a thirsty man dreameth, and, behold, he drinketh; but he awaketh, and, behold, he is faint.
Isa. 29:8

The prophet that hath a dream, let him tell a dream; and he that hath My word, let him speak My word faithfully.
Jer. 23:28

Show me the dream, and the interpretation thereof.
Nebuchadnezzar
Dan. 2:6

There is a God in heaven that revealeth secrets.
Dan. 2:28

Your old men shall dream dreams, your young men shall see visions.
Joel 2:28
See also Acts 2:17

DRUNKENNESS

I have drunk neither wine nor strong drink, but have poured out my soul before the Lord.
1 Sam. 1:15

The drunkard and the glutton shall come to poverty.
Prov. 23:21

Woe unto them that rise up early in the morning, that they may follow strong drink.
Isa. 5:11

As a drunken man staggereth in his vomit.
Isa. 19:14

They are drunken, but not with wine; they stagger, but not with strong drink.
Isa. 29:9

Woe unto him that giveth his neighbour drink.
Hab. 2:15

Be not drunk with wine, wherein is excess; but be filled with the Spirit.
Eph. 5:18

[*See also* Liquor]

DUTY

What doth the Lord thy God require of thee, but to fear the Lord thy God, to walk in all His ways, and to love Him, and to serve the Lord thy God with all thy heart and with all thy soul.
Deut. 10:12

Fear God, and keep His commandments: for this is the whole duty of man.
Eccl. 12:13

Say not, I am a child: for thou shalt go to all that I shall send thee, and whatsoever I command thee thou shalt speak.
God to Jeremiah
Jer. 1:7

What doth the Lord require of thee, but to do justly, and to love mercy, and to walk humbly with thy God?
Mic. 6:8

It becometh us to fulfil all righteousness.
Jesus
Matt. 3:15

Wist ye not that I must be about my Father's business?
Jesus
Luke 2:49

Go thou and preach the kingdom of God.
Jesus
Luke 9:60

This is the work of God, that ye believe on Him whom He hath sent.
Jesus
John 6:29

I must work the works of Him that sent me, while it is day.
Jesus
John 9:4

The cup which my Father hath given me, shall I not drink it?
Jesus
John 18:11

It shall be told thee what thou must do.
Jesus to Saul
Acts 9:6

I go bound in the spirit unto Jerusalem, not knowing the things that shall befall me there.
Acts 20:22

Feed the church of God, which He hath purchased with His own blood.
Paul
Acts 20:28

As the Lord hath called every one, so let him walk.
1 Cor. 7:17

Woe is unto me, if I preach not the gospel!
1 Cor. 9:16

If I yet pleased men, I should not be the servant of Christ.
Gal. 1:10

Walk worthy of the vocation wherewith ye are called.
Eph. 4:1

[*See also* Goals, Mission, Responsibility]

DUTY, NEGLECT OF

Why abodest thou among the sheepfolds, to hear the bleatings of the flocks?
Judg. 5:16

Curse ye bitterly the inhabitants thereof; because they came not to the help of the Lord.
Judg. 5:23

This thing is not good that thou hast done.
David to Abner
1 Sam. 26:16

As the Lord liveth, ye are worthy to die.
1 Sam. 26:16
See also 1 Sam. 26:10

What doest thou here, Elijah?
God
E.g., 1 Kings 19:9

The stork in the heaven knoweth her appointed times; and the turtle and the crane and the swallow observe the time of their coming; but My people know not the judgment of the Lord.
God to Jews
Jer. 8:7

Cursed be he that doeth the work of the Lord deceitfully.
Jer. 48:10

Woe be to the shepherds of Israel that do feed themselves! should not the shepherds feed the flocks?
Ezek. 34:2

My flock was scattered upon all the face of the earth, and none did search or seek after them.
Ezek. 34:6

EARTH

And God called the dry land Earth; and the gathering together of the waters called He Seas.
Gen. 1:10

All the earth is Mine.
Ex. 19:5

The pillars of the earth are the Lord's, and He hath set the world upon them.
1 Sam. 2:8

Who laid the corner stone thereof?
Job 38:6

The earth is the Lord's, and the fulness thereof; the world, and they that dwell therein.
Ps. 24:1
See also 1 Cor. 10:26

The earth is full of the goodness of the Lord.
Ps. 33:5

One generation passeth away, and another generation cometh: but the earth abideth for ever.
Eccl. 1:4

He hath established it, He created it not in vain, He formed it to be inhabited.
Isa. 45:18

He hath made the earth by His power, He hath established the world by His wisdom.
Jer. 51:15

[*See also* Creation, God's Presence, Heaven and Earth, Nature, Oceans]

EDUCATION

And thou shalt teach them diligently unto thy children, and shalt talk of them when thou sittest in thine house, and when thou walkest by the way, and when thou liest down, and when thou risest up.
Deut. 6:7
See also Deut. 11:19

Teach them the good way wherein they should walk.
1 Kings 8:36

Fools despise wisdom and instruction.
Prov. 1:7

Let her not go: keep her; for she is thy life. (her: instruction)
Prov. 4:13

Receive my instruction, and not silver; and knowledge rather than choice gold.
Prov. 8:10

Hear instruction, and be wise, and refuse it not.
Prov. 8:33

Give instruction to a wise man, and he will be yet wiser: teach a just man, and he will increase in learning.
Prov. 9:9

When the scorner is punished, the simple is made wise.
Prov. 21:11

Train up a child in the way he should go: and when he is old, he will not depart from it.
Prov. 22:6

Much study is a weariness of the flesh.
Eccl. 12:12

Precept must be upon precept, precept upon precept; line upon line, line upon line; here a little, and there a little.
Isa. 28:10

All thy children shall be taught of the Lord; and great shall be the peace of thy children.
Isa. 54:13

Understandest thou what thou readest?
Acts 8:30

How can I, except some man should guide me?
Acts 8:31

Paul, thou art beside thyself; much learning doth make thee mad.
Festus
Acts 26:24

How shall they hear without a preacher?
Rom. 10:14

I have fed you with milk, and not with meat.
1 Cor. 3:2

Beware lest any man spoil you through philosophy and vain deceit.
Col. 2:8

Let the woman learn in silence with all subjection.
1 Tim. 2:11

I suffer not a woman to teach, nor to usurp authority over the man, but to be in silence.
1 Tim. 2:12

[*See also* Child-Rearing, Enlightenment, Guidance, Instruction, Knowledge, Teaching, Wisdom]

EFFORT

Let not your hands be weak: for your work shall be rewarded.
  2 Chron. 15:7

Thou shalt eat the labour of thine hands.
  Ps. 128:2

Where no oxen are, the crib is clean: but much increase is by the strength of the ox.
  Prov. 14:4

Whatsoever thy hand findeth to do, do it with thy might.
  Eccl. 9:10

Cast thy bread upon the waters: for thou shalt find it after many days.
  Eccl. 11:1

Blessed are ye that sow beside all waters.
  Isa. 32:20

Sow ye, and reap.
  Isa. 37:30, 2 Kings 19:29

They have sown the wind, and they shall reap the whirlwind.
  Hos. 8:7

Thou shalt sow, but thou shalt not reap.
  Mic. 6:15

Ye have sown much, and bring in little; ye eat, but ye have not enough; ye drink, but ye are not filled.
  Hag. 1:6

Whosoever shall compel thee to go a mile, go with him twain.
  Jesus
  Matt. 5:41

He that seeketh findeth.
  Jesus
  Matt. 7:8, Luke 11:10

To him that knocketh it shall be opened.
  Jesus
  Matt. 7:8, Luke 11:10

With what measure ye mete, it shall be measured to you.
  Jesus
  Mark 4:24
  See also Luke 6:38

He which soweth sparingly shall reap also sparingly.
  2 Cor. 9:6

Whatsoever a man soweth, that shall he also reap.
  Gal. 6:7

Whatsoever ye do, do it heartily, as to the Lord, and not unto men.
  Col. 3:23

I have fought a good fight, I have finished my course, I have kept the faith.
  2 Tim. 4:7

[*See also* Diligence, Patience, Work]

EGO

See Arrogance, Conceit, Humility.

ELOQUENCE

I am slow of speech, and of a slow tongue.
  Moses
  Ex. 4:10

Go, and I will be with thy mouth, and teach thee what thou shalt say.
  God to Moses
  Ex. 4:12

My speech shall distil as the dew, as the small rain upon the tender herb, and as the showers upon the grass.
  Deut. 32:2

The words of his mouth were smoother than butter, but war was in his heart.
  Ps. 55:21

His words were softer than oil, yet were they drawn swords.
  Ps. 55:21

The lips of the wise shall preserve them.
  Prov. 14:3

The heart of the wise teacheth his mouth, and addeth learning to his lips.
  Prov. 16:23

Excellent speech becometh not a fool: much less do lying lips a prince.
  Prov. 17:7

A word fitly spoken is like apples of gold in pictures of silver.
  Prov. 25:11

I will make My words in thy mouth fire, and this people wood.
  Jer. 5:14

Paul, Almost thou persuadest me to be a Christian.
Agrippa
Acts 26:28

Though I speak with the tongues of men and of angels, and have not charity, I am become as sounding brass, or a tinkling cymbal.
(charity: love)
1 Cor. 13:1

Though I be rude in speech, yet not in knowledge.
2 Cor. 11:6

[*See also* Silence, Speech, Verbosity]

EMBARRASSMENT

See Shame.

EMOTIONS

See Fear, Happiness, Hatred, Love, Sorrow.

EMPATHY

As thou livest, and as thy soul liveth, I will not do this thing.
Uriah to David
2 Sam. 11:11

Rejoice with them that do rejoice, and weep with them that weep.
Rom. 12:15

Absent in body, but present in spirit.
1 Cor. 5:3

Who is weak, and I am not weak? who is offended, and I burn not?
2 Cor. 11:29

Though I be absent in the flesh, yet am I with you in the spirit.
Col. 2:5

[*See also* Compassion, Sympathy]

EMPLOYEES

Thou shalt not oppress an hired servant that is poor and needy.
Deut. 24:14

Thou shalt not muzzle the ox when he treadeth out the corn.
Deut. 25:4
See also 1 Cor. 9:9

A wicked messenger falleth into mischief: but a faithful ambassador is health.
Prov. 13:17

The king's favour is toward a wise servant: but his wrath is against him that causeth shame.
Prov. 14:35

I will be a swift witness against the sorcerers, and against the adulterers, and against false swearers, and against those that oppress the hireling in his wages.
Mal. 3:5

The workman is worthy of his meat.
Jesus
Matt. 10:10
See also Luke 10:7, 1 Tim. 5:18

Every man shall receive his own reward according to his own labour.
1 Cor. 3:8

Give unto your servants that which is just and equal; knowing that ye also have a Master in heaven.
Col. 4:1

[*See also* Reward, Wages, Work]

EMPLOYERS

See Business, Work.

ENCOURAGEMENT

Fear ye not, stand still, and see the salvation of the Lord, which He will show to you to-day.
Ex. 14:13

The Lord shall fight for you, and ye shall hold your peace.
Ex. 14:14

Rebel not ye against the Lord, neither fear ye the people of the land.
Num. 14:9

Fear not, neither be discouraged.
E.g., Deut. 1:21

Dread not, neither be afraid of them. The

Lord your God which goeth before you, He shall fight for you.
Deut. 1:29–30

Be strong and of a good courage.
E.g., Deut. 31:6

Fear not, neither be dismayed.
E.g., Deut. 31:8

Get thee up; wherefore liest thou thus upon thy face?
God to Joshua
Josh. 7:10

Go up; for to morrow I will deliver them into thine hand.
God to Israelites
Judg. 20:28

Do all that is in thine heart; for the Lord is with thee.
2 Sam. 7:3

Be not afraid of the words which thou hast heard.
2 Kings 19:6
See also Isa. 37:6

Let not your hands be weak: for your work shall be rewarded.
2 Chron. 15:7

Be not afraid nor dismayed by reason of this great multitude; for the battle is not your's, but God's.
2 Chron. 20:15

Be strong and courageous, be not afraid nor dismayed.
E.g., 2 Chron. 32:7

Be of good courage, and do it.
Ezra 10:4

Fear not, neither be fainthearted.
Isa. 7:4

It shall not stand, neither shall it come to pass.
Isa. 7:7

Strengthen ye the weak hands, and confirm the feeble knees.
Isa. 35:3

Be strong, fear not: behold, your God will come with vengeance.
Isa. 35:4

Be not afraid of their faces: for I am with thee to deliver thee, saith the Lord.
Jer. 1:8

Be not afraid of him, saith the Lord: for I am with you to save you.
Jer. 42:11

Do not My words do good to him that walketh uprightly?
Mic. 2:7

Be of good cheer; thy sins be forgiven thee.
Jesus
Matt. 9:2
See also Mark 2:5

When thou art converted, strengthen thy brethren.
Jesus
Luke 22:32

Be not afraid, but speak, and hold not thy peace: For I am with thee.
Jesus to Paul
Acts 18:9–10

Exhort one another daily, while it is called To day.
Heb. 3:13

Lift up the hands which hang down, and the feeble knees.
Heb. 12:12

[*See also* Courage, Fear, God's Protection, God's Support, Hope]

END DAYS

The wolf also shall dwell with the lamb, and the leopard shall lie down with the kid; and the calf and the young lion and the fatling together.
Isa. 11:6

At the time of the end shall be the vision.
Dan. 8:17

Many of them that sleep in the dust of the earth shall awake, some to everlasting life, and some to shame and everlasting contempt.
Dan. 12:2

Watch ye therefore: for ye know not when the master of the house cometh.
Jesus
Mark 13:35

When ye shall see Jerusalem compassed

with armies, then know that the desolation thereof is nigh.
Jesus
Luke 21:20

The sun shall be turned into darkness, and the moon into blood, before that great and notable day of the Lord come.
Acts 2:20

[*See also* Apocalypse, Judgment Day, Second Coming]

ENDINGS

He that goeth down to the grave shall come up no more.
Job 7:9

The words of Job are ended.
Job 31:40

Better is the end of a thing than the beginning thereof.
Eccl. 7:8

Of His kingdom there shall be no end.
(His: Jesus)
Luke 1:33

The night cometh, when no man can work.
Jesus
John 9:4

I have fought a good fight, I have finished my course, I have kept the faith.
2 Tim. 4:7

[*See also* Apocalypse, Beginnings, Death, Permanence]

ENDURANCE

See Diligence, Fortitude, Perseverance, Strength.

ENEMIES

His hand will be against every man, and every man's hand against him.
(him: Ishmael)
Gen. 16:12

Ye shall chase your enemies, and they shall fall before you by the sword.
Lev. 26:7

Let them that hate Thee flee before Thee.
Num. 10:35

Dread not, neither be afraid of them. The Lord your God which goeth before you, He shall fight for you.
Deut. 1:29–30

Ye shall not fear them: for the Lord your God He shall fight for you.
Deut. 3:22

They shall be as thorns in your sides, and their gods shall be a snare unto you.
Judg. 2:3

Who is this uncircumcised Philistine, that he should defy the armies of the living God?
David, about Goliath
1 Sam. 17:26

He that seeketh my life seeketh thy life.
David to Abiathar
1 Sam. 22:23

If a man find his enemy, will he let him go well away?
Saul to David
1 Sam. 24:19

The souls of thine enemies, them shall He sling out.
1 Sam. 25:29

They prevented me in the day of my calamity: but the Lord was my stay.
2 Sam. 22:19, Ps. 18:18

Save Thou us out of his hand, that all the kingdoms of the earth may know that Thou art the Lord God, even Thou only.
2 Kings 19:19
See also *Isa. 37:20*

I will subdue all thine enemies.
1 Chron. 17:10

Because thou didst rely on the Lord, He delivered them into thine hand.
2 Chron. 16:8

They that hate thee shall be clothed with shame; and the dwelling place of the wicked shall come to nought.
Job 8:22

Destroy Thou them, O God; let them fall by their own counsels.
Ps. 5:10

They cried, but there was none to save

them: even unto the Lord, but He answered them not.
Ps. 18:41

Thine hand shall find out all Thine enemies: Thy right hand shall find out those that hate Thee.
Ps. 21:8

Thou preparest a table before me in the presence of mine enemies: Thou anointest my head with oil; my cup runneth over.
Ps. 23:5

Let me not be ashamed, let not mine enemies triumph over me.
Ps. 25:2

Let them be as chaff before the wind: and let the angel of the Lord chase them.
Ps. 35:5

Let their way be dark and slippery.
Ps. 35:6

Let not them that are mine enemies wrongfully rejoice over me.
Ps. 35:19

Deliver me from mine enemies, O my God.
Ps. 59:1

They that hate me without a cause are more than the hairs of mine head.
Ps. 69:4

Deliver me because of mine enemies.
Ps. 69:18

Let them be blotted out of the book of the living, and not be written with the righteous.
Ps. 69:28

Let his prayer become sin.
Ps. 109:7

Let mine adversaries be clothed with shame, and let them cover themselves with their own confusion.
Ps. 109:29

Rejoice not when thine enemy falleth.
Prov. 24:17

If thine enemy be hungry, give him bread to eat; and if he be thirsty, give him water to drink.
Prov. 25:21
See also Rom. 12:20

They that war against thee shall be as nothing, and as a thing of nought.
Isa. 41:12

They shall fight against thee; but they shall not prevail against thee; for I am with thee, saith the Lord.
Jer. 1:19

Let me see Thy vengeance on them: for unto Thee have I opened my cause.
Jeremiah to God
Jer. 20:12
See also Jer. 11:20

Our persecutors are swifter than the eagles of the heaven: they pursued us upon the mountains, they laid wait for us in the wilderness.
Lam. 4:19

Thus saith the Lord God; Behold, I, even I, am against thee.
Ezek. 5:8

Love your enemies.
Jesus
Matt. 5:44, Luke 6:27
See also Luke 6:35

Bless them that curse you, do good to them that hate you.
Jesus
Matt. 5:44

If ye love them which love you, what reward have ye? do not even the publicans the same?
Jesus
Matt. 5:46
See also Luke 6:32

If ye do good to them which do good to you, what thank have ye? for sinners also do even the same.
Jesus
Luke 6:33

He that hateth me hateth my Father also.
Jesus
John 15:23

If God be for us, who can be against us?
Rom. 8:31

We wrestle not against flesh and blood, but against principalities, against powers, against the rulers of the darkness.
Eph. 6:12

[*See also* Allies, Brotherhood, Gloating,

God's Protection, Hatred, Persecution, Revenge]

ENLIGHTENMENT

Your eyes shall be opened, and ye shall be as gods, knowing good and evil.
Gen. 3:5

The Lord will lighten my darkness.
2 Sam. 22:29

Lord, I pray Thee, open his eyes, that he may see.
2 Kings 6:17

The testimony of the Lord is sure, making wise the simple.
Ps. 19:7

Thy word is a lamp unto my feet, and a light unto my path.
Ps. 119:105

The people that walked in darkness have seen a great light.
Isa. 9:2
See also Matt. 4:16

I will bring the blind by a way that they knew not; I will lead them in paths that they have not known.
God
Isa. 42:16

I will make darkness light before them, and crooked things straight.
Isa. 42:16

To give light to them that sit in darkness.
Luke 1:79

He hath anointed me to preach the gospel to the poor.
Jesus
Luke 4:18
See also Isa. 61:1

The light shineth in darkness; and the darkness comprehended it not.
John 1:5

I am come a light into the world, that whosoever believeth on me should not abide in darkness.
Jesus
John 12:46

Open their eyes.
Jesus to Paul
Acts 26:18

Ye are all the children of light, and the children of the day.
1 Thess. 5:5

The darkness is past, and the true light now shineth.
1 John 2:8

[*See also* Education, Knowledge, Light and Darkness]

ENTHUSIASM

With all thy heart and with all thy soul.
E.g., Deut. 10:12
See also Deut. 11:13

What ye shall say, that will I do for you.
2 Sam. 21:4

Thou shouldest have smitten five or six times.
2 Kings 13:19

Whatsoever ye do, do it heartily, as to the Lord, and not unto men.
Col. 3:23

I know thy works, that thou art neither cold nor hot: I would thou wert cold or hot.
Jesus
Rev. 3:15
See also Rev. 3:16

I heard as it were the voice of a great multitude, and as the voice of many waters, and as the voice of mighty thunderings.
Rev. 19:6

[*See also* Contentment, Zeal]

ENVIRONMENT

See Nature.

ENVY

Thou shalt not covet.
Tenth Commandment
Ex. 20:17, Rom. 13:9
See also Deut. 5:21

Thou shalt not covet thy neighbour's house, thou shalt not covet thy neighbour's wife, nor his manservant, nor his maidser-

vant, nor his ox, nor his ass, nor any thing that is thy neighbour's.
> *Ex. 20:17*
> *See also Deut. 5:21*

Enviest thou for my sake?
> Moses to Joshua
> *Num. 11:29*

Hath the Lord indeed spoken only by Moses?
> *Num. 12:2*

Make us a king to judge us like all the nations.
> *1 Sam. 8:5*

Give me thy vineyard, that I may have it for a garden of herbs.
> Ahab to Naboth
> *1 Kings 21:2*

Wrath killeth the foolish man, and envy slayeth the silly one.
> *Job 5:2*

A little that a righteous man hath is better than the riches of many wicked.
> *Ps. 37:16*

Be not thou afraid when one is made rich, when the glory of his house is increased; For when he dieth he shall carry nothing away.
> *Ps. 49:16–17*

I was envious at the foolish, when I saw the prosperity of the wicked.
> *Ps. 73:3*

Is thine eye evil, because I am good?
> Jesus
> *Matt. 20:15*

For envy they had delivered Him.
> Pilate
> *Matt. 27:18*

Thou art in the gall of bitterness, and in the bond of iniquity.
> *Acts 8:23*

I had not known lust, except the law had said, Thou shalt not covet.
> *Rom. 7:7*

Where envying and strife is, there is confusion and every evil work.
> *James 3:16*

[*See also* Contentment, Greed, Jealousy]

Riches certainly make themselves wings; they fly away as an eagle toward heaven.
> *Prov. 23:5*

They shall be as the morning cloud, and as the early dew that passeth away, as the chaff that is driven with the whirlwind out of the floor, and as the smoke out of the chimney.
> *Hos. 13:3*

[*See also* Mortality, Permanence]

EQUALITY

One law shall be to him that is homeborn, and unto the stranger that sojourneth among you.
> *Ex. 12:49*

Ye shall have one ordinance, both for the stranger, and for him that was born in the land.
> *Num. 9:14*
> *See also Lev. 24:22*

The Lord commanded Moses to give us an inheritance among our brethren.
> (us: Zelophehad's daughters)
> *Josh. 17:4*

Are they not all my lord's servants?
> *1 Chron. 21:3*

They shall lie down alike in the dust, and the worms shall cover them.
> *Job 21:26*

Did not He that made me in the womb make him?
> *Job 31:15*

They all are the work of His hands.
> *Job 34:19*

The rich and poor meet together: the Lord is the maker of them all.
> *Prov. 22:2*

That which befalleth the sons of men befalleth beasts.
> *Eccl. 3:19*

All are of the dust, and all turn to dust again.
> *Eccl. 3:20*

All things come alike to all.
> *Eccl. 9:2*

As is the good, so is the sinner; and he that sweareth, as he that feareth an oath.
Eccl. 9:2

The race is not to the swift, nor the battle to the strong, neither yet bread to the wise, nor yet riches to men of understanding, nor yet favour to men of skill; but time and chance happeneth to them all.
Eccl. 9:11

As with the people, so with the priest; as with the servant, so with his master; as with the maid, so with her mistress; as with the buyer, so with the seller; as with the lender, so with the borrower; as with the taker of usury, so with the giver of usury to him.
Isa. 24:2

The last shall be first, and the first last.
Jesus
Matt. 20:16
See also Matt. 19:30, Mark 10:31

The servant is not greater than his lord; neither he that is sent greater than he that sent him.
Jesus
John 13:16
See also John 15:20, Matt. 10:24

There is no difference between the Jew and the Greek: for the same Lord over all is rich unto all that call upon Him.
Rom. 10:12

We shall all stand before the judgment seat of Christ.
Rom. 14:10
See also 2 Cor. 5:10

Ye are all the children of God by faith in Christ Jesus.
Gal. 3:26

There is neither Jew nor Greek, there is neither bond nor free, there is neither male nor female: for ye are all one in Christ Jesus.
Gal. 3:28

Be as I am; for I am as ye are.
Gal. 4:12

There is neither Greek nor Jew, circumcision nor uncircumcision, Barbarian, Scythian, bond nor free: but Christ is all, and in all.
Col. 3:11

[*See also* Brotherhood, Foreigners, Humility, Impartiality]

ESCAPE

The children of Israel walked upon dry land in the midst of the sea; and the waters were a wall unto them on their right hand, and on their left.
Ex. 14:29

Arise, and let us flee.
2 Sam. 15:14

I am escaped with the skin of my teeth.
Job 19:20

There is no darkness, nor shadow of death, where the workers of iniquity may hide themselves.
Job 34:22

Oh that I had wings, like a dove! for then would I fly away, and be at rest.
Ps. 55:6

If I ascend up into heaven, Thou art there: if I make my bed in hell, behold, Thou art there.
Ps. 139:8

The darkness hideth not from Thee; but the night shineth as the day.
Ps. 139:12

Enter into the rock, and hide thee in the dust, for fear of the Lord.
Isa. 2:10

To whom will ye flee for help? and where will ye leave your glory?
Isa. 10:3

There is no peace, saith the Lord, unto the wicked.
Isa. 48:22
See also Ps. 57:21

Can any hide himself in secret places that I shall not see him? saith the Lord. Do not I fill heaven and earth?
Jer. 23:24

Thy life I will give unto thee for a prey in all places whither thou goest.
Jer. 45:5

He that fleeth from the fear shall fall into

the pit; and he that getteth up out of the pit shall be taken in the snare.
Jer. 48:44
See also Isa. 24:18

Though thou shouldest make thy nest as high as the eagle, I will bring thee down from thence, saith the Lord.
Jer. 49:16

Flee out of the midst of Babylon, and deliver every man his soul.
Jer. 51:6

They pursued us upon the mountains, they laid wait for us in the wilderness.
Lam. 4:19

They shall go out from one fire, and another fire shall devour them.
Ezek. 15:7

Shall he escape that doeth such things?
Ezek. 17:15

He that taketh warning shall deliver his soul.
Ezek. 33:5

And who is that God that shall deliver you out of my hands?
Nebuchadnezzar
Dan. 3:15

Our God whom we serve is able to deliver us from the burning fiery furnace.
Dan. 3:17

He that is swift of foot shall not deliver himself: neither shall he that rideth the horse.
Amos 2:15

He that fleeth of them shall not flee away, and he that escapeth of them shall not be delivered.
Amos 9:1

Though they dig into hell, thence shall Mine hand take them; though they climb up to heaven, thence will I bring them down.
Amos 9:2

O generation of vipers, who hath warned you to flee from the wrath to come?
Matt. 3:7, Luke 3:7

Whosoever shall seek to save his life shall lose it; and whosoever shall lose his life shall preserve it.
Jesus
Luke 17:33
See also Matt. 16:25, Mark 8:35

Save yourselves from this untoward generation.
Acts 2:40

Behold, the men whom ye put in prison are standing in the temple.
Acts 5:25

[*See also* Defeat, Deliverance, Safety, Sanctuary, Survival]

ESTRANGEMENT

Because ye have forsaken the Lord, He hath also forsaken you.
2 Chron. 24:20
See also 2 Chron. 15:2

Why standest Thou afar off, O Lord? why hidest Thou Thyself in times of trouble?
Ps. 10:1

I am become a stranger unto my brethren, and an alien unto my mother's children.
Ps. 69:8

I have gone astray like a lost sheep; seek Thy servant.
Ps. 119:176
See also Isa. 53:6

What iniquity have your fathers found in Me, that they are gone far from Me?
Jer. 2:5

[*See also* Abandonment, Backsliding]

ETERNAL LIFE

Thou wilt not leave my soul in hell; neither wilt Thou suffer Thine Holy One to see corruption.
Ps. 16:10

He that loseth his life for my sake shall find it.
Jesus
Matt. 10:39

There be some standing here, which shall

not taste of death, till they see the Son of man coming in His kingdom.
Jesus
Matt. 16:28
See also Mark 9:1, Luke 9:27

If thou wilt enter into life, keep the commandments.
Jesus
Matt. 19:17

Go and sell that thou hast, and give to the poor, and thou shalt have treasure in heaven.
Jesus
Matt. 19:21
See also Mark 10:21, Luke 18:22

Thou knowest the commandments, Do not commit adultery, Do not kill, Do not steal, Do not bear false witness, Defraud not, Honour thy father and mother.
Jesus
Mark 10:19
See also Matt. 19:18–19, Luke 18:20

Come, take up the cross, and follow me.
Jesus
Mark 10:21
See also Matt. 19:21, Luke 18:22

How hard is it for them that trust in riches to enter into the kingdom of God!
Jesus
Mark 10:24
See also Matt. 19:23, Luke 18:24

Many that are first shall be last; and the last first.
Jesus
Mark 10:31
See also Matt. 19:30, Matt. 20:16

Whosoever believeth in Him should not perish, but have eternal life.
Jesus
John 3:15

For God so loved the world, that He gave His only begotten Son, that whosoever believeth in Him should not perish, but have everlasting life.
Jesus
John 3:16
See also John 3:36, John 6:47

Living water.
John 4:11

Whosoever drinketh of this water shall thirst again: But whosoever drinketh of the water that I shall give him shall never thirst.
Jesus
John 4:13–14

He that reapeth receiveth wages, and gathereth fruit unto life eternal.
Jesus
John 4:36

He that heareth my word, and believeth on Him that sent me, hath everlasting life.
Jesus
John 5:24

I am the living bread which came down from heaven: if any man eat of this bread, he shall live for ever.
Jesus
John 6:51
See also John 6:58

Whoso eateth my flesh, and drinketh my blood, hath eternal life; and I will raise him up at the last day.
Jesus
John 6:54

If a man keep my saying, he shall never see death.
Jesus
John 8:51

I am the resurrection, and the life.
Jesus
John 11:25

Whosoever liveth and believeth in me shall never die.
Jesus
John 11:26

I go to prepare a place for you.
Jesus
John 14:2

The wages of sin is death; but the gift of God is eternal life through Jesus Christ our Lord.
Rom. 6:23

Thanks be to God, which giveth us the victory through our Lord Jesus Christ.
1 Cor. 15:57

He that soweth to the Spirit shall of the Spirit reap life everlasting.
Gal. 6:8

Lay hold on eternal life, whereunto thou art also called.
1 Tim. 6:12

The world passeth away, and the lust thereof: but he that doeth the will of God abideth for ever.
1 John 2:17

God hath given to us eternal life, and this life is in His Son.
1 John 5:11

Be thou faithful unto death, and I will give thee a crown of life.
Jesus
Rev. 2:10

I will give unto him that is athirst of the fountain of the water of life freely.
Jesus
Rev. 21:6

Let him that is athirst come. And whosoever will, let him take the water of life freely.
Rev. 22:17

[*See also* Bread of Life, Christ Eternal, Life, Resurrection, Reward, Salvation]

ETERNITY

The Lord shall reign for ever and ever.
E.g., Ex. 15:18

This God is our God for ever and ever: He will be our guide even unto death.
Ps. 48:14

But Thou, O Lord, shalt endure for ever.
Ps. 102:12
See also, e.g., Ps. 9:7

Thou art the same, and Thy years shall have no end.
Ps. 102:27

Thou, O Lord, remainest for ever; Thy throne from generation to generation.
Lam. 5:19

For Thine is the kingdom, and the power, and the glory, for ever.
Jesus
Matt. 6:13

Holy, holy, holy, Lord God Almighty, which was, and is, and is to come.
Rev. 4:8

[*See also* Christ Eternal, Eternal Life, Permanence]

ETHICS

See Behavior, Honesty, Law.

EVANGELISM

I will publish the name of the Lord: ascribe ye greatness unto our God.
Deut. 32:3

Declare His glory among the heathen; His marvellous works among all nations.
1 Chron. 16:24
See also Ps. 96:3

Say among the heathen that the Lord reigneth.
Ps. 96:10

Make known His deeds among the people.
Ps. 105:1, 1 Chron. 16:8

I shall not die, but live, and declare the works of the Lord.
Ps. 118:17

Praise the Lord, call upon His name, declare His doings among the people, make mention that His name is exalted.
Isa. 12:4

The voice of him that crieth in the wilderness.
Isa. 40:3
See also, e.g., Matt. 3:3

I am sought of them that asked not for Me; I am found of them that sought Me not.
Isa. 65:1
See also Rom. 10:20

They shall declare My glory among the Gentiles.
Isa. 66:19

Hear the word of the Lord, O ye nations, and declare it in the isles afar off.
Jer. 31:10

My name shall be great among the heathen, saith the Lord of hosts.
Mal. 1:11

Follow me, and I will make you fishers of men.
Jesus
Matt. 4:19
See also Mark 1:17

Why eateth your Master with publicans and sinners?
Matt. 9:11
See also Luke 5:30

The harvest truly is plenteous, but the labourers are few.
Jesus
Matt. 9:37
See also Luke 10:2

I send you forth as sheep in the midst of wolves: be ye therefore wise as serpents, and harmless as doves.
Jesus
Matt. 10:16

I am not sent but unto the lost sheep of the house of Israel.
Jesus
Matt. 15:24

Go ye therefore, and teach all nations, baptizing them in the name of the Father, and of the Son, and of the Holy Ghost.
Jesus
Matt. 28:19

The sower soweth the word.
Jesus
Mark 4:14

The gospel must first be published among all nations.
Jesus
Mark 13:10

Go ye into all the world, and preach the gospel to every creature.
Jesus
Mark 16:15

Go thou and preach the kingdom of God.
Jesus
Luke 9:60

Repentance and remission of sins should be preached in His name among all nations.
Jesus
Luke 24:47

He that reapeth receiveth wages, and gathereth fruit unto life eternal.
Jesus
John 4:36

Other sheep I have, which are not of this fold.
Jesus
John 10:16

He that receiveth whomsoever I send receiveth me.
Jesus
John 13:20

Go and bring forth fruit.
Jesus
John 15:16

Ye also shall bear witness, because ye have been with me from the beginning.
Jesus
John 15:27

He is a chosen vessel unto me, to bear my name.
Jesus, about Saul
Acts 9:15

The hand of the Lord was with them: and a great number believed.
Acts 11:21

The word of God grew and multiplied.
Acts 12:24

Open their eyes.
Jesus to Paul
Acts 26:18

Turn them from darkness to light, and from the power of Satan unto God.
Jesus to Paul
Acts 26:18

The salvation of God is sent unto the Gentiles.
Acts 28:28

How shall they believe in Him of whom they have not heard?
Rom. 10:14

To whom He was not spoken of, they shall see: and they that have not heard shall understand.
Rom. 15:21
See also Isa. 52:15

Christ sent me not to baptize, but to preach the gospel.
1 Cor. 1:17

I seek not your's, but you.
2 Cor. 12:14

[*See also* Gospel, Ministry, Mission, Praise of God, Preaching, Testimony]

See Capital Punishment, Judging, Perjury, Proof.

EVIL

The imagination of man's heart is evil from his youth.
Gen. 8:21

Sodom and Gomorrah.
Gen. 18:20, Gen. 19:28

I will not justify the wicked.
God
Ex. 23:7

Thou knowest the people, that they are set on mischief.
Aaron to Moses
Ex. 32:22

Put the evil away from the midst of thee.
Deut. 13:5

Sons of Belial.
E.g., Judg. 19:22

The thing that David had done displeased the Lord.
2 Sam. 11:27

Thou knowest all the wickedness which thine heart is privy to.
1 Kings 2:44

There was none like unto Ahab, which did sell himself to work wickedness in the sight of the Lord.
1 Kings 21:25

Keep me from evil, that it may not grieve me!
1 Chron. 4:10

The triumphing of the wicked is short, and the joy of the hypocrite but for a moment.
Job 20:5

To depart from evil is understanding.
Job 28:28

Far be it from God, that He should do wickedness.
Job 34:10

God will not do wickedly, neither will the Almighty pervert judgment.
Job 34:12

Depart from evil.
E.g., Ps. 34:14
See also *Prov. 3:7, Prov. 16:6*

Spreading himself like a green bay tree.
Ps. 37:35

Ye that love the Lord, hate evil.
Ps. 97:10

Avoid it, pass not by it, turn from it, and pass away.
Prov. 4:15

The fear of the Lord is to hate evil.
Prov. 8:13

He that pursueth evil pursueth it to his own death.
Prov. 11:19

Evil pursueth sinners.
Prov. 13:21

A wise man feareth, and departeth from evil: but the fool rageth, and is confident.
Prov. 14:16

The thoughts of the wicked are an abomination to the Lord.
Prov. 15:26

The heart of the sons of men is full of evil, and madness is in their heart while they live.
Eccl. 9:3

He that diggeth a pit shall fall into it.
Eccl. 10:8

Wickedness burneth as the fire.
Isa. 9:18

I will punish the world for their evil, and the wicked for their iniquity.
Isa. 13:11

Out of the serpent's root shall come forth a cockatrice, and his fruit shall be a fiery flying serpent.
Isa. 14:29

How long shall thy vain thoughts lodge within thee?
Jer. 4:14

The heart is deceitful above all things, and desperately wicked: who can know it?
Jer. 17:9

They have sown the wind, and they shall reap the whirlwind.
Hos. 8:7

Woe to them that devise iniquity, and work evil upon their beds!
Mic. 2:1

Turn ye now from your evil ways, and from your evil doings.
Zech. 1:4

Let none of you imagine evil in your hearts against his neighbour.
Zech. 8:17
See also Zech. 7:10

O generation of vipers.
E.g., Matt. 3:7, Luke 3:7

Lead us not into temptation, but deliver us from evil.
Jesus
Matt. 6:13, Luke 11:4

If thine eye be evil, thy whole body shall be full of darkness.
Jesus
Matt. 6:23
See also Luke 11:34

Wherefore think ye evil in your hearts?
Jesus
Matt. 9:4
See also Luke 6:22

When the unclean spirit is gone out of a man, he walketh through dry places, seeking rest, and findeth none.
Jesus
Matt. 12:43
See also Luke 11:24

My name is Legion: for we are many.
Mark 5:9

This is an evil generation: they seek a sign.
Jesus
Luke 11:29
See also Matt. 12:39, Matt. 16:4

Depart from me, all ye workers of iniquity.
Jesus
Luke 13:27
See also Matt. 7:23

Men loved darkness rather than light, because their deeds were evil.
Jesus
John 3:19

Every one that doeth evil hateth the light.
Jesus
John 3:20

Ye are of your father the devil, and the lusts of your father ye will do.
Jesus
John 8:44

If I have spoken evil, bear witness of the evil.
Jesus
John 18:23

Thou child of the devil, thou enemy of all righteousness.
Acts 13:10

Their feet are swift to shed blood.
Rom. 3:15

A little leaven leaveneth the whole lump.
1 Cor. 5:6, Gal. 5:9

In malice be ye children, but in understanding be men.
1 Cor. 14:20

Evil communications corrupt good manners.
1 Cor. 15:33

Abstain from all appearance of evil.
1 Thess. 5:22

The love of money is the root of all evil.
1 Tim. 6:10

The tongue is a fire, a world of iniquity.
James 3:6

He that will love life, and see good days, let him refrain his tongue from evil.
1 Pet. 3:10
See also Ps. 34:13

The face of the Lord is against them that do evil.
1 Pet. 3:12

He that biddeth him God speed is partaker of his evil deeds.
2 John 11

Let him that hath understanding count the number of the beast.
Rev. 13:18

His number is Six hundred threescore and six.
Rev. 13:18

The Lamb shall overcome them: for He is Lord of lords, and King of kings.
Rev. 17:14

Receive not of her plagues.
(her: Babylon)
Rev. 18:4

Reward her even as she rewarded you, and double unto her double according to her works.
(her: Babylon)
Rev. 18:6

By thy sorceries were all nations deceived.
Rev. 18:23

[*See also* Behavior, Depravity, Godlessness, Good and Evil, Immorality, Purity, Righteousness, Satan, Sin, Wicked People, Wickedness]

EXALTATION

Thou, Lord, art high above all the earth: Thou art exalted far above all gods.
Ps. 97:9

Hereafter shall the Son of man sit on the right hand of the power of God.
Jesus
Luke 22:69
See also Matt. 26:64, Mark 14:62

Sit Thou on my right hand, Until I make Thy foes Thy footstool.
Acts 2:34–35

EXASPERATION

How long refuse ye to keep My commandments and My laws?
Ex. 16:28

How long will this people provoke Me?
Num. 14:11

Ye have forsaken Me, and served other gods: wherefore I will deliver you no more.
Judg. 10:13

Have I need of mad men, that ye have brought this fellow to play the mad man in my presence?
1 Sam. 21:15

They have done that which was evil in My sight, and have provoked Me to anger, since the day their fathers came forth out of Egypt.
2 Kings 21:15

Am I a sea, or a whale, that Thou settest a watch over me?
Job 7:12

Hast Thou eyes of flesh? or seest Thou as man seest?
Job 10:4

How long will ye vex my soul, and break me in pieces with words?
Job 19:2

O ye sons of men, how long will ye turn My glory into shame?
Ps. 4:2

Is it a small thing for you to weary men, but will ye weary my God also?
Isa. 7:13

I am weary with repenting.
God to Jeremiah
Jer. 15:6

Ye have wearied the Lord with your words.
Mal. 2:17

O faithless and perverse generation, how long shall I be with you? how long shall I suffer you?
Jesus
Matt. 17:17
See also Mark 9:19, Luke 9:41

From henceforth I will go unto the Gentiles.
Acts 18:6

[*See also* Anger, God's Anger, Impatience, Patience, Temper]

EXCESS

Thou wilt surely wear away, both thou, and this people that is with thee.
Jethro to Moses
Ex. 18:18

After whom dost thou pursue? after a dead dog, after a flea.
David to Saul
1 Sam. 24:14

The king of Israel is come out to seek a flea, as when one doth hunt a partridge in the mountains.
1 Sam. 26:20

Be not righteous over much; neither make thyself over wise.
Eccl. 7:16

Much study is a weariness of the flesh.
Eccl. 12:12

Be not drunk with wine, wherein is excess; but be filled with the Spirit.
Eph. 5:18

[*See also* Abundance, Gluttony]

EXCUSES

I was afraid, because I was naked.
Adam
Gen. 3:10

The serpent beguiled me, and I did eat.
Eve
Gen. 3:13

I did but taste a little honey with the end of the rod.
1 Sam. 14:43

I feared the people, and obeyed their voice.
Saul to Samuel
1 Sam. 15:24

Their gods are gods of the hills; therefore they were stronger than we.
1 Kings 20:23

The slothful man saith, There is a lion without, I shall be slain in the streets.
Prov. 22:13
See also Prov. 26:13

Say not, I am a child: for thou shalt go to all that I shall send thee, and whatsoever I command thee thou shalt speak.
God to Jeremiah
Jer. 1:7

They say, The Lord seeth us not; the Lord hath forsaken the earth.
Ezek. 8:12

Now they have no cloak for their sin.
Jesus
John 15:22

EXERCISE

See Physical Fitness.

EXILE

He made them wander in the wilderness forty years, until all the generation, that had done evil in the sight of the Lord, was consumed.
Num. 32:13

The Lord shall scatter you among the nations, and ye shall be left few in number among the heathen.
Moses to Israelites
Deut. 4:27

The children of Israel walked forty years in the wilderness.
Josh. 5:6
See also Num. 14:33

Let him turn to his own house, and let him not see my face.
(him: Absalom)
2 Sam. 14:24

How shall we sing the Lord's song in a strange land?
Ps. 137:4

My people are gone into captivity, because they have no knowledge.
Isa. 5:13

As ye have forsaken Me, and served strange gods in your land, so shall ye serve strangers in a land that is not your's.
Jer. 5:19

Weep sore for him that goeth away: for he shall return no more, nor see his native country.
Jer. 22:10

To the land whereunto they desire to return, thither shall they not return.
Jer. 22:27

Ye have sinned against the Lord, and have not obeyed His voice, therefore this thing is come upon you.
Jer. 40:3

I will scatter thee among the heathen, and disperse thee in the countries.
Ezek. 22:15

I will sow them among the people: and they shall remember Me in far countries.
Zech. 10:9

I will carry you away beyond Babylon.
Acts 7:43

[See also Captivity, Freedom, Outcast]

EXORCISM

How can Satan cast out Satan?
Jesus
Mark 3:23

Come out of the man, thou unclean spirit.
Jesus
Mark 5:8

In my name shall they cast out devils.
Jesus
Mark 16:17

I command thee in the name of Jesus Christ to come out of her.
Acts 16:18

EXPECTATION

The desire of the righteous is only good: but the expectation of the wicked is wrath.
Prov. 11:23

We looked for peace, but no good came; and for a time of health, and behold trouble!
Jer. 8:15

The harvest is past, the summer is ended, and we are not saved.
Jer. 8:20

Ye looked for much, and, lo, it came to little.
Hag. 1:9

To whom men have committed much, of him they will ask the more.
Jesus
Luke 12:48

[See also Disappointment, Hope]

EXPERIENCE

Thou mayest be to us instead of eyes.
Moses to Hobab
Num. 10:31

Remember the days of old, consider the years of many generations: ask thy father,

and he will show thee; thy elders, and they will tell thee.
Deut. 32:7

Let not him that girdeth on his harness boast himself as he that putteth it off.
1 Kings 20:11

With the ancient is wisdom; and in length of days understanding.
Job 12:12

Days should speak, and multitude of years should teach wisdom.
Job 32:7

Hast thou perceived the breadth of the earth? declare if thou knowest it all.
God to Job
Job 38:18

Hast thou entered into the treasures of the snow? or hast thou seen the treasures of the hail?
Job 38:22

I understand more than the ancients, because I keep Thy precepts.
Ps. 119:100

The glory of young men is their strength: and the beauty of old men is the grey head.
Prov. 20:29

All things have I seen in the days of my vanity.
Eccl. 7:15

Thou hast not remembered the days of thy youth, when thou wast naked and bare.
Ezek. 16:22

Whether He be a sinner or no, I know not: one thing I know, that, whereas I was blind, now I see.
John 9:25

[See also Age, Maturity, Wisdom, Youth]

EXPOSURE

The voice of thy brother's blood crieth unto Me from the ground.
Gen. 4:10

The morning is to them even as the shadow of death.
Job 24:17

That which ye have spoken in the ear in

closets shall be proclaimed upon the house-tops.
Jesus
Luke 12:3
See also Matt. 10:27

All things that are reproved are made manifest by the light.
Eph. 5:13

[*See also* Criminals, Light and Darkness, Secrecy]

FAILURE

If thou doest not well, sin lieth at the door.
Gen. 4:7

By the way that he came, by the same shall he return.
2 Kings 19:33, Isa. 37:34

He that trusteth in his riches shall fall.
Prov. 11:28

Pride goeth before destruction, and an haughty spirit before a fall.
Prov. 16:18

[*See also* Acceptance, Defeat, Success, Victory]

FAIRNESS

Wilt Thou also destroy the righteous with the wicked?
Abraham to God
Gen. 18:23

He that gathered much had nothing over, and he that gathered little had no lack.
Ex. 16:18

God do so and more also: for thou shalt surely die, Jonathan.
1 Sam. 14:44

He shall not judge after the sight of his eyes, neither reprove after the hearing of his ears.
Isa. 11:3

As with the buyer, so with the seller; as with the lender, so with the borrower; as with the taker of usury, so with the giver of usury to him.
Isa. 24:2

Is not My way equal? are not your ways unequal?
God to Israelites
Ezek. 18:25

With what judgment ye judge, ye shall be judged.
Jesus
Matt. 7:2

All things whatsoever ye would that men should do to you, do ye even so to them.
Jesus
Matt. 7:12
See also Luke 6:31

Whatsoever is right, that shall ye receive.
Jesus
Matt. 20:7

With what measure ye mete, it shall be measured to you.
Jesus
Mark 4:24
See also Luke 6:38

Sittest thou to judge me after the law, and commandest me to be smitten contrary to the law?
Paul to Ananias
Acts 23:3

Give unto your servants that which is just and equal; knowing that ye also have a Master in heaven.
Col. 4:1

The labourer is worthy of his reward.
1 Tim. 5:18
See also Luke 10:7

[*See also* Impartiality, Judging, Justice]

FAITH

Is any thing too hard for the Lord?
Gen. 18:14

If the Lord delight in us, then He will bring us into this land.
Joshua and Caleb
Num. 14:8

How long will it be ere they believe Me, for

all the signs which I have showed among them?
Num. 14:11

Speak ye unto the rock before their eyes; and it shall give forth his water.
God to Moses
Num. 20:8

He will not fail thee, neither forsake thee: fear not, neither be dismayed.
Deut. 31:8

The Lord that delivered me out of the paw of the lion, and out of the paw of the bear, He will deliver me out of the hand of this Philistine.
David
1 Sam. 17:37

Thou comest to me with a sword, and with a spear, and with a shield: but I come to thee in the name of the Lord of hosts.
David to Goliath
1 Sam. 17:45

This day will the Lord deliver thee into mine hand.
David to Goliath
1 Sam. 17:46

The Lord saveth not with sword and spear: for the battle is the Lord's.
David to Goliath
1 Sam. 17:47
See also 2 Chron. 20:15

There was no sword in the hand of David.
1 Sam. 17:50

Thou art my lamp, O Lord.
2 Sam. 22:29

Let the Lord do that which is good in His sight.
1 Chron. 19:13

If thou seek Him, He will be found of thee.
1 Chron. 28:9
See also 2 Chron. 15:2

Believe in the Lord your God, so shall ye be established; believe His prophets, so shall ye prosper.
2 Chron. 20:20

The Lord gave, and the Lord hath taken away; blessed be the name of the Lord.
Job 1:21

Though He slay me, yet will I trust in Him.
Job 13:15

My friends scorn me: but mine eye poureth out tears unto God.
Job 16:20

I know that my redeemer liveth, and that He shall stand at the latter day upon the earth.
Job 19:25

When Thou saidst, Seek ye My face; my heart said unto Thee, Thy face, Lord, will I seek.
Ps. 27:8

Be of good courage, and He shall strengthen your heart, all ye that hope in the Lord.
Ps. 31:24
See also Ps. 27:14

Many sorrows shall be to the wicked: but he that trusteth in the Lord, mercy shall compass him about.
Ps. 32:10

A mighty man is not delivered by much strength.
Ps. 33:16

Those that wait upon the Lord, they shall inherit the earth.
Ps. 37:9

Trust in Him at all times.
Ps. 62:8

Pour out your heart before Him: God is a refuge for us.
Ps. 62:8

Whom have I in heaven but Thee?
Ps. 73:25

Blessed is the man whose strength is in Thee.
Ps. 84:5

Let me not be ashamed of my hope.
Ps. 119:116

Happy is he that hath the God of Jacob for his help, whose hope is in the Lord his God.
Ps. 146:5

Whoso putteth his trust in the Lord shall be safe.
Prov. 29:25

God is my salvation; I will trust, and not be afraid.
Isa. 12:2

In quietness and in confidence shall be your strength.
Isa. 30:15

Blessed are all they that wait for Him.
Isa. 30:18

My judgment is with the Lord, and my work with my God.
Isa. 49:4

They shall not be ashamed that wait for Me.
Isa. 49:23

Let him that glorieth glory in this, that he understandeth and knoweth Me, that I am the Lord.
Jer. 9:24
See also, e.g., 1 Cor. 1:31

The Lord is good unto them that wait for Him, to the soul that seeketh Him.
Lam. 3:25

I called upon Thy name, O Lord, out of the low dungeon.
Lam. 3:55

Our God whom we serve is able to deliver us from the burning fiery furnace.
Dan. 3:17

The people that do know their God shall be strong.
Dan. 11:32

Turn thou to thy God: keep mercy and judgment, and wait on thy God continually.
Hos. 12:6

When my soul fainted within me I remembered the Lord.
Jonah 2:7

I will look unto the Lord; I will wait for the God of my salvation.
Mic. 7:7

When I sit in darkness, the Lord shall be a light unto me.
Mic. 7:8

The just shall live by his faith.
Hab. 2:4

If Thou wilt, Thou canst make me clean.
Leper to Jesus
Matt. 8:2, Mark 1:40, Luke 5:12

Speak the word only, and my servant shall be healed.
Centurion to Jesus
Matt. 8:8

Verily I say unto you, I have not found so great faith, no, not in Israel.
Jesus, about the centurion
Matt. 8:10
See also Luke 7:9

As thou hast believed, so be it done unto thee.
Jesus
Matt. 8:13

Why are ye fearful, O ye of little faith?
Jesus
Matt. 8:26
See also Mark 4:40

If I may but touch His garment, I shall be whole.
Matt. 9:21
See also Mark 5:28

Thy faith hath made thee whole.
Jesus
Matt. 9:22, Mark 5:34,
Mark 10:52, Luke 8:48
See also Luke 17:19

According to your faith be it unto you.
Jesus
Matt. 9:29

As many as touched were made perfectly whole.
Matt. 14:36
See also Mark 6:56

Great is thy faith: be it unto thee even as thou wilt.
Jesus
Matt. 15:28

O ye of little faith.
Jesus
E.g., Matt. 16:8

If ye have faith as a grain of mustard seed, ye shall say unto this mountain, Remove hence to yonder place; and it shall remove.
Jesus
Matt. 17:20

Nothing shall be impossible unto you.
Jesus
Matt. 17:20

If ye shall say unto this mountain, Be thou

removed, and be thou cast into the sea; it shall be done.
>Jesus
>*Matt. 21:21*
>*See also Mark 11:23*

Be not afraid, only believe.
>Jesus
>*Mark 5:36*

All things are possible to him that believeth.
>Jesus
>*Mark 9:23*

Whosoever shall offend one of these little ones that believe in me, it is better for him that a millstone were hanged about his neck, and he were cast into the sea.
>Jesus
>*Mark 9:42*
>*See also Matt. 18:6, Luke 17:2*

Have faith in God.
>Jesus
>*Mark 11:22*

What things soever ye desire, when ye pray, believe that ye receive them, and ye shall have them.
>Jesus
>*Mark 11:24*
>*See also Matt. 21:22*

Thy faith hath saved thee.
>Jesus
>*E.g., Luke 7:50*

Increase our faith.
>Apostles to Jesus
>*Luke 17:5*

Father, into Thy hands I commend my spirit.
>Jesus
>*Luke 23:46*

For God so loved the world, that He gave His only begotten Son, that whosoever believeth in Him should not perish, but have everlasting life.
>Jesus
>*John 3:16*
>*See also John 3:36, John 6:47*

Blessed are they that have not seen, and yet have believed.
>Jesus
>*John 20:29*

The just shall live by faith.
>*E.g., Rom. 1:17*

A man is justified by faith without the deeds of the law.
>*Rom. 3:28*

Do we then make void the law through faith? God forbid.
>*Rom. 3:31*

The righteousness of faith.
>*Rom. 4:13*

Ye are not in the flesh, but in the Spirit.
>*Rom. 8:9*

All things work together for good to them that love God.
>*Rom. 8:28*

Faith cometh by hearing, and hearing by the word of God.
>*Rom. 10:17*

Him that is weak in the faith receive ye, but not to doubtful disputations.
>*Rom. 14:1*

Hast thou faith? have it to thyself before God.
>*Rom. 14:22*

Whatsoever is not of faith is sin.
>*Rom. 14:23*

Faith should not stand in the wisdom of men, but in the power of God.
>*1 Cor. 2:5*

Be not deceived.
>*E.g., 1 Cor. 6:9*

Though I have all faith, so that I could remove mountains, and have not charity, I am nothing.
>(charity: love)
>*1 Cor. 13:2*

And now abideth faith, hope, charity, these three; but the greatest of these is charity.
>(charity: love)
>*1 Cor. 13:13*

If Christ be not raised, your faith is vain; ye are yet in your sins.
>*1 Cor. 15:17*

Stand fast in the faith.
>*1 Cor. 16:13*

By faith ye stand.
>*2 Cor. 1:24*

We walk by faith, not by sight.
2 Cor. 5:7

Having nothing, and yet possessing all things.
2 Cor. 6:10

A man is not justified by the works of the law, but by the faith of Jesus Christ.
Gal. 2:16

I am crucified with Christ: nevertheless I live.
Gal. 2:20

Before faith came, we were kept under the law.
Gal. 3:23

The law was our schoolmaster to bring us unto Christ, that we might be justified by faith.
Gal. 3:24

By grace are ye saved through faith.
Eph. 2:8

The shield of faith, wherewith ye shall be able to quench all the fiery darts of the wicked.
Eph. 6:16

Stand fast in the Lord, my dearly beloved.
Phil. 4:1

Now we live, if ye stand fast in the Lord.
1 Thess. 3:8

Quench not the Spirit.
1 Thess. 5:19

Be not soon shaken in mind.
2 Thess. 2:2

Stand fast, and hold the traditions which ye have been taught.
2 Thess. 2:15

All men have not faith.
2 Thess. 3:2

Fight the good fight of faith.
1 Tim. 6:12

I am not ashamed: for I know whom I have believed.
2 Tim. 1:12

I have fought a good fight, I have finished my course, I have kept the faith.
2 Tim. 4:7

Let us hold fast the profession of our faith without wavering.
Heb. 10:23

We are not of them who draw back unto perdition; but of them that believe to the saving of the soul.
Heb. 10:39

Faith is the substance of things hoped for, the evidence of things not seen.
Heb. 11:1

Without faith it is impossible to please Him.
Heb. 11:6

Ask in faith, nothing wavering.
James 1:6

Faith without works is dead.
James 2:20
See also James 2:17, James 2:26

By works was faith made perfect.
James 2:22

Draw nigh to God, and He will draw nigh to you.
James 4:8

Add to your faith virtue; and to virtue knowledge.
2 Pet. 1:5

Earnestly contend for the faith which was once delivered unto the saints.
Jude 3

Buy of me gold tried in the fire, that thou mayest be rich; and white raiment, that thou mayest be clothed.
Jesus
Rev. 3:18

Here is the patience and the faith of the saints.
Rev. 13:10

He that overcometh shall inherit all things.
Rev. 21:7

[*See also* Belief, Doubt, Fear of God, Healing, Jesus (Acceptance of), Monotheism, Sin, Trust]

Hath He said, and shall He not do it? or hath He spoken, and shall He not make it good?
Num. 23:19

Beware lest thou forget the Lord.
Deut. 6:12
See also Deut. 8:11

Him shalt thou serve, and to Him shalt thou cleave, and swear by His name.
Deut. 10:20

Cleave unto the Lord your God, as ye have done unto this day.
Josh. 23:8
See also Josh. 22:5

But as for me and my house, we will serve the Lord.
Josh. 24:15

God forbid that we should forsake the Lord, to serve other gods.
Josh. 24:16

Thy people shall be my people, and thy God my God.
Ruth 1:16

There hath not failed one word of all His good promise.
1 Kings 8:56

Remember now how I have walked before Thee in truth and with a perfect heart.
2 Kings 20:3
See also Isa. 38:3

Walk after the Lord.
2 Kings 23:3

Be ye mindful always of His covenant.
1 Chron. 16:15

Are they not all my lord's servants?
1 Chron. 21:3

As for us, the Lord is our God, and we have not forsaken Him.
2 Chron. 13:10

The Lord is with you, while ye be with Him.
2 Chron. 15:2

Touch all that he hath, and he will curse Thee to Thy face.
Satan to God, about Job
Job 1:11

Shall we receive good at the hand of God, and shall we not receive evil?
Job 2:10

The Lord preserveth the faithful, and plentifully rewardeth the proud doer.
Ps. 31:23

The Lord loveth judgment, and forsaketh not His saints.
Ps. 37:28

This God is our God for ever and ever: He will be our guide even unto death.
Ps. 48:14

I am small and despised: yet do not I forget Thy precepts.
Ps. 119:141

The earth shall be full of the knowledge of the Lord, as the waters cover the sea.
Isa. 11:9

Thy counsels of old are faithfulness and truth.
Isa. 25:1

They may forget, yet will I not forget thee.
God, about parents
Isa. 49:15

Examine yourselves, whether ye be in the faith.
2 Cor. 13:5

As ye have therefore received Christ Jesus the Lord, so walk ye in Him.
Col. 2:6

The Lord is faithful, who shall stablish you, and keep you from evil.
2 Thess. 3:3

Be thou faithful unto death, and I will give thee a crown of life.
Jesus
Rev. 2:10

They that are with Him are called, and chosen, and faithful.
Rev. 17:14

Behold a white horse; and he that sat upon him was called Faithful and True.
Rev. 19:11

[*See also* Allegiance, Devotion, Faith, Loyalty]

FAITHLESSNESS

We be not able to go up against the people; for they are stronger than we.
Num. 13:31

He will not be slack to him that hateth Him, He will repay him to his face.
Deut. 7:10

They would not hearken unto their judges, but they went a whoring after other gods.
Judg. 2:17
See also 1 Chron. 5:25

He forsook the Lord God of his fathers, and walked not in the way of the Lord.
2 Kings 21:22

The hypocrite's hope shall perish.
Job 8:13

If I forget thee, O Jerusalem, let my right hand forget her cunning.
Ps. 137:5

Who art thou, that thou shouldest be afraid of a man that shall die, and of the son of man which shall be made as grass; And forgettest the Lord thy maker.
Isa. 51:12–13

Can a maid forget her ornaments, or a bride her attire? yet My people have forgotten Me days without number.
Jer. 2:32

[*See also* Atheism, Godlessness]

FALSE GODS

Take heed to yourselves, that your heart be not deceived.
Deut. 11:16

If he be a god, let him plead for himself, because one hath cast down his altar.
Judg. 6:31

Go and cry unto the gods which ye have chosen; let them deliver you.
God to Israelites
Judg. 10:14

Call ye on the name of your gods, and I will call on the name of the Lord.
Elijah
1 Kings 18:24

There was no voice, nor any that answered.
1 Kings 18:26

Have the gods of the nations delivered them which my fathers have destroyed?
Sennacherib to Hezekiah
2 Kings 19:12, Isa. 37:12

All the gods of the people are idols: but the Lord made the heavens.
1 Chron. 16:26
See also Ps. 96:5

To whom then will ye liken Me, or shall I be equal? saith the Holy One.
Isa. 40:25
See also Isa. 46:5

They that observe lying vanities forsake their own mercy.
Jonah 2:8

[*See also* Idolatry, Idols]

FALSE PROPHETS

Thou shalt not hearken unto the words of that prophet, or that dreamer of dreams: for the Lord your God proveth you, to know whether ye love the Lord your God with all your heart and with all your soul.
Deut. 13:3

When a prophet speaketh in the name of the Lord, if the thing follow not, nor come to pass, that is the thing which the Lord hath not spoken.
Deut. 18:22

I am a prophet also as thou art; and an angel spake unto me by the word of the Lord.
1 Kings 13:18

I will go forth, and I will be a lying spirit in the mouth of all his prophets.
1 Kings 22:22

If thou return at all in peace, the Lord hath not spoken by me.
1 Kings 22:28
See also 2 Chron. 18:27

By sword and famine shall those prophets be consumed.
Jer. 14:15

They speak a vision of their own heart, and not out of the mouth of the Lord.
Jer. 23:16

I have not sent these prophets, yet they ran: I have not spoken to them, yet they prophesied.
Jer. 23:21

The prophet that hath a dream, let him tell a dream; and he that hath My word, let him speak My word faithfully.
Jer. 23:28

I am against the prophets, saith the Lord, that use their tongues, and say, He saith.
Jer. 23:31

Hearken not ye to your prophets, nor to your diviners, nor to your dreamers, nor to your enchanters.
Jer. 27:9

If they be prophets, and if the word of the Lord be with them, let them now make intercession to the Lord of hosts.
Jer. 27:18

They prophesy falsely unto you in My name: I have not sent them, saith the Lord.
Jer. 29:9

Woe unto the foolish prophets, that follow their own spirit, and have seen nothing!
Ezek. 13:3

Ye say, The Lord saith it; albeit I have not spoken.
Ezek. 13:7

Will ye pollute Me among My people for handfuls of barley and for pieces of bread?
Ezek. 13:19

With lies ye have made the heart of the righteous sad.
Ezek. 13:22

Thou speakest lies in the name of the Lord.
Zech. 13:3

The prophets shall be ashamed every one of his vision.
Zech. 13:4

Beware of false prophets, which come to you in sheep's clothing, but inwardly they are ravening wolves.
Jesus
Matt. 7:15

Take heed that no man deceive you. For many shall come in my name, saying, I am Christ.
Jesus
Matt. 24:4–5
See also Mark 13:6, Luke 21:8

Thou child of the devil, thou enemy of all righteousness.
Acts 13:10

Wilt thou not cease to pervert the right ways of the Lord?
Acts 13:10

Many shall follow their pernicious ways.
2 Pet. 2:2

These are wells without water, clouds that are carried with a tempest.
2 Pet. 2:17

They are of the world: therefore speak they of the world.
1 John 4:5

[*See also* Heresy, Prophecy]

FAME

His fame was noised throughout all the country.
Josh. 6:27

Saul hath slain his thousands, and David his ten thousands.
E.g., 1 Sam. 18:7

Riches and honour come of Thee.
1 Chron. 29:12

His remembrance shall perish from the earth, and he shall have no name in the street.
(His: wicked people)
Job 18:17

I am forgotten as a dead man out of mind: I am like a broken vessel.
Ps. 31:12

His name shall endure for ever: his name shall be continued as long as the sun.
Ps. 72:17

The seed of evildoers shall never be renowned.
Isa. 14:20

Make sweet melody, sing many songs, that thou mayest be remembered.
Isa. 23:16

I will make you a name and a praise among all people of the earth, when I turn back your captivity before your eyes.
Zeph. 3:20

A city that is set on an hill cannot be hid.
Jesus
Matt. 5:14

[*See also* Boasting, Deeds, Glory, God's Glory, Modesty, Reputation, Respect, Shame]

FAMILY

Be fruitful, and multiply.
E.g., Gen. 1:28

In thee and in thy seed shall all the families of the earth be blessed.
God to Jacob
Gen. 28:14

He that troubleth his own house shall inherit the wind.
Prov. 11:29

He that loveth father or mother more than me is not worthy of me: and he that loveth son or daughter more than me is not worthy of me.
Jesus to disciples
Matt. 10:37

Whosoever shall do the will of my Father which is in heaven, the same is my brother, and sister, and mother.
Jesus
Matt. 12:50
See also Mark 3:35

My mother and my brethren are these which hear the word of God, and do it.
Jesus
Luke 8:21

The father shall be divided against the son, and the son against the father; the mother against the daughter, and the daughter against the mother.
Jesus
Luke 12:53
See also Matt. 10:35

[*See also* Building, Children, Incest, Parents, Siblings, Strife]

FAMINE

The famine shall consume the land.
Gen. 41:30

Famine was over all the face of the earth.
Gen. 41:56

When the poor and needy seek water, and there is none, and their tongue faileth for thirst, I the Lord will hear them, I the God of Israel will not forsake them.
Isa. 41:17

The young children ask bread, and no man breaketh it unto them.
Lam. 4:4

They that be slain with the sword are better than they that be slain with hunger.
Lam. 4:9

They shall eat bread by weight, and with care; and they shall drink water by measure, and with astonishment.
Ezek. 4:16

The fathers shall eat the sons in the midst of thee, and the sons shall eat their fathers.
Ezek. 5:10

He that is far off shall die of the pestilence; and he that is near shall fall by the sword; and he that remaineth and is besieged shall die by the famine.
Ezek. 6:12

The sword is without, and the pestilence and the famine within.
Ezek. 7:15

That which the locust hath left hath the cankerworm eaten; and that which the cankerworm hath left hath the caterpillar eaten.
Joel 1:4

I will send a famine in the land, not a famine of bread, nor a thirst for water, but of hearing the words of the Lord.
Amos 8:11

[*See also* Deprivation, Food, Hunger, Thirst]

FARMING

See Animals, Cultivation, Growth.

FASHION

See Appearance, Beauty, Change, Materialism.

FASTING

I humbled my soul with fasting.
Ps. 35:13

In the day of your fast ye find pleasure.
Isa. 58:3

Is not this the fast that I have chosen? to loose the bands of wickedness, to undo the heavy burdens, and to let the oppressed go free.
Isa. 58:6

When they fast, I will not hear their cry.
Jer. 14:12

When thou fastest, anoint thine head, and wash thy face.
Jesus
Matt. 6:17

Appear not unto men to fast, but unto thy Father.
Jesus
Matt. 6:18

FAVORITISM

He was the son of his old age.
(He: Joseph)
Gen. 37:3

He made him a coat of many colours.
Gen. 37:3

Thou shalt not respect the person of the poor, nor honour the person of the mighty.
Lev. 19:15

Though he was not the firstborn, yet his father made him the chief.
1 Chron. 26:10

There is no respect of persons with God.
Rom. 2:11
See also Acts 10:34

[*See also* Equality, Impartiality]

FEAR

Fear not, for I am with thee, and will bless thee, and will multiply thy seed.
God to Isaac
Gen. 26:24

Deliver me, I pray Thee, from the hand of my brother.
Jacob to God, about Esau
Gen. 32:11

It had been better for us to serve the Egyptians, than that we should die in the wilderness.
Ex. 14:12

Ye shall flee when none pursueth you.
Lev. 26:17

We were in our own sight as grasshoppers.
Num. 13:33

Ye shall not fear them: for the Lord your God He shall fight for you.
Deut. 3:22

Be not afraid, neither be thou dismayed: for the Lord thy God is with thee whithersoever thou goest.
Josh. 1:9

Whosoever is fearful and afraid, let him return and depart early.
Gideon to his soldiers
Judg. 7:3

Thou seest the shadow of the mountains as if they were men.
Judg. 9:36

Do what seemeth good unto thee.
Israelites to Saul
1 Sam. 14:40

The hair of my flesh stood up.
Job 4:15

Let not Thy dread make me afraid.
Job 13:21

Yea, though I walk through the valley of the shadow of death, I will fear no evil: for Thou art with me.
Ps. 23:4

The Lord is my light and my salvation; whom shall I fear? the Lord is the strength of my life; of whom shall I be afraid?
Ps. 27:1

In God I have put my trust; I will not fear what flesh can do unto me.
Ps. 56:4
See also Ps. 56:11

Thou shalt not be afraid for the terror by night; nor for the arrow that flieth by day.
Ps. 91:5

The wicked flee when no man pursueth.
Prov. 28:1

Every man hath his sword upon his thigh because of fear in the night.
Song 3:8

Woe is me! for I am undone.
Isa. 6:5

Let Him be your fear, and let Him be your dread.
Isa. 8:13

One thousand shall flee at the rebuke of one.
Isa. 30:17

Who art thou, that thou shouldest be afraid of a man that shall die, and of the son of man which shall be made as grass?
Isa. 51:12

Be not afraid of him, saith the Lord: for I am with you to save you.
Jer. 42:11

Fear them not, neither be dismayed at their looks, though they be a rebellious house.
Ezek. 3:9

Why are ye fearful, O ye of little faith?
Jesus
Matt. 8:26
See also Mark 4:40

Fear not them which kill the body, but are not able to kill the soul.
Jesus
Matt. 10:28
See also Luke 12:4

Be of good cheer; it is I; be not afraid.
Jesus
Matt. 14:27, Mark 6:50
See also John 6:20

Be not afraid, only believe.
Jesus
Mark 5:36

Fear Him, which after He hath killed hath

power to cast into hell; yea, I say unto you, Fear Him.
Jesus
Luke 12:5
See also Matt. 10:28

Let not your heart be troubled, neither let it be afraid.
Jesus
John 14:27
See also John 14:1

If thou do that which is evil, be afraid; for he beareth not the sword in vain.
(he: civil authorities)
Rom. 13:4

Tribute to whom tribute is due; custom to whom custom; fear to whom fear; honour to whom honour.
Rom. 13:7

The Lord is my helper, and I will not fear what man shall do unto me.
Heb. 13:6
See also Ps. 118:6

Perfect love casteth out fear.
1 John 4:18

[*See also* Courage, Cowardice, Encouragement, God's Protection, Terror, Timidity]

FEAR OF GOD

O that there were such an heart in them, that they would fear Me, and keep all My commandments always.
Deut. 5:29

Fear the Lord thy God.
E.g., Deut. 10:12

Fear before Him, all the earth.
1 Chron. 16:30

The fear of the Lord, that is wisdom.
Job 28:28

The secret of the Lord is with them that fear Him.
Ps. 25:14

When He slew them, then they sought Him.
Ps. 78:34

God is greatly to be feared in the assembly of the saints.
Ps. 89:7

He is to be feared above all gods.
Ps. 96:4

The fear of the Lord is the beginning of wisdom.
Ps. 111:10, Prov. 9:10

Blessed is the man that feareth the Lord.
Ps. 112:1

Ye that fear the Lord, trust in the Lord: He is their help and their shield.
Ps. 115:11

Blessed is every one that feareth the Lord; that walketh in His ways.
Ps. 128:1

The fear of the Lord is the beginning of knowledge.
Prov. 1:7

The fear of the Lord is to hate evil.
Prov. 8:13

The fear of the Lord prolongeth days: but the years of the wicked shall be shortened.
Prov. 10:27

The fear of the Lord is a fountain of life.
Prov. 14:27

By the fear of the Lord men depart from evil.
Prov. 16:6

Be thou in the fear of the Lord all the day long.
Prov. 23:17

Favour is deceitful, and beauty is vain: but a woman that feareth the Lord, she shall be praised.
Prov. 31:30

Fear ye not Me? saith the Lord: will ye not tremble at My presence?
Jer. 5:22

His mercy is on them that fear Him from generation to generation.
Mary, mother of Jesus
Luke 1:50

Whosoever among you feareth God, to you is the word of this salvation sent.
Acts 13:26

The devils also believe, and tremble.
James 2:19

[See also Awe, Reverence]

Behold, how good and how pleasant it is for brethren to dwell together in unity!
Ps. 133:1

Have we not all one father? hath not one God created us?
Mal. 2:10

Whosoever shall do the will of my Father which is in heaven, the same is my brother, and sister, and mother.
Jesus
Matt. 12:50
See also Mark 3:35

Where two or three are gathered together in my name, there am I in the midst of them.
Jesus
Matt. 18:20

Have salt in yourselves, and have peace one with another.
Jesus
Mark 9:50

He that loveth me shall be loved of my Father.
Jesus
John 14:21

I am the vine, ye are the branches.
Jesus
John 15:5

Woman, behold thy son!
Jesus (son: John)
John 19:26

We, being many, are one body in Christ, and every one members one of another.
Rom. 12:5

Him that is weak in the faith receive ye, but not to doubtful disputations.
Rom. 14:1

Receive ye one another, as Christ also received us to the glory of God.
Rom. 15:7

We being many are one bread, and one body: for we are all partakers of that one bread.
1 Cor. 10:17

Ye are no more strangers and foreigners, but fellowcitizens with the saints.
Eph. 2:19

Speak every man truth with his neighbour:
for we are members one of another.
Eph. 4:25

Though I be absent in the flesh, yet am I
with you in the spirit.
Col. 2:5
See also 1 Cor. 5:3

Not now as a servant, but above a servant,
a brother beloved.
Philem. 16

Greet ye one another with a kiss of charity.
1 Pet. 5:14

Our fellowship is with the Father, and with
His Son Jesus Christ.
1 John 1:3

If we walk in the light, as He is in the light,
we have fellowship one with another.
1 John 1:7

See also Brotherhood, Companions,
Friendship]

FERTILITY

Be fruitful, and multiply.
E.g., Gen. 1:28

I will make thy seed as the dust of the
earth: so that if a man can number the dust
of the earth, then shall thy seed also be
numbered.
God to Abram
Gen. 13:16
See also Gen. 28:14

Shall a child be born unto him that is an
hundred years old? and shall Sarah, that is
ninety years old, bear?
Gen. 17:17

Thou art barren, and bearest not: but thou
shalt conceive, and bear a son.
Angel to Samson's mother
Judg. 13:3

The Lord make the woman that is come
into thine house like Rachel and like Leah.
Ruth 4:11

Elkanah knew Hannah his wife; and the
Lord remembered her.
1 Sam. 1:19

Nay, my lord, thou man of God, do not lie
unto thine handmaid.
2 Kings 4:16

He maketh the barren woman to keep
house, and to be a joyful mother of children.
Ps. 113:9

Give them, O Lord: what wilt Thou give?
give them a miscarrying womb and dry
breasts.
Hos. 9:14

[*See also* Birth, Childlessness]

FIDELITY

See Commitment, Faithfulness, Loyalty.

FINANCE

See Borrowing.

FIRSTBORN

The elder shall serve the younger.
Gen. 25:23, Rom. 9:12

His younger brother shall be greater than
he.
Gen. 48:19

My firstborn, my might, and the beginning
of my strength.
Gen. 49:3

I will pass through the land of Egypt this
night, and will smite all the firstborn in the
land of Egypt, both man and beast.
Ex. 12:12

Sanctify unto Me all the firstborn.
Ex. 13:2

The firstborn of thy sons shalt thou give
unto Me.
Ex. 22:29

All the firstborn are Mine.
Num. 3:13

Though he was not the firstborn, yet his
father made him the chief.
1 Chron. 26:10

Every male that openeth the womb shall be called holy to the Lord.
>
> *Luke 2:23*
> *See also Ex. 13:2, 12*

FLATTERY

As thou art, so were they; each one resembled the children of a king.
>
> *Judg. 8:18*

The half was not told me.
>
> Queen of Sheba to Solomon
> *1 Kings 10:7*

With flattering lips and with a double heart do they speak.
>
> *Ps. 12:2*

He that hideth hatred with lying lips, and he that uttereth a slander, is a fool.
>
> *Prov. 10:18*

Meddle not with him that flattereth with his lips.
>
> *Prov. 20:19*

A flattering mouth worketh ruin.
>
> *Prov. 26:28*

Faithful are the wounds of a friend; but the kisses of an enemy are deceitful.
>
> *Prov. 27:6*

A man that flattereth his neighbour spreadeth a net for his feet.
>
> *Prov. 29:5*

It is better to hear the rebuke of the wise, than for a man to hear the song of fools.
>
> *Eccl. 7:5*

Get thee behind me, Satan: thou art an offence unto me.
>
> Jesus
> *Matt. 16:23*
> *See also Matt. 4:10, Mark 8:33, Luke 4:8*

Woe unto you, when all men shall speak well of you!
>
> Jesus
> *Luke 6:26*

FLAVOR

Can that which is unsavoury be eaten without salt?
>
> *Job 6:6*

Is there any taste in the white of an egg?
>
> *Job 6:6*

Eat thou honey, because it is good; and the honeycomb, which is sweet to thy taste.
>
> *Prov. 24:13*

If the salt have lost his savour, wherewith shall it be salted? it is thenceforth good for nothing.
>
> Jesus
> *Matt. 5:13*
> *See also Mark 9:50, Luke 14:34*

It shall make thy belly bitter, but it shall be in thy mouth sweet as honey.
>
> *Rev. 10:9*

FLOOD

Of every living thing of all flesh, two of every sort shalt thou bring into the ark, to keep them alive with thee.
>
> *Gen. 6:19*

And the rain was upon the earth forty days and forty nights.
>
> *Gen. 7:12*

Neither shall there any more be a flood to destroy the earth.
>
> *Gen. 9:11*

FOLLY

But he forsook the counsel which the old men gave him.
>
> *2 Chron. 10:8*

In his disease he sought not to the Lord, but to the physicians.
>
> *2 Chron. 16:12*

Forsake the foolish, and live.
>
> *Prov. 9:6*

The foolishness of fools is folly.
>
> *Prov. 14:24*

He that is hasty of spirit exalteth folly.
>
> *Prov. 14:29*

Folly is joy to him that is destitute of wisdom.
>
> *Prov. 15:21*

The foolishness of man perverteth his way.
>
> *Prov. 19:3*

Wisdom excelleth folly, as far as light
excelleth darkness.
Eccl. 2:13

My people is foolish, they have not known
Me.
Jer. 4:22

Every one that heareth these sayings of
mine, and doeth them not, shall be likened
unto a foolish man, which built his house
upon the sand.
Jesus
Matt. 7:26
See also Luke 6:49

God hath chosen the foolish things of the
world to confound the wise.
1 Cor. 1:27

Walk circumspectly, not as fools, but as
wise.
Eph. 5:15

Shun profane and vain babblings: for they
will increase unto more ungodliness.
2 Tim. 2:16

Avoid foolish questions.
Titus 3:9

[*See also* Fools, Wisdom]

FOOD

Every moving thing that liveth shall be
meat for you.
Gen. 9:3

Eat, that thou mayest have strength, when
thou goest on thy way.
Spiritualist to Saul
1 Sam. 28:22

He hath given meat unto them that fear
Him.
Ps. 111:5

It is good and comely for one to eat and to
drink, and to enjoy the good of all his
labour.
Eccl. 5:18
See also Eccl. 3:13

Eat thy bread with joy, and drink thy wine
with a merry heart.
Eccl. 9:7

Give us this day our daily bread.
Jesus
Matt. 6:11
See also Luke 11:3

Not that which goeth into the mouth de-
fileth a man; but that which cometh out of
the mouth, this defileth a man.
Jesus
Matt. 15:11
See also Mark 7:15

Take no thought for your life, what ye shall
eat; neither for the body, what ye shall put
on.
Jesus
Luke 12:22
See also Matt. 6:25

Labour not for the meat which perisheth,
but for that meat which endureth unto
everlasting life.
Jesus
John 6:27

Rise, Peter; kill, and eat.
Acts 10:13

Every creature of God is good, and nothing to be refused, if it be received with
thanksgiving.
1 Tim. 4:4

[*See also* Bread of Life, Celebration, Deprivation, Famine, Flavor, Gluttony, Hunger, Materialism, Pleasure, Thirst]

FOOLS

The fool hath said in his heart, There is no
God.
Ps. 14:1, Ps. 53:1

The foolish man reproacheth Thee daily.
Ps. 74:22

Fools despise wisdom and instruction.
Prov. 1:7

Scorners delight in their scorning, and
fools hate knowledge.
Prov.1:22

He that walketh with wise men shall be
wise: but a companion of fools shall be
destroyed.
Prov. 13:20

A wise man feareth, and departeth from evil: but the fool rageth, and is confident.
Prov. 14:16

A reproof entereth more into a wise man than an hundred stripes into a fool.
Prov. 17:10

Let a bear robbed of her whelps meet a man, rather than a fool in his folly.
Prov. 17:12

The father of a fool hath no joy.
Prov. 17:21

A foolish son is a grief to his father, and bitterness to her that bare him.
Prov. 17:25

Even a fool, when he holdeth his peace, is counted wise.
Prov. 17:28

A fool's mouth is his destruction, and his lips are the snare of his soul.
Prov. 18:7

Every fool will be meddling.
Prov. 20:3

As snow in summer, and as rain in harvest, so honour is not seemly for a fool.
Prov. 26:1

A whip for the horse, a bridle for the ass, and a rod for the fool's back.
Prov. 26:3

Answer not a fool according to his folly, lest thou also be like unto him.
Prov. 26:4

Answer a fool according to his folly, lest he be wise in his own conceit.
Prov. 26:5

As a dog returneth to his vomit, so a fool returneth to his folly.
Prov. 26:11
See also 2 Pet. 2:22

Though thou shouldest bray a fool in a mortar among wheat with a pestle, yet will not his foolishness depart from him.
Prov. 27:22

The wise man's eyes are in his head; but the fool walketh in darkness.
Eccl. 2:14

A fool's voice is known by multitude of words.
Eccl. 5:3

For He hath no pleasure in fools.
Eccl. 5:4

The heart of the wise is in the house of mourning; but the heart of fools is in the house of mirth.
Eccl. 7:4

For ye suffer fools gladly, seeing ye yourselves are wise.
2 Cor. 11:19

[*See also* Folly]

FOREIGNERS

I have been a stranger in a strange land.
Moses
Ex. 2:22

One law shall be to him that is homeborn, and unto the stranger that sojourneth among you.
Ex. 12:49
See also Lev. 24:22, Num. 9:14

Thou shalt neither vex a stranger, nor oppress him: for ye were strangers in the land of Egypt.
Ex. 22:21
See also Ex. 23:9

Thou shalt love him as thyself.
Lev. 19:34

Love ye therefore the stranger: for ye were strangers in the land of Egypt.
Deut. 10:19

Unto a stranger thou mayest lend upon usury; but unto thy brother thou shalt not lend upon usury.
Deut. 23:20

Learn not the way of the heathen.
Jer. 10:2

FORGIVENESS

Hear Thou in heaven Thy dwelling place: and when Thou hearest, forgive.
1 Kings 8:30
See also, e.g., 1 Kings 8:39

Render unto every man according unto all his ways, whose heart Thou knowest.
2 Chron. 6:30

They have humbled themselves; therefore I will not destroy them.
2 Chron. 12:7

Nevertheless there are good things found in thee.
2 Chron. 19:3

Serve the Lord your God, that the fierceness of His wrath may turn away from you.
2 Chron. 30:8

The good Lord pardon every one That prepareth his heart to seek God.
2 Chron. 30:18–19

Remember not the sins of my youth.
Ps. 25:7

According to Thy mercy remember Thou me for Thy goodness' sake.
Ps. 25:7

Blessed is he whose transgression is forgiven.
Ps. 32:1

He remembered that they were but flesh; a wind that passeth away, and cometh not again.
Ps. 78:39

Wilt Thou be angry for ever? shall Thy jealousy burn like fire?
Ps. 79:5

He will not always chide: neither will He keep His anger for ever.
Ps. 103:9

Hatred stirreth up strifes: but love covereth all sins.
Prov. 10:12

A brother offended is harder to be won than a strong city.
Prov. 18:19

Though your sins be as scarlet, they shall be as white as snow.
Isa. 1:18

Thou hast played the harlot with many lovers; yet return again to Me, saith the Lord.
Jer. 3:1

I am merciful, saith the Lord, and I will not keep anger for ever.
God to Jews
Jer. 3:12

I will forgive their iniquity, and I will remember their sin no more.
Jer. 31:34
See also, e.g., Heb. 8:12

I repent Me of the evil that I have done unto you.
Jer. 42:10

I will pardon them whom I reserve.
Jer. 50:20

Though they cry in Mine ears with a loud voice, yet will I not hear them.
Ezek. 8:18

In his righteousness that he hath done he shall live.
Ezek. 18:22

O Lord, hear; O Lord, forgive; O Lord, hearken and do.
Dan. 9:19

Defer not, for Thine own sake, O my God: for Thy city and Thy people are called by Thy name.
Dan. 9:19

Spare Thy people, O Lord, and give not Thine heritage to reproach.
Joel 2:17

I will restore to you the years that the locust hath eaten.
Joel 2:25

Who can tell if God will turn and repent, and turn away from His fierce anger?
Jonah 3:9

God repented of the evil, that He had said that He would do unto them; and He did it not.
Jonah 3:10

He retaineth not His anger for ever, because He delighteth in mercy.
Mic. 7:18

Whosoever shall smite thee on thy right cheek, turn to him the other also.
Jesus
Matt. 5:39

Pray for them which despitefully use you, and persecute you.
Jesus
Matt. 5:44
See also Luke 6:28

Forgive us our debts, as we forgive our debtors.
>Jesus
>*Matt. 6:12*
>*See also Luke 11:4*

If ye forgive men their trespasses, your heavenly Father will also forgive you.
>Jesus
>*Matt. 6:14*

Be of good cheer; thy sins be forgiven thee.
>Jesus
>*Matt. 9:2*
>*See also Mark 2:5*

The Son of man hath power on earth to forgive sins.
>Jesus
>*Matt. 9:6, Mark 2:10*
>*See also Luke 5:24*

All manner of sin and blasphemy shall be forgiven unto men: but the blasphemy against the Holy Ghost shall not be forgiven unto men.
>Jesus
>*Matt. 12:31*
>*See also Matt. 12:32, Mark 3:29,*
>   *Luke 12:10*

Until seventy times seven.
>Jesus
>*Matt. 18:22*

Unto him that smiteth thee on the one cheek offer also the other.
>Jesus
>*Luke 6:29*
>*See also Matt. 5:39*

Forgive, and ye shall be forgiven.
>Jesus
>*Luke 6:37*

To whom little is forgiven, the same loveth little.
>Jesus
>*Luke 7:47*

Forgive us our sins.
>Jesus
>*Luke 11:4*

If thy brother trespass against thee, rebuke him; and if he repent, forgive him.
>Jesus
>*Luke 17:3*

If he trespass against thee seven times in a day, and seven times in a day turn again to thee, saying, I repent; thou shalt forgive him.
>Jesus
>*Luke 17:4*

Father, forgive them; for they know not what they do.
>Jesus
>*Luke 23:34*

To day shalt thou be with me in paradise.
>Jesus to malefactor on cross
>*Luke 23:43*

Him that cometh to me I will in no wise cast out.
>Jesus
>*John 6:37*

Lord, lay not this sin to their charge.
>Stephen, dying
>*Acts 7:60*

Whosoever believeth in Him shall receive remission of sins.
>*Acts 10:43*

Through this man is preached unto you the forgiveness of sins.
>Paul, about Jesus
>*Acts 13:38*

Blessed are they whose iniquities are forgiven, and whose sins are covered.
>*Rom. 4:7*

Blessed is the man to whom the Lord will not impute sin.
>*Rom. 4:8*

As by one man's disobedience many were made sinners, so by the obedience of one shall many be made righteous.
>*Rom. 5:19*

Where sin abounded, grace did much more abound.
>*Rom. 5:20*

Bless them which persecute you: bless, and curse not.
>*Rom. 12:14*

If thine enemy hunger, feed him; if he thirst, give him drink.
>*Rom. 12:20*
>*See also Prov. 25:21*

Let not the sun go down upon your wrath.
>*Eph. 4:26*

God for Christ's sake hath forgiven you.
>*Eph. 4:32*

We have redemption through His blood, even the forgiveness of sins.
Col. 1:14

Even as Christ forgave you, so also do ye.
Col. 3:13

Without shedding of blood is no remission.
Heb. 9:22

It is not possible that the blood of bulls and of goats should take away sins.
Heb. 10:4

Your sins are forgiven you for His name's sake.
1 John 2:12

[*See also* Anger, Confession, God's Anger, Grudges, Intercession, Repentance, Retribution, Revenge, Sin]

FORNICATION

The body is not for fornication, but for the Lord.
1 Cor. 6:13

Flee fornication.
1 Cor. 6:18

He that committeth fornication sinneth against his own body.
1 Cor. 6:18

To avoid fornication, let every man have his own wife, and let every woman have her own husband.
1 Cor. 7:2

[*See also* Adultery, Carnality, Immorality, Incest, Lust, Sex]

FORTITUDE

Thou wilt surely wear away, both thou, and this people that is with thee.
Jethro to Moses
Ex. 18:18

I am as strong this day as I was in the day that Moses sent me.
Josh. 14:11

As my strength was then, even so is my strength now.
Josh. 14:11

God is my strength and power: and He maketh my way perfect.
2 Sam. 22:33

O God, strengthen my hands.
Neh. 6:9

Is my strength the strength of stones? or is my flesh of brass?
Job 6:12

God is our refuge and strength, a very present help in trouble.
Ps. 46:1

God is the strength of my heart, and my portion for ever.
Ps. 73:26

They go from strength to strength.
Ps. 84:7

They that wait upon the Lord shall renew their strength; they shall mount up with wings as eagles; they shall run, and not be weary.
Isa. 40:31

If thou hast run with the footmen, and they have wearied thee, then how canst thou contend with horses?
Jer. 12:5

The spirit indeed is willing, but the flesh is weak.
Jesus
Matt. 26:41
See also Mark 14:38

Being reviled, we bless; being persecuted, we suffer it.
1 Cor. 4:12

Though our outward man perish, yet the inward man is renewed day by day.
2 Cor. 4:16

Be strong in the Lord, and in the power of His might.
Eph. 6:10

Fight the good fight of faith.
1 Tim. 6:12

Be strong in the grace that is in Christ Jesus.
2 Tim. 2:1

Lift up the hands which hang down, and the feeble knees.
Heb. 12:12

Hold fast till I come.
Jesus
Rev. 2:25

[*See also* Diligence, Patience, Perseverance, Strength, Temptation]

FRAILTY

Remember, I beseech Thee, that Thou hast made me as the clay.
Job 10:9

Have mercy upon me, O Lord; for I am weak.
Ps. 6:2

Every man at his best state is altogether vanity.
Ps. 39:5

If thou faint in the day of adversity, thy strength is small.
Prov. 24:10

We all do fade as a leaf.
Isa. 64:6

The law maketh men high priests which have infirmity.
Heb. 7:28

[*See also* Fortitude, Mortality, Strength]

FREEDOM

When ye go, ye shall not go empty.
God to Moses
Ex. 3:21

Thus saith the Lord God of Israel, Let My people go.
E.g., Ex. 5:1
See also, e.g., Ex. 8:20

It is a night to be much observed unto the Lord.
Ex. 12:42

Remember this day, in which ye came out from Egypt, out of the house of bondage.
Ex. 13:3

It had been better for us to serve the Egyptians, than that we should die in the wilderness.
Ex. 14:12

Proclaim liberty throughout all the land unto all the inhabitants thereof.
Lev. 25:10

The Lord brought us forth out of Egypt with a mighty hand, and with an outstretched arm.
Deut. 26:8

The small and great are there; and the servant is free from his master.
Job, speaking of death
Job 3:19

He bringeth out those which are bound with chains.
Ps. 68:6

They shall take them captives, whose captives they were.
Isa. 14:2

The ransomed of the Lord shall return, and come to Zion with songs and everlasting joy.
Isa. 35:10

Ye shall not go out with haste, nor go by flight: for the Lord will go before you.
Isa. 52:12

Behold, all the land is before thee: whither it seemeth good and convenient for thee to go, thither go.
Jer. 40:4

I will make you a name and a praise among all people of the earth, when I turn back your captivity before your eyes.
Zeph. 3:20

Ye shall know the truth, and the truth shall make you free.
Jesus
John 8:32

If the Son therefore shall make you free, ye shall be free indeed.
John 8:36

But I was free born.
Paul
Acts 22:28

He that is called in the Lord, being a servant, is the Lord's freeman.
1 Cor. 7:22

He that is called, being free, is Christ's servant.
1 Cor. 7:22

Ye are bought with a price; be not ye the servants of men.
1 Cor. 7:23

Where the Spirit of the Lord is, there is liberty.
2 Cor. 3:17

Christ hath made us free.
Gal. 5:1

Use not liberty for an occasion to the flesh.
Gal. 5:13

Of whom a man is overcome, of the same is he brought in bondage.
2 Pet. 2:19

[*See also* Captivity, Deliverance, Exile, Slavery]

FRIENDSHIP

The Lord do so to me, and more also, if ought but death part thee and me.
Ruth 1:17

The soul of Jonathan was knit with the soul of David, and Jonathan loved him as his own soul.
1 Sam. 18:1

Whatsoever thy soul desireth, I will even do it for thee.
Jonathan to David
1 Sam. 20:4

He loved him as he loved his own soul. (spoken of Jonathan and David)
1 Sam. 20:17

Thy love to me was wonderful, passing the love of women.
David, about Jonathan
2 Sam. 1:26

Thou lovest thine enemies, and hatest thy friends.
2 Sam. 19:6

As the Lord liveth, and as thy soul liveth, I will not leave thee.
E.g., 2 Kings 2:2

Miserable comforters are ye all.
Job to his friends
Job 16:2

My friends scorn me: but mine eye poureth out tears unto God.
Job 16:20

It was not an enemy that reproached me; then I could have borne it.
Ps. 55:12

A talebearer revealeth secrets: but he that is of a faithful spirit concealeth the matter.
Prov. 11:13

The poor is hated even of his own neighbour: but the rich hath many friends.
Prov. 14:20

A friend loveth at all times, and a brother is born for adversity.
Prov. 17:17

There is a friend that sticketh closer than a brother.
Prov. 18:24

Wealth maketh many friends; but the poor is separated from his neighbour.
Prov. 19:4

Every man is a friend to him that giveth gifts.
Prov. 19:6

Make no friendship with an angry man.
Prov. 22:24

Faithful are the wounds of a friend; but the kisses of an enemy are deceitful.
Prov. 27:6

Thine own friend, and thy father's friend, forsake not.
Prov. 27:10

Better is a neighbour that is near than a brother far off.
Prov. 27:10

Iron sharpeneth iron; so a man sharpeneth the countenance of his friend.
Prov. 27:17

Woe to him that is alone when he falleth; for he hath not another to help him up.
Eccl. 4:10

Greater love hath no man than this, that a man lay down his life for his friends.
Jesus
John 15:13

I have called you friends; for all things that I have heard of my Father I have made known unto you.
Jesus
John 15:15

Salute one another with an holy kiss.
Rom. 16:16

If thou count me therefore a partner, receive him as myself.
Philem. 17

[*See also* Brotherhood, Companions, Fellowship]

FRUSTRATION

The Lord bringeth the counsel of the heathen to nought.
Ps. 33:10

They have sown wheat, but shall reap thorns: they have put themselves to pain, but shall not profit.
Jer. 12:13

She shall follow after her lovers, but she shall not overtake them.
Hos. 2:7

Thou shalt eat, but not be satisfied.
Mic. 6:14

Thou shalt sow, but thou shalt not reap.
Mic. 6:15

They shall also build houses, but not inhabit them; and they shall plant vineyards, but not drink the wine thereof.
Zeph. 1:13
See also Amos 5:11

In those days shall men seek death, and shall not find it; and shall desire to die, and death shall flee from them.
Rev. 9:6

[*See also* Disappointment, Futility]

FULFILLMENT

He satisfieth the longing soul, and filleth the hungry soul with goodness.
Ps. 107:9

Surely as I have thought, so shall it come to pass; and as I have purposed, so shall it stand.
God
Isa. 14:24

Every one that thirsteth, come ye to the waters, and he that hath no money; come ye, buy, and eat.
Isa. 55:1

I am not come to destroy, but to fulfil.
Jesus
Matt. 5:17

Ye are complete in Him, which is the head of all principality and power.
(Him: Jesus)
Col. 2:10

[*See also* Contentment, Reward, Satisfaction]

FUTILITY

Ye shall sow your seed in vain, for your enemies shall eat it.
Lev. 26:16

Wherefore then dost thou ask of me, seeing the Lord is departed from thee, and is become thine enemy?
Samuel to Saul
1 Sam. 28:16

Knowest thou not that it will be bitterness in the latter end?
2 Sam. 2:26

The Lord hath said unto him, Curse David. Who shall then say, Wherefore hast thou done so?
2 Sam. 16:10

Fight ye not against the Lord God of your fathers; for ye shall not prosper.
2 Chron. 13:12

Call now, if there be any that will answer thee.
Job 5:1

If I be wicked, why then labour I in vain?
Job 9:29

Your remembrances are like unto ashes.
Job 13:12

They cried, but there was none to save them: even unto the Lord, but He answered them not.
Ps. 18:41

Vain is the help of man.
Ps. 60:11

The Lord knoweth the thoughts of man, that they are vanity.
Ps. 94:11
See also 1 Cor. 3:20

Vanity of vanities; all is vanity.
Eccl. 1:2
See also Eccl. 12:8

What profit hath a man of all his labour which he taketh under the sun?
Eccl. 1:3

Behold, all is vanity and vexation of spirit.
Eccl. 1:14
See also, e.g., Eccl. 2:17

What hath man of all his labour, and of the vexation of his heart, wherein he hath laboured under the sun?
Eccl. 2:22

As he came forth of his mother's womb, naked shall he return to go as he came, and shall take nothing of his labour.
Eccl. 5:15

What profit hath he that hath laboured for the wind?
Eccl. 5:16

All that cometh is vanity.
Eccl. 11:8

In vain is salvation hoped for from the hills, and from the multitude of mountains.
Jer. 3:23

Though thou deckest thee with ornaments of gold, though thou rentest thy face with painting, in vain shalt thou make thyself fair.
Jer. 4:30

They have sown the wind, and they shall reap the whirlwind.
Hos. 8:7

He that is swift of foot shall not deliver himself: neither shall he that rideth the horse.
Amos 2:15

They shall run to and fro to seek the word of the Lord, and shall not find it.
Amos 8:12

Ye have sown much, and bring in little; ye eat, but ye have not enough; ye drink, but ye are not filled.
Hag. 1:6

They shall build, but I will throw down.
God, about Edom
Mal. 1:4

[*See also* Disappointment, Frustration]

FUTURE

What God is about to do He showeth unto Pharaoh.
Gen. 41:28

Hast thou not heard long ago how I have done it, and of ancient times that I have formed it?
God
2 Kings 19:25, Isa. 37:26

Boast not thyself of to morrow; for thou knowest not what a day may bring forth.
Prov. 27:1

Shut thou up the vision; for it shall be for many days.
Dan. 8:26

Take therefore no thought for the morrow: for the morrow shall take thought for the things of itself.
Jesus
Matt. 6:34

Sufficient unto the day is the evil thereof.
Jesus
Matt. 6:34

It is not for you to know the times or the seasons.
Jesus
Acts 1:7

Known unto God are all His works from the beginning of the world.
Acts 15:18

Ye know not what shall be on the morrow.
James 4:14

Ye ought to say, If the Lord will, we shall live, and do this, or that.
James 4:15

[*See also* Ambition, Dreams, Posterity, Visions, Worry]

G

GENEROSITY

Every man shall give as he is able, according to the blessing of the Lord thy God which He hath given thee.
Deut. 16:17

Let her glean even among the sheaves, and reproach her not.
Ruth 2:15

Ask what I shall give thee.
God to Solomon
1 Kings 3:5, 2 Chron. 1:7

Send portions unto them for whom nothing is prepared.
Neh. 8:10

The righteous showeth mercy, and giveth.
Ps. 37:21

A good man showeth favour, and lendeth.
Ps. 112:5

He that watereth shall be watered also himself.
Prov. 11:25

If any man will sue thee at the law, and take away thy coat, let him have thy cloak also.
Jesus
Matt. 5:40

Whosoever shall compel thee to go a mile, go with him twain.
Jesus
Matt. 5:41

Give to him that asketh thee, and from him that would borrow of thee turn not thou away.
Jesus
Matt. 5:42
See also Luke 6:30

If ye then, being evil, know how to give good gifts unto your children, how much more shall your Father which is in heaven give good things to them that ask Him?
Jesus
Matt. 7:11
See also Luke 11:13

Freely ye have received, freely give.
Jesus
Matt. 10:8

If ye lend to them of whom ye hope to receive, what thank have ye? for sinners also lend to sinners, to receive as much again.
Jesus
Luke 6:34

Of a truth I say unto you, that this poor widow hath cast in more than they all.
Jesus
Luke 21:3
See also Mark 12:43

Silver and gold have I none; but such as I have give I thee.
Acts 3:6

It is more blessed to give than to receive.
Jesus
Acts 20:35

He which soweth sparingly shall reap also sparingly.
2 Cor. 9:6

[*See also* Altruism, Charity, Greed, Selfishness, Selflessness, Sharing]

GIFTS

He made him a coat of many colours.
Gen. 37:3

A gift in secret pacifieth anger.
Prov. 21:14

They presented unto Him gifts; gold, and frankincense, and myrrh.
Matt. 2:11

[*See also* Altruism, Bribery, Generosity]

GLOATING

Let not them that are mine enemies wrongfully rejoice over me.
Ps. 35:19

Rejoice not when thine enemy falleth, and let not thine heart be glad when he stumbleth.
Prov. 24:17

All mine enemies have heard of my trouble; they are glad that Thou hast done it.
Lam. 1:21

[*See also* Arrogance, Boasting, Conceit, Humility, Pride]

GLORY

The journey that thou takest shall not be for thine honour.
Judg. 4:9

Let them that love Him be as the sun when he goeth forth in his might.
Judg. 5:31

A chariot of fire.
2 Kings 2:11

He died in a good old age, full of days, riches, and honour.
(He: David)
1 Chron. 29:28

In Thy light shall we see light.
Ps. 36:9

In God is my salvation and my glory.
Ps. 62:7

Not unto us, O Lord, not unto us, but unto Thy name give glory.
Ps. 115:1

The wise shall inherit glory: but shame shall be the promotion of fools.
Prov. 3:35

For men to search their own glory is not glory.
Prov. 25:27

Ye are our glory and joy.
1 Thess. 2:20

All flesh is as grass, and all the glory of man as the flower of grass.
1 Pet. 1:24
See also Isa. 40:6

[*See also* Fame, God's Glory, Respect]

GLUTTONY

Put a knife to thy throat, if thou be a man given to appetite.
Prov. 23:2

The drunkard and the glutton shall come to poverty.
Prov. 23:21

Let us eat and drink; for to morrow we shall die.
Isa. 22:13, 1 Cor. 15:32

[*See also* Food]

GOALS

The Lord thy God hath set the land before thee: go up and possess it.
Deut. 1:21

Give me now wisdom and knowledge.
Solomon to God
2 Chron. 1:10

Seek ye first the kingdom of God, and His righteousness.
Jesus
Matt. 6:33
See also Luke 12:31

Great is thy faith: be it unto thee even as thou wilt.
Jesus
Matt. 15:28

Not as I will, but as Thou wilt.
Jesus
Matt. 26:39
See also Mark 14:36, Luke 22:42

What things soever ye desire, when ye pray, believe that ye receive them, and ye shall have them.
Jesus
Mark 11:24
See also Matt. 21:22

A man can receive nothing, except it be given him from heaven.
John 3:27

I seek not mine own will, but the will of the Father.
Jesus
John 5:30

He that planteth and he that watereth are one.
1 Cor. 3:8

Run, that ye may obtain.
1 Cor. 9:24

We should not lust after evil things.
1 Cor. 10:6

Be ye stedfast, unmoveable, always abounding in the work of the Lord.
1 Cor. 15:58

Whether in pretence, or in truth, Christ is preached; and I therein do rejoice.
Phil. 1:18

I press toward the mark for the prize of the high calling of God in Christ Jesus.
Phil. 3:14

Seek those things which are above, where Christ sitteth on the right hand of God.
Col. 3:1

Walk worthy of God, who hath called you unto His kingdom and glory.
1 Thess. 2:12

Follow after righteousness, godliness, faith, love, patience, meekness.
1 Tim. 6:11

[*See also* Ambition, Duty, Mission, Values]

GOD

I am the God of thy father, the God of Abraham, the God of Isaac, and the God of Jacob.
Ex. 3:6
See also, e.g., Mark 12:26

I Am That I Am.
Ex. 3:14

I am the Lord.
E.g., Ex. 6:2

The Lord shall reign for ever and ever.
E.g., Ex. 15:18

I am the Lord thy God, which have brought thee out of the land of Egypt, out of the house of bondage.
Ex. 20:2
See also, e.g., Ex. 29:46, Deut. 5:6

Thou shalt find Him, if thou seek Him with all thy heart and with all thy soul.
Deut. 4:29

He is thy praise.
Deut. 10:21

He is thy life, and the length of thy days.
Deut. 30:20

He is the Rock, His work is perfect.
Deut. 32:4

The Lord liveth.
2 Sam. 22:47, Ps. 18:46

The Lord is God.
1 Kings 8:60

Him shall ye fear, and Him shall ye worship, and to Him shall ye do sacrifice.
2 Kings 17:36

Lord, Thou art God.
1 Chron. 17:26

If thou seek Him, He will be found of thee.
1 Chron. 28:9
See also 2 Chron. 15:2

The Lord shall endure for ever.
Ps. 9:7
See also, e.g., Ps. 102:12

As for God, His way is perfect.
Ps. 18:30, 2 Sam. 22:31

Blessed be the Lord.
E.g., Ps. 31:21

Blessed be God.
E.g., Ps. 68:35

Thou art my father, my God, and the rock of my salvation.
Ps. 89:26

Blessed be the name of the Lord from this time forth and for evermore.
Ps. 113:2

Remember now thy Creator in the days of thy youth.
Eccl. 12:1

The Lord is our judge, the Lord is our lawgiver, the Lord is our king; He will save us.
Isa. 33:22

I am the Lord thy God, that divided the sea, whose waves roared: The Lord of hosts is His name.
Isa. 51:15

I the Lord am thy Saviour and thy Redeemer.
Isa. 60:16

O Lord, Thou art our Father.
Isa. 64:8

The Lord is the true God, He is the living God, and an everlasting king.
Jer. 10:10

All that forsake Thee shall be ashamed.
Jer. 17:13

The Lord, the fountain of living waters.
Jer. 17:13

Behold, all souls are Mine.
Ezek. 18:4

Blessed be the name of God for ever and ever.
Dan. 2:20
See also Ps. 145:1

He giveth wisdom unto the wise, and knowledge to them that know understanding.
Dan. 2:21

The Lord our God is righteous in all His works which He doeth.
Dan. 9:14

The ways of the Lord are right, and the just shall walk in them: but the transgressors shall fall therein.
Hos. 14:9

I am the Lord, I change not.
Mal. 3:6

Our Father which art in heaven, Hallowed be Thy name. Thy kingdom come. Thy will be done in earth, as it is in heaven.
Jesus
Matt. 6:9–10
See also Luke 11:2

God is not the God of the dead, but of the living.
Jesus
Matt. 22:32
See also Mark 12:27, Luke 20:38

Call no man your father upon the earth: for one is your Father, which is in heaven.
Jesus
Matt. 23:9

God is true.
John 3:33

He that sent me is true, whom ye know not.
Jesus
John 7:28

He giveth to all life, and breath, and all things.
Acts 17:25

Is He the God of the Jews only? is He not also of the Gentiles?
Rom. 3:29

The same Lord over all is rich unto all that call upon Him.
Rom. 10:12

There is no power but of God.
Rom. 13:1

The things of God knoweth no man.
1 Cor. 2:11

Faithful is He that calleth you.
1 Thess. 5:24

The foundation of God standeth sure.
2 Tim. 2:19

He that cometh to God must believe that He is, and that He is a rewarder of them that diligently seek Him.
Heb. 11:6

There is one lawgiver, who is able to save and to destroy: who art thou that judgest another?
James 4:12

God is light, and in Him is no darkness at all.
1 John 1:5

God is love.
1 John 4:8, 16

We love Him, because He first loved us.
1 John 4:19

Holy, holy, holy, Lord God Almighty, which was, and is, and is to come.
Rev. 4:8

[*See also* Conduct toward God, Fear of God, Goodness, Holiness, Jesus, Knowledge of God, Love of God, Praise of God, Reverence, Service to God, Sovereignty, Trust, and the categories which follow]

GOD'S ANGER

How long will it be ere they believe Me, for all the signs which I have showed among them?
Num. 14:11

Shall one man sin, and wilt Thou be wroth with all the congregation?
Num. 16:22

Let not Thine anger be hot against me, and I will speak but this once.
Judg. 6:39

They provoked Him to jealousy with their sins.
1 Kings 14:22

Great is the wrath of the Lord that is kindled against us, because our fathers have not hearkened unto the words of this book.
2 Kings 22:13

The anger of the Lord was kindled against Uzza, and He smote him.
1 Chron. 13:10

His power and His wrath is against all them that forsake Him.
Ezra 8:22

He shall drink of the wrath of the Almighty.
Job 21:20

Rebuke me not in Thine anger, neither chasten me in Thy hot displeasure.
Ps. 6:1
See also Ps. 38:1

His anger endureth but a moment.
Ps. 30:5

Wilt Thou be angry for ever? shall Thy jealousy burn like fire?
Ps. 79:5

Wilt Thou be angry with us for ever? wilt Thou draw out Thine anger to all generations?
Ps. 85:5

He will not always chide: neither will He keep His anger for ever.
Ps. 103:9

For all this His anger is not turned away, but His hand is stretched out still.
E.g., Isa. 9:12

His hand is stretched out, and who shall turn it back?
Isa. 14:27

Lest My fury come forth like fire, and burn that none can quench it.
Jer. 4:4
See also 2 Kings 22:17, Jer. 7:20

The whirlwind of the Lord goeth forth with fury, a continuing whirlwind: it shall fall with pain upon the head of the wicked.
Jer. 30:23

Ye provoke Me unto wrath with the works of your hands.
Jer. 44:8
See also Jer. 25:6

Behold, I will watch over them for evil, and not for good.
Jer. 44:27

In the day of the Lord's anger none escaped nor remained.
Lam. 2:22

Thus saith the Lord God; Behold, I, even I, am against thee.
Ezek. 5:8

I will cause My fury to rest upon them, and I will be comforted.
Ezek. 5:13

I will execute great vengeance upon them with furious rebukes.
Ezek. 25:17

I will pour out My wrath upon them like water.
Hos. 5:10

I will execute vengeance in anger and fury upon the heathen, such as they have not heard.
Mic. 5:15

He reserveth wrath for His enemies.
Nah. 1:2

Who can stand before His indignation? and who can abide in the fierceness of His anger?
Nah. 1:6

His fury is poured out like fire.
Nah. 1:6

Neither their silver nor their gold shall be able to deliver them in the day of the Lord's wrath.
Zeph. 1:18
See also Ezek. 7:19

All the earth shall be devoured with the fire of My jealousy.
Zeph. 3:8

O generation of vipers, who hath warned you to flee from the wrath to come?
Matt. 3:7, Luke 3:7

The wrath of God cometh on the children of disobedience.
Col. 3:6

It is a fearful thing to fall into the hands of the living God.
Heb. 10:31

Our God is a consuming fire.
Heb. 12:29
See also Deut. 4:24

The great day of His wrath is come; and who shall be able to stand?
Rev. 6:17

The great winepress of the wrath of God.
Rev. 14:19

Pour out the vials of the wrath of God upon the earth.
Rev. 16:1

[*See also* Exasperation, Forgiveness, Judgment]

GOD'S GLORY

As truly as I live, all the earth shall be filled with the glory of the Lord.
God
Num. 14:21

Declare His glory among the heathen; His marvellous works among all nations.
1 Chron. 16:24
See also Ps. 96:3

O ye sons of men, how long will ye turn My glory into shame?
Ps. 4:2

The heavens declare the glory of God; and the firmament showeth His handywork.
Ps. 19:1

I will be exalted among the heathen, I will be exalted in the earth.
Ps. 46:10

The heavens declare His righteousness, and all the people see His glory.
Ps. 97:6

He saved them for His name's sake, that He might make His mighty power to be known.
Ps. 106:8

Great is the glory of the Lord.
Ps. 138:5

The whole earth is full of His glory.
Isa. 6:3

I am the Lord: that is My name: and My glory will I not give to another.
Isa. 42:8

Do not abhor us, for Thy name's sake, do not disgrace the throne of Thy glory.
Jer. 14:21

I wrought for My name's sake, that it should not be polluted before the heathen.
Ezek. 20:9, 14

I do not this for your sakes, O house of Israel, but for Mine holy name's sake, which ye have profaned.
Ezek. 36:22
See also Ezek. 36:32

I will set My glory among the heathen, and all the heathen shall see My judgment that I have executed.
Ezek. 39:21

I will be glorified, saith the Lord.
Hag. 1:8

My name shall be great among the heathen, saith the Lord of hosts.
Mal. 1:11

Peace in heaven, and glory in the highest.
Luke 19:38

Ye shall see heaven open, and the angels of God ascending and descending upon the Son of man.
Jesus
John 1:51

This sickness is not unto death, but for the glory of God.
Jesus
John 11:4

The hour is come, that the Son of man should be glorified.
Jesus
John 12:23

Father, glorify Thy name.
Jesus
John 12:28

Now is the Son of man glorified, and God is glorified in Him.
Jesus
John 13:31

Whatsoever ye shall ask in my name, that

will I do, that the Father may be glorified in the Son.

Jesus
John 14:13
See also John 14:14

Glorify Thy Son, that Thy Son also may glorify Thee.

Jesus
John 17:1

The city had no need of the sun, neither of the moon, to shine in it: for the glory of God did lighten it, and the Lamb is the light thereof.

Rev. 21:23

GOD'S GOODNESS

See Goodness.

GOD'S GREATNESS

I know that the Lord is greater than all gods.

Ex. 18:11

What God is there in heaven or in earth, that can do according to Thy works?

Deut. 3:24

Thou art great, O Lord God: for there is none like Thee, neither is there any God beside Thee.

2 Sam. 7:22

Let it be known this day that Thou art God in Israel, and that I am Thy servant.

Elijah
1 Kings 18:36

Thine, O Lord, is the greatness, and the power, and the glory, and the victory, and the majesty.

1 Chron. 29:11

The house which I build is great: for great is our God above all gods.

Solomon
2 Chron. 2:5

Heaven and the heaven of heavens cannot contain Thee; how much less this house which I have built!

Solomon
2 Chron. 6:18
See also 1 Kings 8:27

Canst thou by searching find out God?

Job 11:7

Is not God in the height of heaven?

Job 22:12

God is great.

Job 36:26

Great things doeth He, which we cannot comprehend.

Job 37:5

Who is like unto Thee, which deliverest the poor from him that is too strong for him?

Ps. 35:10

Great is the Lord, and greatly to be praised.

E.g., Ps. 48:1

Who is so great a God as our God?

Ps. 77:13

Our Lord is above all gods.

Ps. 135:5

Great is our Lord, and of great power: His understanding is infinite.

Ps. 147:5

Hear, ye that are far off, what I have done; and, ye that are near, acknowledge My might.

Isa. 33:13

Have ye not known? have ye not heard? hath it not been told you from the beginning?

Isa. 40:21

For Thine is the kingdom, and the power, and the glory, for ever.

Jesus
Matt. 6:13

My Father is greater than I.

Jesus
John 14:28

Every house is builded by some man; but He that built all things is God.

Heb. 3:4

Great and marvellous are Thy works, Lord God Almighty.

Rev. 15:3

GOD'S KNOWLEDGE

Thou, even Thou only, knowest the hearts of all the children of men.
1 Kings 8:39

I know thy abode, and thy going out, and thy coming in, and thy rage against Me.
2 Kings 19:27, Isa. 37:28

The Lord searcheth all hearts.
1 Chron. 28:9

Doth not He see my ways, and count all my steps?
Job 31:4

His eyes are upon the ways of man, and He seeth all his goings.
Job 34:21

The Lord knoweth the way of the righteous: but the way of the ungodly shall perish.
Ps. 1:6

He that teacheth man knowledge, shall not He know?
Ps. 94:10

There is not a word in my tongue, but, lo, O Lord, Thou knowest it altogether.
Ps. 139:4

The ways of man are before the eyes of the Lord, and He pondereth all his goings.
Prov. 5:21

I know the things that come into your mind, every one of them.
Ezek. 11:5

Your Father knoweth what things ye have need of, before ye ask Him.
Jesus
Matt. 6:8

Are not five sparrows sold for two farthings, and not one of them is forgotten before God?
Jesus
Luke 12:6
See also Matt. 10:29

Even the very hairs of your head are all numbered.
Jesus
Luke 12:7
See also Matt. 10:30

God knoweth your hearts.
Jesus
Luke 16:15

Known unto God are all His works from the beginning of the world.
Acts 15:18

He that searcheth the hearts knoweth what is the mind of the Spirit.
Rom. 8:27

How unsearchable are His judgments, and His ways past finding out!
Rom. 11:33

Who hath known the mind of the Lord, that he may instruct Him?
1 Cor. 2:16

The Lord knoweth the thoughts of the wise, that they are vain.
1 Cor. 3:20

God is greater than our heart, and knoweth all things.
1 John 3:20

[*See also* God's Presence, Secrecy]

GOD'S LOVE

The Lord did not set His love upon you, nor choose you, because ye were more in number than any people; for ye were the fewest of all people: But because the Lord loved you.
Deut. 7:7–8

I know that Thou favourest me, because mine enemy doth not triumph over me.
Ps. 41:11

Thy mercy is great unto the heavens, and Thy truth unto the clouds.
Ps. 57:10
See also Ps. 108:4

Thy lovingkindness is better than life.
Ps. 63:3

Cause Thy face to shine; and we shall be saved.
Ps. 80:3, 7, 19

Whoso is wise, and will observe these things, even they shall understand the lovingkindness of the Lord.
Ps. 107:43

The Lord loveth the righteous.
Ps. 146:8

Whom the Lord loveth He correcteth.
Prov. 3:12

The mountains shall depart, and the hills be removed; but My kindness shall not depart from thee.
Isa. 54:10

For God so loved the world, that He gave His only begotten Son, that whosoever believeth in Him should not perish, but have everlasting life.
Jesus
John 3:16
See also John 3:36, John 6:47

Whom the Lord loveth He chasteneth.
Heb. 12:6

Draw nigh to God, and He will draw nigh to you.
James 4:8

[*See also* God's Mercy, Love]

GOD'S MERCY

Shall not the Judge of all the earth do right?
Abraham to God
Gen. 18:25

I have looked upon My people, because their cry is come unto Me.
1 Sam. 9:16

My mercy shall not depart away from him.
God to David, about Solomon
2 Sam. 7:15

The Lord your God is gracious and merciful, and will not turn away His face from you, if ye return unto Him.
2 Chron. 30:9

Thou art a God ready to pardon.
Neh. 9:17

Spare me according to the greatness of Thy mercy.
Neh. 13:22

Thou, O Lord, art a God full of compassion, and gracious, longsuffering, and plenteous in mercy and truth.
Ps. 86:15

His mercy is everlasting.
Ps. 100:5

As the heaven is high above the earth, so

great is His mercy toward them that fear Him.
Ps. 103:11

His mercy endureth for ever.
E.g., Ps. 118:1

With the Lord there is mercy.
Ps. 130:7

I will not pity, nor spare, nor have mercy, but destroy them.
Jer. 13:14

His mercy is on them that fear Him from generation to generation.
Mary, mother of Jesus
Luke 1:50

I will have mercy on whom I will have mercy, and I will have compassion on whom I will have compassion.
Rom. 9:15
See also Ex. 33:19

[*See also* Compassion, God's Love, Mercy]

GOD'S PEOPLE

In thee shall all families of the earth be blessed.
God to Abram
Gen. 12:3
See also Gen. 28:14

Ye are the children of the Lord your God.
Deut. 14:1

The Lord will not forsake His people for His great name's sake.
1 Sam. 12:22

Thou didst separate them from among all the people of the earth, to be Thine inheritance.
1 Kings 8:53

Blessed is the nation whose God is the Lord.
Ps. 33:12

We are the people of His pasture, and the sheep of His hand.
Ps. 95:7
See also Ps. 100:3

As the mountains are round about Jerusalem, so the Lord is round about His people.
Ps. 125:2

The Lord taketh pleasure in His people.
Ps. 149:4

Thou art My servant; I have chosen thee, and not cast thee away.
Isa. 41:9

Fear not: for I have redeemed thee, I have called thee by thy name; thou art Mine.
Isa. 43:1

I have created him for My glory, I have formed him; yea, I have made him.
Isa. 43:7

I have chosen thee in the furnace of affliction.
Isa. 48:10

The redeemed of the Lord shall return, and come with singing unto Zion.
Isa. 51:11

As the days of a tree are the days of My people, and Mine elect shall long enjoy the work of their hands.
Isa. 65:22

Obey My voice, and I will be your God, and ye shall be My people.
Jer. 7:23

Though I make a full end of all nations whither I have scattered thee, yet will I not make a full end of thee.
Jer. 30:11

Ye My flock, the flock of My pasture, are men, and I am your God.
Ezek. 34:31

They shall be as the stones of a crown, lifted up as an ensign upon His land.
Zech. 9:16

I will say, It is My people: and they shall say, The Lord is my God.
Zech. 13:9

God is able of these stones to raise up children unto Abraham.
Matt. 3:9, Luke 3:8

As many as received Him, to them gave He power to become the sons of God.
John 1:12

He that is of God heareth God's words.
Jesus
John 8:47

Other sheep I have, which are not of this fold.
Jesus
John 10:16

I will call them My people, which were not My people; and her beloved, which was not beloved.
Rom. 9:25
See also Hos. 2:25

I will be their God, and they shall be My people.
2 Cor. 6:16
See also Lev. 26:12

Ye are all the children of God by faith in Christ Jesus.
Gal. 3:26

Ye who sometimes were far off are made nigh by the blood of Christ.
Eph. 2:13

Unto us was the gospel preached, as well as unto them.
Heb. 4:2

I will be to them a God, and they shall be to Me a people.
Heb. 8:10
See also Jer. 31:33

[*See also* Believers, Chosen People, Christians]

GOD'S POWER

And God said, Let there be light: and there was light.
Gen. 1:3

Is any thing too hard for the Lord?
Gen. 18:14

Fear ye not, stand still, and see the salvation of the Lord, which He will show to you to-day.
Ex. 14:13

Is the Lord's hand waxed short?
Num. 11:23

Speak ye unto the rock before their eyes; and it shall give forth his water.
God to Moses
Num. 20:8

Alas, who shall live when God doeth this!
  Balaam
Num. 24:23

As a consuming fire He shall destroy them, and He shall bring them down before thy face.
  Deut. 9:3

The Lord brought us forth out of Egypt with a mighty hand, and with an outstretched arm.
  Deut. 26:8

There is no god with Me: I kill, and I make alive; I wound, and I heal: neither is there any that can deliver out of My hand.
  Deut. 32:39

The sun stood still in the midst of heaven, and hasted not to go down about a whole day.
  Josh. 10:13

The Lord killeth, and maketh alive: He bringeth down to the grave, and bringeth up.
  1 Sam. 2:6

The Lord maketh poor, and maketh rich: He bringeth low, and lifteth up.
  1 Sam. 2:7

Who is able to stand before this holy Lord God?
  1 Sam. 6:20

There is no restraint to the Lord to save by many or by few.
  Jonathan
  1 Sam. 14:6

I exalted thee out of the dust, and made thee prince over My people Israel.
  1 Kings 16:2

Hast thou not heard long ago how I have done it, and of ancient times that I have formed it?
  God
  2 Kings 19:25, Isa. 37:26

In Thine hand is power and might.
  1 Chron. 29:12

The cause was of God, that the Lord might perform His word.
  2 Chron. 10:15

God hath power to help, and to cast down.
  2 Chron. 25:8

He disappointeth the devices of the crafty,

so that their hands cannot perform their enterprise.
  Job 5:12

He maketh sore, and bindeth up: He woundeth, and His hands make whole.
  Job 5:18

He taketh away, who can hinder Him? who will say unto Him, What doest Thou?
  Job 9:12

Speak to the earth, and it shall teach thee: and the fishes of the sea shall declare unto thee.
  Job 12:8

What His soul desireth, even that He doeth.
  Job 23:13

Hell is naked before Him, and destruction hath no covering.
  Job 26:6

The thunder of His power who can understand?
  Job 26:14

Whatsoever is under the whole heaven is Mine.
  Job 41:11

He maketh the deep to boil like a pot.
  Job 41:31

I know that Thou canst do every thing, and that no thought can be withholden from Thee.
  Job to God
  Job 42:2

Who is this King of glory? The Lord strong and mighty, the Lord mighty in battle.
  Ps. 24:8

He spake, and it was done; He commanded, and it stood fast.
  Ps. 33:9

The world is Mine, and the fulness thereof.
  Ps. 50:12
  See also Ex. 19:5

The Lord on high is mightier than the noise of many waters, yea, than the mighty waves of the sea.
  Ps. 93:4

The Lord reigneth; let the earth rejoice.
  Ps. 97:1

He saved them for His name's sake, that He might make His mighty power to be known.
Ps. 106:8

Our God is in the heavens: He hath done whatsoever He hath pleased.
Ps. 115:3

Who can stand before His cold?
Ps. 147:17

Who can make that straight, which He hath made crooked?
Eccl. 7:13

Surely as I have thought, so shall it come to pass; and as I have purposed, so shall it stand.
God
Isa. 14:24

He shall cry, yea, roar; He shall prevail against His enemies.
Isa. 42:13

I have spoken it, I will also bring it to pass.
Isa. 46:11

I will cause them to know Mine hand and My might; and they shall know that My name is The Lord.
Jer. 16:21

As the clay is in the potter's hand, so are ye in Mine hand, O house of Israel.
Jer. 18:6
See also Rom. 9:21

I am the Lord, the God of all flesh: is there any thing too hard for Me?
Jer. 32:27

Like as I have brought all this great evil upon this people, so will I bring upon them all the good that I have promised.
Jer. 32:42

That which I have built will I break down, and that which I have planted I will pluck up, even this whole land.
Jer. 45:4

Who is like Me? and who will appoint Me the time? and who is that shepherd that will stand before Me?
Jer. 49:19, Jer. 50:44

He doeth according to His will in the army of heaven, and among the inhabitants of the earth: and none can stay His hand.
Dan. 4:35

None can stay His hand, or say unto Him, What doest Thou?
Dan. 4:35

He hath torn, and He will heal us; He hath smitten, and He will bind us up.
Hos. 6:1

The Lord is His name.
E.g., Amos 9:6

The Lord hath His way in the whirlwind and in the storm, and the clouds are the dust of His feet.
Nah. 1:3

God is able of these stones to raise up children unto Abraham.
Matt. 3:9, Luke 3:8

For Thine is the kingdom, and the power, and the glory, for ever.
Jesus
Matt. 6:13

Father, all things are possible unto Thee.
Jesus
Mark 14:36

With God nothing shall be impossible.
Luke 1:37

All things are delivered to me of my Father.
Jesus
Luke 10:22
See also Matt. 11:27

Without Him was not any thing made.
John 1:3

The Son can do nothing of Himself, but what He seeth the Father do.
Jesus
John 5:19

If it be of God, ye cannot overthrow it.
Acts 5:39

What was I, that I could withstand God?
Peter
Acts 11:17

All things are of God.
2 Cor. 5:18

To Him be glory and dominion for ever and ever.
1 Pet. 5:11

The Lamb shall overcome them: for He is Lord of lords, and King of kings.
Rev. 17:14

Alleluia: for the Lord God omnipotent reigneth.
Rev. 19:6

[*See also* God's Knowledge]

GOD'S PRESENCE

And the Spirit of God moved upon the face of the waters.
Gen. 1:2

Surely the Lord is in this place; and I knew it not.
Gen. 28:16

I have seen God face to face, and my life is preserved.
Jacob
Gen. 32:30

Behold, the bush burned with fire, and the bush was not consumed.
Ex. 3:2

There shall no man see Me, and live.
Ex. 33:20

I will walk among you, and will be your God, and ye shall be My people.
Lev. 26:12
See also 2 Cor. 6:16

We have seen this day that God doth talk with man, and he liveth.
Deut. 5:24

The Lord thy God is among you, a mighty God and terrible.
Deut. 7:21

The Lord thy God is with thee whithersoever thou goest.
Josh. 1:9

The Lord your God, He is God in heaven above, and in earth beneath.
Josh. 2:11

We shall surely die, because we have seen God.
Judg. 13:22

The Lord our God be with us, as He was with our fathers.
1 Kings 8:57

Let Him not leave us, nor forsake us.
1 Kings 8:57

Mine eyes and Mine heart shall be there perpetually.
1 Kings 9:3

Who is able to build Him an house, seeing the heaven and heaven of heavens cannot contain Him?
2 Chron. 2:6

The eyes of the Lord run to and fro throughout the whole earth.
2 Chron. 16:9

Upon whom doth not His light arise?
Job 25:3

He hideth His face, who then can behold Him?
Job 34:29

The voice of the Lord is upon the waters.
Ps. 29:3

He that planted the ear, shall He not hear? He that formed the eye, shall He not see?
Ps. 94:9

He is the Lord our God: His judgments are in all the earth.
Ps. 105:7, 1 Chron. 16:14

If I ascend up into heaven, Thou art there: if I make my bed in hell, behold, Thou art there.
Ps. 139:8

The Lord is nigh unto all them that call upon Him, to all that call upon Him in truth.
Ps. 145:18

The eyes of the Lord are in every place, beholding the evil and the good.
Prov. 15:3

The heaven is My throne, and the earth is My footstool.
Isa. 66:1
See also Matt. 5:34–35

Am I a God at hand, saith the Lord, and not a God afar off?
Jer. 23:23

Can any hide himself in secret places that I shall not see him? saith the Lord. Do not I fill heaven and earth?
Jer. 23:24

My spirit remaineth among you: fear ye not.
Hag. 2:5

Lo, I come, and I will dwell in the midst of thee, saith the Lord.
    Zech. 2:10

Thy Father which seeth in secret shall reward thee openly.
    Jesus
    Matt. 6:6, Matt. 6:18

Where two or three are gathered together in my name, there am I in the midst of them.
    Jesus
    Matt. 18:20

God that made the world and all things therein, seeing that He is Lord of heaven and earth, dwelleth not in temples made with hands.
    Acts 17:24

He be not far from every one of us.
    Acts 17:27

Ye are the temple of the living God.
    2 Cor. 6:16

The Lord is at hand.
    Phil 4:5

[*See also* Awe, Churches, God's Temple]

GOD'S PROTECTION

Whosoever slayeth Cain, vengeance shall be taken on him sevenfold.
    Gen. 4:15

The Lord set a mark upon Cain.
    Gen. 4:15

I will bless them that bless thee, and curse him that curseth thee.
    God to Abram
    Gen. 12:3

I am thy shield, and thy exceeding great reward.
    God to Abram
    Gen. 15:1

Deliver me, I pray Thee, from the hand of my brother.
    Jacob to God, about Esau
    Gen. 32:11

Against any of the children of Israel shall not a dog move his tongue.
    Ex. 11:7

The Lord went before them by day in a pillar of a cloud, to lead them the way; and by night in a pillar of fire, to give them light.
    Ex. 13:21
    See also, e.g., Num. 14:14

Let us flee from the face of Israel; for the Lord fighteth for them.
    Ex. 14:25

I will be an enemy unto thine enemies, and an adversary unto thine adversaries.
    God
    Ex. 23:22

The Lord thy God is among you, a mighty God and terrible.
    Deut. 7:21

All people of the earth shall see that thou art called by the name of the Lord; and they shall be afraid of thee.
    Deut. 28:10

As I was with Moses, so I will be with thee.
    God to Joshua
    Josh. 1:5, Josh. 3:7

The Lord saveth not with sword and spear: for the battle is the Lord's.
    David to Goliath
    1 Sam. 17:47
    See also 2 Chron. 20:15

He is my shield, and the horn of my salvation, my high tower, and my refuge.
    David
    2 Sam. 22:3

They prevented me in the day of my calamity: but the Lord was my stay.
    2 Sam. 22:19, Ps. 18:18

He is a buckler to all them that trust in Him.
    2 Sam. 22:31
    See also Ps. 18:30

He shall deliver you out of the hand of all your enemies.
    2 Kings 17:39

On whom dost thou trust, that thou rebellest against me?
    King of Assyria to King of Judah
    2 Kings 18:20, Isa. 36:5

He shall not come into this city, nor shoot an arrow there.
    2 Kings 19:32, Isa. 37:33

I will defend this city, to save it, for Mine

own sake, and for My servant David's sake.

   2 Kings 19:34, Isa. 37:35
   See also 2 Kings 20:6

I will subdue all thine enemies.
   1 Chron. 17:10

The hand of our God is upon all them for good that seek Him.
   Ezra 8:22

Hast not Thou made an hedge about him, and about his house?
   Satan to God, of Job
   Job 1:10

He saveth the poor from the sword, from their mouth, and from the hand of the mighty.
   Job 5:15

Am I a sea, or a whale, that Thou settest a watch over me?
   Job 7:12

Thou, O Lord, art a shield for me; my glory, and the lifter up of mine head.
   Ps. 3:3

O God, lift up Thine hand: forget not the humble.
   Ps. 10:12

In the Lord put I my trust.
   Ps. 11:1
   See also, e.g., Ps. 71:1

Thou wilt not leave my soul in hell; neither wilt Thou suffer Thine Holy One to see corruption.
   Ps. 16:10

Keep me as the apple of the eye, hide me under the shadow of Thy wings.
   Ps. 17:8

The Lord is my rock, and my fortress, and my deliverer; my God, my strength, in whom I will trust.
   Ps. 18:2

Be not far from me; for trouble is near; for there is none to help.
   Ps. 22:11

The Lord is my shepherd; I shall not want.
   Ps. 23:1

Thy rod and Thy staff they comfort me.
   Ps. 23:4

The Lord is my strength and my shield.
   Ps. 28:7

The eye of the Lord is upon them that fear Him.
   Ps. 33:18

The eyes of the Lord are upon the righteous, and His ears are open unto their cry.
   Ps. 34:15

Who is like unto Thee, which deliverest the poor from him that is too strong for him?
   Ps. 35:10

The Lord loveth judgment, and forsaketh not His saints.
   Ps. 37:28

Deliver me from the deceitful and unjust man.
   Ps. 43:1

God is my defence.
   Ps. 59:17
   See also Ps. 94:22

Give us help from trouble: for vain is the help of man.
   Ps. 60:11

He only is my rock and my salvation: He is my defence; I shall not be moved.
   Ps. 62:6

His truth shall be thy shield and buckler.
   Ps. 91:4

Thou shalt not be afraid for the terror by night; nor for the arrow that flieth by day.
   Ps. 91:5

A thousand shall fall at thy side, and ten thousand at thy right hand; but it shall not come nigh thee.
   Ps. 91:7

He suffered no man to do them wrong.
   Ps. 105:14, 1 Chron. 16:21

Touch not Mine anointed, and do My prophets no harm.
   Ps. 105:15, 1 Chron. 16:22

Sit thou at My right hand, until I make thine enemies thy footstool.
   Ps. 110:1
   See also, e.g., Matt. 22:44

Ye that fear the Lord, trust in the Lord: He is their help and their shield.
   Ps. 115:11

He that keepeth thee will not slumber.
Ps. 121:3

The Lord is thy keeper.
Ps. 121:5

The sun shall not smite thee by day, nor the moon by night.
Ps. 121:6

Our help is in the name of the Lord.
Ps. 124:8

Thy right hand shall save me. '
Ps. 138:7

My goodness, and my fortress; my high tower, and my deliverer; my shield, and He in whom I trust.
Ps. 144:2

The name of the Lord is a strong tower: the righteous runneth into it, and is safe.
Prov. 18:10

He is a shield unto them that put their trust in Him.
Prov. 30:5

Awake, awake, put on strength, O arm of the Lord; awake, as in the ancient days, in the generations of old.
Isa. 51:9

He that scattered Israel will gather him, and keep him, as a shepherd doth his flock.
Jer. 31:10

I will surely deliver thee.
Jer. 39:18

Come not near any man upon whom is the mark.
Ezek. 9:6

I will feed My flock, and I will cause them to lie down, saith the Lord God.
Ezek. 34:15

My God hath sent His angel, and hath shut the lions' mouths.
Dan. 6:22

The Lord is good, a strong hold in the day of trouble.
Nah. 1:7

Thy strong holds shall be like fig trees with the firstripe figs: if they be shaken, they shall even fall into the mouth of the eater.
Nah. 3:12

His arrow shall go forth as the lightning: and the Lord God shall blow the trumpet.
Zech. 9:14

I commend you to God, and to the word of His grace.
Paul
Acts 20:32

Shall their unbelief make the faith of God without effect?
Rom. 3:3

If God be for us, who can be against us?
Rom. 8:31

Take unto you the whole armour of God, that ye may be able to withstand in the evil day.
Eph. 6:13

The shield of faith, wherewith ye shall be able to quench all the fiery darts of the wicked.
Eph. 6:16

The Lord is faithful, who shall stablish you, and keep you from evil.
2 Thess. 3:3

The eyes of the Lord are over the righteous, and His ears are open unto their prayers.
1 Pet. 3:12

The face of the Lord is against them that do evil.
1 Pet. 3:12

They shall hunger no more, neither thirst any more; neither shall the sun light on them, nor any heat.
Rev. 7:16

[*See also* Assistance, Enemies, Fear, God's Presence, God's Support, Reliance, Security, Trust, and the Appendix at p. 420]

GOD'S SUPPORT

The Lord bless thee, and keep thee.
Num. 6:24

Go not up, neither fight; for I am not among you.
Deut. 1:42

He will not fail thee, nor forsake thee.
Deut. 31:6
See also Josh. 1:5, Heb. 13:5

Be not afraid, neither be thou dismayed: for the Lord thy God is with thee whithersoever thou goest.
Josh. 1:9

The living God is among you.
Josh. 3:10

The sun stood still, and the moon stayed, until the people had avenged themselves upon their enemies.
Josh. 10:13

The Lord fought for Israel.
Josh. 10:14

The Lord your God, He it is that fighteth for you.
Josh. 23:10
See also Josh. 23:3

Is not the Lord gone out before thee?
Judg. 4:14

They fought from heaven; the stars in their courses fought against Sisera.
Judg. 5:20

I will deliver thine enemy into thine hand, that thou mayest do to him as it shall seem good unto thee.
God to David
1 Sam. 24:4

I will be his father, and he shall be My son.
God to David about Solomon
2 Sam. 7:14, 1 Chron. 17:13

Fear not: for they that be with us are more than they that be with them.
2 Kings 6:16

Go up; for I will deliver them into thine hand.
1 Chron. 14:10

Seek His face continually.
1 Chron. 16:11

O Lord, Thou art our God; let not man prevail against Thee.
2 Chron. 14:11

Forbear thee from meddling with God, who is with me, that He destroy thee not.
2 Chron. 35:21

Our God shall fight for us.
Neh. 4:20

Their clothes waxed not old, and their feet swelled not.
Neh. 9:21

God will not cast away a perfect man, neither will He help the evil doers.
Job 8:20

My witness is in heaven, and my record is on high.
Job 16:19

Thou preparest a table before me in the presence of mine enemies: Thou anointest my head with oil; my cup runneth over.
Ps. 23:5

Into Thine hand I commit my spirit.
Ps. 31:5

Thou art the God of my strength: why dost Thou cast me off?
Ps. 43:2

God is our refuge and strength, a very present help in trouble.
Ps. 46:1

Cast thy burden upon the Lord, and He shall sustain thee.
Ps. 55:22

Thou art my help and my deliverer; O Lord, make no tarrying.
Ps. 70:5
See also Ps. 40:17

Whom have I in heaven but Thee?
Ps. 73:25

He is my refuge and my fortress: my God; in Him will I trust.
Ps. 91:2
See also Ps. 71:3

When I said, My foot slippeth; Thy mercy, O Lord, held me up.
Ps. 94:18

The Lord preserveth the simple.
Ps. 116:6

The Lord upholdeth all that fall, and raiseth up all those that be bowed down.
Ps. 145:14

The Lord is far from the wicked: but He heareth the prayer of the righteous.
Prov. 15:29

Strengthen ye the weak hands, and confirm the feeble knees.
Isa. 35:3

He giveth power to the faint; and to them that have no might He increaseth strength.
Isa. 40:29

I am thy God: I will strengthen thee; yea, I will help thee; yea, I will uphold thee with the right hand of My righteousness.
Isa. 41:10

I will help thee, saith the Lord.
Isa. 41:14

When the poor and needy seek water, and there is none, and their tongue faileth for thirst, I the Lord will hear them, I the God of Israel will not forsake them.
Isa. 41:17

Even to your old age I am He; and even to hoar hairs will I carry you.
Isa. 46:4

O Israel, thou hast destroyed thyself; but in Me is thine help.
Hos. 13:9

I am with you, saith the Lord.
Hag. 1:13, Hag. 2:4

Consider the lilies of the field, how they grow; they toil not, neither do they spin: And yet I say unto you, That even Solomon in all his glory was not arrayed like one of these.
Jesus
Matt. 6:28–29
See also Luke 12:27

No man can do these miracles that Thou doest, except God be with him.
John 3:2

The Lamb which is in the midst of the throne shall feed them, and shall lead them unto living fountains of waters.
Rev. 7:17

[*See also* Abandonment, Encouragement, Faith, God's Protection]

GOD'S TEMPLE

He is my God, and I will prepare Him an habitation; my father's God, and I will exalt Him.
Ex. 15:2

Mine eyes and Mine heart shall be there perpetually.
1 Kings 9:3

Let her not be slain in the house of the Lord.
2 Kings 11:15
See also 2 Chron. 23:14

He shall build Me an house, and I will stablish his throne for ever.
(He: Solomon)
1 Chron. 17:12

The house which I build is great: for great is our God above all gods.
Solomon
2 Chron. 2:5

But will God in very deed dwell with men on the earth?
2 Chron. 6:18
See also 1 Kings 8:27

Whatsoever is commanded by the God of heaven, let it be diligently done for the house of the God of heaven.
Ezra 7:23

The Lord is in His holy temple: let all the earth keep silence before Him.
Hab. 2:20

The temple of God is holy, which temple ye are.
1 Cor. 3:17

Behold, the tabernacle of God is with men, and He will dwell with them.
Rev. 21:3

I saw no temple therein: for the Lord God Almighty and the Lamb are the temple of it.
Rev. 21:22

[*See also* Churches]

GOD'S UNIQUENESS

There is none like Me in all the earth.
Ex. 9:14

Who is like unto Thee, O Lord, among the gods? who is like Thee, glorious in holiness, fearful in praises, doing wonders?
Ex. 15:11

What God is there in heaven or in earth, that can do according to Thy works?
Deut. 3:24

The Lord He is God in heaven above, and
upon the earth beneath: there is none else.
  Deut. 4:39

See now that I, even I, am He.
  Deut. 32:39

There is no god with Me: I kill, and I make
alive; I wound, and I heal: neither is there
any that can deliver out of My hand.
  Deut. 32:39

Who is God, save the Lord?
  2 Sam. 22:32, Ps. 18:31

There is no God like Thee, in heaven
above, or on earth beneath.
  1 Kings 8:23

Thou, even Thou, art Lord alone.
  Neh. 9:6

O God, who is like unto Thee!
  Ps. 71:19

To whom then will ye liken God? or what
likeness will ye compare unto Him?
  Isa. 40:18
  See also, e.g., Isa. 46:5

I, even I, am the Lord; and beside Me
there is no saviour.
  Isa. 43:11

I am the first, and I am the last; and beside
Me there is no God.
  Isa. 44:6
  See also Isa. 48:12

I am God, and there is none else; I am
God, and there is none like Me.
  E.g., Isa. 46:9

I am He; I am the first, I also am the last.
  Isa. 48:12

Who is like Me? and who will appoint Me
the time? and who is that shepherd that
will stand before Me?
  Jer. 49:19, Jer. 50:44

To us there is but one God, the Father, of
whom are all things, and we in Him.
  1 Cor. 8:6

God is one.
  Gal. 3:20

There is one God, and one mediator between God and men, the man Christ Jesus.
  1 Tim. 2:5

[*See also* Monotheism]

GOD'S WILL

It is the Lord: let Him do what seemeth
Him good.
  1 Sam. 3:18
  See also 2 Sam. 15:26

Our Father which art in heaven, Hallowed
be Thy name. Thy kingdom come. Thy
will be done in earth, as it is in heaven.
  Jesus
  Matt. 6:9–10
  See also Luke 11:2

Not my will, but Thine, be done.
  Jesus
  Luke 22:42
  See also Mark 14:36

The will of the Lord be done.
  Acts 21:14

Ye ought to say, If the Lord will, we shall
live, and do this, or that.
  James 4:15

The world passeth away, and the lust
thereof: but he that doeth the will of God
abideth for ever.
  1 John 2:17

[*See also* Certainty]

GOD'S WORD

The word is very nigh unto thee, in thy
mouth, and in thy heart.
  Deut. 30:14
  See also Rom. 10:8

Thus saith the Lord.
  E.g., 1 Kings 12:24

Good is the word of the Lord which thou
hast spoken.
  2 Kings 20:19, Isa. 39:8

In His word do I hope.
  Ps. 130:5

Every one that thirsteth, come ye to the
waters, and he that hath no money; come
ye, buy, and eat.
  Isa. 55:1

I the Lord have spoken it.
  Ezek. 5:13, 17

They shall run to and fro to seek the word
of the Lord, and shall not find it.
  Amos 8:12

My doctrine is not mine, but His that sent me.
>Jesus
>*John 7:16*

Thy word is truth.
>Jesus to God
>*John 17:17*

Let the word of Christ dwell in you.
>*Col. 3:16*

The word of God is quick, and powerful, and sharper than any twoedged sword.
>*Heb. 4:12*

The grass withereth, and the flower thereof falleth away: But the word of the Lord endureth forever.
>*1 Pet. 1:24–25*
>*See also Isa. 40:8*

As newborn babes, desire the sincere milk of the word, that ye may grow thereby.
>*1 Pet. 2:2*

[*See also* Commandments, Gospel, Scripture]

GOD, NAMES OF

I am God Almighty.
>*E.g., Gen. 35:11*

I Am That I Am.
>*Ex. 3:14*

The Lord your God is God of gods, and Lord of lords.
>*Deut. 10:17*

The Most High.
>*Deut. 32:8*

Lord God of Israel.
>*1 Chron. 29:10*

The Lord of hosts, He is the King of glory.
>*Ps. 24:10*

Thou, whose name alone is JEHOVAH.
>*Ps. 83:18*

Know ye that the Lord He is God.
>*Ps. 100:3*
>*See also 1 Kings 18:39*

The Lord of hosts is His name.
>*Jer. 31:35*

Their Redeemer is strong; the Lord of hosts is His name.
>*Jer. 50:34*

The Lord is His name.
>*E.g., Amos 9:6*

Our Father.
>Jesus
>*Matt. 6:9*

GOD, TRAITS OF

The Lord is a man of war: the Lord is His name.
>*Ex. 15:3*

Who is like unto Thee, O Lord, among the gods? who is like Thee, glorious in holiness, fearful in praises, doing wonders?
>*Ex. 15:11*

I the Lord thy God am a jealous God.
>*E.g., Ex. 20:5*

The Lord, The Lord God, merciful and gracious, longsuffering, and abundant in goodness and truth.
>*Ex. 34:6*

The Lord, whose name is Jealous, is a jealous God.
>*Ex. 34:14*

God is not a man, that He should lie; neither the son of man, that He should repent: hath He said, and shall He not do it? or hath He spoken, and shall He not make it good?
>*Num. 23:19*

The Lord thy God is a consuming fire, even a jealous God.
>*Deut. 4:24*
>*See also Heb. 12:29*

The Lord thy God is a merciful God.
>*Deut. 4:31*

A God of truth and without iniquity, just and right is He.
>*Deut. 32:4*

He is an holy God; He is a jealous God; He will not forgive your transgressions nor your sins.
>*Josh. 24:19*

With the merciful Thou wilt show Thyself

merciful, and with the upright man Thou wilt show Thyself upright.
2 Sam. 22:26
See also Ps. 18:25

The Lord is righteous.
2 Chron. 12:6

God will not do wickedly, neither will the Almighty pervert judgment.
Job 34:12

All the paths of the Lord are mercy and truth unto such as keep His covenant.
Ps. 25:10

Thy mercy is great unto the heavens, and Thy truth unto the clouds.
Ps. 57:10
See also Ps. 108:4

The Lord is good; His mercy is everlasting; and His truth endureth to all generations.
Ps. 100:5

Thou art the same, and Thy years shall have no end.
Ps. 102:27

The Lord is merciful and gracious, slow to anger, and plenteous in mercy.
Ps. 103:8

The works of His hands are verity and judgment; all His commandments are sure.
Ps. 111:7

The Lord is gracious, and full of compassion; slow to anger, and of great mercy.
Ps. 145:8

The Lord is righteous in all His ways, and holy in all His works.
Ps. 145:17

The Lord is a God of judgment: blessed are all they that wait for Him.
Isa. 30:18

To the Lord our God belong mercies and forgivenesses, though we have rebelled against Him.
Dan. 9:9

He is gracious and merciful, slow to anger, and of great kindness.
Joel 2:13
See also Jonah 4:2

We ought not to think that the Godhead is like unto gold, or silver, or stone, graven by art and man's device.
Acts 17:29

God is faithful.
E.g., 1 Cor. 1:9

The Father of mercies, and the God of all comfort.
2 Cor. 1:3

GODLESSNESS

I know not the Lord, neither will I let Israel go.
Pharaoh
Ex. 5:2

Come not among these nations, these that remain among you.
Josh. 23:7

There arose another generation after them, which knew not the Lord.
Judg. 2:10

What profit should we have, if we pray unto Him?
Job 21:15

The hypocrites in heart heap up wrath: they cry not when He bindeth them.
Job 36:13

The way of the ungodly shall perish.
Ps. 1:6

The wicked shall be turned into hell, and all the nations that forget God.
Ps. 9:17

How long shall the adversary reproach? shall the enemy blaspheme Thy name for ever?
Ps. 74:10

The foolish man reproacheth Thee daily.
Ps. 74:22

The tumult of those that rise up against Thee increaseth continually.
Ps. 74:23

A stubborn and rebellious generation; a generation that set not their heart aright, and whose spirit was not stedfast with God.
Ps. 78:8

Wherefore should the heathen say, Where is now their God?
Ps. 115:2
See also Ps. 79:10

It is time for Thee, Lord, to work: for they have made void Thy law.
Ps. 119:126

The ox knoweth his owner, and the ass his master's crib: but Israel doth not know, My people doth not consider.
Isa. 1:3

Seeing many things, but thou observest not; opening the ears, but he heareth not.
Isa. 42:20
See also, e.g., Matt. 13:13

Of whom hast thou been afraid or feared, that thou hast lied, and hast not remembered Me?
Isa. 57:11

My people is foolish, they have not known Me.
Jer. 4:22

Shall not My soul be avenged on such a nation as this?
Jer. 5:9

Learn not the way of the heathen.
Jer. 10:2

Pour out Thy fury upon the heathen that know Thee not, and upon the families that call not on Thy name.
Jer. 10:25

Walk ye not in the statutes of your fathers, neither observe their judgments, nor defile yourselves with their idols.
Ezek. 20:18

I will send a famine in the land, not a famine of bread, nor a thirst for water, but of hearing the words of the Lord.
Amos 8:11

The day of the Lord is near upon all the heathen.
Obad. 15

I will execute vengeance in anger and fury upon the heathen, such as they have not heard.
Mic. 5:15

The good man is perished out of the earth: and there is none upright among men.
Mic. 7:2

O faithless and perverse generation.
Jesus
Matt. 17:17

It shall be more tolerable for Sodom and Gomorrha in the day of judgment than for that city.
Jesus
Mark 6:11
See also Matt. 10:15

He that denieth me before men shall be denied before the angels of God.
Jesus
Luke 12:9
See also Matt. 10:33

Ye are of your father the devil, and the lusts of your father ye will do.
Jesus
John 8:44

Ye stiffnecked and uncircumcised in heart and ears, ye do always resist the Holy Ghost.
Acts 7:51

Wilt thou not cease to pervert the right ways of the Lord?
Acts 13:10

Turn them from darkness to light, and from the power of Satan unto God.
Jesus to Paul
Acts 26:18

When they knew God, they glorified Him not as God.
Rom 1:21

Shall their unbelief make the faith of God without effect?
Rom. 3:3

If the unbelieving depart, let him depart.
1 Cor. 7:15

The things which the Gentiles sacrifice, they sacrifice to devils, and not to God.
1 Cor. 10:20

If any man love not the Lord Jesus Christ, let him be Anathema.
1 Cor. 16:22

If our gospel be hid, it is hid to them that are lost.
2 Cor. 4:3

Strangers from the covenants of promise, having no hope, and without God in the world.
Eph. 2:12

The enemies of the cross of Christ: Whose

end is destruction, whose God is their belly, and whose glory is in their shame.
Phil. 3:18–19

They that sleep sleep in the night; and they that be drunken are drunken in the night.
1 Thess. 5:7

The Lord Jesus shall be revealed from heaven with His mighty angels, In flaming fire taking vengeance on them that know not God, and that obey not the gospel.
2 Thess. 1:7–8

All men have not faith.
2 Thess. 3:2

Shun profane and vain babblings: for they will increase unto more ungodliness.
2 Tim. 2:16

Unto them that are defiled and unbelieving is nothing pure; but even their mind and conscience is defiled.
Titus 1:15

Ye were as sheep going astray; but are now returned unto the Shepherd.
1 Pet. 2:25

If the righteous scarcely be saved, where shall the ungodly and the sinner appear?
1 Pet. 4:18

Whosoever denieth the Son, the same hath not the Father.
1 John 2:23

The world knoweth us not, because it knew Him not.
1 John 3:1

He that believeth not God hath made Him a liar.
(Him: Jesus)
1 John 5:10

Woe unto them! for they have gone in the way of Cain.
Jude 11

Clouds they are without water, carried about of winds; trees whose fruit withereth.
Jude 12

Murmurers, complainers, walking after their own lusts.
Jude 16

Babylon the Great, the Mother of Harlots and Abominations of the Earth.
Rev. 17:5

Babylon the great is fallen, is fallen, and is become the habitation of devils.
Rev. 18:2

Her sins have reached unto heaven, and God hath remembered her iniquities.
(her: Babylon)
Rev. 18:5

With violence shall that great city Babylon be thrown down.
Rev. 18:21

[*See also* Atheism, Backsliding, Faith, Godliness, Idolatry, Rebellion, Sin]

GODLINESS

Happy is that people, whose God is the Lord.
Ps. 144:15

Though a sinner do evil an hundred times, and his days be prolonged, yet surely I know that it shall be well with them that fear God.
Eccl. 8:12

Ye cannot serve God and mammon.
Jesus
Matt. 6:24, Luke 16:13

None of us liveth to himself.
Rom. 14:7

The unbelieving husband is sanctified by the wife, and the unbelieving wife is sanctified by the husband.
1 Cor. 7:14

He that soweth to the Spirit shall of the Spirit reap life everlasting.
Gal. 6:8

Great is the mystery of godliness.
1 Tim. 3:16

Bodily exercise profiteth little: but godliness is profitable unto all things.
1 Tim. 4:8

Godliness with contentment is great gain.
1 Tim. 6:6

All that will live godly in Christ Jesus shall suffer persecution.
2 Tim. 3:12

Whosoever is born of God doth not commit sin.
1 John 3:9

Whosoever shall confess that Jesus is the Son of God, God dwelleth in him, and he in God.
1 John 4:15

If a man say, I love God, and hateth his brother, he is a liar.
1 John 4:20

Whatsoever is born of God overcometh the world.
1 John 5:4

I have no greater joy than to hear that my children walk in truth.
3 John 4

He that doeth good is of God: but he that doeth evil hath not seen God.
3 John 11

Keep yourselves in the love of God, looking for the mercy of our Lord Jesus Christ.
Jude 21

[*See also* Righteousness]

GOOD AND EVIL

Of every tree of the garden thou mayest freely eat: But of the tree of the knowledge of good and evil, thou shalt not eat.
Gen. 2:16–17

Your eyes shall be opened, and ye shall be as gods, knowing good and evil.
Gen. 3:5

The Lord God said, Behold, the man is become as one of us, to know good and evil.
Gen. 3:22

I have set before thee this day life and good, and death and evil.
Deut. 30:15

Give therefore Thy servant an understanding heart to judge Thy people, that I may discern between good and bad.
Solomon
1 Kings 3:9

When I looked for good, then evil came unto me: and when I waited for light, there came darkness.
Job 30:26

They have rewarded me evil for good, and hatred for my love.
Ps. 109:5
See also 1 Sam. 25:21

The eyes of the Lord are in every place, beholding the evil and the good.
Prov. 15:3

Whoso rewardeth evil for good, evil shall not depart from his house.
Prov. 17:13

Woe unto them that call evil good, and good evil.
Isa. 5:20

Butter and honey shall he eat, that he may know to refuse the evil, and choose the good.
Isa. 7:15

I make peace, and create evil: I the Lord do all these things.
Isa. 45:7

They are wise to do evil, but to do good they have no knowledge.
Jer. 4:22

Can the Ethiopian change his skin, or the leopard his spots? then may ye also do good, that are accustomed to do evil.
Jer. 13:23

I have set My face against this city for evil, and not for good, saith the Lord.
(city: Jerusalem)
Jer. 21:10

Out of the mouth of the most High proceedeth not evil and good?
Lam. 3:38

Seek good, and not evil, that ye may live.
Amos 5:14

Hate the evil, and love the good, and establish judgment in the gate.
Amos 5:15

Discern between the righteous and the wicked, between him that serveth God and him that serveth Him not.
Mal. 3:18

He maketh His sun to rise on the evil and on the good, and sendeth rain on the just and on the unjust.
Jesus
Matt. 5:45

Every good tree bringeth forth good fruit;
but a corrupt tree bringeth forth evil fruit.
  Jesus
  Matt. 7:17
  See also Luke 6:43

How can ye, being evil, speak good things?
  Jesus
  Matt. 12:34

A good man out of the good treasure of the
heart bringeth forth good things: and an
evil man out of the evil treasure bringeth
forth evil things.
  Jesus
  Matt. 12:35

They that have done good, unto the resurrection of life; and they that have done
evil, unto the resurrection of damnation.
  Jesus
  John 5:29

Ye are from beneath; I am from above: ye
are of this world; I am not of this world.
  Jesus
  John 8:23

Abhor that which is evil; cleave to that
which is good.
  Rom. 12:9

Be not overcome of evil, but overcome evil
with good.
  Rom. 12:21

Let us therefore cast off the works of
darkness, and let us put on the armour of
light.
  Rom. 13:12

I would have you wise unto that which is
good, and simple concerning evil.
  Rom. 16:19

To him that knoweth to do good, and doeth
it not, to him it is sin.
  James 4:17

Eschew evil, and do good.
  1 Pet. 3:11

We know that we are of God, and the
whole world lieth in wickedness.
  1 John 5:19

Follow not that which is evil, but that
which is good.
  3 John 11

He that doeth good is of God: but he that
doeth evil hath not seen God.
  3 John 11

[See also Corruption, Evil, Wickedness]

GOODNESS

Thou art not a God that hath pleasure in
wickedness.
  Ps. 5:4

Surely goodness and mercy shall follow me
all the days of my life: and I will dwell in
the house of the Lord for ever.
  Ps. 23:6

The earth is full of the goodness of the
Lord.
  Ps. 33:5

The Lord is good.
  Ps. 100:5

Give thanks unto the Lord; for He is good:
for His mercy endureth for ever.
  E.g., Ps. 106:1

Your goodness is as a morning cloud, and
as the early dew it goeth away.
  Hos. 6:4

The good man is perished out of the earth:
and there is none upright among men.
  Mic. 7:2

The Lord is good, a strong hold in the day
of trouble.
  Nah. 1:7

He maketh His sun to rise on the evil and
on the good, and sendeth rain on the just
and on the unjust.
  Jesus
  Matt. 5:45

Why callest thou me good? there is none
good but one, that is, God.
  Jesus
  Matt. 19:17, Mark 10:18
  See also Luke 18:19

Is thine eye evil, because I am good?
  Jesus
  Matt. 20:15

If ye do good to them which do good to

you, what thank have ye? for sinners also
do even the same.
Jesus
Luke 6:33
See also Matt. 5:46

Take care of him; and whatsoever thou
spendest more, when I come again, I will
repay thee.
(I: The Good Samaritan)
Luke 10:35

Go, and do thou likewise.
Jesus
Luke 10:37

The goodness of God leadeth thee to repentance.
Rom. 2:4

Whatsoever good thing any man doeth, the
same shall he receive of the Lord.
Eph. 6:8

Hold fast to that which is good.
1 Thess. 5:21

Do good.
1 Tim. 6:18

Every good gift and every perfect gift is
from above.
James 1:17

[*See also* Altruism, Good and Evil, Kindness, Righteousness, Virtue]

GOSPEL

The care of this world, and the deceitful-
ness of riches, choke the word.
Jesus
Matt. 13:22
See also Mark 4:19

Repent ye, and believe the gospel.
Jesus
Mark 1:15

Whosoever shall lose his life for my sake
and the gospel's, the same shall save it.
Jesus
Mark 8:35
See also Matt. 16:25, Luke 9:24

The gospel must first be published among
all nations.
Jesus
Mark 13:10

Go ye into all the world, and preach the
gospel to every creature.
Jesus
Mark 16:15

Man shall not live by bread alone, but by
every word of God.
Jesus
Luke 4:4
See also Deut. 8:3, Matt. 4:4

He hath anointed me to preach the gospel
to the poor.
Jesus
Luke 4:18
See also Isa. 61:1

Whosoever shall be ashamed of me and of
my words, of him shall the Son of man be
ashamed.
Jesus
Luke 9:26

Blessed are they that hear the word of
God, and keep it.
Jesus
Luke 11:28

He that heareth my word, and believeth on
Him that sent me, hath everlasting life.
Jesus
John 5:24

The promise which was made unto the
fathers, God hath fulfilled the same unto us
their children.
Acts 13:32–33

Seeing ye put it from you, and judge
yourselves unworthy of everlasting life, lo,
we turn to the Gentiles.
Paul to Jews
Acts 13:46

Remember the words of the Lord Jesus.
Acts 20:35

I am not ashamed of the gospel of Christ.
Rom. 1:16

It is the power of God unto salvation to
every one that believeth.
Rom. 1:16

The word is nigh thee.
Rom. 10:8

How shall they hear without a preacher?
Rom. 10:14

How beautiful are the feet of them that preach the gospel of peace.
Rom. 10:15

In Christ Jesus I have begotten you through the gospel.
1 Cor. 4:15

If our gospel be hid, it is hid to them that are lost.
2 Cor. 4:3

The gospel which was preached of me is not after man.
Gal. 1:11

I neither received it of man, neither was I taught it, but by the revelation of Jesus Christ.
Gal. 1:12

I am set for the defence of the gospel.
Phil. 1:17

Whether in pretence, or in truth, Christ is preached; and I therein do rejoice.
Phil. 1:18

Be not moved away from the hope of the gospel.
Col. 1:23

The word of God is not bound.
2 Tim. 2:9

Preach the word.
2 Tim. 4:2

Unto us was the gospel preached, as well as unto them.
Heb. 4:2

[*See also* Evangelism, God's Word, Preaching, Scripture]

GOSSIP

Thou shalt not go up and down as a talebearer among thy people.
Lev. 19:16

A talebearer revealeth secrets.
Prov. 11:13

A whisperer separateth chief friends.
Prov. 16:28

The words of a talebearer are as wounds.
Prov. 18:8, Prov. 26:22

Meddle not with him that flattereth with his lips.
Prov. 20:19

Where no wood is, there the fire goeth out. so where there is no talebearer, the strife ceaseth.
Prov. 26:20

[*See also* Secrecy, Slander, Speech]

GOVERNMENT

Provide out of all the people able men. such as fear God, men of truth, hating covetousness.
Jethro to Moses
Ex. 18:21

They are a nation void of counsel, neither is there any understanding in them.
Deut. 32:28

I will not rule over you, neither shall my son rule over you: the Lord shall over you.
Gideon
Judg. 8:23

He that ruleth over men must be just. ruling in the fear of God.
2 Sam. 23:3

The kingdom is the Lord's.
Ps. 22:28

Blessed is the nation whose God is the Lord.
Ps. 33:12

It is better to trust in the Lord than to put confidence in princes.
Ps. 118:9

By me kings reign, and princes decree justice. By me princes rule, and nobles, even all the judges of the earth.
(me: wisdom)
Prov. 8:15–16

In the multitude of people is the king's honour: but in the want of people is the destruction of the prince.
Prov. 14:28

Righteousness exalteth a nation: but sin is a reproach to any people.
Prov. 14:34

When the righteous are in authority, the

people rejoice: but when the wicked beareth rule, the people mourn.
Prov. 29:2

Woe unto them that decree unrighteous decrees.
Isa. 10:1

The nations are as a drop of a bucket, and are counted as the small dust of the balance.
Isa. 40:15

All nations before Him are as nothing.
Isa. 40:17

Woe to him that buildeth a town with blood.
Hab. 2:12

If a kingdom be divided against itself, that kingdom cannot stand.
Jesus
Mark 3:24
See also Matt. 12:25, Luke 11:17

Whether it be right in the sight of God to hearken unto you more than unto God, judge ye.
Acts 4:19

Thou shalt not speak evil of the ruler of thy people.
Acts 23:5
See also Ex. 22:28

Let every soul be subject unto the higher powers.
Rom. 13:1

The powers that be are ordained of God.
Rom. 13:1

Rulers are not a terror to good works, but to the evil.
Rom. 13:3

He is the minister of God, a revenger to execute wrath upon him that doeth evil.
Rom. 13:4

Fear God. Honour the king.
1 Pet. 2:17

[*See also* Church and State, Independence, Leadership, Monarchy, Obedience, Rebellion, Taxation]

GRACE

The law was given by Moses, but grace and truth came by Jesus Christ.
John 1:17

No man can come unto me, except it were given unto him of my Father.
Jesus
John 6:65

Where sin abounded, grace did much more abound.
Rom. 5:20

Sin shall not have dominion over you: for ye are not under the law, but under grace.
Rom. 6:14

The gift of God is eternal life through Jesus Christ our Lord.
Rom. 6:23

If by grace, then is it no more of works: otherwise grace is no more grace.
Rom. 11:6

By grace are ye saved through faith.
Eph. 2:8

It is the gift of God.
Eph. 2:8

Grace be with all them that love our Lord Jesus Christ in sincerity.
Eph. 6:24

GRANDCHILDREN

He shall be unto thee a restorer of thy life, and a nourisher of thine old age.
Ruth 4:15

A good man leaveth an inheritance to his children's children.
Prov. 13:22

Children's children are the crown of old men.
Prov. 17:6

[*See also* Children]

GRATITUDE

Remember this day, in which ye came out from Egypt, out of the house of bondage.
Ex. 13:3

What goodness the Lord shall do unto us, the same will we do unto thee.
> *Num. 10:32*

Praise ye the Lord for the avenging of Israel.
> *Judg. 5:2*

If thou wilt offer a burnt offering, thou must offer it unto the Lord.
> *Judg. 13:16*

Let me find favour in thy sight, my lord; for that thou hast comforted me.
> *Ruth 2:13*

Blessed be ye of the Lord; for ye have compassion on me.
> Saul
> *1 Sam. 23:21*

When the Lord had delivered me into thine hand, thou killedst me not.
> Saul to David
> *1 Sam. 24:18*

When the Lord shall have dealt well with my lord, then remember thine handmaid.
> Abigail to David
> *1 Sam. 25:31*

Whatsoever thou shalt require of me, that will I do for thee.
> *2 Sam. 19:38*

Let them be of those that eat at thy table.
> *1 Kings 2:7*

Blessed be the Lord, that hath given rest unto His people Israel.
> *1 Kings 8:56*

Good is the word of the Lord which thou hast spoken.
> *2 Kings 20:19, Isa. 39:8*

My cup runneth over.
> *Ps. 23:5*

Blessed be the Lord, because He hath heard the voice of my supplications.
> *Ps. 28:6*

Give unto the Lord the glory due unto His name.
> *Ps. 29:2*

O Lord my God, I will give thanks unto Thee for ever.
> *Ps. 30:12*

Blessed be the Lord.
> *E.g., Ps. 31:21*

I will praise the name of God with a song, and will magnify Him with thanksgiving.
> *Ps. 69:30*

It is a good thing to give thanks unto the Lord.
> *Ps. 92:1*

Give thanks unto the Lord; call upon His name.
> *Ps. 105:1, 1 Chron. 16:8*

Give thanks unto the Lord; for He is good: for His mercy endureth for ever.
> *E.g., Ps. 106:1*

In all thy ways acknowledge Him.
> *Prov. 3:6*

Withhold not good from them to whom it is due, when it is in the power of thine hand to do it.
> *Prov. 3:27*

He that is mighty hath done to me great things; and holy is His name.
> Mary
> *Luke 1:49*

To whom little is forgiven, the same loveth little.
> Jesus
> *Luke 7:47*

All things are delivered to me of my Father.
> Jesus
> *Luke 10:22*
> *See also Matt. 11:27*

Thanks be to God, which giveth us the victory through our Lord Jesus Christ.
> *1 Cor. 15:57*

Thanks be unto God for His unspeakable gift.
> *2 Cor. 9:15*

In every thing give thanks: for this is the will of God in Christ Jesus.
> *1 Thess. 5:18*

Every creature of God is good, and nothing to be refused, if it be received with thanksgiving.
> *1 Tim. 4:4*

[*See also* Appreciation, Ingratitude, Praise of God]

GREATNESS

Great men are not always wise: neither do the aged understand judgment.
Job 32:9

God is greater than man.
Job 33:12

He that cometh after me is mightier than I, whose shoes I am not worthy to bear.
John the Baptist
Matt. 3:11
See also Mark 1:7, Luke 3:16

Whosoever shall do and teach them, the same shall be called great in the kingdom of heaven.
Jesus (them: commandments)
Matt. 5:19

He that is least among you all, the same shall be great.
Jesus
Luke 9:48

The servant is not greater than his lord; neither he that is sent greater than he that sent him.
Jesus
John 13:16
See also John 15:20, Matt. 10:24

[*See also* God's Greatness, Size, Status]

GREED

There shall cleave nought of the cursed thing to thine hand.
Deut. 13:17

Is it a time to receive money?
2 Kings 5:26

Will ye even sell your brethren?
Neh. 5:8

Better is a little with righteousness than great revenues without right.
Prov. 16:8

Hell and destruction are never full; so the eyes of man are never satisfied.
Prov. 27:20

He that maketh haste to be rich shall not be innocent.
Prov. 28:20

The horseleach hath two daughters, crying, Give, give.
Prov. 30:15

He that loveth silver shall not be satisfied with silver; nor he that loveth abundance with increase.
Eccl. 5:10

Will ye pollute Me among My people for handfuls of barley and for pieces of bread?
Ezek. 13:19

Exact no more than that which is appointed you.
Luke 3:13

Beware of covetousness.
Jesus
Luke 12:15

Having food and raiment let us be therewith content.
1 Tim. 6:8

The love of money is the root of all evil.
1 Tim. 6:10

Be content with such things as ye have.
Heb. 13:5

[*See also* Ambition, Contentment, Envy, Jealousy, Satisfaction]

GREETINGS

See Salutations.

GRIEF

If I be bereaved of my children, I am bereaved.
Gen. 43:14

How long wilt thou mourn for Saul, seeing I have rejected him?
God to Samuel
1 Sam. 16:1

They had no more power to weep.
1 Sam. 30:4

Tell it not in Gath, publish it not in the streets of Askelon.
2 Sam. 1:20

Would God I had died for thee, O Absalom, my son, my son!
2 Sam. 18:33

The victory that day was turned into mourning.
2 Sam. 19:2

O my son Absalom, O Absalom, my son, my son!
2 Sam. 19:4

My friends scorn me: but mine eye poureth out tears unto God.
Job 16:20

The Lord is nigh unto them that are of a broken heart; and saveth such as be of a contrite spirit.
Ps. 34:18

Pour out your heart before Him: God is a refuge for us.
Ps. 62:8

Thou feedest them with the bread of tears.
Ps. 80:5

To the sinner He giveth travail, to gather and to heap up.
Eccl. 2:26

Teach your daughters wailing, and every one her neighbour lamentation.
Jer. 9:20

Her sun is gone down while it was yet day.
Jer. 15:9

Behold, and see if there be any sorrow like unto my sorrow.
Lam. 1:12

Ye shall pine away for your iniquities, and mourn one toward another.
Ezek. 24:23

Lament like a virgin girded with sackcloth for the husband of her youth.
Joel 1:8

I will wail and howl, I will go stripped and naked.
Mic. 1:8

Weep not for me, but weep for yourselves, and for your children.
Jesus
Luke 23:28

Ye shall weep and lament, but the world shall rejoice.
Jesus
John 16:20

[*See also* Anguish, Mourning, Sorrow, Tears]

GROWTH

Can the rush grow up without mire? can the flag grow without water?
Job 8:11

Spreading himself like a green bay tree.
Ps. 37:35

The righteous shall flourish like the palm tree: he shall grow like a cedar in Lebanon.
Ps. 92:12

Thou hast multiplied the nation, and not increased the joy.
Isa. 9:3

A little one shall become a thousand, and a small one a strong nation.
Isa. 60:22

Being planted, shall it prosper?
Ezek. 17:10

First the blade, then the ear, after that the full corn in the ear.
Jesus
Mark 4:28

It is like a grain of mustard seed, which a man took, and cast into his garden; and it grew, and waxed a great tree.
Jesus
Luke 13:19
See also Matt. 13:31, Mark 4:31

I have fed you with milk, and not with meat.
1 Cor. 3:2

[*See also* Cultivation, Maturity]

GRUDGES

He that repeateth a matter separateth very friends.
Prov. 17:9

Agree with thine adversary quickly, whiles thou art in the way with him.
Jesus
Matt. 5:25

When ye stand praying, forgive, if ye have ought against any: that your Father also

which is in heaven may forgive you your trespasses.
Jesus
Mark 11:25

If ye do not forgive, neither will your Father which is in heaven forgive your trespasses.
Jesus
Mark 11:26

Let not the sun go down upon your wrath.
Eph. 4:26

[*See also* Anger, Arguments, Forgiveness, Temper]

GUIDANCE

The Lord went before them by day in a pillar of a cloud, to lead them the way; and by night in a pillar of fire, to give them light.
Ex. 13:21
See also, e.g., Num. 14:14

If I have found grace in Thy sight, show me now Thy way, that I may know Thee.
Moses to God
Ex. 33:13

Thou mayest be to us instead of eyes.
Moses to Hobab
Num. 10:31

Thou art my lamp, O Lord.
2 Sam. 22:29

Enquire of the Lord for me, and for the people.
2 Kings 22:13

He maketh me to lie down in green pastures: He leadeth me beside the still waters. He restoreth my soul.
Ps. 23:2–3

Show me Thy ways, O Lord; teach me Thy paths.
Ps. 25:4

The meek will He guide in judgment: and the meek will He teach His way.
Ps. 25:9

The steps of a good man are ordered by the Lord: and He delighteth in his way.
Ps. 37:23

Send out Thy light and Thy truth: let them lead me.
Ps. 43:3

This God is our God for ever and ever: He will be our guide even unto death.
Ps. 48:14

Teach me Thy way, O Lord; I will walk in Thy truth.
Ps. 86:11

Thy word is a lamp unto my feet, and a light unto my path.
Ps. 119:105

Cause me to know the way wherein I should walk.
Ps. 143:8

Attend to my words; incline thine ear unto my sayings.
(thine: children)
Prov. 4:20

The commandment is a lamp; and the law is light.
Prov. 6:23

Where no counsel is, the people fall.
Prov. 11:14

Where there is no vision, the people perish.
Prov. 29:18

The words of the wise are as goads.
Eccl. 12:11

This is the way, walk ye in it.
Isa. 30:21

I will also give thee for a light to the Gentiles.
Isa. 49:6

The Lord shall be unto thee an everlasting light.
Isa. 60:19

O Lord, correct me, but with judgment.
Jer. 10:24

When I sit in darkness, the Lord shall be a light unto me.
Mic. 7:8

I am the light of the world.
Jesus
John 8:12

I am the way, the truth, and the life: no man cometh unto the Father, but by me.
Jesus
John 14:6

Lord, what wilt Thou have me to do?
Saul to Jesus
Acts 9:6

It shall be told thee what thou must do.
Jesus to Saul
Acts 9:6

Remember the words of the Lord Jesus.
Acts 20:35

Let the word of Christ dwell in you.
Col. 3:16

Make straight paths for your feet, lest that which is lame be turned out of the way.
Heb. 12:13

[*See also* Advice, Behavior, Instruction]

GUILT

Who told thee that thou wast naked?
Gen. 3:11

The voice of thy brother's blood crieth unto Me from the ground.
Gen. 4:10

I have sinned this time: the Lord is righteous, and I and my people are wicked.
Pharaoh
Ex. 9:27

Thy blood be upon thy head.
2 Sam. 1:16

Hast thou killed, and also taken possession?
(thou: Ahab)
1 Kings 21:19

Every man shall be put to death for his own sin.
E.g., 2 Kings 14:6

If I be wicked, woe unto me.
Job 10:15

Thy mouth uttereth thine iniquity.
Job 15:5

Thine own mouth condemneth thee, and not I.
Job 15:6

Thine own lips testify against thee.
Job 15:6
See also 2 Sam. 1:16

Your hands are full of blood.
Isa. 1:15

The show of their countenance doth witness against them.
Isa. 3:9

Our sins testify against us.
Isa. 59:12

Though thou wash thee with nitre, and take thee much soap, yet thine iniquity is marked before Me.
Jer. 2:22

His blood shall be upon him.
E.g., Ezek. 18:13

The stone shall cry out of the wall, and the beam out of the timber shall answer it.
Hab. 2:11

He that is without sin among you, let him first cast a stone.
Jesus
John 8:7

Woman, where are those thine accusers?
Jesus
John 8:10

Ye are not all clean.
Jesus
John 13:11

He that delivered me unto thee hath the greater sin.
Jesus
John 19:11

Your blood be upon your own heads; I am clean.
Acts 18:6

If I build again the things which I destroyed, I make myself a transgressor.
Gal. 2:18

Whosoever shall keep the whole law, and yet offend in one point, he is guilty of all.
James 2:10

[*See also* Blame, Innocence, Justice, Responsibility, Restitution, Self-Incrimination]

HABIT

As a dog returneth to his vomit, so a fool returneth to his folly.
Prov. 26:11
See also 2 Pet. 2:22

Can the Ethiopian change his skin, or the leopard his spots? then may ye also do good, that are accustomed to do evil.
Jer. 13:23

HANDICAPPED

Who hath made man's mouth? or who maketh the dumb, or deaf, or the seeing, or the blind? have not I the Lord?
Ex. 4:11

Thou shalt not curse the deaf, nor put a stumblingblock before the blind.
Lev. 19:14

He maketh both the deaf to hear, and the dumb to speak.
(He: Jesus)
Mark 7:37

The blind see, the lame walk, the lepers are cleansed, the deaf hear, the dead are raised, to the poor the gospel is preached.
Jesus
Luke 7:22
See also Matt. 11:5

When thou makest a feast, call the poor, the maimed, the lame, the blind: And thou shalt be blessed; for they cannot recompense thee.
Jesus
Luke 14:13–14

[*See also* Blindness, Healing, Obstacles, Sight]

HANGING

He that is hanged is accursed of God.
Deut. 21:23
See also Gal. 3:13

HAPPINESS

My heart rejoiceth in the Lord.
1 Sam. 2:1

Happy is the man whom God correcteth.
Job 5:17

The triumphing of the wicked is short, and the joy of the hypocrite but for a moment.
Job 20:5

Let all those that put their trust in Thee rejoice: let them ever shout for joy.
Ps. 5:11

Surely goodness and mercy shall follow me all the days of my life: and I will dwell in the house of the Lord for ever.
Ps. 23:6

Weeping may endure for a night, but joy cometh in the morning.
Ps. 30:5

Be glad in the Lord.
Ps. 32:11

Shout for joy, all ye that are upright in heart.
Ps. 32:11

Blessed is that man that maketh the Lord his trust.
Ps. 40:4
See also, e.g., Ps. 34:8

Shout unto God with the voice of triumph.
Ps. 47:1

Blessed is the man whom Thou choosest, and causest to approach unto Thee.
Ps. 65:4

Light is sown for the righteous, and gladness for the upright in heart.
Ps. 97:11

Glory ye in His holy name.
Ps. 105:3, 1 Chron. 16:10

Let the heart of them rejoice that seek the Lord.
Ps. 105:3

Thy law is my delight.
Ps. 119:77, 174
See also Ps. 119:143

They that sow in tears shall reap in joy.
Ps. 126:5

Happy is that people, whose God is the Lord.
Ps. 144:15

Happy is he that hath the God of Jacob for his help, whose hope is in the Lord his God.
Ps. 146:5

Happy is the man that findeth wisdom, and the man that getteth understanding.
Prov. 3:13

When it goeth well with the righteous, the city rejoiceth.
Prov. 11:10

When the wicked perish, there is shouting.
Prov. 11:10

A merry heart maketh a cheerful countenance.
Prov. 15:13

He that is of a merry heart hath a continual feast.
Prov. 15:15

Whoso trusteth in the Lord, happy is he.
Prov. 16:20

A merry heart doeth good like a medicine: but a broken spirit drieth the bones.
Prov. 17:22

A time to weep, and a time to laugh; a time to mourn, and a time to dance.
Eccl. 3:4

Blessed is the man that trusteth in the Lord, and whose hope the Lord is.
Jer. 17:7

Their soul shall be as a watered garden; and they shall not sorrow any more at all.
Jer. 31:12

I will rejoice in the Lord, I will joy in the God of my salvation.
Hab. 3:18

I bring you good tidings of great joy.
Luke 2:10

Rejoice not, that the spirits are subject unto you; but rather rejoice, because your names are written in heaven.
Jesus
Luke 10:20

Rejoice with me; for I have found my sheep which was lost.
Jesus
Luke 15:6

If ye know these things, happy are ye if ye do them.
Jesus
John 13:17

Ask, and ye shall receive, that your joy may be full.
Jesus
John 16:24

Rejoice with them that do rejoice, and weep with them that weep.
Rom. 12:15

Rejoice in the Lord.
E.g., Phil. 3:1

We count them happy which endure.
James 5:11

He that will love life, and see good days, let him refrain his tongue from evil.
1 Pet. 3:10
See also Ps. 34:13

Let us be glad and rejoice, and give honour to Him.
Rev. 19:7

Blessed are they which are called unto the marriage supper of the Lamb.
Rev. 19:9

[*See also* Celebration, Contentment, Laughter, Pleasure, Satisfaction]

HATRED

My soul shall abhor you.
Lev. 26:30

Let them that hate Thee flee before Thee.
Num. 10:35

The hatred wherewith he hated her was greater than the love wherewith he had loved her.
2 Sam. 13:15

They that hate me without a cause are more than the hairs of mine head.
Ps. 69:4

He that hideth hatred with lying lips, and he that uttereth a slander, is a fool.
Prov. 10:18

He that despiseth his neighbour sinneth.
Prov. 14:21

A time to love, and a time to hate.
Eccl. 3:8

Do good to them that hate you.
Jesus
Matt. 5:44
See also Luke 6:27

If the world hate you, ye know that it hated me before it hated you.
Jesus
John 15:18

The poison of asps is under their lips.
Rom. 3:13
See also Ps. 140:3

He that saith he is in the light, and hateth his brother, is in darkness even until now.
1 John 2:9

Whosoever hateth his brother is a murderer.
1 John 3:15

He that loveth not knoweth not God; for God is love.
1 John 4:8

If a man say, I love God, and hateth his brother, he is a liar.
1 John 4:20

[*See also* Brotherhood, Contempt, Enemies, Love, Persecution, Self-Hatred]

HEALING

There is no god with Me: I kill, and I make alive; I wound, and I heal: neither is there any that can deliver out of My hand.
Deut. 32:39

Am I God, to kill and to make alive?
2 Kings 5:7

If the prophet had bid thee do some great thing, wouldest thou not have done it?
2 Kings 5:13

In his disease he sought not to the Lord, but to the physicians.
2 Chron. 16:12

He maketh sore, and bindeth up: He woundeth, and His hands make whole.
Job 5:18

A merry heart doeth good like a medicine: but a broken spirit drieth the bones.
Prov. 17:22

A time to kill, and a time to heal; a time to break down, and a time to build up.
Eccl. 3:3

A time to rend, and a time to sew.
Eccl. 3:7

Then shall the lame man leap as an hart, and the tongue of the dumb sing.
Isa. 35:6

I have heard thy prayer, I have seen thy tears: behold, I will add unto thy days fifteen years.
God to Hezekiah
Isa. 38:5
See also 2 Kings 20:5-6

With his stripes we are healed.
Isa. 53:5

Is there no balm in Gilead? is there no physician there?
Jer. 8:22

Heal me, O Lord, and I shall be healed; save me, and I shall be saved.
Jer. 17:14

In vain shalt thou use many medicines; for thou shalt not be cured.
Jer. 46:11

I will seek that which was lost, and bring again that which was driven away, and will bind up that which was broken, and will strengthen that which was sick.
Ezek. 34:16

He hath torn, and He will heal us; He hath smitten, and He will bind us up.
Hos. 6:1

If Thou wilt, Thou canst make me clean.
Leper to Jesus
Matt. 8:2, Mark 1:40,
Luke 5:12

They that be whole need not a physician, but they that are sick.
Jesus
Matt. 9:12
See also Mark 2:17, Luke 5:31

If I may but touch His garment, I shall be whole.
Matt. 9:21
See also Mark 5:28

Thy faith hath made thee whole.
Jesus
Matt. 9:22, Mark 5:34,
Mark 10:52, Luke 8:48
See also Luke 17:19

Heal the sick, cleanse the lepers, raise the dead, cast out devils.
Jesus
Matt. 10:8

As many as touched were made perfectly whole.
Matt. 14:36
See also Mark 6:56

Ephphatha, that is, Be opened.
Jesus
Mark 7:34

He maketh both the deaf to hear, and the dumb to speak.
(He: Jesus)
Mark 7:37

They shall lay hands on the sick, and they shall recover.
Jesus
Mark 16:18

He hath sent me to heal the brokenhearted, to preach deliverance to the captives.
Jesus
Luke 4:18
See also Isa. 61:1

Physician, heal thyself.
Luke 4:23

He laid His hands on every one of them, and healed them.
Luke 4:40

Go thy way; thy son liveth.
Jesus
John 4:50

Rise, take up thy bed, and walk.
Jesus
John 5:8
See also Matt. 9:6, Mark 2:9, Luke 5:24

Go, wash in the pool of Siloam.
Jesus
John 9:7

In the name of Jesus Christ of Nazareth rise up and walk.
Acts 3:6

By Him doth this man stand here before you whole.
Acts 4:10

And they were healed every one.
Acts 5:16

Jesus Christ maketh thee whole: arise, and make thy bed.
Acts 9:34

He had faith to be healed.
Acts 14:9

And he leaped and walked.
Acts 14:10

The prayer of faith shall save the sick.
James 5:15

[*See also* Faith, Miracles, Restoration]

HEALTH

See Handicapped, Healing.

HEAVEN

If I ascend up into heaven, Thou art there: if I make my bed in hell, behold, Thou art there.
Ps. 139:8

It is better for thee to enter into the kingdom of God with one eye, than having two eyes to be cast into hell fire.
Jesus
Mark 9:47
See also Matt. 18:9

In my Father's house are many mansions.
Jesus
John 14:2

I go to prepare a place for you.
Jesus
John 14:2

Whither I go ye know, and the way ye know.
Jesus
John 14:4

Heaven is My throne, and earth is My footstool: what house will ye build Me? saith the Lord.
Acts 7:49
See also Isa. 66:1

The gates of it shall not be shut at all by day: for there shall be no night there.
Rev. 21:25

[*See also* Creation, Damnation, Eternal Life, God's Presence, Kingdom of God, Kingdom of Heaven]

HEAVEN AND EARTH

And God called the firmament Heaven.
Gen. 1:8

In six days the Lord made heaven and earth, the sea, and all that in them is.
Ex. 20:11

All that is in the heaven and in the earth is Thine.
1 Chron. 29:11

The heavens declare the glory of God; and the firmament showeth His handywork.
Ps. 19:1

The world is Mine, and the fulness thereof.
Ps. 50:12
See also Ex. 19:5

The heavens are Thine, the earth also is Thine.
Ps. 89:11

The heavens declare His righteousness, and all the people see His glory.
Ps. 97:6

They shall perish, but Thou shalt endure.
Ps. 102:26

The heaven, even the heavens, are the Lord's: but the earth hath He given to the children of men.
Ps. 115:16

He telleth the number of the stars; He calleth them all by their names.
Ps. 147:4

The heaven is My throne, and the earth is My footstool.
Isa. 66:1
See also Matt. 5:34–35

He hath established the world by His wisdom, and hath stretched out the heavens by His discretion.
Jer. 10:12

One star differeth from another star in glory.
1 Cor. 15:41

They shall perish; but Thou remainest.
Heb. 1:11

I saw a new heaven and a new earth: for the first heaven and the first earth were passed away.
Rev. 21:1

[*See also* Creation, Earth]

HEEDFULNESS

Speak, Lord; for Thy servant heareth.
1 Sam. 3:9

Hold thy peace, and I shall teach thee wisdom.
Job 33:33

A wise man will hear, and will increase learning.
Prov. 1:5

I spake unto thee in thy prosperity; but thou saidst, I will not hear.
Jer. 22:21

I have spoken unto them, but they have not heard; and I have called unto them, but they have not answered.
Jer. 35:17

They hearkened not, nor inclined their ear to turn from their wickedness.
Jer. 44:5

Thus saith the Lord God; He that heareth, let him hear; and he that forbeareth, let him forebear.
Ezek. 3:27

They hear thy words, but they do them not.
God to Ezekiel
Ezek. 33:32

Hear the word of the Lord, ye children of Israel.
Hos. 4:1

We have piped unto you, and ye have not danced; we have mourned unto you, and ye have not lamented.
Jesus
Matt. 11:17
See also Luke 7:32

Who hath ears to hear, let him hear.
Jesus
Matt. 13:9, Matt. 13:43
See also, e.g., Matt. 11:15, Mark 4:9,
Rev. 13:9

Hear, and understand.
Jesus
Matt. 15:10

Ye that fear God, give audience.
Acts 13:16

Let every man be swift to hear, slow to speak, slow to wrath.
James 1:19

He that hath an ear, let him hear what the Spirit saith unto the churches.
Jesus
E.g., Rev. 2:7

[*See also* Obedience, Pleas, Prayer, Preaching, Warning]

HEIGHT

See Size.

HELL

Hell and destruction are never full.
Prov. 27:20

Hell hath enlarged herself, and opened her mouth without measure.
Isa. 5:14

Hell from beneath is moved for thee to meet thee at thy coming.
Isa. 14:9

The fire that never shall be quenched.
Jesus
Mark 9:43, 45

Where their worm dieth not, and the fire is not quenched.
Jesus
Mark 9:44, 46, 48

I am tormented in this flame.
Luke 16:24

Between us and you there is a great gulf fixed: so that they which would pass from hence to you cannot.
Luke 16:26

I looked, and behold a pale horse: and his name that sat on him was Death, and Hell followed with him.
Rev. 6:8

The bottomless pit.
Rev. 9:1

Death and hell were cast into the lake of fire. This is the second death.
Rev. 20:14

[*See also* Damnation, Death, Torment]

HELP

See Assistance, Deliverance.

HERESY

Thou shalt not hearken unto the words of that prophet, or that dreamer of dreams: for the Lord your God proveth you, to know whether ye love the Lord your God with all your heart and with all your soul.
Deut. 13:3

Put the evil away from the midst of thee.
Deut. 13:5

Woe unto him that striveth with his Maker!
Isa. 45:9

I am against the prophets, saith the Lord, that use their tongues, and say, He saith.
Jer. 23:31

Thou shalt die, because thou hast taught rebellion against the Lord.
Jer. 28:16

In vain they do worship me, teaching for doctrines the commandments of men.
Jesus
Matt. 15:9, Mark 7:7
See also Isa. 29:13

False Christs and false prophets shall rise, and shall show signs and wonders, to seduce, if it were possible, even the elect.
Jesus
Mark 13:22
See also Matt. 24:24

After the way which they call heresy, so worship I the God of my fathers.
Paul
Acts 24:14

If any man preach any other gospel unto

you than that ye have received, let him be accursed.
Gal. 1:9

Beware lest any man spoil you through philosophy and vain deceit.
Col. 2:8

A man that is an heretick after the first and second admonition reject.
Titus 3:10

There shall be false teachers among you.
2 Pet. 2:1

He that biddeth him God speed is partaker of his evil deeds.
2 John 11

Woe unto them! for they have gone in the way of Cain.
Jude 11

[*See also* Blasphemy, False Prophets]

HERITAGE

My covenant is with thee, and thou shalt be a father of many nations.
God to Abram
Gen. 17:4

In thee and in thy seed shall all the families of the earth be blessed.
God to Jacob
Gen. 28:14

I am the God of thy father, the God of Abraham, the God of Isaac, and the God of Jacob.
Ex. 3:6
See also, e.g., Mark 12:26

He is my God, and I will prepare Him an habitation; my father's God, and I will exalt Him.
Ex. 15:2

Why should the name of our father be done away from among his family, because he hath no son?
Num. 27:4

The Lord made not this covenant with our fathers, but with us, even us, who are all of us here alive this day.
Deut. 5:3

Let a double portion of thy spirit be upon me.
Elisha to Elijah
2 Kings 2:9

The lines are fallen unto me in pleasant places; yea, I have a goodly heritage.
Ps. 16:6

As is the mother, so is her daughter.
Ezek. 16:44

The fathers have eaten sour grapes, and the children's teeth are set on edge.
Ezek. 18:2
See also Jer. 31:29

Who shall declare His generation? for His life is taken from the earth.
Acts 8:33
See also Isa. 53:8

I am a Pharisee, the son of a Pharisee.
Paul
Acts 23:6

I am debtor both to the Greeks, and to the Barbarians; both to the wise, and to the unwise.
Rom. 1:14

If the root be holy, so are the branches.
Rom. 11:16

We are not children of the bondwoman, but of the free.
Gal. 4:31

[*See also* Character, Inheritance, Tradition]

HEROISM

See Courage, Leadership.

HIERARCHY

See Authority, Leadership.

HISTORY

Remember the days of old, consider the years of many generations: ask thy father, and he will show thee; thy elders, and they will tell thee.
Deut. 32:7

Write it before them in a table, and note it

in a book, that it may be for the time to
come for ever and ever.
Isa. 30:8

Have ye forgotten the wickedness of your
fathers?
Jer. 44:9

He that saw it bare record, and his record
is true.
John 19:35

If they should be written every one, I
suppose that even the world itself could not
contain the books that should be written.
John 21:25

That which we have seen and heard declare
we unto you.
1 John 1:3

[*See also* Testimony]

HOLIDAYS

It is a night to be much observed unto the
Lord.
Ex. 12:42

This day is holy unto the Lord your God;
mourn not, nor weep.
Neh. 8:9

[*See also* Celebration, Sabbath]

HOLINESS

Put off thy shoes from off thy feet, for the
place whereon thou standest is holy
ground.
Ex. 3:5
See also Josh. 5:15

I will be sanctified in them that come nigh
Me.
Lev. 10:3

Ye shall be holy: for I the Lord your God
am holy.
E.g., Lev. 19:2
See also 1 Pet. 1:16

Every devoted thing is most holy unto the
Lord.
Lev. 27:28

There is none holy as the Lord.
1 Sam. 2:2

Who shall ascend into the hill of the Lord?
or who shall stand in His holy place? He
that hath clean hands, and a pure heart;
who hath not lifted up his soul unto vanity,
nor sworn deceitfully.
Ps. 24:3–4

Holy, holy, holy, is the Lord of hosts: the
whole earth is full of His glory.
Isa. 6:3

Before thou camest forth out of the womb
I sanctified thee.
God to Jeremiah
Jer. 1:5

They shall teach My people the difference
between the holy and profane.
Ezek. 44:23

Holiness unto the Lord.
Zech. 14:20

Now ye are clean through the word which I
have spoken unto you.
Jesus
John 15:3

Sanctify them through Thy truth.
Jesus
John 17:17

If the root be holy, so are the branches.
Rom. 11:16

The temple of God is holy, which temple
ye are.
1 Cor. 3:17

God hath not called us unto uncleanness,
but unto holiness.
1 Thess. 4:7

Both He that sanctifieth and they who are
sanctified are all of one.
Heb. 2:11

As He which hath called you is holy, so be
ye holy.
1 Pet. 1:15

Holy, holy, holy, Lord God Almighty,
which was, and is, and is to come.
Rev. 4:8

Thou only art holy.
Rev. 15:4

[*See also* Consecration]

HOLY SPIRIT

And the Spirit of God moved upon the face of the waters.
Gen. 1:2

The Spirit of the Lord God is upon me.
Isa. 61:1

The Spirit of God descending like a dove.
Matt. 3:16
See also Mark 1:10

Whosoever speaketh against the Holy Ghost, it shall not be forgiven him, neither in this world, neither in the world to come.
Jesus
Matt. 12:32
See also Mark 3:29, Luke 12:10

I indeed have baptized you with water: but He shall baptize you with the Holy Ghost.
John the Baptist
Mark 1:8
See also Matt. 3:11, Luke 3:16

I saw the Spirit descending from heaven like a dove, and it abode upon Him.
John 1:32

Except a man be born of water and of the Spirit, he cannot enter into the kingdom of God.
Jesus
John 3:5

It is the Spirit that quickeneth; the flesh profiteth nothing.
Jesus
John 6:63

He shall give you another Comforter, that He may abide with you for ever.
Jesus
John 14:16

The Comforter, which is the Holy Ghost.
Jesus
John 14:26

If I go not away, the Comforter will not come unto you.
Jesus
John 16:7

Receive ye the Holy Ghost.
Jesus
John 20:22

Wait for the promise of the Father.
Jesus
Acts 1:4

The promise is unto you, and to your children, and to all that are afar off.
Acts 2:39

They that are after the flesh do mind the things of the flesh; but they that are after the Spirit the things of the Spirit.
Rom. 8:5

Ye are not in the flesh, but in the Spirit.
Rom. 8:9

As many as are led by the Spirit of God, they are the sons of God.
Rom. 8:14

The kingdom of God is not meat and drink; but righteousness, and peace, and joy in the Holy Ghost.
Rom. 14:17

The Spirit searcheth all things.
1 Cor. 2:10

The Spirit of God dwelleth in you.
1 Cor. 3:16

There are diversities of gifts, but the same Spirit.
1 Cor. 12:4

Walk in the Spirit, and ye shall not fulfil the lust of the flesh.
Gal. 5:16

The fruit of the Spirit is love, joy, peace, longsuffering, gentleness, goodness, faith, meekness, temperance.
Gal. 5:22–23

If we live in the Spirit, let us also walk in the Spirit.
Gal. 5:25

Be not drunk with wine, wherein is excess; but be filled with the Spirit.
Eph. 5:18

Quench not the Spirit.
1 Thess. 5:19

It is the Spirit that beareth witness, because the Spirit is truth.
1 John 5:6

Out of His mouth goeth a sharp sword, that with it He should smite the nations.
Rev. 19:15

[*See also* Spiritualism]

HOMAGE

He that sacrificeth unto any god, save unto the Lord only, he shall be utterly destroyed.
Ex. 22:20

What shall be done unto the man whom the king delighteth to honour?
Esther 6:6

Give unto the Lord the glory due unto His name.
Ps. 29:2

Worship Him, all ye gods.
Ps. 97:7

Come ye, and let us go up to the mountain of the Lord.
Isa. 2:3

I am sought of them that asked not for Me; I am found of them that sought Me not.
Isa. 65:1
See also Rom. 10:20

We have seen His star in the east, and are come to worship Him.
Matt. 2:2

Whosoever shall receive me, receiveth not me, but Him that sent me.
Jesus
Mark 9:37
See also Luke 9:48

He that honoureth not the Son honoureth not the Father which hath sent Him.
Jesus
John 5:23

I receive not honour from men.
Jesus
John 5:41

He that receiveth whomsoever I send receiveth me.
Jesus
John 13:20

He that regardeth the day, regardeth it unto the Lord.
Rom. 14:6

He that eateth, eateth to the Lord, for he giveth God thanks.
Rom. 14:6

At the name of Jesus every knee should bow.
Phil. 2:10

[*See also* Fear of God, Respect]

HOME

Bury me not, I pray thee, in Egypt.
Jacob to Joseph
Gen. 47:29

How goodly are thy tents, O Jacob, and thy tabernacles, O Israel!
Num. 24:5

By the rivers of Babylon, there we sat down, yea, we wept, when we remembered Zion.
Ps. 137:1

Every wise woman buildeth her house: but the foolish plucketh it down with her hands.
Prov. 14:1

Foxes have holes, and birds of the air have nests; but the Son of man hath not where to lay His head.
Jesus
Luke 9:58
See also Matt. 8:20

[*See also* Building, Children, Family, Marriage]

HOMELESS

See Exile.

HOMOSEXUALITY

Thou shalt not lie with mankind, as with womankind: it is abomination.
Lev. 18:22
See also Lev. 20:13

They shall surely be put to death.
Lev. 20:13

Sons of Belial.
E.g., Judg. 19:22

Their women did change the natural use into that which is against nature.
Rom. 1:26

Men, leaving the natural use of the woman, burned in their lust one toward another.
Rom. 1:27

Men with men working that which is unseemly.
Rom. 1:27

HONESTY

If thou meet thine enemy's ox or his ass going astray, thou shalt surely bring it back to him again.
Ex. 23:4

Keep thee far from a false matter.
Ex. 23:7

Ye shall not steal, neither deal falsely, neither lie one to another.
Lev. 19:11

Ye shall do no unrighteousness in judgment, in meteyard, in weight, or in measure.
Lev. 19:35

Must I not take heed to speak that which the Lord hath put in my mouth?
Num. 23:12

A gift doth blind the eyes of the wise, and pervert the words of the righteous.
Deut. 16:19
See also Ex. 23:8

Thou shalt not have in thy bag divers weights, a great and a small.
Deut. 25:13

All that do unrighteously, are an abomination unto the Lord thy God.
Deut. 25:16

Serve Him in sincerity and in truth.
Josh. 24:14

Walk before Me, as David thy father walked, in integrity of heart, and in uprightness.
1 Kings 9:4

How forcible are right words!
Job 6:25

He that hath clean hands, and a pure heart.
Ps. 24:4

Keep thy tongue from evil, and thy lips from speaking guile.
Ps. 34:13
See also 1 Pet. 3:10

The wicked borroweth, and payeth not again: but the righteous showeth mercy, and giveth.
Ps. 37:21

He that walketh uprightly walketh surely.
Prov. 10:9

The tongue of the just is as choice silver: the heart of the wicked is little worth.
Prov. 10:20

A false balance is abomination to the Lord: but a just weight is His delight.
Prov. 11:1
See also Prov. 20:10, 23

He that speaketh truth showeth forth righteousness.
Prov. 12:17

A true witness delivereth souls.
Prov. 14:25

The just man walketh in his integrity.
Prov. 20:7

Be not a witness against thy neighbour without cause.
Prov. 24:28

Deceive not with thy lips.
Prov. 24:28

Better is the poor that walketh in his uprightness, than he that is perverse in his ways, though he be rich.
Prov. 28:6

Ye shall have just balances.
Ezek. 45:10

Speak ye every man the truth to his neighbour.
Zech. 8:16

The law of truth was in his mouth, and iniquity was not found in his lips.
Mal. 2:6

Exact no more than that which is appointed you.
Luke 3:13

He that is faithful in that which is least is faithful also in much.
Jesus
Luke 16:10

God is my witness.
Rom. 1:9

Speak every man truth with his neighbour: for we are members one of another.
Eph. 4:25

Lie not one to another.
Col. 3:9

Ye know that our record is true.
3 John 12

[*See also* Candor, Corruption, Dishonesty, Integrity, Lies, Truth]

HONOR

See Glory, Respect.

HOPE

The poor hath hope.
Job 5:16

The hypocrite's hope shall perish.
Job 8:13

The needy shall not always be forgotten: the expectation of the poor shall not perish for ever.
Ps. 9:18

Those that wait upon the Lord, they shall inherit the earth.
Ps. 37:9

Thou art my hope, O Lord God: Thou art my trust from my youth.
Ps. 71:5

I will lift up mine eyes unto the hills, from whence cometh my help.
Ps. 121:1

I wait for the Lord, my soul doth wait.
Ps. 130:5

In His word do I hope.
Ps. 130:5

My soul waiteth for the Lord more than they that watch for the morning.
Ps. 130:6

In Thee is my trust; leave not my soul destitute.
Ps. 141:8

The eyes of all wait upon Thee.
Ps. 145:15

Hope deferred maketh the heart sick: but when the desire cometh, it is a tree of life.
Prov. 13:12

A living dog is better than a dead lion.
Eccl. 9:4

Awake and sing, ye that dwell in dust.
Isa. 26:19

Fear thou not; for I am with thee: be not dismayed; for I am thy God.
Isa. 41:10

Be not a terror unto me: Thou art my hope in the day of evil.
Jer. 17:17

Ye prisoners of hope.
Zech. 9:12

The last shall be first.
Jesus
Matt. 19:30
See also, e.g., Mark 10:31

Ye shall be sorrowful, but your sorrow shall be turned into joy.
Jesus
John 16:20

Tribulation worketh patience; And patience, experience; and experience, hope.
Rom. 5:3–4

Hope maketh not ashamed.
Rom. 5:5

We are saved by hope.
Rom. 8:24

Hope that is seen is not hope.
Rom. 8:24

And now abideth faith, hope, charity, these three; but the greatest of these is charity.
(charity: love)
1 Cor. 13:13

We are perplexed, but not in despair; Persecuted, but not forsaken; cast down, but not destroyed.
2 Cor. 4:8–9

Be not moved away from the hope of the gospel.
Col. 1:23

Faith is the substance of things hoped for, the evidence of things not seen.
Heb. 11:1

I will give unto him that is athirst of the fountain of the water of life freely.
Jesus
Rev. 21:6

[*See also* Depression, Despair, Disappointment, Encouragement, Expectation, Prayer, Restoration]

HOSPITALITY

Thou shalt neither vex a stranger, nor oppress him: for ye were strangers in the land of Egypt.
Ex. 22:21
See also Ex. 23:9

Comfort thine heart with a morsel of bread, and afterward go your way.
Judg. 19:5

Let all thy wants lie upon me; only lodge not in the street.
Judg. 19:20

Eat, that thou mayest have strength, when thou goest on thy way.
Spiritualist to Saul
1 Sam. 28:22

The stranger did not lodge in the street: but I opened my doors to the traveller.
Job 31:32

Withdraw thy foot from thy neighbour's house; lest he be weary of thee, and so hate thee.
Prov. 25:17

If the house be worthy, let your peace come upon it: but if it be not worthy, let your peace return to you.
Jesus
Matt. 10:13

He that receiveth a prophet in the name of a prophet shall receive a prophet's reward.
Jesus
Matt. 10:41

He that receiveth a righteous man in the name of a righteous man shall receive a righteous man's reward.
Jesus
Matt. 10:41

For I was an hungred, and ye gave me meat: I was thirsty, and ye gave me drink: I was a stranger, and ye took me in: Naked, and ye clothed me: I was sick, and ye visited me: I was in prison, and ye came unto me.
Jesus
Matt. 25:35–36

Inasmuch as ye have done it unto one of the least of these my brethren, ye have done it unto me.
Jesus
Matt. 25:40
See also Matt. 25:45

Whosoever shall give you a cup of water to drink in my name, because ye belong to Christ, verily I say unto you, he shall not lose his reward.
Jesus
Mark 9:41

Every man at the beginning doth set forth good wine.
John 2:10

He that receiveth whomsoever I send receiveth me.
Jesus
John 13:20

Be not forgetful to entertain strangers: for thereby some have entertained angels unawares.
Heb. 13:2

Use hospitality one to another without grudging.
1 Pet. 4:9

[*See also* Brotherhood, Kindness]

HUMAN BODY

See Body, Physical Fitness.

HUMAN NATURE

The imagination of man's heart is evil from his youth.
Gen. 8:21

The heart of the sons of men is full of evil, and madness is in their heart while they live.
Eccl. 9:3

Destruction and misery are in their ways: And the way of peace have they not known.
Rom. 3:16–17
See also Isa. 59:7–8

The law is spiritual: but I am carnal.
Rom. 7:14

In me (that is, in my flesh,) dwelleth no good thing.
    Rom. 7:18

The flesh lusteth against the Spirit, and the Spirit against the flesh.
    Gal. 5:17

[*See also* Behavior, Carnality, Mankind, Sin]

HUMILIATION

Upon thy belly shalt thou go, and dust shalt thou eat all the days of thy life.
    God to serpent
    Gen. 3:14

Thus shall the Lord do to all your enemies against whom ye fight.
    Josh. 10:25

Draw thy sword, and slay me, that men say not of me, A woman slew him.
    Judg. 9:54

The glory is departed from Israel: for the ark of God is taken.
    1 Sam. 4:22

He shall lie with thy wives in the sight of this sun.
    (He: David's neighbor)
    2 Sam. 12:11

Thou didst it secretly: but I will do this thing before all Israel, and before the sun.
    God to David
    2 Sam. 12:12

The carcase of Jezebel shall be as dung upon the face of the field.
    2 Kings 9:37

I will put My hook in thy nose, and My bridle in thy lips, and I will turn thee back by the way by which thou camest.
    2 Kings 19:28, Isa. 37:29

They shall be eunuchs in the palace of the king of Babylon.
    2 Kings 20:18, Isa. 39:7

They shall become a prey and a spoil to all their enemies.
    2 Kings 21:14

His enemies shall lick the dust.
    Ps. 72:9

The mean man shall be brought down, and the mighty man shall be humbled.
    Isa. 5:15

Thy pomp is brought down to the grave, and the noise of thy viols.
    Isa. 14:11

Thy nakedness shall be uncovered, yea, thy shame shall be seen.
    Isa. 47:3

He was despised, and we esteemed him not.
    Isa. 53:3

Though thou shouldest make thy nest as high as the eagle, I will bring thee down from thence, saith the Lord.
    Jer. 49:16

They shall become as women.
    Jer. 50:37

She that was great among the nations, and princess among the provinces, how is she become tributary!
    Lam. 1:1

They that did feed delicately are desolate in the streets: they that were brought up in scarlet embrace dunghills.
    Lam. 4:5

Those that be near, and those that be far from thee, shall mock thee.
    Ezek. 22:5

I will deliver thee into the hand of them whom thou hatest.
    Ezek. 23:28

Wherefore should they say among the people, Where is their God?
    Joel 2:17
    See also, e.g., Ps. 79:10

They shall lick the dust like a serpent, they shall move out of their holes like worms of the earth: they shall be afraid of the Lord our God.
    Mic. 7:17

I will show the nations thy nakedness, and the kingdoms thy shame.
    (thy: Nineveh)
    Nah. 3:5

I will corrupt your seed, and spread dung upon your faces.
    God to wayward priests
    Mal. 2:3

God hath chosen the foolish things of the world to confound the wise.
1 Cor. 1:27

[*See also* Contempt, Defeat, Outcast, Shame]

HUMILITY

Who am I, that I should go unto Pharaoh, and that I should bring forth the children of Israel out of Egypt?
Moses
Ex. 3:11

I am slow of speech, and of a slow tongue.
Moses
Ex. 4:10

I will not rule over you, neither shall my son rule over you: the Lord shall rule over you.
Gideon
Judg. 8:23

Who am I, O Lord God? and what is my house, that Thou hast brought me hither-to?
David
2 Sam. 7:18

Is this the manner of man, O Lord God?
2 Sam. 7:19

I am but a little child: I know not how to go out or come in.
Solomon to God
1 Kings 3:7

Am I God, to kill and to make alive?
2 Kings 5:7

Shall any teach God knowledge?
Job 21:22

He shall save the humble person.
Job 22:29

Serve the Lord with fear, and rejoice with trembling.
Ps. 2:11

The Lord is nigh unto them that are of a broken heart; and saveth such as be of a contrite spirit.
Ps. 34:18

I am poor and sorrowful: let Thy salvation, O God, set me up on high.
Ps. 69:29

I had rather be a doorkeeper in the house of my God, than to dwell in the tents of wickedness.
Ps. 84:10

Not unto us, O Lord, not unto us, but unto Thy name give glory.
Ps. 115:1

The Lord preserveth the simple.
Ps. 116:6

Before honour is humility.
Prov. 15:33, Prov. 18:12

Better it is to be of an humble spirit with the lowly, than to divide the spoil with the proud.
Prov. 16:19

A man hath no preeminence above a beast: for all is vanity.
Eccl. 3:19

God is in heaven, and thou upon earth: therefore let thy words be few.
Eccl. 5:2

Let not the wise man glory in his wisdom, neither let the mighty man glory in his might, let not the rich man glory in his riches.
Jer. 9:23

We do not present our supplications before Thee for our righteousnesses, but for Thy great mercies.
Dan. 9:18

Walk humbly with thy God.
Mic. 6:8

Behold, thy King cometh unto thee: he is just, and having salvation; lowly, and riding upon an ass.
Zech. 9:9

He that cometh after me is mightier than I, whose shoes I am not worthy to bear.
John the Baptist
Matt. 3:11
See also Mark 1:7, Luke 3:16

Blessed are the poor in spirit: for their's is the kingdom of heaven.
Jesus
Matt. 5:3
See also Luke 6:20

Blessed are the meek: for they shall inherit the earth.
Jesus
Matt. 5:5
See also Ps. 37:11

I am meek and lowly in heart: and ye shall find rest unto your souls.
Jesus
Matt. 11:29

Except ye be converted, and become as little children, ye shall not enter into the kingdom of heaven.
Jesus
Matt. 18:3

Whosoever will be great among you, let him be your minister.
Jesus
Matt. 20:26
See also Mark 10:43

Whosoever will be chief among you, let him be your servant.
Jesus
Matt. 20:27
See also Matt. 23:11, Mark 10:44

Whosoever shall exalt himself shall be abased; and he that shall humble himself shall be exalted.
Jesus
Matt. 23:12
See also Luke 14:11

If any man desire to be first, the same shall be last of all, and servant of all.
Jesus
Mark 9:35

He that is least among you all, the same shall be great.
Jesus
Luke 9:48

I am among you as He that serveth.
Jesus
Luke 22:27

I can of mine own self do nothing.
Jesus
John 5:30

The servant is not greater than his lord; neither he that is sent greater than he that sent him.
Jesus
John 13:16
See also John 15:20, Matt. 10:24

Stand up; I myself also am a man.
Acts 10:26

What was I, that I could withstand God?
Peter
Acts 11:17

Serving the Lord with all humility of mind, and with many tears.
Acts 20:19

In me (that is, in my flesh,) dwelleth no good thing.
Rom. 7:18

Think soberly.
Rom. 12:3

I have planted, Apollos watered; but God gave the increase.
1 Cor. 3:6

Let him become a fool, that he may be wise.
1 Cor. 3:18

I know nothing by myself.
1 Cor. 4:4

By the grace of God I am what I am: and His grace which was bestowed upon me was not in vain.
1 Cor. 15:10

Our sufficiency is of God.
2 Cor. 3:5

My strength is made perfect in weakness.
Jesus
2 Cor. 12:9

God resisteth the proud, but giveth grace unto the humble.
James 4:6

Humble yourselves in the sight of the Lord, and He shall lift you up.
James 4:10

Confess your faults one to another.
James 5:16

Be clothed with humility.
1 Pet. 5:5

God resisteth the proud, and giveth grace to the humble.
1 Pet. 5:5

Remember therefore from whence thou art fallen, and repent.
Jesus
Rev. 2:5

[*See also* Arrogance, Audacity, Conceit, Equality, Gloating, Meekness, Modesty, Pride]

HUNGER

Behold, I am at the point to die: and what profit shall this birthright do to me?
> Esau to Jacob
> *Gen. 25:32*

They that were full have hired out themselves for bread.
> *1 Sam. 2:5*

Men do not despise a thief, if he steal to satisfy his soul when he is hungry.
> *Prov. 6:30*

If thine enemy be hungry, give him bread to eat; and if he be thirsty, give him water to drink.
> *Prov. 25:21*
> *See also Rom. 12:20*

Thou shalt eat, but not be satisfied.
> *Mic. 6:14*

He that cometh to me shall never hunger; and he that believeth on me shall never thirst.
> Jesus
> *John 6:35*

If any would not work, neither should he eat.
> *2 Thess. 3:10*

[*See also* Bread of Life, Deprivation, Famine, Food, Thirst]

HUSBAND AND WIFE

See Marriage.

HYPOCRISY

How canst thou say, I love thee, when thine heart is not with me?
> Delilah to Samson
> *Judg. 16:15*

The triumphing of the wicked is short, and the joy of the hypocrite but for a moment.
> *Job 20:5*

What is the hope of the hypocrite, though he hath gained, when God taketh away his soul?
> *Job 27:8*

The workers of iniquity, which speak peace to their neighbours, but mischief is in their hearts.
> *Ps. 28:3*

They bless with their mouth, but they curse inwardly.
> *Ps. 62:4*

This people draw near Me with their mouth, and with their lips do honour Me, but have removed their heart far from Me.
> *Isa. 29:13*
> *See also Matt. 15:8*

Their fear toward Me is taught by the precept of men.
> *Isa. 29:13*

In the day of your fast ye find pleasure.
> *Isa. 58:3*

One speaketh peaceably to his neighbour with his mouth, but in heart he layeth his wait.
> *Jer. 9:8*

With their mouth they show much love, but their heart goeth after their covetousness.
> *Ezek. 33:31*

They love to pray standing in the synagogues and in the corners of the streets, that they may be seen of men.
> Jesus
> *Matt. 6:5*

They have their reward.
> Jesus
> *Matt. 6:5*

They disfigure their faces, that they may appear unto men to fast.
> Jesus
> *Matt. 6:16*

Why beholdest thou the mote that is in thy brother's eye, but considerest not the beam that is in thine own eye?
> Jesus
> *Matt. 7:3*
> *See also Luke 6:41*

In vain they do worship me, teaching for doctrines the commandments of men.
> Jesus
> *Matt. 15:9, Mark 7:7*
> *See also Isa. 29:13*

O ye hypocrites, ye can discern the face of the sky; but can ye not discern the signs of the times?
Jesus
Matt. 16:3
See also Luke 12:56

Do not ye after their works: for they say, and do not.
Jesus
Matt. 23:3

They bind heavy burdens and grievous to be borne, and lay them on men's shoulders; but they themselves will not move them with one of their fingers.
Jesus
Matt. 23:4
See also Luke 11:46

All their works they do for to be seen of men.
Jesus
Matt. 23:5

Woe unto you, scribes and Pharisees, hypocrites!
Jesus
E.g., Matt. 23:14

Ye blind guides, which strain at a gnat, and swallow a camel.
Jesus
Matt. 23:24

Ye also outwardly appear righteous unto men, but within ye are full of hypocrisy and iniquity.
Jesus
Matt. 23:28

This people honoureth me with their lips, but their heart is far from me.
Jesus
Mark 7:6
See also Matt. 15:8

Ye reject the commandment of God, that ye may keep your own tradition.
Jesus
Mark 7:9
See also Matt. 15:3

Beware of the scribes, which love to go in long clothing, and love salutations in the marketplaces, And the chief seats in the synagogues, and the uppermost rooms at feasts.
Jesus
Mark 12:38–40
See also Matt. 23:5–6, Luke 20:46–47

Woe unto you also, ye lawyers!
Jesus
Luke 11:46

Beware ye of the leaven of the Pharisees, which is hypocrisy.
Jesus
Luke 12:1
See also Matt. 16:6, Mark 8:15

He that is without sin among you, let him first cast a stone.
Jesus
John 8:7

If ye were Abraham's children, ye would do the works of Abraham.
Jesus
John 8:39

Thou that sayest a man should not commit adultery, dost thou commit adultery?
Rom. 2:22

The name of God is blasphemed among the Gentiles through you.
(you: hypocrites)
Rom. 2:24

They profess that they know God; but in works they deny Him.
Titus 1:16

Out of the same mouth proceedeth blessing and cursing.
James 3:10

Doth a fountain send forth at the same place sweet water and bitter?
James 3:11

If we say that we have not sinned, we make Him a liar.
1 John 1:10

He that saith, I know Him, and keepeth not His commandments, is a liar.
(Him: Jesus)
1 John 2:4

He that saith he is in the light, and hateth his brother, is in darkness even until now.
1 John 2:9

If a man say, I love God, and hateth his brother, he is a liar.
    1 John 4:20

[*See also* Deception, Lies, Rituals, Sincerity]

IDOLATRY

Thou shalt have no other gods before Me.
    First Commandment
    Ex. 20:3
    See also Deut. 5:7

Thou shalt not make unto thee any graven image.
    Second Commandment
    Ex. 20:4
    See also Deut. 5:8

He that sacrificeth unto any god, save unto the Lord only, he shall be utterly destroyed.
    Ex. 22:20

Make no mention of the name of other gods.
    Ex. 23:13

In the day when I visit I will visit their sin upon them.
    God to Moses
    Ex. 32:34

The Lord, whose name is Jealous, is a jealous God.
    Ex. 34:14

All the curses that are written in this book shall lie upon him.
    Deut. 29:20

Put away the gods which your fathers served on the other side of the flood.
    Josh. 24:14

God forbid that we should forsake the Lord, to serve other gods.
    Josh. 24:16

They would not hearken unto their judges, but they went a whoring after other gods.
    Judg. 2:17
    See also 1 Chron. 5:25

Ye have forsaken Me, and served other gods: wherefore I will deliver you no more.
    Judg. 10:13

If the Lord be God, follow Him: but if Baal, then follow him.
    1 Kings 18:21

But the high places were not taken away: the people still sacrificed and burnt incense.
    2 Kings 12:3

They caused their sons and their daughters to pass through the fire.
    2 Kings 17:17

As did their fathers, so do they unto this day.
    2 Kings 17:41

My wrath shall be kindled against this place, and shall not be quenched.
    2 Kings 22:17

The land was polluted with blood.
    Ps. 106:38

They that make them are like unto them; so is every one that trusteth in them.
    Ps. 115:8, Ps. 135:18

They worship the work of their own hands, that which their own fingers have made.
    Isa. 2:8

They shall be greatly ashamed, that trust in graven images, that say to the molten images, Ye are our gods.
    Isa. 42:17

They have turned their back unto Me, and not their face.
    Jer. 2:27

As ye have forsaken Me, and served strange gods in your land, so shall ye serve strangers in a land that is not your's.
    Jer. 5:19

Go not after other gods to serve them.
    Jer. 25:6, Jer. 35:15

They give gifts to all whores: but thou givest thy gifts to all thy lovers.
    Ezek. 16:33

Woe unto him that saith to the wood, Awake; to the dumb stone, Arise.
    Hab. 2:19

We ought not to think that the Godhead is

like unto gold, or silver, or stone, graven by art and man's device.
Acts 17:29

Served the creature more than the Creator.
Rom. 1:25

Flee from idolatry.
1 Cor. 10:14

Little children, keep yourselves from idols.
1 John 5:21

They have no rest day nor night, who worship the beast and his image.
Rev. 14:11

[*See also* Backsliding, False Gods, Godlessness, Monotheism, Worship]

IDOLS

Against all the gods of Egypt I will execute judgment: I am the Lord.
Ex. 12:12

Ye shall not make with Me gods of silver, neither shall ye make unto you gods of gold.
Ex. 20:23

Turn ye not unto idols, nor make to yourselves molten gods.
Lev. 19:4

The work of men's hands, wood and stone, which neither see, nor hear, nor eat, nor smell.
Deut. 4:28

Thou shalt not make thee any graven image.
Deut. 5:8

The graven images of their gods shall ye burn with fire.
Deut. 7:25

It is an abomination to the Lord.
E.g., Deut. 7:25

Ye shall throw down their altars.
Judg. 2:2

Peradventure he sleepeth, and must be awaked.
Elijah, about Baal
1 Kings 18:27

Ye shall not fear other gods.
2 Kings 17:37

They were no gods, but the work of men's hands, wood and stone.
2 Kings 19:18, Isa. 37:19

Their idols are silver and gold, the work of men's hands.
Ps. 115:4
See also Ps. 135:15

They have mouths, but they speak not: eyes have they, but they see not.
Ps. 115:5, Ps. 135:16
See also Rev. 9:20

They have ears, but they hear not: noses have they, but they smell not.
Ps. 115:6

Feet have they, but they walk not: neither speak they through their throat.
Ps. 115:7

The idols He shall utterly abolish.
Isa. 2:18

Thou shalt cast them away as a menstruous cloth.
Isa. 30:22

Ye are of nothing, and your work of nought: an abomination is he that chooseth you.
Isa. 41:24

Their works are nothing: their molten images are wind and confusion.
Isa. 41:29

Let them arise, if they can save thee in the time of thy trouble.
God to Jews
Jer. 2:28

They are vanity, and the work of errors: in the time of their visitation they shall perish.
Jer. 10:15, Jer. 51:18

Ye provoke Me unto wrath with the works of your hands.
Jer. 44:8
See also Jer. 25:6

Your altars shall be desolate, and your images shall be broken: and I will cast down your slain men before your idols.
Ezek. 6:4

Pollute ye My holy name no more with your gifts, and with your idols.
Ezek. 20:39

The workman made it; therefore it is not God.
Hos. 8:6

What profiteth the graven image that the maker thereof hath graven it?
Hab. 2:18

They comfort in vain.
Zech. 10:2

Turn from these vanities unto the living God.
Acts 14:15

They be no gods, which are made with hands.
Acts 19:26

[*See also* False Gods, Godlessness, Idolatry, Monotheism, Worship]

IGNORANCE

They were both naked, the man and his wife, and were not ashamed.
Gen. 2:25

If a soul sin, and commit any of these things which are forbidden to be done by the commandments of the Lord; though he wist it not, yet is he guilty.
Lev. 5:17

They are a nation void of counsel, neither is there any understanding in them.
Deut. 32:28

He multiplieth words without knowledge.
Job 35:16

Who is this that darkeneth counsel by words without knowledge?
Job 38:2

A brutish man knoweth not; neither doth a fool understand this.
Ps. 92:6

Ye fools, when will ye be wise?
Ps. 94:8

Fools die for want of wisdom.
Prov. 10:21

Folly is joy to him that is destitute of wisdom.
Prov. 15:21

My people are gone into captivity, because they have no knowledge.
Isa. 5:13

Who is blind as he that is perfect, and blind as the Lord's servant?
Isa. 42:19

Every man is brutish in his knowledge.
Jer. 10:14

The people that doth not understand shall fall.
Hos. 4:14

They seeing see not; and hearing they hear not, neither do they understand.
Jesus
Matt. 13:13
See also Isa. 6:9, Isa. 42:20, Acts 28:26

If the blind lead the blind, both shall fall into the ditch.
Jesus
Matt. 15:14
See also Luke 6:39

O ye hypocrites, ye can discern the face of the sky; but can ye not discern the signs of the times?
Jesus
Matt. 16:3
See also Luke 12:56

Father, forgive them; for they know not what they do.
Jesus
Luke 23:34

He was in the world, and the world was made by Him, and the world knew Him not.
John 1:10

Art thou a master of Israel, and knoweth not these things?
Jesus
John 3:10

Ye worship ye know not what.
Jesus
John 4:22

He that followeth me shall not walk in darkness.
Jesus
John 8:12

He that walketh in darkness knoweth not whither he goeth.
Jesus
John 12:35

Who art Thou, Lord?
Saul to Jesus
Acts 9:5

Whom therefore ye ignorantly worship, Him declare I unto you.
Acts 17:23

The heart of this people is waxed gross, and their ears are dull of hearing, and their eyes have they closed.
Acts 28:27

I had not known sin, but by the law.
Rom. 7:7
See also Rom. 3:20, Rom. 4:15

They have a zeal of God, but not according to knowledge.
Rom. 10:2

How shall they believe in Him of whom they have not heard?
Rom. 10:14

Had they known it, they would not have crucified the Lord.
1 Cor. 2:8

We know in part, and we prophesy in part.
1 Cor. 13:9

Foolish and unlearned questions avoid, knowing that they do gender strifes.
2 Tim. 2:23

Every one that useth milk is unskilful in the word of righteousness: for he is a babe.
Heb. 5:13

[*See also* Knowledge, Naivete, Understanding, Wisdom]

IMAGINATION

See Dreams, Future, Visions.

IMMINENCE

The time is come, the day draweth near.
Ezek. 7:12
See also Ezek. 7:7

The day of the Lord is near.
Ezek. 30:3

My time is at hand.
Jesus
Matt. 26:18

Behold, the hour is at hand, and the Son of man is betrayed into the hands of sinners.
Jesus
Matt. 26:45
See also Mark 14:41

The hour is coming, in the which all that are in the graves shall hear His voice.
Jesus
John 5:28

The hour is come, that the Son of man should be glorified.
Jesus
John 12:23

Yet a little while, and the world seeth me no more.
Jesus
John 14:19

Behold, the hour cometh.
Jesus
John 16:32

The Lord is at hand.
Phil 4:5

The coming of the Lord draweth nigh.
James 5:8

Behold, the judge standeth before the door.
James 5:9

The end of all things is at hand: be ye therefore sober, and watch unto prayer.
1 Pet. 4:7

The time is at hand.
E.g., Rev. 1:3

[*See also* Second Coming, Time]

IMMORALITY

Do not prostitute thy daughter, to cause her to be a whore; lest the land fall to whoredom, and the land become full of wickedness.
Lev. 19:29

How is the faithful city become an harlot!
Isa. 1:21

Thy silver is become dross, thy wine mixed with water.
Isa. 1:22

Thou hast polluted the land with thy whoredoms and with thy wickedness.
Jer. 3:2

As is the mother, so is her daughter.
Ezek. 16:44

Flee fornication.
1 Cor. 6:18

She that liveth in pleasure is dead while she liveth.
1 Tim. 5:6

Whoremongers and adulterers God will judge.
Heb. 13:4

Woe unto them! for they have gone in the way of Cain.
Jude 11

[*See also* Carnality, Decadence, Depravity, Fornication, Lust, Prostitution, Sin]

IMMORTALITY

See Death, Eternal Life, Resurrection.

IMPARTIALITY

Neither shalt thou countenance a poor man in his cause.
Ex. 23:3

Thou shalt not wrest the judgment of thy poor in his cause.
Ex. 23:6

Thou shalt not respect the person of the poor, nor honour the person of the mighty.
Lev. 19:15

Ye shall not respect persons in judgment.
Deut. 1:17
See also Deut. 16:19

Ye shall hear the small as well as the great.
Deut. 1:17

Though it be in Jonathan my son, he shall surely die.
Saul
1 Sam. 14:39

He maketh His sun to rise on the evil and on the good, and sendeth rain on the just and on the unjust.
Jesus
Matt. 5:45

God is no respecter of persons.
Acts 10:34
See also Rom. 2:11

God accepteth no man's person.
Gal. 2:6

If ye have respect to persons, ye commit sin.
James 2:9

[*See also* Equality, Fairness, Justice, Neutrality]

IMPATIENCE

How long will it be ere ye make an end of words?
Job 18:2

Lord, how long wilt Thou look on?
Ps. 35:17

How long shall the adversary reproach? shall the enemy blaspheme Thy name for ever?
Ps. 74:10

How long, Lord?
Ps. 79:5, Ps. 89:46

He that maketh haste to be rich shall not be innocent.
Prov. 28:20

O thou sword of the Lord, how long will it be ere thou be quiet?
Jer. 47:6

O Lord, how long shall I cry, and Thou wilt not hear!
Hab. 1:2

[*See also* Exasperation, Patience]

IMPENITENCE

And the children of Israel did evil again in the sight of the Lord.
E.g., Judg. 3:12

This is a rebellious people, lying children,

children that will not hear the law of the Lord.
Isa. 30:9

They have made their faces harder than a rock.
Jer. 5:3

They hearkened not, nor inclined their ear to turn from their wickedness.
Jer. 44:5

Thou hast not remembered the days of thy youth, when thou wast naked and bare.
Ezek. 16:22

All this evil is come upon us: yet made we not our prayer before the Lord our God.
Dan. 9:13

They made their hearts as an adamant stone, lest they should hear the law.
Zech. 7:12

It shall be more tolerable for the land of Sodom in the day of judgment, than for thee.
Jesus
Matt. 11:24
See also Luke 10:14

Harden not your hearts.
E.g., Heb. 3:8

[*See also* Repentance, Stubbornness]

IMPOSSIBILITY

See God's Power, Possibility.

IMPRISONMENT

He bringeth out those which are bound with chains.
Ps. 68:6

Let the sighing of the prisoner come before Thee.
Ps. 79:11

The Lord looseth the prisoners.
Ps. 146:7

To proclaim liberty to the captives, and the opening of the prison to them that are bound.
Isa. 61:1

They have cut off my life in the dungeon, and cast a stone upon me.
Lam. 3:53

The earth with her bars was about me for ever: yet hast Thou brought up my life from corruption.
Jonah 2:6

For the hope of Israel I am bound with this chain.
Acts 28:20

I am an ambassador in bonds.
Eph. 6:20

Remember my bonds.
Col. 4:18

Remember them that are in bonds, as bound with them; and them which suffer adversity, as being yourselves also in the body.
Heb. 13:3

[*See also* Captivity, Persecution]

INCEST

The nakedness of thy father, or the nakedness of thy mother, shalt thou not uncover.
Lev. 18:7
See also Lev. 18:8–17

For their's is thine own nakedness.
Lev. 18:10

Cursed be he that lieth with his father's wife.
Deut. 27:20

Cursed be he that lieth with his sister.
Deut. 27:22

Do not thou this folly.
2 Sam. 13:12

Whither shall I cause my shame to go?
2 Sam. 13:13

INDECISION

Choose you this day whom ye will serve.
Josh. 24:15

How long halt ye between two opinions?
1 Kings 18:21

As a drunken man staggereth in his vomit.
Isa. 19:14

No man, having put his hand to the plough, and looking back, is fit for the kingdom of God.
Jesus
Luke 9:62

We henceforth be no more children, tossed to and fro, and carried about with every wind of doctrine, by the sleight of men, and cunning craftiness, whereby they lie in wait to deceive.
Eph. 4:14

He that wavereth is like a wave of the sea driven with the wind.
James 1:6

A double minded man is unstable in all his ways.
James 1:8

[*See also* Certainty, Decisions, Laziness, Neutrality]

INDEPENDENCE

Thou shalt lend unto many nations, but thou shalt not borrow.
Deut. 15:6
See also Deut. 28:12

Thou shalt reign over many nations, but they shall not reign over thee.
Deut. 15:6

Every one turned to his course, as the horse rusheth into the battle.
Jer. 8:6

[*See also* Freedom]

INDIVIDUAL, IMPORTANCE OF

I will judge you every one after his ways.
Ezek. 33:20

Ye are of more value than many sparrows.
Jesus
Matt. 10:31, Luke 12:7

Are not five sparrows sold for two farthings, and not one of them is forgotten before God?
Jesus
Luke 12:6
See also Matt. 10:29

Rejoice with me; for I have found my sheep which was lost.
Jesus
Luke 15:6

Joy shall be in heaven over one sinner that repenteth, more than over ninety and nine just persons, which need no repentance.
Jesus
Luke 15:7

There is joy in the presence of the angels of God over one sinner that repenteth.
Jesus
Luke 15:10

By one man sin entered into the world.
Rom. 5:12

As by one man's disobedience many were made sinners, so by the obedience of one shall many be made righteous.
Rom. 5:19

Every man hath his proper gift of God.
1 Cor. 7:7

One star differeth from another star in glory.
1 Cor. 15:41

I seek not your's, but you.
2 Cor. 12:14

What is man, that Thou art mindful of him? or the son of man, that Thou visitest him?
Heb. 2:6
See also Ps. 8:4

[*See also* Mankind]

INEVITABILITY

See Certainty, Death, Mortality.

INFINITY

I will multiply thy seed as the stars of the heaven, and as the sand which is upon the sea shore.
God to Abraham
Gen. 22:17

They came as grasshoppers for multitude; for both they and their camels were without number.
Judg. 6:5

They that hate me without a cause are more than the hairs of mine head.
Ps. 69:4

He telleth the number of the stars; He calleth them all by their names.
Ps. 147:4

The number of the children of Israel shall be as the sand of the sea, which cannot be measured nor numbered.
Hos. 1:10

Even the very hairs of your head are all numbered.
Jesus
Luke 12:7
See also Matt. 10:30

[*See also* Abundance]

INGRATITUDE

Wherefore have ye rewarded evil for good?
Gen. 44:4

Hast thou taken us away to die in the wilderness?
Israelites to Moses
Ex. 14:11
See also Num. 21:5

It had been better for us to serve the Egyptians, than that we should die in the wilderness.
Ex. 14:12

Ye have wept in the ears of the Lord.
Num. 11:18

Would God that we had died in the land of Egypt!
Num. 14:2

Do ye thus requite the Lord, O foolish people and unwise? is not He thy father that hath bought thee? hath He not made thee, and established thee?
Deut. 32:6

Wherefore kick ye at My sacrifice and at Mine offering?
1 Sam. 2:29

Art thou come unto me to call my sin to remembrance?
1 Kings 17:18

Wilt thou condemn Him that is most just?
Job 34:17

They have rewarded me evil for good, and hatred for my love.
Ps. 109:5
See also 1 Sam. 25:21

Whoso rewardeth evil for good, evil shall not depart from his house.
Prov. 17:13

They were as fed horses in the morning: every one neighed after his neighbour's wife.
Jer. 5:8

I have loved you, saith the Lord. Yet ye say, Wherein hast Thou loved us?
Mal. 1:2

Give not that which is holy unto the dogs, neither cast ye your pearls before swine, lest they trample them under their feet, and turn again and rend you.
Jesus
Matt. 7:6

When they knew God, they glorified Him not as God.
Rom 1:21

[*See also* Gratitude]

INHERITANCE

He sold his birthright unto Jacob.
(He: Esau)
Gen. 25:33

If a man die, and have no son, then ye shall cause his inheritance to pass unto his daughter.
Num. 27:8

Behold, I have set the land before you: go in and possess the land which the Lord sware unto your fathers.
Deut. 1:8

The Lord commanded Moses to give us an inheritance among our brethren.
(us: Zelophehad's daughters)
Josh. 17:4

The Lord is the portion of mine inheritance.
Ps. 16:5

He heapeth up riches, and knoweth not who shall gather them.
Ps. 39:6

A good man leaveth an inheritance to his children's children.
Prov. 13:22

House and riches are the inheritance of fathers: and a prudent wife is from the Lord.
Prov. 19:14

Who knoweth whether he shall be a wise man or a fool?
Eccl. 2:19

Our inheritance is turned to strangers, our houses to aliens.
Lam. 5:2

[*See also* Heritage, Reward]

INJUSTICE

Keep thee far from a false matter.
Ex. 23:7

He destroyeth the perfect and the wicked.
Job 9:22

The earth is given into the hand of the wicked: He covereth the faces of the judges thereof.
Job 9:24

I cry aloud, but there is no judgment.
Job 19:7

Wherefore do the wicked live, become old, yea, are mighty in power?
Job 21:7

How oft is the candle of the wicked put out! and how oft cometh their destruction upon them!
Job 21:17

Far be it from God, that He should do wickedness.
Job 34:10

Lord, how long shall the wicked, how long shall the wicked triumph?
Ps. 94:3

We wait for light, but behold obscurity; for brightness, but we walk in darkness.
Isa. 59:9

They judge not the cause, the cause of the fatherless, yet they prosper.
Jer. 5:28

Wherefore doth the way of the wicked prosper? wherefore are all they happy that deal very treacherously?
Jeremiah to God
Jer. 12:1

Wherefore lookest Thou upon them that deal treacherously, and holdest Thy tongue when the wicked devoureth the man that is more righteous than he?
Hab. 1:13

Sittest thou to judge me after the law, and commandest me to be smitten contrary to the law?
Paul to Ananias
Acts 23:3

Remember my bonds.
Col. 4:18

If, when ye do well, and suffer for it, ye take it patiently, this is acceptable with God.
1 Pet. 2:20

[*See also* Corruption, Judgment, Justice, Lawlessness]

INNOCENCE

They were both naked, the man and his wife, and were not ashamed.
Gen. 2:25

Behold, his daughter came out to meet him with timbrels and with dances.
(his: Jephthah)
Judg. 11:34

Now shall I be more blameless than the Philistines, though I do them a displeasure.
Judg. 15:3

I did but taste a little honey with the end of the rod.
1 Sam. 14:43

What have I done? what is mine iniquity?
David
1 Sam. 20:1

If there be in me iniquity, slay me thyself.
David to Jonathan
1 Sam. 20:8

Wherefore shall he be slain? what hath he done?
> Jonathan to Saul, about David
> *1 Sam. 20:32*

Wickedness proceedeth from the wicked: but mine hand shall not be upon thee.
> *1 Sam. 24:13*

What evil is in mine hand?
> *1 Sam. 26:18*

I and my kingdom are guiltless before the Lord.
> *2 Sam. 3:28*

As a man falleth before wicked men, so fellest thou.
> *2 Sam. 3:34*

They went in their simplicity, and they knew not any thing.
> *2 Sam. 15:11*

As for these sheep, what have they done?
> *1 Chron. 21:17*
> *See also 2 Sam. 24:17*

If thou wert pure and upright; surely now He would awake for thee.
> *Job 8:6*

God will not cast away a perfect man, neither will He help the evil doers.
> *Job 8:20*

Make me to know my transgression and my sin.
> Job to God
> *Job 13:23*

My witness is in heaven, and my record is on high.
> *Job 16:19*

Till I die I will not remove mine integrity from me.
> *Job 27:5*

Let me be weighed in an even balance, that God may know mine integrity.
> *Job 31:6*

Then let mine arm fall from my shoulder blade, and mine arm be broken from the bone.
> *Job 31:22*

Oh that one would hear me!
> *Job 31:35*

Let thistles grow instead of wheat, and cockle instead of barley.
> *Job 31:40*

He was righteous in his own eyes.
> (He: Job)
> *Job 32:1*

False witnesses did rise up; they laid to my charge things that I knew not.
> *Ps. 35:11*

A little child shall lead them.
> *Isa. 11:6*

He is brought as a lamb to the slaughter.
> *Isa. 53:7*
> *See also Jer. 11:19, Acts 8:32*

Thou hast not remembered the days of thy youth, when thou wast naked and bare.
> *Ezek. 16:22*

If ye were blind, ye should have no sin.
> Jesus
> *John 9:41*

Whom seek ye?
> Jesus to His captors
> *John 18:4, 7*

Neither against the law of the Jews, neither against the temple, nor yet against Caesar, have I offended any thing at all.
> *Acts 25:8*

I stand at Caesar's judgment seat, where I ought to be judged: to the Jews have I done no wrong.
> Paul
> *Acts 25:10*

If I be an offender, or have committed any thing worthy of death, I refuse not to die.
> *Acts 25:11*

Unto the pure all things are pure.
> *Titus 1:15*

If we say that we have no sin, we deceive ourselves.
> *1 John 1:8*

If we say that we have not sinned, we make Him a liar.
> *1 John 1:10*

In their mouth was found no guile: for they are without fault before the throne of God.
> *Rev. 14:5*

[*See also* Guilt, Naivete]

INNOVATION

There is no new thing under the sun.
Eccl. 1:9

That which hath been is now; and that which is to be hath already been.
Eccl. 3:15

That which hath been is named already.
Eccl. 6:10

No man also having drunk old wine straightway desireth new.
Jesus
Luke 5:39

INSANITY

See Madness.

INSINCERITY

See Hypocrisy, Sincerity.

INSPIRATION

Go, and I will be with thy mouth, and teach thee what thou shalt say.
God to Moses
Ex. 4:12

The word that God putteth in my mouth, that shall I speak.
Num. 22:38

The Spirit of the Lord came upon Gideon, and he blew a trumpet.
Judg. 6:34

The Spirit of the Lord will come upon thee.
Samuel to Saul
1 Sam. 10:6

The Spirit of the Lord spake by me, and His word was in my tongue.
2 Sam. 23:2

The hand of the Lord was upon me.
Ezek. 37:1

Your old men shall dream dreams, your young men shall see visions.
Joel 2:28
See also Acts 2:17

It is not ye that speak, but the Spirit of your Father which speaketh in you.
Jesus
Matt. 10:20

A man can receive nothing, except it be given him from heaven.
John 3:27

He was a burning and a shining light: and ye were willing for a season to rejoice in his light.
Jesus (He: John the Baptist)
John 5:35

Write the things which thou hast seen, and the things which are, and the things which shall be hereafter.
Jesus
Rev. 1:19

INSTABILITY

Unstable as water, thou shalt not excel.
Gen. 49:4

Your goodness is as a morning cloud, and as the early dew it goeth away.
Hos. 6:4

[*See also* Indecision]

INSTIGATION

And the serpent said unto the woman, Ye shall not surely die.
Gen. 3:4

Entice him, and see wherein his great strength lieth.
Philistines to Delilah
Judg. 16:5

Doth Job fear God for nought?
Satan to God
Job 1:9

Touch all that he hath, and he will curse Thee to Thy face.
Satan to God, about Job
Job 1:11

These six things doth the Lord hate: yea, seven are an abomination unto Him: A proud look, a lying tongue, and hands that shed innocent blood, An heart that deviseth wicked imaginations, feet that be swift in running to mischief, A false witness that speaketh lies, and he that soweth discord among brethren.
Prov. 6:16–19

Woe to that man by whom the offence cometh!
Jesus
Matt. 18:7

[*See also* Provocation]

INSTINCT

The stork in the heaven knoweth her appointed times; and the turtle and the crane and the swallow observe the time of their coming; but My people know not the judgment of the Lord.
God to Jews
Jer. 8:7

INSTRUCTION

God exalteth by His power: who teacheth like Him?
Job 36:22

Make me to understand the way of Thy precepts: so shall I talk of Thy wondrous works.
Ps. 119:27

How sweet are Thy words unto my taste! yea, sweeter than honey to my mouth!
Ps. 119:103

He will teach us of His ways, and we will walk in His paths.
Isa. 2:3, Mic. 4:2

He that hath ears to hear, let him hear.
Jesus
Luke 14:35
See also, e.g., Matt. 13:9

Though ye have ten thousand instructors in Christ, yet have ye not many fathers.
1 Cor. 4:15

[*See also* Criticism, Education, Guidance, Heedfulness, Knowledge]

INSULTS

Am I a dog, that thou comest to me with staves?
Goliath to David
1 Sam. 17:43

Am I a dog's head?
2 Sam. 3:8

A fool's wrath is presently known: but a prudent man covereth shame.
Prov. 12:16

A brother offended is harder to be won than a strong city.
Prov. 18:19

Take no heed unto all words that are spoken; lest thou hear thy servant curse thee.
Eccl. 7:21

INTEGRITY

Though I should receive a thousand shekels of silver in mine hand, yet would I not put forth mine hand against the king's son.
2 Sam. 18:12

If thou wilt give me half thine house, I will not go in with thee, neither will I eat bread nor drink water in this place.
1 Kings 13:8

What the Lord saith unto me, that will I speak.
1 Kings 22:14
See also 2 Chron. 18:13

Dost thou still retain thine integrity? curse God, and die.
Job's wife to Job
Job 2:9

Till I die I will not remove mine integrity from me.
Job 27:5

My righteousness I hold fast, and will not let it go: my heart shall not reproach me so long as I live.
Job 27:6

As for me, I will walk in mine integrity.
Ps. 26:11

The integrity of the upright shall guide them.
Prov. 11:3

They hate him that rebuketh in the gate, and they abhor him that speaketh uprightly.
Amos 5:10

What shall a man give in exchange for his soul?
    Jesus
    Matt. 16:26, Mark 8:37

What shall it profit a man, if he shall gain the whole world, and lose his own soul?
    Jesus
    Mark 8:36
    See also Matt. 16:26, Luke 9:25

I have coveted no man's silver, or gold, or apparel.
    Acts 20:33

I have lived in all good conscience before God until this day.
    Acts 23:1

Walk as children of light.
    Eph. 5:8

Unto the pure all things are pure.
    Titus 1:15

Swear not, neither by heaven, neither by the earth, neither by any other oath: but let your yea be yea; and your nay, nay.
    James 5:12

[*See also* Character, Conscience, Corruption, Honesty, Righteousness]

INTELLIGENCE

See Education, Ignorance, Knowledge, Understanding.

INTENTIONS

They shall not deliver the slayer up into his hand; because he smote his neighbour unwittingly, and hated him not beforetime.
    Josh. 20:5

Man looketh on the outward appearance, but the Lord looketh on the heart.
    1 Sam. 16:7

Thou didst well in that it was in thine heart.
    God to David
    2 Chron. 6:8

Whosoever looketh on a woman to lust after her hath committed adultery with her already in his heart.
    Jesus
    Matt. 5:28

Wherefore think ye evil in your hearts?
    Jesus
    Matt. 9:4
    See also Luke 6:22

The good that I would I do not: but the evil which I would not, that I do.
    Rom. 7:19

[*See also* Motivation, Purpose]

INTERCESSION

Speak thou with us, and we will hear: but let not God speak with us, lest we die.
    Israelites to Moses
    Ex. 20:19

He stood between the dead and the living; and the plague was stayed.
    (He: Aaron)
    Num. 16:48

Enquire of the Lord for me, and for the people.
    2 Kings 22:13

All things are delivered unto me of my Father.
    Jesus
    Matt. 11:27
    See also Luke 10:22

No man cometh unto the Father, but by me.
    Jesus
    John 14:6

There is one God, and one mediator between God and men, the man Christ Jesus.
    1 Tim. 2:5

If any man sin, we have an advocate with the Father.
    1 John 2:1

INTERMARRIAGE

They will turn away thy son from following Me, that they may serve other gods.
    Deut. 7:4

Come not among these nations, these that remain among you.
    Josh. 23:7

Is there never a woman among the daughters of thy brethren, or among all my

people, that thou goest to take a wife of the uncircumcised Philistines?
> (thou: Samson)
> *Judg. 14:3*

Ye shall not go in to them, neither shall they come in unto you: for surely they will turn away your heart after their gods.
> *1 Kings 11:2*

I rent my garment and my mantle, and plucked off the hair of my head and of my beard.
> *Ezra 9:3*

Give not your daughters unto their sons, neither take their daughters unto your sons.
> *Ezra 9:12*

Did not Solomon king of Israel sin by these things?
> *Neh. 13:26*

INTOXICATION

See Drunkenness.

ISRAEL

A land flowing with milk and honey.
> *E.g., Ex. 3:8*

I am the Lord your God, which brought you forth out of the land of Egypt, to give you the land of Canaan, and to be your God.
> *E.g., Lev. 25:38*

If the Lord delight in us, then He will bring us into this land.
> Joshua and Caleb
> *Num. 14:8*

I have given you the land to possess it.
> God to Israelites
> *Num. 33:53*

Behold, I have set the land before you: go in and possess the land which the Lord sware unto your fathers.
> *Deut. 1:8*

It is a good land which the Lord our God doth give us.
> *Deut. 1:25*

A land which the Lord thy God careth for:

the eyes of the Lord thy God are always upon it.
> *Deut. 11:12*

Every place whereon the soles of your feet shall tread shall be your's.
> *Deut. 11:24*
> *See also Josh. 1:3*

Behold the land of Canaan, which I give unto the children of Israel for a possession.
> God to Moses
> *Deut. 32:49*

Divide thou it by lot unto the Israelites for an inheritance.
> *Josh. 13:6*

Ye shall possess their land, as the Lord your God hath promised unto you.
> *Josh. 23:5*

I have given you a land for which ye did not labour.
> *Josh. 24:13*

Unto thee will I give the land of Canaan, the lot of your inheritance.
> *1 Chron. 16:18, Ps. 105:11*

I will ordain a place for My people Israel.
> *1 Chron. 17:9*

They shall dwell in their place, and shall be moved no more.
> *1 Chron. 17:9*

He will make her wilderness like Eden, and her desert like the garden of the Lord.
> *Isa. 51:3*

Ye shall know that I am the Lord, when I shall bring you into the land of Israel.
> *Ezek. 20:42*

[*See also* Chosen People, Jerusalem]

JEALOUSY

Give me children, or else I die.
> Rachel to Jacob
> *Gen. 30:1*

They hated him yet the more for his dreams, and for his words.
(They: Joseph's brothers)
Gen. 37:8

They have ascribed unto David ten thousands, and to me they have ascribed but thousands.
Saul
1 Sam. 18:8

What can he have more but the kingdom?
Saul about David
1 Sam. 18:8

Saul eyed David from that day and forward.
1 Sam. 18:9

Fret not thyself because of him who prospereth.
Ps. 37:7

Jealousy is the rage of a man.
Prov. 6:34

Let not thine heart envy sinners.
Prov. 23:17

Wrath is cruel, and anger is outrageous; but who is able to stand before envy?
Prov. 27:4

Better is the sight of the eyes than the wandering of the desire.
Eccl. 6:9

Jealousy is cruel as the grave: the coals thereof are coals of fire, which hath a most vehement flame.
Song 8:6

Charity envieth not.
(charity: love)
1 Cor. 13:4

[*See also* Envy, Greed, Zeal]

JERUSALEM

The city of David, which is Zion.
1 Kings 8:1

Jerusalem, the city which I have chosen Me to put My name.
1 Kings 11:36
See also 2 Kings 21:4

Jerusalem, the city which the Lord did choose out of all the tribes of Israel, to put His name there.
1 Kings 14:21

I have chosen Jerusalem, that My name might be there.
2 Chron. 6:6
See also 1 Kings 8:29

In Jerusalem shall My name be for ever.
2 Chron. 33:4

Come, and let us build up the wall of Jerusalem, that we be no more a reproach.
Neh. 2:17

God is in the midst of her; she shall not be moved.
Ps. 46:5

The joy of the whole earth, is mount Zion.
Ps. 48:2

The city of the great King.
Ps. 48:2, Matt. 5:35

The Lord loveth the gates of Zion more than all the dwellings of Jacob.
Ps. 87:2

When the Lord shall build up Zion, He shall appear in His glory.
Ps. 102:16

They shall prosper that love thee.
Ps. 122:6

As the mountains are round about Jerusalem, so the Lord is round about His people.
Ps. 125:2

The Lord hath chosen Zion; He hath desired it for His habitation.
Ps. 132:13

This is My rest for ever: here will I dwell.
Ps. 132:14

By the rivers of Babylon, there we sat down, yea, we wept, when we remembered Zion.
Ps. 137:1

If I forget thee, O Jerusalem, let my right hand forget her cunning.
Ps. 137:5

If I do not remember thee, let my tongue cleave to the roof of my mouth.
Ps. 137:6

The city of righteousness, the faithful city.
Isa. 1:26

Zion shall be redeemed with judgment, and her converts with righteousness.
Isa. 1:27

Out of Zion shall go forth the law, and the word of the Lord from Jerusalem.
Isa. 2:3

The Lord hath founded Zion, and the poor of His people shall trust in it.
Isa. 14:32

The Lord shall comfort Zion: He will comfort all her waste places.
Isa. 51:3

In My wrath I smote thee, but in My favour have I had mercy on thee.
Isa. 60:10

The nation and kingdom that will not serve thee shall perish.
Isa. 60:12

The Lord shall be unto thee an everlasting light.
Isa. 60:19

For Zion's sake will I not hold My peace, and for Jerusalem's sake I will not rest.
Isa. 62:1

Keep not silence, And give Him no rest, till He establish, and till He make Jerusalem a praise in the earth.
Isa. 62:6–7

Rejoice ye with Jerusalem, and be glad with her, all ye that love her.
Isa. 66:10

How doth the city sit solitary, that was full of people! how is she become as a widow!
Lam. 1:1
See also Lam. 1:2–22

She that was great among the nations, and princess among the provinces, how is she become tributary!
Lam. 1:1

Among all her lovers she hath none to comfort her.
Lam. 1:2

Her friends have dealt treacherously with her, they are become her enemies.
Lam. 1:2

From the daughter of Zion all her beauty is departed: her princes are become like harts that find no pasture.
Lam. 1:6

All that honoured her despise her, because they have seen her nakedness.
Lam. 1:8

Is this the city that men call The perfection of beauty, The joy of the whole earth?
Lam. 2:15

The Lord dwelleth in Zion.
Joel 3:21

The law shall go forth of Zion, and the word of the Lord from Jerusalem.
Mic. 4:2

The Lord shall yet comfort Zion, and shall yet choose Jerusalem.
Zech. 1:17

O Jerusalem, Jerusalem, thou that killest the prophets, and stonest them which are sent unto thee.
Jesus
Matt. 23:37
See also Luke 13:34

[*See also* Covenant, Israel]

JESUS

He shall save His people from their sins.
Matt. 1:21

We have seen His star in the east, and are come to worship Him.
Matt. 2:2

He that cometh after me is mightier than I, whose shoes I am not worthy to bear.
John the Baptist
Matt. 3:11
See also Mark 1:7, Luke 3:16

This is My beloved Son, in whom I am well pleased.
Matt. 3:17
See also Mark 1:11, Luke 3:22

What manner of man is this, that even the winds and the sea obey Him!
Matt. 8:27
See also Mark 4:41, Luke 8:25

The Son of man hath power on earth to forgive sins.
Jesus
Matt. 9:6, Mark 2:10
See also Luke 5:24

Whosoever therefore shall confess me be-

fore men, him will I confess also before my Father which is in heaven. But whosoever shall deny me before men, him will I also deny before my Father which is in heaven.
Jesus
Matt. 10:32–33

He that taketh not his cross, and followeth after me, is not worthy of me.
Jesus
Matt. 10:38
See also Luke 14:27

In His name shall the Gentiles trust.
Matt. 12:21

He that is not with me is against me.
Jesus
Matt. 12:30, Luke 11:23

Behold, a greater than Solomon is here.
Jesus
Matt. 12:42, Luke 11:31

Is not this the carpenter's son?
Matt. 13:55
See also Mark 6:3, John 6:42

The Son of man is come to save that which was lost.
Jesus
Matt. 18:11

Art Thou the King of the Jews?
Pilate to Jesus
Matt. 27:11, Mark 15:2,
Luke 23:3, John 18:33

Come, take up the cross, and follow me.
Jesus
Mark 10:21
See also Matt. 19:21, Luke 18:22

In my name shall they cast out devils.
Jesus
Mark 16:17

A great prophet is risen up among us.
Luke 7:16

The Son of man is come to seek and to save that which was lost.
Jesus
Luke 19:10

In the beginning was the Word, and the Word was with God, and the Word was God.
John 1:1

Without Him was not any thing made.
John 1:3

In Him was life; and the life was the light of men.
John 1:4

He was in the world, and the world was made by Him, and the world knew Him not.
John 1:10

The Word was made flesh, and dwelt among us.
John 1:14

Behold the Lamb of God, which taketh away the sin of the world.
John the Baptist
John 1:29

Whosoever believeth in Him should not perish, but have eternal life.
Jesus
John 3:15

For God so loved the world, that He gave His only begotten Son, that whosoever believeth in Him should not perish, but have everlasting life.
Jesus
John 3:16
See also John 3:36, John 6:47

God sent not His Son into the world to condemn the world; but that the world through Him might be saved.
Jesus
John 3:17

He that believeth not the Son shall not see life; but the wrath of God abideth on him.
John 3:36

He told me all that ever I did.
Woman of Samaria
John 4:39

Know that this is indeed the Christ, the Saviour of the world.
John 4:42

He that was healed wist not who it was.
John 5:13

He that honoureth not the Son honoureth not the Father which hath sent Him.
Jesus
John 5:23

He that heareth my word, and believeth on Him that sent me, hath everlasting life.
Jesus
John 5:24

I came down from heaven, not to do mine own will, but the will of Him that sent me.
Jesus
John 6:38

He that eateth my flesh, and drinketh my blood, dwelleth in me, and I in him.
Jesus
John 6:56

If any man thirst, let him come unto me, and drink.
Jesus
John 7:37

If ye had known me, ye should have known my Father also.
Jesus
John 8:19

If God were your Father, ye would love me: for I proceeded forth and came from God.
Jesus
John 8:42

As long as I am in the world, I am the light of the world.
Jesus
John 9:5

I am the door: by me if any man enter in, he shall be saved.
Jesus
John 10:9

I am the resurrection, and the life.
Jesus
John 11:25

He that believeth in me, though he were dead, yet shall he live.
Jesus
John 11:25

I am come a light into the world, that whosoever believeth on me should not abide in darkness.
Jesus
John 12:46

I am the way, the truth, and the life.
Jesus
John 14:6

If ye shall ask any thing in my name, I will do it.
Jesus
John 14:14

If ye love me, keep my commandments.
Jesus
John 14:15
See also John 14:23

Whatsoever ye shall ask the Father in my name, He will give it you.
Jesus
John 16:23

I am He.
Jesus
John 18:5

Follow me.
Jesus
John 21:19

Him hath God exalted with His right hand to be a Prince and a Saviour.
Acts 5:31

Who shall declare His generation? for His life is taken from the earth.
Acts 8:33
See also Isa. 53:8

Whosoever believeth in Him shall receive remission of sins.
Acts 10:43

Through this man is preached unto you the forgiveness of sins.
Paul, about Jesus
Acts 13:38

I have set thee to be a light of the Gentiles, that thou shouldest be for salvation unto the ends of the earth.
Acts 13:47
See also Isa. 49:6

We have peace with God through our Lord Jesus Christ.
Rom. 5:1

In that He died, He died unto sin once: but in that He liveth, He liveth unto God.
Rom. 6:10

The wages of sin is death; but the gift of God is eternal life through Jesus Christ our Lord.
Rom. 6:23

Whosoever believeth on Him shall not be ashamed.
Rom. 9:33, Rom. 10:11

Ye are Christ's; and Christ is God's.
1 Cor. 3:23

In Christ Jesus I have begotten you through the gospel.
1 Cor. 4:15

We being many are one bread, and one body: for we are all partakers of that one bread.
1 Cor. 10:17

Maranatha.
1 Cor. 16:22

Though He was rich, yet for your sakes He became poor, that ye through His poverty might be rich.
2 Cor. 8:9

Thanks be unto God for His unspeakable gift.
2 Cor. 9:15

Christ liveth in me.
Gal. 2:20

The Son of God, who loved me, and gave Himself for me.
Gal. 2:20

Ye are all one in Christ Jesus.
Gal. 3:28

Christ hath made us free.
Gal. 5:1

He is our peace.
Eph. 2:14

God for Christ's sake hath forgiven you.
Eph. 4:32

We are members of His body, of His flesh, and of His bones.
Eph. 5:30

At the name of Jesus every knee should bow.
Phil. 2:10

He is before all things, and by Him all things consist.
Col. 1:17

He is the head of the body, the church.
Col. 1:18

Ye are complete in Him, which is the head of all principality and power.
Col. 2:10

Christ is all, and in all.
Col. 3:11

Let the word of Christ dwell in you.
Col. 3:16

Christ Jesus came into the world to save sinners.
1 Tim. 1:15

God was manifest in the flesh, justified in the Spirit, seen of angels, preached unto the Gentiles, believed on in the world, received up into glory.
1 Tim. 3:16

Be not thou therefore ashamed of the testimony of our Lord.
2 Tim. 1:8

Be strong in the grace that is in Christ Jesus.
2 Tim. 2:1

If we be dead with Him, we shall also live with Him.
2 Tim. 2:11

If we deny Him, He also will deny us.
2 Tim. 2:12

If we believe not, yet He abideth faithful: He cannot deny Himself.
2 Tim. 2:13

Though He were a Son, yet learned He obedience by the things which He suffered.
Heb. 5:8

Jesus the author and finisher of our faith.
Heb. 12:2

Ye should follow His steps: Who did no sin.
1 Pet. 2:21–22

To Him be glory both now and for ever.
2 Pet. 3:18

Whosoever denieth the Son, the same hath not the Father.
1 John 2:23

In Him is no sin.
1 John 3:5

Whosoever sinneth hath not seen Him, neither known Him.
1 John 3:6

Greater is He that is in you, than he that is in the world.
1 John 4:4

God sent His only begotten Son into the world, that we might live through Him.
1 John 4:9

The Father sent the Son to be the Saviour of the world.
1 John 4:14

To Him be glory and dominion for ever and ever.
Rev. 1:6

I am He which searcheth the reins and hearts.
Jesus
Rev. 2:23

The marriage of the Lamb is come, and His wife hath made herself ready.
Rev. 19:7

I will give unto him that is athirst of the fountain of the water of life freely.
Jesus
Rev. 21:6

I am the root and the offspring of David, and the bright and morning star.
Jesus
Rev. 22:16

[*See also* Authority, Bread of Life, Christ Eternal, Crucifixion, Intercession, Messiah, Messianic Hopes and Prophecies, Redemption, Resurrection, Revelation, Sacrifice, Second Coming, and the categories which follow]

JESUS, ACCEPTANCE OF

Take my yoke upon you, and learn of me; for I am meek and lowly in heart: and ye shall find rest unto your souls.
Jesus
Matt. 11:29

Flesh and blood hath not revealed it unto thee, but my Father which is in heaven.
Jesus
Matt. 16:17

Whosoever will come after me, let him deny himself, and take up his cross, and follow me.
Jesus
Mark 8:34
See also Matt. 16:24, Luke 9:23

Whosoever shall confess me before men, him shall the Son of man also confess before the angels of God.
Jesus
Luke 12:8
See also Matt. 10:32

Whosoever he be of you that forsaketh not all that he hath, he cannot be my disciple.
Jesus
Luke 14:33

As many as received Him, to them gave He power to become the sons of God.
John 1:12

Ye must be born again.
Jesus
John 3:7

This is the work of God, that ye believe on Him whom He hath sent.
Jesus
John 6:29

He that cometh to me shall never hunger; and he that believeth on me shall never thirst.
Jesus
John 6:35

No man can come to me, except the Father which hath sent me draw him.
Jesus
John 6:44
See also John 6:65

Lord, I believe.
John 9:38

I believe that Thou art the Christ, the Son of God.
John 11:27

He that believeth on me, believeth not on me, but on Him that sent me.
Jesus
John 12:44

He that receiveth me receiveth Him that sent me.
Jesus
John 13:20

Ye believe in God, believe also in me.
Jesus
John 14:1

He that loveth me shall be loved of my Father.
Jesus
John 14:21

If a man love me, he will keep my words.
    Jesus
    John 14:23

If thou shalt confess with thy mouth the Lord Jesus, and shalt believe in thine heart that God hath raised Him from the dead, thou shalt be saved.
    Rom. 10:9

To whom He was not spoken of, they shall see: and they that have not heard shall understand.
    Rom. 15:21
    See also Isa. 52:15

Ye were sometimes darkness, but now are ye light in the Lord.
    Eph. 5:8

Every tongue should confess that Jesus Christ is Lord.
    Phil. 2:11

What things were gain to me, those I counted loss for Christ.
    Phil. 3:7

Ye are dead, and your life is hid with Christ in God.
    Col. 3:3

He that acknowledgeth the Son hath the Father also.
    1 John 2:23

Whosoever shall confess that Jesus is the Son of God, God dwelleth in him, and he in God.
    1 John 4:15

He that hath the Son hath life.
    1 John 5:12

If any man hear my voice, and open the door, I will come in to him.
    Jesus
    Rev. 3:20

[*See also* Born Again, Conversion, Faith, Redemption]

JESUS, BIRTH OF

She shall bring forth a son, and thou shalt call His name JESUS.
    Matt. 1:21

Behold, a virgin shall be with child, and shall bring forth a son.
    Matt. 1:23
    See also Isa. 7:14

They presented unto Him gifts; gold, and frankincense, and myrrh.
    Matt. 2:11

The Lord is with thee: blessed art thou among women.
    Angel to Mary
    Luke 1:28

Behold, thou shalt conceive in thy womb, and bring forth a son, and shalt call His name JESUS.
    Luke 1:31

How shall this be, seeing I know not a man?
    Luke 1:34

With God nothing shall be impossible.
    Luke 1:37

He that is mighty hath done to me great things; and holy is His name.
    Mary
    Luke 1:49

There was no room for them in the inn.
    Luke 2:7

Unto you is born this day in the city of David a Saviour, which is Christ the Lord.
    Luke 2:11

His name was called JESUS.
    Luke 2:21

To this end was I born, and for this cause came I into the world, that I should bear witness unto the truth.
    Jesus
    John 18:37

JESUS, LAST WORDS ON THE CROSS

Eli, Eli, lama sabachthani?
    Matt. 27:46
    See also Mark 15:34

My God, my God, why hast Thou forsaken me?
    Matt. 27:46, Mark 15:34
    See also Ps. 22:1

Father, forgive them; for they know not what they do.
    Luke 23:34

Verily I say unto thee, To day shalt thou be with me in paradise.
> *Luke 23:43*

Father, into Thy hands I commend my spirit.
> *Luke 23:46*

Woman, behold thy son!
> (son: John)
> *John 19:26*

Behold thy mother!
> Jesus to his disciple
> *John 19:27*

I thirst.
> *John 19:28*

It is finished.
> *John 19:30*

JESUS, TITLES OF

His name shall be called Wonderful, Counsellor, The mighty God, The everlasting Father, The Prince of Peace.
> *Isa. 9:6*

They shall call His name Emmanuel.
> *Matt. 1:23*
> *See also Isa. 7:14*

Thou art the Christ, the Son of the living God.
> Simon Peter
> *Matt. 16:16*
> *See also Mark 8:29, Luke 9:20, John 6:69*

A Saviour, which is Christ the Lord.
> *Luke 2:11*

His name was called JESUS.
> *Luke 2:21*

The Lamb of God.
> *E.g., John 1:29*

The Son of God.
> *E.g., John 1:34*

The Messiah.
> *John 1:41, Dan. 9:25*

The Son of man.
> Jesus
> *E.g., John 1:51*

The bread of life.
> Jesus
> *E.g., John 6:35*

I am the light of the world.
> Jesus
> *John 8:12*

I am the door.
> Jesus
> *E.g., John 10:9*

The good shepherd.
> Jesus
> *John 10:11*

I am the way, the truth, and the life.
> Jesus
> *John 14:6*

I am the true vine.
> Jesus
> *John 15:1*

Jesus of Nazareth the King of the Jews.
> *John 19:19*
> *See also Matt. 27:37, Mark 15:26, Luke 23:38*

The Holy One and the Just.
> *Acts 3:14*

The Deliverer.
> *Rom. 11:26*

That great shepherd of the sheep.
> *Heb. 13:20*

The judge.
> *James 5:9*

The chief Shepherd.
> *1 Pet. 5:4*

The true light.
> *1 John 2:8*

The faithful witness.
> *Rev. 1:5*

The prince of the kings of the earth.
> *Rev. 1:5*

The morning star.
> Jesus
> *Rev. 2:28*

The Word of God.
> *Rev. 19:13*

KING OF KINGS, AND LORD OF LORDS.
> *Rev. 19:16*

I am Alpha and Omega, the beginning and the end, the first and the last.
> Jesus
> *Rev. 22:13*
> *See also Rev. 1:8, 11, Rev. 21:6*

The lost sheep of the house of Israel.
Jesus
Matt. 15:24

He came unto His own, and His own received Him not.
John 1:11

Forty years suffered He their manners in the wilderness.
Acts 13:18

I am a Pharisee, the son of a Pharisee.
Paul
Acts 23:6

He is not a Jew, which is one outwardly.
Rom. 2:28

What advantage then hath the Jew? or what profit is there of circumcision?
Rom. 3:1

Unto them were committed the oracles of God.
Rom. 3:2

They have a zeal of God, but not according to knowledge.
Rom. 10:2

Hath God cast away His people? God forbid.
Rom. 11:1

I also am an Israelite, of the seed of Abraham.
Paul
Rom. 11:1

Through their fall salvation is come unto the Gentiles.
Rom. 11:11

Unto the Jews I became as a Jew, that I might gain the Jews.
1 Cor. 9:20

Are they Hebrews? so am I. Are they Israelites? so am I. Are they the seed of Abraham? so am I.
Paul
2 Cor. 11:22

[*See also* Chosen People]

Elias is come already, and they knew him not.
Jesus
Matt. 17:12

One mightier than I cometh, the latchet of whose shoes I am not worthy to unloose.
Luke 3:16
See also Matt. 3:11, Mark 1:7, John 1:27

He was not that Light, but was sent to bear witness of that Light.
John 1:8

I am the voice of one crying in the wilderness, Make straight the way of the Lord.
John the Baptist
John 1:23
See also Matt. 3:3, Mark 1:3, Luke 3:4

He was a burning and a shining light: and ye were willing for a season to rejoice in his light.
Jesus
John 5:35

JOY

See Happiness, Laughter, Tears.

JUDAS

None of them is lost, but the son of perdition.
Jesus
John 17:12

[*See also* Betrayal]

JUDGING

Thou shalt not respect the person of the poor, nor honour the person of the mighty.
Lev. 19:15

In righteousness shalt thou judge thy neighbour.
Lev. 19:15

Judge righteously between every man and his brother, and the stranger that is with him.
Deut. 1:16

Ye shall not be afraid of the face of man; for the judgment is God's.
Deut. 1:17

Thou shalt not respect persons, neither take a gift.
Deut. 16:19
See also Deut. 1:17

A gift doth blind the eyes of the wise, and pervert the words of the righteous.
Deut. 16:19
See also Ex. 23:8

Take heed what ye do: for ye judge not for man, but for the Lord.
2 Chron. 19:6

Let the fear of the Lord be upon you.
2 Chron. 19:7

[*See also* Fairness, Justice]

JUDGMENT

Shall not the Judge of all the earth do right?
Abraham to God
Gen. 18:25

The Lord shall judge His people.
E.g., Deut. 32:36

I will render vengeance to Mine enemies, and will reward them that hate Me.
Deut. 32:41

The Lord shall judge the ends of the earth.
1 Sam. 2:10

If one man sin against another, the judge shall judge him: but if a man sin against the Lord, who shall intreat for him?
1 Sam. 2:25

Let me be weighed in an even balance, that God may know mine integrity.
Job 31:6

Judgment is before Him; therefore trust thou in Him.
Job 35:14

God judgeth the righteous, and God is angry with the wicked every day.
Ps. 7:11

He that planted the ear, shall He not hear? He that formed the eye, shall He not see?
Ps. 94:9

He shall judge the world with righteousness, and the people with His truth.
Ps. 96:13

With righteousness shall He judge the world.
Ps. 98:9

If Thou, Lord, shouldest mark iniquities, O Lord, who shall stand?
Ps. 130:3

Enter not into judgment with Thy servant: for in Thy sight shall no man living be justified.
Ps. 143:2

God shall judge the righteous and the wicked.
Eccl. 3:17

God shall bring every work into judgment.
Eccl. 12:14

Howl ye; for the day of the Lord is at hand.
Isa. 13:6

By fire and by His sword will the Lord plead with all flesh: and the slain of the Lord shall be many.
Isa. 66:16

I have set My face against this city for evil, and not for good, saith the Lord.
(city: Jerusalem)
Jer. 21:10

And they shall know that I am the Lord.
Ezek. 6:10

I will judge thee according to thy ways, and will recompense thee for all thine abominations.
Ezek. 7:8

I will judge you every one after his ways.
Ezek. 33:20

I will destroy the fat and the strong; I will feed them with judgment.
Ezek. 34:16

Multitudes, multitudes in the valley of decision: for the day of the Lord is near.
Joel 3:14

The day of the Lord is near upon all the heathen.
Obad. 15

I will be a swift witness against the sorcerers, and against the adulterers, and against

false swearers, and against those that oppress the hireling in his wages.
Mal. 3:5

By thy words thou shalt be justified, and by thy words thou shalt be condemned.
Jesus
Matt. 12:37

He shall reward every man according to his works.
Jesus
Matt. 16:27

It shall be more tolerable for Sodom and Gomorrha in the day of judgment than for that city.
Jesus
Mark 6:11
See also Matt. 10:15

The Father judgeth no man, but hath committed all judgment unto the Son.
Jesus
John 5:22

As I hear, I judge: and my judgment is just.
Jesus
John 5:30

If I judge, my judgment is true: for I am not alone.
Jesus
John 8:16

Now is the judgment of this world: now shall the prince of this world be cast out.
Jesus
John 12:31

I came not to judge the world, but to save the world.
Jesus
John 12:47

He will judge the world in righteousness.
Acts 17:31

As many as have sinned in the law shall be judged by the law.
Rom. 2:12

We shall all stand before the judgment seat of Christ.
Rom. 14:10
See also 2 Cor. 5:10

He that judgeth me is the Lord.
1 Cor. 4:4

The saints shall judge the world.
1 Cor. 6:2

God hath not appointed us to wrath, but to obtain salvation.
1 Thess. 5:9

Whoremongers and adulterers God will judge.
Heb. 13:4

There is one lawgiver, who is able to save and to destroy: who art thou that judgest another?
James 4:12

Behold, the judge standeth before the door.
James 5:9

Judgment must begin at the house of God.
1 Pet. 4:17

If the righteous scarcely be saved, where shall the ungodly and the sinner appear?
1 Pet. 4:18

Thrust in Thy sickle, and reap.
Rev. 14:15

Gather the clusters of the vine of the earth; for her grapes are fully ripe.
Rev. 14:18

Pour out the vials of the wrath of God upon the earth.
Rev. 16:1

With violence shall that great city Babylon be thrown down.
Rev. 18:21

True and righteous are His judgments.
Rev. 19:2
See also Rev. 16:7

In righteousness He doth judge and make war.
Rev. 19:11

[*See also* Criticism, Judgment Day, Misjudgment, Punishment, Responsibility, Retribution]

JUDGMENT DAY

Alas for the day! for the day of the Lord is at hand.
Joel 1:15

The day of the Lord cometh.
E.g., Joel 2:1

The day of the Lord is great and very
terrible; and who can abide it?
Joel 2:11

Woe unto you that desire the day of the
Lord!
Amos 5:18

Behold, the day cometh, that shall burn as
an oven; and all the proud, yea, and all
that do wickedly, shall be stubble.
Mal. 4:1

He shall separate them one from another,
as a shepherd divideth his sheep from the
goats.
Jesus
Matt. 25:32

These be the days of vengeance, that all
things which are written may be fulfilled.
Luke 21:22

He hath appointed a day, in the which He
will judge the world in righteousness.
Acts 17:31

We must all appear before the judgment
seat of Christ.
2 Cor. 5:10

The great day of His wrath is come; and
who shall be able to stand?
Rev. 6:17

Fear God, and give glory to Him; for the
hour of His judgment is come.
Rev. 14:7

I saw the dead, small and great, stand
before God.
Rev. 20:12

Death and hell delivered up the dead
which were in them: and they were judged
every man according to their works.
Rev. 20:13

Whosoever was not found written in the
book of life was cast into the lake of fire.
Rev. 20:15

[*See also* Apocalypse, End Days, Second
Coming]

Whoso sheddeth man's blood, by man shall
his blood be shed.
Gen. 9:6

One law shall be to him that is homeborn,
and unto the stranger that sojourneth
among you.
Ex. 12:49

Thou shalt give life for life, Eye for eye,
tooth for tooth, hand for hand, foot for
foot, Burning for burning, wound for
wound, stripe for stripe.
Ex. 21:23–25
See also Lev. 24:20, Deut. 19:21

Thou shalt not wrest the judgment of thy
poor in his cause.
Ex. 23:6

I will not justify the wicked.
God
Ex. 23:7

Ye shall have one manner of law, as well
for the stranger, as for one of your own
country.
Lev. 24:22
See also Num. 9:14

The murderer shall surely be put to death.
E.g., Num. 35:16
See also Ex. 21:12, Lev. 24:17

Ye shall hear the small as well as the great.
Deut. 1:17

At the mouth of two witnesses, or three
witnesses, shall he that is worthy of death
be put to death; but at the mouth of one
witness he shall not be put to death.
Deut. 17:6

Justify the righteous, and condemn the
wicked.
Deut. 25:1

As I have done, so God hath requited me.
Judg. 1:7

If he will show himself a worthy man, there
shall not an hair of him fall to the earth.
1 Kings 1:52

Divide the living child in two, and give half
to the one, and half to the other.
1 Kings 3:25

Give her the living child, and in no wise
slay it: she is the mother thereof.
1 Kings 3:27

Hast thou found me, O mine enemy?
Ahab to Elijah
1 Kings 21:20

I will cause him to fall by the sword in his own land.
2 Kings 19:7, Isa. 37:7

Render unto every man according unto all his ways, whose heart Thou knowest.
2 Chron. 6:30

They hanged Haman on the gallows that he had prepared for Mordecai.
Esther 7:10

Unto God would I commit my cause.
Job 5:8

O that one might plead for a man with God, as a man pleadeth for his neighbour!
Job 16:21

The light of the wicked shall be put out, and the spark of his fire shall not shine.
Job 18:5

The triumphing of the wicked is short, and the joy of the hypocrite but for a moment.
Job 20:5

They are exalted for a little while, but are gone and brought low.
(they: the wicked)
Job 24:24

Oh that one would hear me!
Job 31:35

God will not do wickedly, neither will the Almighty pervert judgment.
Job 34:12

Let them be taken in the devices that they have imagined.
Ps. 10:2

Give them after the work of their hands; render to them their desert.
Ps. 28:4

Evil shall slay the wicked.
Ps. 34:21

I have been young, and now am old; yet have I not seen the righteous forsaken.
Ps. 37:25

Thou renderest to every man according to his work.
Ps. 62:12
See also, e.g., Matt. 16:27

Defend the poor and fatherless: do justice to the afflicted and needy.
Ps. 82:3

Justice and judgment are the habitation of Thy throne: mercy and truth shall go before Thy face.
Ps. 89:14

As he loved cursing, so let it come unto him: as he delighted not in blessing, so let it be far from him.
Ps. 109:17

The wicked shall fall by his own wickedness.
Prov. 11:5

To do justice and judgment is more acceptable to the Lord than sacrifice.
Prov. 21:3

Many seek the ruler's favour; but every man's judgment cometh from the Lord.
Prov. 29:26

Open thy mouth, judge righteously, and plead the cause of the poor and needy.
Prov. 31:9

He shall not fail nor be discouraged, till he have set judgment in the earth.
Isa. 42:4

I the Lord love judgment.
Isa. 61:8

To subvert a man in his cause, the Lord approveth not.
Lam. 3:36

O Lord, Thou hast seen my wrong: judge Thou my cause.
Lam. 3:59

According to their deserts will I judge them.
Ezek. 7:27

The Lord our God is righteous in all His works which He doeth.
Dan. 9:14

Ye have plowed wickedness, ye have reaped iniquity.
Hos. 10:13

Let judgment run down as waters, and righteousness as a mighty stream.
Amos 5:24

Thy reward shall return upon thine own head.
Obad. 15

Do justly.
Mic. 6:8

Though it tarry, wait for it; because it will surely come.
Hab. 2:3
See also Heb. 10:37

Execute true judgment, and show mercy and compassions every man to his brother.
Zech. 7:9

Oppress not the widow, nor the fatherless, the stranger, nor the poor.
Zech. 7:10

Execute the judgment of truth and peace in your gates.
Zech. 8:16

He hath filled the hungry with good things; and the rich He hath sent empty away.
Luke 1:53

Judge not according to the appearance, but judge righteous judgment.
Jesus
John 7:24

Doth our law judge any man, before it hear him, and know what he doeth?
Nicodemus
John 7:51

Men, brethren, and fathers, hear ye my defence.
Paul
Acts 22:1

Is it lawful for you to scourge a man that is a Roman, and uncondemned?
Acts 22:25

Take heed what thou doest: for this man is a Roman.
Acts 22:26

I appeal unto Caesar.
Acts 25:11

He shall have judgment without mercy, that hath showed no mercy.
James 2:13

He that leadeth into captivity shall go into captivity.
Rev. 13:10

[*See also* Fairness, Guilt, Impartiality, Injustice, Innocence, Judging, Judgment, Law, Restitution, Wickedness]

JUSTIFICATION

By Him all that believe are justified.
Acts 13:39

A man is justified by faith without the deeds of the law.
Rom. 3:28

It is God that justifieth.
Rom. 8:33

Ye are justified in the name of the Lord Jesus, and by the Spirit of our God.
1 Cor. 6:11

No man is justified by the law in the sight of God.
Gal. 3:11

KINDNESS

Drink, and I will give thy camels drink also.
Rebekah
Gen. 24:14

The Lord deal kindly with you, as ye have dealt with the dead, and with me.
Naomi
Ruth 1:8

Let her glean even among the sheaves, and reproach her not.
Ruth 2:15

Thou hast showed more kindness in the latter end than at the beginning.
Ruth 3:10

Let them be of those that eat at thy table.
1 Kings 2:7

The merciful man doeth good to his own soul: but he that is cruel troubleth his own flesh.
Prov. 11:17

The tender mercies of the wicked are cruel.
Prov. 12:10

If thine enemy be hungry, give him bread to eat; and if he be thirsty, give him water to drink.
   Prov. 25:21
   See also Rom. 12:20

Even the sea monsters draw out the breast, they give suck to their young ones.
   Lam. 4:3

Let none of you imagine evil against his brother in your heart.
   Zech. 7:10
   See also Zech. 8:17

What man is there of you, whom if his son ask bread, will he give him a stone?
   Jesus
   Matt. 7:9
   See also Luke 11:11

Be ye kind one to another.
   Eph. 4:32

Be gentle unto all men, apt to teach, patient.
   2 Tim. 2:24

[*See also* Altruism, Compassion, Cruelty, Generosity, Hospitality, Humility]

KINGDOM OF GOD

It is easier for a camel to go through the eye of a needle, than for a rich man to enter into the kingdom of God.
   Jesus
   Matt. 19:24, Mark 10:25
   See also Luke 18:25

Whosoever shall not receive the kingdom of God as a little child, he shall not enter therein.
   Jesus
   Mark 10:15
   See also Luke 18:17

No man, having put his hand to the plough, and looking back, is fit for the kingdom of God.
   Jesus
   Luke 9:62

The kingdom of God is come nigh unto you.
   Jesus
   Luke 10:9

Seek ye the kingdom of God; and all these things shall be added unto you.
   Jesus
   Luke 12:31
   See also Matt. 6:33

Fear not, little flock; for it is your Father's good pleasure to give you the kingdom.
   Jesus
   Luke 12:32

It is like a grain of mustard seed, which a man took, and cast into his garden; and it grew, and waxed a great tree.
   Jesus
   Luke 13:19
   See also Matt. 13:31, Mark 4:31

The law and the prophets were until John: since that time the kingdom of God is preached.
   Jesus
   Luke 16:16

The kingdom of God cometh not with observation.
   Jesus
   Luke 17:20

The kingdom of God is within you.
   Jesus
   Luke 17:21

Except a man be born again, he cannot see the kingdom of God.
   Jesus
   John 3:3

Except a man be born of water and of the Spirit, he cannot enter into the kingdom of God.
   Jesus
   John 3:5

We must through much tribulation enter into the kingdom of God.
   Acts 14:22

The kingdom of God is not meat and drink; but righteousness, and peace, and joy in the Holy Ghost.
   Rom. 14:17

The kingdom of God is not in word, but in power.
   1 Cor. 4:20

The unrighteous shall not inherit the kingdom of God.
   1 Cor. 6:9

Flesh and blood cannot inherit the kingdom of God.
1 Cor. 15:50

[*See also* Heaven, Kingdom of Heaven, Salvation]

KINGDOM OF HEAVEN

Repent, for the kingdom of heaven is at hand.
Jesus
Matt. 4:17
See also Matt. 3:2, Matt. 10:7, Mark 1:15

Blessed are the poor in spirit: for their's is the kingdom of heaven.
Jesus
Matt. 5:3
See also Luke 6:20

Blessed are they which are persecuted for righteousness' sake: for their's is the kingdom of heaven.
Jesus
Matt. 5:10

Not every one that saith unto me, Lord, Lord, shall enter into the kingdom of heaven.
Jesus
Matt. 7:21

The kingdom of heaven is like unto treasure hid in a field.
Jesus
Matt. 13:44

I will give unto thee the keys of the kingdom of heaven.
Jesus to Peter
Matt. 16:19

Except ye be converted, and become as little children, ye shall not enter into the kingdom of heaven.
Jesus
Matt. 18:3

A rich man shall hardly enter into the kingdom of heaven.
Jesus
Matt. 19:23
See also Mark 10:24

[*See also* Heaven, Kingdom of God, Salvation]

KINGS

See Monarchy.

KNOWLEDGE

Of every tree of the garden thou mayest freely eat: But of the tree of the knowledge of good and evil, thou shalt not eat.
Gen. 2:16–17

Ye shall not eat of it, neither shall ye touch it, lest ye die.
(it: tree of knowledge)
Gen. 3:3

Your eyes shall be opened, and ye shall be as gods, knowing good and evil.
Gen. 3:5

And the eyes of them both were opened, and they knew that they were naked.
Gen. 3:7

Who told thee that thou wast naked?
Gen. 3:11

The Lord God said, Behold, the man is become as one of us, to know good and evil.
Gen. 3:22

The secret things belong unto the Lord our God: but those things which are revealed belong unto us and to our children for ever.
Deut. 29:29

The Lord is a God of knowledge, and by Him actions are weighed.
1 Sam. 2:3

Canst thou by searching find out God?
Job 11:7

Shall any teach God knowledge?
Job 21:22

Let us choose to us judgment: let us know among ourselves what is good.
Job 34:4

Have the gates of death been opened unto thee? or hast thou seen the doors of the shadow of death?
God to Job
Job 38:17

I am a stranger in the earth: hide not Thy commandments from me.
Ps. 119:19

I understand more than the ancients, because I keep Thy precepts.
Ps. 119:100

A wise man will hear, and will increase learning.
Prov. 1:5

The fear of the Lord is the beginning of knowledge.
Prov. 1:7

Get wisdom, get understanding: forget it not.
Prov. 4:5

Wise men lay up knowledge.
Prov. 10:14

Through knowledge shall the just be delivered.
Prov. 11:9

Knowledge is easy unto him that understandeth.
Prov. 14:6

The heart of him that hath understanding seeketh knowledge.
Prov. 15:14

The ear of the wise seeketh knowledge.
Prov. 18:15

He that increaseth knowledge increaseth sorrow.
Eccl. 1:18

Have ye not known? have ye not heard? hath it not been told you from the beginning?
Isa. 40:21

Thy wisdom and thy knowledge, it hath perverted thee; and thou hast said in thine heart, I am, and none else beside me.
Isa. 47:10

The stork in the heaven knoweth her appointed times; and the turtle and the crane and the swallow observe the time of their coming; but My people know not the judgment of the Lord.
God to Jews
Jer. 8:7

Because thou hast rejected knowledge, I will also reject thee.
God
Hos. 4:6

Hear, and understand.
Jesus
Matt. 15:10

Flesh and blood hath not revealed it unto thee, but my Father which is in heaven.
Jesus
Matt. 16:17

If ye were blind, ye should have no sin.
Jesus
John 9:41

Walk while ye have the light, lest darkness come upon you.
Jesus
John 12:35

It is not for you to know the times or the seasons.
Jesus
Acts 1:7

I had not known lust, except the law had said, Thou shalt not covet.
Rom. 7:7

I would have you wise unto that which is good, and simple concerning evil.
Rom. 16:19

I know nothing by myself.
1 Cor. 4:4

If any man think that he knoweth any thing, he knoweth nothing yet as he ought to know.
1 Cor. 8:2

Though I be rude in speech, yet not in knowledge.
2 Cor. 11:6

Ye know not what shall be on the morrow.
James 4:14

To him that knoweth to do good, and doeth it not, to him it is sin.
James 4:17

As newborn babes, desire the sincere milk of the word, that ye may grow thereby.
1 Pet. 2:2

Add to your faith virtue; and to virtue knowledge.
2 Pet. 1:5

[*See also* Education, Experience, God's Knowledge, Ignorance, Understanding, Wisdom]

And they shall know that I am the Lord their God, that brought them forth out of the land of Egypt.
Ex. 29:46

And ye shall know that I am the Lord.
1 Kings 20:28

Know thou the God of thy father.
1 Chron. 28:9

We know Him not, neither can the number of His years be searched out.
Job 36:26

The secret of the Lord is with them that fear Him.
Ps. 25:14

Be still, and know that I am God.
Ps. 46:10

The earth shall be full of the knowledge of the Lord, as the waters cover the sea.
Isa. 11:9

They shall all know Me, from the least of them unto the greatest.
Jer. 31:34
See also Heb. 8:11

Ye shall know that I am the Lord, when I set My face against them.
Ezek. 15:7

I will be known in the eyes of many nations, and they shall know that I am the Lord.
Ezek. 38:23

No man knoweth the Son, but the Father; neither knoweth any man the Father, save the Son, and he to whomsoever the Son will reveal Him.
Jesus
Matt. 11:27
See also Luke 10:22

I know Him: for I am from Him, and He hath sent me.
Jesus
John 7:29

If ye had known me, ye should have known my Father also.
Jesus
John 8:19

If I should say, I know Him not, I shall be a liar like unto you: but I know Him, and keep His saying.
Jesus
John 8:55

As the Father knoweth me, even so know I the Father.
Jesus
John 10:15

They know not Him that sent me.
Jesus
John 15:21

Who hath known the mind of the Lord? or who hath been His counsellor?
Rom. 11:34

They profess that they know God; but in works they deny Him.
Titus 1:16

Grace and peace be multiplied unto you through the knowledge of God, and of Jesus our Lord.
2 Pet. 1:2

Grow in grace, and in the knowledge of our Lord.
2 Pet. 3:18

[*See also* Acknowledgment, Disobedience, Salvation, Testimony]

LABOR

See Business, Work.

LAMENT

How are the mighty fallen!
E.g., 2 Sam. 1:19

Tell it not in Gath, publish it not in the streets of Askelon.
2 Sam. 1:20

I have no son to keep my name in remembrance.
2 Sam. 18:18

How doth the city sit solitary, that was full of people! how is she become as a widow!
Lam. 1:1
See also Lam. 1:2–22

Alas for the day! for the day of the Lord is
at hand.
Joel 1:15

Woe is me!
E.g., Mic. 7:1

O faithless and perverse generation.
Jesus
Matt. 17:17

[*See also* Anguish, Grief, Jerusalem,
Mourning]

LANGUAGE

See Communication, Eloquence, Speech.

LAST JUDGMENT

See Apocalypse, Judgment Day.

LAUGHTER

Even in laughter the heart is sorrowful.
Prov. 14:13

I said of laughter, It is mad: and of mirth,
What doeth it?
Eccl. 2:2

A time to weep, and a time to laugh.
Eccl. 3:4

Sorrow is better than laughter: for by the
sadness of the countenance the heart is
made better.
Eccl. 7:3

As the crackling of thorns under a pot, so is
the laughter of the fool.
Eccl. 7:6

Blessed are ye that weep now: for ye shall
laugh.
Jesus
Luke 6:21

Woe unto you that laugh now! for ye shall
mourn and weep.
Jesus
Luke 6:25

Let your laughter be turned to mourning,
and your joy to heaviness.
James 4:9

LAW

Ye shall have one manner of law, as well
for the stranger, as for one of your own
country.
Lev. 24:22
See also Ex. 12:49, Num. 9:14

If any man will sue thee at the law, and
take away thy coat, let him have thy cloak
also.
Jesus
Matt. 5:40

Woe unto you also, ye lawyers!
Jesus
Luke 11:46

What things soever the law saith, it saith to
them who are under the law.
Rom. 3:19

Where no law is, there is no transgression.
Rom. 4:15
See also Rom. 3:20

Sin is not imputed when there is no law.
Rom. 5:13

Brother goeth to law with brother, and that
before the unbelievers.
1 Cor. 6:6

There is utterly a fault among you, because
ye go to law one with another.
1 Cor. 6:7

It was added because of transgressions.
Gal. 3:19

The law is good, if a man use it lawfully.
1 Tim. 1:8

The law is not made for a righteous man,
but for the lawless and disobedient, for the
ungodly and for sinners.
1 Tim. 1:9

Submit yourselves to every ordinance of
man for the Lord's sake.
1 Pet. 2:13

[*See also* Commandments, Judging, Justice, Scripture]

LAWLESSNESS

The earth is given into the hand of the
wicked: He covereth the faces of the judges
thereof.
Job 9:24

If the foundations be destroyed, what can the righteous do?
Ps. 11:3

The wicked watcheth the righteous, and seeketh to slay him.
Ps. 37:32

Deliver me from the workers of iniquity, and save me from bloody men.
Ps. 59:2

When the wicked spring as the grass, and when all the workers of iniquity do flourish; it is that they shall be destroyed for ever.
Ps. 92:7

Rivers of waters run down mine eyes, because they keep not Thy law.
Ps. 119:136

A wise king scattereth the wicked.
Prov. 20:26

There shall be no reward to the evil man; the candle of the wicked shall be put out.
Prov. 24:20

Judgment is turned away backward, and justice standeth afar off.
Isa. 59:14

Truth is fallen in the street, and equity cannot enter.
Isa. 59:14

The law is no more.
Lam. 2:9

The land is full of bloody crimes, and the city is full of violence.
Ezek. 7:23

Wherefore lookest Thou upon them that deal treacherously, and holdest Thy tongue when the wicked devoureth the man that is more righteous than he?
Hab. 1:13

[*See also* Corruption, Crime, Injustice, Wickedness]

LAZINESS

He becometh poor that dealeth with a slack hand: but the hand of the diligent maketh rich.
Prov. 10:4

He that sleepeth in harvest is a son that causeth shame.
Prov. 10:5

As vinegar to the teeth, and as smoke to the eyes, so is the sluggard to them that send him.
Prov. 10:26

In all labour there is profit: but the talk of the lips tendeth only to penury.
Prov. 14:23

An idle soul shall suffer hunger.
Prov. 19:15

Love not sleep, lest thou come to poverty.
Prov. 20:13

The slothful man saith, There is a lion without, I shall be slain in the streets.
Prov. 22:13
See also Prov. 26:13

Drowsiness shall clothe a man with rags.
Prov. 23:21

The sluggard is wiser in his own conceit than seven men that can render a reason.
Prov. 26:16

The fool foldeth his hands together, and eateth his own flesh.
Eccl. 4:5

By much slothfulness the building decayeth.
Eccl. 10:18

He that observeth the wind shall not sow, and he that regardeth the clouds shall not reap.
Eccl. 11:4

Their strength is to sit still.
Isa. 30:7

If any would not work, neither should he eat.
2 Thess. 3:10

[*See also* Diligence, Work]

LEADERSHIP

Can we find such a one as this is, a man in whom the Spirit of God is?
Pharaoh to Joseph
Gen. 41:38

The sceptre shall not depart from Judah

nor a lawgiver from between his feet, until Shiloh come.
>Jacob to Judah
Gen. 49:10

Who made thee a prince and a judge over us?
>(thee: Moses)
Ex. 2:14

The children of Israel have not hearkened unto me; how then shall Pharaoh hear me?
>Moses to God
Ex. 6:12

What shall I do unto this people? they be almost ready to stone me.
>Moses
Ex. 17:4

Thou wilt surely wear away, both thou, and this people that is with thee.
>Jethro to Moses
Ex. 18:18

Show them the way wherein they must walk, and the work that they must do.
Ex. 18:20

Provide out of all the people able men, such as fear God, men of truth, hating covetousness.
>Jethro to Moses
Ex. 18:21

Every great matter they shall bring unto thee, but every small matter they shall judge.
Ex. 18:22
See also Ex. 18:26

Wherefore have I not found favour in Thy sight, that Thou layest the burden of all this people upon me?
>Moses to God
Num. 11:11

Have I conceived all this people? have I begotten them, that Thou shouldest say unto me, Carry them in thy bosom, as a nursing father beareth the sucking child?
>Moses to God
Num. 11:12

The man whom the Lord doth choose, he shall be holy.
Num. 16:7

The cause that is too hard for you, bring it unto me, and I will hear it.
>Moses
Deut. 1:17

Whithersoever thou sendest us, we will go.
Josh. 1:16

They feared him, as they feared Moses, all the days of his life.
Josh. 4:14

Follow after me: for the Lord hath delivered your enemies.
Judg. 3:28

The Spirit of the Lord came upon Gideon, and he blew a trumpet.
Judg. 6:34

They have not rejected thee, but they have rejected Me, that I should not reign over them.
>God to Samuel
1 Sam. 8:7

Because thou hast rejected the word of the Lord, He hath also rejected thee from being king.
>Samuel to Saul
1 Sam. 15:23

Arise, anoint him; for this is he.
>God to Samuel, about David
1 Sam. 16:12

Who am I, O Lord God? and what is my house, that Thou hast brought me hitherto?
>David
2 Sam. 7:18

Give therefore Thy servant an understanding heart to judge Thy people, that I may discern between good and bad.
>Solomon
1 Kings 3:9

Walk before Me, as David thy father walked, in integrity of heart, and in uprightness.
1 Kings 9:4

Happy are thy men, happy are these thy servants, which stand continually before thee.
>Queen of Sheba to Solomon
1 Kings 10:8

Because the Lord loved Israel for ever, therefore made He thee king.
> Queen of Sheba to Solomon
> *1 Kings 10:9*

Elijah passed by him, and cast his mantle upon him.
> *1 Kings 19:19*
> *See also 2 Kings 2:13*

Let a double portion of thy spirit be upon me.
> Elisha to Elijah
> *2 Kings 2:9*

As thou hast said, so must we do.
> *Ezra 10:12*

Where no counsel is, the people fall.
> *Prov. 11:14*

Excellent speech becometh not a fool: much less do lying lips a prince.
> *Prov. 17:7*

Where there is no vision, the people perish.
> *Prov. 29:18*

Better is a poor and a wise child than an old and foolish king, who will no more be admonished.
> *Eccl. 4:13*

Woe to thee, O land, when thy king is a child.
> *Eccl. 10:16*

Thou hast clothing, be thou our ruler.
> *Isa. 3:6*

A little child shall lead them.
> *Isa. 11:6*

I will bring the blind by a way that they knew not; I will lead them in paths that they have not known.
> God
> *Isa. 42:16*

Woe be unto the pastors that destroy and scatter the sheep of My pasture!
> *Jer. 23:1*

My people hath been lost sheep: their shepherds have caused them to go astray.
> *Jer. 50:6*

Woe be to the shepherds of Israel that do feed themselves! should not the shepherds feed the flocks?
> *Ezek. 34:2*

Smite the shepherd, and the sheep shall be scattered.
> *Zech. 13:7*
> *See also Matt. 26:31, Mark 14:27*

Ye are the light of the world. A city that is set on an hill cannot be hid.
> Jesus
> *Matt. 5:14*

Let your light so shine before men, that they may see your good works.
> Jesus
> *Matt. 5:16*

Follow me.
> Jesus
> *Matt. 9:9, Luke 5:27*
> *See also Matt. 4:19, Mark 1:17*

If the blind lead the blind, both shall fall into the ditch.
> Jesus
> *Matt. 15:14*
> *See also Luke 6:39*

Whosoever will be chief among you, let him be your servant.
> Jesus
> *Matt. 20:27*
> *See also Mark 10:44*

He that is greatest among you shall be your servant.
> Jesus
> *Matt. 23:11*

As a hen gathereth her chickens under her wings.
> Jesus
> *Matt. 23:37*

As sheep not having a shepherd.
> *Mark 6:34*

He that entereth in by the door is the shepherd of the sheep.
> Jesus
> *John 10:2*

The good shepherd giveth his life for the sheep.
> Jesus
> *John 10:11*

My sheep hear my voice, and I know them, and they follow me.
> Jesus
> *John 10:27*

Ye have not chosen me, but I have chosen you.
Jesus
John 15:16

He is the minister of God, a revenger to execute wrath upon him that doeth evil.
Rom. 13:4

Who then is Paul, and who is Apollos, but ministers by whom ye believed?
1 Cor. 3:5

If a man desire the office of a bishop, he desireth a good work.
1 Tim. 3:1

If a man know not how to rule his own house, how shall he take care of the church of God?
1 Tim. 3:5

Let the elders that rule well be counted worthy of double honour.
1 Tim. 5:17

Them that sin rebuke before all, that others also may fear.
(Them: church leaders)
1 Tim. 5:20

A bishop must be blameless, as the steward of God.
Titus 1:7

For love's sake I rather beseech thee.
Philem. 9

Feed the flock of God which is among you.
1 Pet. 5:2

There shall be false teachers among you.
2 Pet. 2:1

[*See also* Ambition, Authority, Corruption, Disciples, Government, Models, Monarchy]

LENIENCY

See Compassion, Forgiveness, Punishment.

LIES

The Strength of Israel will not lie.
1 Sam. 15:29

Should thy lies make men hold their peace?
Job 11:3

Ye are forgers of lies, ye are all physicians of no value.
Job to his friends
Job 13:4

I said in my haste, All men are liars.
Ps. 116:11

These six things doth the Lord hate: yea, seven are an abomination unto Him: A proud look, a lying tongue, and hands that shed innocent blood, An heart that deviseth wicked imaginations, feet that be swift in running to mischief, A false witness that speaketh lies, and he that soweth discord among brethren.
Prov. 6:16–19

The wicked is snared by the transgression of his lips.
Prov. 12:13

A lying tongue is but for a moment.
Prov. 12:19

Lying lips are abomination to the Lord.
Prov. 12:22

A righteous man hateth lying.
Prov. 13:5

Excellent speech becometh not a fool: much less do lying lips a prince.
Prov. 17:7

Woe unto them that call evil good, and good evil; that put darkness for light, and light for darkness; that put bitter for sweet, and sweet for bitter!
Isa. 5:20

Their tongue is deceitful in their mouth.
Mic. 6:12

Thou speakest lies in the name of the Lord.
Zech. 13:3

He is a liar, and the father of it.
Jesus (He: Satan)
John 8:44

Thou hast not lied unto men, but unto God.
Acts 5:4

The poison of asps is under their lips.
Rom. 3:13
See also Ps. 140:3

No lie is of the truth.
1 John 2:21

Who is a liar but he that denieth that Jesus is the Christ?
1 John 2:22

[*See also* Deception, Dishonesty, Honesty, Hypocrisy, Perjury, Truth]

LIFE

The Lord God formed man of the dust of the ground, and breathed into his nostrils the breath of life.
Gen. 2:7

The life of all flesh is the blood thereof.
Lev. 17:14

Wherefore is light given to him that is in misery, and life unto the bitter in soul?
Job 3:20

What is mine end, that I should prolong my life?
Job 6:11

Wherefore then hast Thou brought me forth out of the womb? Oh that I had given up the ghost, and no eye had seen me!
Job 10:18

Man that is born of a woman is of few days, and full of trouble.
Job 14:1

The spirit of God hath made me, and the breath of the Almighty hath given me life.
Job 33:4

We spend our years as a tale that is told.
Ps. 90:9

The days of our years are threescore years and ten; and if by reason of strength they be fourscore years, yet is their strength labour and sorrow.
Ps. 90:10

Teach us to number our days, that we may apply our hearts unto wisdom.
Ps. 90:12

Give me understanding, and I shall live.
Ps. 119:144

Let my soul live, and it shall praise Thee.
Ps. 119:175

The fear of the Lord prolongeth days: but the years of the wicked shall be shortened.
Prov. 10:27

The fear of the Lord is a fountain of life.
Prov. 14:27

Vanity of vanities; all is vanity.
Eccl. 1:2
See also Eccl. 12:8

Therefore I hated life.
Eccl. 2:17

All his days are sorrows, and his travail grief; yea, his heart taketh not rest in the night.
Eccl. 2:23

A pleasant thing it is for the eyes to behold the sun.
Eccl. 11:7

Cursed be the day wherein I was born: let not the day wherein my mother bare me be blessed.
Jer. 20:14

Wherefore came I forth out of the womb to see labour and sorrow?
Jer. 20:18

Ye shall live; and ye shall know that I am the Lord.
Ezek. 37:6

Seek the Lord, and ye shall live.
Amos 5:6
See also Amos 5:4

Seek good, and not evil, that ye may live.
Amos 5:14

In Him was life; and the life was the light of men.
John 1:4

Except ye eat the flesh of the Son of man, and drink His blood, ye have no life in you.
Jesus
John 6:53
See also John 6:54

It is the Spirit that quickeneth; the flesh profiteth nothing.
Jesus
John 6:63

As long as I am in the world, I am the light of the world.
Jesus
John 9:5

He that loveth his life shall lose it; and he that hateth his life in this world shall keep it unto life eternal.
Jesus
John 12:25

I am the way, the truth, and the life: no man cometh unto the Father, but by me.
Jesus
John 14:6

Because I live, ye shall live also.
Jesus
John 14:19

In Him we live, and move, and have our being.
Acts 17:28

None of us liveth to himself.
Rom. 14:7

Now we live, if ye stand fast in the Lord.
1 Thess. 3:8

God sent His only begotten Son into the world, that we might live through Him.
1 John 4:9

He that hath the Son hath life.
1 John 5:12

Blessed are they that do His commandments, that they may have right to the tree of life.
Rev. 22:14

[*See also* Age, Death, Eternal Life, Mortality]

LIFE AND DEATH

I have set before you life and death, blessing and cursing: therefore choose life, that both thou and thy seed may live.
Deut. 30:19

There is no god with Me: I kill, and I make alive; I wound, and I heal: neither is there any that can deliver out of My hand.
Deut. 32:39

The Lord killeth, and maketh alive: He bringeth down to the grave, and bringeth up.
1 Sam. 2:6

Naked came I out of my mother's womb, and naked shall I return hither.
Job 1:21

Unto God the Lord belong the issues from death.
Ps. 68:20

According to the greatness of Thy power preserve Thou those that are appointed to die.
Ps. 79:11

Shall Thy lovingkindness be declared in the grave? or Thy faithfulness in destruction?
Ps. 88:11

Take me not away in the midst of my days.
Ps. 102:24

I shall not die, but live, and declare the works of the Lord.
Ps. 118:17

Man is like to vanity: his days are as a shadow that passeth away.
Ps. 144:4

He that keepeth the commandment keepeth his own soul; but he that despiseth His ways shall die.
Prov. 19:16

A time to be born, and a time to die.
Eccl. 3:2

I praised the dead which are already dead more than the living which are yet alive.
Eccl. 4:2

A good name is better than precious ointment; and the day of death than the day of one's birth.
Eccl. 7:1

Why shouldest thou die before thy time?
Eccl. 7:17

There is one event to the righteous, and to the wicked; to the good and to the clean, and to the unclean.
Eccl. 9:2

A living dog is better than a dead lion.
Eccl. 9:4

The living know that they shall die: but the dead know not any thing.
Eccl. 9:5

As the days of a tree are the days of My people, and Mine elect shall long enjoy the work of their hands.
Isa. 65:22

Behold, I set before you the way of life, and the way of death.
Jer. 21:8

Make you a new heart and a new spirit: for why will ye die?
Ezek. 18:31

Whosoever will save his life shall lose it: and whosoever will lose his life for my sake shall find it.
Jesus
Matt. 16:25
See also Mark 8:35, Luke 9:24

God is not the God of the dead, but of the living.
Jesus
Matt. 22:32
See also Mark 12:27, Luke 20:38

The damsel is not dead, but sleepeth.
Jesus
Mark 5:39
See also Matt. 9:24

He that believeth in me, though he were dead, yet shall he live.
Jesus
John 11:25

If I will that he tarry till I come, what is that to thee?
Jesus to Peter, about John
John 21:22

In that He died, He died unto sin once: but in that He liveth, He liveth unto God.
Rom. 6:10

The wages of sin is death; but the gift of God is eternal life through Jesus Christ our Lord.
Rom. 6:23

Whether we live therefore, or die, we are the Lord's.
Rom. 14:8

As in Adam all die, even so in Christ shall all be made alive.
1 Cor. 15:22

Whilst we are at home in the body, we are absent from the Lord.
2 Cor. 5:6

I through the law am dead to the law, that I might live unto God.
Gal. 2:19

To live is Christ, and to die is gain.
Phil. 1:21

Ye are dead, and your life is hid with Christ in God.
Col. 3:3

If we be dead with Him, we shall also live with Him.
2 Tim. 2:11

[*See also* Christ Eternal, Death, Eternal Life, Life, Mortality]

LIGHT AND DARKNESS

And God said, Let there be light: and there was light.
Gen. 1:3

Darkness which may be felt.
Ex. 10:21

The people that walked in darkness have seen a great light.
Isa. 9:2
See also Matt. 4:16, Luke 1:79

Ye are the light of the world. A city that is set on an hill cannot be hid.
Jesus
Matt. 5:14

Take heed therefore that the light which is in thee be not darkness.
Jesus
Luke 11:35

The light shineth in darkness; and the darkness comprehended it not.
John 1:5

Men loved darkness rather than light, because their deeds were evil.
Jesus
John 3:19

Every one that doeth evil hateth the light.
Jesus
John 3:20

As long as I am in the world, I am the light of the world.
Jesus
John 9:5

Turn them from darkness to light, and from the power of Satan unto God.
Jesus to Paul
Acts 26:18

All things that are reproved are made manifest by the light.
Eph. 5:13

God is light, and in Him is no darkness at all.
1 John 1:5

The city had no need of the sun, neither of the moon, to shine in it: for the glory of God did lighten it, and the Lamb is the light thereof.
Rev. 21:23

[*See also* Enlightenment, Nature, Night, Spirituality]

LIQUOR

Wine that maketh glad the heart of man.
Ps. 104:15

Wine is a mocker, strong drink is raging.
Prov. 20:1

Look not thou upon the wine when it is red.
Prov. 23:31

It biteth like a serpent, and stingeth like an adder.
Prov. 23:32

Give strong drink unto him that is ready to perish, and wine unto those that be of heavy hearts.
Prov. 31:6

Let him drink, and forget his poverty, and remember his misery no more.
Prov. 31:7

Eat thy bread with joy, and drink thy wine with a merry heart.
Eccl. 9:7

Whoredom and wine and new wine take away the heart.
Hos. 4:11

No man also having drunk old wine straightway desireth new.
Jesus
Luke 5:39

Use a little wine for thy stomach's sake.
1 Tim. 5:23

[*See also* Drunkenness]

LISTENING

See Heedfulness.

LONELINESS

It is not good that the man should be alone; I will make him an help meet for him.
Gen. 2:18

My kinsfolk have failed, and my familiar friends have forgotten me.
Job 19:14

I am a brother to dragons, and a companion to owls.
Job 30:29

How long wilt Thou forget me, O Lord? for ever? how long wilt Thou hide Thy face from me?
Ps. 13:1

When my father and my mother forsake me, then the Lord will take me up.
Ps. 27:10

I am forgotten as a dead man out of mind: I am like a broken vessel.
Ps. 31:12

I looked for some to take pity, but there was none; and for comforters, but I found none.
Ps. 69:20

Woe to him that is alone when he falleth; for he hath not another to help him up.
Eccl. 4:10

Among all her lovers she hath none to comfort her.
(her: Jerusalem)
Lam. 1:2

They shall be desolate in the midst of the countries that are desolate.
Ezek. 30:7

I am not alone, because the Father is with me.
Jesus
John 16:32

None of us liveth to himself.
Rom. 14:7

[*See also* Abandonment, Desolation, Fellowship, Friendship]

See Age, Mortality.

LOSS

The Lord gave, and the Lord hath taken away; blessed be the name of the Lord.
Job 1:21

A time to get, and a time to lose.
Eccl. 3:6

I will restore to you the years that the locust hath eaten.
Joel 2:25

If the salt have lost his savour, wherewith shall it be salted? it is thenceforth good for nothing.
Jesus
Matt. 5:13
See also Mark 9:50, Luke 14:34

The last shall be first.
Jesus
Matt. 19:30
See also, e.g., Mark 10:31

Many are called, but few are chosen.
Jesus
Matt. 22:14
See also Matt. 20:16

From him that hath not shall be taken away even that which he hath.
Jesus
Matt. 25:29

He that hath, to him shall be given: and he that hath not, from him shall be taken even that which he hath.
Jesus
Mark 4:25
See also Matt. 13:12, Luke 8:18, Luke 19:26

What shall it profit a man, if he shall gain the whole world, and lose his own soul?
Jesus
Mark 8:36
See also Matt. 16:26, Luke 9:25

The fruits that thy soul lusted after are departed from thee.
Rev. 18:14

[*See also* Acceptance, Profit, Reward]

Jacob served seven years for Rachel; and they seemed unto him but a few days, for the love he had to her.
Gen. 29:20

Israel loved Joseph more than all his children, because he was the son of his old age.
Gen. 37:3

Now let me die, since I have seen thy face, because thou art yet alive.
Jacob to Joseph
Gen. 46:30

Thou shalt love thy neighbour as thyself.
E.g., Lev. 19:18, Matt. 19:19

The apple of His eye.
Deut. 32:10

How canst thou say, I love thee, when thine heart is not with me?
Delilah to Samson
Judg. 16:15

Am not I better to thee than ten sons?
(I: Hannah's husband)
1 Sam. 1:8

In their death they were not divided.
(they: Saul and Jonathan)
2 Sam. 1:23

Would God I had died for thee, O Absalom, my son, my son!
2 Sam. 18:33

O my Lord, give her the living child, and in no wise slay it.
1 Kings 3:26

Hatred stirreth up strifes: but love covereth all sins.
Prov. 10:12

Better is a dinner of herbs where love is, than a stalled ox and hatred therewith.
Prov. 15:17

A time to love, and a time to hate.
Eccl. 3:8

Let him kiss me with the kisses of his mouth: for thy love is better than wine.
Song 1:2

His banner over me was love.
Song 2:4

Stay me with flagons, comfort me with apples: for I am sick of love.
Song 2:5

I sought him, but I found him not.
Song 3:1, 2

In the broad ways I will seek him whom my soul loveth.
Song 3:2

How much better is thy love than wine! and the smell of thine ointments than all spices!
Song 4:10

Let my beloved come into his garden, and eat his pleasant fruits.
Song 4:16

I am my beloved's, and my beloved is mine.
Song 6:3

I am my beloved's, and his desire is toward me.
Song 7:10

Set me as a seal upon thine heart, as a seal upon thine arm.
Song 8:6

Love is strong as death.
Song 8:6

Many waters cannot quench love, neither can the floods drown it.
Song 8:7

She shall follow after her lovers, but she shall not overtake them.
Hos. 2:7

Your goodness is as a morning cloud, and as the early dew it goeth away.
Hos. 6:4

I have loved you, saith the Lord. Yet ye say, Wherein hast Thou loved us?
Mal. 1:2

Was not Esau Jacob's brother? saith the Lord: yet I loved Jacob.
Mal. 1:2
See also Rom. 9:13

Love your enemies.
Jesus
Matt. 5:44, Luke 6:27
See also Luke 6:35

Bless them that curse you, do good to them that hate you.
Jesus
Matt. 5:44

If ye love them which love you, what reward have ye? do not even the publicans the same?
Jesus
Matt. 5:46
See also Luke 6:32

He that loveth father or mother more than me is not worthy of me: and he that loveth son or daughter more than me is not worthy of me.
Jesus to disciples
Matt. 10:37

This do, and thou shalt live.
Jesus
Luke 10:28

A new commandment I give unto you, That ye love one another.
Jesus
John 13:34

By this shall all men know that ye are my disciples, if ye have love one to another.
Jesus
John 13:35

He that loveth me shall be loved of my Father.
Jesus
John 14:21

This is my commandment, That ye love one another, as I have loved you.
Jesus
John 15:12

Greater love hath no man than this, that a man lay down his life for his friends.
Jesus
John 15:13

Let love be without dissimulation.
Rom. 12:9

Owe no man any thing, but to love one another.
Rom. 13:8

He that loveth another hath fulfilled the law.
Rom. 13:8
See also Rom. 13:10

Love worketh no ill to his neighbour.
Rom. 13:10

Shall I come unto you with a rod, or in love?
1 Cor. 4:21

[Note: The following quotations from 1

Corinthians contain the word "charity." This is an Elizabethan translation from the Latin "caritas" and the Greek "agape." Recent versions of the Bible translate the word more accurately, as "love." See Appendix, p. 424]

Knowledge puffeth up, but charity edifieth.
1 Cor. 8:1

Though I speak with the tongues of men and of angels, and have not charity, I am become as sounding brass, or a tinkling cymbal.
1 Cor. 13:1

Though I have all faith, so that I could remove mountains, and have not charity, I am nothing.
1 Cor. 13:2

And though I bestow all my goods to feed the poor, and though I give my body to be burned, and have not charity, it profiteth me nothing.
1 Cor. 13:3

Charity suffereth long, and is kind; charity envieth not; charity vaunteth not itself, is not puffed up.
1 Cor. 13:4

Charity envieth not.
1 Cor. 13:4

Beareth all things, believeth all things, hopeth all things, endureth all things.
1 Cor. 13:7

Charity never faileth.
1 Cor. 13:8

And now abideth faith, hope, charity, these three; but the greatest of these is charity.
1 Cor. 13:13

Let all your things be done with charity.
1 Cor. 16:14

By love serve one another.
Gal. 5:13

All the law is fulfilled in one word, even in this; Thou shalt love thy neighbour as thyself.
Gal. 5:14

Walk in love, as Christ also hath loved us.
Eph. 5:2

Husbands, love your wives, even as Christ also loved the church.
Eph. 5:25

He that loveth his wife loveth himself.
Eph. 5:28

Above all these things put on charity, which is the bond of perfectness.
(charity: love)
Col. 3:14

The end of the commandment is charity out of a pure heart, and of a good conscience, and of faith unfeigned.
1 Tim. 1:5

Above all things have fervent charity among yourselves.
1 Pet. 4:8

Charity shall cover the multitude of sins.
(charity: love)
1 Pet. 4:8

He that loveth his brother abideth in the light.
1 John 2:10

This is the message that ye heard from the beginning, that we should love one another.
1 John 3:11

Let us not love in word, neither in tongue; but in deed and in truth.
1 John 3:18

Let us love one another: for love is of God.
1 John 4:7

Every one that loveth is born of God, and knoweth God.
1 John 4:7

He that loveth not knoweth not God.
1 John 4:8

God is love.
1 John 4:8, 16

If God so loved us, we ought also to love one another.
1 John 4:11

If we love one another, God dwelleth in us.
1 John 4:12

He that dwelleth in love dwelleth in God, and God in him.
1 John 4:16

Perfect love casteth out fear.
1 John 4:18

We love Him, because He first loved us.
1 John 4:19

As many as I love, I rebuke and chasten.
Jesus
Rev. 3:19

[*See also* Brotherhood, Friendship, God's Love, God's Mercy, Hatred, and the Appendix at p. 424]

LOVE OF GOD

Thou shalt love the Lord thy God with all thine heart, and with all thy soul, and with all thy might.
Deut. 6:5

Love Him.
Deut. 10:12

Love the Lord thy God.
E.g., Deut. 19:9

Take good heed therefore unto yourselves, that ye love the Lord your God.
Josh. 23:11
See also Deut. 4:15

Let them that love Him be as the sun when he goeth forth in his might.
Judg. 5:31

As the hart panteth after the water brooks, so panteth my soul after Thee, O God.
Ps. 42:1

My soul thirsteth after Thee, as a thirsty land.
Ps. 143:6

Thou shalt love the Lord thy God with all thy heart, and with all thy soul, and with all thy mind. This is the first and great commandment.
Jesus
Matt. 22:37–38
See also Mark 12:29–30, Luke 10:27

All things work together for good to them that love God.
Rom. 8:28

Who shall separate us from the love of Christ? shall tribulation, or distress, or persecution, or famine, or nakedness, or peril, or sword?
Rom. 8:35

Eye hath not seen, nor ear heard, neither have entered into the heart of man, the things which God hath prepared for them that love Him.
1 Cor. 2:9
See also Isa. 64:4

Whosoever therefore will be a friend of the world is the enemy of God.
James 4:4

If any man love the world, the love of the Father is not in him.
1 John 2:15

He that loveth not his brother whom he hath seen, how can he love God whom he hath not seen?
1 John 4:20

He who loveth God love his brother also.
1 John 4:21

We love the children of God, when we love God, and keep His commandments.
1 John 5:2

Keep yourselves in the love of God, looking for the mercy of our Lord Jesus Christ.
Jude 21

[*See also* Reverence]

LOYALTY

Enviest thou for my sake?
Moses to Joshua
Num. 11:29

He will not forsake thee, neither destroy thee, nor forget the covenant of thy fathers which He sware unto them.
Deut. 4:31

He left nothing undone of all that the Lord commanded Moses.
Josh. 11:15

Intreat me not to leave thee.
Ruth 1:16

Whither thou goest, I will go; and where thou lodgest, I will lodge: thy people shall be my people, and thy God my God.
Ruth 1:16

Where thou diest, will I die, and there will I be buried.
Ruth 1:17

I will raise Me up a faithful priest.
1 Sam. 2:35

Who is so faithful among all thy servants as David?
1 Sam. 22:14

Blessed be ye of the Lord; for ye have compassion on me.
Saul
1 Sam. 23:21

In what place my lord the king shall be, whether in death or life, even there also will thy servant be.
2 Sam. 15:21

Hast not Thou made an hedge about him, and about his house?
Satan to God, of Job
Job 1:10

The Lord will not cast off His people, neither will He forsake His inheritance.
Ps. 94:14

A faithful man who can find?
Prov. 20:6

Thine own friend, and thy father's friend, forsake not.
Prov. 27:10

Where your treasure is, there will your heart be also.
Jesus
Matt. 6:21, Luke 12:34

Ye cannot serve God and mammon.
Jesus
Matt. 6:24, Luke 16:13

No man can serve two masters: for either he will hate the one, and love the other; or else he will hold to the one, and despise the other.
Jesus
Matt. 6:24, Luke 16:13

He that is not with me is against me.
Jesus
Matt. 12:30, Luke 11:23

Render therefore unto Caesar the things which are Caesar's; and unto God the things that are God's.
Jesus
Matt. 22:21
See also Mark 12:17, Luke 20:25

Though I should die with Thee, yet will I not deny Thee.
Peter to Jesus
Matt. 26:35
See also Mark 14:31

We have no king but Caesar.
John 19:15

God is faithful.
E.g., 1 Cor. 1:9

Faithful is He that calleth you.
1 Thess. 5:24

All men have not faith. But the Lord is faithful.
2 Thess. 3:2–3

The Lord knoweth them that are His.
2 Tim. 2:19

I will never leave thee, nor forsake thee.
(I: God)
Heb. 13:5
See also Deut. 31:6, Josh. 1:5

They went out from us, but they were not of us.
1 John 2:19

[*See also* Allegiance, Allies, Betrayal, Faithfulness]

LUCK

See Chance.

LUST

Keep thee from the evil woman, from the flattery of the tongue of a strange woman.
Prov. 6:24

Lust not after her beauty in thine heart; neither let her take thee with her eyelids.
Prov. 6:25

Can a man take fire in his bosom, and his clothes not be burned?
Prov. 6:27

Can one go upon hot coals, and his feet not be burned?
Prov. 6:28

He goeth after her straightway, as an ox goeth to the slaughter.
Prov. 7:22

Give not thy strength unto women, nor thy ways to that which destroyeth kings.
Prov. 31:3

They were as fed horses in the morning: every one neighed after his neighbour's wife.
　　Jer. 5:8

Whosoever looketh on a woman to lust after her hath committed adultery with her already in his heart.
　　Jesus
　　Matt. 5:28

I had not known lust, except the law had said, Thou shalt not covet.
　　Rom. 7:7

To be carnally minded is death; but to be spiritually minded is life and peace.
　　Rom. 8:6

Use not liberty for an occasion to the flesh.
　　Gal. 5:13

Walk in the Spirit, and ye shall not fulfil the lust of the flesh.
　　Gal. 5:16

The flesh lusteth against the Spirit, and the Spirit against the flesh.
　　Gal. 5:17

He that soweth to his flesh shall of the flesh reap corruption.
　　Gal. 6:8

Abstain from fleshly lusts, which war against the soul.
　　1 Pet. 2:11

[*See also* Adultery, Carnality, Desire, Fornication, Immorality]

MADNESS

Have I need of mad men, that ye have brought this fellow to play the mad man in my presence?
　　1 Sam. 21:15

Surely oppression maketh a wise man mad.
　　Eccl. 7:7

They say, He hath a devil.
　　Jesus (He: John the Baptist)
　　Matt. 11:18
　　See also Luke 7:33

These are not the words of him that hath a devil.
　　John 10:21

Paul, thou art beside thyself; much learning doth make thee mad.
　　Festus
　　Acts 26:24

I am not mad, most noble Festus; but speak forth the words of truth and soberness.
　　Paul
　　Acts 26:25

[*See also* Exorcism]

MAN AND WOMAN

One man among a thousand have I found; but a woman among all those have I not.
　　Eccl. 7:28

He is the image and glory of God: but the woman is the glory of the man.
　　1 Cor. 11:7

The man is not of the woman; but the woman of the man.
　　1 Cor. 11:8

Neither was the man created for the woman; but the woman for the man.
　　1 Cor. 11:9

I suffer not a woman to teach, nor to usurp authority over the man, but to be in silence.
　　1 Tim. 2:12

For Adam was first formed, then Eve.
　　1 Tim. 2:13

[*See also* Family, Mankind, Marriage, Women]

MANAGEMENT

See Business, Leadership.

Let them have dominion over the fish of the sea, and over the fowl of the air, and over the cattle, and over all the earth, and over every creeping thing that creepeth.
Gen. 1:26

God created man in His own image, in the image of God created He him; male and female created He them.
Gen. 1:27

Be fruitful, and multiply, and replenish the earth, and subdue it.
Gen. 1:28

The Lord God formed man of the dust of the ground, and breathed into his nostrils the breath of life.
Gen. 2:7

Dust thou art, and unto dust shalt thou return.
Gen. 3:19

God created man, in the likeness of God made He him.
Gen. 5:1

Male and female created He them; and blessed them.
Gen. 5:2

It repented the Lord that He had made man on the earth.
Gen. 6:6

There is no man that sinneth not.
1 Kings 8:46, 2 Chron. 6:36

All the people, both small and great.
2 Kings 23:2

Shall mortal man be more just than God? shall a man be more pure than his maker?
Job 4:17

Man is born unto trouble.
Job 5:7

What is man, that Thou shouldest magnify him? and that Thou shouldest set Thine heart upon him?
Job 7:17

Man that is born of a woman is of few days, and full of trouble.
Job 14:1

Can a man be profitable unto God, as he that is wise may be profitable unto himself?
Job 22:2

How can he be clean that is born of a woman?
Job 25:4

Yea, the stars are not pure in His sight. How much less man, that is a worm? and the son of man, which is a worm?
Job 25:5–6

God is greater than man.
Job 33:12

They all are the work of His hands.
Job 34:19

If thou sinnest, what doest thou against Him?
Job 35:6

Canst thou draw out leviathan with an hook? or his tongue with a cord which thou lettest down?
God to Job
Job 41:1

What is man, that Thou art mindful of him? and the son of man, that Thou visitest him?
Ps. 8:4
See also Heb. 2:6

Thou hast made him a little lower than the angels, and hast crowned him with glory and honour.
Ps. 8:5

Every man at his best state is altogether vanity.
Ps. 39:5

Surely men of low degree are vanity, and men of high degree are a lie.
Ps. 62:9

He remembered that they were but flesh; a wind that passeth away, and cometh not again.
Ps. 78:39

They are like grass which groweth up. In the morning it flourisheth, and groweth up; in the evening it is cut down, and withereth.
Ps. 90:5–6

It is He that hath made us, and not we ourselves.
Ps. 100:3

As for man, his days are as grass: as a flower of the field, so he flourisheth.
Ps. 103:15

I will praise Thee; for I am fearfully and wonderfully made.
> Ps. 139:14

Lord, what is man, that Thou takest knowledge of him! or the son of man, that Thou makest account of him!
> Ps. 144:3

All his days are sorrows, and his travail grief; yea, his heart taketh not rest in the night.
> Eccl. 2:23

A man hath no preeminence above a beast: for all is vanity.
> Eccl. 3:19

All nations before Him are as nothing.
> Isa. 40:17

Who art thou, that thou shouldest be afraid of a man that shall die, and of the son of man which shall be made as grass?
> Isa. 51:12

We are the clay, and Thou our potter.
> Isa. 64:8

We all are the work of Thy hand.
> Isa. 64:8

With men it is impossible, but not with God.
> Jesus
> Mark 10:27
> See also Matt. 19:26, Luke 18:27

That which is born of the flesh is flesh; and that which is born of the Spirit is spirit.
> Jesus
> John 3:6

They are all under sin.
> Rom. 3:9

There is none righteous, no, not one.
> Rom. 3:10
> See also Ps. 14:3, Ps. 53:3

All have sinned, and come short of the glory of God.
> Rom. 3:23

Ye are the temple of God.
> 1 Cor. 3:16

The Spirit of God dwelleth in you.
> 1 Cor. 3:16

There is neither Jew nor Greek, there is neither bond nor free, there is neither male nor female: for ye are all one in Christ Jesus.
> Gal. 3:28

There is neither Greek nor Jew, circumcision nor uncircumcision, Barbarian, Scythian, bond nor free: but Christ is all, and in all.
> Col. 3:11

Thou crownedst him with glory and honour, and didst set him over the works of Thy hands.
> Heb. 2:7

All flesh is as grass, and all the glory of man as the flower of grass.
> 1 Pet. 1:24
> See also Isa. 40:6

[See also Human Nature, Individual (Importance of), Man and Woman, Mortality]

MANNERS

See Courtesy.

MARRIAGE

And they shall be one flesh.
> Gen. 2:24

Thy desire shall be to thy husband, and he shall rule over thee.
> God to Eve
> Gen. 3:16

Are there yet any more sons in my womb, that they may be your husbands?
> Naomi to Ruth and Orpah
> Ruth 1:11

Would ye tarry for them till they were grown?
> Ruth 1:13

Rejoice with the wife of thy youth.
> Prov. 5:18

A virtuous woman is a crown to her husband.
> Prov. 12:4

Whoso findeth a wife findeth a good thing, and obtaineth favour of the Lord.
> Prov. 18:22

House and riches are the inheritance of

fathers: and a prudent wife is from the Lord.
Prov. 19:14

A faithful man who can find?
Prov. 20:6

It is better to dwell in a corner of the housetop, than with a brawling woman in a wide house.
Prov. 21:9
See also Prov. 25:24

It is better to dwell in the wilderness, than with a contentious and an angry woman.
Prov. 21:19

Who can find a virtuous woman? for her price is far above rubies.
Prov. 31:10

She looketh well to the ways of her household, and eateth not the bread of idleness. (she: wife)
Prov. 31:27

Many daughters have done virtuously, but thou excellest them all.
Prov. 31:29

Let us be called by thy name, to take away our reproach.
Isa. 4:1

Let none deal treacherously against the wife of his youth.
Mal. 2:15

Take heed to your spirit, that ye deal not treacherously.
Mal. 2:16

What therefore God hath joined together, let not man put asunder.
Jesus
Matt. 19:6, Mark 10:9

They twain shall be one flesh.
Jesus
Mark 10:8
See also Matt. 19:6, Eph. 5:31

To avoid fornication, let every man have his own wife, and let every woman have her own husband.
1 Cor. 7:2

Let the husband render unto the wife due benevolence: and likewise also the wife unto the husband.
1 Cor. 7:3

It is better to marry than to burn.
1 Cor. 7:9

The woman which hath an husband that believeth not, and if he be pleased to dwell with her, let her not leave him.
1 Cor. 7:13

The unbelieving husband is sanctified by the wife, and the unbelieving wife is sanctified by the husband.
1 Cor. 7:14

If the unbelieving depart, let him depart.
1 Cor. 7:15

Such shall have trouble in the flesh.
1 Cor. 7:28

He that is unmarried careth for the things that belong to the Lord, how he may please the Lord: But he that is married careth for the things that are of the world, how he may please his wife.
1 Cor. 7:32–33

She that is married careth for the things of the world, how she may please her husband.
1 Cor. 7:34

He that giveth her in marriage doeth well; but he that giveth her not in marriage doeth better.
1 Cor. 7:38

Wives, submit yourselves unto your own husbands, as unto the Lord.
Eph. 5:22
See also Col. 3:18

The husband is the head of the wife, even as Christ is the head of the church.
Eph. 5:23

As the church is subject unto Christ, so let the wives be to their own husbands in every thing.
Eph. 5:24

Husbands, love your wives, even as Christ also loved the church.
Eph. 5:25

He that loveth his wife loveth himself.
Eph. 5:28

Husbands, love your wives, and be not bitter against them.
Col. 3:19

Teach the young women to be sober, to love their husbands, to love their children.
Titus 2:4

Wives, be in subjection to your own husbands.
1 Pet. 3:1

Giving honour unto the wife, as unto the weaker vessel.
1 Pet. 3:7

[*See also* Adultery, Divorce, Family, Strife, Women]

MARTYRDOM

Let me die the death of the righteous, and let my last end be like his!
Num. 23:10

For Thy sake are we killed all the day long; we are counted as sheep for the slaughter.
Ps. 44:22

Precious in the sight of the Lord is the death of His saints.
Ps. 116:15

The Lord hath laid on him the iniquity of us all.
Isa. 53:6

Blessed are they which are persecuted for righteousness' sake: for their's is the kingdom of heaven.
Jesus
Matt. 5:10

Great is your reward in heaven.
Jesus
Matt. 5:12

Whosoever shall lose his life for my sake and the gospel's, the same shall save it.
Jesus
Mark 8:35
See also Matt. 16:25, Luke 9:24

If we let Him thus alone, all men will believe on Him.
John 11:48

Behold, I see the heavens opened, and the Son of man standing on the right hand of God.
Stephen
Acts 7:56

Lord Jesus, receive my spirit.
Stephen
Acts 7:59

I am ready not to be bound only, but also to die at Jerusalem for the name of the Lord Jesus.
Acts 21:13

And though I bestow all my goods to feed the poor, and though I give my body to be burned, and have not charity, it profiteth me nothing.
(charity: love)
1 Cor. 13:3

I am set for the defence of the gospel.
Phil. 1:17

All that will live godly in Christ Jesus shall suffer persecution.
2 Tim. 3:12

They shall hunger no more, neither thirst any more; neither shall the sun light on them, nor any heat.
Rev. 7:16

The Lamb which is in the midst of the throne shall feed them, and shall lead them unto living fountains of waters.
Rev. 7:17

Blessed are the dead which die in the Lord from henceforth.
Rev. 14:13

They have shed the blood of saints and prophets, and Thou hast given them blood to drink.
Rev. 16:6

I saw the souls of them that were beheaded for the witness of Jesus, and for the word of God.
Rev. 20:4

[*See also* Persecution, Sacrifice]

MATERIALISM

Man doth not live by bread only, but by every word that proceedeth out of the mouth of the Lord.
Deut. 8:3
See also, e.g., Matt. 4:4

Lay not up for yourselves treasures upon

earth, where moth and rust doth corrupt, and where thieves break through and steal.
Jesus
Matt. 6:19

Ye cannot serve God and mammon.
Jesus
Matt. 6:24, Luke 16:13

Take no thought for your life, what ye shall eat, or what ye shall drink; nor yet for your body, what ye shall put on.
Jesus
Matt. 6:25
See also Luke 12:22

Is not the life more than meat, and the body than raiment?
Jesus
Matt. 6:25
See also Luke 12:23

Why take ye thought for raiment?
Jesus
Matt. 6:28

What shall it profit a man, if he shall gain the whole world, and lose his own soul?
Jesus
Mark 8:36
See also Matt. 16:26, Luke 9:25

Man shall not live by bread alone, but by every word of God.
Jesus
Luke 4:4
See also Matt. 4:4

A man's life consisteth not in the abundance of the things which he possesseth.
Jesus
Luke 12:15

That which is highly esteemed among men is abomination in the sight of God.
Jesus
Luke 16:15

Labour not for the meat which perisheth, but for that meat which endureth unto everlasting life.
Jesus
John 6:27

The kingdom of God is not meat and drink; but righteousness, and peace, and joy in the Holy Ghost.
Rom. 14:17

He that is unmarried careth for the things that belong to the Lord, how he may please the Lord: But he that is married careth for the things that are of the world, how he may please his wife.
1 Cor. 7:32–33

She that is married careth for the things of the world, how she may please her husband.
1 Cor. 7:34

The things which are seen are temporal; but the things which are not seen are eternal.
2 Cor. 4:18

Set your affection on things above, not on things on the earth.
Col. 3:2

Having food and raiment let us be therewith content.
1 Tim. 6:8

Love not the world, neither the things that are in the world.
1 John 2:15

Thou sayest, I am rich, and increased with goods, and have need of nothing; and knowest not that thou art wretched, and miserable, and poor, and blind, and naked.
Jesus
Rev. 3:17

[*See also* Greed, Spirituality, Wealth, Worldliness]

MATURITY

He is of age; ask him.
John 9:21, 23

When I was a child, I spake as a child, I understood as a child, I thought as a child: but when I became a man, I put away childish things.
1 Cor. 13:11

Be not children in understanding.
1 Cor. 14:20

In malice be ye children, but in understanding be men.
1 Cor. 14:20

We henceforth be no more children, tossed to and fro, and carried about with every wind of doctrine, by the sleight of men,

and cunning craftiness, whereby they lie in wait to deceive.
> *Eph. 4:14*

Flee also youthful lusts: but follow righteousness, faith, charity, peace.
> *2 Tim. 2:22*

Strong meat belongeth to them that are of full age.
> *Heb. 5:14*

Grow in grace, and in the knowledge of our Lord.
> *2 Pet. 3:18*

The time is come for Thee to reap; for the harvest of the earth is ripe.
> *Rev. 14:15*

Gather the clusters of the vine of the earth; for her grapes are fully ripe.
> *Rev. 14:18*

[*See also* Age, Children, Experience, Growth]

MEDIATION

A mediator is not a mediator of one.
> *Gal. 3:20*

Jesus the mediator of the new covenant.
> *Heb. 12:24*

[*See also* Compromise, Intercession]

MEDICINE

See Healing.

MEEKNESS

The meek shall eat and be satisfied: they shall praise the Lord that seek Him.
> *Ps. 22:26*

The meek will He guide in judgment: and the meek will He teach His way.
> *Ps. 25:9*

The meek shall inherit the earth.
> *Ps. 37:11*
> *See also, e.g., Matt. 5:5*

The Lord lifteth up the meek: He casteth the wicked down to the ground.
> *Ps. 147:6*

He is brought as a lamb to the slaughter.
> *Isa. 53:7*
> *See also Jer. 11:19*

Seek righteousness, seek meekness: it may be ye shall be hid in the day of the Lord's anger.
> *Zeph. 2:3*

Behold, I send you forth as lambs among wolves.
> Jesus
> *Luke 10:3*
> *See also Matt. 10:16*

Like a lamb dumb before His shearer, so opened He not His mouth.
> *Acts 8:32*

[*See also* Humility]

MEMORIALS

See Burial, Remembrance.

MEMORY

See Remembrance.

MENSTRUATION

The custom of women is upon me.
> *Gen. 31:35*

MERCY

Let not our hand be upon him; for he is our brother and our flesh.
> Judah to his brothers
> *Gen. 37:27*

And God Almighty give you mercy before the man.
> Jacob to his sons
> *Gen. 43:14*

The Lord thy God is a merciful God.
> *Deut. 4:31*

Show us, we pray thee, the entrance into the city, and we will show thee mercy.
> *Judg. 1:24*

Some bade me kill thee: but mine eye spared thee.
> David to Saul
> *1 Sam. 24:10*

If a man find his enemy, will he let him go well away?
Saul to David
1 Sam. 24:19

Go up in peace to thine house.
1 Sam. 25:35

Let him turn to his own house, and let him not see my face.
(him: Absalom)
2 Sam. 14:24

It is enough: stay now thine hand.
God to an angel
2 Sam. 24:16, 1 Chron. 21:15

In thy days I will not do it for David thy father's sake: but I will rend it out of the hand of thy son.
God to Solomon
1 Kings 11:12

Let me fall now into the hand of the Lord; for very great are His mercies: but let me not fall into the hand of man.
1 Chron. 21:13
See also 2 Sam. 24:14

God hast punished us less than our iniquities deserve.
Ezra 9:13
See also Job 11:6

Rebuke me not in Thine anger, neither chasten me in Thy hot displeasure.
Ps. 6:1
See also Ps. 38:1

Have mercy upon me, O Lord; for I am weak.
Ps. 6:2

Be merciful unto me, O God: for man would swallow me up.
Ps. 56:1

God be merciful unto us, and bless us; and cause His face to shine upon us.
Ps. 67:1

If Thou, Lord, shouldest mark iniquities, O Lord, who shall stand?
Ps. 130:3

Enter not into judgment with Thy servant: for in Thy sight shall no man living be justified.
Ps. 143:2

O Lord, be gracious unto us; we have waited for Thee.
Isa. 33:2

I am merciful, saith the Lord, and I will not keep anger for ever.
God to Jews
Jer. 3:12

Thy life I will give unto thee for a prey in all places whither thou goest.
Jer. 45:5

Though He cause grief, yet will He have compassion.
Lam. 3:32

Mine eye shall not spare thee, neither will I have pity: but I will recompense thy ways.
E.g., Ezek. 7:4
See also Ezek. 9:5

Not for your sakes do I this, saith the Lord God.
Ezek. 36:32
See also Ezek. 36:22

To the Lord our God belong mercies and forgivenesses, though we have rebelled against Him.
Dan. 9:9

I am God, and not man.
Hos. 11:9

God repented of the evil, that He had said that He would do unto them; and He did it not.
Jonah 3:10

In wrath remember mercy.
Hab. 3:2

I will spare them, as a man spareth his own son that serveth him.
God to Israelites
Mal. 3:17

Blessed are the merciful: for they shall obtain mercy.
Jesus
Matt. 5:7

Be ye therefore merciful, as your Father also is merciful.
Jesus
Luke 6:36

It is not of him that willeth, nor of him that runneth, but of God that showeth mercy.
Rom. 9:16

[See also Compassion, Forgiveness, God's Mercy, Kindness, Suffering]

MERIT

See Justice, Reward, Success, Worthiness.

MESSENGERS

See News, Reliability.

MESSIAH

Art thou He that should come, or do we look for another?
Matt. 11:3
See also Luke 7:19

But whom say ye that I am?
Jesus
Matt. 16:15, Mark 8:29,
Luke 9:20

This is My beloved Son, in whom I am well pleased; hear ye Him.
Matt. 17:5
See also Mark 9:7, Luke 9:35

Blessed is He that cometh in the name of the Lord.
Matt. 21:9, Matt. 23:39
See also Mark 11:9, John 12:13, Ps. 118:26

Take heed that no man deceive you. For many shall come in my name, saying, I am Christ.
Jesus
Matt. 24:4–5
See also Mark 13:6, Luke 21:8

If Thou be the Son of God, come down from the cross.
Passersby to Jesus
Matt. 27:40
See also Mark 15:30

Truly this was the Son of God.
Matt. 27:54
See also Mark 15:39

False Christs and false prophets shall rise, and shall show signs and wonders, to seduce, if it were possible, even the elect.
Jesus
Mark 13:22
See also Matt. 24:24

Mine eyes have seen Thy salvation, Which Thou hast prepared before the face of all people.
Simeon
Luke 2:30–31

The Son of man is not come to destroy men's lives, but to save them.
Jesus
Luke 9:56

He was not that Light, but was sent to bear witness of that Light.
(He: John the Baptist)
John 1:8

I am the voice of one crying in the wilderness, Make straight the way of the Lord.
John the Baptist
John 1:23
See also Matt. 3:3, Mark 1:3, Luke 3:4

He whom God hath sent speaketh the words of God.
John 3:34

I that speak unto thee am He.
Jesus
John 4:26

Whom He hath sent, Him ye believe not.
Jesus
John 5:38

The bread of God is He which cometh down from heaven, and giveth life unto the world.
Jesus
John 6:33

If ye believe not that I am He, ye shall die in your sins.
Jesus
John 8:24

It is He that talketh with thee.
Jesus
John 9:37

This Jesus, whom I preach unto you, is Christ.
Acts 17:3

Who is a liar but he that denieth that Jesus is the Christ?
1 John 2:22

Whosoever believeth that Jesus is the Christ is born of God.
1 John 5:1

[See also False Prophets, Jesus, Second Coming]

MESSIANIC HOPES AND PROPHECIES

The sceptre shall not depart from Judah, nor a lawgiver from between his feet, until Shiloh come.
> Jacob to Judah
> *Gen. 49:10*

Neither shall ye break a bone thereof.
> *Ex. 12:46*

I shall see him, but not now: I shall behold him, but not nigh: there shall come a Star out of Jacob, and a Sceptre shall rise out of Israel.
> *Num. 24:17*

The Lord thy God will raise up unto thee a Prophet from the midst of thee, of thy brethren, like unto me; unto him ye shall hearken.
> Moses
> *Deut. 18:15*
> *See also Deut. 18:18*

Thou wilt not leave my soul in hell; neither wilt Thou suffer Thine Holy One to see corruption.
> *Ps. 16:10*

He keepeth all his bones: not one of them is broken.
> *Ps. 34:20*

I looked for some to take pity, but there was none; and for comforters, but I found none.
> *Ps. 69:20*

In my thirst they gave me vinegar to drink.
> *Ps. 69:21*

A virgin shall conceive, and bear a son, and shall call his name Immanuel.
> *Isa. 7:14*

Unto us a child is born, unto us a son is given.
> *Isa. 9:6*

Of the increase of his government and peace there shall be no end.
> *Isa. 9:7*

There shall come forth a rod out of the stem of Jesse, and a Branch shall grow out of his roots.
> *Isa. 11:1*

The spirit of the Lord shall rest upon him, the spirit of wisdom and understanding, the spirit of counsel and might, the spirit of knowledge and of the fear of the Lord.
> *Isa. 11:2*

He shall not judge after the sight of his eyes, neither reprove after the hearing of his ears.
> *Isa. 11:3*

With righteousness shall he judge the poor.
> *Isa. 11:4*

Prepare ye the way of the Lord, make straight in the desert a highway for our God.
> *Isa. 40:3*
> *See also, e.g., Matt. 3:3*

He shall not fail nor be discouraged, till he have set judgment in the earth.
> *Isa. 42:4*

I will also give thee for a light to the Gentiles.
> *Isa. 49:6*

He is despised and rejected of men; a man of sorrows, and acquainted with grief.
> *Isa. 53:3*

He was despised, and we esteemed him not.
> *Isa. 53:3*

He hath borne our griefs, and carried our sorrows: yet we did esteem him stricken, smitten of God, and afflicted.
> *Isa. 53:4*

He was wounded for our transgressions, he was bruised for our iniquities.
> *Isa. 53:5*

The Lord hath laid on him the iniquity of us all.
> *Isa. 53:6*

He was oppressed, and he was afflicted, yet he opened not his mouth.
> *Isa. 53:7*

He bare the sin of many, and made intercession for the transgressors.
> *Isa. 53:12*

I will raise unto David a righteous Branch, and a King shall reign and prosper.
> *Jer. 23:5*

Behold, thy King cometh unto thee: he is

just, and having salvation; lowly, and riding upon an ass.
Zech. 9:9

I will send My messenger, and he shall prepare the way before Me.
Mal. 3:1

Who may abide the day of his coming? and who shall stand when he appeareth?
Mal. 3:2

Behold, I will send you Elijah the prophet before the coming of the great and dreadful day of the Lord.
Mal. 4:5

I am not come to destroy, but to fulfil.
Jesus
Matt. 5:17

This is he, of whom it is written, Behold, I send my messenger before Thy face, which shall prepare Thy way before Thee.
Jesus (he: John the Baptist)
Matt. 11:10, Luke 7:27

All this was done, that the scriptures of the prophets might be fulfilled.
Jesus
Matt. 26:56

Every valley shall be filled, and every mountain and hill shall be brought low.
Luke 3:5
See also Isa. 40:5

This day is this scripture fulfilled in your ears.
Jesus
Luke 4:21

We have found Him, of whom Moses in the law, and the prophets, did write.
John 1:45

Search the scriptures.
Jesus
John 5:39

Had ye believed Moses, ye would have believed me: for he wrote of me.
Jesus
John 5:46

Of a truth this is the Prophet.
John 7:40

These things were done, that the scripture should be fulfilled.
John 19:36

Of whom speaketh the prophet this? of himself, or of some other man?
Acts 8:34

They have fulfilled them in condemning Him.
(them: Scripture)
Acts 13:27

The promise which was made unto the fathers, God hath fulfilled the same unto us their children.
Acts 13:32–33

[*See also* Jesus, Messiah]

MINISTRY

Serve Him in sincerity and in truth.
Josh. 24:14

Blessed be he that cometh in the name of the Lord.
Ps. 118:26
See also, e.g., Matt. 21:9

Here am I; send me.
Isaiah to God
Isa. 6:8

Cursed be he that doeth the work of the Lord deceitfully.
Jer. 48:10

The harvest truly is plenteous, but the labourers are few.
Jesus
Matt. 9:37
See also Luke 10:2

Freely ye have received, freely give.
Jesus
Matt. 10:8

Feed my lambs.
Jesus
John 21:15

Feed my sheep.
Jesus
John 21:16, 17

It is not reason that we should leave the word of God, and serve tables.
Acts 6:2

Serving the Lord with all humility of mind, and with many tears.
Acts 20:19

Feed the church of God, which He hath purchased with His own blood.
    Paul
    Acts 20:28

We are labourers together with God.
    1 Cor. 3:9

We are fools for Christ's sake.
    1 Cor. 4:10

Being reviled, we bless; being persecuted, we suffer it.
    1 Cor. 4:12

Are not ye my work in the Lord?
    1 Cor. 9:1

Though I be free from all men, yet have I made myself servant unto all.
    1 Cor. 9:19

I am made all things to all men, that I might by all means save some.
    1 Cor. 9:22

Let all things be done decently and in order.
    1 Cor. 14:40

Be ye stedfast, unmoveable, always abounding in the work of the Lord.
    1 Cor. 15:58

We are ambassadors for Christ.
    2 Cor. 5:20

As we have therefore opportunity, let us do good unto all men.
    Gal. 6:10

If any man minister, let him do it as of the ability which God giveth.
    1 Pet. 4:11

Feed the flock of God which is among you.
    1 Pet. 5:2

[*See also* Clergy, Disciples, Evangelism, Preaching, Service to God, Underprivileged]

MIRACLES

Behold, the bush burned with fire, and the bush was not consumed.
    Ex. 3:2

The children of Israel walked upon dry land in the midst of the sea; and the waters were a wall unto them on their right hand, and on their left.
    Ex. 14:29

Speak ye unto the rock before their eyes; and it shall give forth his water.
    God to Moses
    Num. 20:8

He smote the rock twice: and the water came out abundantly.
    (He: Moses)
    Num. 20:11

Your eyes have seen what I have done in Egypt.
    Josh. 24:7

Where be all His miracles which our fathers told us of?
    Judg. 6:13

An evil and adulterous generation seeketh after a sign; and there shall no sign be given to it, but the sign of the prophet Jonas.
    Jesus
    Matt. 12:39
    See also Matt. 16:4, Mark 8:12, Luke 11:29

We have here but five loaves, and two fishes.
    His disciples to Jesus
    Matt. 14:17
    See also Luke 9:13

Jesus went unto them, walking on the sea.
    Matt. 14:25
    See also Mark 6:48

In my name shall they cast out devils.
    Jesus
    Mark 16:17

He laid His hands on every one of them, and healed them.
    Luke 4:40

We have seen strange things to day.
    Luke 5:26

The blind see, the lame walk, the lepers are cleansed, the deaf hear, the dead are raised, to the poor the gospel is preached.
    Jesus
    Luke 7:22
    See also Matt. 11:5

No man can do these miracles that Thou doest, except God be with him.
    John 3:2

Go thy way; thy son liveth.
Jesus
John 4:50

How can a man that is a sinner do such miracles?
Pharisees, about Jesus
John 9:16

Whether He be a sinner or no, I know not: one thing I know, that, whereas I was blind, now I see.
John 9:25

Can a devil open the eyes of the blind?
John 10:21

If they should be written every one, I suppose that even the world itself could not contain the books that should be written.
John 21:25

Why marvel ye at this?
Acts 3:12

And he leaped and walked.
Acts 14:10

The gods are come down to us in the likeness of men.
Acts 14:11

[*See also* God's Power, Healing, Wonders]

MISERY

See Anguish.

MISJUDGMENT

Call for Samson, that he may make us sport.
Judg. 16:25

Make us a king to judge us like all the nations.
1 Sam. 8:5

Nay; but we will have a king over us.
1 Sam. 8:19

Surely the bitterness of death is past.
Agag, king of the Amalekites
1 Sam. 15:32

Thou art but a youth, and he a man of war.
Saul to David about Goliath
1 Sam. 17:33

I will give thy flesh unto the fowls of the air, and to the beasts of the field.
Goliath to David
1 Sam. 17:44

The king of Israel is come out to seek a flea, as when one doth hunt a partridge in the mountains.
1 Sam. 26:20

Behold, I have played the fool, and have erred exceedingly.
1 Sam. 26:21

There is nothing among my treasures that I have not showed them.
2 Kings 20:15, Isa. 39:4

But he forsook the counsel which the old men gave him.
2 Chron. 10:8

In his disease he sought not to the Lord, but to the physicians.
2 Chron. 16:12

He hath borne our griefs, and carried our sorrows: yet we did esteem him stricken, smitten of God, and afflicted.
Isa. 53:4

How can a man that is a sinner do such miracles?
Pharisees, about Jesus
John 9:16

[*See also* Rashness]

MISSION

Whom shall I send, and who will go for us? Then said I, Here am I; send me.
God to Isaiah, and response
Isa. 6:8

I will also give thee for a light to the Gentiles.
Isa. 49:6

To proclaim liberty to the captives, and the opening of the prison to them that are bound.
Isa. 61:1

Arise, go to Nineveh.
Jonah 1:2, Jonah 3:2

And ye shall know that the Lord of hosts hath sent me.
Zech. 2:9

Heal the sick, cleanse the lepers, raise the dead, cast out devils.
Jesus
Matt. 10:8

He hath sent me to heal the brokenhearted, to preach deliverance to the captives.
Jesus
Luke 4:18
See also Isa. 61:1

Behold, I send you forth as lambs among wolves.
Jesus
Luke 10:3
See also Matt. 10:16

My meat is to do the will of Him that sent me, and to finish His work.
Jesus
John 4:34

I came down from heaven, not to do mine own will, but the will of Him that sent me.
Jesus
John 6:38

I know Him: for I am from Him, and He hath sent me.
Jesus
John 7:29

But for this cause came I unto this hour.
Jesus
John 12:27

To this end was I born, and for this cause came I into the world, that I should bear witness unto the truth.
Jesus
John 18:37

As my Father hath sent me, even so send I you.
Jesus
John 20:21

Arise, and go into Damascus.
Jesus to Saul
Acts 22:10
See also Acts 9:6

I have appeared unto thee for this purpose, to make thee a minister and a witness.
Jesus to Saul
Acts 26:16

Let us run with patience the race that is set before us.
Heb. 12:1

[*See also* Duty, Goals, Purpose]

MISSIONARIES

See Evangelism.

MOBS

Thou shalt not follow a multitude to do evil.
Ex. 23:2

The multitude of many people, which make a noise like the noise of the seas.
Isa. 17:12

Not this man, but Barabbas.
John 18:40
See also Luke 23:18

They cried out, saying, Crucify Him, crucify Him.
John 19:6, Luke 23:21
See also, e.g., Matt. 27:23, Mark 15:13

Take ye Him, and crucify Him: for I find no fault in Him.
Pilate
John 19:6
See also Luke 23:4

They stoned Stephen.
Acts 7:59

[*See also* Public Opinion]

MOCKERY

Behold, this dreamer cometh.
(dreamer: Joseph)
Gen. 37:19

Thou seest the shadow of the mountains as if they were men.
Judg. 9:36

Go and cry unto the gods which ye have chosen; let them deliver you.
God to Israelites
Judg. 10:14

Call for Samson, that he may make us sport.
Judg. 16:25

Peradventure he sleepeth, and must be awaked.
    Elijah, about Baal
    1 Kings 18:27

Go up, thou bald head; go up, thou bald head.
    2 Kings 2:23

No doubt but ye are the people, and wisdom shall die with you.
    Job to his friends
    Job 12:2

The just upright man is laughed to scorn.
    Job 12:4

Art thou the first man that was born? or wast thou made before the hills?
    Job 15:7

After that I have spoken, mock on.
    Job 21:3

Wherefore should the heathen say, Where is now their God?
    Ps. 115:2
    See also Ps. 79:10

Scorners delight in their scorning, and fools hate knowledge.
    Prov. 1:22

He that is void of wisdom despiseth his neighbour: but a man of understanding holdeth his peace.
    Prov. 11:12

Be ye not mockers.
    Isa. 28:22

Let now the astrologers, the stargazers, the monthly prognosticators, stand up, and save thee from these things.
    Isa. 47:13

Is this the city that men call The perfection of beauty, The joy of the whole earth?
    Lam. 2:15

If Thou be the Son of God, come down from the cross.
    Passersby to Jesus
    Matt. 27:40
    See also Mark 15:30

He saved others; Himself He cannot save.
    Matt. 27:42, Mark 15:31
    See also Luke 23:35

Can there any good thing come out of Nazareth?
    John 1:46

Art thou also of Galilee?
    John 7:52

God is not mocked.
    Gal. 6:7

[*See also* Contempt, Scorn]

MODELS

Surely this great nation is a wise and understanding people.
    Deut. 4:6

There was not among the children of Israel a goodlier person than he.
    (he: Saul)
    1 Sam. 9:2

Like unto him was there no king before him, that turned to the Lord with all his heart.
    (him: Josiah)
    2 Kings 23:25

And the Lord said unto Satan, Hast thou considered my servant Job?
    Job 1:8

There is none like him in the earth, a perfect and an upright man, one that feareth God, and escheweth evil.
    (him: Job)
    Job 1:8, Job 2:3

Mark the perfect man, and behold the upright: for the end of that man is peace.
    Ps. 37:37

Ye are the light of the world. A city that is set on an hill cannot be hid.
    Jesus
    Matt. 5:14

Let your light so shine before men, that they may see your good works.
    Jesus
    Matt. 5:16

It is enough for the disciple that he be as his master, and the servant as his lord.
    Jesus
    Matt. 10:25

Do not ye after their works: for they say, and do not.
    Jesus
    Matt. 23:3

Go, and do thou likewise.
>Jesus
>*Luke 10:37*

He was a burning and a shining light: and ye were willing for a season to rejoice in his light.
>Jesus (He: John the Baptist)
>*John 5:35*

Do as I have done to you.
>Jesus
>*John 13:15*

Be ye followers of me, even as I also am of Christ.
>*1 Cor. 11:1*

Be as I am; for I am as ye are.
>*Gal. 4:12*

Be ye therefore followers of God, as dear children.
>*Eph. 5:1*

Mark them which walk so as ye have us for an ensample.
>*Phil. 3:17*

Ye should follow His steps: Who did no sin.
>*1 Pet. 2:21–22*

[*See also* Leadership]

MODESTY

Few and evil have the days of the years of my life been.
>Jacob to Pharaoh
>*Gen. 47:9*

Seemeth it to you a light thing to be a king's son in law?
>*1 Sam. 18:23*

Let another man praise thee, and not thine own mouth.
>*Prov. 27:2*

When thou doest thine alms, do not sound a trumpet before thee, as the hypocrites do.
>Jesus
>*Matt. 6:2*

Appear not unto men to fast, but unto thy Father.
>Jesus
>*Matt. 6:18*

See that no man know it.
>Jesus to blind men He healed
>*Matt. 9:30*

Thou sayest it.
>Jesus to Pilate
>*Mark 15:2, Luke 23:3*
>*See also Matt. 27:11*

He must increase, but I must decrease.
>John the Baptist
>*John 3:30*

[*See also* Conceit, Humility, Ostentation, Pride, Publicity]

MONARCHY

Make us a king to judge us like all the nations.
>*1 Sam. 8:5*

He will take your fields, and your vineyards, and your oliveyards, even the best of them, and give them to his servants.
>*1 Sam. 8:14*

Nay; but we will have a king over us.
>*1 Sam. 8:19*

Hearken unto their voice, and make them a king.
>God to Samuel
>*1 Sam. 8:22*

Seemeth it to you a light thing to be a king's son in law?
>*1 Sam. 18:23*

I will not put forth mine hand against my lord; for he is the Lord's anointed.
>David to Saul
>*1 Sam. 24:10*

Because the Lord loved Israel for ever, therefore made He thee king.
>Queen of Sheba to Solomon
>*1 Kings 10:9*

I exalted thee out of the dust, and made thee prince over My people Israel.
>*1 Kings 16:2*

Like unto him was there no king before him, that turned to the Lord with all his heart.
>(him: Josiah)
>*2 Kings 23:25*

God save the king.
2 Chron. 23:11

Serve the Lord with fear, and rejoice with trembling.
Ps. 2:11

There is no king saved by the multitude of an host.
Ps. 33:16

It is He that giveth salvation unto kings.
Ps. 144:10

By me kings reign, and princes decree justice.
(me: wisdom)
Prov. 8:15

The wrath of a king is as messengers of death.
Prov. 16:14

The king's wrath is as the roaring of a lion; but his favour is as dew upon the grass.
Prov. 19:12

A wise king scattereth the wicked.
Prov. 20:26

Mercy and truth preserve the king.
Prov. 20:28

Fear thou the Lord and the king: and meddle not with them that are given to change.
Prov. 24:21

The honour of kings is to search out a matter.
Prov. 25:2

The heart of kings is unsearchable.
Prov. 25:3

Take away the wicked from before the king, and his throne shall be established in righteousness.
Prov. 25:5

The king that faithfully judgeth the poor, his throne shall be established for ever.
Prov. 29:14

Many seek the ruler's favour; but every man's judgment cometh from the Lord.
Prov. 29:26

Keep the king's commandment.
Eccl. 8:2

Where the word of a king is, there is power.
Eccl. 8:4

In mercy shall the throne be established: and he shall sit upon it in truth.
Isa. 16:5

We have no king but Caesar.
John 19:15

Fear God. Honour the king.
1 Pet. 2:17

[*See also* Assassination, Government, Leadership, Sovereignty]

MONEY

Money answereth all things.
Eccl. 10:19

Ye cannot serve God and mammon.
Jesus
Matt. 6:24, Luke 16:13

Thy money perish with thee, because thou hast thought that the gift of God may be purchased with money.
Acts 8:20

Filthy lucre.
E.g., 1 Tim. 3:3

The love of money is the root of all evil.
1 Tim. 6:10

[*See also* Borrowing, Materialism, Usury, Wealth]

MONOTHEISM

Hear, O Israel: The Lord our God is one Lord.
Deut. 6:4
See also, e.g., Mark 12:29

Rebel not against the Lord, nor rebel against us, in building you an altar beside the altar of the Lord.
Josh. 22:19

There is none beside Thee.
1 Sam. 2:2

There is none else.
1 Kings 8:60

How long halt ye between two opinions? if the Lord be God, follow Him: but if Baal, then follow him.
Elijah to Israelites
1 Kings 18:21

Thou art the God, even Thou alone.
2 Kings 19:15, Isa. 37:16

Be still, and know that I am God.
Ps. 46:10

I will be exalted among the heathen, I will be exalted in the earth.
Ps. 46:10

Know ye that the Lord He is God.
Ps. 100:3
See also 1 Kings 18:39

And ye shall know that I am the Lord.
E.g., Ezek. 25:5

Thou shalt know no god but Me: for there is no saviour beside Me.
Hos. 13:4

Thou shalt worship the Lord thy God, and Him only shalt thou serve.
Jesus
Matt. 4:10
See also Deut. 6:13

The devils also believe, and tremble.
James 2:19

[*See also* False Gods, God's Uniqueness, Idolatry]

MORALITY

See Decadence, Depravity, Immorality, Righteousness.

MORTALITY

Dust thou art, and unto dust shalt thou return.
Gen. 3:19

We must needs die, and are as water spilt on the ground, which cannot be gathered up again.
2 Sam. 14:14

My days are swifter than a weaver's shuttle, and are spent without hope.
Job 7:6

Our days upon earth are a shadow.
Job 8:9
See also 1 Chron. 29:15

Remember, I beseech Thee, that Thou hast made me as the clay.
Job 10:9

Are not my days few? cease then, and let me alone, that I may take comfort a little.
Job 10:20

Man that is born of a woman is of few days, and full of trouble.
Job 14:1

He cometh forth like a flower, and is cut down.
Job 14:2

What is man, that Thou art mindful of him? and the son of man, that Thou visitest him?
Ps. 8:4
See also Heb. 2:6

None can keep alive his own soul.
Ps. 22:29

Lord, make me to know mine end, and the measure of my days.
Ps. 39:4

Mine age is as nothing before Thee.
Ps. 39:5

Wise men die, likewise the fool and the brutish person perish, and leave their wealth to others.
Ps. 49:10

He remembered that they were but flesh; a wind that passeth away, and cometh not again.
Ps. 78:39

Remember how short my time is: wherefore hast Thou made all men in vain?
Ps. 89:47

What man is he that liveth, and shall not see death?
Ps. 89:48

They are like grass which groweth up. In the morning it flourisheth, and groweth up; in the evening it is cut down, and withereth.
Ps. 90:5–6

My days are like a shadow that declineth; and I am withered like grass.
Ps. 102:11

But Thou, O Lord, shalt endure for ever.
Ps. 102:12
See also, e.g., Ps. 9:7

He knoweth our frame; He remembereth that we are dust.
Ps. 103:14

As for man, his days are as grass: as a flower of the field, so he flourisheth.
>   *Ps. 103:15*

Man is like to vanity: his days are as a shadow that passeth away.
>   *Ps. 144:4*

His breath goeth forth, he returneth to his earth; in that very day his thoughts perish.
>   *Ps. 146:4*

One generation passeth away, and another generation cometh: but the earth abideth for ever.
>   *Eccl. 1:4*

All are of the dust, and all turn to dust again.
>   *Eccl. 3:20*

It is better to go to the house of mourning, than to go to the house of feasting: for that is the end of all men; and the living will lay it to his heart.
>   *Eccl. 7:2*

There is no man that hath power over the spirit to retain the spirit.
>   *Eccl. 8:8*

Thou shalt be a man, and no God, in the hand of him that slayeth thee.
>   *Ezek. 28:9*
>   *See also Ezek. 28:2*

Your fathers, where are they? and the prophets, do they live for ever?
>   *Zech. 1:5*

Which of you by taking thought can add one cubit unto his stature?
>   Jesus
>   *Matt. 6:27*
>   *See also Luke 12:25*

Be not afraid of them that kill the body, and after that have no more that they can do.
>   Jesus
>   *Luke 12:4*
>   *See also Matt. 10:28*

For what is your life? It is even a vapour, that appeareth for a little time, and then vanisheth away.
>   *James 4:14*

All flesh is as grass, and all the glory of man as the flower of grass.
>   *1 Pet. 1:24*
>   *See also Isa. 40:6*

The grass withereth, and the flower thereof falleth away: But the word of the Lord endureth forever.
>   *1 Pet. 1:24–25*
>   *See also Isa. 40:8*

[*See also* Age, Death, Eternal Life, Frailty, Life, Life and Death, Mankind]

MOTHERHOOD

See Birth, Childlessness, Children, Fertility, Jesus (Birth of), Parents.

MOTIVATION

Every way of a man is right in his own eyes: but the Lord pondereth the hearts.
>   *Prov. 21:2*

I do not this for your sakes, O house of Israel, but for Mine holy name's sake, which ye have profaned.
>   *Ezek. 36:22*
>   *See also Ezek. 36:32*

Will a lion roar in the forest, when he hath no prey?
>   *Amos 3:4*

Out of the heart proceed evil thoughts, murders, adulteries, fornications, thefts, false witness, blasphemies.
>   Jesus
>   *Matt. 15:19*
>   *See also Mark 7:21*

Ye ask, and receive not, because ye ask amiss.
>   *James 4:3*

Not for filthy lucre.
>   *1 Pet. 5:2*

[*See also* Attitude, Behavior, Intentions, Self-Interest]

MOURNING

Rend your clothes, and gird you with sackcloth, and mourn.
>   *2 Sam. 3:31*

Now he is dead, wherefore should I fast? can I bring him back again?
> David, about his son
> 2 Sam. 12:23

I rent my garment and my mantle, and plucked off the hair of my head and of my beard.
> Ezra 9:3

A time to weep, and a time to laugh; a time to mourn, and a time to dance.
> Eccl. 3:4

The heart of the wise is in the house of mourning; but the heart of fools is in the house of mirth.
> Eccl. 7:4

On all their heads shall be baldness, and every beard cut off.
> Isa. 15:2

Gird you with sackcloth, lament and howl: for the fierce anger of the Lord is not turned back.
> Jer. 4:8

Gird thee with sackcloth, and wallow thyself in ashes: make thee mourning, as for an only son.
> Jer. 6:26

Blessed are they that mourn: for they shall be comforted.
> Jesus
> Matt. 5:4

We have piped unto you, and ye have not danced; we have mourned unto you, and ye have not lamented.
> Jesus
> Matt. 11:17
> See also Luke 7:32

[See also Anguish, Death, Grief, Lament, Sorrow]

MURDER

Whoso sheddeth man's blood, by man shall his blood be shed.
> Gen. 9:6

Let not our hand be upon him; for he is our brother and our flesh.
> Judah to his brothers
> Gen. 37:27

Thou shalt not kill.
> Sixth Commandment
> Ex. 20:13, Deut. 5:17
> See also, e.g., Matt. 19:18

The murderer shall surely be put to death
> E.g., Num. 35:16
> See also Ex. 21:12, Lev. 24:17

Ye shall take no satisfaction for the life of a murderer, which is guilty of death: but he shall be surely put to death.
> Num. 35:31

The land cannot be cleansed of the blood that is shed therein, but by the blood of him that shed it.
> Num. 35:33

Thine eye shall not pity him.
> Deut. 19:13

Cursed be he that taketh reward to slay an innocent person.
> Deut. 27:25

They shall not deliver the slayer up into his hand; because he smote his neighbour unwittingly, and hated him not beforetime.
> Josh. 20:5

Wherefore then wilt thou sin against innocent blood?
> Jonathan to King Saul
> 1 Sam. 19:5

As a man falleth before wicked men, so fellest thou.
> 2 Sam. 3:34

Thou art a wise man, and knowest what thou oughtest to do unto him.
> 1 Kings 2:9

The land was polluted with blood.
> Ps. 106:38

These six things doth the Lord hate: yea seven are an abomination unto Him: A proud look, a lying tongue, and hands that shed innocent blood, An heart that deviseth wicked imaginations, feet that be swift in running to mischief, A false witness that speaketh lies, and he that soweth discord among brethren.
> Prov. 6:16–19

They hunt every man his brother with a net.
> Mic. 7:2

No murderer hath eternal life abiding in him.
1 John 3:15

[*See also* Assassination, Capital Punishment, Death, Violence]

MUSIC

Praise the Lord with harp: sing unto Him with the psaltery and an instrument of ten strings.
Ps. 33:2

Praise Him with the sound of the trumpet: praise Him with the psaltery and harp.
Ps. 150:3

Praise Him with the timbrel and dance: praise Him with stringed instruments and organs.
Ps. 150:4

Praise Him upon the loud cymbals: praise Him upon the high sounding cymbals.
Ps. 150:5

[*See also* Dance, Song]

MYSTERY

The way of an eagle in the air; the way of a serpent upon a rock; the way of a ship in the midst of the sea; and the way of a man with a maid.
Prov. 30:19

Watchman, what of the night?
Isa. 21:11

There is a God in heaven that revealeth secrets.
Dan. 2:28

Mene, Mene, Tekel, Upharsin.
Dan. 5:25

The wind bloweth where it listeth, and thou hearest the sound thereof, but canst not tell whence it cometh, and whither it goeth.
Jesus
John 3:8

He that was healed wist not who it was.
John 5:13

Who is worthy to open the book, and to loose the seals thereof?
Rev. 5:2

When He had opened the seventh seal, there was silence in heaven about the space of half an hour.
Rev. 8:1

[*See also* Riddles, Secrecy, Wonders]

MYTH

Refuse profane and old wives' fables.
1 Tim. 4:7

NAGGING

Thou dost but hate me, and lovest me not.
Samson's wife
Judg. 14:16

His soul was vexed unto death.
(His: Samson)
Judg. 16:16

If I be shaven, then my strength will go from me.
Judg. 16:17

It is better to dwell in a corner of the housetop, than with a brawling woman in a wide house.
Prov. 21:9
See also Prov. 25:24

It is better to dwell in the wilderness, than with a contentious and an angry woman.
Prov. 21:19

A continual dropping in a very rainy day and a contentious woman are alike.
Prov. 27:15

[*See also* Strife]

NAIVETE

Behold the fire and the wood: but where is the lamb for a burnt offering?
    Isaac to Abraham
    Gen. 22:7

Wherefore have ye beguiled us?
    Josh. 9:22

Who is this uncircumcised Philistine, that he should defy the armies of the living God?
    David, about Goliath
    1 Sam. 17:26

What is my sin before thy father, that he seeketh my life?
    David to Jonathan
    1 Sam. 20:1

There is nothing among my treasures that I have not showed them.
    2 Kings 20:15, Isa. 39:4

Wherefore doeth the Lord our God all these things unto us?
    Jer. 5:19

Ye know not what ye ask.
    Jesus
    Matt. 20:22, Mark 10:38

Sir, Thou hast nothing to draw with, and the well is deep.
    John 4:11

Whither will He go, that we shall not find Him?
    Pharisees about Jesus
    John 7:35

Who art Thou, Lord?
    Saul to Jesus
    Acts 9:5

We henceforth be no more children, tossed to and fro, and carried about with every wind of doctrine, by the sleight of men, and cunning craftiness, whereby they lie in wait to deceive.
    Eph. 4:14

[*See also* Innocence]

NAKEDNESS

They were both naked, the man and his wife, and were not ashamed.
    Gen. 2:25

And the eyes of them both were opened, and they knew that they were naked.
    Gen. 3:7

I was afraid, because I was naked.
    Adam
    Gen. 3:10

For their's is thine own nakedness.
    Lev. 18:10

Naked came I out of my mother's womb, and naked shall I return hither.
    Job 1:21

Thy nakedness shall be uncovered, yea, thy shame shall be seen.
    Isa. 47:3

NAMES

Whatsoever Adam called every living creature, that was the name thereof.
    Gen. 2:19

As his name is, so is he.
    1 Sam. 25:25

That which hath been is named already.
    Eccl. 6:10

[*See also* Reputation]

NATURE

And God made two great lights; the greater light to rule the day, and the lesser light to rule the night.
    Gen. 1:16

Ye shall not pollute the land wherein ye are.
    Num. 35:33

Defile not therefore the land which ye shall inhabit.
    Num. 35:34

The tree of the field is man's life.
    Deut. 20:19

Can the rush grow up without mire? can the flag grow without water?
    Job 8:11

Speak to the earth, and it shall teach thee: and the fishes of the sea shall declare unto thee.
    Job 12:8

Stand still, and consider the wondrous works of God.
Job 37:14

The trees of the Lord are full of sap.
Ps. 104:16

How manifold are Thy works! in wisdom hast Thou made them all.
Ps. 104:24

The earth is full of Thy riches.
Ps. 104:24

He commandeth, and raiseth the stormy wind, which lifteth up the waves thereof.
Ps. 107:25

The works of the Lord are great.
Ps. 111:2

The mountains skipped like rams, and the little hills like lambs.
Ps. 114:4

All are Thy servants.
Ps. 119:91

Let them praise the name of the Lord: for He commanded, and they were created.
Ps. 148:5

The sun also ariseth.
Eccl. 1:5

To every thing there is a season, and a time to every purpose under the heaven.
Eccl. 3:1

A time to be born, and a time to die; a time to plant, and a time to pluck up that which is planted.
Eccl. 3:2

A pleasant thing it is for the eyes to behold the sun.
Eccl. 11:7

For the mountains will I take up a weeping and wailing, and for the habitations of the wilderness a lamentation.
Jer. 9:10

The Lord hath His way in the whirlwind and in the storm, and the clouds are the dust of His feet.
Nah. 1:3

Consider the lilies of the field, how they grow; they toil not, neither do they spin: And yet I say unto you, That even Solomon in all his glory was not arrayed like one of these.
Jesus
Matt. 6:28–29
See also Luke 12:27

The wind bloweth where it listeth, and thou hearest the sound thereof, but canst not tell whence it cometh, and whither it goeth.
Jesus
John 3:8

Hath not My hand made all these things?
Acts 7:50
See also Isa. 66:2

The earth is the Lord's, and the fulness thereof.
1 Cor. 10:26, 28
See also Ps. 24:1

Can the fig tree, my brethren, bear olive berries?
James 3:12

The grass withereth, and the flower thereof falleth away: But the word of the Lord endureth forever.
1 Pet. 1:24–25
See also Isa. 40:8

[*See also* Creation, Cultivation, Earth, Heaven and Earth, Instinct, Night and Day, Oceans, Rain, Seasons]

NEED

Your Father knoweth what things ye have need of, before ye ask Him.
Jesus
Matt. 6:8

They that be whole need not a physician, but they that are sick.
Jesus
Matt. 9:12
See also Mark 2:17, Luke 5:31

Let him that is athirst come. And whosoever will, let him take the water of life freely.
Rev. 22:17

[*See also* Charity, Poverty, Underprivileged]

NEGOTIATION

Wilt Thou also destroy the righteous with the wicked?
>Abraham to God
>*Gen. 18:23*

Peradventure there shall lack five of the fifty righteous: wilt Thou destroy all the city for lack of five?
>*Gen. 18:28*

Our life for your's, if ye utter not this our business.
>*Josh. 2:14*

It is naught, it is naught, saith the buyer: but when he is gone his way, then he boasteth.
>*Prov. 20:14*

Come now, and let us reason together, saith the Lord.
>*Isa. 1:18*

If ye think good, give me my price; and if not, forbear.
>*Zech. 11:12*

[*See also* Compromise]

NEIGHBORS

Thou shalt not covet thy neighbour's house, thou shalt not covet thy neighbour's wife, nor his manservant, nor his maidservant, nor his ox, nor his ass, nor any thing that is thy neighbour's.
>*Ex. 20:17*
>*See also Deut. 5:21*

Thou shalt love thy neighbour as thyself.
>*E.g., Lev. 19:18, Matt. 19:19*

He that is void of wisdom despiseth his neighbour: but a man of understanding holdeth his peace.
>*Prov. 11:12*

Let none of you imagine evil in your hearts against his neighbour.
>*Zech. 8:17*
>*See also Zech. 7:10*

Love worketh no ill to his neighbour.
>*Rom. 13:10*

[*See also* Brotherhood, Fellowship]

NEUTRALITY

Curse ye bitterly the inhabitants thereof; because they came not to the help of the Lord.
>*Judg. 5:23*

He that is not with me is against me.
>Jesus
>*Matt. 12:30, Luke 11:23*

He that is not against us is for us.
>Jesus
>*Luke 9:50*
>*See also Mark 9:40*

I know thy works, that thou art neither cold nor hot: I would thou wert cold or hot.
>Jesus
>*Rev. 3:15*

Because thou art lukewarm, and neither cold nor hot, I will spue thee out of my mouth.
>Jesus
>*Rev. 3:16*

[*See also* Choice, Impartiality]

NEW TESTAMENT

See Gospel, Scripture.

NEWS

It is no good report that I hear.
>*1 Sam. 2:24*

Tell it not in Gath, publish it not in the streets of Askelon.
>*2 Sam. 1:20*

I am sent to thee with heavy tidings.
>*1 Kings 14:6*

He shall hear a rumour, and shall return to his own land.
>(He: Sennacherib)
>*2 Kings 19:7*
>*See also Isa. 37:7*

As cold waters to a thirsty soul, so is good news from a far country.
>*Prov. 25:25*

He that sendeth a message by the hand of a fool cutteth off the feet.
>*Prov. 26:6*

How beautiful upon the mountains are the feet of him that bringeth good tidings, that publisheth peace.
Isa. 52:7
See also Nah. 1:15, Rom. 10:15

Publish, and set up a standard; publish, and conceal not.
Jer. 50:2

I bring you good tidings of great joy.
Luke 2:10

NIGHT

A thick darkness in all the land of Egypt three days.
Ex. 10:22

Desire not the night, when people are cut off in their place.
Job 36:20

Watchman, what of the night?
Isa. 21:11

I clothe the heavens with blackness, and I make sackcloth their covering.
Isa. 50:3

They that sleep sleep in the night; and they that be drunken are drunken in the night.
1 Thess. 5:7

NIGHT AND DAY

And God called the light Day, and the darkness He called Night. And the evening and the morning were the first day.
Gen. 1:5

The day is Thine, the night also is Thine: Thou hast prepared the light and the sun.
Ps. 74:16

The morning cometh, and also the night.
Isa. 21:12

[*See also* Light and Darkness, Nature]

NOISE

The multitude of many people, which make a noise like the noise of the seas.
Isa. 17:12

A rushing like the rushing of mighty waters!
Isa. 17:12

The suburbs shall shake at the sound of the cry of thy pilots.
Ezek. 27:28

NOVELTY

See Innovation.

OATHS

Swear unto me by the Lord.
Josh. 2:12

As the Lord thy God liveth.
1 Kings 18:10

So let the gods do to me, and more.
Jezebel to Elijah
1 Kings 19:2
See also 1 Sam. 14:44

Thus saith the Lord God; As I live.
E.g., Ezek. 33:27

Swear not at all; neither by heaven; for it is God's throne: Nor by the earth; for it is His footstool: neither by Jerusalem; for it is the city of the great King.
Jesus
Matt. 5:34–35

Neither shalt thou swear by thy head, because thou canst not make one hair white or black.
Jesus
Matt. 5:36

He that shall swear by heaven, sweareth by the throne of God, and by Him that sitteth thereon.
Jesus
Matt. 23:22

Swear not, neither by heaven, neither by the earth, neither by any other oath: but let your yea be yea; and your nay, nay.
James 5:12

[*See also* Profanity, Promises]

OBEDIENCE

Of every tree of the garden thou mayest freely eat: But of the tree of the knowledge of good and evil, thou shalt not eat.
Gen. 2:16–17

Walk before Me, and be thou perfect.
God to Abram
Gen. 17:1

In thy seed shall all the nations of the earth be blessed; because thou hast obeyed My voice.
God to Abraham
Gen. 22:18

Upon me be thy curse, my son: only obey my voice.
Rebekah to Jacob
Gen. 27:13

If ye will obey My voice indeed, and keep My covenant, then ye shall be a peculiar treasure unto Me above all people: for all the earth is Mine.
Ex. 19:5

All that the Lord hath spoken we will do.
Ex. 19:8
See also Ex. 24:3

Keep My statutes, and do them: I am the Lord which sanctify you.
Lev. 20:8

If ye walk in My statutes, and keep My commandments, and do them; Then I will give you rain in due season, and the land shall yield her increase, and the trees of the field shall yield their fruit.
Lev. 26:3–4

If Balak would give me his house full of silver and gold, I cannot go beyond the word of the Lord my God, to do less or more.
Num. 22:18
See also Num. 24:13

The word that God putteth in my mouth, that shall I speak.
Num. 22:38

Must I not take heed to speak that which the Lord hath put in my mouth?
Num. 23:12

All that the Lord speaketh, that I must do.
Num. 23:26

Take heed to thyself, and keep thy soul diligently, lest thou forget the things which thine eyes have seen.
Deut. 4:9

O that there were such an heart in them, that they would fear Me, and keep all My commandments always.
Deut. 5:29

Ye shall not turn aside to the right hand or to the left.
Deut. 5:32
See also Josh. 23:6

Thou shalt keep the commandments of the Lord thy God, to walk in His ways, and to fear Him.
Deut. 8:6

Serve the Lord thy God with all thy heart and with all thy soul.
Deut. 10:12
See also, e.g., Josh. 22:5

Circumcise therefore the foreskin of your heart, and be no more stiffnecked.
Deut. 10:16

Serve Him with all your heart and with all your soul.
Deut. 11:13

Behold, I set before you this day a blessing and a curse; A blessing, if ye obey the commandments of the Lord your God, which I command you this day: And a curse, if ye will not obey.
Deut. 11:26–28

What thing soever I command you, observe to do it: thou shalt not add thereto, nor diminish from it.
Deut. 12:32

The Lord shall make thee the head, and not the tail; and thou shalt be above only, and thou shalt not be beneath.
Deut. 28:13

This book of the law shall not depart out of thy mouth.
Josh. 1:8

All that thou commandest us we will do, and whithersoever thou sendest us, we will go.
Israelites to Joshua
Josh. 1:16

According to the commandment of the Lord shall ye do.
Josh. 8:8

He left nothing undone of all that the Lord commanded Moses.
Josh. 11:15

Walk in all His ways.
E.g., Josh. 22:5
See also Deut. 19:9

Keep His commandments.
E.g., Josh. 22:5

The Lord our God will we serve, and His voice will we obey.
Josh. 24:24

Do to me according to that which hath proceeded out of thy mouth.
Judg. 11:36

All that thou sayest unto me I will do.
Ruth 3:5

Fear the Lord, and serve Him, and obey His voice.
1 Sam. 12:14

Fear the Lord, and serve Him in truth with all your heart.
1 Sam. 12:24

Hearken thou unto the voice of the words of the Lord.
Samuel to Saul
1 Sam. 15:1

Hath the Lord as great delight in burnt offerings and sacrifices, as in obeying the voice of the Lord?
1 Sam. 15:22

To obey is better than sacrifice, and to hearken than the fat of rams.
1 Sam. 15:22

Keep the charge of the Lord thy God, to walk in His ways.
1 Kings 2:3

Let your heart therefore be perfect with the Lord our God.
1 Kings 8:61

Walk before Me, as David thy father walked, in integrity of heart, and in uprightness.
1 Kings 9:4

He did that which was right in the sight of the Lord.
2 Kings 14:3

Keep His commandments and His testimonies and His statutes.
2 Kings 23:3

Set your heart and your soul to seek the Lord your God.
1 Chron. 22:19

Know thou the God of thy father.
1 Chron. 28:9

Walk after the Lord.
2 Chron. 34:31

Let it be done according to the law.
Ezra 10:3

As thou hast said, so must we do.
Ezra 10:12

Lay up His words in thine heart.
Job 22:22

All the paths of the Lord are mercy and truth unto such as keep His covenant.
Ps. 25:10

When Thou saidst, Seek ye My face; my heart said unto Thee, Thy face, Lord, will I seek.
Ps. 27:8

Teach me, O Lord, the way of Thy statutes; and I shall keep it unto the end.
Ps. 119:33

Give me understanding, and I shall keep Thy law.
Ps. 119:34
See also Ps. 119:73

Blessed is every one that feareth the Lord; that walketh in His ways.
Ps. 128:1

Teach me to do Thy will.
Ps. 143:10

The way of the Lord is strength to the upright.
Prov. 10:29

Whoso despiseth the word shall be destroyed: but he that feareth the commandment shall be rewarded.
Prov. 13:13

Whoso keepeth the law is a wise son.
Prov. 28:7

He that keepeth the law, happy is he.
Prov. 29:18

Keep the king's commandment.
Eccl. 8:2

Fear God, and keep His commandments: for this is the whole duty of man.
Eccl. 12:13

If ye be willing and obedient, ye shall eat the good of the land.
Isa. 1:19

O that thou hadst hearkened to My commandments! then had thy peace been as a river, and thy righteousness as the waves of the sea.
Isa. 48:18

Obey My voice, and I will be your God, and ye shall be My people.
Jer. 7:23

Amend your ways and your doings, and obey the voice of the Lord your God.
Jer. 26:13

Obey, I beseech thee, the voice of the Lord.
Jer. 38:20

I am the Lord your God; walk in My statutes, and keep My judgments.
Ezek. 20:19

The lion hath roared, who will not fear? the Lord God hath spoken, who can but prophesy?
Amos 3:8

Whosoever heareth these sayings of mine, and doeth them, I will liken him unto a wise man, which built his house upon a rock.
Jesus
Matt. 7:24

Whosoever shall do the will of my Father which is in heaven, the same is my brother, and sister, and mother.
Jesus
Matt. 12:50
See also Mark 3:35

Blessed are they that hear the word of God, and keep it.
Jesus
Luke 11:28

Not my will, but Thine, be done.
Jesus
Luke 22:42
See also Mark 14:36

My meat is to do the will of Him that sent me, and to finish His work.
Jesus
John 4:34

If ye continue in my word, then are ye my disciples indeed.
Jesus
John 8:31

He that is of God heareth God's words.
Jesus
John 8:47

If a man keep my saying, he shall never see death.
Jesus
John 8:51

If ye know these things, happy are ye if ye do them.
Jesus
John 13:17

If ye love me, keep my commandments.
Jesus
John 14:15
See also John 14:23

If ye keep my commandments, ye shall abide in my love.
Jesus
John 15:10

Follow me.
Jesus
John 21:19

Whether it be right in the sight of God to hearken unto you more than unto God, judge ye.
Acts 4:19

We ought to obey God rather than men.
Acts 5:29

Not the hearers of the law are just before God, but the doers of the law shall be justified.
Rom. 2:13

As by one man's disobedience many were made sinners, so by the obedience of one shall many be made righteous.
Rom. 5:19

With the mind I myself serve the law of God; but with the flesh the law of sin.
Rom. 7:25

Let every soul be subject unto the higher powers.
Rom. 13:1

Circumcision is nothing, and uncircumcision is nothing, but the keeping of the commandments of God.
1 Cor. 7:19

Children, obey your parents in the Lord.
Eph. 6:1

Let us walk by the same rule, let us mind the same thing.
Phil. 3:16

Children, obey your parents in all things: for this is well pleasing unto the Lord.
Col. 3:20

Though He were a Son, yet learned He obedience by the things which He suffered.
Heb. 5:8

We put bits in the horses' mouths, that they may obey us.
James 3:3

Submit yourselves to every ordinance of man for the Lord's sake.
1 Pet. 2:13

Servants, be subject to your masters with all fear; not only to the good and gentle.
1 Pet. 2:18
See also *Eph. 6:5*

Whoso keepeth His word, in him verily is the love of God perfected.
(His: Jesus)
1 John 2:5

Whosoever abideth in Him sinneth not.
1 John 3:6

He that keepeth His commandments dwelleth in Him.
1 John 3:24

We love the children of God, when we love God, and keep His commandments.
1 John 5:2

He that hath an ear, let him hear what the Spirit saith unto the churches.
Jesus
E.g., Rev. 2:7

Blessed is he that keepeth the sayings of the prophecy of this book.
Rev. 22:7

Blessed are they that do His command-ments, that they may have right to the tree of life.
Rev. 22:14

[*See also* Acceptance, Authority, Backsliding, Commandments, Disobedience, Law, Rebellion, Reward, Sin]

OBLIGATION

Unto whomsoever much is given, of him shall be much required.
Jesus
Luke 12:48

To whom men have committed much, of him they will ask the more.
Jesus
Luke 12:48

Owe no man any thing, but to love one another.
Rom. 13:8

Though I be free from all men, yet have I made myself servant unto all.
1 Cor. 9:19

[*See also* Borrowing, Duty]

OBSTACLES

The way of the wicked is as darkness: they know not at what they stumble.
Prov. 4:19

I will break in pieces the gates of brass, and cut in sunder the bars of iron.
Isa. 45:2

Prepare the way, take up the stumblingblock out of the way of My people.
Isa. 57:14

I will lay stumblingblocks before this people, and the fathers and the sons together shall fall upon them.
Jer. 6:21

I will hedge up thy way with thorns, and make a wall, that she shall not find her paths.
Hos. 2:6

Every valley shall be filled, and every mountain and hill shall be brought low.
Luke 3:5
See also *Isa. 40:5*

The crooked shall be made straight, and the rough ways shall be made smooth.
Luke 3:5
See also Isa. 40:4

Make straight paths for your feet, lest that which is lame be turned out of the way.
Heb. 12:13

OCEANS

The gathering together of the waters called He Seas.
Gen. 1:10

He maketh the deep to boil like a pot.
Job 41:31

The voice of the Lord is upon the waters.
Ps. 29:3

They that go down to the sea in ships, that do business in great waters; These see the works of the Lord, and His wonders in the deep.
Ps. 107:23–24

All the rivers run into the sea; yet the sea is not full.
Eccl. 1:7

OLD AGE

See Age.

OLD TESTAMENT

See Scripture.

OMENS

Shall the shadow go forward ten degrees, or go back?
2 Kings 20:9

Let the shadow return backward ten degrees.
2 Kings 20:10

He delivereth and rescueth, and He worketh signs and wonders in heaven and in earth.
Dan. 6:27

An evil and adulterous generation seeketh after a sign; and there shall no sign be given to it, but the sign of the prophet Jonas.
Jesus
Matt. 12:39
See also Matt. 16:4, Mark 8:12, Luke 11:29

O ye hypocrites, ye can discern the face of the sky; but can ye not discern the signs of the times?
Jesus
Matt. 16:3
See also Luke 12:56

[*See also* Astrology]

OMNIPOTENCE

See God's Power.

OMNISCIENCE

See God's Knowledge.

OPPORTUNISM

Why are ye come unto me now when ye are in distress?
Jephthah to his stepbrothers
Judg. 11:7

Let us build with you: for we seek your God, as ye do.
Ezra 4:2

Wealth maketh many friends; but the poor is separated from his neighbour.
Prov. 19:4

Every man is a friend to him that giveth gifts.
Prov. 19:6

O generation of vipers, who hath warned you to flee from the wrath to come?
Matt. 3:7, Luke 3:7

Wheresoever the carcase is, there will the eagles be gathered together.
Jesus
Matt. 24:28
See also Luke 17:37

OPPORTUNITY

The Lord thy God hath set the land before thee: go up and possess it.
Deut. 1:21

Seek ye the Lord while He may be found, call ye upon Him while He is near.
Isa. 55:6

I called you, but ye answered not.
God
Jer. 7:13

Seek, and ye shall find.
Jesus
Matt. 7:7, Luke 11:9

Knock, and it shall be opened unto you.
Jesus
Matt. 7:7, Luke 11:9

Many are called, but few are chosen.
Jesus
Matt. 22:14
See also Matt. 20:16

Lift up your eyes, and look on the fields; for they are white already to harvest.
Jesus
John 4:35

I must work the works of Him that sent me, while it is day.
Jesus
John 9:4

The night cometh, when no man can work.
Jesus
John 9:4

I am the door: by me if any man enter in, he shall be saved.
Jesus
John 10:9

This sickness is not unto death, but for the glory of God.
Jesus
John 11:4

Walk while ye have the light, lest darkness come upon you.
Jesus
John 12:35

The time is short.
1 Cor. 7:29

Behold, I have set before thee an open door, and no man can shut it.
Jesus
Rev. 3:8

If any man hear my voice, and open the door, I will come in to him.
Jesus
Rev. 3:20

Thrust in Thy sickle, and reap.
Rev. 14:15

The time is come for Thee to reap; for the harvest of the earth is ripe.
Rev. 14:15

Let him that is athirst come. And whosoever will, let him take the water of life freely.
Rev. 22:17

OPPRESSION

Ye shall no more give the people straw to make brick.
Ex. 5:7

Fulfil your works, your daily tasks, as when there was straw.
Ex. 5:13

My father chastised you with whips, but I will chastise you with scorpions.
2 Chron. 10:11, 14
See also 1 Kings 12:11

Let not the proud oppress me.
Ps. 119:122

Deliver me from the oppression of man.
Ps. 119:134

The Lord looseth the prisoners.
Ps. 146:7

He that oppresseth the poor reproacheth his Maker.
Prov. 14:31

Rob not the poor, because he is poor: neither oppress the afflicted in the gate.
Prov. 22:22

Relieve the oppressed.
Isa. 1:17

He looked for judgment, but behold oppression; for righteousness, but behold a cry.
Isa. 5:7

They shall cry unto the Lord because of the oppressors, and He shall send them a saviour.
Isa. 19:20

Our necks are under persecution: we labour, and have no rest.
Lam. 5:5

I will make thy grave; for thou art vile.
(thy: Nineveh)
Nah. 1:14

The word of God is not bound.
2 Tim. 2:9

[*See also* Burdens, Cruelty, Persecution, Tyranny]

OPTIMISM

See Hope.

ORATORY

See Preaching, Speech.

ORPHANS

See Widows and Orphans.

OSTENTATION

Though thou deckest thee with ornaments of gold, though thou rentest thy face with painting, in vain shalt thou make thyself fair.
Jer. 4:30

Do not your alms before men, to be seen of them: otherwise ye have no reward of your Father which is in heaven.
Jesus
Matt. 6:1

They love to pray standing in the synagogues and in the corners of the streets, that they may be seen of men.
Jesus (they: hypocrites)
Matt. 6:5

All their works they do for to be seen of men.
Jesus
Matt. 23:5

Beware of the scribes, which love to go in long clothing, and love salutations in the marketplaces, And the chief seats in the synagogues, and the uppermost rooms at feasts.
Jesus
Mark 12:38–40
See also Matt. 23:5–6, Luke 20:46–47

[*See also* Boasting, Humility, Modesty]

OUTCAST

The Lord God sent him forth from the garden of Eden, to till the ground from whence he was taken. So He drove out the man.
Gen. 3:23–24

A fugitive and a vagabond shalt thou be in the earth.
Gen. 4:12

And Cain went out from the presence of the Lord, and dwelt in the land of Nod, on the east of Eden.
Gen. 4:16

His hand will be against every man, and every man's hand against him.
(him: Ishmael)
Gen. 16:12

I am a brother to dragons, and a companion to owls.
Job 30:29

I am a worm, and no man; a reproach of men, and despised of the people.
Ps. 22:6

I am become a stranger unto my brethren, and an alien unto my mother's children.
Ps. 69:8

The stone which the builders refused is become the head stone of the corner.
Ps. 118:22
See also, e.g., Matt. 21:42

I am small and despised: yet do not I forget Thy precepts.
Ps. 119:141

He is despised and rejected of men; a man of sorrows, and acquainted with grief.
Isa. 53:3

If any man love not the Lord Jesus Christ, let him be Anathema.
1 Cor. 16:22

He was cast out into the earth, and his angels were cast out with him.
    Rev. 12:9

[*See also* Estrangement, Exile, Rejection]

PAGANISM

See Idolatry.

PAIN

See Anguish, Birth, Healing, Suffering.

PARADISE

The garden of Eden.
    Gen. 3:23

[*See also* Heaven, Kingdom of God]

PARENTS

Shall a child be born unto him that is an hundred years old? and shall Sarah, that is ninety years old, bear?
    Gen. 17:17

I am Joseph; doth my father yet live?
    Gen. 45:3

Honour thy father and thy mother.
    Fifth Commandment
    Ex. 20:12
    See also, e.g., Matt. 19:19

He that smiteth his father, or his mother, shall be surely put to death.
    Ex. 21:15

He that curseth his father, or his mother, shall surely be put to death.
    Ex. 21:17
    See also, e.g., Lev. 20:9, Matt. 15:4

Ye shall fear every man his mother, and his father.
    Lev. 19:3

Honour thy father and thy mother, as the

Lord thy God hath commanded thee; that thy days may be prolonged.
    Deut. 5:16
    See also Ex. 20:12, Eph. 6:2–3

Would God I had died for thee, O Absalom, my son, my son!
    2 Sam. 18:33

Ask on, my mother: for I will not say thee nay.
    1 Kings 2:20

O my Lord, give her the living child, and in no wise slay it.
    1 Kings 3:26

When my father and my mother forsake me, then the Lord will take me up.
    Ps. 27:10

Receive my sayings; and the years of thy life shall be many.
    (thy: children)
    Prov. 4:10

Attend to my words; incline thine ear unto my sayings.
    (thine: children)
    Prov. 4:20

A wise son maketh a glad father: but a foolish man despiseth his mother.
    Prov. 15:20

He that begetteth a fool doeth it to his sorrow.
    Prov. 17:21

Hearken unto thy father that begat thee, and despise not thy mother when she is old.
    Prov. 23:22

Her children arise up, and call her blessed.
    Prov. 31:28

Can a woman forget her sucking child, that she should not have compassion on the son of her womb?
    Isa. 49:15

They may forget, yet will I not forget thee.
    God, about parents
    Isa. 49:15

A son honoureth his father, and a servant his master: if then I be a father, where is Mine honour?
    Mal. 1:6

What man is there of you, whom if his son ask bread, will he give him a stone?
Jesus
Matt. 7:9
See also Luke 11:11

Call no man your father upon the earth: for one is your Father, which is in heaven.
Jesus
Matt. 23:9

The children ought not to lay up for the parents, but the parents for the children.
2 Cor. 12:14

Children, obey your parents in all things: for this is well pleasing unto the Lord.
Col. 3:20

[*See also* Age, Children, Family, Marriage]

PASSION

See Carnality, Desire, Love, Lust.

PASSWORD

Say now Shibboleth.
Judg. 12:6

PATIENCE

How long shall I bear with this evil congregation, which murmur against Me?
Num. 14:27

Their foot shall slide in due time.
Deut. 32:35

Let not Thine anger be hot against me, and I will speak but this once.
Judg. 6:39

Would ye tarry for them till they were grown?
Ruth 1:13

His day shall come to die.
1 Sam. 26:10

After that I have spoken, mock on.
Job 21:3

I gave ear to your reasons, whilst ye searched out what to say.
Job 32:11

Wait on the Lord.
Ps. 27:14

Our soul waiteth for the Lord: He is our help and our shield.
Ps. 33:20

I wait for the Lord, my soul doth wait.
Ps. 130:5

My soul waiteth for the Lord more than they that watch for the morning.
Ps. 130:6

He that is slow to wrath is of great understanding.
Prov. 14:29

A soft answer turneth away wrath.
Prov. 15:1

He that is slow to anger is better than the mighty.
Prov. 16:32

The patient in spirit is better than the proud in spirit.
Eccl. 7:8

This is our God; we have waited for Him, and He will save us: this is the Lord.
Isa. 25:9

Blessed are all they that wait for Him.
Isa. 30:18

Shall a nation be born at once?
Isa. 66:8

It is good that a man should both hope and quietly wait for the salvation of the Lord.
Lam. 3:26

It is good for a man that he bear the yoke in his youth.
Lam. 3:27

Blessed is he that waiteth.
Dan. 12:12

Though it tarry, wait for it; because it will surely come.
Hab. 2:3
See also Heb. 10:37

Wait ye upon Me, saith the Lord, until the day that I rise up to the prey.
Zeph. 3:8

The end is not yet.
Jesus
Matt. 24:6
See also Mark 13:7

If he trespass against thee seven times in a day, and seven times in a day turn again to

thee, saying, I repent; thou shalt forgive him.
> Jesus
> *Luke 17:4*

Wait for the promise of the Father.
> Jesus
> *Acts 1:4*

Forty years suffered He their manners in the wilderness.
> *Acts 13:18*

Tribulation worketh patience; And patience, experience; and experience, hope.
> *Rom. 5:3–4*

Let us not be weary in well doing: for in due season we shall reap.
> *Gal. 6:9*
> *See also 2 Thess. 3:13*

Be patient toward all men.
> *1 Thess. 5:14*

The servant of the Lord must not strive.
> *2 Tim. 2:24*

Be gentle unto all men, apt to teach, patient.
> *2 Tim. 2:24*

Reprove, rebuke, exhort with all longsuffering and doctrine.
> *2 Tim. 4:2*

Ye have need of patience, that, after ye have done the will of God, ye might receive the promise.
> *Heb. 10:36*

Let every man be swift to hear, slow to speak, slow to wrath.
> *James 1:19*

The coming of the Lord draweth nigh.
> *James 5:8*

The patience of Job.
> *James 5:11*

What glory is it, if, when ye be buffeted for your faults, ye shall take it patiently?
> *1 Pet. 2:20*

If, when ye do well, and suffer for it, ye take it patiently, this is acceptable with God.
> *1 Pet. 2:20*

One day is with the Lord as a thousand years, and a thousand years as one day.
> *2 Pet. 3:8*

The longsuffering of our Lord is salvation.
> *2 Pet. 3:15*

Rest yet for a little season.
> *Rev. 6:11*

The patience of the saints.
> *Rev. 14:12*
> *See also Rev. 13:10*

[*See also* Anger, Exasperation, Fortitude, Impatience, Restraint, Temper]

PEACE

If thou wilt take the left hand, then I will go to the right; or if thou depart to the right hand, then I will go to the left.
> *Gen. 13:9*

Go in peace.
> *E.g., Ex. 4:18*

And the land rested from war.
> *Josh. 11:23*

How long shall it be then, ere thou bid the people return from following their brethren?
> *2 Sam. 2:26*

Is it not good, if peace and truth be in my days?
> *2 Kings 20:19*

Ye shall not go up, nor fight against your brethren.
> *2 Chron. 11:4, 1 Kings 12:24*

He maketh peace in His high places.
> *Job 25:2*

Seek peace, and pursue it.
> *Ps. 34:14*

Behold, how good and how pleasant it is for brethren to dwell together in unity!
> *Ps. 133:1*

To the counsellors of peace is joy.
> *Prov. 12:20*

When a man's ways please the Lord, he maketh even his enemies to be at peace with him.
> *Prov. 16:7*

It is an honour for a man to cease from strife.
> *Prov. 20:3*

They shall beat their swords into plow-

shares, and their spears into pruninghooks: nation shall not lift up sword against nation, neither shall they learn war any more.
Isa. 2:4
See also Mic. 4:3

The wolf also shall dwell with the lamb, and the leopard shall lie down with the kid; and the calf and the young lion and the fatling together.
Isa. 11:6

A little child shall lead them.
Isa. 11:6

The earth shall be full of the knowledge of the Lord, as the waters cover the sea.
Isa. 11:9

How beautiful upon the mountains are the feet of him that bringeth good tidings, that publisheth peace.
Isa. 52:7
See also Nah. 1:15, Rom. 10:15

The wolf and the lamb shall feed together, and the lion shall eat straw like the bullock.
Isa. 65:25

We looked for peace, but no good came; and for a time of health, and behold trouble!
Jer. 8:15

They shall sit every man under his vine and under his fig tree; and none shall make them afraid.
Mic. 4:4

Love the truth and peace.
Zech. 8:19

Blessed are the peacemakers: for they shall be called the children of God.
Jesus
Matt. 5:9

Agree with thine adversary quickly, whiles thou art in the way with him.
Jesus
Matt. 5:25

Have salt in yourselves, and have peace one with another.
Jesus
Mark 9:50

On earth peace, good will toward men.
Luke 2:14

Suppose ye that I am come to give peace on earth? I tell you, Nay; but rather division.
Jesus
Luke 12:51
See also Matt. 10:34

Peace in heaven, and glory in the highest.
Luke 19:38

Peace I leave with you, my peace I give unto you.
Jesus
John 14:27

We have peace with God through our Lord Jesus Christ.
Rom. 5:1

God is not the author of confusion, but of peace.
1 Cor. 14:33

He is our peace.
(He: Jesus)
Eph. 2:14

Let the peace of God rule in your hearts.
Col. 3:15

Be at peace among yourselves.
1 Thess. 5:13

The fruit of righteousness is sown in peace of them that make peace.
James 3:18

[*See also* Brotherhood, Serenity, War, War and Peace]

PEDANTRY

Ye blind guides, which strain at a gnat, and swallow a camel.
Jesus
Matt. 23:24

The letter killeth, but the spirit giveth life.
2 Cor. 3:6

If righteousness come by the law, then Christ is dead in vain.
Gal. 2:21

Strive not about words to no profit.
2 Tim. 2:14

PERFECTION

He is the Rock, His work is perfect.
Deut. 32:4

And the Lord said unto Satan, Hast thou considered my servant Job?
Job 1:8

There is none like him in the earth, a perfect and an upright man, one that feareth God, and escheweth evil.
(him: Job)
Job 1:8, Job 2:3

As for God, His way is perfect.
Ps. 18:30, 2 Sam. 22:31

Every man at his best state is altogether vanity.
Ps. 39:5

That which is crooked cannot be made straight: and that which is wanting cannot be numbered.
Eccl. 1:15

There is not a just man upon earth, that doeth good, and sinneth not.
Eccl. 7:20

I am the rose of Sharon, and the lily of the valleys.
Song 2:1

Be ye therefore perfect, even as your Father which is in heaven is perfect.
Jesus
Matt. 5:48

If thou wilt be perfect, go and sell that thou hast, and give to the poor, and thou shalt have treasure in heaven: and come and follow me.
Jesus
Matt. 19:21
See also Mark 10:21, Luke 18:22

The crooked shall be made straight, and the rough ways shall be made smooth.
Luke 3:5
See also Isa. 40:4

Every good gift and every perfect gift is from above.
James 1:17

Whosoever shall keep the whole law, and yet offend in one point, he is guilty of all.
James 2:10

I have not found thy works perfect before God.
Jesus
Rev. 3:2

[*See also* Models]

PERJURY

Thou shalt not bear false witness.
Ninth Commandment
Ex. 20:16
See also, e.g., Deut. 5:20, Matt. 19:18

Do unto him, as he had thought to have done unto his brother.
Deut. 19:19

A false witness will utter lies.
Prov. 14:5

Every one that sweareth shall be cut off.
Zech. 5:3

Love no false oath.
Zech. 8:17

[*See also* Dishonesty, Honesty, Lies]

PERMANENCE

It is a covenant of salt for ever before the Lord.
Num. 18:19

Oh that my words were now written! oh that they were printed in a book!
Job 19:23

The counsel of the Lord standeth for ever.
Ps. 33:11

Riches are not for ever.
Prov. 27:24

One generation passeth away, and another generation cometh: but the earth abideth for ever.
Eccl. 1:4

That which now is in the days to come shall all be forgotten.
Eccl. 2:16

Whatsoever God doeth, it shall be for ever.
Eccl. 3:14

Write it before them in a table, and note it in a book, that it may be for the time to come for ever and ever.
Isa. 30:8

Written with a pen of iron, and with the

point of a diamond: it is graven upon the table of their heart.
Jer. 17:1

I am the Lord, I change not.
Mal. 3:6

If this counsel or this work be of men, it will come to nought: But if it be of God, ye cannot overthrow it.
Acts 5:38–39

If it be of God, ye cannot overthrow it.
Acts 5:39

Not in tables of stone, but in fleshy tables of the heart.
2 Cor. 3:3

The foundation of God standeth sure.
2 Tim. 2:19

Jesus Christ the same yesterday, and to day, and for ever.
Heb. 13:8

The grass withereth, and the flower thereof falleth away: But the word of the Lord endureth forever.
1 Pet. 1:24–25
See also Isa. 40:8

The world passeth away, and the lust thereof: but he that doeth the will of God abideth for ever.
1 John 2:17

[*See also* Christ Eternal, Ephemera, Eternal Life, Eternity, Mortality]

PERSECUTION

I have not sinned against thee; yet thou huntest my soul to take it.
David to Saul
1 Sam. 24:11

I, even I only, am left; and they seek my life, to take it away.
1 Kings 19:10, 14
See also Rom. 11:3

Think not with thyself that thou shalt escape in the king's house, more than all the Jews.
Mordecai to Esther
Esther 4:13

How can I endure to see the evil that shall come unto my people?
Esther 8:6

Behold, He findeth occasions against me, He counteth me for His enemy.
Job 33:10

The wicked in his pride doth persecute the poor.
Ps. 10:2

The assembly of the wicked have inclosed me: they pierced my hands and my feet.
Ps. 22:16

Deliver me not over unto the will of mine enemies: for false witnesses are risen up against me.
Ps. 27:12

The wicked watcheth the righteous, and seeketh to slay him.
Ps. 37:32

The plowers plowed upon my back: they made long their furrows.
Ps. 129:3

I hid not my face from shame and spitting.
Isa. 50:6

They hunt our steps, that we cannot go in our streets: our end is near, our days are fulfilled.
Lam. 4:18

Our persecutors are swifter than the eagles of the heaven: they pursued us upon the mountains, they laid wait for us in the wilderness.
Lam. 4:19

Blessed are they which are persecuted for righteousness' sake: for their's is the kingdom of heaven.
Jesus
Matt. 5:10

Blessed are ye, when men shall revile you, and persecute you, and shall say all manner of evil against you falsely, for my sake.
Jesus
Matt. 5:11

Pray for them which despitefully use you, and persecute you.
Jesus
Matt. 5:44
See also Luke 6:28

Ye shall be hated of all men for my name's

sake: but he that endureth to the end shall be saved.
>Jesus
Matt. 10:22
See also Mark 13:13, Luke 21:17

Fear not them which kill the body, but are not able to kill the soul.
>Jesus
Matt. 10:28
See also Luke 12:4

O Jerusalem, Jerusalem, thou that killest the prophets, and stonest them which are sent unto thee.
>Jesus
Matt. 23:37
See also Luke 13:34

They shall mock Him, and shall scourge Him, and shall spit upon Him, and shall kill Him: and the third day He shall rise again.
>Jesus
Mark 10:34
See also Luke 18:33

In the synagogues ye shall be beaten: and ye shall be brought before rulers and kings for my sake.
>Jesus
Mark 13:9

He that despiseth you despiseth me; and he that despiseth me despiseth Him that sent me.
>Jesus
Luke 10:16

For which of those works do ye stone me?
>Jesus
John 10:32

If we let Him thus alone, all men will believe on Him.
John 11:48

If the world hate you, ye know that it hated me before it hated you.
>Jesus
John 15:18

If they have persecuted me, they will also persecute you.
>Jesus
John 15:20

They know not Him that sent me.
>Jesus
John 15:21

He that hateth me hateth my Father also.
>Jesus
John 15:23

The time cometh, that whosoever killeth you will think that he doeth God service.
>Jesus
John 16:2

He that delivered me unto thee hath the greater sin.
>Jesus
John 19:11

He bearing His cross went forth.
(He: Jesus)
John 19:17

As your fathers did, so do ye.
Acts 7:51

Which of the prophets have not your fathers persecuted?
Acts 7:52

Saul, Saul, why persecutest thou me?
>Jesus
E.g., Acts 9:4

I am Jesus whom thou persecutest.
>Jesus to Saul
Acts 9:5, Acts 26:15

If a spirit or an angel hath spoken to him, let us not fight against God.
>Pharisees, about Paul
Acts 23:9

I stand at Caesar's judgment seat, where I ought to be judged: to the Jews have I done no wrong.
>Paul
Acts 25:10

I stand and am judged for the hope of the promise made of God unto our fathers.
>Paul
Acts 26:6

Many of the saints did I shut up in prison.
>Paul
Acts 26:10

I persecuted them even unto strange cities.
>Paul
Acts 26:11

Bless them which persecute you: bless, and curse not.
Rom. 12:14

Being reviled, we bless; being persecuted, we suffer it.
1 Cor. 4:12

Why stand we in jeopardy every hour?
1 Cor. 15:30

In labours more abundant, in stripes above measure, in prisons more frequent, in deaths oft.
2 Cor. 11:23

Let no man trouble me: for I bear in my body the marks of the Lord Jesus.
Gal. 6:17

I am an ambassador in bonds.
Eph. 6:20

Endure hardness, as a good soldier of Jesus Christ.
2 Tim. 2:3

All that will live godly in Christ Jesus shall suffer persecution.
2 Tim. 3:12

If ye be reproached for the name of Christ, happy are ye.
1 Pet. 4:14

If any man suffer as a Christian, let him not be ashamed.
1 Pet. 4:16

Marvel not, my brethren, if the world hate you.
1 John 3:13

Fear none of those things which thou shalt suffer.
Jesus
Rev. 2:10

Behold, the devil shall cast some of you into prison, that ye may be tried.
Jesus
Rev. 2:10

[*See also* Martyrdom, Suffering]

PERSEVERANCE

O God, strengthen my hands.
Neh. 6:9

The Lord gave Job twice as much as he had before.
Job 42:10

We went through fire and through water.
Ps. 66:12

Harder than flint have I made thy forehead.
Ezek. 3:9

Blessed is he that waiteth.
Dan. 12:12

Ye shall be hated of all men for my name's sake: but he that endureth to the end shall be saved.
Jesus
Matt. 10:22
See also Mark 13:13, Luke 21:17

Tribulation worketh patience; And patience, experience; and experience, hope.
Rom. 5:3–4

Who shall separate us from the love of Christ? shall tribulation, or distress, or persecution, or famine, or nakedness, or peril, or sword?
Rom. 8:35

Let us not be weary in well doing: for in due season we shall reap.
Gal. 6:9
See also 2 Thess. 3:13

Endure hardness, as a good soldier of Jesus Christ.
2 Tim. 2:3

Let us hold fast the profession of our faith without wavering.
Heb. 10:23

Let us run with patience the race that is set before us.
Heb. 12:1

We count them happy which endure.
James 5:11

The patience of Job.
James 5:11

Hope to the end.
1 Pet. 1:13

He that overcometh shall inherit all things.
Rev. 21:7

[*See also* Determination, Diligence, Effort, Fortitude, Strength]

Behold, I am at the point to die: and what profit shall this birthright do to me?
Esau to Jacob
Gen. 25:32

O that they were wise, that they understood this, that they would consider their latter end!
Deut. 32:29

Is not the gleaning of the grapes of Ephraim better than the vintage of Abiezer?
Judg. 8:2

After whom dost thou pursue? after a dead dog, after a flea.
David to Saul
1 Sam. 24:14

How long have I to live, that I should go up with the king unto Jerusalem?
2 Sam. 19:34

Shall we receive good at the hand of God, and shall we not receive evil?
Job 2:10

Our days upon earth are a shadow.
Job 8:9
See also 1 Chron. 29:15

Mine age is as nothing before Thee.
Ps. 39:5

A thousand years in Thy sight are but as yesterday when it is past.
Ps. 90:4

Better is a dinner of herbs where love is, than a stalled ox and hatred therewith.
Prov. 15:17

What hath the wise more than the fool?
Eccl. 6:8

It is better to go to the house of mourning, than to go to the house of feasting: for that is the end of all men; and the living will lay it to his heart.
Eccl. 7:2

In the day of prosperity be joyful, but in the day of adversity consider.
Eccl. 7:14

The nations are as a drop of a bucket, and are counted as the small dust of the balance.
Isa. 40:15

They that be slain with the sword are better than they that be slain with hunger.
Lam. 4:9

If thy right eye offend thee, pluck it out, and cast it from thee: for it is profitable for thee that one of thy members should perish, and not that thy whole body should be cast into hell.
Jesus
Matt. 5:29
See also Matt. 18:9

If a man have an hundred sheep, and one of them be gone astray, doth he not leave the ninety and nine, and goeth into the mountains, and seeketh that which is gone astray?
Jesus
Matt. 18:12
See also Luke 15:4

The last shall be first, and the first last.
Jesus
Matt. 20:16
See also Matt. 19:30, Mark 10:31

If thy foot offend thee, cut it off: it is better for thee to enter halt into life, than having two feet to be cast into hell.
Jesus
Mark 9:45
See also Matt. 18:8

Woe unto you that laugh now! for ye shall mourn and weep.
Jesus
Luke 6:25

Ye shall be sorrowful, but your sorrow shall be turned into joy.
Jesus
John 16:20

Be of good cheer; I have overcome the world.
Jesus
John 16:33

[*See also* Attitude]

PERSUASION

Stand still, that I may reason with you before the Lord.
1 Sam. 12:7

How forcible are right words!
Job 6:25

Produce your cause, saith the Lord; bring forth your strong reasons.
Isa. 41:21

If they hear not Moses and the prophets, neither will they be persuaded, though one rose from the dead.
Jesus
Luke 16:31

Paul, Almost thou persuadest me to be a Christian.
Agrippa
Acts 26:28

Some believed the things which were spoken, and some believed not.
Acts 28:24

Let no man deceive you with vain words.
Eph. 5:6

For love's sake I rather beseech thee.
Philem. 9

[*See also* Eloquence, Proof]

PESSIMISM

See Despair, Hope.

PHILANTHROPY

See Charity, Generosity.

PHYSICAL FITNESS

Bodily exercise profiteth little: but godliness is profitable unto all things.
1 Tim. 4:8

[*See also* Body]

PITY

See Compassion, Mercy.

PLAGUE

The waters that were in the river were turned to blood.
Ex. 7:20

The frogs came up, and covered the land.
Ex. 8:6

All the dust of the land became lice.
Ex. 8:17

This is the finger of God.
Ex. 8:19

There came a grievous swarm of flies into the house of Pharaoh, and into his servants' houses, and into all the land.
Ex. 8:24

All the cattle of Egypt died: but of the cattle of the children of Israel died not one.
Ex. 9:6

A boil breaking forth with blains upon man, and upon beast.
Ex. 9:10

I will stretch out My hand, that I may smite thee and thy people with pestilence.
Ex. 9:15

The hail shall come down upon them, and they shall die.
Ex. 9:19

There was hail, and fire mingled with the hail, very grievous.
Ex. 9:24

And when it was morning, the east wind brought the locusts.
Ex. 10:13

A thick darkness in all the land of Egypt three days.
Ex. 10:22

I will pass through the land of Egypt this night, and will smite all the firstborn in the land of Egypt, both man and beast.
Ex. 12:12

The sword is without, and the pestilence and the famine within.
Ezek. 7:15

Heal the sick, cleanse the lepers.
Jesus
Matt. 10:8

Pour out the vials of the wrath of God upon the earth.
Rev. 16:1

Receive not of her plagues.
(her: Babylon)
Rev. 18:4

Therefore shall her plagues come in one day, death, and mourning, and famine.
(her: Babylon)
Rev. 18:8

If any man shall add unto these things, God shall add unto him the plagues that are written in this book.
Rev. 22:18

[*See also* Healing]

PLANNING

Consider of it, take advice, and speak your minds.
Judg. 19:30

The Lord bringeth the counsel of the heathen to nought.
Ps. 33:10

The counsel of the Lord standeth for ever.
Ps. 33:11

Ponder the path of thy feet.
Prov. 4:26

There is a way which seemeth right unto a man, but the end thereof are the ways of death.
Prov. 14:12, Prov. 16:25

A man's heart deviseth his way: but the Lord directeth his steps.
Prov. 16:9

Where there is no vision, the people perish.
Prov. 29:18

The ants are a people not strong, yet they prepare their meat in the summer.
Prov. 30:25

A time to plant, and a time to pluck up.
Eccl. 3:2

Better is the end of a thing than the beginning thereof.
Eccl. 7:8

Thy counsels of old are faithfulness and truth.
Isa. 25:1

They shall also build houses, but not inhabit them; and they shall plant vineyards, but not drink the wine thereof.
Zeph. 1:13
See also Amos 5:11

A wise man, which built his house upon a rock.
Jesus
Matt. 7:24

A foolish man, which built his house upon the sand.
Jesus
Matt. 7:26

Which of you, intending to build a tower, sitteth not down first, and counteth the cost, whether he have sufficient to finish it?
Jesus
Luke 14:28

Let all things be done decently and in order.
1 Cor. 14:40

[*See also* Building, Cooperation, Readiness, Scheming]

PLEAS

Hast thou not reserved a blessing for me?
Esau to Isaac
Gen. 27:36

Do Thou unto us whatsoever seemeth good unto Thee; deliver us only, we pray Thee, this day.
Judg. 10:15

Hear, O our God; for we are despised.
Neh. 4:4

Are not my days few? cease then, and let me alone, that I may take comfort a little.
Job 10:20

Oh that one would hear me!
Job 31:35

Lord, be Thou my helper.
Ps. 30:10

Hide not Thy face from Thy servant; for I am in trouble.
Ps. 69:17
See also Ps. 102:2

Keep not Thou silence, O God: hold not Thy peace.
Ps. 83:1

They cry unto the Lord in their trouble, and He saveth them out of their distresses.
Ps. 107:19

Help me, O Lord my God: O save me according to Thy mercy.
Ps. 109:26

Do not abhor us, for Thy name's sake, do not disgrace the throne of Thy glory.
Jer. 14:21

Heal me, O Lord, and I shall be healed; save me, and I shall be saved.
Jer. 17:14

Be not a terror unto me: Thou art my hope in the day of evil.
Jer. 17:17

Remember, O Lord, what is come upon us: consider, and behold our reproach.
Lam. 5:1

Men, brethren, and fathers, hear ye my defence.
Paul
Acts 22:1

Maranatha.
1 Cor. 16:22

[See also Prayer]

PLEASURE

Can that which is unsavoury be eaten without salt?
Job 6:6

Is there any taste in the white of an egg?
Job 6:6

Stolen waters are sweet, and bread eaten in secret is pleasant.
Prov. 9:17

He that loveth pleasure shall be a poor man.
Prov. 21:17

He that loveth wine and oil shall not be rich.
Prov. 21:17

I said of laughter, It is mad: and of mirth, What doeth it?
Eccl. 2:2

Every man should eat and drink, and enjoy the good of all his labour, it is the gift of God.
Eccl. 3:13
See also Eccl. 5:18

A man hath no better thing under the sun, than to eat, and to drink, and to be merry.
Eccl. 8:15

Eat thy bread with joy, and drink thy wine with a merry heart.
Eccl. 9:7

Let us eat and drink; for to morrow we shall die.
Isa. 22:13, 1 Cor. 15:32

She that liveth in pleasure is dead while she liveth.
1 Tim. 5:6

Lovers of pleasures more than lovers of God.
2 Tim. 3:4

[See also Happiness, Laughter]

POPULATION

See Covenant, Fertility, Growth.

POSSIBILITY

Is any thing too hard for the Lord?
Gen. 18:14

If Balak would give me his house full of silver and gold, I cannot go beyond the word of the Lord my God, to do less or more.
Num. 22:18
See also Num. 24:13

Shall the shadow go forward ten degrees, or go back?
2 Kings 20:9

Who can make that straight, which He hath made crooked?
Eccl. 7:13

I am the Lord, the God of all flesh: is there any thing too hard for Me?
Jer. 32:27

It is a rare thing that the king requireth.
Dan. 2:11

If ye have faith as a grain of mustard seed, ye shall say unto this mountain, Remove hence to yonder place; and it shall remove.
Jesus
Matt. 17:20

It is easier for a camel to go through the

eye of a needle, than for a rich man to enter into the kingdom of God.
Jesus
Matt. 19:24, Mark 10:25
See also Luke 18:25

With God all things are possible.
Jesus
Matt. 19:26, Mark 10:27
See also Luke 18:27

Ye know not what ye ask.
Jesus
Matt. 20:22, Mark 10:38

If ye shall say unto this mountain, Be thou removed, and be thou cast into the sea; it shall be done.
Jesus
Matt. 21:21
See also Mark 11:23

All things are possible to him that believeth.
Jesus
Mark 9:23

With men it is impossible, but not with God.
Jesus
Mark 10:27
See also Matt. 19:26, Luke 18:27

With God nothing shall be impossible.
Luke 1:37

[*See also* Ability, God's Power, Skepticism]

POSTERITY

I will make thy seed as the dust of the earth: so that if a man can number the dust of the earth, then shall thy seed also be numbered.
God to Abram
Gen. 13:16
See also Gen. 28:14

A nation and a company of nations shall be of thee, and kings shall come out of thy loins.
Gen. 35:11

Who shall declare his generation?
Isa. 53:8

The promise is unto you, and to your children, and to all that are afar off.
Acts 2:39

[*See also* Heritage]

POTENTIAL

A little cloud out of the sea, like a man's hand.
1 Kings 18:44

Other sheep I have, which are not of this fold.
Jesus
John 10:16

A little leaven leaveneth the whole lump.
1 Cor. 5:6, Gal. 5:9

Behold, how great a matter a little fire kindleth!
James 3:5

POVERTY

The poor shall never cease out of the land.
Deut. 15:11

He raiseth up the poor out of the dust, and lifteth up the beggar from the dunghill.
1 Sam. 2:8
See also Ps. 113:7

Naked came I out of my mother's womb, and naked shall I return hither.
Job 1:21

He saveth the poor from the sword, from their mouth, and from the hand of the mighty.
(He: God)
Job 5:15

The poor hath hope.
Job 5:16

The needy shall not always be forgotten: the expectation of the poor shall not perish for ever.
Ps. 9:18

The wicked in his pride doth persecute the poor.
Ps. 10:2

Who is like unto Thee, which deliverest the poor from him that is too strong for him?
Ps. 35:10

A little that a righteous man hath is better than the riches of many wicked.
Ps. 37:16

I am poor and needy; yet the Lord thinketh upon me.
Ps. 40:17

Blessed is he that considereth the poor: the Lord will deliver him in time of trouble.
Ps. 41:1

The Lord heareth the poor, and despiseth not His prisoners.
Ps. 69:33

I am poor and needy: make haste unto me, O God.
Ps. 70:5

Yet a little sleep, a little slumber, a little folding of the hands to sleep: So shall thy poverty come.
Prov. 6:10–11

The destruction of the poor is their poverty.
Prov. 10:15

The poor is hated even of his own neighbour: but the rich hath many friends.
Prov. 14:20

He that oppresseth the poor reproacheth his Maker.
Prov. 14:31

He that honoureth Him hath mercy on the poor.
Prov. 14:31

Better it is to be of an humble spirit with the lowly, than to divide the spoil with the proud.
Prov. 16:19

Whoso mocketh the poor reproacheth his Maker.
Prov. 17:5

He that hath pity upon the poor lendeth unto the Lord; and that which he hath given will He pay him again.
Prov. 19:17

Whoso stoppeth his ears at the cry of the poor, he also shall cry himself, but shall not be heard.
Prov. 21:13

Drowsiness shall clothe a man with rags.
Prov. 23:21

The righteous considereth the cause of the poor: but the wicked regardeth not to know it.
Prov. 29:7

The king that faithfully judgeth the poor, his throne shall be established for ever.
Prov. 29:14

The poor man's wisdom is despised, and his words are not heard.
Eccl. 9:16

Ye have the poor always with you; but me ye have not always.
Jesus
Matt. 26:11
See also Mark 14:7, John 12:8

Having nothing, and yet possessing all things.
2 Cor. 6:10

Remember the poor.
Gal. 2:10

[See also Charity, Underprivileged, Wealth]

POWER

How shall I curse, whom God hath not cursed? or how shall I defy, whom the Lord hath not defied?
Balaam to Balak
Num. 23:8

He will take your fields, and your vineyards, and your oliveyards, even the best of them, and give them to his servants.
(He: a king)
1 Sam. 8:14

Am I God, to kill and to make alive?
2 Kings 5:7

Canst thou bind the sweet influences of Pleiades, or loose the bands of Orion?
God to Job
Job 38:31

Canst thou draw out leviathan with an hook? or his tongue with a cord which thou lettest down?
God to Job
Job 41:1

Power belongeth unto God.
Ps. 62:11

The king's wrath is as the roaring of a lion; but his favour is as dew upon the grass.
Prov. 19:12

Where the word of a king is, there is power.
Eccl. 8:4

He shall open, and none shall shut; and he shall shut, and none shall open.
Isa. 22:22

A little one shall become a thousand, and a small one a strong nation.
Isa. 60:22

What manner of man is this, that even the winds and the sea obey Him!
Matt. 8:27
See also Mark 4:41, Luke 8:25

Whatsoever thou shalt bind on earth shall be bound in heaven.
Jesus to Peter
Matt. 16:19
See also Matt. 18:18

If ye have faith as a grain of mustard seed, ye shall say unto this mountain, Remove hence to yonder place; and it shall remove.
Jesus
Matt. 17:20

If Thou be the Son of God, come down from the cross.
Passersby to Jesus
Matt. 27:40
See also Mark 15:30

Rejoice not, that the spirits are subject unto you; but rather rejoice, because your names are written in heaven.
Jesus
Luke 10:20

Thou couldest have no power at all against me, except it were given thee from above.
Jesus
John 19:11

Hath not the potter power over the clay?
Rom. 9:21

The kingdom of God is not in word, but in power.
1 Cor. 4:20

Of whom a man is overcome, of the same is he brought in bondage.
2 Pet. 2:19

[See also Authority, God's Power, Strength]

PRAISE

Saul hath slain his thousands, and David his ten thousands.
E.g., 1 Sam. 18:7

Because the Lord loved Israel for ever, therefore made He thee king.
Queen of Sheba to Solomon
1 Kings 10:9

A man shall be commended according to his wisdom.
Prov. 12:8

Out of the mouth of babes and sucklings Thou hast perfected praise.
Jesus
Matt. 21:16
See also Ps. 8:2

If I honour myself, my honour is nothing: it is my Father that honoureth me.
Jesus
John 8:54

Hosanna.
John 12:13

They loved the praise of men more than the praise of God.
John 12:43

Nor of men sought we glory, neither of you, nor yet of others.
1 Thess. 2:6

I heard as it were the voice of a great multitude, and as the voice of many waters, and as the voice of mighty thunderings.
Rev. 19:6

[See also Flattery]

PRAISE OF GOD

I will sing unto the Lord, for He hath triumphed gloriously: the horse and his rider hath He thrown into the sea.
Ex. 15:1
See also Ex. 15:21

I will publish the name of the Lord: ascribe ye greatness unto our God.
Deut. 32:3

Give, I pray thee, glory to the Lord God.
Josh. 7:19

Bless ye the Lord.
Judg. 5:9

Speak, ye that ride on white asses, ye that sit in judgment, and walk by the way.
Judg. 5:10

The pillars of the earth are the Lord's, and He hath set the world upon them.
1 Sam. 2:8

Exalted be the God of the rock of my salvation.
2 Sam. 22:47

I will give thanks unto Thee, O Lord, among the heathen, and I will sing praises unto Thy name.
2 Sam. 22:50
See also Ps. 18:49

Blessed be the Lord God of Israel for ever and ever.
1 Chron. 16:36

Praise the Lord; for His mercy endureth for ever.
E.g., 2 Chron. 20:21

Stand up and bless the Lord your God for ever and ever.
Neh. 9:5

Blessed be Thy glorious name, which is exalted above all blessing and praise.
Neh. 9:5

In death there is no remembrance of Thee: in the grave who shall give Thee thanks?
Ps. 6:5

Give unto the Lord, O ye mighty, give unto the Lord glory and strength.
Ps. 29:1

Many, O Lord my God, are Thy wonderful works.
Ps. 40:5

I will be exalted among the heathen, I will be exalted in the earth.
Ps. 46:10

God is the King of all the earth: sing ye praises with understanding.
Ps. 47:7

O Lord, open Thou my lips; and my mouth shall show forth Thy praise.
Ps. 51:15

Blessed be God.
E.g., Ps. 68:35

I will praise the name of God with a song, and will magnify Him with thanksgiving.
Ps. 69:30

Let the heaven and earth praise Him, the seas, and every thing that moveth therein.
Ps. 69:34

Shall Thy lovingkindness be declared in the grave? or Thy faithfulness in destruction?
Ps. 88:11

Give unto the Lord the glory due unto His name.
Ps. 96:8, 1 Chron. 16:29

Make a joyful noise unto the Lord.
Ps. 100:1

All that is within me, bless His holy name.
Ps. 103:1

Praise ye the Lord.
E.g., Ps. 104:35

Make known His deeds among the people.
Ps. 105:1, 1 Chron. 16:8

Oh that men would praise the Lord for His goodness, and for His wonderful works to the children of men!
E.g., Ps. 107:8

From the rising of the sun unto the going down of the same the Lord's name is to be praised.
Ps. 113:3

Not unto us, O Lord, not unto us, but unto Thy name give glory.
Ps. 115:1

The dead praise not the Lord.
Ps. 115:17

Praise the Lord, all ye nations: praise Him, all ye people.
Ps. 117:1
See also Rom. 15:11

Praise ye the name of the Lord; praise Him, O ye servants of the Lord.
Ps. 135:1

Ye that fear the Lord, bless the Lord.
Ps. 135:20

I will bless Thy name for ever and ever.
Ps. 145:1

While I live will I praise the Lord.
Ps. 146:2

It is good to sing praises unto our God.
Ps. 147:1

Praise ye the Lord from the heavens: praise Him in the heights.
Ps. 148:1

Let every thing that hath breath praise the Lord.
Ps. 150:6

Praise the Lord, call upon His name, declare His doings among the people, make mention that His name is exalted.
Isa. 12:4

I will exalt Thee, I will praise Thy name; for Thou hast done wonderful things.
Isa. 25:1

Publish ye, praise ye, and say, O Lord, save Thy people.
Jer. 31:7

Glory to God in the highest, and on earth peace, good will toward men.
Luke 2:14

Unto God and our Father be glory for ever.
Phil. 4:20

Who shall not fear Thee, O Lord, and glorify Thy name?
Rev. 15:4

Alleluia: for the Lord God omnipotent reigneth.
Rev. 19:6

Let us be glad and rejoice, and give honour to Him.
Rev. 19:7

[*See also* Gratitude, Song, Testimony]

PRAYER

Remember me, I pray Thee, and strengthen me, I pray Thee, only this once, O God.
Samson
Judg. 16:28

For this child I prayed; and the Lord hath given me my petition.
Hannah
1 Sam 1:27

God forbid that I should sin against the Lord in ceasing to pray for you.
Samuel to Israelites
1 Sam. 12:23

In my distress I called upon the Lord.
2 Sam. 22:7, Ps. 18:6

He did hear my voice out of His temple, and my cry did enter into His ears.
2 Sam. 22:7

Hear Thou in heaven Thy dwelling place: and when Thou hearest, forgive.
1 Kings 8:30
See also, e.g., 1 Kings 8:39

Hearken unto them in all that they call for unto Thee.
1 Kings 8:52

Let these my words, wherewith I have made supplication before the Lord, be nigh unto the Lord our God day and night.
1 Kings 8:59

Lift up thy prayer for the remnant that are left.
2 Kings 19:4
See also Isa. 37:4

Remember now how I have walked before Thee in truth and with a perfect heart.
2 Kings 20:3
See also Isa. 38:3

I have heard thy prayer, I have seen thy tears: behold, I will heal thee.
2 Kings 20:5

Keep me from evil, that it may not grieve me!
1 Chron. 4:10

Turn not away the face of thine anointed.
2 Chron. 6:42

The good Lord pardon every one That prepareth his heart to seek God.
2 Chron. 30:18–19

Let Thine ear now be attentive, and Thine eyes open.
Neh. 1:6

Think upon me, my God, for good.
Neh. 5:19
See also Neh. 12:31

I cry unto Thee, and Thou dost not hear me: I stand up, and Thou regardest me not.
Job 30:20

He heareth the cry of the afflicted.
Job 34:28

The Lord will hear when I call unto Him.
Ps. 4:3

He forgetteth not the cry of the humble.
Ps. 9:12

Why standest Thou afar off, O Lord? why hidest Thou Thyself in times of trouble?
Ps. 10:1

Let the words of my mouth, and the meditation of my heart, be acceptable in Thy sight, O Lord, my strength, and my redeemer.
Ps. 19:14

I cry in the daytime, but Thou hearest not; and in the night season, and am not silent.
Ps. 22:2

Be not far from me; for trouble is near; for there is none to help.
Ps. 22:11

Unto Thee, O Lord, do I lift up my soul.
Ps. 25:1

Blessed be the Lord, because He hath heard the voice of my supplications.
Ps. 28:6

I sought the Lord, and He heard me, and delivered me from all my fears.
Ps. 34:4

The righteous cry, and the Lord heareth.
Ps. 34:17

O Lord: keep not silence: O Lord, be not far from me.
Ps. 35:22

Forsake me not, O Lord: O my God, be not far from me.
Ps. 38:21
See also Ps. 71:12

Deliver me from the deceitful and unjust man.
Ps. 43:1

Call upon Me in the day of trouble: I will deliver thee, and thou shalt glorify Me.
Ps. 50:15

As for me, I will call upon God; and the Lord shall save me.
Ps. 55:16

He shall deliver the needy when he crieth; the poor also, and him that hath no helper.
Ps. 72:12

In the day of my trouble I will call upon Thee.
Ps. 86:7

He shall call upon Me, and I will answer him: I will be with him in trouble.
Ps. 91:15

Hear my prayer, O Lord, and let my cry come unto Thee.
Ps. 102:1

Because He hath inclined His ear unto me, therefore will I call upon Him as long as I live.
Ps. 116:2

In my distress I cried unto the Lord, and He heard me.
Ps. 120:1

Out of the depths have I cried unto Thee, O Lord.
Ps. 130:1

Grant not, O Lord, the desires of the wicked.
Ps. 140:8

The Lord is nigh unto all them that call upon Him, to all that call upon Him in truth.
Ps. 145:18

The sacrifice of the wicked is an abomination to the Lord: but the prayer of the upright is His delight.
Prov. 15:8

The Lord is far from the wicked: but He heareth the prayer of the righteous.
Prov. 15:29

God is in heaven, and thou upon earth: therefore let thy words be few.
Eccl. 5:2

When ye spread forth your hands, I will hide Mine eyes from you.
Isa. 1:15

O Lord, be gracious unto us; we have waited for Thee.
Isa. 33:2

Incline Thine ear, O Lord, and hear; open Thine eyes, O Lord, and see.
Isa. 37:17
See also 2 Kings 19:16

Seek ye the Lord while He may be found, call ye upon Him while He is near.
Isa. 55:6

Your sins have hid His face from you, that He will not hear.
Isa. 59:2

Ye shall seek Me, and find Me, when ye shall search for Me with all your heart.
Jer. 29:13

Call unto Me, and I will answer thee.
Jer. 33:3

Pour out thine heart like water before the face of the Lord.
Lam. 2:19

I called upon Thy name, O Lord, out of the low dungeon.
Lam. 3:55

Thou hast heard my voice: hide not Thine ear.
Lam. 3:56

Though they cry in Mine ears with a loud voice, yet will I not hear them.
Ezek. 8:18

O my God, incline Thine ear, and hear; open Thine eyes, and behold our desolations.
Dan. 9:18

We do not present our supplications before Thee for our righteousnesses, but for Thy great mercies.
Dan. 9:18

O Lord, hear; O Lord, forgive; O Lord, hearken and do.
Dan. 9:19

Defer not, for Thine own sake, O my God: for Thy city and Thy people are called by Thy name.
Dan. 9:19

Whosoever shall call on the name of the Lord shall be delivered.
Joel 2:32

Out of the belly of hell cried I, and Thou heardest my voice.
Jonah 2:2

O Lord, how long shall I cry, and Thou wilt not hear!
Hab. 1:2

As He cried, and they would not hear; so they cried, and I would not hear, saith the Lord of hosts.
Zech. 7:13

They shall call on My name, and I will hear them.
Zech. 13:9

They love to pray standing in the synagogues and in the corners of the streets, that they may be seen of men.
Jesus (they: hypocrites)
Matt. 6:5

When thou prayest, enter into thy closet.
Jesus
Matt. 6:6

Use not vain repetitions, as the heathen do.
Jesus
Matt. 6:7

They think that they shall be heard for their much speaking.
Jesus (they: heathens praying)
Matt. 6:7

Your Father knoweth what things ye have need of, before ye ask Him.
Jesus
Matt. 6:8

Our Father which art in heaven, Hallowed be Thy name. Thy kingdom come. Thy will be done in earth, as it is in heaven.
Jesus
Matt. 6:9–10
See also Luke 11:2

Ask, and it shall be given you; seek, and ye shall find; knock, and it shall be opened unto you.
Jesus
Matt. 7:7, Luke 11:9

Every one that asketh receiveth.
Jesus
Matt. 7:8, Luke 11:10

If ye then, being evil, know how to give good gifts unto your children, how much more shall your Father which is in heaven give good things to them that ask Him?
Jesus
Matt. 7:11
See also Luke 11:13

Where two or three are gathered together

in my name, there am I in the midst of
them.
Jesus
Matt. 18:20

Whatsoever ye shall ask in prayer, believ-
ing, ye shall receive.
Jesus
Matt. 21:22
See also Mark 11:24

When ye stand praying, forgive, if ye have
ought against any: that your Father also
which is in heaven may forgive you your
trespasses.
Jesus
Mark 11:25

Take ye heed, watch and pray: for ye know
not when the time is.
Jesus
Mark 13:33
See also Matt. 13:23

Not what I will, but what Thou wilt.
Jesus
Mark 14:36
See also Matt. 26:39, Luke 22:42

Men ought always to pray.
Luke 18:1

Watch ye therefore, and pray always.
Jesus
Luke 21:36

Whatsoever ye shall ask in my name, that
will I do, that the Father may be glorified in
the Son.
Jesus
John 14:13
See also John 14:14

Whatsoever ye shall ask the Father in my
name, He will give it you.
Jesus
John 16:23

Ask, and ye shall receive, that your joy
may be full.
Jesus
John 16:24

Whosoever shall call on the name of the
Lord shall be saved.
E.g., Acts 2:21

Lord Jesus, receive my spirit.
Stephen
Acts 7:59

The same Lord over all is rich unto all tha
call upon Him.
Rom. 10:12

If I pray in an unknown tongue, my spiri
prayeth, but my understanding is unfruit
ful.
1 Cor. 14:14

By prayer and supplication with thanksgiv
ing let your requests be made known unto
God.
Phil. 4:6

Pray without ceasing.
1 Thess. 5:17

Pray every where, lifting up holy hands
without wrath and doubting.
1 Tim. 2:8

Ask in faith, nothing wavering.
James 1:6

Ye fight and war, yet ye have not, becaus
ye ask not.
James 4:2

Ye ask, and receive not, because ye ask
amiss.
James 4:3

The prayer of faith shall save the sick.
James 5:15

Pray one for another, that ye may b
healed.
James 5:16

The effectual fervent prayer of a righteou
man availeth much.
James 5:16

The eyes of the Lord are over the righ
teous, and His ears are open unto thei
prayers.
1 Pet. 3:12

Whatsoever we ask, we receive of Him
because we keep His commandments.
1 John 3:22

[*See also* Assistance, Pleas, Worship, an
the Appendix at p. 423]

PREACHIN

Hear, O Israel: The Lord our God is on
Lord.
Deut. 6:4
See also, e.g., Mark 12:29

The Lord gave the word: great was the company of those that published it.
Ps. 68:11

Give ye ear, and hear my voice; hearken, and hear my speech.
Isa. 28:23

Blessed are ye that sow beside all waters.
Isa. 32:20

Let the earth hear, and all that is therein; the world, and all things that come forth of it.
Isa. 34:1

Lift up thy voice with strength; lift it up, be not afraid.
Isa. 40:9

Lift up thy voice like a trumpet, and show My people their transgression.
Isa. 58:1

Thou shalt go to all that I shall send thee, and whatsoever I command thee thou shalt speak.
Jer. 1:7

Hear ye the word of the Lord.
Jer. 21:11

O earth, earth, earth, hear the word of the Lord.
Jer. 22:29

Thou shalt say unto them, Thus saith the Lord God.
E.g., Ezek. 2:4

If thou warn the wicked, and he turn not from his wickedness, nor from his wicked way, he shall die in his iniquity; but thou hast delivered thy soul.
Ezek. 3:19, 21

Thus saith the Lord God; He that heareth, let him hear; and he that forbeareth, let him forebear.
Ezek. 3:27

Cause Jerusalem to know her abominations.
Ezek. 16:2

I am not come to call the righteous, but sinners to repentance.
Jesus
Matt. 9:13
See also Mark 2:17, Luke 5:32

Preach ye upon the housetops.
Jesus
Matt. 10:27
See also Luke 12:3

Who hath ears to hear, let him hear.
Jesus
Matt. 13:9, Matt. 13:43
See also, e.g., Matt. 11:15, Mark 4:9, Rev. 13:9

He hath anointed me to preach the gospel to the poor.
Jesus
Luke 4:18
See also Isa. 61:1

He whom God hath sent speaketh the words of God.
John 3:34

Ye that fear God, give audience.
Acts 13:16

From henceforth I will go unto the Gentiles.
Acts 18:6

Be not afraid, but speak, and hold not thy peace: For I am with thee.
Jesus to Paul
Acts 18:9–10

How shall they hear without a preacher?
Rom. 10:14

How beautiful are the feet of them that preach the gospel of peace.
Rom. 10:15

Faith cometh by hearing, and hearing by the word of God.
Rom. 10:17

We preach Christ crucified.
1 Cor. 1:23

Woe is unto me, if I preach not the gospel!
1 Cor. 9:16

We preach not ourselves, but Christ Jesus the Lord.
2 Cor. 4:5

We are ambassadors for Christ.
2 Cor. 5:20

If any man preach any other gospel unto you than that ye have received, let him be accursed.
Gal. 1:9

Give attendance to reading, to exhortation, to doctrine.
1 Tim. 4:13

Fight the good fight of faith.
1 Tim. 6:12

Preach the word.
2 Tim. 4:2

If any man speak, let him speak as the oracles of God.
1 Pet. 4:11

He that hath an ear, let him hear what the Spirit saith unto the churches.
Jesus
E.g., Rev. 2:7

[*See also* Communication, Evangelism, God's Word, Ministry, Speech, Testimony]

PREDICTIONS

See Future, Prophecy.

PREJUDICE

See Brotherhood, Equality.

PREPAREDNESS

See Readiness, Second Coming, Vigilance.

PRIDE

How are the mighty fallen!
E.g., 2 Sam. 1:19

Pride compasseth them about as a chain; violence covereth them as a garment.
(them: the wicked)
Ps. 73:6

When pride cometh, then cometh shame.
Prov. 11:2

Pride goeth before destruction, and an haughty spirit before a fall.
Prov. 16:18

A man's pride shall bring him low.
Prov. 29:23

The patient in spirit is better than the proud in spirit.
Eccl. 7:8

Let him that glorieth glory in this, that he understandeth and knoweth Me, that I am the Lord.
Jer. 9:24
See also, e.g., 1 Cor. 1:31

Be not proud.
Jer. 13:15

Those that walk in pride He is able to abase.
Dan. 4:37

Though thou set thy nest among the stars, thence will I bring thee down, saith the Lord.
Obad. 4

Whosoever shall exalt himself shall be abased; and he that shall humble himself shall be exalted.
Jesus
Matt. 23:12
See also Luke 14:11

If I honour myself, my honour is nothing.
Jesus
John 8:54

God resisteth the proud, and giveth grace to the humble.
1 Pet. 5:5

[*See also* Arrogance, Boasting, Conceit, Confidence, Humility]

PRIESTHOOD

All the firstborn are Mine.
Num. 3:13

The priesthood of the Lord is their inheritance.
Josh. 18:7

I have lent him to the Lord.
Hannah, of her child
1 Sam. 1:28

As long as he liveth he shall be lent to the Lord.
1 Sam. 1:28

They shall go in, for they are holy.
2 Chron. 23:6

I am their inheritance.
Ezek. 44:28

He is the messenger of the Lord of hosts.
Mal. 2:7

PRINCIPLES

PRIORITIES

PRISON

PROCRASTINATION

If we tarry till the morning light, some mischief will come upon us.
2 Kings 7:9

He that observeth the wind shall not sow; and he that regardeth the clouds shall not reap.
Eccl. 11:4

Seek ye the Lord while He may be found, call ye upon Him while He is near.
Isa. 55:6

Exhort one another daily, while it is called To day.
Heb. 3:13

PROFANITY

Put off all these; anger, wrath, malice, blasphemy, filthy communication out of your mouth.
Col. 3:8

PROFIT

Shall I drink the blood of these men that have put their lives in jeopardy?
David
1 Chron. 11:19

Treasures of wickedness profit nothing.
Prov. 10:2

In all labour there is profit.
Prov. 14:23

What hath man of all his labour, and of the vexation of his heart, wherein he hath laboured under the sun?
Eccl. 2:22

What profit hath he that worketh in that wherein he laboureth?
Eccl. 3:9

By thy great wisdom and by thy traffick hast thou increased thy riches.
Ezek. 28:5

Ye have sown much, and bring in little; ye eat, but ye have not enough; ye drink, but ye are not filled.
Hag. 1:6

Godliness is profitable unto all things.
1 Tim. 4:8

PROGRESS

PROMISES

Is the Lord's hand waxed short?
Num. 11:23

Hath He said, and shall He not do it? or hath He spoken, and shall He not make it good?
Num. 23:19

When thou shalt vow a vow unto the Lord thy God, thou shalt not slack to pay it.
Deut. 23:21

If thou shalt forbear to vow, it shall be no sin in thee.
Deut. 23:22

All are come to pass unto you, and not one thing hath failed thereof.
Joshua to Israelites
Josh. 23:14

The Lord be witness between us, if we do not so according to thy words.
Judg. 11:10

I have opened my mouth unto the Lord, and I cannot go back.
Judg. 11:35

When I begin, I will also make an end.
God to Samuel
1 Sam. 3:12

When thou vowest a vow unto God, defer not to pay it.
Eccl. 5:4

Better is it that thou shouldest not vow, than that thou shouldest vow and not pay.
Eccl. 5:5

Shall I bring to the birth, and not cause to bring forth?
Isa. 66:9

I will do it; I will not go back, neither will I spare, neither will I repent.
Ezek. 24:14

Whatsoever thou shalt ask of me, I will give it thee, unto the half of my kingdom.
Herod to his daughter
Mark 6:23

If ye shall ask any thing in my name, I will do it.
Jesus
John 14:14

The Lord is not slack concerning His promise.
2 Pet. 3:9

[*See also* Covenant, Oaths]

PROOF

Hear now, ye rebels; must we fetch you water out of this rock?
Num. 20:10

The God that answereth by fire, let Him be God.
1 Kings 18:24

Hear me, O Lord, hear me, that this people may know that Thou art the Lord God, and that Thou hast turned their heart back again.
1 Kings 18:37

And ye shall know that I am the Lord.
1 Kings 20:28

Thou shalt see it with thine eyes, but shalt not eat thereof.
2 Kings 7:2

I will not ask, neither will I tempt the Lord.
Isa. 7:12

An evil and adulterous generation seeketh after a sign; and there shall no sign be given to it, but the sign of the prophet Jonas.
Jesus
Matt. 12:39
See also Matt. 16:4, Mark 8:12, Luke 11:29

Why doth this generation seek after a sign?
Jesus about Pharisees
Mark 8:12

Physician, heal thyself.
Luke 4:23

If they hear not Moses and the prophets, neither will they be persuaded, though one rose from the dead.
Jesus
Luke 16:31

Search the scriptures.
Jesus
John 5:39

Whether He be a sinner or no, I know not: one thing I know, that, whereas I was blind, now I see.
John 9:25

Though ye believe not me, believe the works.
Jesus
John 10:38

Reach hither thy hand, and thrust it into my side: and be not faithless, but believing.
Jesus
John 20:27

Him God raised up the third day, and showed Him openly; Not to all the people, but unto witnesses chosen before of God.
Acts 10:40–41

God is my witness.
Rom. 1:9

The Jews require a sign, and the Greeks seek after wisdom.
1 Cor. 1:22

Prove all things; hold fast that which is good.
1 Thess. 5:21

Where a testament is, there must also of necessity be the death of the testator.
Heb. 9:16

[See also Doubt, Testimony]

PROPERTY

The land shall not be sold for ever: for the land is Mine; for ye are strangers and sojourners with Me.
Lev. 25:23

Cursed be he that removeth his neighbour's landmark.
Deut. 27:17
See also Deut. 19:14

The world is Mine, and the fulness thereof.
Ps. 50:12
See also Ex. 19:5

Remove not the ancient landmark, which thy fathers have set.
Prov. 22:28
See also Prov. 23:10

[See also Materialism, Wealth]

PROPHECY

Would God that all the Lord's people were prophets, and that the Lord would put His spirit upon them!
Moses to Joshua
Num. 11:29

When a prophet speaketh in the name of the Lord, if the thing follow not, nor come to pass, that is the thing which the Lord hath not spoken.
Deut. 18:22

I hate him; for he doth not prophesy good concerning me, but evil.
1 Kings 22:8

Speak that which is good.
1 Kings 22:13

Hear ye the word of the Lord.
E.g., 2 Kings 7:1

Good is the word of the Lord which thou hast spoken.
2 Kings 20:19, Isa. 39:8

Believe in the Lord your God, so shall ye be established; believe His prophets, so shall ye prosper.
2 Chron. 20:20

I have set thee for a tower and a fortress among My people.
God to Jeremiah
Jer. 6:27

I am the Lord: I will speak, and the word that I shall speak shall come to pass.
Ezek. 12:25

This is the day whereof I have spoken.
Ezek. 39:8

The day of the Lord cometh.
E.g., Joel 2:1

Write the vision, and make it plain.
Hab. 2:2

And ye shall know that the Lord of hosts hath sent me.
Zech. 2:9

The voice of one crying in the wilderness.
Matt. 3:3, Mark 1:3,
Luke 3:4, John 1:23
See also Isa. 40:3

A prophet is not without honour, save in his own country, and in his own house.
Jesus
Matt. 13:57
See also Mark 6:4, Luke 4:24, John 4:44

Behold, I have foretold you all things.
Jesus
Mark 13:23

O fools, and slow of heart to believe all that the prophets have spoken.
Jesus
Luke 24:25

Well spake the Holy Ghost by Esaias the prophet unto our fathers.
Acts 28:25

Greater is he that prophesieth than he that speaketh with tongues.
1 Cor. 14:5

Prophesying serveth not for them that believe not, but for them which believe.
1 Cor. 14:22

Despise not prophesyings.
1 Thess. 5:20

No prophecy of the Scripture is of any private interpretation.
2 Pet. 1:20

Blessed is he that readeth, and they that hear the words of this prophecy.
Rev. 1:3

What thou seest, write in a book, and send it unto the seven churches.
Jesus
Rev. 1:11

Write the things which thou hast seen, and the things which are, and the things which shall be hereafter.
Jesus
Rev. 1:19

If any man have an ear, let him hear.
E.g., Rev. 13:9

The testimony of Jesus is the spirit of prophecy.
Rev. 19:10

Blessed is he that keepeth the sayings of the prophecy of this book.
Rev. 22:7

If any man shall add unto these things, God shall add unto him the plagues that are written in this book.
Rev. 22:18

If any man shall take away from the words of the book of this prophecy, God shall take away his part out of the book of life.
Rev. 22:19

[*See also* False Prophets, Messiah, Messianic Hopes and Prophecies, Scripture]

PROSELYTIZATION

See Evangelism.

PROSPERITY

If ye walk in My statutes, and keep My commandments, and do them; Then I will give you rain in due season, and the land shall yield her increase, and the trees of the field shall yield their fruit.
Lev. 26:3–4

The Lord make His face shine upon thee, and be gracious unto thee.
Num. 6:25

The Lord maketh poor, and maketh rich: He bringeth low, and lifteth up.
1 Sam. 2:7

Give rain upon Thy land, which Thou hast given to Thy people.
1 Kings 8:36

The Lord was with him; and he prospered whithersoever he went forth.
2 Kings 18:7

Acquaint now thyself with Him, and be at peace: thereby good shall come unto thee.
Job 22:21

If they obey and serve Him, they shall spend their days in prosperity, and their years in pleasures.
Job 36:11

The righteous shall flourish like the palm tree: he shall grow like a cedar in Lebanon.
Ps. 92:12

In the day of prosperity be joyful, but in the day of adversity consider.
Eccl. 7:14

The parched ground shall become a pool, and the thirsty land springs of water.
Isa. 35:7

All thy children shall be taught of the Lord; and great shall be the peace of thy children.
Isa. 54:13

In the peace thereof shall ye have peace.
Jer. 29:7

Like as I have brought all this great evil upon this people, so will I bring upon them all the good that I have promised.
Jer. 32:42

The plowman shall overtake the reaper, and the treader of grapes him that soweth seed.
Amos 9:13

The streets of the city shall be full of boys and girls playing in the streets.
Zech. 8:5

Corn shall make the young men cheerful, and new wine the maids.
Zech. 9:17

[*See also* Abundance, Adversity, Reward, Success, Wealth]

PROSTITUTION

Do not prostitute thy daughter, to cause her to be a whore; lest the land fall to whoredom, and the land become full of wickedness.
Lev. 19:29

Thou shalt not bring the hire of a whore, or the price of a dog, into the house of the Lord.
Deut. 23:18

The lips of a strange woman drop as an honeycomb, and her mouth is smoother than oil.
Prov. 5:3

Keep thee from the evil woman, from the flattery of the tongue of a strange woman.
Prov. 6:24

By means of a whorish woman a man is brought to a piece of bread.
Prov. 6:26

Her house is the way to hell.
Prov. 7:27

A whore is a deep ditch; and a strange woman is a narrow pit.
Prov. 23:27

They give gifts to all whores: but thou givest thy gifts to all thy lovers.
Ezek. 16:33

Whoredom and wine and new wine take away the heart.
Hos. 4:11

[*See also* Adultery, Carnality, Fornication, Immorality, Sin]

PROTECTION

See Deliverance, God's Protection, Safety, Vigilance.

PROVOCATION

Now shall I be more blameless than the Philistines, though I do them a displeasure.
Judg. 15:3

They provoked Him to jealousy with their sins.
1 Kings 14:22

Provoke Me not to anger with the works of your hands; and I will do you no hurt.
Jer. 25:6
See also Jer. 44:8

[*See also* God's Anger, Instigation]

PRUDENCE

He that is surety for a stranger shall smart for it.
Prov. 11:15

He that keepeth his mouth keepeth his life: but he that openeth wide his lips shall have destruction.
Prov. 13:3

The wisdom of the prudent is to understand his way.
Prov. 14:8

Whoso keepeth his mouth and his tongue keepeth his soul from troubles.
Prov. 21:23

A prudent man forseeth the evil, and hideth himself: but the simple pass on, and are punished.
Prov. 22:3

A fool uttereth all his mind: but a wise man keepeth it in till afterwards.
Prov. 29:11

A time to keep silence, and a time to speak.
Eccl. 3:7

Be not rash with thy mouth.
Eccl. 5:2

Be not over much wicked, neither be thou foolish: why shouldest thou die before thy time?
Eccl. 7:17

Yielding pacifieth great offences.
Eccl. 10:4

A bird of the air shall carry the voice, and that which hath wings shall tell the matter.
Eccl. 10:20

The prudent shall keep silence in that time; for it is an evil time.
Amos 5:13

Keep the doors of thy mouth from her that lieth in thy bosom.
Mic. 7:5

Let him that thinketh he standeth take heed lest he fall.
1 Cor. 10:12

[*See also* Rashness, Warning]

PUBLIC OPINION

Ye shall not be afraid of the face of man; for the judgment is God's.
Deut. 1:17

Hearken unto their voice, and make them a king.
God to Samuel
1 Sam. 8:22

I feared the people, and obeyed their voice.
Saul to Samuel
1 Sam. 15:24

No doubt but ye are the people, and wisdom shall die with you.
Job to his friends
Job 12:2

Hath he not sent me to the men that sit upon the wall?
Isa. 36:12
See also 2 Kings 18:27

They feared the people, lest they should have been stoned.
(they: apostles)
Acts 5:26

[*See also* Mobs]

PUBLICITY

His fame was noised throughout all the country.
Josh. 6:27

For men to search their own glory is not glory.
Prov. 25:27

A city that is set on an hill cannot be hid.
Jesus
Matt. 5:14

Neither do men light a candle, and put it under a bushel, but on a candlestick.
Jesus
Matt. 5:15
See also Mark 4:21, Luke 11:33

Let your light so shine before men, that they may see your good works.
Jesus
Matt. 5:16

He that doeth truth cometh to the light, that his deeds may be made manifest.
Jesus
John 3:21

PUNISHMENT

Upon thy belly shalt thou go, and dust shalt thou eat all the days of thy life.
God to serpent
Gen. 3:14

In sorrow thou shalt bring forth children.
God to Eve
Gen. 3:16

In the sweat of thy face shalt thou eat bread, till thou return unto the ground.
Gen. 3:19

A fugitive and a vagabond shalt thou be in the earth.
Gen. 4:12

My punishment is greater than I can bear.
Cain to God
Gen. 4:13

He that curseth his father, or his mother, shall surely be put to death.
Ex. 21:17
See also, e.g., Lev. 20:9, Matt. 15:4

Thou shalt give life for life, Eye for eye, tooth for tooth, hand for hand, foot for foot, Burning for burning, wound for wound, stripe for stripe.
Ex. 21:23–25
See also Lev. 24:20, Deut. 19:21

Whosoever hath sinned against Me, him will I blot out of My book.
Ex. 32:33

In the day when I visit I will visit their sin upon them.
God to Moses
Ex. 32:34

His blood shall be upon him.
Lev. 20:9

He that killeth a beast, he shall restore it: and he that killeth a man, he shall be put to death.
Lev. 24:21

Ye shall sow your seed in vain, for your enemies shall eat it.
Lev. 26:16

They that hate you shall reign over you; and ye shall flee when none pursueth you.
Lev. 26:17

If her father had but spit in her face, should she not be ashamed seven days?
Num. 12:14

Surely they shall not see the land which I sware unto their fathers, neither shall any of them that provoked Me.
Num. 14:23

Your carcases shall fall in this wilderness.
God to Israelites
Num. 14:29

Because ye are turned away from the Lord, therefore the Lord will not be with you.
Num. 14:43

Shall one man sin, and wilt Thou be wroth with all the congregation?
Num. 16:22

He made them wander in the wilderness forty years, until all the generation, that had done evil in the sight of the Lord, was consumed.
Num. 32:13

The land cannot be cleansed of the blood that is shed therein, but by the blood of him that shed it.
Num. 35:33

But I must die in this land, I must not go over Jordan.
Moses
Deut. 4:22

The Lord shall scatter you among the nations, and ye shall be left few in number among the heathen.
Moses to Israelites
Deut. 4:27

I the Lord thy God am a jealous God, visiting the iniquity of the fathers upon the children unto the third and fourth generation of them that hate Me, And showing mercy unto thousands of them that love Me and keep My commandments.
Deut. 5:9–10

He will not be slack to him that hateth Him, He will repay him to his face.
Deut. 7:10

Cursed shalt thou be in the city, and cursed shalt thou be in the field.
Deut. 28:16

Thou shalt become an astonishment, a proverb, and a byword, among all nations.
Deut. 28:37
See also 1 Kings 9:7

Ye shall be left few in number, whereas ye were as the stars of heaven for multitude.
Deut. 28:62

Thou shalt fear day and night, and shalt have none assurance of thy life.
Deut. 28:66

The sword without, and terror within, shall destroy both the young man and the virgin, the suckling also with the man of gray hairs.
Deut. 32:25

Their foot shall slide in due time.
Deut. 32:35

The day of their calamity is at hand, and the things that shall come upon them make haste.
Deut. 32:35

Thou shalt see the land before thee; but thou shalt not go thither.
God to Moses
Deut. 32:52

The children of Israel walked forty years in the wilderness.
Josh. 5:6
See also Num. 14:33

He that is taken with the accursed thing shall be burnt with fire, he and all that he hath.
Josh. 7:15

Let them be hewers of wood and drawers of water.
Josh. 9:21

As I have done, so God hath requited me.
Judg. 1:7

The Lord hath testified against me.
Ruth 1:21

It is the Lord: let Him do what seemeth Him good.
1 Sam. 3:18
See also 2 Sam. 15:26

The Lord will not hear you in that day.
1 Sam. 8:18

Thy kingdom shall not continue.
Samuel to Saul
1 Sam. 13:14

Though it be in Jonathan my son, he shall surely die.
Saul
1 Sam. 14:39

His day shall come to die.
1 Sam. 26:10

As the Lord liveth, ye are worthy to die.
1 Sam. 26:16
See also 1 Sam. 26:10

The Lord shall reward the doer of evil according to his wickedness.
2 Sam. 3:39

I will not put thee to death with the sword.
1 Kings 2:8

And they shall answer, Because they forsook the Lord their God.
1 Kings 9:9

In thy days I will not do it for David thy father's sake: but I will rend it out of the hand of thy son.
God to Solomon
1 Kings 11:12

Thy carcase shall not come unto the sepulchre of thy fathers.
1 Kings 13:22

Get thee to thine own house: and when thy feet enter into the city, the child shall die.
1 Kings 14:12

Because he humbleth himself before Me, I will not bring the evil in his days: but in his son's days will I bring the evil.
1 Kings 21:29

There came forth two she bears out of the wood, and tare forty and two children.
2 Kings 2:24

Thou shalt not build an house unto My name, because thou hast shed much blood upon the earth.
God to David
1 Chron. 22:8

The fathers shall not die for the children, neither shall the children die for the fathers, but every man shall die for his own sin.
2 Chron. 25:4
See also, e.g., Deut. 24:16

His power and His wrath is against all them that forsake Him.
Ezra 8:22

God hast punished us less than our iniquities deserve.
Ezra 9:13
See also Job 11:6

He taketh the wise in their own craftiness.
Job 5:13

He destroyeth the perfect and the wicked.
Job 9:22

The eyes of the wicked shall fail, and they shall not escape.
Job 11:20

God distributeth sorrows in His anger.
Job 21:17

He shall drink of the wrath of the Almighty.
Job 21:20

Drought and heat consume the snow waters: so doth the grave those which have sinned.
Job 24:19

Then let mine arm fall from my shoulder blade, and mine arm be broken from the bone.
Job 31:22

Let thistles grow instead of wheat, and cockle instead of barley.
Job 31:40

The Lord knoweth the way of the righteous: but the way of the ungodly shall perish.
Ps. 1:6

Break Thou the arm of the wicked and the evil man.
Ps. 10:15

Evil shall slay the wicked.
Ps. 34:21

As wax melteth before the fire, so let the wicked perish at the presence of God.
Ps. 68:2

When the wicked spring as the grass, and when all the workers of iniquity do flourish; it is that they shall be destroyed for ever.
Ps. 92:7

Let the sinners be consumed out of the earth, and let the wicked be no more.
Ps. 104:35

Let his days be few; and let another take his office.
(his: the wicked)
Ps. 109:8

It is time for Thee, Lord, to work: for they have made void Thy law.
Ps. 119:126

The Lord preserveth all them that love Him: but all the wicked will He destroy.
Ps. 145:20

The curse of the Lord is in the house of the wicked: but He blesseth the habitation of the just.
Prov. 3:33

The lamp of the wicked shall be put out.
Prov. 13:9

A reproof entereth more into a wise man than an hundred stripes into a fool.
Prov. 17:10

When the scorner is punished, the simple is made wise.
Prov. 21:11

Woe unto the wicked! it shall be ill with him: for the reward of his hands shall be given him.
Isa. 3:11

The mean man shall be brought down, and the mighty man shall be humbled.
Isa. 5:15

Lord, how long?
Isa. 6:11

What will ye do in the day of visitation, and in the desolation which shall come from far?
Isa. 10:3

Her time is near to come, and her days shall not be prolonged.
(Her: Babylon)
Isa. 13:22

Fear, and the pit, and the snare, are upon thee, O inhabitant of the earth.
Isa. 24:17

The wisdom of their wise men shall perish,

and the understanding of their prudent men shall be hid.
Isa. 29:14
See also 1 Cor. 1:19

Thou shalt not know from whence it riseth.
Isa. 47:11

With his stripes we are healed.
Isa. 53:5

According to their deeds, accordingly He will repay.
Isa. 59:18

As ye have forsaken Me, and served strange gods in your land, so shall ye serve strangers in a land that is not your's.
Jer. 5:19

They have sown wheat, but shall reap thorns: they have put themselves to pain, but shall not profit.
Jer. 12:13

Such as are for death, to death; and such as are for the sword, to the sword.
Jer. 15:2

He will give them that are wicked to the sword, saith the Lord.
Jer. 25:31

Their dead bodies shall be for meat unto the fowls of the heaven, and to the beasts of the earth.
Jer. 34:20

Behold, I will set My face against you for evil.
Jer. 44:11

He that fleeth from the fear shall fall into the pit; and he that getteth up out of the pit shall be taken in the snare.
Jer. 48:44
See also Isa. 24:18

They whose judgment was not to drink of the cup have assuredly drunken.
Jer. 49:12

I will make thee small among the heathen, and despised among men.
Jer. 49:15

He that is far off shall die of the pestilence; and he that is near shall fall by the sword; and he that remaineth and is besieged shall die by the famine.
Ezek. 6:12

The time is come, the day draweth near.
Ezek. 7:12
See also Ezek. 7:7

They shall go out from one fire, and another fire shall devour them.
Ezek. 15:7

Shall he escape that doeth such things?
Ezek. 17:15

I will execute great vengeance upon them with furious rebukes.
Ezek. 25:17

I will pour out My wrath upon them like water.
Hos. 5:10

They consider not in their hearts that I remember all their wickedness.
Hos. 7:2

Thorns shall be in their tabernacles.
Hos. 9:6

Give them, O Lord: what wilt Thou give? give them a miscarrying womb and dry breasts.
Hos. 9:14

I will set Mine eyes upon them for evil, and not for good.
Amos 9:4

Thy reward shall return upon thine own head.
Obad. 15

Thou shalt sow, but thou shalt not reap.
Mic. 6:15

The Lord is slow to anger, and great in power, and will not at all acquit the wicked.
Nah. 1:3

They shall also build houses, but not inhabit them; and they shall plant vineyards, but not drink the wine thereof.
Zeph. 1:13
See also Amos 5:11

It shall be more tolerable for the land of Sodom in the day of judgment, than for thee.
Jesus
Matt. 11:24
See also Luke 10:14

God sent not His Son into the world to condemn the world; but that the world through Him might be saved.
Jesus
John 3:17

As many as have sinned without law shall also perish without law.
Rom. 2:12

If thou do that which is evil, be afraid; for he beareth not the sword in vain.
(he: civil authorities)
Rom. 13:4

The Lord reward him according to his works.
2 Tim. 4:14

It is a fearful thing to fall into the hands of the living God.
Heb. 10:31

God spared not the angels that sinned, but cast them down to hell.
2 Pet. 2:4

Behold, the Lord cometh with ten thousands of His saints, To execute judgment upon all.
Jude 14–15

The time is come for Thee to reap; for the harvest of the earth is ripe.
Rev. 14:15

True and righteous are Thy judgments.
Rev. 16:7
See also Rev. 19:2

Great Babylon came in remembrance before God.
Rev. 16:19

How much she hath glorified herself, and lived deliciously, so much torment and sorrow give her.
(she: Babylon)
Rev. 18:7

Strong is the Lord God who judgeth her.
(her: Babylon)
Rev. 18:8

The lake of fire and brimstone.
Rev. 20:10

If any man shall add unto these things, God shall add unto him the plagues that are written in this book.
Rev. 22:18

If any man shall take away from the words

of the book of this prophecy, God shall take away his part out of the book of life.
Rev. 22:19

[*See also* Capital Punishment, Desolation, Discipline, Forgiveness, God's Anger, Judgment, Plague, Retribution, Revenge, Reward, Sin]

PURITY

Neither will I be with you any more, except ye destroy the accursed from among you.
God to Joshua
Josh. 7:12

Sanctify yourselves against to morrow.
Josh. 7:13
See also Josh. 3:5

Thou canst not stand before thine enemies, until ye take away the accursed thing from among you.
Josh. 7:13

Who can bring a clean thing out of an unclean? not one.
Job 14:4

Yea, the stars are not pure in His sight. How much less man, that is a worm? and the son of man, which is a worm?
Job 25:5–6

Who shall ascend into the hill of the Lord? or who shall stand in His holy place? He that hath clean hands, and a pure heart; who hath not lifted up his soul unto vanity, nor sworn deceitfully.
Ps. 24:3–4

Wash me, and I shall be whiter than snow.
Ps. 51:7

Be ye clean, that bear the vessels of the Lord.
Isa. 52:11

Thou art of purer eyes than to behold evil.
Habakkuk to God
Hab. 1:13

Blessed are the pure in heart: for they shall see God.
Jesus
Matt. 5:8

Not that which goeth into the mouth defileth a man; but that which cometh out of the mouth, this defileth a man.
Jesus
Matt. 15:11
See also Mark 7:15

To eat with unwashen hands defileth not a man.
Jesus
Matt. 15:20

If thy foot offend thee, cut it off: it is better for thee to enter halt into life, than having two feet to be cast into hell.
Jesus
Mark 9:45
See also Matt. 18:8

Now ye are clean through the word which I have spoken unto you.
Jesus
John 15:3

What God hath cleansed, that call not thou common.
Acts 10:15, Acts 11:9

There is nothing unclean of itself: but to him that esteemeth any thing to be unclean, to him it is unclean.
Rom. 14:14

The temple of God is holy, which temple ye are.
1 Cor. 3:17

Glorify God in your body, and in your spirit.
1 Cor. 6:20

God hath not called us unto uncleanness, but unto holiness.
1 Thess. 4:7

Keep thyself pure.
1 Tim. 5:22

Cleanse your hands, ye sinners; and purify your hearts, ye double minded.
James 4:8

They shall walk with me in white: for they are worthy.
Jesus
Rev. 3:4

[*See also* Contamination, Corruption, Evil]

God did send me before you to preserve life.

> Joseph to his brothers
> *Gen. 45:5*

The Lord hath made all things for Himself: yea, even the wicked for the day of evil.
> *Prov. 16:4*

I will give them one heart, and one way, that they may fear Me for ever.
> *Jer. 32:39*

The thief cometh not, but for to steal, and to kill, and to destroy.
> Jesus
> *John 10:10*

Do all to the glory of God.
> *1 Cor. 10:31*

[*See also* Duty, Goals, Intentions, Mission]

QUALITY

The excellency of dignity.
> *Gen. 49:3*

None were of silver.
> *1 Kings 10:21*

Thy silver is become dross, thy wine mixed with water.
> *Isa. 1:22*

Reprobate silver shall men call them, because the Lord hath rejected them.
> *Jer. 6:30*

Every good tree bringeth forth good fruit; but a corrupt tree bringeth forth evil fruit.
> Jesus
> *Matt. 7:17*
> *See also Luke 6:43*

No man also having drunk old wine straightway desireth new.
> Jesus
> *Luke 5:39*

Of thorns men do not gather figs, nor of a bramble bush gather they grapes.
> Jesus
> *Luke 6:44*

[*See also* Perfection, Purity, Value]

QUANTITY

The Lord did not set His love upon you, nor choose you, because ye were more in number than any people; for ye were the fewest of all people: But because the Lord loved you.
> *Deut. 7:7–8*

There is no restraint to the Lord to save by many or by few.
> Jonathan
> *1 Sam. 14:6*

As the sand that is by the sea for multitude.
> *2 Sam. 17:11*
> *See also, e.g., Judg. 7:12*

My name is Legion: for we are many.
> *Mark 5:9*

Behold, how great a matter a little fire kindleth!
> *James 3:5*

[*See also* Abundance, Infinity, Size]

QUESTIONING

See Authority, Doctrine, Skepticism.

QUOTATIONS

Every one that useth proverbs shall use this proverb against thee.
> *Ezek. 16:44*

This is a faithful saying and worthy of all acceptation.
> *1 Tim. 4:9*

[*See also* Speech]

RAIN

A little cloud out of the sea, like a man's hand.
1 Kings 18:44

Hath the rain a father? or who hath begotten the drops of dew?
Job 38:28

He watereth the hills from His chambers.
Ps. 104:13

A continual dropping in a very rainy day and a contentious woman are alike.
Prov. 27:15

If the clouds be full of rain, they empty themselves upon the earth.
Eccl. 11:3

He causeth the vapours to ascend from the ends of the earth: He maketh lightnings with rain, and bringeth forth the wind out of His treasures.
Jer. 51:16
See also Ps. 135:7

He maketh His sun to rise on the evil and on the good, and sendeth rain on the just and on the unjust.
Jesus
Matt. 5:45

He left not Himself without witness, in that He did good, and gave us rain from heaven.
Acts 14:17

RAINBOW

I do set My bow in the cloud, and it shall be for a token of a covenant between Me and the earth.
God to Noah
Gen. 9:13

RASHNESS

Whatsoever cometh forth of the doors of my house to meet me, when I return in peace from the children of Ammon, shall surely be the Lord's.
Judg. 11:31

I have opened my mouth unto the Lord, and I cannot go back.
Judg. 11:35

Uzza put forth his hand to hold the ark; for the oxen stumbled. And the anger of the Lord was kindled against Uzza, and He smote him.
1 Chron. 13:9–10
See also 2 Sam. 6:6–7

Set a watch, O Lord, before my mouth; keep the door of my lips.
Ps. 141:3

He that is hasty of spirit exalteth folly.
Prov. 14:29

He that hasteth with his feet sinneth.
Prov. 19:2

Seest thou a man that is hasty in his words? there is more hope of a fool than of him.
Prov. 29:20

Let not thine heart be hasty to utter any thing before God.
Eccl. 5:2

Every one turned to his course, as the horse rusheth into the battle.
Jer. 8:6

Whatsoever thou shalt ask of me, I will give it thee, unto the half of my kingdom.
Herod to his daughter
Mark 6:23

[*See also* Misjudgment, Prudence]

READINESS

Sanctify yourselves against to morrow.
Josh. 7:13
See also Josh. 3:5

Is not the Lord gone out before thee?
Judg. 4:14

Speak, Lord; for Thy servant heareth.
1 Sam. 3:9

Set thine house in order; for thou shalt die, and not live.
2 Kings 20:1, Isa. 38:1

Every man hath his sword upon his thigh because of fear in the night.
Song 3:8

Prepare ye the way of the Lord, make straight in the desert a highway for our God.
Isa. 40:3

They have blown the trumpet, even to make all ready; but none goeth to the battle.
Ezek. 7:14

Be thou prepared.
Ezek. 38:7

Prepare to meet thy God, O Israel.
Amos 4:12

I will send My messenger, and he shall prepare the way before Me.
Mal. 3:1

Prepare ye the way of the Lord, make His paths straight.
Matt. 3:3, Mark 1:3, Luke 3:4

This is he, of whom it is written, Behold, I send my messenger before Thy face, which shall prepare Thy way before Thee.
Jesus (he: John the Baptist)
Matt. 11:10, Luke 7:27

Elias is come already, and they knew him not.
Jesus
Matt. 17:12

Every valley shall be filled, and every mountain and hill shall be brought low.
Luke 3:5
See also Isa. 40:5

Be ye therefore ready also: for the Son of man cometh at an hour when ye think not.
Jesus
Luke 12:40
See also Matt. 24:44

I am the voice of one crying in the wilderness, Make straight the way of the Lord.
John the Baptist
John 1:23
See also Matt. 3:3, Mark 1:3, Luke 3:4

Lift up your eyes, and look on the fields; for they are white already to harvest.
Jesus
John 4:35

Be instant in season, out of season.
2 Tim. 4:2

Gird up the loins of your mind.
1 Pet. 1:13

[*See also* Vigilance]

REBELLION

Thou hast overthrown them that rose up against Thee: Thou sentest forth Thy wrath, which consumed them as stubble.
Ex. 15:7

Your murmurings are not against us, but against the Lord.
Moses to Israelites
Ex. 16:8

Wherefore do ye tempt the Lord?
Moses
Ex. 17:2

Hath the Lord indeed spoken only by Moses?
Num. 12:2

Rebel not ye against the Lord, neither fear ye the people of the land.
Num. 14:9

How long shall I bear with this evil congregation, which murmur against Me?
Num. 14:27

Ye have been rebellious against the Lord from the day that I knew you.
Deut. 9:24

They are a perverse and crooked generation.
Deut. 32:5

God forbid that we should rebel against the Lord.
Josh. 22:29

They turned quickly out of the way which their fathers walked in.
Judg. 2:17

Rebellion is as the sin of witchcraft.
Samuel to Saul
1 Sam. 15:23

I will raise up evil against thee out of thine own house.
God to David
2 Sam. 12:11

All Israel stoned him with stones.
1 Kings 12:18

Fight ye not against the Lord God of your fathers; for ye shall not prosper.
2 Chron. 13:12

Why dost thou strive against Him? for He giveth not account of any of His matters.
Job 33:13

He addeth rebellion unto his sin.
Job 34:37

Fear thou the Lord and the king: and meddle not with them that are given to change.
Prov. 24:21

Keep the king's commandment.
Eccl. 8:2

Woe unto him that striveth with his Maker!
Isa. 45:9

Be not thou rebellious like that rebellious house.
Ezek. 2:8

Woe unto them! for they have fled from Me: destruction unto them! because they have transgressed against Me.
Hos. 7:13

Whosoever therefore resisteth the power, resisteth the ordinance of God.
Rom. 13:2

They that resist shall receive to themselves damnation.
Rom. 13:2

[*See also* Disobedience, Godlessness, Government, Strife]

REBIRTH

See Born Again, Jesus (Acceptance of).

RECIPROCITY

Thou shalt give life for life, Eye for eye, tooth for tooth, hand for hand, foot for foot, Burning for burning, wound for wound, stripe for stripe.
Ex. 21:23–25
See also Lev. 24:20, Deut. 19:21

Blessed is he that blesseth thee, and cursed is he that curseth thee.
Num. 24:9

Do unto him, as he had thought to have done unto his brother.
Deut. 19:19

As they did unto me, so have I done unto them.
Samson
Judg. 15:11

Them that honour Me I will honour, and they that despise Me shall be lightly esteemed.
1 Sam. 2:30

As thy sword hath made women childless, so shall thy mother be childless among women.
Samuel to Amalekite king
1 Sam. 15:33

The Lord is with you, while ye be with Him.
2 Chron. 15:2

Because ye have forsaken the Lord, He hath also forsaken you.
2 Chron. 24:20
See also 2 Chron. 15:2

He that watereth shall be watered also himself.
Prov. 11:25

They shall be My people, and I will be their God.
E.g., Jer. 24:7

Take vengeance upon her; as she hath done, do unto her.
Jer. 50:15

Because they trespassed against Me, therefore hid I My face from them.
Ezek. 39:23

Turn ye unto Me, saith the Lord of hosts, and I will turn unto you.
Zech. 1:3

All things whatsoever ye would that men should do to you, do ye even so to them.
Jesus
Matt. 7:12
See also Luke 6:31

He shall have judgment without mercy, that hath showed no mercy.
James 2:13

[*See also* Consequences, Retribution]

REDEMPTION

Redeem us for Thy mercies' sake.
Ps. 44:26

Zion shall be redeemed with judgment, and her converts with righteousness.
Isa. 1:27

Fear not: for I have redeemed thee, I have called thee by thy name; thou art Mine.
Isa. 43:1

The redeemed of the Lord shall return, and come with singing unto Zion.
Isa. 51:11

With his stripes we are healed.
Isa. 53:5

Ye shall know that I am the Lord, when I shall bring you into the land of Israel.
Ezek. 20:42

I will seek that which was lost, and bring again that which was driven away, and will bind up that which was broken, and will strengthen that which was sick.
Ezek. 34:16

Behold the Lamb of God, which taketh away the sin of the world.
John the Baptist
John 1:29

The bread that I will give is my flesh, which I will give for the life of the world.
Jesus
John 6:51

Sin shall not have dominion over you: for ye are not under the law, but under grace.
Rom. 6:14

Christ hath redeemed us from the curse of the law.
Gal. 3:13

Thou art no more a servant, but a son.
Gal. 4:7

We have redemption through His blood, even the forgiveness of sins.
Col. 1:14

The blood of Jesus Christ His Son cleanseth us from all sin.
1 John 1:7

[*See also* Kingdom of God, Salvation]

REFUGE

See Safety.

REGRET

It repented the Lord that He had made man on the earth.
Gen. 6:6

It repenteth Me that I have set up Saul to be king.
1 Sam. 15:11

Wherefore then hast Thou brought me forth out of the womb? Oh that I had given up the ghost, and no eye had seen me!
Job 10:18

O that thou hadst hearkened to My commandments! then had thy peace been as a river, and thy righteousness as the waves of the sea.
Isa. 48:18

Cursed be the day wherein I was born: let not the day wherein my mother bare me be blessed.
Jer. 20:14

Thou shalt remember thy ways, and be ashamed.
Ezek. 16:61

Ye shall lothe yourselves in your own sight for all your evils that ye have committed.
Ezek. 20:43

There shall be weeping and gnashing of teeth.
Jesus
E.g., Matt. 24:51

He found no place of repentance, though he sought it carefully with tears.
(He: Esau)
Heb. 12:17

REHABILITATION

Put on the new man.
Eph. 4:24

Let him that stole steal no more: but rather let him labour, working with his hands.
Eph. 4:28

He which converteth the sinner from the error of his way shall save a soul from death.
James 5:20

[*See also* Renewal]

REJECTION

I will not return with thee: for thou hast rejected the word of the Lord.
1 Sam. 15:26

The Spirit of the Lord departed from Saul.
1 Sam. 16:14

Israel shall be a proverb and a byword among all people.
1 Kings 9:7
See also Deut. 28:37

If thou forsake Him, He will cast thee off for ever.
1 Chron. 28:9

I cry unto Thee, and Thou dost not hear me: I stand up, and Thou regardest me not.
Job 30:20

Thou art the God of my strength: why dost Thou cast me off?
Ps. 43:2

Turn not away the face of Thine anointed.
Ps. 132:10

They have turned their back unto Me, and not their face.
Jer. 2:27

Reprobate silver shall men call them, because the Lord hath rejected them.
Jer. 6:30

I called you, but ye answered not.
God
Jer. 7:13

Though they shall cry unto Me, I will not hearken unto them.
Jer. 11:11

I spake unto thee in thy prosperity; but thou saidst, I will not hear.
Jer. 22:21

They have turned unto Me the back, and not the face.
Jer. 32:33

From the daughter of Zion all her beauty is departed: her princes are become like harts that find no pasture.
Lam. 1:6

Thus saith the Lord God; Behold, I, even I, am against thee.
Ezek. 5:8

Ye are not My people, and I will not be your God.
Hos. 1:9

He that despiseth you despiseth me; and he that despiseth me despiseth Him that sent me.
Jesus
Luke 10:16

He that denieth me before men shall be denied before the angels of God.
Jesus
Luke 12:9
See also Matt. 10:33

Depart from me, all ye workers of iniquity.
Jesus
Luke 13:27
See also Matt. 7:23

He came unto His own, and His own received Him not.
John 1:11

Whom He hath sent, Him ye believe not.
Jesus
John 5:38

I am come in my Father's name, and ye receive me not.
Jesus
John 5:43

Hath God cast away His people? God forbid.
Rom. 11:1

[*See also* Abandonment, God's Anger]

RELIABILITY

It is better to trust in the Lord than to put confidence in man.
Ps. 118:8

It is better to trust in the Lord than to put confidence in princes.
Ps. 118:9

As vinegar to the teeth, and as smoke to

the eyes, so is the sluggard to them that send him.
Prov. 10:26

A wicked messenger falleth into mischief: but a faithful ambassador is health.
Prov. 13:17

He that sendeth a message by the hand of a fool cutteth off the feet.
Prov. 26:6

The mountains shall depart, and the hills be removed; but My kindness shall not depart from thee.
Isa. 54:10

RELIANCE

If the Lord do not help thee, whence shall I help thee?
2 Kings 6:27

Let not him that is deceived trust in vanity: for vanity shall be his recompence.
Job 15:31

Some trust in chariots, and some in horses: but we will remember the name of the Lord our God.
Ps. 20:7

The Lord is my shepherd; I shall not want.
Ps. 23:1

Unto Thee, O Lord, do I lift up my soul.
Ps. 25:1

The Lord is my light and my salvation; whom shall I fear? the Lord is the strength of my life; of whom shall I be afraid?
Ps. 27:1

In Thee, O Lord, do I put my trust; let me never be ashamed.
Ps. 31:1

There is no king saved by the multitude of an host.
Ps. 33:16

Our soul waiteth for the Lord: He is our help and our shield.
Ps. 33:20

Blessed is that man that maketh the Lord his trust.
Ps. 40:4
See also, e.g., Ps. 34:8

Surely men of low degree are vanity, and men of high degree are a lie.
Ps. 62:9

Ye that fear the Lord, trust in the Lord: He is their help and their shield.
Ps. 115:11

In Thee is my trust; leave not my soul destitute.
Ps. 141:8

Put not your trust in princes, nor in the son of man.
Ps. 146:3

Confidence in an unfaithful man in time of trouble is like a broken tooth, and a foot out of joint.
Prov. 25:19

Trust ye not in lying words.
Jer. 7:4

The way of man is not in himself: it is not in man that walketh to direct his steps.
Jer. 10:23

Cursed be the man that trusteth in man, and maketh flesh his arm, and whose heart departeth from the Lord.
Jer. 17:5

Let me see Thy vengeance on them: for unto Thee have I opened my cause.
Jeremiah to God
Jer. 20:12
See also Jer. 11:20

But thou didst trust in thine own beauty.
Ezek. 16:15

Without me ye can do nothing.
Jesus
John 15:5

Our sufficiency is of God.
2 Cor. 3:5

[*See also* God's Protection, God's Support, Trust]

REMEMBRANCE

Remember this day, in which ye came out from Egypt, out of the house of bondage.
Ex. 13:3

Take heed to thyself, and keep thy soul

diligently, lest thou forget the things which thine eyes have seen.
Deut. 4:9

Forget not the Lord thy God.
Deut. 8:11
See also Deut. 6:12

What mean ye by these stones?
Josh. 4:6

Behold, this stone shall be a witness unto us.
Josh. 24:27

They shall not say, This is Jezebel.
2 Kings 9:37

Their memorial is perished with them.
Ps. 9:6

If I forget thee, O Jerusalem, let my right hand forget her cunning.
Ps. 137:5

There is no remembrance of the wise more than of the fool for ever.
Eccl. 2:16

That which now is in the days to come shall all be forgotten.
Eccl. 2:16

Remember ye not the former things, neither consider the things of old.
Isa. 43:18

They may forget, yet will I not forget thee.
God, about parents
Isa. 49:15

They shall not take of thee a stone for a corner, nor a stone for foundations; but thou shalt be desolate for ever, saith the Lord.
Jer. 51:26

Wherefore dost Thou forget us for ever, and forsake us so long time?
Lam. 5:20

They consider not in their hearts that I remember all their wickedness.
Hos. 7:2

This is my body, which is broken for you: this do in remembrance of me.
Jesus
1 Cor. 11:24
See also Luke 22:19

This cup is the new testament in my blood:

this do ye, as oft as ye drink it, in remembrance of me.
Jesus
1 Cor. 11:25
See also Luke 22:20

[*See also* Abandonment, Fame, History]

RENEWAL

Be fruitful, and multiply, and replenish the earth.
God to Noah, after the flood
Gen. 9:1

He restoreth my soul.
Ps. 23:3

A time to break down, and a time to build up.
Eccl. 3:3

They that wait upon the Lord shall renew their strength.
Isa. 40:31

Awake, awake; put on thy strength, O Zion; put on thy beautiful garments, O Jerusalem.
Isa. 52:1

I create new heavens and a new earth: and the former shall not be remembered, nor come into mind.
Isa. 65:17

Come, and let us join ourselves to the Lord.
Jer. 50:5

Turn Thou us unto Thee, O Lord, and we shall be turned; renew our days as of old.
Lam. 5:21

I will take the stony heart out of their flesh, and will give them an heart of flesh.
Ezek. 11:19
See also Ezek. 36:26

Old things are passed away; behold, all things are become new.
2 Cor. 5:17

Be renewed in the spirit of your mind.
Eph. 4:23

Ye were as sheep going astray; but are now returned unto the Shepherd.
1 Pet. 2:25

I saw a new heaven and a new earth: for

the first heaven and the first earth were passed away.
Rev. 21:1

Behold, I make all things new.
Rev. 21:5

[*See also* Born Again, Rehabilitation]

REPENTANCE

I have sinned this time: the Lord is righteous, and I and my people are wicked.
Pharaoh
Ex. 9:27

Forgive, I pray thee, my sin only this once.
Pharaoh to Moses
Ex. 10:17

It is the blood that maketh an atonement for the soul.
Lev. 17:11

Make confession unto Him.
Josh. 7:19

Do Thou unto us whatsoever seemeth good unto Thee; deliver us only, we pray Thee, this day.
Judg. 10:15

He is not a man, that He should repent.
1 Sam. 15:29

Turn ye from your evil ways, and keep My commandments and My statutes.
2 Kings 17:13

Turn again unto the Lord.
2 Chron. 30:9

The Lord your God is gracious and merciful, and will not turn away His face from you, if ye return unto Him.
2 Chron. 30:9

Make confession unto the Lord God of your fathers, and do His pleasure.
Ezra 10:11

To depart from evil is understanding.
Job 28:28

I abhor myself, and repent in dust and ashes.
Job 42:6

When He slew them, then they sought Him.
Ps. 78:34

Fear the Lord, and depart from evil.
Prov. 3:7
See also Ps. 34:14, Ps. 37:27

By the fear of the Lord men depart from evil.
Prov. 16:6

Put away the evil of your doings from before Mine eyes.
Isa. 1:16

Cease to do evil.
Isa. 1:16

Turn ye unto Him from whom the children of Israel have deeply revolted.
Isa. 31:6

Let him return unto the Lord, and He will have mercy upon him.
Isa. 55:7

Is not this the fast that I have chosen? to loose the bands of wickedness, to undo the heavy burdens, and to let the oppressed go free.
Isa. 58:6

Turn thou unto Me.
Jer. 3:7
See also Jer. 4:1

Break up your fallow ground, and sow not among thorns.
Jer. 4:3

Take away the foreskins of your heart.
Jer. 4:4

Wash thine heart from wickedness, that thou mayest be saved.
Jer. 4:14

Can the Ethiopian change his skin, or the leopard his spots? then may ye also do good, that are accustomed to do evil.
Jer. 13:23

I am weary with repenting.
God to Jeremiah
Jer. 15:6

Return ye now every one from his evil way.
Jer. 18:11

Amend your ways and your doings, and obey the voice of the Lord your God.
Jer. 26:13

Return ye now every man from his evil way, and amend your doings.
Jer. 35:15

Let us search and try our ways, and turn again to the Lord.
Lam. 3:40

If the wicked will turn from all his sins that he hath committed, and keep all My statutes, and do that which is lawful and right, he shall surely live.
Ezek. 18:21
See also Ezek. 33:19

Repent, and turn yourselves from all your transgressions; so iniquity shall not be your ruin.
Ezek. 18:30

Make you a new heart and a new spirit: for why will ye die?
Ezek. 18:31

Turn yourselves, and live ye.
Ezek. 18:32

He that taketh warning shall deliver his soul.
Ezek. 33:5

Turn ye, turn ye from your evil ways; for why will ye die?
Ezek. 33:11
See also Jonah 3:8

Come, and let us return unto the Lord.
Hos. 6:1

It is time to seek the Lord.
Hos. 10:12

Rend your heart, and not your garments, and turn unto the Lord.
Joel 2:13

Seek the Lord, and ye shall live.
Amos 5:6
See also Amos 5:4

Turn ye unto Me, saith the Lord of hosts, and I will turn unto you.
Zech. 1:3

Turn ye now from your evil ways, and from your evil doings.
Zech. 1:4

Return unto Me, and I will return unto you, saith the Lord of hosts.
Mal. 3:7

Repent, for the kingdom of heaven is at hand.
Jesus
Matt. 4:17
See also Matt. 3:2, Matt. 10:7, Mark 1:15

I am not come to call the righteous, but sinners to repentance.
Jesus
Matt. 9:13
See also Mark 2:17, Luke 5:32

Bring forth therefore fruits worthy of repentance.
Luke 3:8

Except ye repent, ye shall all likewise perish.
Jesus
Luke 13:3

Rejoice with me; for I have found my sheep which was lost.
Jesus
Luke 15:6

Joy shall be in heaven over one sinner that repenteth, more than over ninety and nine just persons, which need no repentance.
Jesus
Luke 15:7

There is joy in the presence of the angels of God over one sinner that repenteth.
Jesus
Luke 15:10

When thou art converted, strengthen thy brethren.
Jesus
Luke 22:32

Repentance and remission of sins should be preached in His name among all nations.
Jesus
Luke 24:47

Repent, and be baptized every one of you in the name of Jesus Christ.
Acts 2:38

Repent ye therefore, and be converted, that your sins may be blotted out.
Acts 3:19

Pray God, if perhaps the thought of thine heart may be forgiven thee.
Acts 8:22

The baptism of repentance.
Acts 13:24

The goodness of God leadeth thee to repentance.
Rom. 2:4

He found no place of repentance, though he sought it carefully with tears.
(He: Esau)
Heb. 12:17

Cleanse your hands, ye sinners; and purify your hearts, ye double minded.
James 4:8

Remember therefore from whence thou art fallen, and repent.
Jesus
Rev. 2:5

Repent; or else I will come unto thee quickly.
Jesus
Rev. 2:16

[*See also* Forgiveness, Punishment, Rehabilitation, Sin]

REPRESENTATIVES

See Reliability, Spokesmen, Status.

REPUTATION

Thou knowest the people, that they are set on mischief.
Aaron to Moses
Ex. 32:22

How are the mighty fallen!
E.g., 2 Sam. 1:19

The half was not told me.
Queen of Sheba to Solomon
1 Kings 10:7

I believed not their words, until I came, and mine eyes had seen it.
Queen of Sheba to Solomon
2 Chron. 9:6
See also 1 Kings 10:7

Behold, the one half of the greatness of thy wisdom was not told me.
2 Chron. 9:6
See also 1 Kings 10:7

The wise shall inherit glory: but shame shall be the promotion of fools.
Prov. 3:35

The memory of the just is blessed: but the name of the wicked shall rot.
Prov. 10:7

A good name is rather to be chosen than great riches.
Prov. 22:1

There is no remembrance of the wise more than of the fool for ever.
Eccl. 2:16

A good name is better than precious ointment.
Eccl. 7:1

A prophet is not without honour, save in his own country, and in his own house.
Jesus
Matt. 13:57
See also Mark 6:4, Luke 4:24

Woe unto you, when all men shall speak well of you!
Jesus
Luke 6:26

A prophet hath no honour in his own country.
John 4:44

Ye know that our record is true.
3 John 12

[*See also* Achievement, Fame, Shame]

RESCUE

See Assistance, Danger, Deliverance.

RESPECT

The excellency of dignity.
Gen. 49:3

Honour the face of the old man.
Lev. 19:32

They feared him, as they feared Moses, all the days of his life.
Josh. 4:14

Loose thy shoe from off thy foot; for the place whereon thou standest is holy.
Josh. 5:15
See also Ex. 3:5

Them that honour Me I will honour, and they that despise Me shall be lightly esteemed.
1 Sam. 2:30

I will not put forth mine hand against my lord; for he is the Lord's anointed.
David to Saul
1 Sam. 24:10

Ask on, my mother: for I will not say thee nay.
1 Kings 2:20

The Lord your God ye shall fear.
2 Kings 17:39

Let him alone; let no man move his bones.
2 Kings 23:18

Before honour is humility.
Prov. 15:33, Prov. 18:12

Despise not thy mother when she is old.
Prov. 23:22

As snow in summer, and as rain in harvest, so honour is not seemly for a fool.
Prov. 26:1

Her children arise up, and call her blessed.
Prov. 31:28

My people shall know My name.
Isa. 52:6

A son honoureth his father, and a servant his master: if then I be a father, where is Mine honour?
Mal. 1:6

A prophet is not without honour, save in his own country, and in his own house.
Jesus
Matt. 13:57
See also Mark 6:4, Luke 4:24

A prophet hath no honour in his own country.
John 4:44

If I honour myself, my honour is nothing: it is my Father that honoureth me.
Jesus
John 8:54

God hath showed me that I should not call any man common or unclean.
Acts 10:28

Thou shalt not speak evil of the ruler of thy people.
Acts 23:5
See also Ex. 22:28

Tribute to whom tribute is due; custom to whom custom; fear to whom fear; honour to whom honour.
Rom. 13:7

Walk honestly toward them that are without.
1 Thess. 4:12

Rebuke not an elder, but intreat him as a father.
1 Tim. 5:1

He who hath builded the house hath more honour than the house.
Heb. 3:3

Honour all men.
1 Pet. 2:17

Fear God. Honour the king.
1 Pet. 2:17

Submit yourselves unto the elder.
1 Pet. 5:5

[*See also* Homage]

RESPONSIBILITY

Am I my brother's keeper?
Cain
Gen. 4:9

Upon me be thy curse, my son: only obey my voice.
Rebekah to Jacob
Gen. 27:13

If thou meet thine enemy's ox or his ass going astray, thou shalt surely bring it back to him again.
Ex. 23:4

Wherefore have I not found favour in Thy sight, that Thou layest the burden of all this people upon me?
Moses to God
Num. 11:11

Have I conceived all this people? have I begotten them, that Thou shouldest say

unto me, Carry them in thy bosom, as a nursing father beareth the sucking child?
Moses to God
Num. 11:12

Shall your brethren go to war, and shall ye sit here?
Num. 32:6

The cause that is too hard for you, bring it unto me, and I will hear it.
Moses
Deut. 1:17

Upon me, my lord, upon me let this iniquity be.
1 Sam. 25:24

Lo, I have sinned, and I have done wickedly: but these sheep, what have they done?
David to God
2 Sam. 24:17
See also 1 Chron. 21:17

If the Lord do not help thee, whence shall I help thee?
2 Kings 6:27

Every man shall be put to death for his own sin.
E.g., 2 Kings 14:6

The fathers shall not die for the children, neither shall the children die for the fathers, but every man shall die for his own sin.
2 Chron. 25:4
See also, e.g., Deut. 24:16

Gird up now thy loins like a man.
Job 38:3

He was wounded for our transgressions, he was bruised for our iniquities.
Isa. 53:5

Hast thou not procured this unto thyself, in that thou hast forsaken the Lord thy God?
God to Jews
Jer. 2:17

Every one shall die for his own iniquity: every man that eateth the sour grape, his teeth shall be set on edge.
Jer. 31:30

Cursed be he that keepeth back his sword from blood.
Jer. 48:10

The soul that sinneth, it shall die.
Ezek. 18:4, 20

His blood shall be upon him.
E.g., Ezek. 18:13

I have set thee a watchman unto the house of Israel.
Ezek. 33:7

O Israel, thou hast destroyed thyself; but in Me is thine help.
Hos. 13:9

Let the dead bury their dead.
Jesus
Matt. 8:22, Luke 9:60

Every idle word that men shall speak, they shall give account thereof in the day of judgment.
Jesus
Matt. 12:36

He took water, and washed his hands.
(He: Pilate)
Matt. 27:24

His blood be on us, and on our children.
Crowd to Pilate
Matt. 27:25

Unto whomsoever much is given, of him shall be much required.
Jesus
Luke 12:48

He that is faithful in that which is least is faithful also in much.
Jesus
Luke 16:10

Father, forgive them; for they know not what they do.
Jesus
Luke 23:34

The hireling fleeth, because he is an hireling, and careth not for the sheep.
Jesus
John 10:13

Take ye Him, and judge Him according to your law.
John 18:31

Take ye Him, and crucify Him: for I find no fault in Him.
Pilate
John 19:6
See also Luke 23:4

Feed my lambs.
Jesus
John 21:15

Feed my sheep.
Jesus
John 21:16, 17

Lord, lay not this sin to their charge.
Stephen, dying
Acts 7:60

Do thyself no harm: for we are all here.
Acts 16:28

Look ye to it; for I will be no judge of such matters.
Acts 18:15

It is no more I that do it, but sin that dwelleth in me.
Rom. 7:17, 20

Every one of us shall give account of himself to God.
Rom. 14:12

When I became a man, I put away childish things.
1 Cor. 13:11

Bear ye one another's burdens.
Gal. 6:2

Every man shall bear his own burden.
Gal. 6:5

If he hath wronged thee, or oweth thee ought, put that on mine account.
Philem. 18

[*See also* Blame, Burdens, Duty, Guilt]

RESTITUTION

When ye go, ye shall not go empty.
God to Moses
Ex. 3:21

If the thief be found, let him pay double.
Ex. 22:7

Whom the judges shall condemn, he shall pay double unto his neighbour.
Ex. 22:9

He shall make amends for the harm that he hath done.
Lev. 5:16

He shall restore that which he took violently away.
Lev. 6:4

He that killeth a beast shall make it good; beast for beast.
Lev. 24:18
See also Lev. 24:21

[*See also* Justice, Restoration, Retribution, Revenge]

RESTORATION

The desert shall rejoice, and blossom as the rose.
Isa. 35:1

The eyes of the blind shall be opened, and the ears of the deaf shall be unstopped.
Isa. 35:5

Then shall the lame man leap as an hart, and the tongue of the dumb sing.
Isa. 35:6

Again I will build thee, and thou shalt be built, O virgin of Israel.
Jer. 31:4

This land that was desolate is become like the garden of Eden.
Ezek. 36:35

I will restore to you the years that the locust hath eaten.
Joel 2:25

The plowman shall overtake the reaper, and the treader of grapes him that soweth seed.
Amos 9:13

The streets of the city shall be full of boys and girls playing in the streets.
Zech. 8:5

[*See also* Redemption, Renewal]

RESTRAINT

Let not the anger of my lord wax hot.
Aaron to Moses
Ex. 32:22

How shall I curse, whom God hath not cursed? or how shall I defy, whom the Lord hath not defied?
Balaam to Balak
Num. 23:8

I will not put forth mine hand against my
lord; for he is the Lord's anointed.
David to Saul
1 Sam. 24:10

The Lord judge between me and thee, and
the Lord avenge me of thee: but mine hand
shall not be upon thee.
David to Saul
1 Sam. 24:12

When the Lord had delivered me into thine
hand, thou killedst me not.
Saul to David
1 Sam. 24:18

Blessed be thy advice, and blessed be thou,
which hast kept me this day from coming to
shed blood.
1 Sam. 25:33

Return every man to his house; for this
thing is from Me.
1 Kings 12:24
See also 2 Chron. 11:4

Ye shall not go up, nor fight against your
brethren.
2 Chron. 11:4, 1 Kings 12:24

He that is void of wisdom despiseth his
neighbour: but a man of understanding
holdeth his peace.
Prov. 11:12

A fool's wrath is presently known: but a
prudent man covereth shame.
Prov. 12:16

He that is slow to anger appeaseth strife.
Prov. 15:18

It is an honour for a man to cease from
strife.
Prov. 20:3

Whoso keepeth his mouth and his tongue
keepeth his soul from troubles.
Prov. 21:23

I will not ask, neither will I tempt the Lord.
Isa. 7:12

Unto him that smiteth thee on the one
cheek offer also the other.
Jesus
Luke 6:29
See also Matt. 5:39

Hast thou faith? have it to thyself before
God.
Rom. 14:22

[*See also* Anger, Forgiveness, Patience,
Prudence, Revenge, Temper, Temptation]

RESURRECTION

If a man die, shall he live again?
Job 14:14

Though after my skin worms destroy this
body, yet in my flesh shall I see God.
Job 19:26

He will swallow up death in victory.
Isa. 25:8

Awake and sing, ye that dwell in dust.
Isa. 26:19

Son of man, can these bones live?
Ezek. 37:3

O ye dry bones, hear the word of the Lord.
Ezek. 37:4

Many of them that sleep in the dust of the
earth shall awake, some to everlasting life,
and some to shame and everlasting contempt.
Dan. 12:2

The third day He shall rise again.
Jesus
Matt. 20:19, Mark 10:34,
Luke 18:33

God is not the God of the dead, but of the
living.
Jesus
Matt. 22:32
See also Mark 12:27, Luke 20:38

He is risen.
Matt. 28:6, Mark 16:6

After that He is killed, He shall rise the
third day.
Jesus
Mark 9:31
See also Matt. 17:23

They shall mock Him, and shall scourge
Him, and shall spit upon Him, and shall
kill Him: and the third day He shall rise
again.
Jesus
Mark 10:34
See also Luke 18:33

They are equal unto the angels; and are the children of God.
Jesus
Luke 20:36

Why seek ye the living among the dead?
Luke 24:5

Destroy this temple, and in three days I will raise it up.
Jesus
John 2:19

The hour is coming, in the which all that are in the graves shall hear His voice.
Jesus
John 5:28

They that have done good, unto the resurrection of life; and they that have done evil, unto the resurrection of damnation.
Jesus
John 5:29

Thy brother shall rise again.
Jesus, about Lazarus
John 11:23

I am the resurrection, and the life.
Jesus
John 11:25

Lazarus, come forth.
Jesus
John 11:43

His soul was not left in hell, neither His flesh did see corruption.
Acts 2:31

Him God raised up the third day, and showed Him openly; Not to all the people, but unto witnesses chosen before of God.
Acts 10:40–41

God raised Him from the dead.
Acts 13:30
See also Acts 17:31

I will give you the sure mercies of David.
Acts 13:34
See also Isa. 55:3

Why should it be thought a thing incredible with you, that God should raise the dead?
Acts 26:8

Who was delivered for our offences, and was raised again for our justification.
Rom. 4:25

If thou shalt confess with thy mouth the

Lord Jesus, and shalt believe in thine heart that God hath raised Him from the dead, thou shalt be saved.
Rom. 10:9

If Christ be not raised, your faith is vain; ye are yet in your sins.
1 Cor. 15:17

If in this life only we have hope in Christ, we are of all men most miserable.
1 Cor. 15:19

As in Adam all die, even so in Christ shall all be made alive.
1 Cor. 15:22

The last enemy that shall be destroyed is death.
1 Cor. 15:26

Death is swallowed up in victory.
1 Cor. 15:54

When Christ, who is our life, shall appear, then shall ye also appear with Him in glory.
Col. 3:4

The dead in Christ shall rise first.
1 Thess. 4:16

Remember that Jesus Christ of the seed of David was raised from the dead.
2 Tim. 2:8

I am He that liveth, and was dead.
Jesus
Rev. 1:18

I am alive for evermore.
Jesus
Rev. 1:18

I saw the souls of them that were beheaded for the witness of Jesus, and for the word of God.
Rev. 20:4

Blessed and holy is he that hath part in the first resurrection: on such the second death hath no power.
Rev. 20:6

I saw the dead, small and great, stand before God.
Rev. 20:12

Death and hell delivered up the dead which were in them: and they were judged every man according to their works.
Rev. 20:13

[See also Christ Eternal, Eternal Life]

RETRIBUTION

Whoso sheddeth man's blood, by man shall his blood be shed.
Gen. 9:6

Eye for eye, tooth for tooth, hand for hand, foot for foot.
Ex. 21:24
See also Matt. 5:38

The land cannot be cleansed of the blood that is shed therein, but by the blood of him that shed it.
Num. 35:33

Why hast thou troubled us? the Lord shall trouble thee this day.
Joshua to Achan
Josh. 7:25

He is an holy God; He is a jealous God; He will not forgive your transgressions nor your sins.
Josh. 24:19

Whithersoever they went out, the hand of the Lord was against them for evil.
Judg. 2:15

The dead which he slew at his death were more than they which he slew in his life.
(he: Samson)
Judg. 16:30

As thy sword hath made women childless, so shall thy mother be childless among women.
Samuel to Amalekite king
1 Sam. 15:33

He shall lie with thy wives in the sight of this sun.
(He: David's neighbor)
2 Sam. 12:11

The Lord shall return thy wickedness upon thine own head.
1 Kings 2:44

In the place where dogs licked the blood of Naboth shall dogs lick thy blood, even thine.
(thy: Ahab)
1 Kings 21:19

I will bring evil upon thee, and will take away thy posterity.
1 Kings 21:21

I will cause him to fall by the sword in his own land.
2 Kings 19:7, Isa. 37:7

Whosoever heareth of it, both his ears shall tingle.
2 Kings 21:12
See also 1 Sam. 3:11

I will wipe Jerusalem as a man wipeth a dish, wiping it, and turning it upside down.
2 Kings 21:13

I will forsake the remnant of Mine inheritance, and deliver them into the hand of their enemies.
2 Kings 21:14

Behold, I will bring evil upon this place, and upon the inhabitants thereof.
2 Kings 22:16

The sword of the Lord.
E.g., 1 Chron. 21:12

They hanged Haman on the gallows that he had prepared for Mordecai.
Esther 7:10

Give them after the work of their hands; render to them their desert.
Ps. 28:4

Let them be blotted out of the book of the living, and not be written with the righteous.
Ps. 69:28

Let his children be fatherless, and his wife a widow.
Ps. 109:9

As he loved cursing, so let it come unto him: as he delighted not in blessing, so let it be far from him.
Ps. 109:17

Let the wicked fall into their own nets.
Ps. 141:10

He that diggeth a pit shall fall into it.
Eccl. 10:8

Thy men shall fall by the sword, and thy mighty in the war.
Isa. 3:25

The sword of the Lord is filled with blood, it is made fat with fatness.
Isa. 34:6

The moth shall eat them up like a garment, and the worm shall eat them like wool.
Isa. 51:8

I will not keep silence, but will recompense.
Isa. 65:6

He shall come up as clouds, and his chariots shall be as a whirlwind.
Jer. 4:13

Mine eye shall not spare thee, neither will I have pity: but I will recompense thy ways.
E.g., Ezek. 7:4
See also Ezek. 9:5

Ye shall know that I am the Lord, when I set My face against them.
Ezek. 15:7

I will destroy the fat and the strong; I will feed them with judgment.
Ezek. 34:16

Their blood shall be poured out as dust, and their flesh as the dung.
Zeph. 1:17

As He cried, and they would not hear; so they cried, and I would not hear, saith the Lord of hosts.
Zech. 7:13

He that killeth with the sword must be killed with the sword.
Rev. 13:10

Reward her even as she rewarded you, and double unto her double according to her works.
(her: Babylon)
Rev. 18:6

Out of His mouth goeth a sharp sword, that with it He should smite the nations.
Rev. 19:15

[*See also* Forgiveness, God's Anger, Judgment, Punishment, Revenge]

REVELATION

Stand thou still a while, that I may show thee the word of God.
Samuel to Saul
1 Sam. 9:27

No man knoweth the Son, but the Father; neither knoweth any man the Father, save the Son, and he to whomsoever the Son will reveal Him.
Jesus
Matt. 11:27
See also Luke 10:22

Flesh and blood hath not revealed it unto thee, but my Father which is in heaven.
Jesus
Matt. 16:17

I that speak unto thee am He.
Jesus
John 4:26

I speak to the world those things which I have heard of Him.
Jesus
John 8:26

I have not spoken of myself; but the Father which sent me.
Jesus
John 12:49
See also John 14:10

He that hath seen me hath seen the Father.
Jesus
John 14:9

All things that I have heard of my Father I have made known unto you.
Jesus
John 15:15

I have appeared unto thee for this purpose, to make thee a minister and a witness.
Jesus to Saul
Acts 26:16

REVENGE

The voice of thy brother's blood crieth unto Me from the ground.
Gen. 4:10

Should he deal with our sister as with an harlot?
Gen. 34:31

Against all the gods of Egypt I will execute judgment: I am the Lord.
Ex. 12:12

Thou shalt give life for life, Eye for eye, tooth for tooth, hand for hand, foot for foot, Burning for burning, wound for wound, stripe for stripe.
Ex. 21:23–25
See also Lev. 24:20, Deut. 19:21

I would make the remembrance of them to cease from among men.
Deut. 32:26

To Me belongeth vengeance, and recompense.
Deut. 32:35

I will render vengeance to Mine enemies, and will reward them that hate Me.
Deut. 32:41

I will make Mine arrows drunk with blood, and My sword shall devour flesh.
Deut. 32:42

As the Lord liveth, if ye had saved them alive, I would not slay you.
Judg. 8:19

Now shall I be more blameless than the Philistines, though I do them a displeasure.
Judg. 15:3

As they did unto me, so have I done unto them.
Samson
Judg. 15:11

Remember me, I pray Thee, and strengthen me, I pray Thee, only this once, O God.
Samson
Judg. 16:28

Slay both man and woman, infant and suckling, ox and sheep, camel and ass.
Samuel to Saul
1 Sam. 15:3

I will deliver thine enemy into thine hand, that thou mayest do to him as it shall seem good unto thee.
God to David
1 Sam. 24:4

Shall the sword devour for ever?
2 Sam. 2:26

Let not his hoar head go down to the grave in peace.
1 Kings 2:6

Hold him not guiltless.
1 Kings 2:9

Thou art a wise man, and knowest what thou oughtest to do unto him.
1 Kings 2:9

The dogs shall eat Jezebel by the wall of Jezreel.
1 Kings 21:23

There came forth two she bears out of the wood, and tare forty and two children.
2 Kings 2:24

Turn their reproach upon their own head.
Neh. 4:4

Let not their sin be blotted out from before Thee.
Neh. 4:5

Destroy Thou them, O God; let them fall by their own counsels.
Ps. 5:10

It is God that avengeth me.
Ps. 18:47, 2 Sam. 22:48

The righteous shall rejoice when he seeth the vengeance: he shall wash his feet in the blood of the wicked.
Ps. 58:10

Keep not Thou silence, O God: hold not Thy peace.
Ps. 83:1

God, to whom vengeance belongeth.
Ps. 94:1

Let his days be few; and let another take his office.
(his: the wicked)
Ps. 109:8

Let mine adversaries be clothed with shame, and let them cover themselves with their own confusion.
Ps. 109:29

Let the high praises of God be in their mouth, and a twoedged sword in their hand; To execute vengeance upon the heathen.
Ps. 149:6–7

Say not, I will do so to him as he hath done to me.
Prov. 24:29

I will ease Me of Mine adversaries, and avenge Me of Mine enemies.
Isa. 1:24

They shall take them captives, whose captives they were.
Isa. 14:2

Awake, awake, put on strength, O arm of the Lord; awake, as in the ancient days, in the generations of old.
Isa. 51:9

Shall not My soul be avenged on such a nation as this?
Jer. 5:9

Pour out Thy fury upon the heathen that know Thee not, and upon the families that call not on Thy name.
Jer. 10:25

Let me see Thy vengeance on them: for unto Thee have I revealed my cause.
Jer. 11:20
See also Jer. 20:12

They that spoil thee shall be a spoil, and all that prey upon thee will I give for a prey.
Jer. 30:16

The sword shall devour, and it shall be satiate and made drunk with their blood.
Jer. 46:10

O thou sword of the Lord, how long will it be ere thou be quiet?
Jer. 47:6

All ye that bend the bow, shoot at her, spare no arrows: for she hath sinned against the Lord.
(her: Babylon)
Jer. 50:14

Take vengeance upon her; as she hath done, do unto her.
Jer. 50:15

According to all that she hath done, do unto her: for she hath been proud against the Lord, against the Holy One of Israel.
Jer. 50:29

He shall come up like a lion from the swelling of Jordan unto the habitation of the strong.
Jer. 50:44
See also Jer. 49:19

Do unto them, as Thou hast done unto me.
Lam. 1:22

I have no pleasure in the death of the wicked.
Ezek. 33:11

As thou hast done, it shall be done unto thee.
Obad. 15

God is jealous, and the Lord revengeth.
Nah. 1:2

The Lord will take vengeance on His adversaries.
Nah. 1:2

Whosoever shall smite thee on thy right cheek, turn to him the other also.
Jesus
Matt. 5:39

Give me here John Baptist's head.
Matt. 14:8
See also Mark 6:25

Unto him that smiteth thee on the one cheek offer also the other.
Jesus
Luke 6:29

The Son of man is not come to destroy men's lives, but to save them.
Jesus
Luke 9:56

Recompense to no man evil for evil.
Rom. 12:17

Avenge not yourselves.
Rom. 12:19

Vengeance is Mine; I will repay, saith the Lord.
Rom. 12:19

Be not overcome of evil, but overcome evil with good.
Rom. 12:21

See that none render evil for evil unto any man.
1 Thess. 5:15

In flaming fire taking vengeance on them that know not God, and that obey not the gospel.
2 Thess. 1:8

Vengeance belongeth unto Me, I will recompense, saith the Lord.
Heb. 10:30

The great winepress of the wrath of God.
Rev. 14:19

They have shed the blood of saints and prophets, and Thou hast given them blood to drink.
Rev. 16:6

Rejoice over her, thou heaven, and ye holy apostles and prophets; for God hath avenged you on her.
(her: Babylon)
Rev. 18:20

[See also Enemies, Forgiveness, Punishment, Restraint, Retribution]

REVERENCE

Put off thy shoes from off thy feet, for the place whereon thou standest is holy ground.
> Ex. 3:5
> See also Josh. 5:15

Thou shalt fear the Lord thy God; Him shalt thou serve, and to Him shalt thou cleave, and swear by His name.
> Deut. 10:20
> See also Deut. 6:13

Fear the Lord, and serve Him, and obey His voice.
> 1 Sam. 12:14

As the heaven is high above the earth, so great is His mercy toward them that fear Him.
> Ps. 103:11

The Lord taketh pleasure in them that fear Him, in those that hope in His mercy.
> Ps. 147:11

Their fear toward Me is taught by the precept of men.
> Isa. 29:13

The Lord is in His holy temple: let all the earth keep silence before Him.
> Hab. 2:20

Every tongue should confess that Jesus Christ is Lord.
> Phil. 2:11

Fear God, and give glory to Him; for the hour of His judgment is come.
> Rev. 14:7

Who shall not fear Thee, O Lord, and glorify Thy name?
> Rev. 15:4

[See also Awe, Fear of God]

REVERSAL

The elder shall serve the younger.
> Gen. 25:23, Rom. 9:12

They that were full have hired out themselves for bread.
> 1 Sam. 2:5

How are the mighty fallen!
> E.g., 2 Sam. 1:19

The victory that day was turned into mourning.
> 2 Sam. 19:2

They shall become a prey and a spoil to all their enemies.
> 2 Kings 21:14

The mean man shall be brought down, and the mighty man shall be humbled.
> Isa. 5:15

A little one shall become a thousand, and a small one a strong nation.
> Isa. 60:22

She that was great among the nations, and princess among the provinces, how is she become tributary!
> Lam. 1:1

The crown is fallen from our head: woe unto us, that we have sinned!
> Lam. 5:16

Exalt him that is low, and abase him that is high.
> Ezek. 21:26

The stone which the builders rejected is become the head of the corner.
> Jesus
> Mark 12:10
> See also Ps. 118:22, Matt. 21:42, Luke 20:17

He that is least among you all, the same shall be great.
> Jesus
> Luke 9:48

Babylon the great is fallen, is fallen, and become the habitation of devils.
> Rev. 18:2

REVOLUTION

See Rebellion, Strife.

If thou doest well, shalt thou not be accepted?
> God to Cain
> *Gen. 4:7*

In thy seed shall all the nations of the earth be blessed; because thou hast obeyed My voice.
> God to Abraham
> *Gen. 22:18*

If ye will obey My voice indeed, and keep My covenant, then ye shall be a peculiar treasure unto Me above all people: for all the earth is Mine.
> *Ex. 19:5*

If ye walk in My statutes, and keep My commandments, and do them; Then I will give you rain in due season, and the land shall yield her increase, and the trees of the field shall yield their fruit.
> *Lev. 26:3–4*

I will walk among you, and will be your God, and ye shall be My people.
> *Lev. 26:12*
> *See also 2 Cor. 6:16*

I the Lord thy God am a jealous God, visiting the iniquity of the fathers upon the children unto the third and fourth generation of them that hate Me, And showing mercy unto thousands of them that love Me and keep My commandments.
> *Deut. 5:9–10*

Blessed shalt thou be in the city, and blessed shalt thou be in the field.
> *Deut. 28:3*

The Lord shall make thee the head, and not the tail; and thou shalt be above only, and thou shalt not be beneath.
> *Deut. 28:13*

I will build him a sure house; and he shall walk before Mine anointed for ever.
> *1 Sam. 2:35*

The Lord render to every man his righteousness and his faithfulness.
> *1 Sam. 26:23*

Ask what I shall give thee.
> God to Solomon
> *1 Kings 3:5, 2 Chron. 1:7*

I have also given thee that which thou hast not asked, both riches, and honour.
> God to Solomon
> *1 Kings 3:13*

Thou shalt be gathered into thy grave in peace.
> *2 Kings 22:20*

Your work shall be rewarded.
> *2 Chron. 15:7*

The Lord is able to give thee much more.
> *2 Chron. 25:9*

Remember me, O my God, for good.
> *Neh. 13:31*
> *See also Neh. 5:19*

What shall be done unto the man whom the king delighteth to honour?
> *Esther 6:6*

What is the hope of the hypocrite, though he hath gained, when God taketh away his soul?
> *Job 27:8*

The Lord gave Job twice as much as he had before.
> *Job 42:10*

The Lord preserveth the faithful, and plentifully rewardeth the proud doer.
> *Ps. 31:23*

Many sorrows shall be to the wicked: but he that trusteth in the Lord, mercy shall compass him about.
> *Ps. 32:10*

Those that wait upon the Lord, they shall inherit the earth.
> *Ps. 37:9*

The meek shall inherit the earth.
> *Ps. 37:11*

The righteous shall inherit the land.
> *Ps. 37:29*

Verily there is a reward for the righteous.
> *Ps. 58:11*

No good thing will He withhold from them that walk uprightly.
> *Ps. 84:11*

Thou shalt eat the labour of thine hands.
> *Ps. 128:2*

The Lord lifteth up the meek: He casteth the wicked down to the ground.
> *Ps. 147:6*

Withhold not good from them to whom it is due, when it is in the power of thine hand to do it.
Prov. 3:27

He that troubleth his own house shall inherit the wind.
Prov. 11:29

The fruit of the righteous is a tree of life.
Prov. 11:30

He that tilleth his land shall have plenty of bread.
Prov. 28:19

Many seek the ruler's favour; but every man's judgment cometh from the Lord.
Prov. 29:26

God giveth to a man that is good in His sight wisdom, and knowledge, and joy.
Eccl. 2:26

Every man should eat and drink, and enjoy the good of all his labour, it is the gift of God.
Eccl. 3:13
See also Eccl. 5:18

Cast thy bread upon the waters: for thou shalt find it after many days.
Eccl. 11:1

Sow ye, and reap.
Isa. 37:30, 2 Kings 19:29

He that putteth his trust in Me shall possess the land, and shall inherit My holy mountain.
Isa. 57:13

As the days of a tree are the days of My people, and Mine elect shall long enjoy the work of their hands.
Isa. 65:22

The hand of the Lord shall be known toward His servants, and His indignation toward His enemies.
Isa. 66:14

Refrain thy voice from weeping, and thine eyes from tears: for thy work shall be rewarded, saith the Lord.
Jer. 31:16

They have sown the wind, and they shall reap the whirlwind.
Hos. 8:7

Sow to yourselves in righteousness, reap in mercy.
Hos. 10:12

What profiteth the graven image that the maker thereof hath graven it?
Hab. 2:18

Blessed are the meek: for they shall inherit the earth.
Jesus
Matt. 5:5

Great is your reward in heaven.
Jesus
Matt. 5:12

Thy Father which seeth in secret shall reward thee openly.
Jesus
Matt. 6:6, Matt. 6:18

Every one that asketh receiveth.
Jesus
Matt. 7:8, Luke 11:10

According to your faith be it unto you.
Jesus
Matt. 9:29

Freely ye have received, freely give.
Jesus
Matt. 10:8

He shall reward every man according to his works.
Jesus
Matt. 16:27

To sit on my right hand, and on my left, is not mine to give, but it shall be given to them for whom it is prepared of my Father.
Jesus
Matt. 20:23
See also Mark 10:40

He that hath, to him shall be given: and he that hath not, from him shall be taken even that which he hath.
Jesus
Mark 4:25
See also Matt. 13:12, Matt. 25:29,
Luke 8:18, Luke 19:26

Seek ye the kingdom of God; and all these things shall be added unto you.
Jesus
Luke 12:31
See also Matt. 6:33

When thou makest a feast, call the poor the maimed, the lame, the blind: And thou

shalt be blessed; for they cannot recompense thee.
Jesus
Luke 14:13–14

Thou shalt be recompensed at the resurrection of the just.
Jesus
Luke 14:14

A man can receive nothing, except it be given him from heaven.
John 3:27

He that reapeth receiveth wages, and gathereth fruit unto life eternal.
Jesus
John 4:36

If any man serve me, him will my Father honour.
Jesus
John 12:26

Glory, honour, and peace, to every man that worketh good.
Rom. 2:10

The wages of sin is death; but the gift of God is eternal life through Jesus Christ our Lord.
Rom. 6:23

All things work together for good to them that love God.
Rom. 8:28

Every man shall receive his own reward according to his own labour.
1 Cor. 3:8

He which soweth bountifully shall reap also bountifully.
2 Cor. 9:6

Whatsoever a man soweth, that shall he also reap.
Gal. 6:7

He that soweth to the Spirit shall of the Spirit reap life everlasting.
Gal. 6:8

In due season we shall reap.
Gal. 6:9

Whatsoever good thing any man doeth, the same shall he receive of the Lord.
Eph. 6:8

Of the Lord ye shall receive the reward of the inheritance.
Col. 3:24

The husbandman that laboureth must be first partaker of the fruits.
2 Tim. 2:6

There is laid up for me a crown of righteousness, which the Lord, the righteous judge, shall give me at that day.
2 Tim. 4:8

Ye have need of patience, that, after ye have done the will of God, ye might receive the promise.
Heb. 10:36

When the chief Shepherd shall appear, ye shall receive a crown of glory that fadeth not away.
1 Pet. 5:4

To him that overcometh will I give to eat of the hidden manna.
Jesus
Rev. 2:17

And I will give him the morning star.
Jesus
Rev. 2:28

They shall walk with me in white: for they are worthy.
Jesus
Rev. 3:4

Him that overcometh will I make a pillar in the temple of my God.
Jesus
Rev. 3:12

[*See also* Blessing, Eternal Life, Profit, Punishment, Success, Victory, Wealth]

RIDDLES

Out of the eater came forth meat, and out of the strong came forth sweetness.
Judg. 14:14

What is sweeter than honey? and what is stronger than a lion?
Judg. 14:18

RIGHTEOUSNESS

Can we find such a one as this is, a man in whom the Spirit of God is?
Pharaoh to Joseph
Gen. 41:38

In righteousness shalt thou judge thy neighbour.
Lev. 19:15

All that do unrighteously, are an abomination unto the Lord thy God.
Deut. 25:16

Thou art more righteous than I: for thou hast rewarded me good, whereas I have rewarded thee evil.
Saul to David
1 Sam. 24:17

He did that which was right in the sight of the Lord.
2 Kings 14:3

One that feared God, and eschewed evil.
(one: Job)
Job 1:1

Shall mortal man be more just than God? shall a man be more pure than his maker?
Job 4:17

How should man be just with God?
Job 9:2

Is it any pleasure to the Almighty, that thou art righteous?
Job 22:3

I was eyes to the blind, and feet was I to the lame.
Job 29:15

With kings are they on the throne.
(they: the righteous)
Job 36:7

His delight is in the law of the Lord; and in His law doth he meditate day and night.
Ps. 1:2

He leadeth me in the paths of righteousness for His name's sake.
Ps. 23:3

Shout for joy, all ye that are upright in heart.
Ps. 32:11

The eyes of the Lord are upon the righteous, and His ears are open unto their cry.
Ps. 34:15

The steps of a good man are ordered by the Lord: and He delighteth in his way.
Ps. 37:23

I have been young, and now am old; yet have I not seen the righteous forsaken.
Ps. 37:25

The righteous shall inherit the land.
Ps. 37:29

Mark the perfect man, and behold the upright: for the end of that man is peace.
Ps. 37:37

The salvation of the righteous is of the Lord: He is their strength in the time of trouble.
Ps. 37:39

Verily there is a reward for the righteous.
Ps. 58:11

No good thing will He withhold from them that walk uprightly.
Ps. 84:11

The righteous shall flourish like the palm tree: he shall grow like a cedar in Lebanon.
Ps. 92:12

Righteousness and judgment are the habitation of His throne.
Ps. 97:2

Light is sown for the righteous, and gladness for the upright in heart.
Ps. 97:11

With righteousness shall He judge the world.
Ps. 98:9

Precious in the sight of the Lord is the death of His saints.
Ps. 116:15

I have done judgment and justice: leave me not to mine oppressors.
Ps. 119:121

The Lord is righteous in all His ways, and holy in all His works.
Ps. 145:17

The Lord loveth the righteous.
Ps. 146:8

The path of the just is as the shining light, that shineth more and more unto the perfect day.
Prov. 4:18

Righteousness delivereth from death.
Prov. 10:2, Prov. 11:4

The labour of the righteous tendeth to life: the fruit of the wicked to sin.
Prov. 10:16

The lips of the righteous feed many.
Prov. 10:21

The mouth of the just bringeth forth wisdom.
Prov. 10:31

When it goeth well with the righteous, the city rejoiceth.
Prov. 11:10

To him that soweth righteousness shall be a sure reward.
Prov. 11:18

The desire of the righteous is only good: but the expectation of the wicked is wrath.
Prov. 11:23

The fruit of the righteous is a tree of life.
Prov. 11:30

The thoughts of the righteous are right: but the counsels of the wicked are deceit.
Prov. 12:5

In the house of the righteous is much treasure: but in the revenues of the wicked is trouble.
Prov. 15:6

To do justice and judgment is more acceptable to the Lord than sacrifice.
Prov. 21:3

God giveth to a man that is good in His sight wisdom, and knowledge, and joy.
Eccl. 2:26

One man among a thousand have I found; but a woman among all those have I not.
Eccl. 7:28

God that is holy shall be sanctified in righteousness.
Isa. 5:16

The way of the just is uprightness.
Isa. 26:7

The work of righteousness shall be peace.
Isa. 32:17

Bread shall be given him; his waters shall be sure.
(him: the righteous)
Isa. 33:16

In righteousness shalt thou be established.
Isa. 54:14

Though these three men, Noah, Daniel, and Job, were in it, they should deliver but their own souls by their righteousness.
Ezek. 14:14

He is just, he shall surely live, saith the Lord God.
Ezek. 18:9

The righteousness of the righteous shall not deliver him in the day of his transgression.
Ezek. 33:12

O Lord, righteousness belongeth unto Thee.
Dan. 9:7

Sow to yourselves in righteousness, reap in mercy.
Hos. 10:12

Do justly.
Mic. 6:8

It becometh us to fulfil all righteousness.
Jesus
Matt. 3:15

Blessed are they which do hunger and thirst after righteousness: for they shall be filled.
Jesus
Matt. 5:6
See also Luke 6:21

Blessed are they which are persecuted for righteousness' sake: for their's is the kingdom of heaven.
Jesus
Matt. 5:10

He that receiveth a righteous man in the name of a righteous man shall receive a righteous man's reward.
Jesus
Matt. 10:41

If ye were Abraham's children, ye would do the works of Abraham.
Jesus
John 8:39

Thy heart is not right in the sight of God.
Acts 8:21

The just shall live by faith.
E.g., Rom. 1:17
See also Hab. 2:4

There is none righteous, no, not one.
Rom. 3:10
See also Ps. 14:3, Ps. 53:3

The unrighteous shall not inherit the kingdom of God.
1 Cor. 6:9

If righteousness come by the law, then Christ is dead in vain.
Gal. 2:21

Ever follow that which is good.
1 Thess. 5:15

Be not weary in well doing.
2 Thess. 3:13
See also Gal. 6:9

Flee also youthful lusts: but follow righteousness, faith, charity, peace.
2 Tim. 2:22

A sceptre of righteousness is the sceptre of Thy kingdom.
Heb. 1:8

The fruit of righteousness is sown in peace of them that make peace.
James 3:18

If ye suffer for righteousness' sake, happy are ye.
1 Pet. 3:14

Every one that doeth righteousness is born of Him.
1 John 2:29

Little children, let no man deceive you: he that doeth righteousness is righteous.
1 John 3:7

All unrighteousness is sin.
1 John 5:17

They shall walk with me in white: for they are worthy.
Jesus
Rev. 3:4

In their mouth was found no guile: for they are without fault before the throne of God.
Rev. 14:5

Just and true are Thy ways, Thou King of saints.
Rev. 15:3

Behold a white horse; and he that sat upon him was called Faithful and True.
Rev. 19:11

[*See also* Evil, Goodness, Integrity, Justice, Self-Righteousness, Sin, Virtue, Wickedness]

RISK

Is not this the blood of the men that went in jeopardy of their lives?
2 Sam. 23:17

With the jeopardy of their lives they brought it.
1 Chron. 11:19

Why stand we in jeopardy every hour?
1 Cor. 15:30

RITUALS

Hath the Lord as great delight in burnt offerings and sacrifices, as in obeying the voice of the Lord?
1 Sam. 15:22

To do justice and judgment is more acceptable to the Lord than sacrifice.
Prov. 21:3

To what purpose is the multitude of your sacrifices unto Me?
Isa. 1:11

Bring no more vain oblations.
Isa. 1:13

I desired mercy, and not sacrifice; and the knowledge of God more than burnt offerings.
Hos. 6:6
See also Matt. 9:13

To eat with unwashen hands defileth not a man.
Jesus
Matt. 15:20

This people honoureth me with their lips, but their heart is far from me.
Jesus
Mark 7:6
See also Matt. 15:8

He is not a Jew, which is one outwardly.
Rom. 2:28

He that eateth, eateth to the Lord, for he giveth God thanks.
Rom. 14:6

The kingdom of God is not meat and

drink; but righteousness, and peace, and joy in the Holy Ghost.
Rom. 14:17

Circumcision is nothing, and uncircumcision is nothing, but the keeping of the commandments of God.
1 Cor. 7:19

The things which the Gentiles sacrifice, they sacrifice to devils, and not to God.
1 Cor. 10:20

It is not possible that the blood of bulls and of goats should take away sins.
Heb. 10:4

[*See also* Circumcision, Sacrifices]

ROBBERY

Thou shalt not steal.
Eighth Commandment
Ex. 20:15
See also Lev. 19:11, Deut. 5:19, Matt. 19:18

If the thief be found, let him pay double.
Ex. 22:7

Rob not the poor, because he is poor: neither oppress the afflicted in the gate.
Prov. 22:22

[*See also* Crime, Criminals]

ROMANCE

The way of an eagle in the air; the way of a serpent upon a rock; the way of a ship in the midst of the sea; and the way of a man with a maid.
Prov. 30:19

Let him kiss me with the kisses of his mouth: for thy love is better than wine.
Song 1:2

Rise up, my love, my fair one, and come away.
Song 2:10

I am my beloved's, and his desire is toward me.
Song 7:10

Set me as a seal upon thine heart, as a seal upon thine arm.
Song 8:6

[*See also* Love]

SABBATH

And God blessed the seventh day, and sanctified it: because that in it He had rested from all His work which God created and made.
Gen. 2:3

Remember the sabbath day, to keep it holy.
Fourth Commandment
Ex. 20:8

Six days shalt thou labour, and do all thy work: But the seventh day is the sabbath of the Lord thy God: in it thou shalt not do any work.
Ex. 20:9–10
See also Ex. 35:2, Deut. 5:13–14

Six days thou shalt do thy work, and on the seventh day thou shalt rest.
Ex. 23:12
See also Ex. 34:21, Ex. 35:2

My sabbaths ye shall keep: for it is a sign between Me and you throughout your generations.
Ex. 31:13

Every one that defileth it shall surely be put to death.
Ex. 31:14

In six days the Lord made heaven and earth, and on the seventh day He rested, and was refreshed.
Ex. 31:17

Keep the sabbath day to sanctify it.
Deut. 5:12

Hallow My sabbaths; and they shall be a sign between Me and you, that ye may know that I am the Lord your God.
Ezek. 20:20

The Son of man is Lord even of the sabbath day.
Jesus
Matt. 12:8
See also Mark 2:28, Luke 6:5

It is lawful to do well on the sabbath days.
Jesus
Matt. 12:12
See also Mark 3:4, Luke 6:5

The sabbath was made for man, and not man for the sabbath.
Jesus
Mark 2:27

He that regardeth the day, regardeth it unto the Lord.
Rom. 14:6

SACRIFICE

He that loseth his life for my sake shall find it.
Jesus
Matt. 10:39

Whosoever will save his life shall lose it: and whosoever will lose his life for my sake shall find it.
Jesus
Matt. 16:25
See also Mark 8:35, Luke 9:24

The Son of man came not to be ministered unto, but to minister, and to give His life a ransom for many.
Jesus
Matt. 20:28, Mark 10:45

For God so loved the world, that He gave His only begotten Son, that whosoever believeth in Him should not perish, but have everlasting life.
Jesus
John 3:16
See also John 3:36, John 6:47

The bread that I will give is my flesh, which I will give for the life of the world.
Jesus
John 6:51

The good shepherd giveth his life for the sheep.
Jesus
John 10:11

Greater love hath no man than this, that a man lay down his life for his friends.
Jesus
John 15:13

Glorify Thy Son, that Thy Son also may glorify Thee.
Jesus
John 17:1

Like a lamb dumb before His shearer, so opened He not His mouth.
Acts 8:32
See also Isa. 53:7

Christ died for the ungodly.
Rom. 5:6

Scarcely for a righteous man will one die: yet peradventure for a good man some would even dare to die.
Rom. 5:7

While we were yet sinners, Christ died for us.
Rom. 5:8

This is my body, which is broken for you: this do in remembrance of me.
Jesus
1 Cor. 11:24
See also Luke 22:19

Christ died for our sins.
1 Cor. 15:3

He died for all.
2 Cor. 5:15

Though He was rich, yet for your sakes He became poor, that ye through His poverty might be rich.
2 Cor. 8:9

Ye would have plucked out your own eyes, and have given them to me.
Gal. 4:15

What things were gain to me, those I counted loss for Christ.
Phil. 3:7

With such sacrifices God is well pleased.
Heb. 13:16

He laid down His life for us: and we ought to lay down our lives for the brethren.
1 John 3:16

God sent His only begotten Son into the world, that we might live through Him.
1 John 4:9

They overcame him by the blood of the Lamb.
(him: Satan)
Rev. 12:11

[*See also* Crucifixion, Martyrdom]

SACRIFICES

Behold the fire and the wood: but where is the lamb for a burnt offering?
Isaac to Abraham
Gen. 22:7

He that sacrificeth unto any god, save unto the Lord only, he shall be utterly destroyed.
Ex. 22:20

If thou wilt offer a burnt offering, thou must offer it unto the Lord.
Judg. 13:16

To obey is better than sacrifice, and to hearken than the fat of rams.
1 Sam. 15:22

I desired mercy, and not sacrifice; and the knowledge of God more than burnt offerings.
Hos. 6:6
See also Matt. 9:13

[*See also* Rituals]

SACRILEGE

Thou shalt not bring the hire of a whore, or the price of a dog, into the house of the Lord.
Deut. 23:18

Why wilt thou swallow up the inheritance of the Lord?
2 Sam. 20:19

Let her not be slain in the house of the Lord.
2 Kings 11:15
See also 2 Chron. 23:14

Uzza put forth his hand to hold the ark; for the oxen stumbled. And the anger of the Lord was kindled against Uzza, and He smote him.
1 Chron. 13:9–10
See also 2 Sam. 6:6–7

I will curse your blessings.
God to wayward priests
Mal. 2:2

My house is the house of prayer: but ye have made it a den of thieves.
Jesus
Luke 19:46
See also Matt. 21:13, Mark 11:17

Make not my Father's house an house of merchandise.
Jesus
John 2:16

If any man defile the temple of God, him shall God destroy.
1 Cor. 3:17

[*See also* Holiness]

SAFETY

The beloved of the Lord shall dwell in safety by Him.
Deut. 33:12

The eternal God is thy refuge.
Deut. 33:27

There shall not one hair of thy son fall to the earth.
2 Sam. 14:11

Thou hast enlarged my steps under me; so that my feet did not slip.
2 Sam. 22:37

The Lord also will be a refuge for the oppressed, a refuge in times of trouble.
Ps. 9:9

Deliver me not over unto the will of mine enemies: for false witnesses are risen up against me.
Ps. 27:12

God is our refuge and strength, a very present help in trouble.
Ps. 46:1

In the shadow of Thy wings will I make my refuge.
Ps. 57:1

Lead me to the rock that is higher than I.
Ps. 61:2

My God is the rock of my refuge.
Ps. 94:22

Hold Thou me up, and I shall be safe.
Ps. 119:117

The Lord shall preserve thee from all evil:
He shall preserve thy soul.
Ps. 121:7

Set up the standard toward Zion.
Jer. 4:6

They shall dwell with confidence, when I
have executed judgments upon all those
that despise them.
Ezek. 28:26

The ways of the Lord are right, and the just
shall walk in them: but the transgressors
shall fall therein.
Hos. 14:9

Seek righteousness, seek meekness: it may
be ye shall be hid in the day of the Lord's
anger.
Zeph. 2:3

He that followeth me shall not walk in
darkness.
Jesus
John 8:12

I am with thee, and no man shall set on
thee to hurt thee.
Jesus to Paul
Acts 18:10

The Lord shall deliver me from every evil
work, and will preserve me unto His heavenly kingdom.
2 Tim. 4:18

The Lord is my helper, and I will not fear
what man shall do unto me.
Heb. 13:6
See also Ps. 118:6

[*See also* God's Protection, God's Support,
Peace, Security]

SALUTATIONS

The Lord be with you.
Ruth 2:4

The Lord bless thee.
Ruth 2:4

Grace be to you and peace from God our
Father.
2 Cor. 1:2

Greet one another with an holy kiss.
2 Cor. 13:12
See also Rom. 16:16

Grace and peace be multiplied unto you
through the knowledge of God, and of
Jesus our Lord.
2 Pet. 1:2

Grace be with you, mercy, and peace.
2 John 3

Mercy unto you, and peace, and love.
Jude 2

[*See also* Blessings, Greetings]

SALVATION

I have waited for Thy salvation, O Lord.
Jacob
Gen. 49:18

The Lord is my strength and song, and He
is become my salvation.
Ex. 15:2

He is my shield, and the horn of my
salvation, my high tower, and my refuge.
David
2 Sam. 22:3

Salvation belongeth unto the Lord.
Ps. 3:8

Save me for Thy mercies' sake.
E.g., Ps. 6:4

He that walketh uprightly, and worketh
righteousness, and speaketh the truth in his
heart.
Ps. 15:2

The salvation of the righteous is of the
Lord: He is their strength in the time of
trouble.
Ps. 37:39

My soul waiteth upon God: from Him
cometh my salvation.
Ps. 62:1

In God is my salvation and my glory.
Ps. 62:7

Cause Thy face to shine; and we shall be
saved.
Ps. 80:3, 7, 19

Salvation is far from the wicked: for they seek not Thy statutes.
Ps. 119:155

They that dwell in the land of the shadow of death, upon them hath the light shined.
Isa. 9:2

To whom will ye flee for help? and where will ye leave your glory?
Isa. 10:3

God is my salvation; I will trust, and not be afraid.
Isa. 12:2

With joy shall ye draw water out of the wells of salvation.
Isa. 12:3

My salvation shall be for ever, and My righteousness shall not be abolished.
Isa. 51:6

In vain is salvation hoped for from the hills, and from the multitude of mountains.
Jer. 3:23

Heal me, O Lord, and I shall be healed; save me, and I shall be saved.
Jer. 17:14

Flee out of the midst of Babylon, and deliver every man his soul.
Jer. 51:6

It is good that a man should both hope and quietly wait for the salvation of the Lord.
Lam. 3:26

If thou warn the wicked, and he turn not from his wickedness, nor from his wicked way, he shall die in his iniquity; but thou hast delivered thy soul.
Ezek. 3:19, 21

Salvation is of the Lord.
Jonah 2:9

I will rejoice in the Lord, I will joy in the God of my salvation.
Hab. 3:18

The Lord thy God in the midst of thee is mighty; He will save, He will rejoice over thee with joy.
Zeph. 3:17

Unto you that fear My name shall the Sun of righteousness arise with healing in his wings.
Mal. 4:2

Strait is the gate, and narrow is the way, which leadeth unto life, and few there be that find it.
Jesus
Matt. 7:14

The kingdom of heaven is at hand.
Jesus
E.g., Matt. 10:7

The keys of the kingdom of heaven.
Jesus
Matt. 16:19

Whosoever will save his life shall lose it: and whosoever will lose his life for my sake shall find it.
Jesus
Matt. 16:25
See also Mark 8:35, Luke 9:24

The Son of man is come to save that which was lost.
Jesus
Matt. 18:11

Who then can be saved?
Matt. 19:25, Mark 10:26,
Luke 18:26

He that shall endure unto the end, the same shall be saved.
Jesus
Matt. 24:13, Mark 13:13

The kingdom of God is at hand: repent ye, and believe the gospel.
Jesus
Mark 1:15
See also Matt. 4:17

Suffer the little children to come unto me, and forbid them not: for of such is the kingdom of God.
Jesus
Mark 10:14
See also Matt. 19:14, Luke 18:16

He that believeth and is baptized shall be saved; but he that believeth not shall be damned.
Jesus
Mark 16:16

The Son of man is not come to destroy men's lives, but to save them.
Jesus
Luke 9:56

The Son of man is come to seek and to save that which was lost.
Jesus
Luke 19:10

For God so loved the world, that He gave His only begotten Son, that whosoever believeth in Him should not perish, but have everlasting life.
Jesus
John 3:16
See also John 3:36, John 6:47

God sent not His Son into the world to condemn the world; but that the world through Him might be saved.
Jesus
John 3:17

Salvation is of the Jews.
Jesus
John 4:22

These things I say, that ye might be saved.
Jesus
John 5:34

I am the door: by me if any man enter in, he shall be saved.
Jesus
John 10:9

I am come a light into the world, that whosoever believeth on me should not abide in darkness.
Jesus
John 12:46

I came not to judge the world, but to save the world.
Jesus
John 12:47

No man cometh unto the Father, but by me.
Jesus
John 14:6

None of them is lost, but the son of perdition.
Jesus (son: Judas)
John 17:12

Whosoever shall call on the name of the Lord shall be saved.
E.g., Acts 2:21
See also Joel 2:32

Whosoever among you feareth God, to you is the word of this salvation sent.
Acts 13:26

I have set thee to be a light of the Gentiles, that thou shouldest be for salvation unto the ends of the earth.
Acts 13:47
See also Isa. 49:6

Through the grace of the Lord Jesus Christ we shall be saved.
Acts 15:11

Believe on the Lord Jesus Christ, and thou shalt be saved.
Acts 16:31

The salvation of God is sent unto the Gentiles.
Acts 28:28

The gift of God is eternal life through Jesus Christ our Lord.
Rom. 6:23

If thou shalt confess with thy mouth the Lord Jesus, and shalt believe in thine heart that God hath raised Him from the dead, thou shalt be saved.
Rom. 10:9

Now it is high time to awake out of sleep.
Rom. 13:11

Now is our salvation nearer than when we believed.
Rom. 13:11

I am made all things to all men, that I might by all means save some.
1 Cor. 9:22

Behold, now is the accepted time; behold, now is the day of salvation.
2 Cor. 6:2

By grace are ye saved through faith.
Eph. 2:8

Work out your own salvation with fear and trembling.
Phil. 2:12

God hath not appointed us to wrath, but to obtain salvation.
1 Thess. 5:9

Christ Jesus came into the world to save sinners.
1 Tim. 1:15

God our Saviour.
1 Tim. 2:3

Not by works of righteousness which we

have done, but according to His mercy He saved us.
> *Titus 3:5*

Ye have need of patience, that, after ye have done the will of God, ye might receive the promise.
> *Heb. 10:36*

He which converteth the sinner from the error of his way shall save a soul from death.
> *James 5:20*

If the righteous scarcely be saved, where shall the ungodly and the sinner appear?
> *1 Pet. 4:18*

The longsuffering of our Lord is salvation.
> *2 Pet. 3:15*

The Father sent the Son to be the Saviour of the world.
> *1 John 4:14*

Without are dogs, and sorcerers, and whoremongers, and murderers, and idolaters, and whosoever loveth and maketh a lie.
> *Rev. 22:15*

[*See also* Eternal Life, Kingdom of God, Redemption]

SANCTUARY

And they shall be your refuge from the avenger of blood.
> (they: cities of refuge)
> *Josh. 20:3*

They shall not deliver the slayer up into his hand; because he smote his neighbour unwittingly, and hated him not beforetime.
> *Josh. 20:5*

Let her not be slain in the house of the Lord.
> *2 Kings 11:15*
> *See also 2 Chron. 23:14*

SARCASM

See Mockery.

SATAN

If Satan cast out Satan, he is divided against himself; how shall then his kingdom stand?
> Jesus
> *Matt. 12:26*
> *See also Mark 3:26, Luke 11:18*

Get thee behind me, Satan: thou art an offence unto me.
> Jesus
> *Matt. 16:23*
> *See also Matt. 4:10, Mark 8:33, Luke 4:8*

How can Satan cast out Satan?
> Jesus
> *Mark 3:23*

What have I to do with Thee, Jesus, Thou Son of the most high God?
> *Mark 5:7*
> *See also Matt. 8:29, Luke 8:28*

Even the devils are subject unto us through Thy name.
> (Thy: Jesus)
> *Luke 10:17*

I beheld Satan as lightning fall from heaven.
> Jesus
> *Luke 10:18*

Ye are of your father the devil, and the lusts of your father ye will do.
> Jesus
> *John 8:44*

There is no truth in him.
> Jesus
> *John 8:44*

He is a liar, and the father of it.
> Jesus
> *John 8:44*

Can a devil open the eyes of the blind?
> *John 10:21*

Now is the judgment of this world: now shall the prince of this world be cast out.
> Jesus
> *John 12:31*

Wilt thou not cease to pervert the right ways of the Lord?
> *Acts 13:10*

Ye cannot drink the cup of the Lord, and the cup of devils.
1 Cor. 10:21

We are not ignorant of his devices.
2 Cor. 2:11

A thorn in the flesh, the messenger of Satan to buffet me.
2 Cor. 12:7

Put on the whole armour of God, that ye may be able to stand against the wiles of the devil.
Eph. 6:11

We wrestle not against flesh and blood, but against principalities, against powers, against the rulers of the darkness.
Eph. 6:12

Resist the devil, and he will flee from you.
James 4:7

Be sober, be vigilant; because your adversary the devil, as a roaring lion, walketh about, seeking whom he may devour.
1 Pet. 5:8

He that committeth sin is of the devil; for the devil sinneth from the beginning.
1 John 3:8

He was cast out into the earth, and his angels were cast out with him.
Rev. 12:9

They overcame him by the blood of the Lamb.
Rev. 12:11

Woe to the inhabiters of the earth and of the sea! for the devil is come down unto you.
Rev. 12:12

[*See also* Evil, Temptation]

SATISFACTION

And God saw the light, that it was good.
Gen. 1:4

And God saw every thing that He had made, and, behold, it was very good.
Gen. 1:31

Glory of this, and tarry at home.
2 Kings 14:10

A good man shall be satisfied from himself.
Prov. 14:14

Hell and destruction are never full; so the eyes of man are never satisfied.
Prov. 27:20

The horseleach hath two daughters, crying, Give, give.
Prov. 30:15

There are three things that are never satisfied, yea, four things say not, It is enough: The grave; and the barren womb; the earth that is not filled with water; and the fire that saith not, It is enough.
Prov. 30:15–16

There is nothing better, than that a man should rejoice in his own works.
Eccl. 3:22

All the labour of man is for his mouth, and yet the appetite is not filled.
Eccl. 6:7

Better is the sight of the eyes than the wandering of the desire.
Eccl. 6:9

Having food and raiment let us be therewith content.
1 Tim. 6:8

Ye fight and war, yet ye have not, because ye ask not.
James 4:2

Thou sayest, I am rich, and increased with goods, and have need of nothing; and knowest not that thou art wretched, and miserable, and poor, and blind, and naked.
Jesus
Rev. 3:17

[*See also* Complaints, Contentment, Greed, Happiness, Serenity]

SCAPEGOAT

One lot for the Lord, and the other lot for the scapegoat.
Lev. 16:8

Let him go for a scapegoat into the wilderness.
Lev. 16:10

The goat shall bear upon him all their iniquities.
Lev. 16:22

[*See also* Blame]

SCHEMING

Let the wicked fall into their own nets.
Ps. 141:10

The way of the wicked He turneth upside down.
Ps. 146:9

The wicked shall fall by his own wickedness.
Prov. 11:5

Whoso diggeth a pit shall fall therein.
Prov. 26:27

Let none of you imagine evil in your hearts against his neighbour.
Zech. 8:17
See also Zech. 7:10

[*See also* Instigation, Strategy]

SCORN

The daughter of Zion hath despised thee, and laughed thee to scorn; the daughter of Jerusalem hath shaken her head at thee.
2 Kings 19:21, Isa. 37:22

Hear, O our God; for we are despised.
Neh. 4:4

When thou mockest, shall no man make thee ashamed?
Job 11:3

Young children despised me; I arose, and they spake against me.
Job 19:18

He addeth rebellion unto his sin.
Job 34:37

Wherefore should the heathen say, Where is their God?
Ps. 79:10
See also, e.g., Ps. 115:2

The stone which the builders refused is become the head stone of the corner.
Ps. 118:22
See also, e.g., Matt. 21:42

I am small and despised: yet do not I forget Thy precepts.
Ps. 119:141

All that honoured her despise her, because they have seen her nakedness.
Lam. 1:8

Nineveh is laid waste: who will bemoan her?
Nah. 3:7

Ye have wearied the Lord with your words.
Mal. 2:17

Is not this the carpenter's son?
Matt. 13:55
See also Mark 6:3

A crown of thorns.
Matt. 27:29, Mark 15:17,
John 19:2

Is not this Jesus, the son of Joseph, whose father and mother we know?
John 6:42

These men are full of new wine.
Acts 2:13

Paul, thou art beside thyself; much learning doth make thee mad.
Festus
Acts 26:24

So is the will of God, that with well doing ye may put to silence the ignorance of foolish men.
1 Pet. 2:15

[*See also* Contempt, Criticism, Mockery]

SCRIPTURE

Ye shall not add unto the word which I command you, neither shall ye diminish ought from it.
Deut. 4:2

Man doth not live by bread only, but by every word that proceedeth out of the mouth of the Lord.
Deut. 8:3
See also, e.g., Matt. 4:4

This book of the law shall not depart out of thy mouth.
Josh. 1:8

Thou shalt meditate therein day and night.
Josh. 1:8

Observe to do according to all that is written therein.
Josh. 1:8

Turn not aside therefrom to the right hand or to the left.
Josh. 23:6

Great is the wrath of the Lord that is kindled against us, because our fathers have not hearkened unto the words of this book.
2 Kings 22:13

His delight is in the law of the Lord; and in His law doth he meditate day and night.
Ps. 1:2

The Lord gave the word: great was the company of those that published it.
Ps. 68:11

How sweet are Thy words unto my taste! yea, sweeter than honey to my mouth!
Ps. 119:103

Thy word is a lamp unto my feet, and a light unto my path.
Ps. 119:105

Thy word is true from the beginning.
Ps. 119:160

Add thou not unto His words.
Prov. 30:6

Seek ye out of the book of the Lord, and read.
Isa. 34:16

Hear ye the word of the Lord.
Jer. 21:11

The law shall go forth of Zion, and the word of the Lord from Jerusalem.
Mic. 4:2

I am not come to destroy, but to fulfil.
Jesus
Matt. 5:17

This day is this scripture fulfilled in your ears.
Jesus
Luke 4:21

The law and the prophets were until John: since that time the kingdom of God is preached.
Jesus
Luke 16:16

If ye believe not his writings, how shall ye believe my words?
Jesus, about Moses
John 5:47

These things were done, that the scripture should be fulfilled.
John 19:36

They have fulfilled them in condemning Him.
Acts 13:27

Give attendance to reading, to exhortation, to doctrine.
1 Tim. 4:13

All Scripture is given by inspiration of God.
2 Tim. 3:16

If that first covenant had been faultless, then should no place have been sought for the second.
Heb. 8:7

In that He saith, A new covenant, He hath made the first old.
Heb. 8:13

Blessed is he that readeth, and they that hear the words of this prophecy.
Rev. 1:3

[*See also* Commandments, God's Word, Gospel, Prophecy]

SEARCHING

Thou shalt find Him, if thou seek Him with all thy heart and with all thy soul.
Deut. 4:29

If thou seek Him, He will be found of thee.
1 Chron. 28:9
See also 2 Chron. 15:2

Canst thou by searching find out God?
Job 11:7

When Thou saidst, Seek ye My face; my heart said unto Thee, Thy face, Lord, will I seek.
Ps. 27:8

In the broad ways I will seek him whom my soul loveth.
Song 3:2

Seek ye the Lord while He may be found, call ye upon Him while He is near.
Isa. 55:6

I am sought of them that asked not for Me; I am found of them that sought Me not.
Isa. 65:1
See also Rom. 10:20

Ye shall seek Me, and find Me, when ye shall search for Me with all your heart.
Jer. 29:13

It is time to seek the Lord.
Hos. 10:12

Seek good, and not evil, that ye may live.
Amos 5:14

Seek ye first the kingdom of God, and His righteousness.
Jesus
Matt. 6:33
See also Luke 12:31

Seek, and ye shall find.
Jesus
Matt. 7:7, Luke 11:9

Ye shall seek me, and shall not find me: and where I am, thither ye cannot come.
Jesus
John 7:34

The Spirit searcheth all things.
1 Cor. 2:10

I am He which searcheth the reins and hearts.
Jesus
Rev. 2:23

[*See also* Devotion]

SEAS

See Oceans.

SEASONS

While the earth remaineth, seedtime and harvest, and cold and heat, and summer and winter, and day and night shall not cease.
Gen. 8:22

By the breath of God frost is given.
Job 37:10

Who can stand before His cold?
Ps. 147:17

To every thing there is a season, and a time to every purpose under the heaven.
Eccl. 3:1

Lo, the winter is past, the rain is over and gone.
Song 2:11

The flowers appear on the earth; the time of the singing of birds is come, and the voice of the turtle is heard in our land.
Song 2:12

The harvest is past, the summer is ended, and we are not saved.
Jer. 8:20

[*See also* Nature and the Appendix at p. 421]

SECOND COMING

The end is not yet.
Jesus
Matt. 24:6
See also Mark 13:7

As the lightning cometh out of the east, and shineth even unto the west; so shall also the coming of the Son of man be.
Jesus
Matt. 24:27
See also Luke 17:24

Of that day and hour knoweth no man, no, not the angels of heaven, but my Father only.
Jesus
Matt. 24:36
See also Mark 13:32

Watch therefore: for ye know not what hour your Lord doth come.
Jesus
Matt. 24:42
See also Matt. 25:13

Be ye also ready.
Jesus
Matt. 24:44

Take ye heed, watch and pray: for ye know not when the time is.
Jesus
Mark 13:33
See also Matt. 13:23

If the goodman of the house had known

what hour the thief would come, he would have watched.
Jesus
Luke 12:39
See also Matt. 24:43

Be ye therefore ready also: for the Son of man cometh at an hour when ye think not.
Jesus
Luke 12:40
See also Matt. 24:44

Then shall they see the Son of man coming in a cloud with power and great glory.
Luke 21:27
See also Matt. 24:30, Mark 13:26

I will come again.
Jesus
John 14:3

If I will that he tarry till I come, what is that to thee?
Jesus to Peter, about John
John 21:22

When Christ, who is our life, shall appear, then shall ye also appear with Him in glory.
Col. 3:4

The Lord Jesus shall be revealed from heaven with His mighty angels, In flaming fire taking vengeance on them that know not God, and that obey not the gospel.
2 Thess. 1:7–8

Let no man deceive you.
2 Thess. 2:3

That day shall not come, except there come a falling away first, and that man of sin be revealed, the son of perdition.
2 Thess. 2:3

Unto them that look for Him shall He appear the second time.
Heb. 9:28

Rejoice, inasmuch as ye are partakers of Christ's sufferings; that, when His glory shall be revealed, ye may be glad also with exceeding joy.
1 Pet. 4:13

When the chief Shepherd shall appear, ye shall receive a crown of glory that fadeth not away.
1 Pet. 5:4

The Lord is not slack concerning His promise.
2 Pet. 3:9

The day of the Lord will come as a thief in the night.
2 Pet. 3:10
See also, e.g., 1 Thess. 5:2

Behold, the Lord cometh with ten thousands of His saints, To execute judgment upon all.
Jude 14–15

I will come on thee as a thief.
Jesus
Rev. 3:3
See also Rev. 16:15

Thou shalt not know what hour I will come upon thee.
Jesus
Rev. 3:3

Blessed is he that watcheth, and keepeth his garments, lest he walk naked, and they see his shame.
Rev. 16:15

I saw a new heaven and a new earth: for the first heaven and the first earth were passed away.
Rev. 21:1

There shall be no more death, neither sorrow, nor crying, neither shall there be any more pain: for the former things are passed away.
Rev. 21:4

Behold, I come quickly.
Jesus
Rev. 22:7, 12

[*See also* Apocalypse, End Days, Imminence, Jesus, Judgment Day]

SECRECY

Be sure your sin will find you out.
Num. 32:23

The secret things belong unto the Lord our God: but those things which are revealed belong unto us and to our children for ever.
Deut. 29:29

Our life for your's, if ye utter not this our business.
Josh. 2:14

If thou utter this our business, then we will be quit of thine oath.
Josh. 2:20

Behold, I have not told it my father nor my mother, and shall I tell it thee?
Samson to his wife
Judg. 14:16

Entice him, and see wherein his great strength lieth.
Philistines to Delilah
Judg. 16:5

The Lord searcheth all hearts.
1 Chron. 28:9

No thought can be withholden from Thee.
Job 42:2

Pour out your heart before Him: God is a refuge for us.
Ps. 62:8

My sins are not hid from Thee.
Ps. 69:5

He that teacheth man knowledge, shall not He know?
Ps. 94:10

A talebearer revealeth secrets: but he that is of a faithful spirit concealeth the matter.
Prov. 11:13

The eyes of the Lord are in every place, beholding the evil and the good.
Prov. 15:3

Discover not a secret to another.
Prov. 25:9

A bird of the air shall carry the voice, and that which hath wings shall tell the matter.
Eccl. 10:20

Woe unto them that seek deep to hide their counsel from the Lord.
Isa. 29:15

Speak, I pray thee, unto thy servants in the Syrian language.
Isa. 36:11
See also 2 Kings 18:26

Can any hide himself in secret places that I shall not see him? saith the Lord. Do not I fill heaven and earth?
Jer. 23:24

Let no man know of these words, and thou shalt not die.
Jer. 38:24

Shut thou up the vision; for it shall be for many days.
Dan. 8:26

See that no man know it.
Jesus to blind men He healed
Matt. 9:30

Nothing is secret, that shall not be made manifest; neither any thing hid, that shall not be known.
Jesus
Luke 8:17

There is nothing covered, that shall not be revealed; neither hid, that shall not be known.
Jesus
Luke 12:2
See also Matt. 10:26, Mark 4:22

That which ye have spoken in the ear in closets shall be proclaimed upon the house-tops.
Jesus
Luke 12:3
See also Matt. 10:27

God knoweth your hearts.
Jesus
Luke 16:15

Every one that doeth evil hateth the light.
Jesus
John 3:20

I have called you friends; for all things that I have heard of my Father I have made known unto you.
Jesus
John 15:15

This thing was not done in a corner.
Acts 26:26

The Spirit searcheth all things.
1 Cor. 2:10

I am He which searcheth the reins and hearts.
Jesus
Rev. 2:23

[*See also* Exposure, God's Knowledge, Mystery]

Against any of the children of Israel shall not a dog move his tongue.
Ex. 11:7

As thy days, so shall thy strength be.
Deut. 33:25

They were a wall unto us both by night and day, all the while we were with them keeping the sheep.
1 Sam. 25:16

The Lord is our defence.
Ps. 89:18

They that trust in the Lord shall be as mount Zion, which cannot be removed.
Ps. 125:1

Except the Lord keep the city, the watchman waketh but in vain.
Ps. 127:1

As arrows are in the hand of a mighty man; so are children of the youth.
Ps. 127:4

Whoso putteth his trust in the Lord shall be safe.
Prov. 29:25

Bread shall be given him; his waters shall be sure.
   (him: the righteous)
Isa. 33:16

Foxes have holes, and birds of the air have nests; but the Son of man hath not where to lay His head.
   Jesus
Luke 9:58
See also Matt. 8:20

[*See also* God's Protection, God's Support, Safety]

SEDUCTION

See Temptation.

SELF-AWARENESS

Let us search and try our ways, and turn again to the Lord.
Lam. 3:40

Why beholdest thou the mote that is in thy brother's eye, but considerest not the beam that is in thine own eye?
   Jesus
Matt. 7:3
See also Luke 6:41

Examine yourselves, whether ye be in the faith.
2 Cor. 13:5

SELF-CONFIDENCE

See Confidence.

SELF-CONTROL

Take ye therefore good heed unto yourselves.
Deut. 4:15

Set a watch, O Lord, before my mouth; keep the door of my lips.
Ps. 141:3

He that hath no rule over his own spirit is like a city that is broken down.
Prov. 25:28

What I hate, that do I.
Rom. 7:15

The good that I would I do not: but the evil which I would not, that I do.
Rom. 7:19

Be sober, be vigilant; because your adversary the devil, as a roaring lion, walketh about, seeking whom he may devour.
1 Pet. 5:8

[*See also* Anger, Temper, Temptation]

SELF-DECEPTION

Knowest thou not yet that Egypt is destroyed?
   Pharaoh's servants to Pharaoh
Ex. 10:7

There is a way which seemeth right unto a man, but the end thereof are the ways of death.
Prov. 14:12, Prov. 16:25

We have made lies our refuge, and under falsehood have we hid ourselves.
Isa. 28:15

They are drunken, but not with wine; they stagger, but not with strong drink.
Isa. 29:9

Deceive not yourselves.
Jer. 37:9

Thy terribleness hath deceived thee, and the pride of thine heart.
Jer. 49:16

Professing themselves to be wise, they became fools.
Rom. 1:22

If any man think that he knoweth any thing, he knoweth nothing yet as he ought to know.
1 Cor. 8:2

Thou sayest, I am rich, and increased with goods, and have need of nothing; and knowest not that thou art wretched, and miserable, and poor, and blind, and naked.
Jesus
Rev. 3:17

[*See also* Deception, Misjudgment]

SELF-DENIAL

As thou livest, and as thy soul liveth, I will not do this thing.
Uriah to David
2 Sam. 11:11

Be it far from me, O Lord, that I should do this.
2 Sam. 23:17

Whosoever will come after me, let him deny himself, and take up his cross, and follow me.
Jesus
Mark 8:34
See also Matt. 16:24, Luke 9:23

Whosoever he be of you that forsaketh not all that he hath, he cannot be my disciple.
Jesus
Luke 14:33

Make not provision for the flesh, to fulfil the lusts thereof.
Rom. 13:14

[*See also* Denial, Self-Control, Temptation, Worldliness]

SELF-HATRED

I abhor myself, and repent in dust and ashes.
Job 42:6

Whoso is partner with a thief hateth his own soul.
Prov. 29:24

Ye shall lothe yourselves in your own sight for all your evils that ye have committed.
Ezek. 20:43

O wretched man that I am! who shall deliver me from the body of this death?
Rom. 7:24

SELF-INCRIMINATION

The man that hath done this thing shall surely die.
David to Nathan
2 Sam. 12:5

Thine own lips testify against thee.
Job 15:6
See also 2 Sam. 1:16

Wherein thou judgest another, thou condemnest thyself.
Rom. 2:1

[*See also* Guilt]

SELF-INTEREST

Doth Job fear God for nought?
Satan to God
Job 1:9

Hast not Thou made an hedge about him, and about his house?
Satan to God, of Job
Job 1:10

Skin for skin, yea, all that a man hath will he give for his life.
Satan to God
Job 2:4

I wrought for My name's sake, that it should not be polluted before the heathen.
Ezek. 20:9, 14

If ye do good to them which do good to

you, what thank have ye? for sinners also
do even the same.
> Jesus
> *Luke 6:33*
> *See also Matt. 5:46*

Sinners also lend to sinners, to receive as
much again.
> Jesus
> *Luke 6:34*

When thou makest a feast, call the poor,
the maimed, the lame, the blind: And thou
shalt be blessed; for they cannot recompense thee.
> Jesus
> *Luke 14:13–14*

We preach not ourselves, but Christ Jesus
the Lord.
> *2 Cor. 4:5*

[*See also* Motivation, Selfishness, Selfless-
ness]

SELF-PITY

Kill me, I pray thee, out of hand, if I have
found favour in Thy sight; and let me not
see my wretchedness.
> Moses to God
> *Num. 11:15*

I have no son to keep my name in remembrance.
> *2 Sam. 18:18*

I should have been as though I had not
been; I should have been carried from the
womb to the grave.
> *Job 10:19*

The just upright man is laughed to scorn.
> *Job 12:4*

My kinsfolk have failed, and my familiar
friends have forgotten me.
> *Job 19:14*

Mark me, and be astonished.
> *Job 21:5*

I am a brother to dragons, and a companion to owls.
> *Job 30:29*

What man is like Job, who drinketh up
scorning like water?
> *Job 34:7*

I am a worm, and no man; a reproach of
men, and despised of the people.
> *Ps. 22:6*

Woe is me now! for the Lord hath added
grief to my sorrow.
> *Jer. 45:3*

[*See also* Depression, Despair]

SELF-RIGHTEOUSNESS

He was righteous in his own eyes.
> (He: Job)
> *Job 32:1*

Wilt thou condemn Me, that thou mayest
be righteous?
> *Job 40:8*

All the ways of a man are clean in his own
eyes; but the Lord weigheth the spirits.
> *Prov. 16:2*

Be not righteous over much; neither make
thyself over wise.
> *Eccl. 7:16*

I am holier than thou.
> *Isa. 65:5*

Why eateth your Master with publicans
and sinners?
> *Matt. 9:11*
> *See also Luke 5:30*

The time cometh, that whosoever killeth
you will think that he doeth God service.
> Jesus
> *John 16:2*

If He were not a malefactor, we would not
have delivered Him up unto thee.
> *John 18:30*

[*See also* Conceit]

SELF-SUFFICIENCY

See Cooperation.

SELFISHNESS

Let it be neither mine nor thine, but divide
it.
> *1 Kings 3:26*

Is it not good, if peace and truth be in my days?
2 Kings 20:19

He that withholdeth corn, the people shall curse him: but blessing shall be upon the head of him that selleth it.
Prov. 11:26

Whoso stoppeth his ears at the cry of the poor, he also shall cry himself, but shall not be heard.
Prov. 21:13

They judge not the cause, the cause of the fatherless, yet they prosper.
Jer. 5:28

I was an hungred, and ye gave me no meat: I was thirsty, and ye gave me no drink.
Jesus
Matt. 25:42

Whosoever shall seek to save his life shall lose it; and whosoever shall lose his life shall preserve it.
Jesus
Luke 17:33
See also Matt. 16:25, Mark 8:35

He that loveth his life shall lose it; and he that hateth his life in this world shall keep it unto life eternal.
Jesus
John 12:25

The merchants of the earth shall weep and mourn over her; for no man buyeth their merchandise any more.
(her: Babylon)
Rev. 18:11

[See also Altruism, Greed, Poverty, Underprivileged]

SELFLESSNESS

Would God that all the Lord's people were prophets, and that the Lord would put His spirit upon them!
Moses to Joshua
Num. 11:29

Thou shalt be king over Israel, and I shall be next unto thee.
Jonathan to David
1 Sam. 23:17

Shall I drink the blood of these men that have put their lives in jeopardy?
David
1 Chron. 11:19

If I go not away, the Comforter will not come unto you.
Jesus
John 16:7

I have coveted no man's silver, or gold, or apparel.
Acts 20:33

Even Christ pleased not Himself.
Rom. 15:3

[See also Altruism, Charity, Generosity, Sacrifice, Self-Interest, Selfishness]

SEPARATION

The Lord do so to me, and more also, if ought but death part thee and me.
Ruth 1:17

In their death they were not divided.
(they: Saul and Jonathan)
2 Sam. 1:23

Whither I go, ye cannot come.
Jesus
John 8:21, John 13:33
See also John 7:34

Who shall separate us from the love of Christ? shall tribulation, or distress, or persecution, or famine, or nakedness, or peril, or sword?
Rom. 8:35

SERENITY

Now let me die, since I have seen thy face, because thou art yet alive.
Jacob to Joseph
Gen. 46:30

The Lord bless thee, and keep thee: The Lord make His face shine upon thee, and be gracious unto thee: The Lord lift up His countenance upon thee, and give thee peace.
Num. 6:24–26

How goodly are thy tents, O Jacob, and thy tabernacles, O Israel!
Num. 24:5

The Lord is my shepherd; I shall not want.
Ps. 23:1

Great peace have they which love Thy law.
Ps. 119:165

Better is a dry morsel, and quietness therewith, than an house full of sacrifices with strife.
Prov. 17:1

There is no peace, saith the Lord, unto the wicked.
Isa. 48:22
See also Ps. 57:21

Take my yoke upon you, and learn of me; for I am meek and lowly in heart: and ye shall find rest unto your souls.
Jesus
Matt. 11:29

Peace be with you all that are in Christ Jesus.
1 Pet. 5:14

[*See also* Contentment, Peace, Satisfaction]

SERVANTS

See Employees, Freedom, Slavery, Work.

SERVICE

See Altruism, Charity, Ministry.

SERVICE TO GOD

Serve the Lord thy God with all thy heart and with all thy soul.
Deut. 10:12
See also, e.g., Josh. 22:5

Serve ye the Lord.
Josh. 24:14

Deliver us out of the hand of our enemies, and we will serve Thee.
1 Sam. 12:10

Let it be known this day that Thou art God in Israel, and that I am Thy servant.
Elijah
1 Kings 18:36

Serve Him with a perfect heart and with a willing mind.
1 Chron. 28:9

Minister unto Him.
2 Chron. 29:11

Serve the Lord your God, that the fierceness of His wrath may turn away from you.
2 Chron. 30:8

Serve the Lord with gladness: come before His presence with singing.
Ps. 100:2

If any man serve me, him will my Father honour.
Jesus
John 12:26

We should serve in newness of spirit, and not in the oldness of the letter.
Rom. 7:6

He that is called, being free, is Christ's servant.
1 Cor. 7:22

There are differences of administrations, but the same Lord.
1 Cor. 12:5

[*See also* Devotion, Ministry]

SEVERITY

My punishment is greater than I can bear.
Cain to God
Gen. 4:13

My little finger shall be thicker than my father's loins.
1 Kings 12:10, 2 Chron. 10:10

Thou hast broken the yokes of wood; but thou shalt make for them yokes of iron.
Jer. 28:13

It shall be more tolerable for the land of Sodom in the day of judgment, than for thee.
Jesus
Matt. 11:24
See also Luke 10:14

[*See also* Cruelty, Oppression]

SEX

See Adultery, Carnality, Celibacy, Fornication, Homosexuality, Immorality, Incest, Lust.

SHAME

If her father had but spit in her face, should she not be ashamed seven days?
Num. 12:14

Thou shalt become an astonishment, a proverb, and a byword, among all nations.
Deut. 28:37
See also 1 Kings 9:7

Why abodest thou among the sheepfolds, to hear the bleatings of the flocks?
Judg. 5:16

Tell it not in Gath, publish it not in the streets of Askelon.
2 Sam. 1:20

Tarry at Jericho until your beards be grown.
2 Sam. 10:5, 1 Chron. 19:5

Thy carcase shall not come unto the sepulchre of thy fathers.
1 Kings 13:22

The dogs shall eat Jezebel.
2 Kings 9:10

There shall be none to bury her.
(her: Jezebel)
2 Kings 9:10

Our iniquities are increased over our head, and our trespass is grown up unto the heavens.
Ezra 9:6

Let me not be ashamed, let not mine enemies triumph over me.
Ps. 25:2

Wherefore should the heathen say, Where is their God?
Ps. 79:10
See also, e.g., Ps. 115:2

When pride cometh, then cometh shame.
Prov. 11:2

Thou shalt heap coals of fire upon his head.
Prov. 25:22
See also Rom. 12:20

They declare their sin as Sodom, they hide it not.
Isa. 3:9

Thou hadst a whore's forehead, thou refusedst to be ashamed.
Jer. 3:3

All that forsake Thee shall be ashamed.
Jer. 17:13

Remember, O Lord, what is come upon us: consider, and behold our reproach.
Lam. 5:1

The crown is fallen from our head: woe unto us, that we have sinned!
Lam. 5:16

Thou shalt remember thy ways, and be ashamed.
Ezek. 16:61

The unjust knoweth no shame.
Zeph. 3:5

Whosoever shall be ashamed of me and of my words, of him shall the Son of man be ashamed.
Jesus
Luke 9:26

Brother goeth to law with brother, and that before the unbelievers.
1 Cor. 6:6

I am not ashamed: for I know whom I have believed.
2 Tim. 1:12

[*See also* Humiliation, Nakedness]

SHAMELESSNESS

See Audacity.

SHARING

What goodness the Lord shall do unto us, the same will we do unto thee.
Num. 10:32

Divide the spoil of your enemies with your brethren.
Joshua
Josh. 22:8

It is not meet to take the children's bread, and to cast it to dogs.
Jesus
Matt. 15:26
See also Mark 7:27

Yet the dogs eat of the crumbs which fall from their masters' table.
Matt. 15:27
See also Mark 7:28

Him they compelled to bear His cross.
(Him: Simon)
Matt. 27:32
See also John 19:17

He that hath two coats, let him impart to him that hath none; and he that hath meat, let him do likewise.
John the Baptist
Luke 3:11

I have called you friends; for all things that I have heard of my Father I have made known unto you.
Jesus
John 15:15

Bear ye one another's burdens.
Gal. 6:2

[*See also* Burdens, Charity, Cooperation, Generosity, Selfishness, Underprivileged]

SHARPNESS

Sharper than any twoedged sword.
Heb. 4:12

SIBLINGS

Am I my brother's keeper?
Cain
Gen. 4:9

The voice of thy brother's blood crieth unto Me from the ground.
Gen. 4:10

The elder shall serve the younger.
Gen. 25:23, Rom. 9:12

He sold his birthright unto Jacob.
(He: Esau)
Gen. 25:33

The voice is Jacob's voice, but the hands are the hands of Esau.
Isaac
Gen. 27:22

They hated him yet the more for his dreams, and for his words.
(They: Joseph's brothers)
Gen. 37:8

Behold, this dreamer cometh.
(dreamer: Joseph)
Gen. 37:19

Let not our hand be upon him; for he is our brother and our flesh.
Judah to his brothers
Gen. 37:27

His younger brother shall be greater than he.
Gen. 48:19

A friend loveth at all times, and a brother is born for adversity.
Prov. 17:17

A brother offended is harder to be won than a strong city.
Prov. 18:19

Was not Esau Jacob's brother? saith the Lord: yet I loved Jacob.
Mal. 1:2
See also Rom. 9:13

SICKNESS

See Healing, Miracles.

SIGHT

Thou seest the shadow of the mountains as if they were men.
Judg. 9:36

Lord, I pray Thee, open his eyes, that he may see.
2 Kings 6:17

Hast Thou eyes of flesh? or seest Thou as man seest?
Job 10:4

Better is the sight of the eyes than the wandering of the desire.
Eccl. 6:9

Mine eye affecteth mine heart.
Lam. 3:51

The light of the body is the eye.
Jesus
Matt. 6:22, Luke 11:34

If thine eye offend thee, pluck it out, and
cast it from thee.
Jesus
Matt. 18:9
See also Matt. 5:29, Mark 9:47

It is better for thee to enter into the
kingdom of God with one eye, than having
two eyes to be cast into hell fire.
Jesus
Mark 9:47
See also Matt. 18:9

There fell from his eyes as it had been
scales: and he received sight forthwith, and
arose, and was baptized.
(he: Saul)
Acts 9:18

Now we see through a glass, darkly; but
then face to face.
1 Cor. 13:12

We walk by faith, not by sight.
2 Cor. 5:7

Anoint thine eyes with eyesalve, that thou
mayest see.
Jesus
Rev. 3:18

[*See also* Blindness]

SILENCE

As people being ashamed steal away when
they flee in battle.
2 Sam. 19:3

If I hold my tongue, I shall give up the
ghost.
Job 13:19

Hold thy peace, and I shall teach thee
wisdom.
Job 33:33

He that refraineth his lips is wise.
Prov. 10:19

Even a fool, when he holdeth his peace, is
counted wise.
Prov. 17:28

A time to keep silence, and a time to
speak.
Eccl. 3:7

He was oppressed, and he was afflicted, yet
he opened not his mouth.
Isa. 53:7

The prudent shall keep silence in that time;
for it is an evil time.
Amos 5:13

As a thief in the night.
1 Thess. 5:2, 2 Pet. 3:10

When He had opened the seventh seal,
there was silence in heaven about the space
of half an hour.
Rev. 8:1

[*See also* Eloquence, Speech, Verbosity]

SIN

She took of the fruit thereof, and did eat.
(She: Eve)
Gen. 3:6

Who told thee that thou wast naked?
Gen. 3:11

If thou doest not well, sin lieth at the door.
Gen. 4:7

Be sure your sin will find you out.
Num. 32:23

And the children of Israel did evil again in
the sight of the Lord.
E.g., Judg. 3:12

It is no good report that I hear.
1 Sam. 2:24

If one man sin against another, the judge
shall judge him: but if a man sin against the
Lord, who shall intreat for him?
1 Sam. 2:25

We have sinned, because we have forsaken
the Lord.
1 Sam. 12:10

Though it be in Jonathan my son, he shall
surely die.
Saul
1 Sam. 14:39

There is no man that sinneth not.
1 Kings 8:46, 2 Chron. 6:36

He walked in all the sins of his father.
E.g., 1 Kings 15:3

Every man shall be put to death for his own sin.
E.g., 2 Kings 14:6

They have done that which was evil in My sight, and have provoked Me to anger, since the day their fathers came forth out of Egypt.
2 Kings 21:15

He did that which was evil in the sight of the Lord his God.
E.g., 2 Chron. 36:12

If iniquity be in thine hand, put it far away.
Job 11:14

Who can bring a clean thing out of an unclean? not one.
Job 14:4

How can he be clean that is born of a woman?
Job 25:4

If thou sinnest, what doest thou against Him?
Job 35:6

There is none that doeth good, no, not one.
Ps. 14:3, Ps. 53:3, Rom. 3:12

Remember not the sins of my youth.
Ps. 25:7

They are more than the hairs of mine head.
Ps. 40:12

In sin did my mother conceive me.
Ps. 51:5

If Thou, Lord, shouldest mark iniquities, O Lord, who shall stand?
Ps. 130:3

Stolen waters are sweet, and bread eaten in secret is pleasant.
Prov. 9:17

The labour of the righteous tendeth to life: the fruit of the wicked to sin.
Prov. 10:16

Fools make a mock at sin.
Prov. 14:9

Righteousness exalteth a nation: but sin is a reproach to any people.
Prov. 14:34

Suffer not thy mouth to cause thy flesh to sin.
Eccl. 5:6

There is not a just man upon earth, that doeth good, and sinneth not.
Eccl. 7:20

He was wounded for our transgressions, he was bruised for our iniquities.
Isa. 53:5

All we like sheep have gone astray.
Isa. 53:6

The Lord hath laid on him the iniquity of us all.
Isa. 53:6

Your sins have hid His face from you, that He will not hear.
Isa. 59:2

Our sins testify against us.
Isa. 59:12

O Lord, why hast Thou made us to err from Thy ways, and hardened our heart from Thy fear?
Isa. 63:17

Though thou wash thee with nitre, and take thee much soap, yet thine iniquity is marked before Me.
Jer. 2:22

The soul that sinneth, it shall die.
Ezek. 18:4, 20

The son shall not bear the iniquity of the father, neither shall the father bear the iniquity of the son.
Ezek. 18:20
See also, e.g., Deut. 24:16

The righteousness of the righteous shall not deliver him in the day of his transgression.
Ezek. 33:12

Because they trespassed against Me, therefore hid I My face from them.
Ezek. 39:23

All manner of sin and blasphemy shall be forgiven unto men: but the blasphemy against the Holy Ghost shall not be forgiven unto men.
Jesus
Matt. 12:31
See also Matt. 12:32, Mark 3:29, Luke 12:10

Not that which goeth into the mouth defileth a man; but that which cometh out of the mouth, this defileth a man.
Jesus
Matt. 15:11
See also Mark 7:15

Out of the heart proceed evil thoughts, murders, adulteries, fornications, thefts, false witness, blasphemies.
Jesus
Matt. 15:19
See also Mark 7:21

The spirit indeed is willing, but the flesh is weak.
Jesus
Matt. 26:41
See also Mark 14:38

All these evil things come from within, and defile the man.
Jesus
Mark 7:23

It is better for thee to enter into the kingdom of God with one eye, than having two eyes to be cast into hell fire.
Jesus
Mark 9:47
See also Matt. 18:9

Forgive us our sins.
Jesus
Luke 11:4

There is nothing covered, that shall not be revealed; neither hid, that shall not be known.
Jesus
Luke 12:2
See also Matt. 10:26, Mark 4:22

Sin no more, lest a worse thing come unto thee.
Jesus
John 5:14

He that is without sin among you, let him first cast a stone.
Jesus
John 8:7

Woman, where are those thine accusers?
Jesus
John 8:10

Go, and sin no more.
Jesus
John 8:11

Whosoever committeth sin is the servant of sin.
Jesus
John 8:34

If ye were blind, ye should have no sin.
Jesus
John 9:41

Now they have no cloak for their sin.
Jesus
John 15:22

Pray God, if perhaps the thought of thine heart may be forgiven thee.
Acts 8:22

Thou art in the gall of bitterness, and in the bond of iniquity.
Acts 8:23

Whosoever believeth in Him shall receive remission of sins.
Acts 10:43

Arise, and be baptized, and wash away thy sins.
Acts 22:16

As many as have sinned without law shall also perish without law.
Rom. 2:12

As many as have sinned in the law shall be judged by the law.
Rom. 2:12

They are all under sin.
Rom. 3:9

By the law is the knowledge of sin.
Rom. 3:20

All have sinned, and come short of the glory of God.
Rom. 3:23

Where no law is, there is no transgression.
Rom. 4:15

By one man sin entered into the world.
Rom. 5:12

Sin is not imputed when there is no law.
Rom. 5:13

Where sin abounded, grace did much more abound.
Rom. 5:20

He that is dead is freed from sin.
Rom. 6:7

Sin shall not have dominion over you: for ye are not under the law, but under grace.
Rom. 6:14

The wages of sin is death; but the gift of God is eternal life through Jesus Christ our Lord.
Rom. 6:23

I had not known sin, but by the law.
Rom. 7:7

When the commandment came, sin revived.
Rom. 7:9

What I hate, that do I.
Rom. 7:15

It is no more I that do it, but sin that dwelleth in me.
Rom. 7:17, 20

In me (that is, in my flesh,) dwelleth no good thing.
Rom. 7:18

With the mind I myself serve the law of God; but with the flesh the law of sin.
Rom. 7:25

Make not provision for the flesh, to fulfil the lusts thereof.
Rom. 13:14

Whatsoever is not of faith is sin.
Rom. 14:23

Christ died for our sins.
1 Cor. 15:3

Awake to righteousness, and sin not.
1 Cor. 15:34

The sting of death is sin; and the strength of sin is the law.
1 Cor. 15:56

Use not liberty for an occasion to the flesh.
Gal. 5:13

He that soweth to his flesh shall of the flesh reap corruption.
Gal. 6:8

When lust hath conceived, it bringeth forth sin.
James 1:15

Sin, when it is finished, bringeth forth death.
James 1:15

To him that knoweth to do good, and doeth it not, to him it is sin.
James 4:17

A multitude of sins.
James 5:20

He that hath suffered in the flesh hath ceased from sin.
1 Pet. 4:1

Charity shall cover the multitude of sins.
(charity: love)
1 Pet. 4:8

The blood of Jesus Christ His Son cleanseth us from all sin.
1 John 1:7

If we say that we have no sin, we deceive ourselves.
1 John 1:8

If we say that we have not sinned, we make Him a liar.
1 John 1:10

If any man sin, we have an advocate with the Father.
1 John 2:1

Whosoever committeth sin transgresseth also the law: for sin is the transgression of the law.
1 John 3:4

In Him is no sin.
1 John 3:5

Whosoever abideth in Him sinneth not.
1 John 3:6

Whosoever is born of God doth not commit sin.
1 John 3:9

All unrighteousness is sin.
1 John 5:17

Be not partakers of her sins.
(her: Babylon)
Rev. 18:4

Her sins have reached unto heaven, and God hath remembered her iniquities.
(her: Babylon)
Rev. 18:5

[*See also* Adultery, Behavior, Carnality, Confession, Decadence, Depravity, Disobedience, Evil, Forgiveness, Godlessness, Immorality, Prostitution, Punishment, Re pentance, Righteousness, Sinners, Wickedness]

SINCERITY

Thou shalt find Him, if thou seek Him with all thy heart and with all thy soul.
Deut. 4:29

What hast thou to do with peace? turn thee behind me.
2 Kings 9:18, 19

If thou seek Him, He will be found of thee.
1 Chron. 28:9
See also 2 Chron. 15:2

With flattering lips and with a double heart do they speak.
Ps. 12:2

Bring no more vain oblations.
Isa. 1:13

Ye shall seek Me, and find Me, when ye shall search for Me with all your heart.
Jer. 29:13

I desired mercy, and not sacrifice; and the knowledge of God more than burnt offerings.
Hos. 6:6
See also Matt. 9:13

Rend your heart, and not your garments, and turn unto the Lord.
Joel 2:13

Not every one that saith unto me, Lord, Lord, shall enter into the kingdom of heaven.
Jesus
Matt. 7:21

Why call ye me, Lord, Lord, and do not the things which I say?
Jesus
Luke 6:46

They that worship Him must worship Him in spirit and in truth.
Jesus
John 4:24

If God were your Father, ye would love me: for I proceeded forth and came from God.
Jesus
John 8:42

Circumcision is that of the heart, in the spirit, and not in the letter; whose praise is not of men, but of God.
Rom. 2:29

With the heart man believeth unto righteousness.
Rom. 10:10

The kingdom of God is not in word, but in power.
1 Cor. 4:20

Not in tables of stone, but in fleshy tables of the heart.
2 Cor. 3:3

Be ye doers of the word, and not hearers only.
James 1:22

Sanctify the Lord God in your hearts.
1 Pet. 3:15

Let us not love in word, neither in tongue; but in deed and in truth.
1 John 3:18

[*See also* Devotion, Hypocrisy, Rituals]

SINNERS

Whosoever hath sinned against Me, him will I blot out of My book.
Ex. 32:33

They are a perverse and crooked generation.
Deut. 32:5

The light of the wicked shall be put out, and the spark of his fire shall not shine.
Job 18:5

Drought and heat consume the snow waters: so doth the grave those which have sinned.
Job 24:19

The Lord knoweth the way of the righteous: but the way of the ungodly shall perish.
Ps. 1:6

Blessed is he whose transgression is forgiven.
Ps. 32:1

Let the sinners be consumed out of the earth, and let the wicked be no more.
Ps. 104:35

Let me not eat of their dainties.
Ps. 141:4

The way of transgressors is hard.
Prov. 13:15

Evil pursueth sinners.
Prov. 13:21

Let not thine heart envy sinners.
Prov. 23:17

To the sinner He giveth travail, to gather and to heap up.
Eccl. 2:26

Though a sinner do evil an hundred times, and his days be prolonged, yet surely I know that it shall be well with them that fear God.
Eccl. 8:12

Woe unto them that draw iniquity with cords of vanity, and sin as it were with a cart rope.
Isa. 5:18

He shall destroy the sinners.
Isa. 13:9

I will not pity, nor spare, nor have mercy, but destroy them.
Jer. 13:14

He that fleeth of them shall not flee away, and he that escapeth of them shall not be delivered.
Amos 9:1

Though they dig into hell, thence shall Mine hand take them; though they climb up to heaven, thence will I bring them down.
Amos 9:2

Their blood shall be poured out as dust, and their flesh as the dung.
Zeph. 1:17

They that be whole need not a physician, but they that are sick.
Jesus
Matt. 9:12
See also Mark 2:17, Luke 5:31

Sinners also lend to sinners, to receive as much again.
Jesus
Luke 6:34

Christ died for the ungodly.
Rom. 5:6

While we were yet sinners, Christ died for us.
Rom. 5:8

By one man's disobedience many were made sinners.
Rom. 5:19

Christ Jesus came into the world to save sinners.
1 Tim. 1:15

Lovers of pleasures more than lovers of God.
2 Tim. 3:4

The devils also believe, and tremble.
James 2:19

Cleanse your hands, ye sinners; and purify your hearts, ye double minded.
James 4:8

He which converteth the sinner from the error of his way shall save a soul from death.
James 5:20

The error of his way.
James 5:20

They think it strange that ye run not with them to the same excess of riot.
1 Pet. 4:4

God spared not the angels that sinned, but cast them down to hell.
2 Pet. 2:4

Whosoever sinneth hath not seen Him, neither known Him.
1 John 3:6

He that committeth sin is of the devil; for the devil sinneth from the beginning.
1 John 3:8

Whosoever is born of God sinneth not.
1 John 5:18

[*See also* Sin, Wicked People]

SIZE

There were giants in the earth in those days.
Gen. 6:4

We were in our own sight as grasshoppers.
Num. 13:33

The ants are a people not strong, yet they prepare their meat in the summer.
Prov. 30:25

Which of you by taking thought can add one cubit unto his stature?
Jesus
Matt. 6:27
See also Luke 12:25

A little leaven leaveneth the whole lump.
1 Cor. 5:6, Gal. 5:9

[*See also* Abundance, Growth, Quantity]

SKEPTICISM

Shall a child be born unto him that is an hundred years old? and shall Sarah, that is ninety years old, bear?
Gen. 17:17

Hear now, ye rebels; must we fetch you water out of this rock?
Num. 20:10

The God that answereth by fire, let Him be God.
1 Kings 18:24

Nay, my lord, thou man of God, do not lie unto thine handmaid.
2 Kings 4:16

If the prophet had bid thee do some great thing, wouldest thou not have done it?
2 Kings 5:13

If the Lord would make windows in heaven, might this thing be?
2 Kings 7:2
See also 2 Kings 7:19

Thou shalt see it with thine eyes, but shalt not eat thereof.
2 Kings 7:2

I believed not their words, until I came, and mine eyes had seen it.
Queen of Sheba to Solomon
2 Chron. 9:6
See also 1 Kings 10:7

I will work a work in your days, which ye will not believe, though it be told you.
Hab. 1:5
See also Acts 13:41

An evil and adulterous generation seeketh after a sign; and there shall no sign be given to it, but the sign of the prophet Jonas.
Jesus
Matt. 12:39
See also Matt. 16:4, Mark 8:12, Luke 11:29

But whom say ye that I am?
Jesus
Matt. 16:15, Mark 8:29,
Luke 9:20

Physician, heal thyself.
Luke 4:23

If they hear not Moses and the prophets, neither will they be persuaded, though one rose from the dead.
Jesus
Luke 16:31

O fools, and slow of heart to believe all that the prophets have spoken.
Jesus
Luke 24:25

If I have told you earthly things, and ye believe not, how shall ye believe, if I tell you of heavenly things?
Jesus
John 3:12

Except ye see signs and wonders, ye will not believe.
Jesus
John 4:48

Had ye believed Moses, ye would have believed me: for he wrote of me.
Jesus
John 5:46

Because I tell you the truth, ye believe me not.
Jesus
John 8:45
See also John 8:46

How can a man that is a sinner do such miracles?
Pharisees, about Jesus
John 9:16

Though ye believe not me, believe the works.
Jesus
John 10:38

Blessed are they that have not seen, and yet have believed.

Jesus
John 20:29

Some believed the things which were spoken, and some believed not.
Acts 28:24

The Jews require a sign, and the Greeks seek after wisdom.
1 Cor. 1:22

Believe not every spirit.
1 John 4:1

[*See also* Belief, Doubt, Faith, Possibility]

SKILL

See Ability, Chance.

SLANDER

Thy tongue deviseth mischiefs; like a sharp razor, working deceitfully.
Ps. 52:2

Swords are in their lips.
Ps. 59:7

Deliver my soul, O Lord, from lying lips, and from a deceitful tongue.
Ps. 120:2

They have sharpened their tongues like a serpent; adders' poison is under their lips.
Ps. 140:3
See also Rom. 3:13

He that hideth hatred with lying lips, and he that uttereth a slander, is a fool.
Prov. 10:18

An hypocrite with his mouth destroyeth his neighbour.
Prov. 11:9

Do violence to no man, neither accuse any falsely.
Luke 3:14

Their throat is an open sepulchre.
Rom. 3:13

Speak evil of no man.
Titus 3:2
See also James 4:11

[*See also* Gossip, Speech]

SLAVERY

I am the Lord thy God, which have brought thee out of the land of Egypt, out of the house of bondage.
Ex. 20:2
See also, e.g., Ex. 29:46, Deut. 5:6

Remember that thou wast a bondman in the land of Egypt, and the Lord thy God redeemed thee.
Deut. 15:15
See also Deut. 5:15, Deut. 24:22

Thou shalt not deliver unto his master the servant which is escaped from his master unto thee.
Deut. 23:15

Will ye even sell your brethren?
Neh. 5:8

We are not children of the bondwoman, but of the free.
Gal. 4:31

Servants, be obedient to them that are your masters.
Eph. 6:5
See also 1 Pet. 2:18

He that leadeth into captivity shall go into captivity.
Rev. 13:10

[*See also* Captivity, Freedom]

SLEEP

All the night make I my bed to swim; I water my couch with my tears.
Ps. 6:6

He that keepeth Israel shall neither slumber nor sleep.
Ps. 121:4

I will not give sleep to mine eyes, or slumber to mine eyelids, Until I find out a place for the Lord.
Ps. 132:4–5

Yet a little sleep, a little slumber, a little folding of the hands to sleep: So shall thy poverty come.
Prov. 6:10–11

Love not sleep, lest thou come to poverty.
  Prov. 20:13

Drowsiness shall clothe a man with rags.
  Prov. 23:21

The sleep of a labouring man is sweet.
  Eccl. 5:12

The abundance of the rich will not suffer
him to sleep.
  Eccl. 5:12

They that sleep sleep in the night; and they
that be drunken are drunken in the night.
  1 Thess. 5:7

SLOTH

See Laziness.

SNAKES

Now the serpent was more subtil than any
beast of the field.
  Gen. 3:1

Thou art cursed above all cattle, and above
every beast of the field.
  Gen. 3:14

Upon thy belly shalt thou go, and dust
shalt thou eat all the days of thy life.
  God to serpent
  Gen. 3:14

Be ye therefore wise as serpents, and
harmless as doves.
  Jesus to disciples
  Matt. 10:16

[*See also* Temptation]

SNOBBERY

See Conceit.

SODOMY

Sodom and Gomorrah.
  Gen. 18:20, Gen. 19:28

Whosoever lieth with a beast shall surely
be put to death.
  Ex. 22:19

Cursed be he that lieth with any manner of
beast.
  Deut. 27:21

[*See also* Homosexuality]

SOLDIERS

See Peace, War, War and Peace, Weapons.

SONG

Hear, O ye kings; give ear, O ye princes; I,
even I, will sing unto the Lord.
  Judg. 5:3

Awake, awake, utter a song.
  Judg. 5:12

With my song will I praise Him.
  Ps. 28:7

Shout unto God with the voice of triumph.
  Ps. 47:1

Make a joyful noise unto God, all ye lands:
Sing forth the honour of His name.
  Ps. 66:1–2

Sing unto God, ye kingdoms of the earth;
O sing praises unto the Lord.
  Ps. 68:32

O come, let us sing unto the Lord: let us
make a joyful noise to the rock of our
salvation.
  Ps. 95:1

Sing unto the Lord, all the earth.
  Ps. 96:1, 1 Chron. 16:23

Make a joyful noise unto the Lord, all the
earth: make a loud noise, and rejoice, and
sing praise.
  Ps. 98:4
  See also Ps. 100:1

Serve the Lord with gladness: come before
His presence with singing.
  Ps. 100:2

I will sing unto the Lord as long as I live: I
will sing praise to my God while I have my
being.
  Ps. 104:33

Sing unto Him, sing psalms unto Him: talk
ye of all His wondrous works.
  Ps. 105:2, 1 Chron. 16:9

Sing praises unto His name; for it is pleasant.
Ps. 135:3

How shall we sing the Lord's song in a strange land?
Ps. 137:4

Sing unto the Lord with thanksgiving.
Ps. 147:7

Let them praise His name in the dance: let them sing praises unto Him with the timbrel and harp.
Ps. 149:3
See also Ps. 150:4

Sing unto the Lord; for He hath done excellent things.
Isa. 12:5

Make sweet melody, sing many songs, that thou mayest be remembered.
Isa. 23:16

Sing unto the Lord a new song, and His praise from the end of the earth.
Isa. 42:10

Sing unto the Lord, praise ye the Lord.
Jer. 20:13

[*See also* Music, Praise of God]

SORROW

I am this day weak, though anointed king.
2 Sam. 3:39

This day is a day of trouble, and of rebuke, and blasphemy.
2 Kings 19:3, Isa. 37:3

It came to pass, when I heard these words, that I sat down and wept.
Neh. 1:4

By the rivers of Babylon, there we sat down, yea, we wept, when we remembered Zion.
Ps. 137:1

He healeth the broken in heart, and bindeth up their wounds.
Ps. 147:3

Even in laughter the heart is sorrowful.
Prov. 14:13

By sorrow of the heart the spirit is broken.
Prov. 15:13

He that increaseth knowledge increaseth sorrow.
Eccl. 1:18

A time to weep, and a time to laugh; a time to mourn, and a time to dance.
Eccl. 3:4

Sorrow is better than laughter: for by the sadness of the countenance the heart is made better.
Eccl. 7:3

The new wine mourneth, the vine languisheth, all the merry hearted do sigh.
Isa. 24:7

They shall not drink wine with a song.
Isa. 24:9

He is despised and rejected of men; a man of sorrows, and acquainted with grief.
Isa. 53:3

More are the children of the desolate than the children of the married wife, saith the Lord.
Isa. 54:1

For the mountains will I take up a weeping and wailing, and for the habitations of the wilderness a lamentation.
Jer. 9:10

Wherefore came I forth out of the womb to see labour and sorrow?
Jer. 20:18

Mine eye affecteth mine heart.
Lam. 3:51

Ye shall be sorrowful, but your sorrow shall be turned into joy.
Jesus
John 16:20

Be of good cheer; I have overcome the world.
Jesus
John 16:33

The voice of the bridegroom and of the bride shall be heard no more at all in thee.
Rev. 18:23

There shall be no more death, neither sorrow, nor crying, neither shall there be any more pain: for the former things are passed away.
Rev. 21:4

[*See also* Anguish, Grief, Mourning, Tears]

SOUL

Thou wilt not leave my soul in hell; neither wilt Thou suffer Thine Holy One to see corruption.
Ps. 16:10

None can keep alive his own soul.
Ps. 22:29

He restoreth my soul.
Ps. 23:3

He satisfieth the longing soul, and filleth the hungry soul with goodness.
Ps. 107:9

He that winneth souls is wise.
Prov. 11:30

A true witness delivereth souls.
Prov. 14:25

He that keepeth the commandment keepeth his own soul; but he that despiseth His ways shall die.
Prov. 19:16

Behold, all souls are Mine.
Ezek. 18:4

Fear not them which kill the body, but are not able to kill the soul.
Jesus
Matt. 10:28
See also Luke 12:4

What shall a man give in exchange for his soul?
Jesus
Matt. 16:26, Mark 8:37

What shall it profit a man, if he shall gain the whole world, and lose his own soul?
Jesus
Mark 8:36
See also Matt. 16:26, Luke 9:25

SOVEREIGNTY

The Lord shall reign for ever and ever.
E.g., Ex. 15:18

Thine is the kingdom, O Lord, and Thou art exalted as head above all.
1 Chron. 29:11

Why dost thou strive against Him? for He giveth not account of any of His matters.
Job 33:13

The kingdom is the Lord's.
Ps. 22:28

God is the King of all the earth: sing ye praises with understanding.
Ps. 47:7

Justice and judgment are the habitation of Thy throne: mercy and truth shall go before Thy face.
Ps. 89:14

The Lord reigneth; let the earth rejoice.
Ps. 97:1

Righteousness and judgment are the habitation of His throne.
Ps. 97:2

Thou, O Lord, remainest for ever; Thy throne from generation to generation.
Lam. 5:19

The kingdom shall be the Lord's.
Obad. 21

Of His kingdom there shall be no end. (His: Jesus)
Luke 1:33

Heaven is My throne, and earth is My footstool: what house will ye build Me? saith the Lord.
Acts 7:49
See also Isa. 66:1

The earth is the Lord's, and the fulness thereof.
1 Cor. 10:26, 28
See also Ps. 24:1

He must reign, till He hath put all enemies under His feet.
1 Cor. 15:25

Thy throne, O God, is for ever and ever.
Heb. 1:8

A sceptre of righteousness is the sceptre of Thy kingdom.
Heb. 1:8

[*See also* Authority, God's Power, Monarchy]

SPEECH

Who hath made man's mouth? or who maketh the dumb, or deaf, or the seeing, or the blind? have not I the Lord?
Ex. 4:11

He shall be to thee instead of a mouth, and thou shalt be to him instead of God.
> God to Moses, about Aaron
> *Ex. 4:16*

The word that God putteth in my mouth, that shall I speak.
> *Num. 22:38*

Give ear, O ye heavens, and I will speak; and hear, O earth, the words of my mouth.
> *Deut. 32:1*

Say now Shibboleth.
> *Judg. 12:6*

What the Lord saith unto me, that will I speak.
> *1 Kings 22:14*
> *See also 2 Chron. 18:13*

How forcible are right words!
> *Job 6:25*

Thy mouth uttereth thine iniquity.
> *Job 15:5*

Thou choosest the tongue of the crafty.
> *Job 15:5*

Who is this that darkeneth counsel by words without knowledge?
> *Job 38:2*

My tongue is the pen of a ready writer.
> *Ps. 45:1*

O Lord, open Thou my lips; and my mouth shall show forth Thy praise.
> *Ps. 51:15*

Set a watch, O Lord, before my mouth; keep the door of my lips.
> *Ps. 141:3*

In the multitude of words there wanteth not sin.
> *Prov. 10:19*

The tongue of the just is as choice silver: the heart of the wicked is little worth.
> *Prov. 10:20*

In all labour there is profit: but the talk of the lips tendeth only to penury.
> *Prov. 14:23*

A soft answer turneth away wrath.
> *Prov. 15:1*

A word spoken in due season, how good is it!
> *Prov. 15:23*

Pleasant words are as an honeycomb, sweet to the soul, and health to the bones.
> *Prov. 16:24*

He that hath a perverse tongue falleth into mischief.
> *Prov. 17:20*

A fool's mouth is his destruction, and his lips are the snare of his soul.
> *Prov. 18:7*

Be not rash with thy mouth.
> *Eccl. 5:2*

Suffer not thy mouth to cause thy flesh to sin.
> *Eccl. 5:6*

How can ye, being evil, speak good things?
> Jesus
> *Matt. 12:34*

Out of the abundance of the heart the mouth speaketh.
> Jesus
> *Matt. 12:34*

A good man out of the good treasure of the heart bringeth forth good things: and an evil man out of the evil treasure bringeth forth evil things.
> Jesus
> *Matt. 12:35*

Every idle word that men shall speak, they shall give account thereof in the day of judgment.
> Jesus
> *Matt. 12:36*

By thy words thou shalt be justified, and by thy words thou shalt be condemned.
> Jesus
> *Matt. 12:37*

Not that which goeth into the mouth defileth a man; but that which cometh out of the mouth, this defileth a man.
> Jesus
> *Matt. 15:11*
> *See also Mark 7:15*

Their throat is an open sepulchre.
> *Rom. 3:13*

Whatsoever ye do in word or deed, do all in the name of the Lord Jesus.
> *Col. 3:17*

Let your speech be alway with grace, sea-

soned with salt, that ye may know how ye ought to answer every man.
Col. 4:6

Shun profane and vain babblings: for they will increase unto more ungodliness.
2 Tim. 2:16

The word of God is quick, and powerful, and sharper than any twoedged sword.
Heb. 4:12

The tongue is a fire, a world of iniquity.
James 3:6

It defileth the whole body, and setteth on fire the course of nature.
(It: the tongue)
James 3:6

The tongue can no man tame; it is an unruly evil, full of deadly poison.
James 3:8

Out of the same mouth proceedeth blessing and cursing.
James 3:10

He that will love life, and see good days, let him refrain his tongue from evil.
1 Pet. 3:10
See also Ps. 34:13

[*See also* Advice, Candor, Communication, Eloquence, Gossip, Lies, Persuasion, Preaching, Profanity, Quotations, Silence, Slander, Verbosity]

SPEED

Come down unto me, tarry not.
Gen. 45:9

They were swifter than eagles, they were stronger than lions.
2 Sam. 1:23

He did fly upon the wings of the wind.
Ps. 18:10

The race is not to the swift, nor the battle to the strong, neither yet bread to the wise, nor yet riches to men of understanding, nor yet favour to men of skill; but time and chance happeneth to them all.
Eccl. 9:11

He shall come up as clouds, and his chariots shall be as a whirlwind.
Jer. 4:13

Our persecutors are swifter than the eagles of the heaven.
Lam. 4:19

The flight shall perish from the swift.
Amos 2:14

He that is swift of foot shall not deliver himself: neither shall he that rideth the horse.
Amos 2:15

They shall fly as the eagle that hasteth to eat.
Hab. 1:8

That thou doest, do quickly.
Jesus
John 13:27

In the twinkling of an eye.
1 Cor. 15:52

[*See also* Urgency]

SPIES

Ye are spies; to see the nakedness of the land ye are come.
Joseph to his brothers
Gen. 42:9

[*See also* Betrayal, Treachery]

SPIRIT

See Holy Spirit, Inspiration.

SPIRITUALISM

Regard not them that have familiar spirits, neither seek after wizards, to be defiled by them.
Lev. 19:31

All that do these things are an abomination unto the Lord.
Deut. 18:12

Bring me up Samuel.
1 Sam. 28:11

Why hast thou disquieted me, to bring me up?
Samuel to Saul
1 Sam. 28:15

SPIRITUALITY

Man doth not live by bread only, but by every word that proceedeth out of the mouth of the Lord.
> *Deut. 8:3*
> *See also, e.g., Matt. 4:4*

In Thy light shall we see light.
> *Ps. 36:9*

Create in me a clean heart, O God; and renew a right spirit within me.
> *Ps. 51:10*

There is that maketh himself rich, yet hath nothing: there is that maketh himself poor, yet hath great riches.
> *Prov. 13:7*

Eat ye that which is good, and let your soul delight itself in fatness.
> *Isa. 55:2*

Lay up for yourselves treasures in heaven, where neither moth nor rust doth corrupt, and where thieves do not break through nor steal.
> Jesus
> *Matt. 6:20*

The light of the body is the eye.
> Jesus
> *Matt. 6:22, Luke 11:34*

Seek ye first the kingdom of God, and His righteousness.
> Jesus
> *Matt. 6:33*
> *See also Luke 12:31*

To give light to them that sit in darkness.
> *Luke 1:79*

Take heed therefore that the light which is in thee be not darkness.
> Jesus
> *Luke 11:35*

Except a man be born again, he cannot see the kingdom of God.
> Jesus
> *John 3:3*

That which is born of the flesh is flesh; and that which is born of the Spirit is spirit.
> Jesus
> *John 3:6*

I have meat to eat that ye know not of.
> Jesus
> *John 4:32*

If any man thirst, let him come unto me, and drink.
> Jesus
> *John 7:37*

The law is spiritual: but I am carnal.
> *Rom. 7:14*

To be carnally minded is death; but to be spiritually minded is life and peace.
> *Rom. 8:6*

The carnal mind is enmity against God.
> *Rom. 8:7*

Flesh and blood cannot inherit the kingdom of God.
> *1 Cor. 15:50*

Though our outward man perish, yet the inward man is renewed day by day.
> *2 Cor. 4:16*

The things which are seen are temporal; but the things which are not seen are eternal.
> *2 Cor. 4:18*

Having nothing, and yet possessing all things.
> *2 Cor. 6:10*

Put on the new man.
> *Eph. 4:24*

Ye were sometimes darkness, but now are ye light in the Lord.
> *Eph. 5:8*

Seek those things which are above, where Christ sitteth on the right hand of God.
> *Col. 3:1*

Bodily exercise profiteth little: but godliness is profitable unto all things.
> *1 Tim. 4:8*

The darkness is past, and the true light now shineth.
> *1 John 2:8*

[*See also* Born Again, God's Presence, Holy Spirit, Light and Darkness, Materialism, Worldliness]

SPOILS OF WAR

There shall cleave nought of the cursed thing to thine hand.
> *Deut. 13:17*

Keep yourselves from the accursed thing, lest ye make yourselves accursed.
Josh. 6:18

Divide the spoil of your enemies with your brethren.
Joshua
Josh. 22:8

Whomsoever the Lord our God shall drive out from before us, them will we possess.
Judg. 11:24

SPOKESMEN

He shall be to thee instead of a mouth, and thou shalt be to him instead of God.
God to Moses, about Aaron
Ex. 4:16

I am come in my Father's name, and ye receive me not.
Jesus
John 5:43

He that receiveth whomsoever I send receiveth me.
Jesus
John 13:20

He is a chosen vessel unto me, to bear my name.
Jesus, about Saul
Acts 9:15

I am an ambassador in bonds.
Eph. 6:20

[*See also* Intercession]

SPORTSMANSHIP

See Competition.

STAMINA

See Fortitude.

STATUS

The Lord maketh poor, and maketh rich: He bringeth low, and lifteth up.
1 Sam. 2:7

I had rather be a doorkeeper in the house of my God, than to dwell in the tents of wickedness.
Ps. 84:10

Thou hast lifted me up, and cast me down.
Ps. 102:10

I will make thee small among the heathen, and despised among men.
Jer. 49:15

The disciple is not above his master, nor the servant above his lord.
Jesus
Matt. 10:24
See also Luke 6:40

The servant is not greater than his lord; neither he that is sent greater than he that sent him.
Jesus
John 13:16
See also John 15:20

God is no respecter of persons.
Acts 10:34
See also Rom. 2:11

As the Lord hath called every one, so let him walk.
1 Cor. 7:17

If ye have respect to persons, ye commit sin.
James 2:9

[*See also* Appearance, Authority]

STEADFASTNESS

Be not moved away from the hope of the gospel.
Col. 1:23

Hold fast to that which is good.
1 Thess. 5:21

We are not of them who draw back unto perdition; but of them that believe to the saving of the soul.
Heb. 10:39

[*See also* Diligence, Perseverance]

STOICISM

See Acceptance.

See Foreigners, Hospitality.

STRATEGY

Let us go down, and there confound their language, that they may not understand one another's speech.
Gen. 11:7

Turn in, my lord, turn in to me; fear not.
Jael to Sisera
Judg. 4:18

Take an heifer with thee, and say, I am come to sacrifice to the Lord.
God to Samuel
1 Sam. 16:2

I will be a lying spirit in the mouth of all his prophets.
1 Kings 22:22

Ahab served Baal a little; but Jehu shall serve him much.
2 Kings 10:18

Be ye therefore wise as serpents, and harmless as doves.
Jesus to disciples
Matt. 10:16

[See also Planning, Traps]

STRENGTH

The Lord is my strength and song, and He is become my salvation.
Ex. 15:2

Thy right hand, O Lord, is become glorious in power: Thy right hand, O Lord, hath dashed in pieces the enemy.
Ex. 15:6

He lay down as a lion, and as a great lion: who shall stir him up?
Num. 24:9

No man hath been able to stand before you unto this day.
Joshua to Israelites
Josh. 23:9

One man of you shall chase a thousand: for the Lord your God, He it is that fighteth for you.
Josh. 23:10

As the man is, so is his strength.
Judg. 8:21

Out of the eater came forth meat, and out of the strong came forth sweetness.
Judg. 14:14

What is sweeter than honey? and what is stronger than a lion?
Judg. 14:18

With the jawbone of an ass, heaps upon heaps, with the jaw of an ass have I slain a thousand men.
Samson
Judg. 15:16

If I be shaven, then my strength will go from me.
Judg. 16:17

By strength shall no man prevail.
1 Sam. 2:9

They were swifter than eagles, they were stronger than lions.
2 Sam. 1:23

He lift up his spear against eight hundred, whom he slew at one time.
2 Sam. 23:8

Be thou strong therefore, and show thyself a man.
David to Solomon
1 Kings 2:2

With him is an arm of flesh; but with us is the Lord our God.
2 Chron. 32:8

The joy of the Lord is your strength.
Neh. 8:10

Will He esteem thy riches? no, not gold, nor all the forces of strength.
Job 36:19

Hast thou an arm like God?
God to Job
Job 40:9

He esteemeth iron as straw, and brass as rotten wood.
Job 41:27

The Lord is my strength and my shield.
Ps. 28:7

There is no king saved by the multitude of an host.
Ps. 33:16

A mighty man is not delivered by much strength.
Ps. 33:16

I will not trust in my bow, neither shall my sword save me.
Ps. 44:6

The Lord is my strength and song, and is become my salvation.
Ps. 118:14

Blessed be the Lord my strength, which teacheth my hands to war, and my fingers to fight.
Ps. 144:1

The way of the Lord is strength to the upright.
Prov. 10:29

A wise man is strong.
Prov. 24:5

Wisdom strengtheneth the wise more than ten mighty men which are in the city.
Eccl. 7:19

The race is not to the swift, nor the battle to the strong, neither yet bread to the wise, nor yet riches to men of understanding, nor yet favour to men of skill; but time and chance happeneth to them all.
Eccl. 9:11

Wisdom is better than strength.
Eccl. 9:16

The Lord Jehovah is my strength and my song; He also is become my salvation.
Isa. 12:2

Trust ye in the Lord for ever: for in the Lord Jehovah is everlasting strength.
Isa. 26:4

In quietness and in confidence shall be your strength.
Isa. 30:15

He shall come up like a lion from the swelling of Jordan unto the habitation of the strong.
Jer. 50:44
See also Jer. 49:19

Wisdom and might are His.
Dan. 2:20

The people that do know their God shall be strong.
Dan. 11:32

The Lord God is my strength.
Hab. 3:19
See also Isa. 49:5

Not by might, nor by power, but by My spirit, saith the Lord of hosts.
Zech. 4:6

Upon this rock I will build my church; and the gates of hell shall not prevail against it.
Jesus
Matt. 16:18

The weakness of God is stronger than men.
1 Cor. 1:25

My strength is made perfect in weakness.
Jesus
2 Cor. 12:9

When I am weak, then am I strong.
2 Cor. 12:10

[*See also* Fortitude, Frailty, Weakness]

STRIFE

Knowest thou not that it will be bitterness in the latter end?
2 Sam. 2:26

He that troubleth his own house shall inherit the wind.
Prov. 11:29

Better is a dinner of herbs where love is, than a stalled ox and hatred therewith.
Prov. 15:17

Better is a dry morsel, and quietness therewith, than an house full of sacrifices with strife.
Prov. 17:1

The beginning of strife is as when one letteth out water: therefore leave off contention.
Prov. 17:14

Every fool will be meddling.
Prov. 20:3

Cast out the scorner, and contention shall go out; yea, strife and reproach shall cease.
Prov. 22:10

Where no wood is, there the fire goeth out: so where there is no talebearer, the strife ceaseth.
Prov. 26:20

A man's foes shall be they of his own household.
Jesus
Matt. 10:36

If a house be divided against itself, that house cannot stand.
Jesus
Mark 3:25
See also Matt. 12:35, Luke 11:17

Suppose ye that I am come to give peace on earth? I tell you, Nay; but rather division.
Jesus
Luke 12:51
See also Matt. 10:34

The father shall be divided against the son, and the son against the father; the mother against the daughter, and the daughter against the mother.
Jesus
Luke 12:53
See also Matt. 10:35

After my departing shall grievous wolves enter in among you, not sparing the flock.
Acts 20:29

Of your own selves shall men arise, speaking perverse things.
Acts 20:30

Brother goeth to law with brother, and that before the unbelievers.
1 Cor. 6:6

Be at peace among yourselves.
1 Thess. 5:13

Where envying and strife is, there is confusion and every evil work.
James 3:16

Ye fight and war, yet ye have not, because ye ask not.
James 4:2

[*See also* Arguments, Nagging, Trouble, Unity, War, War and Peace]

STUBBORNNESS

I will harden his heart, that he shall not let the people go.
Ex. 4:21

I know not the Lord, neither will I let Israel go.
Pharaoh
Ex. 5:2

How long wilt thou refuse to humble thyself before Me? let My people go.
God to Pharaoh
Ex. 10:3

Thou art a stiffnecked people.
E.g., Ex. 33:3

Circumcise therefore the foreskin of your heart, and be no more stiffnecked.
Deut. 10:16

They ceased not from their own doings, nor from their stubborn way.
Judg. 2:19

Stubbornness is as iniquity and idolatry.
1 Sam. 15:23

They would not hear, but hardened their necks.
2 Kings 17:14

They have done that which was evil in My sight, and have provoked Me to anger, since the day their fathers came forth out of Egypt.
2 Kings 21:15

Be ye not stiffnecked, as your fathers were.
2 Chron. 30:8

If ye will hear His voice, Harden not your heart.
Ps. 95:7–8
See also, e.g., Heb. 3:15

If ye refuse and rebel, ye shall be devoured with the sword: for the mouth of the Lord hath spoken it.
Isa. 1:20

Hear ye indeed, but understand not; and see ye indeed, but perceive not.
Isa. 6:9
See also, e.g., Matt. 13:14

Hear, ye deaf; and look, ye blind, that ye may see.
Isa. 42:18

Who is blind, but My servant? or deaf, as My messenger that I sent?
Isa. 42:19

Who is blind as he that is perfect, and blind as the Lord's servant?
Isa. 42:19

Thou art obstinate, and thy neck is an iron sinew, and thy brow brass.
Isa. 48:4

Take away the foreskins of your heart.
Jer. 4:4

They are brass and iron; they are all corrupters.
Jer. 6:28

I will take the stony heart out of their flesh, and will give them an heart of flesh.
Ezek. 11:19
See also Ezek. 36:26

Having eyes, see ye not? and having ears, hear ye not?
Jesus
Mark 8:18

What I have written I have written.
Pilate
John 19:22

Ye stiffnecked and uncircumcised in heart and ears, ye do always resist the Holy Ghost.
Acts 7:51

The heart of this people is waxed gross, and their ears are dull of hearing, and their eyes have they closed.
Acts 28:27

[*See also* Impenitence]

SUBMISSION

See Acceptance, Authority, Marriage.

SUCCESS

The Lord shall make thee the head, and not the tail; and thou shalt be above only, and thou shalt not be beneath.
Deut. 28:13

I exalted thee out of the dust, and made thee prince over My people Israel.
1 Kings 16:2

Believe in the Lord your God, so shall ye be established; believe His prophets, so shall ye prosper.
2 Chron. 20:20

God hath power to help, and to cast down.
2 Chron. 25:8

As long as he sought the Lord, God made him to prosper.
2 Chron. 26:5

The God of heaven, He will prosper us.
Neh. 2:20

What is the hope of the hypocrite, though he hath gained, when God taketh away his soul?
Job 27:8

He shall be like a tree planted by the rivers of water, that bringeth forth his fruit in his season.
Ps. 1:3

The righteous shall inherit the land.
Ps. 37:29

Promotion cometh neither from the east, nor from the west, nor from the south. But God is the judge: He putteth down one, and setteth up another.
Ps. 75:6–7

They go from strength to strength.
Ps. 84:7

This is the Lord's doing; it is marvellous in our eyes.
Ps. 118:23
See also, e.g., Matt. 21:42

He becometh poor that dealeth with a slack hand: but the hand of the diligent maketh rich.
Prov. 10:4

Commit thy works unto the Lord, and thy thoughts shall be established.
Prov. 16:3

The race is not to the swift, nor the battle to the strong, neither yet bread to the wise, nor yet riches to men of understanding, nor yet favour to men of skill; but time and chance happeneth to them all.
Eccl. 9:11

If ye will not believe, surely ye shall not be established.
Isa. 7:9

Being planted, shall it prosper?
Ezek. 17:10

Not by might, nor by power, but by My spirit, saith the Lord of hosts.
Zech. 4:6

Many that are first shall be last; and the last first.
Jesus
Mark 10:31
See also Matt. 19:30, Matt. 20:16

The stone which the builders rejected is become the head of the corner.
Jesus
Mark 12:10
See also Ps. 118:22, Matt. 21:42, Luke 20:17

A man's life consisteth not in the abundance of the things which he possesseth.
Jesus
Luke 12:15

Unto whomsoever much is given, of him shall be much required.
Jesus
Luke 12:48

The hand of the Lord was with them: and a great number believed.
Acts 11:21

The word of God grew and multiplied.
Acts 12:24

It is not of him that willeth, nor of him that runneth, but of God that showeth mercy.
Rom. 9:16

What hast thou that thou didst not receive?
1 Cor. 4:7

[*See also* Achievement, Defeat, Failure, Prosperity, Reward, Victory, Wealth]

SUDDENNESS

As the lightning cometh out of the east, and shineth even unto the west; so shall also the coming of the Son of man be.
Jesus
Matt. 24:27
See also Luke 17:24

[*See also* Second Coming]

SUFFERING

Lord, wherefore hast Thou so evil entreated this people?
Moses
Ex. 5:22

He breaketh me with a tempest, and multiplieth my wounds without cause.
Job 9:17

Are not my days few? cease then, and let me alone, that I may take comfort a little.
Job 10:20

The wicked man travaileth with pain all his days.
Job 15:20

He delivereth the poor in his affliction.
Job 36:15

For Thy sake are we killed all the day long; we are counted as sheep for the slaughter.
Ps. 44:22

Thou feedest them with the bread of tears.
Ps. 80:5

Thou hast lifted me up, and cast me down.
Ps. 102:10

I praised the dead which are already dead more than the living which are yet alive.
Eccl. 4:2

I have chosen thee in the furnace of affliction.
Isa. 48:10

He was wounded for our transgressions, he was bruised for our iniquities.
Isa. 53:5

He was oppressed, and he was afflicted, yet he opened not his mouth.
Isa. 53:7

He bare the sin of many, and made intercession for the transgressors.
Isa. 53:12

My sighs are many, and my heart is faint.
Lam. 1:22

Though He cause grief, yet will He have compassion.
Lam. 3:32

Remember, O Lord, what is come upon us: consider, and behold our reproach.
Lam. 5:1

Shall there be evil in a city, and the Lord hath not done it?
Amos 3:6

Let this cup pass from me.
Jesus
Matt. 26:39

We must through much tribulation enter into the kingdom of God.
Acts 14:22

For the hope of Israel I am bound with this chain.
Acts 28:20

Tribulation worketh patience; And patience, experience; and experience, hope.
Rom. 5:3–4

We are fools for Christ's sake.
1 Cor. 4:10

If in this life only we have hope in Christ, we are of all men most miserable.
1 Cor. 15:19

As ye are partakers of the sufferings, so shall ye be also of the consolation.
2 Cor. 1:7

In labours more abundant, in stripes above measure, in prisons more frequent, in deaths oft.
2 Cor. 11:23

A thorn in the flesh, the messenger of Satan to buffet me.
2 Cor. 12:7

If we suffer, we shall also reign with Him.
2 Tim. 2:12

Though He were a Son, yet learned He obedience by the things which He suffered.
Heb. 5:8

Without shedding of blood is no remission.
Heb. 9:22

Whom the Lord loveth He chasteneth.
Heb. 12:6

We count them happy which endure.
James 5:11

What glory is it, if, when ye be buffeted for your faults, ye shall take it patiently?
1 Pet. 2:20

If, when ye do well, and suffer for it, ye take it patiently, this is acceptable with God.
1 Pet. 2:20

If ye suffer for righteousness' sake, happy are ye.
1 Pet. 3:14

It is better, if the will of God be so, that ye suffer for well doing, than for evil doing.
1 Pet. 3:17

He that hath suffered in the flesh hath ceased from sin.
1 Pet. 4:1

Rejoice, inasmuch as ye are partakers of Christ's sufferings; that, when His glory shall be revealed, ye may be glad also with exceeding joy.
1 Pet. 4:13

[*See also* Anguish, Compassion, Grief, Mercy, Persecution, Torment]

SUPERSTITION

Be not dismayed at the signs of heaven; for the heathen are dismayed at them.
Jer. 10:2

The gods are come down to us in the likeness of men.
Acts 14:11

[*See also* Idols, Omens]

SUPPORT

See God's Support.

SURVIVAL

Of every living thing of all flesh, two of every sort shalt thou bring into the ark, to keep them alive with thee.
Gen. 6:19

The more they afflicted them, the more they multiplied and grew.
(them: Hebrews in Egypt)
Ex. 1:12

The remnant that is escaped of the house of Judah shall yet again take root downward, and bear fruit upward.
2 Kings 19:30
See also Isa. 37:31

Out of Jerusalem shall go forth a remnant.
2 Kings 19:31, Isa. 37:32

Skin for skin, yea, all that a man hath will he give for his life.
Satan to God
Job 2:4

I am escaped with the skin of my teeth.
Job 19:20

The Lord blessed the latter end of Job more than his beginning.
Job 42:12

Unless the Lord had been my help, my soul had almost dwelt in silence.
Ps. 94:17

Except the Lord of hosts had left unto us a very small remnant, we should have been as Sodom.
Isa. 1:9
See also Rom. 9:29

We are left but a few of many.
Jer. 42:2

Can thine heart endure, or can thine hands be strong, in the days that I shall deal with thee?
Ezek. 22:14

I send you forth as sheep in the midst of wolves: be ye therefore wise as serpents, and harmless as doves.
Jesus
Matt. 10:16

If we suffer, we shall also reign with Him.
2 Tim. 2:12

[*See also* Life and Death, Perseverance]

SUSTENANCE

See Bread of Life, Food.

SWEARING

Swear not at all; neither by heaven; for it is God's throne: Nor by the earth; for it is His footstool: neither by Jerusalem; for it is the city of the great King.
Jesus
Matt. 5:34–35

[*See also* Blasphemy, Oaths, Profanity, Promises]

SYMBOLISM

See Omens.

SYMPATHY

Miserable comforters are ye all.
Job to his friends
Job 16:2

Though they shall cry unto Me, I will not hearken unto them.
Jer. 11:11

Is it nothing to you, all ye that pass by?
Lam. 1:12

He that despiseth you despiseth me; and he that despiseth me despiseth Him that sent me.
Jesus
Luke 10:16

Jesus wept.
John 11:35

Remember them that are in bonds, as bound with them; and them which suffer adversity, as being yourselves also in the body.
Heb. 13:3

[*See also* Comfort, Compassion]

TACT

A soft answer turneth away wrath.
Prov. 15:1

Pleasant words are as an honeycomb, sweet to the soul, and health to the bones.
Prov. 16:24

A soft tongue breaketh the bone.
Prov. 25:15

[*See also* Prudence, Restraint]

TAINT

See Contamination.

TALENT

See Ability.

See Discernment, Flavor.

If ye love them which love you, what reward have ye? do not even the publicans the same?
>Jesus
>*Matt. 5:46*
>*See also Luke 6:32*

Of whom do the kings of the earth take custom or tribute? of their own children, or of strangers?
>Jesus
>*Matt. 17:25*

Take, and give unto them for me and thee.
>Jesus
>*Matt. 17:27*

Render therefore unto Caesar the things which are Caesar's; and unto God the things that are God's.
>Jesus
>*Matt. 22:21*
>*See also Mark 12:17, Luke 20:25*

Exact no more than that which is appointed you.
>*Luke 3:13*

Pay ye tribute also: for they are God's ministers.
>*Rom. 13:6*

Tribute to whom tribute is due.
>*Rom. 13:7*

Show them the way wherein they must walk, and the work that they must do.
>*Ex. 18:20*

My speech shall distil as the dew, as the small rain upon the tender herb, and as the showers upon the grass.
>*Deut. 32:2*

Whosoever shall do and teach them, the same shall be called great in the kingdom of heaven.
>Jesus (them: commandments)
>*Matt. 5:19*

My doctrine is not mine, but His that sent me.
>Jesus
>*John 7:16*

Thou therefore which teachest another, teachest thou not thyself?
>*Rom. 2:21*

Be gentle unto all men, apt to teach, patient.
>*2 Tim. 2:24*

Reprove, rebuke, exhort with all long-suffering and doctrine.
>*2 Tim. 4:2*

Speak thou the things which become sound doctrine.
>*Titus 2:1*

We put bits in the horses' mouths, that they may obey us.
>*James 3:3*

[*See also* Child-Rearing, Education, Guidance, Instruction]

All the night make I my bed to swim; I water my couch with my tears.
>*Ps. 6:6*

Weeping may endure for a night, but joy cometh in the morning.
>*Ps. 30:5*

Rivers of waters run down mine eyes, because they keep not Thy law.
>*Ps. 119:136*

They that sow in tears shall reap in joy.
>*Ps. 126:5*

He that goeth forth and weepeth, bearing precious seed, shall doubtless come again with rejoicing, bringing his sheaves with him.
>*Ps. 126:6*

A time to weep, and a time to laugh.
>*Eccl. 3:4*

Oh that my head were waters, and mine eyes a fountain of tears, that I might weep day and night.
>*Jer. 9:1*

Refrain thy voice from weeping, and thine

eyes from tears: for thy work shall be rewarded, saith the Lord.
Jer. 31:16

Mine eye runneth down with water, because the comforter that should relieve my soul is far from me.
Lam. 1:16

Blessed are ye that weep now: for ye shall laugh.
Jesus
Luke 6:21

Woman, why weepest thou?
Jesus to Mary Magdalene
John 20:15

What mean ye to weep and to break mine heart?
Acts 21:13

Rejoice with them that do rejoice, and weep with them that weep.
Rom. 12:15

He found no place of repentance, though he sought it carefully with tears.
(He: Esau)
Heb. 12:17

God shall wipe away all tears from their eyes.
Rev. 7:17

[*See also* Grief, Happiness, Joy, Sorrow]

TEMPER

Let not the anger of my lord wax hot.
Aaron to Moses
Ex. 32:22

Cease from anger, and forsake wrath.
Ps. 37:8

A fool's wrath is presently known: but a prudent man covereth shame.
Prov. 12:16

He that is soon angry dealeth foolishly.
Prov. 14:17

For a small moment have I forsaken thee; but with great mercies will I gather thee.
Isa. 54:7

[*See also* Anger, Patience, Restraint]

TEMPERANCE

See Behavior, Excess.

TEMPTATION

And the serpent said unto the woman, Ye shall not surely die.
Gen. 3:4

Your eyes shall be opened, and ye shall be as gods, knowing good and evil.
Gen. 3:5

She took of the fruit thereof, and did eat.
(She: Eve)
Gen. 3:6

The serpent beguiled me, and I did eat.
Eve
Gen. 3:13

If thou doest not well, sin lieth at the door.
Gen. 4:7

Look not behind thee.
Angel to Lot and his wife
Gen. 19:17

His wife looked back from behind him, and she became a pillar of salt.
Gen. 19:26

Ye shall not tempt the Lord your God.
Deut. 6:16

Take heed to yourselves, that your heart be not deceived.
Deut. 11:16

Tell me, I pray thee, wherein thy great strength lieth.
Delilah
Judg. 16:6

And the Lord said unto Satan, Hast thou considered my servant Job?
Job 1:8

Dost thou still retain thine integrity? curse God, and die.
Job's wife to Job
Job 2:9

As for me, I will walk in mine integrity.
Ps. 26:11

If sinners entice thee, consent thou not.
Prov. 1:10

Discretion shall preserve thee, understanding shall keep thee.
Prov. 2:11

Enter not into the path of the wicked, and go not in the way of evil men.
Prov. 4:14

The lips of a strange woman drop as an honeycomb, and her mouth is smoother than oil.
Prov. 5:3

Keep thee from the evil woman, from the flattery of the tongue of a strange woman.
Prov. 6:24

Lust not after her beauty in thine heart; neither let her take thee with her eyelids.
Prov. 6:25

Can a man take fire in his bosom, and his clothes not be burned?
Prov. 6:27

As a bird hasteth to the snare, and knoweth not that it is for his life.
Prov. 7:23

Let not thine heart decline to her ways, go not astray in her paths.
Prov. 7:25

She hath cast down many wounded: yea, many strong men have been slain by her.
Prov. 7:26

Look not thou upon the wine when it is red.
Prov. 23:31

Woe unto him that giveth his neighbour drink.
Hab. 2:15

If Thou be the Son of God, command that these stones be made bread.
Devil to Jesus
Matt. 4:3
See also Luke 4:3

Thou shalt not tempt the Lord thy God.
Jesus
Matt. 4:7, Luke 4:12

Lead us not into temptation, but deliver us from evil.
Jesus
Matt. 6:13, Luke 11:4

Wide is the gate, and broad is the way, that leadeth to destruction.
Jesus
Matt. 7:13

Get thee behind me, Satan: thou art an offence unto me.
Jesus
Matt. 16:23
See also Matt. 4:10, Mark 8:33, Luke 4:8

Woe to that man by whom the offence cometh!
Jesus
Matt. 18:7

Why tempt ye me, ye hypocrites?
Jesus
Matt. 22:18
See also Mark 12:15, Luke 20:23

Watch and pray, that ye enter not into temptation.
Jesus
Matt. 26:41
See also Luke 22:40, 46

The spirit indeed is willing, but the flesh is weak.
Jesus
Matt. 26:41
See also Mark 14:38

He that is dead is freed from sin.
Rom. 6:7

Yield yourselves unto God.
Rom. 6:13

What I hate, that do I.
Rom. 7:15

It is no more I that do it, but sin that dwelleth in me.
Rom. 7:17, 20

With the mind I myself serve the law of God; but with the flesh the law of sin.
Rom. 7:25

To avoid fornication, let every man have his own wife, and let every woman have her own husband.
1 Cor. 7:2

We are not ignorant of his devices.
(his: Satan)
2 Cor. 2:11

The flesh lusteth against the Spirit, and the Spirit against the flesh.
Gal. 5:17

Put on the whole armour of God, that ye

may be able to stand against the wiles of the devil.
Eph. 6:11

Blessed is the man that endureth temptation.
James 1:12

God cannot be tempted with evil, neither tempteth He any man.
James 1:13

Resist the devil, and he will flee from you.
James 4:7

The Lord knoweth how to deliver the godly out of temptations.
2 Pet. 2:9

[*See also* Fortitude, Restraint, Self-Control, Self-Denial]

TEN COMMANDMENTS, THE

And he was there with the Lord forty days and forty nights.
(he: Moses)
Ex. 34:28

Two tables of stone written with the finger of God.
Deut. 9:10

[*See also* Commandments and the Appendix at p. 419]

TERROR

The sword without, and terror within, shall destroy both the young man and the virgin, the suckling also with the man of gray hairs.
Deut. 32:25

The ears of every one that heareth it shall tingle.
1 Sam. 3:11
See also *2 Kings 21:12*

Let not Thy dread make me afraid.
Job 13:21

The terrors of the shadow of death.
Job 24:17

Pangs and sorrows shall take hold of them;

they shall be in pain as a woman that travaileth.
Isa. 13:8

Howl, O gate; cry, O city; thou, whole Palestina, art dissolved.
Isa. 14:31

They shall clothe themselves with trembling.
Ezek. 26:16

The suburbs shall shake at the sound of the cry of thy pilots.
Ezek. 27:28

I have caused My terror in the land of the living.
Ezek. 32:32

The abomination of desolation.
Jesus
Matt. 24:15, Mark 13:14

Every island fled away, and the mountains were not found.
Rev. 16:20

[*See also* Destruction, Fear, Violence]

TESTIMONY

Speak ye unto the rock before their eyes; and it shall give forth his water.
God to Moses
Num. 20:8

Your eyes have seen what I have done in Egypt.
Josh. 24:7

Ye are witnesses against yourselves that ye have chosen you the Lord, to serve Him.
Josh. 24:22

Behold, this stone shall be a witness unto us.
Josh. 24:27

Stand still, that I may reason with you before the Lord.
1 Sam. 12:7

Let it be known this day that Thou art God in Israel, and that I am Thy servant.
Elijah
1 Kings 18:36

Let the shadow return backward ten degrees.
2 Kings 20:10

Declare His glory among the heathen; His marvellous works among all nations.
1 Chron. 16:24
See also Ps. 96:3

Make known His deeds among the people.
Ps. 105:1, 1 Chron. 16:8

In all thy ways acknowledge Him.
Prov. 3:6

Praise the Lord, call upon His name, declare His doings among the people, make mention that His name is exalted.
Isa. 12:4

Lift up thy voice with strength; lift it up, be not afraid.
Isa. 40:9

Ye are My witnesses, saith the Lord.
Isa. 43:10, 12

Whosoever therefore shall confess me before men, him will I confess also before my Father which is in heaven. But whosoever shall deny me before men, him will I also deny before my Father which is in heaven.
Jesus
Matt. 10:32–33

The blind see, the lame walk, the lepers are cleansed, the deaf hear, the dead are raised, to the poor the gospel is preached.
Jesus
Luke 7:22
See also Matt. 11:5

Whosoever shall confess me before men, him shall the Son of man also confess before the angels of God.
Jesus
Luke 12:8

I saw, and bare record that this is the Son of God.
John 1:34

If I bear witness of myself, my witness is not true.
Jesus
John 5:31

The works that I do in my Father's name, they bear witness of me.
Jesus
John 10:25

Ye also shall bear witness, because ye have been with me from the beginning.
Jesus
John 15:27

To this end was I born, and for this cause came I into the world, that I should bear witness unto the truth.
Jesus
John 18:37

He that saw it bare record, and his record is true.
John 19:35

If they should be written every one, I suppose that even the world itself could not contain the books that should be written.
John 21:25

Ye shall be witnesses unto me.
Jesus
Acts 1:8

We cannot but speak the things which we have seen and heard.
Acts 4:20

To Him give all the prophets witness.
Acts 10:43

He left not Himself without witness, in that He did good, and gave us rain from heaven.
Acts 14:17

Thou shalt be His witness unto all men.
Acts 22:15

As thou hast testified of me in Jerusalem, so must thou bear witness also at Rome.
Jesus
Acts 23:11

I continue unto this day, witnessing both to small and great.
Paul
Acts 26:22

God is my witness.
Rom. 1:9

Ye are our epistle written in our hearts, known and read of all men.
2 Cor. 3:2

Not in tables of stone, but in fleshy tables of the heart.
2 Cor. 3:3

Walk in wisdom toward them that are without.
Col. 4:5

Be not thou therefore ashamed of the testimony of our Lord.
2 Tim. 1:8

That which we have seen and heard declare we unto you.
  1 John 1:3

It is the Spirit that beareth witness, because the Spirit is truth.
  1 John 5:6

There are three that bear witness in earth, the Spirit, and the water, and the blood: and these three agree in one.
  1 John 5:8

If we receive the witness of men, the witness of God is greater.
  1 John 5:9

What thou seest, write in a book, and send it unto the seven churches.
  Jesus
  Rev. 1:11

Write the things which thou hast seen, and the things which are, and the things which shall be hereafter.
  Jesus
  Rev. 1:19

[*See also* Evangelism, Praise of God]

TESTING

Through them I may prove Israel, whether they will keep the way of the Lord to walk therein.
  Judg. 2:22

Thou art weighed in the balances, and art found wanting.
  Dan. 5:27

[*See also* Competition]

THANKSGIVING

See Gratitude.

THIRST

Oh that one would give me drink of the water of the well of Bethlehem.
  2 Sam. 23:15, 1 Chron. 11:17

In my thirst they gave me vinegar to drink.
  Ps. 69:21

The tongue of the sucking child cleaveth to the roof of his mouth for thirst.
  Lam. 4:4

Whosoever drinketh of this water shall thirst again: But whosoever drinketh of the water that I shall give him shall never thirst.
  Jesus
  John 4:13–14

I thirst.
  Jesus, on the cross
  John 19:28

[*See also* Bread of Life, Deprivation, Famine, Hunger]

THOUGHTS

Thou, even Thou only, knowest the hearts of all the children of men.
  1 Kings 8:39

The Lord knoweth the thoughts of man, that they are vanity.
  Ps. 94:11

There is not a word in my tongue, but, lo, O Lord, Thou knowest it altogether.
  Ps. 139:4

The thoughts of the wicked are an abomination to the Lord.
  Prov. 15:26

My thoughts are not your thoughts, neither are your ways My ways, saith the Lord.
  Isa. 55:8

How long shall thy vain thoughts lodge within thee?
  Jer. 4:14

I know the things that come into your mind, every one of them.
  Ezek. 11:5

Think soberly.
  Rom. 12:3

The Lord knoweth the thoughts of the wise, that they are vain.
  1 Cor. 3:20

Gird up the loins of your mind.
  1 Pet. 1:13

I am He which searcheth the reins and hearts.
Jesus
Rev. 2:23

[*See also* Attitude, Contemplation, Secrecy]

THREAT

Intendest thou to kill me, as thou killedst the Egyptian?
Ex. 2:14

Neither will I be with you any more, except ye destroy the accursed from among you.
God to Joshua
Josh. 7:12

Show us, we pray thee, the entrance into the city, and we will show thee mercy.
Judg. 1:24

The ears of every one that heareth it shall tingle.
1 Sam. 3:11
See also 2 Kings 21:12

So let the gods do to me, and more.
Jezebel to Elijah
1 Kings 19:2
See also 1 Sam. 14:44

In the place where dogs licked the blood of Naboth shall dogs lick thy blood, even thine.
(thy: Ahab)
1 Kings 21:19

My father chastised you with whips, but I will chastise you with scorpions.
2 Chron. 10:11, 14
See also 1 Kings 12:11

I have not said in vain that I would do this evil unto them.
Ezek. 6:10

If thou let this man go, thou art not Caesar's friend.
John 19:12

TIME

And God called the light Day, and the darkness He called Night. And the evening and the morning were the first day.
Gen. 1:5

Jacob served seven years for Rachel; and they seemed unto him but a few days, for the love he had to her.
Gen. 29:20

The sun stood still, and the moon stayed, until the people had avenged themselves upon their enemies.
Josh. 10:13

The sun stood still in the midst of heaven, and hasted not to go down about a whole day.
Josh. 10:13

Shall the shadow go forward ten degrees, or go back?
2 Kings 20:9

Our days upon earth are a shadow.
Job 8:9
See also 1 Chron. 29:15

Waters wear the stones.
Job 14:19

A thousand years in Thy sight are but as yesterday when it is past.
Ps. 90:4

One generation passeth away, and another generation cometh: but the earth abideth for ever.
Eccl. 1:4

That which now is in the days to come shall all be forgotten.
Eccl. 2:16

To every thing there is a season, and a time to every purpose under the heaven.
Eccl. 3:1

A time to be born, and a time to die; a time to plant, and a time to pluck up that which is planted.
Eccl. 3:2

A time to kill, and a time to heal; a time to break down, and a time to build up.
Eccl. 3:3

That which hath been is now; and that which is to be hath already been.
Eccl. 3:15

The race is not to the swift, nor the battle to the strong, neither yet bread to the wise, nor yet riches to men of understanding, nor yet favour to men of skill; but time and chance happeneth to them all.
Eccl. 9:11

Lord, how long?
Isa. 6:11

Remember ye not the former things, neither consider the things of old.
Isa. 43:18

I will restore to you the years that the locust hath eaten.
Joel 2:25

Mine hour is not yet come.
Jesus
John 2:4
See also John 7:6

Lift up your eyes, and look on the fields; for they are white already to harvest.
Jesus
John 4:35

The night cometh, when no man can work.
Jesus
John 9:4

The fashion of this world passeth away.
1 Cor. 7:31

One day is with the Lord as a thousand years, and a thousand years as one day.
2 Pet. 3:8

Thrust in Thy sickle, and reap.
Rev. 14:15

The time is come for Thee to reap; for the harvest of the earth is ripe.
Rev. 14:15

[*See also* Imminence, Procrastination, Second Coming and the Appendix at p. 421]

TIMIDITY

The children of Israel have not hearkened unto me; how then shall Pharaoh hear me?
Moses to God
Ex. 6:12

If thou wilt go with me, then I will go.
Barak to Deborah
Judg. 4:8

When I have a convenient season, I will call for thee.
Felix to Paul
Acts 24:25

God hath not given us the spirit of fear; but

of power, and of love, and of a sound mind.
2 Tim. 1:7

[*See also* Confidence, Cowardice, Fear]

TITHE

Of all that Thou shalt give me I will surely give the tenth unto Thee.
Gen. 28:22

The tithe of the land, whether of the seed of the land, or of the fruit of the tree, is the Lord's.
Lev. 27:30

Honour the Lord with thy substance, and with the firstfruits of all thine increase.
Prov. 3:9

[*See also* Charity]

TOLERANCE

Love ye therefore the stranger: for ye were strangers in the land of Egypt.
Deut. 10:19

Thou shalt not muzzle the ox when he treadeth out the corn.
Deut. 25:4
See also 1 Cor. 9:9

Shouldest thou help the ungodly, and love them that hate the Lord?
2 Chron. 19:2

For all this His anger is not turned away, but His hand is stretched out still.
E.g., Isa. 5:25, Isa. 9:17

Thou art of purer eyes than to behold evil.
Habakkuk to God
Hab. 1:13

Why eateth your Master with publicans and sinners?
Matt. 9:11
See also Luke 5:30

O faithless and perverse generation, how long shall I be with you? how long shall I suffer you?
Jesus
Matt. 17:17
See also Mark 9:19, Luke 9:41

Judge not, and ye shall not be judged: condemn not, and ye shall not be condemned.
Jesus
Luke 6:37
See also Matt. 7:1

Forgive, and ye shall be forgiven.
Jesus
Luke 6:37

Let not him which eateth not judge him that eateth.
Rom. 14:3

One man esteemeth one day above another: another esteemeth every day alike. Let every man be fully persuaded in his own mind.
Rom. 14:5

We then that are strong ought to bear the infirmities of the weak.
Rom. 15:1

Receive ye one another, as Christ also received us to the glory of God.
Rom. 15:7

Let no man think me a fool; if otherwise, yet as a fool receive me.
2 Cor. 11:16

For ye suffer fools gladly, seeing ye yourselves are wise.
2 Cor. 11:19

[*See also* Equality, Forgiveness]

TONGUES

The Spirit gave them utterance.
Acts 2:4

We do hear them speak in our tongues the wonderful works of God.
Acts 2:11

These men are full of new wine.
Acts 2:13

He that speaketh in an unknown tongue speaketh not unto men, but unto God: for no man understandeth him.
1 Cor. 14:2

He that speaketh in an unknown tongue edifieth himself; but he that prophesieth edifieth the church.
1 Cor. 14:4

Except ye utter by the tongue words easy to be understood, how shall it be known what is spoken? for ye shall speak into the air.
1 Cor. 14:9

Tongues are for a sign, not to them that believe, but to them that believe not.
1 Cor. 14:22

TORMENT

In the morning thou shalt say, Would God it were even! and at even thou shalt say, Would God it were morning!
Deut. 28:67

Let not his hoar head go down to the grave in peace.
1 Kings 2:6

How long will ye vex my soul, and break me in pieces with words?
Job 19:2

In those days shall men seek death, and shall not find it; and shall desire to die, and death shall flee from them.
Rev. 9:6

They have no rest day nor night, who worship the beast and his image.
Rev. 14:11

The lake of fire and brimstone.
Rev. 20:10

[*See also* Anguish, Grief, Suffering]

TRADITION

He did evil in the sight of the Lord, and walked in the way of his father.
E.g., 1 Kings 15:26

As did their fathers, so do they unto this day.
2 Kings 17:41

Remove not the ancient landmark, which thy fathers have set.
Prov. 22:28
See also Prov. 23:10

Ask for the old paths, where is the good way, and walk therein, and ye shall find rest for your souls.
Jer. 6:16

Laying aside the commandment of God, ye hold the tradition of men.
    Jesus
    Mark 7:8

Ye reject the commandment of God, that ye may keep your own tradition.
    Jesus
    Mark 7:9
    See also Matt. 15:3

As your fathers did, so do ye.
    Acts 7:51

[*See also* Heritage, Inheritance, Posterity, Rituals]

TRAITORS

See Betrayal, Loyalty, Treachery.

TRANSVESTITES

The woman shall not wear that which pertaineth unto a man, neither shall a man put on a woman's garment: for all that do so are abomination unto the Lord thy God.
    Deut. 22:5

[*See also* Homosexuals]

TRAPS

Say now Shibboleth.
    Judg. 12:6

As a bird hasteth to the snare, and knoweth not that it is for his life.
    Prov. 7:23

I will spread My net upon him, and he shall be taken in My snare.
    Ezek. 17:20

[*See also* Strategy]

TREACHERY

Let not mine hand be upon him, but let the hand of the Philistines be upon him.
    Saul about David
    1 Sam. 18:17

The words of his mouth were smoother than butter, but war was in his heart.
    Ps. 55:21

His words were softer than oil, yet were they drawn swords.
    Ps. 55:21

One speaketh peaceably to his neighbour with his mouth, but in heart he layeth his wait.
    Jer. 9:8

By thy sorceries were all nations deceived.
    Rev. 18:23

[*See also* Betrayal, Loyalty]

TRIBULATION

See Suffering.

TRINITY

Go ye therefore, and teach all nations, baptizing them in the name of the Father, and of the Son, and of the Holy Ghost.
    Jesus
    Matt. 28:19

The grace of the Lord Jesus Christ, and the love of God, and the communion of the Holy Ghost, be with you all.
    2 Cor. 13:14

There are three that bear record in heaven, the Father, the Word, and the Holy Ghost: and these three are one.
    1 John 5:7

There are three that bear witness in earth, the Spirit, and the water, and the blood: and these three agree in one.
    1 John 5:8

[*See also* God, Holy Spirit, Jesus]

TROUBLE

Evil will befall you in the latter days.
    Deut. 31:29

Let Him deliver me out of all tribulation.
    1 Sam. 26:24

Man is born unto trouble.
    Job 5:7

The Lord also will be a refuge for the oppressed, a refuge in times of trouble.
Ps. 9:9

Many are the afflictions of the righteous: but the Lord delivereth him out of them all.
Ps. 34:19

Give us help from trouble: for vain is the help of man.
Ps. 60:11

In the day of my trouble I will call upon Thee.
Ps. 86:7

My soul is full of troubles: and my life draweth nigh unto the grave.
Ps. 88:3

The days of our years are threescore years and ten; and if by reason of strength they be fourscore years, yet is their strength labour and sorrow.
Ps. 90:10

Hide not Thy face from me in the day when I am in trouble.
Ps. 102:2
See also Ps. 69:17

I was brought low, and He helped me.
Ps. 116:6

He that seeketh mischief, it shall come unto him.
Prov. 11:27

A prudent man forseeth the evil, and hideth himself: but the simple pass on, and are punished.
Prov. 22:3

If thou faint in the day of adversity, thy strength is small.
Prov. 24:10

All his days are sorrows, and his travail grief; yea, his heart taketh not rest in the night.
Eccl. 2:23

We looked for peace, but no good came; and for a time of health, and behold trouble!
Jer. 8:15

All mine enemies have heard of my trouble; they are glad that Thou hast done it.
Lam. 1:21

The Lord is good, a strong hold in the day of trouble.
Nah. 1:7

Sufficient unto the day is the evil thereof.
Jesus
Matt. 6:34

This sickness is not unto death, but for the glory of God.
Jesus
John 11:4

Give none offence.
1 Cor. 10:32

[*See also* Anguish, Assistance, Danger, Escape, God's Protection, God's Support, Safety]

TRUST

Let Him do to me as seemeth good unto Him.
2 Sam. 15:26

Our eyes are upon Thee.
2 Chron. 20:12

Blessed are all they that put their trust in Him.
Ps. 2:12

Let all those that put their trust in Thee rejoice: let them ever shout for joy.
Ps. 5:11

The Lord is my rock, and my fortress, and my deliverer; my God, my strength, in whom I will trust.
Ps. 18:2

Some trust in chariots, and some in horses: but we will remember the name of the Lord our God.
Ps. 20:7

Into Thine hand I commit my spirit.
Ps. 31:5

Commit thy way unto the Lord; trust also in Him.
Ps. 37:5

Blessed is that man that maketh the Lord his trust.
Ps. 40:4
See also, e.g., Ps. 34:8

As for me, I will call upon God; and the Lord shall save me.
> *Ps. 55:16*

In God I have put my trust; I will not fear what flesh can do unto me.
> *Ps. 56:4*
> *See also Ps. 56:11*

In Thee, O Lord, do I put my trust.
> *Ps. 71:1*
> *See also, e.g., 1 Sam. 22:3*

Trust thou in the Lord.
> *Ps. 115:9*

Hold Thou me up, and I shall be safe.
> *Ps. 119:117*

Trust in the Lord with all thine heart.
> *Prov. 3:5*

Whoso trusteth in the Lord, happy is he.
> *Prov. 16:20*

Trust ye in the Lord for ever: for in the Lord Jehovah is everlasting strength.
> *Isa. 26:4*

He that putteth his trust in Me shall possess the land, and shall inherit My holy mountain.
> *Isa. 57:13*

Blessed is the man that trusteth in the Lord, and whose hope the Lord is.
> *Jer. 17:7*

I will look unto the Lord; I will wait for the God of my salvation.
> *Mic. 7:7*

He knoweth them that trust in Him.
> *Nah. 1:7*

We trust in the living God, who is the Saviour of all men.
> *1 Tim. 4:10*

Cast not away therefore your confidence, which hath great recompence of reward.
> *Heb. 10:35*

[*See also* Betrayal, Faith, God's Protection, God's Support, Reliability, Reliance, Safety]

What the Lord saith unto me, that will I speak.
> *1 Kings 22:14*
> *See also 2 Chron. 18:13*

The ear trieth words, as the mouth tasteth meat.
> *Job 34:3*

His truth endureth to all generations.
> *Ps. 100:5*

The works of His hands are verity and judgment; all His commandments are sure.
> *Ps. 111:7*

The truth of the Lord endureth for ever.
> *Ps. 117:2*

Thy law is the truth.
> *Ps. 119:142*

Thy word is true from the beginning.
> *Ps. 119:160*

Every way of a man is right in his own eyes: but the Lord pondereth the hearts.
> *Prov. 21:2*

Buy the truth, and sell it not.
> *Prov. 23:23*

Thy counsels of old are faithfulness and truth.
> *Isa. 25:1*

Truth is fallen in the street, and equity cannot enter.
> *Isa. 59:14*

Truth is perished, and is cut off from their mouth.
> *Jer. 7:28*

The law shall go forth of Zion, and the word of the Lord from Jerusalem.
> *Mic. 4:2*

Love the truth and peace.
> *Zech. 8:19*

Heaven and earth shall pass away, but my words shall not pass away.
> Jesus
> *Matt. 24:35, Mark 13:31,*
> *Luke 21:33*

The law was given by Moses, but grace and truth came by Jesus Christ.
> *John 1:17*

He that doeth truth cometh to the light, that his deeds may be made manifest.
Jesus
John 3:21

God is true.
John 3:33

He that sent me is true, whom ye know not.
Jesus
John 7:28

Ye shall know the truth, and the truth shall make you free.
Jesus
John 8:32

Because I tell you the truth, ye believe me not.
Jesus
John 8:45
See also John 8:46

These are not the words of him that hath a devil.
John 10:21

I am the way, the truth, and the life: no man cometh unto the Father, but by me.
Jesus
John 14:6

Sanctify them through Thy truth.
Jesus
John 17:17

Thy word is truth.
Jesus to God
John 17:17

To this end was I born, and for this cause came I into the world, that I should bear witness unto the truth.
Jesus
John 18:37

Every one that is of the truth heareth my voice.
Jesus
John 18:37

What is truth?
Pilate
John 18:38

We cannot but speak the things which we have seen and heard.
Acts 4:20

Well spake the Holy Ghost by Esaias the prophet unto our fathers.
Acts 28:25

Let God be true, but every man a liar.
Rom. 3:4

We can do nothing against the truth, but for the truth.
2 Cor. 13:8

Behold, before God, I lie not.
Gal. 1:20

Am I therefore become your enemy, because I tell you the truth?
Gal. 4:16

The truth is in Jesus.
Eph. 4:21

Whatsoever things are true, whatsoever things are honest, whatsoever things are just, whatsoever things are pure, whatsoever things are lovely, whatsoever things are of good report; if there be any virtue, and if there be any praise, think on these things.
Phil. 4:8

I have not written unto you because ye know not the truth, but because ye know it.
1 John 2:21

It is the Spirit that beareth witness, because the Spirit is truth.
1 John 5:6

I have no greater joy than to hear that my children walk in truth.
3 John 4

Just and true are Thy ways, Thou King of saints.
Rev. 15:3

Behold a white horse; and he that sat upon him was called Faithful and True.
Rev. 19:11

[*See also* Candor, Credibility, Dishonesty, Honesty, Lies]

TYRANTS

This is the day in which the Lord hath delivered Sisera into thine hand.
Deborah to Barak
Judg. 4:14

My little finger shall be thicker than my father's loins.
1 Kings 12:10, 2 Chron. 10:10

Give me thy vineyard, that I may have it for a garden of herbs.
Ahab to Naboth
1 Kings 21:2

Princes have persecuted me without a cause: but my heart standeth in awe of Thy word.
Ps. 119:161

Envy thou not the oppressor, and choose none of his ways.
Prov. 3:31

Woe unto them that decree unrighteous decrees.
Isa. 10:1

Thy pomp is brought down to the grave, and the noise of thy viols.
Isa. 14:11

The worm is spread under thee, and the worms cover thee.
Isa. 14:11

How art thou fallen from heaven, O Lucifer, son of the morning!
Isa. 14:12

They that spoil thee shall be a spoil, and all that prey upon thee will I give for a prey.
Jer. 30:16

The prince shall not take of the people's inheritance by oppression.
Ezek. 46:18

He shall come to his end, and none shall help him.
Dan. 11:45

As thou hast done, it shall be done unto thee.
Obad. 15

[*See also* Oppression]

U

UNCERTAINTY

See Decisions, Doubt.

UNDERPRIVILEGED

Thou shalt open thine hand wide unto thy brother, to thy poor, and to thy needy, in thy land.
Deut. 15:11

Remember that thou wast a bondman in the land of Egypt.
Deut. 24:22
See also Deut. 5:15

He heareth the cry of the afflicted.
Job 34:28

He forgetteth not the cry of the humble.
Ps. 9:12

O God, lift up Thine hand: forget not the humble.
Ps. 10:12

He shall deliver the needy when he crieth the poor also, and him that hath no helper
Ps. 72:12

Precious shall their blood be in His sight.
Ps. 72:14

Defend the poor and fatherless: do justice to the afflicted and needy.
Ps. 82:3

Though the Lord be high, yet hath He respect unto the lowly.
Ps. 138:6

The Lord upholdeth all that fall, and raiseth up all those that be bowed down.
Ps. 145:14

Rob not the poor, because he is poor neither oppress the afflicted in the gate.
Prov. 22:22

Open thy mouth, judge righteously, and plead the cause of the poor and needy.
Prov. 31:9

Relieve the oppressed, judge the fatherless, plead for the widow.
Isa. 1:17

I the God of Israel will not forsake them.
Isa. 41:17

Ye have the poor with you always.
Jesus
Mark 14:7
See also Matt. 26:11, John 12:8

He hath filled the hungry with good things and the rich He hath sent empty away.
Luke 1:53

Support the weak.
1 Thess. 5:14

[*See also* Charity, Poverty, Wealth, Widows and Orphans]

The thunder of His power who can understand?
Job 26:14

Man knoweth not the price thereof.
Job 28:13

To depart from evil is understanding.
Job 28:28

The ear trieth words, as the mouth tasteth meat.
Job 34:3

Great things doeth He, which we cannot comprehend.
Job 37:5

Be ye not as the horse, or as the mule, which have no understanding.
Ps. 32:9

Teach me, O Lord, the way of Thy statutes; and I shall keep it unto the end.
Ps. 119:33

Give me understanding, and I shall keep Thy law.
Ps. 119:34
See also Ps. 119:73

Give me understanding, and I shall live.
Ps. 119:144

Wisdom is the principal thing; therefore get wisdom: and with all thy getting get understanding.
Prov. 4:7

O ye simple, understand wisdom: and, ye fools, be ye of an understanding heart.
Prov. 8:5

In the lips of him that hath understanding wisdom is found.
Prov. 10:13

A man of understanding hath wisdom.
Prov. 10:23

The wisdom of the prudent is to understand his way.
Prov. 14:8

He that is slow to wrath is of great understanding.
Prov. 14:29

Understanding is a wellspring of life unto him that hath it: but the instruction of fools is folly.
Prov. 16:22

Hear ye indeed, but understand not; and see ye indeed, but perceive not.
Isa. 6:9
See also, e.g., Matt. 13:14

In the latter days ye shall consider it.
Jer. 30:24

Who hath ears to hear, let him hear.
Jesus
Matt. 13:9, Matt. 13:43
See also, e.g., Matt. 11:15, Mark 4:9,
Rev. 13:9

They seeing see not; and hearing they hear not, neither do they understand.
Jesus
Matt. 13:13
See also Isa. 42:20, Acts 28:26

Having eyes, see ye not? and having ears, hear ye not?
Jesus
Mark 8:18

We do hear them speak in our tongues the wonderful works of God.
Acts 2:11

When I was a child, I spake as a child, I understood as a child, I thought as a child: but when I became a man, I put away childish things.
1 Cor. 13:11

Now we see through a glass, darkly; but then face to face.
1 Cor. 13:12

Be not children in understanding.
1 Cor. 14:20

The peace of God, which passeth all understanding.
Phil. 4:7

Anoint thine eyes with eyesalve, that thou mayest see.
Jesus
Rev. 3:18

Let him that hath understanding count the number of the beast.
Rev. 13:18

[*See also* Clarity, Compassion, Education, Folly, Ignorance, Knowledge, Wisdom]

The whole earth was of one language, and of one speech.
Gen. 11:1

Now nothing will be restrained from them, which they have imagined to do.
Gen. 11:6

Behold, how good and how pleasant it is for brethren to dwell together in unity!
Ps. 133:1

A threefold cord is not quickly broken.
Eccl. 4:12

If a kingdom be divided against itself, that kingdom cannot stand.
Jesus
Mark 3:24
See also Matt. 12:25, Luke 11:17

If a house be divided against itself, that house cannot stand.
Jesus
Mark 3:25
See also Matt. 12:35, Luke 11:17

I and my Father are one.
Jesus
John 10:30

All that believed were together, and had all things common.
Acts 2:44

We, being many, are one body in Christ, and every one members one of another.
Rom. 12:5

Is Christ divided?
1 Cor. 1:13

We being many are one bread, and one body: for we are all partakers of that one bread.
1 Cor. 10:17

One Lord, one faith, one baptism.
Eph. 4:5

Both He that sanctifieth and they who are sanctified are all of one.
Heb. 2:11

[*See also* Cooperation]

There shall be one fold, and one shepherd
Jesus
John 10:16

Is He the God of the Jews only? is He no also of the Gentiles?
Rom. 3:29

I am made all things to all men, that might by all means save some.
1 Cor. 9:22

There is neither Jew nor Greek, there i neither bond nor free, there is neither mal nor female: for ye are all one in Chris Jesus.
Gal. 3:28

[*See also* Brotherhood]

UNIVERS

See Earth, Heaven and Earth, Nature.

URGENC

Thou art my help and my deliverer; (Lord, make no tarrying.
Ps. 70:5
See also Ps. 40:17

I must work the works of Him that sei me, while it is day.
Jesus
John 9:4

The time is short.
1 Cor. 7:29

[*See also* Speed]

USUR

Thou shalt not give him thy money upo usury, nor lend him thy victuals for ii crease.
Lev. 25:37

Thou shalt not lend upon usury to th brother; usury of money, usury of victual usury of any thing that is lent upon usur
Deut. 23:19

Unto a stranger thou mayest lend upo

usury; but unto thy brother thou shalt not lend upon usury.
Deut. 23:20

[*See also* Borrowing]

VALUE

Take away the dross from the silver, and there shall come forth a vessel for the finer.
Prov. 25:4

They shall be as the stones of a crown, lifted up as an ensign upon His land.
Zech. 9:16

Ye are the salt of the earth.
Jesus
Matt. 5:13

If the salt have lost his savour, wherewith shall it be salted? it is thenceforth good for nothing.
Jesus
Matt. 5:13
See also Mark 9:50, Luke 14:34

Give not that which is holy unto the dogs, neither cast ye your pearls before swine.
Jesus
Matt. 7:6

Ye are of more value than many sparrows.
Jesus
Matt. 10:31, Luke 12:7

If a man have an hundred sheep, and one of them be gone astray, doth he not leave the ninety and nine, and goeth into the mountains, and seeketh that which is gone astray?
Jesus
Matt. 18:12
See also Luke 15:4

[*See also* Quality]

VALUES

Behold, I am at the point to die: and what profit shall this birthright do to me?
Esau to Jacob
Gen. 25:32

He that killeth a beast, he shall restore it: and he that killeth a man, he shall be put to death.
Lev. 24:21

Man looketh on the outward appearance, but the Lord looketh on the heart.
1 Sam. 16:7

I dwell in an house of cedar, but the ark of God dwelleth within curtains.
David
2 Sam. 7:2

Thou lovest thine enemies, and hatest thy friends.
2 Sam. 19:6

If the foundations be destroyed, what can the righteous do?
Ps. 11:3

Teach us to number our days, that we may apply our hearts unto wisdom.
Ps. 90:12

The law of Thy mouth is better unto me than thousands of gold and silver.
Ps. 119:72

Wisdom is the principal thing; therefore get wisdom: and with all thy getting get understanding.
Prov. 4:7

Where no oxen are, the crib is clean: but much increase is by the strength of the ox.
Prov. 14:4

In the house of the righteous is much treasure: but in the revenues of the wicked is trouble.
Prov. 15:6

Labour not to be rich.
Prov. 23:4

Wherefore do ye spend money for that which is not bread?
Isa. 55:2

Eat ye that which is good, and let your soul delight itself in fatness.
Isa. 55:2

Let him that glorieth glory in this, that he understandeth and knoweth Me, that I am the Lord.
Jer. 9:24
See also, e.g., 1 Cor. 1:31

Lay up for yourselves treasures in heaven, where neither moth nor rust doth corrupt,

and where thieves do not break through nor steal.
> Jesus
> *Matt. 6:20*

Is not the life more than meat, and the body than raiment?
> Jesus
> *Matt. 6:25*
> *See also Luke 12:23*

He that loveth father or mother more than me is not worthy of me: and he that loveth son or daughter more than me is not worthy of me.
> Jesus to disciples
> *Matt. 10:37*

Thou savourest not the things that be of God, but those that be of men.
> Jesus
> *Matt. 16:23*
> *See also Mark 8:33*

What shall a man give in exchange for his soul?
> Jesus
> *Matt. 16:26, Mark 8:37*

What shall it profit a man, if he shall gain the whole world, and lose his own soul?
> Jesus
> *Mark 8:36*
> *See also Matt. 16:26, Luke 9:25*

If thy foot offend thee, cut it off: it is better for thee to enter halt into life, than having two feet to be cast into hell.
> Jesus
> *Mark 9:45*
> *See also Matt. 18:8*

It is better for thee to enter into the kingdom of God with one eye, than having two eyes to be cast into hell fire.
> Jesus
> *Mark 9:47*
> *See also Matt. 18:9*

Take no thought for your life, what ye shall eat; neither for the body, what ye shall put on.
> Jesus
> *Luke 12:22*
> *See also Matt. 6:25*

That which is highly esteemed among men is abomination in the sight of God.
> Jesus
> *Luke 16:15*

Labour not for the meat which perisheth, but for that meat which endureth unto everlasting life.
> Jesus
> *John 6:27*

They loved the praise of men more than the praise of God.
> *John 12:43*

The things which are seen are temporal; but the things which are not seen are eternal.
> *2 Cor. 4:18*

What things were gain to me, those I counted loss for Christ.
> *Phil. 3:7*

Above all these things put on charity, which is the bond of perfectness.
> (charity: love)
> *Col. 3:14*

Hold fast to that which is good.
> *1 Thess. 5:21*

He that said, Do not commit adultery, said also, Do not kill.
> *James 2:11*

Know ye not that the friendship of the world is enmity with God?
> *James 4:4*

Buy of me gold tried in the fire, that thou mayest be rich; and white raiment, that thou mayest be clothed.
> Jesus
> *Rev. 3:18*

[*See also* Goals, Materialism, Spirituality]

VANITY

See Arrogance, Conceit, Futility.

VENGEANCE

See Revenge.

VERBOSITY

Should a wise man utter vain knowledge, and fill his belly with the east wind?
> *Job 15:2*

How long will it be ere ye make an end of
words?
Job 18:2

He multiplieth words without knowledge.
Job 35:16

He that hath knowledge spareth his words.
Prov. 17:27

A fool uttereth all his mind: but a wise man
keepeth it in till afterwards.
Prov. 29:11

A fool's voice is known by multitude of
words.
Eccl. 5:3

They think that they shall be heard for
their much speaking.
Jesus (they: heathens praying)
Matt. 6:7

[*See also* Eloquence, Silence, Speech]

VICTIMS

See Innocence, Martyrdom, Persecution,
Sacrifice.

VICTORY

Let us flee from the face of Israel; for the
Lord fighteth for them.
Ex. 14:25

I will sing unto the Lord, for He hath
triumphed gloriously: the horse and his
rider hath He thrown into the sea.
Ex. 15:1
See also Ex. 15:21

Thy right hand, O Lord, is become glorious in power: Thy right hand, O Lord,
hath dashed in pieces the enemy.
Ex. 15:6

Thou hast overthrown them that rose up
against Thee: Thou sentest forth Thy
wrath, which consumed them as stubble.
Ex. 15:7

Ye shall chase your enemies, and they shall
fall before you by the sword.
Lev. 26:7

Ye shall be saved from your enemies.
Num. 10:9

Not for thy righteousness, or for the uprightness of thine heart, dost thou go to
possess their land: but for the wickedness
of these nations the Lord thy God doth
drive them out.
Deut. 9:5

Every place whereon the soles of your feet
shall tread shall be your's.
Deut. 11:24
See also Josh. 1:3

Shout; for the Lord hath given you the city.
Joshua, at Jericho
Josh. 6:16

Fear them not: for I have delivered them
into thine hand.
God to Joshua
Josh. 10:8

The Lord fought for Israel.
Josh. 10:14

No man hath been able to stand before you
unto this day.
Joshua to Israelites
Josh. 23:9

The Lord your God, He it is that fighteth
for you.
Josh. 23:10
See also Josh. 23:3

The Lord shall sell Sisera into the hand of a
woman.
Judg. 4:9

With the jawbone of an ass, heaps upon
heaps, with the jaw of an ass have I slain a
thousand men.
Samson
Judg. 15:16

Go up; for to morrow I will deliver them
into thine hand.
God to Israelites
Judg. 20:28

My mouth is enlarged over mine enemies;
because I rejoice in Thy salvation.
1 Sam. 2:1

David prevailed over the Philistine with a
sling and with a stone.
1 Sam. 17:50

The victory that day was turned into
mourning.
2 Sam. 19:2

I beat them as small as the dust of the

earth, I did stamp them as the mire of the street.
2 Sam. 22:43

The God that answereth by fire, let Him be God.
1 Kings 18:24

Have the gods of the nations delivered them which my fathers have destroyed?
Sennacherib to Hezekiah
2 Kings 19:12, Isa. 37:12

When they arose early in the morning, behold, they were all dead corpses.
2 Kings 19:35, Isa. 37:36

I know that Thou favorest me, because mine enemy doth not triumph over me.
Ps. 41:11

His enemies shall lick the dust.
Ps. 72:9

Sit thou at My right hand, until I make thine enemies thy footstool.
Ps. 110:1
See also, e.g., Matt. 22:44

This is the day which the Lord hath made; we will rejoice and be glad in it.
Ps. 118:24

It is He that giveth salvation unto kings.
Ps. 144:10

The horse is prepared against the day of battle: but safety is of the Lord.
Prov. 21:31

He shall cry, yea, roar; He shall prevail against His enemies.
Isa. 42:13

A little one shall become a thousand, and a small one a strong nation.
Isa. 60:22

He shall array himself with the land of Egypt, as a shepherd putteth on his garment.
Jer. 43:12

Their mighty ones are beaten down, and are fled apace, and look not back.
Jer. 46:5

Let not the swift flee away, nor the mighty man escape.
Jer. 46:6

The kingdom shall be the Lord's.
Obad. 21

Thine hand shall be lifted up upon thine adversaries, and all thine enemies shall be cut off.
Mic. 5:9

Be of good cheer; I have overcome the world.
Jesus
John 16:33

Sit Thou on my right hand, Until I make Thy foes Thy footstool.
Acts 2:34–35

They which run in a race run all, but one receiveth the prize.
1 Cor. 9:24

Thanks be to God, which giveth us the victory through our Lord Jesus Christ.
1 Cor. 15:57

Whatsoever is born of God overcometh the world.
1 John 5:4

To him that overcometh will I give to eat of the hidden manna.
Jesus
Rev. 2:17

They overcame him by the blood of the Lamb.
(him: Satan)
Rev. 12:11

The Lamb shall overcome them: for He is Lord of lords, and King of kings.
Rev. 17:14

Alleluia: for the Lord God omnipotent reigneth.
Rev. 19:6

He that overcometh shall inherit all things.
Rev. 21:7

[*See also* Confidence, Defeat, Reward, Success]

VIEWPOINT

See Attitude, Perspective.

VIGILANCE

He that keepeth Israel shall neither slumber nor sleep.
Ps. 121:4

Except the Lord keep the city, the watchman waketh but in vain.
> Ps. 127:1

Go, set a watchman, let him declare what he seeth.
> Isa. 21:6

Awake, awake, stand up, O Jerusalem.
> Isa. 51:17

Take heed that no man deceive you. For many shall come in my name, saying, I am Christ.
> Jesus
> Matt. 24:4–5
> See also Mark 13:6, Luke 21:8

Watch therefore: for ye know not what hour your Lord doth come.
> Jesus
> Matt. 24:42
> See also Matt. 25:13

What, could ye not watch with me one hour?
> Jesus
> Matt. 26:40
> See also Mark 14:37

Watch and pray, that ye enter not into temptation.
> Jesus
> Matt. 26:41
> See also Luke 22:40, 46

Take heed to yourselves.
> Jesus
> Mark 13:9

Take ye heed, watch and pray: for ye know not when the time is.
> Jesus
> Mark 13:33
> See also Matt. 13:23

Watch ye therefore: for ye know not when the master of the house cometh.
> Jesus
> Mark 13:35

If the goodman of the house had known what hour the thief would come, he would have watched.
> Jesus
> Luke 12:39
> See also Matt. 24:43

Watch ye therefore, and pray always.
> Jesus
> Luke 21:36

Take heed therefore unto yourselves, and to all the flock.
> Acts 20:28

Now it is high time to awake out of sleep.
> Rom. 13:11

Let us not sleep, as do others; but let us watch and be sober.
> 1 Thess. 5:6

They that sleep sleep in the night; and they that be drunken are drunken in the night.
> 1 Thess. 5:7

Be sober, be vigilant; because your adversary the devil, as a roaring lion, walketh about, seeking whom he may devour.
> 1 Pet. 5:8

Look to yourselves, that we lose not those things which we have wrought.
> 2 John 8

Blessed is he that watcheth, and keepeth his garments, lest he walk naked, and they see his shame.
> Rev. 16:15

[See also Deception, Readiness]

VINDICATION

Why are ye come unto me now when ye are in distress?
> Jephthah to his stepbrothers
> Judg. 11:7

The stone which the builders refused is become the head stone of the corner.
> Ps. 118:22
> See also, e.g., Matt. 21:42

Where are now your prophets which prophesied unto you, saying, The king of Babylon shall not come?
> Jer. 37:19

They shall lick the dust like a serpent, they shall move out of their holes like worms of the earth: they shall be afraid of the Lord our God.
> Mic. 7:17

Many that are first shall be last; and the last first.
> Jesus
> Mark 10:31
> See also Matt. 19:30, Matt. 20:16

Sit Thou on my right hand, Until I make Thy foes Thy footstool.
Acts 2:34–35

VIOLENCE

He that smiteth his father, or his mother, shall be surely put to death.
Ex. 21:15

He smote them hip and thigh.
Judg. 15:8

The sword shall never depart from thine house.
(thine: David)
2 Sam. 12:10

Thou shalt not build an house unto My name, because thou hast shed much blood upon the earth.
God to David
1 Chron. 22:8

The Lord trieth the righteous: but the wicked and him that loveth violence His soul hateth.
Ps. 11:5

Evil shall hunt the violent man to overthrow him.
Ps. 140:11

Envy thou not the oppressor, and choose none of his ways.
Prov. 3:31

The land is full of bloody crimes, and the city is full of violence.
Ezek. 7:23

Woe to the bloody city! it is all full of lies and robbery.
(it: Nineveh)
Nah. 3:1

Woe to him that buildeth a town with blood.
Hab. 2:12

All they that take the sword shall perish with the sword.
Jesus
Matt. 26:52
See also Rev. 13:10

Do violence to no man, neither accuse any falsely.
Luke 3:14

Be ye come out, as against a thief, with swords and staves?
Jesus
Luke 22:52

Their feet are swift to shed blood.
Rom. 3:15

Destruction and misery are in their ways: And the way of peace have they not known.
Rom. 3:16–17
See also Isa. 59:7–8

With violence shall that great city Babylon be thrown down.
Rev. 18:21

[*See also* Desolation, Destruction, Murder, Terror, War]

VIRTUE

A virtuous woman is a crown to her husband.
Prov. 12:4

Who can find a virtuous woman? for her price is far above rubies.
Prov. 31:10

Many daughters have done virtuously, but thou excellest them all.
Prov. 31:29

Whatsoever things are true, whatsoever things are honest, whatsoever things are just, whatsoever things are pure, whatsoever things are lovely, whatsoever things are of good report; if there be any virtue, and if there be any praise, think on these things.
Phil. 4:8

Add to your faith virtue; and to virtue knowledge.
2 Pet. 1:5

[*See also* Goodness, Honesty, Integrity, Kindness, Righteousness]

VISION

See Sight.

The word of the Lord was precious in those days.
> *1 Sam. 3:1*

O ye dry bones, hear the word of the Lord.
> *Ezek. 37:4*

Your old men shall dream dreams, your young men shall see visions.
> *Joel 2:28*
> *See also Acts 2:17*

Behold, I see the heavens opened, and the Son of man standing on the right hand of God.
> Stephen
> *Acts 7:56*

They heard not the voice of Him that spake to me.
> Paul
> *Acts 22:9*

If a spirit or an angel hath spoken to him, let us not fight against God.
> Pharisees, about Paul
> *Acts 23:9*

Who is worthy to open the book, and to loose the seals thereof?
> *Rev. 5:2*

[*See also* Dreams, Future]

VITALITY

The life of all flesh is the blood thereof.
> *Lev. 17:14*

The trees of the Lord are full of sap.
> *Ps. 104:16*

Whatsoever thy hand findeth to do, do it with thy might.
> *Eccl. 9:10*

Lift up the hands which hang down, and the feeble knees.
> *Heb. 12:12*

[*See also* Fortitude]

VOLUNTEERS

Let no man's heart fail because of him; thy servant will go and fight with this Philistine.
> David, about Goliath
> *1 Sam. 17:32*

Who is there among you of all His people? The Lord his God be with him, and let him go up.
> *2 Chron. 36:23, Ezra 1:3*

Whom shall I send, and who will go for us? Then said I, Here am I; send me.
> God to Isaiah, and response
> *Isa. 6:8*

WAGES

Because thou art my brother, shouldest thou therefore serve me for nought? tell me, what shall thy wages be?
> Laban to Jacob
> *Gen. 29:15*

Did not I serve with thee for Rachel?
> Jacob to Laban
> *Gen. 29:25*

Let them deliver it into the hand of the doers of the work.
> *2 Kings 22:5*

The recompence of a man's hands shall be rendered unto him.
> *Prov. 12:14*

Whatsoever is right, that shall ye receive.
> Jesus
> *Matt. 20:7*

Be content with your wages.
> John the Baptist to soldiers
> *Luke 3:14*

The labourer is worthy of his reward.
> *1 Tim. 5:18*
> *See also Luke 10:7*

[*See also* Employees]

WAR

Ye shall be saved from your enemies.
> *Num. 10:9*

Go not up, for the Lord is not among you.
> *Num. 14:42*
> *See also Deut. 1:42*

Because ye are turned away from the Lord, therefore the Lord will not be with you.
Num. 14:43

Shall your brethren go to war, and shall ye sit here?
Num. 32:6

Dread not, neither be afraid of them. The Lord your God which goeth before you, He shall fight for you.
Deut. 1:29–30

As a consuming fire He shall destroy them, and He shall bring them down before thy face.
Deut. 9:3

All that thou commandest us we will do, and whithersoever thou sendest us, we will go.
Israelites to Joshua
Josh. 1:16

Joshua drew not his hand back, wherewith he stretched out the spear.
Josh. 8:26

Stay ye not, but pursue after your enemies.
Josh. 10:19

Whosoever is fearful and afraid, let him return and depart early.
Gideon to his soldiers
Judg. 7:3

The Lord saveth not with sword and spear: for the battle is the Lord's.
David to Goliath
1 Sam. 17:47

Shall the sword devour for ever?
2 Sam. 2:26

The sword devoureth one as well as another.
David, about Bathsheba's husband
2 Sam. 11:25

The wood devoured more people that day than the sword.
2 Sam. 18:8

Let not him that girdeth on his harness boast himself as he that putteth it off.
1 Kings 20:11

This day is a day of trouble, and of rebuke, and blasphemy.
2 Kings 19:3, Isa. 37:3

The battle is not your's, but God's.
2 Chron. 20:15

With him is an arm of flesh; but with us is the Lord our God.
2 Chron. 32:8

Forbear thee from meddling with God, who is with me, that He destroy thee not.
2 Chron. 35:21

Blessed be the Lord my strength, which teacheth my hands to war, and my fingers to fight.
Ps. 144:1

Let the high praises of God be in their mouth, and a twoedged sword in their hand; To execute vengeance upon the heathen.
Ps. 149:6–7

By wise counsel thou shalt make thy war.
Prov. 24:6

Nation shall not lift up sword against nation, neither shall they learn war any more.
Isa. 2:4

They shall have no pity on the fruit of the womb; their eye shall not spare children.
Isa. 13:18

They shall fight every one against his brother, and every one against his neighbour; city against city, and kingdom against kingdom.
Isa. 19:2

Go not forth into the field, nor walk by the way; for the sword of the enemy and fear is on every side.
Jer. 6:25

Let not the swift flee away, nor the mighty man escape.
Jer. 46:6

The sword shall devour, and it shall be satiate and made drunk with their blood.
Jer. 46:10

They have blown the trumpet, even to make all ready; but none goeth to the battle.
Ezek. 7:14

He that is in the field shall die with the sword; and he that is in the city, famine and pestilence shall devour him.
Ezek. 7:15

By the swords of the mighty will I cause thy multitude to fall.
Ezek. 32:12

Beat your plowshares into swords, and your pruninghooks into spears: let the weak say, I am strong.
Joel 3:10

All they that take the sword shall perish with the sword.
Jesus
Matt. 26:52
See also Rev. 13:10

Such things must needs be.
Jesus
Mark 13:7

Armageddon.
Rev. 16:16

In righteousness He doth judge and make war.
Rev. 19:11

[*See also* Battle Calls, Conquest, Defeat, God's Protection, Peace, Spoils of War, Strife, Violence, Weapons]

WAR AND PEACE

Go not up, neither fight; for I am not among you.
Deut. 1:42

When thou comest nigh unto a city to fight against it, then proclaim peace unto it.
Deut. 20:10

Thou doest me wrong to war against me.
Judg. 11:27

What hast thou to do with peace? turn thee behind me.
2 Kings 9:18, 19

Why shouldest thou meddle to thy hurt?
2 Kings 14:10

The words of his mouth were smoother than butter, but war was in his heart.
Ps. 55:21

Scatter Thou the people that delight in war.
Ps. 68:30

I am for peace: but when I speak, they are for war.
Ps. 120:7

Except the Lord keep the city, the watchman waketh but in vain.
Ps. 127:1

With good advice make war.
Prov. 20:18

A time to kill, and a time to heal; a time to break down, and a time to build up.
Eccl. 3:3

A time to love, and a time to hate; a time of war, and a time of peace.
Eccl. 3:8

Wisdom is better than weapons of war.
Eccl. 9:18

They shall beat their swords into plowshares, and their spears into pruninghooks: nation shall not lift up sword against nation, neither shall they learn war any more.
Isa. 2:4
See also Mic. 4:3

Saying, Peace, peace; when there is no peace.
Jer. 6:14, Jer. 8:11

O thou sword of the Lord, how long will it be ere thou be quiet?
Jer. 47:6

They shall seek peace, and there shall be none.
Ezek. 7:25

They have seduced My people, saying, Peace; and there was no peace.
Ezek. 13:10

Think not that I am come to send peace on earth: I came not to send peace, but a sword.
Jesus
Matt. 10:34
See also Luke 12:51

[*See also* Peace, War]

WARNING

The Lord set a mark upon Cain.
Gen. 4:15

Look not behind thee.
Angel to Lot and his wife
Gen. 19:17

Go not up, for the Lord is not among you.
Num. 14:42
See also Deut. 1:42

Beware lest thou forget the Lord.
Deut. 6:12
See also Deut. 8:11

Ye shall not tempt the Lord your God.
Deut. 6:16

Evil will befall you in the latter days.
Deut. 31:29

The Lord will not hear you in that day.
1 Sam. 8:18

If ye shall still do wickedly, ye shall be consumed.
1 Sam. 12:25

If thou save not thy life to night, to morrow thou shalt be slain.
Michal to David
1 Sam. 19:11

A little cloud out of the sea, like a man's hand.
1 Kings 18:44

Why shouldest thou meddle to thy hurt?
2 Kings 14:10

Turn ye from your evil ways, and keep My commandments and My statutes.
2 Kings 17:13

Fight ye not against the Lord God of your fathers; for ye shall not prosper.
2 Chron. 13:12

Forbear thee from meddling with God, who is with me, that He destroy thee not.
2 Chron. 35:21

Let the earth hear, and all that is therein; the world, and all things that come forth of it.
Isa. 34:1

Let not your prophets and your diviners, that be in the midst of you, deceive you.
Jer. 29:8

I have spoken unto them, but they have not heard; and I have called unto them, but they have not answered.
Jer. 35:17

Deceive not yourselves.
Jer. 37:9

Be not thou rebellious like that rebellious house.
Ezek. 2:8

The time is come, the day of trouble is near.
Ezek. 7:7
See also Ezek. 7:12

Hear ye the word of the Lord.
E.g., Ezek. 13:2

He that taketh warning shall deliver his soul.
Ezek. 33:5

Mene, Mene, Tekel, Upharsin.
Dan. 5:25

The day of the Lord cometh.
E.g., Joel 2:1

Prepare to meet thy God, O Israel.
Amos 4:12

Behold, I have foretold you all things.
Jesus
Mark 13:23

If the goodman of the house had known what hour the thief would come, he would have watched.
Jesus
Luke 12:39
See also Matt. 24:43

Ye can discern the face of the sky and of the earth; but how is it that ye do not discern this time?
Jesus
Luke 12:56
See also Matt. 16:3

Sin no more, lest a worse thing come unto thee.
Jesus
John 5:14

If this counsel or this work be of men, it will come to nought: But if it be of God, ye cannot overthrow it.
Acts 5:38–39

Antichrist shall come.
1 John 2:18

Even now are there many antichrists.
1 John 2:18

Receive not of her plagues.
(her: Babylon)
Rev. 18:4

[*See also* Heedfulness, Prudence, Vigilance]

Give not that which is holy unto the dogs, neither cast ye your pearls before swine.
> Jesus
> *Matt. 7:6*

It is not meet to take the children's bread, and to cast it to dogs.
> Jesus
> *Matt. 15:26*
> *See also Mark 7:27*

Gather up the fragments that remain, that nothing be lost.
> Jesus
> *John 6:12*

Unstable as water, thou shalt not excel.
> *Gen. 49:4*

Can the rush grow up without mire? can the flag grow without water?
> *Job 8:11*

Waters wear the stones.
> *Job 14:19*

He maketh me to lie down in green pastures: He leadeth me beside the still waters. He restoreth my soul.
> *Ps. 23:2–3*

Stolen waters are sweet, and bread eaten in secret is pleasant.
> *Prov. 9:17*

He that watereth shall be watered also himself.
> *Prov. 11:25*

Cast thy bread upon the waters: for thou shalt find it after many days.
> *Eccl. 11:1*

Many waters cannot quench love, neither can the floods drown it.
> *Song 8:7*

Blessed are ye that sow beside all waters.
> *Isa. 32:20*

I will make the wilderness a pool of water, and the dry land springs of water.
> *Isa. 41:18*

Every one that thirsteth, come ye to the waters, and he that hath no money; come ye, buy, and eat.
> *Isa. 55:1*

Doth a fountain send forth at the same place sweet water and bitter?
> *James 3:11*

[*See also* Oceans, Thirst]

The children are come to the birth, and there is not strength to bring forth.
> *2 Kings 19:3, Isa. 37:3*

My days are like a shadow that declineth; and I am withered like grass.
> *Ps. 102:11*

He giveth power to the faint; and to them that have no might He increaseth strength.
> *Isa. 40:29*

They shall become as women.
> *Jer. 50:37*

All hands shall be feeble, and all knees shall be weak as water.
> *Ezek. 7:17*

Thy strong holds shall be like fig trees with the firstripe figs: if they be shaken, they shall even fall into the mouth of the eater.
> *Nah. 3:12*

God hath chosen the weak things of the world to confound the things which are mighty.
> *1 Cor. 1:27*

Who is weak, and I am not weak? who is offended, and I burn not?
> *2 Cor. 11:29*

Support the weak.
> *1 Thess. 5:14*

[*See also* Fortitude, Strength]

Thou shalt remember the Lord thy God: for it is He that giveth thee power to get wealth.
> *Deut. 8:18*

The Lord maketh poor, and maketh rich: He bringeth low, and lifteth up.
> *1 Sam. 2:7*

I have also given thee that which thou hast not asked, both riches, and honour.
God to Solomon
1 Kings 3:13

None were of silver.
1 Kings 10:21

All that is in the heaven and in the earth is Thine.
1 Chron. 29:11

Riches and honour come of Thee.
1 Chron. 29:12

All things come of Thee.
1 Chron. 29:14

King Solomon passed all the kings of the earth in riches and wisdom.
2 Chron. 9:22

Will He esteem thy riches? no, not gold, nor all the forces of strength.
Job 36:19

A little that a righteous man hath is better than the riches of many wicked.
Ps. 37:16

He heapeth up riches, and knoweth not who shall gather them.
Ps. 39:6

Wise men die, likewise the fool and the brutish person perish, and leave their wealth to others.
Ps. 49:10

Be not thou afraid when one is made rich, when the glory of his house is increased; For when he dieth he shall carry nothing away.
Ps. 49:16–17

If riches increase, set not your heart upon them.
Ps. 62:10

I was envious at the foolish, when I saw the prosperity of the wicked.
Ps. 73:3

Riches profit not in the day of wrath.
Prov. 11:4

He that trusteth in his riches shall fall.
Prov. 11:28

There is that maketh himself rich, yet hath nothing: there is that maketh himself poor, yet hath great riches.
Prov. 13:7

He that gathereth by labour shall increase.
Prov. 13:11

Better is little with the fear of the Lord than great treasure and trouble therewith.
Prov. 15:16

How much better is it to get wisdom than gold!
Prov. 16:16

Better is a dry morsel, and quietness therewith, than an house full of sacrifices with strife.
Prov. 17:1

Wealth maketh many friends; but the poor is separated from his neighbour.
Prov. 19:4

Riches certainly make themselves wings; they fly away as an eagle toward heaven.
Prov. 23:5

Riches are not for ever.
Prov. 27:24

Give me neither poverty nor riches; feed me with food convenient for me.
Prov. 30:8

The abundance of the rich will not suffer him to sleep.
Eccl. 5:12

As he came forth of his mother's womb, naked shall he return to go as he came, and shall take nothing of his labour.
Eccl. 5:15

It is the stumblingblock of their iniquity.
Ezek. 7:19

Ye have built houses of hewn stone, but ye shall not dwell in them; ye have planted pleasant vineyards, but ye shall not drink wine of them.
Amos 5:11
See also Zeph. 1:13

Neither their silver nor their gold shall be able to deliver them in the day of the Lord's wrath.
Zeph. 1:18
See also Ezek. 7:19

The silver is Mine, and the gold is Mine, saith the Lord of hosts.
Hag. 2:8

Lay up for yourselves treasures in heaven, where neither moth nor rust doth corrupt,

and where thieves do not break through nor steal.
>Jesus
>*Matt. 6:20*

Where your treasure is, there will your heart be also.
>Jesus
>*Matt. 6:21, Luke 12:34*

The care of this world, and the deceitfulness of riches, choke the word.
>Jesus
>*Matt. 13:22*
>*See also Mark 4:19*

If thou wilt be perfect, go and sell that thou hast, and give to the poor, and thou shalt have treasure in heaven: and come and follow me.
>Jesus
>*Matt. 19:21*
>*See also Mark 10:21, Luke 18:22*

A rich man shall hardly enter into the kingdom of heaven.
>Jesus
>*Matt. 19:23*

It is easier for a camel to go through the eye of a needle, than for a rich man to enter into the kingdom of God.
>Jesus
>*Matt. 19:24, Mark 10:25*
>*See also Luke 18:25*

How hard is it for them that trust in riches to enter into the kingdom of God!
>Jesus
>*Mark 10:24*
>*See also Luke 18:24*

Woe unto you that are rich! for ye have received your consolation.
>Jesus
>*Luke 6:24*

Though He was rich, yet for your sakes He became poor, that ye through His poverty might be rich.
>*2 Cor. 8:9*

We brought nothing into this world, and it is certain we can carry nothing out.
>*1 Tim. 6:7*

They that will be rich fall into temptation and a snare.
>*1 Tim. 6:9*

Be rich in good works.
>*1 Tim. 6:18*

Ye rich men, weep and howl for your miseries that shall come upon you.
>*James 5:1*

The merchants of the earth are waxed rich through the abundance of her delicacies.
>(her: Babylon)
>*Rev. 18:3*

[*See also* Greed, Materialism, Money, Poverty, Profit, Prosperity, Sharing, Underprivileged, Values, Worldliness]

WEAPONS

Thou comest to me with a sword, and with a spear, and with a shield: but I come to thee in the name of the Lord of hosts.
>David to Goliath
>*1 Sam. 17:45*

The Lord saveth not with sword and spear: for the battle is the Lord's.
>David to Goliath
>*1 Sam. 17:47*
>*See also 2 Chron. 20:15*

David prevailed over the Philistine with a sling and with a stone.
>*1 Sam. 17:50*

How are the mighty fallen, and the weapons of war perished!
>*2 Sam. 1:27*

I will not trust in my bow, neither shall my sword save me.
>*Ps. 44:6*

They shall beat their swords into plowshares, and their spears into pruninghooks: nation shall not lift up sword against nation, neither shall they learn war any more.
>*Isa. 2:4*
>*See also Mic. 4:3*

Their arrows shall be as of a mighty expert man; none shall return in vain.
>*Jer. 50:9*

Beat your plowshares into swords, and your pruninghooks into spears: let the weak say, I am strong.
>*Joel 3:10*

The shield of faith, wherewith ye shall be able to quench all the fiery darts of the wicked.
>*Eph. 6:16*

He that killeth with the sword must be killed with the sword.
Rev. 13:10

[*See also* War, War and Peace]

WICKED PEOPLE

The wicked man travaileth with pain all his days.
Job 15:20

His remembrance shall perish from the earth, and he shall have no name in the street.
Job 18:17

His bones are full of the sin of his youth.
Job 20:11

They are as stubble before the wind, and as chaff that the storm carrieth away.
Job 21:18

The worm shall feed sweetly on him; he shall be no more remembered.
Job 24:20

They are exalted for a little while, but are gone and brought low.
Job 24:24

If his children be multiplied, it is for the sword.
Job 27:14

Let them be taken in the devices that they have imagined.
Ps. 10:2

Break Thou the arm of the wicked and the evil man.
Ps. 10:15

They shall soon be cut down like the grass, and wither as the green herb.
Ps. 37:2

The wicked borroweth, and payeth not again.
Ps. 37:21

They say, Who shall see them?
Ps. 64:5

As wax melteth before the fire, so let the wicked perish at the presence of God.
Ps. 68:2

Pride compasseth them about as a chain; violence covereth them as a garment.
Ps. 73:6

Let his days be few; and let another take his office.
Ps. 109:8

As he loved cursing, so let it come unto him: as he delighted not in blessing, so let it be far from him.
Ps. 109:17

Salvation is far from the wicked: for they seek not Thy statutes.
Ps. 119:155

Grant not, O Lord, the desires of the wicked.
Ps. 140:8

Let me not eat of their dainties.
Ps. 141:4

The Lord preserveth all them that love Him: but all the wicked will He destroy.
Ps. 145:20

The wicked shall be cut off from the earth.
Prov. 2:22

They sleep not, except they have done mischief.
Prov. 4:16

When the wicked perish, there is shouting.
Prov. 11:10

The tender mercies of the wicked are cruel.
Prov. 12:10

A wicked man is loathsome, and cometh to shame.
Prov. 13:5

Let him return unto the Lord, and He will have mercy upon him.
Isa. 55:7

The wicked are like the troubled sea, when it cannot rest, whose waters cast up mire and dirt.
Isa. 57:20

As a cage is full of birds, so are their houses full of deceit.
Jer. 5:27

Prophesy against them, prophesy, O son of man.
Ezek. 11:4

O generation of vipers.
E.g., Matt. 3:7, Luke 3:7

The Lord reward him according to his works.
2 Tim. 4:14

[See also Evil, Punishment, Sinners, Wickedness]

WICKEDNESS

Thou shalt not follow a multitude to do evil.
Ex. 23:2

Not for thy righteousness, or for the uprightness of thine heart, dost thou go to possess their land: but for the wickedness of these nations the Lord thy God doth drive them out.
Deut. 9:5

Count not thine handmaid for a daughter of Belial.
1 Sam. 1:16

The children of Belial.
E.g., 1 Sam. 10:27

If ye shall still do wickedly, ye shall be consumed.
1 Sam. 12:25

He walked in all the sins of his father.
E.g., 1 Kings 15:3

He disappointeth the devices of the crafty, so that their hands cannot perform their enterprise.
(He: God)
Job 5:12

They that hate thee shall be clothed with shame; and the dwelling place of the wicked shall come to nought.
Job 8:22

There is no darkness, nor shadow of death, where the workers of iniquity may hide themselves.
Job 34:22

The way of the ungodly shall perish.
Ps. 1:6

The wicked shall be turned into hell, and all the nations that forget God.
Ps. 9:17

The wicked in his pride doth persecute the poor.
Ps. 10:2

The Lord trieth the righteous: but the wicked and him that loveth violence His soul hateth.
Ps. 11:5

Many sorrows shall be to the wicked: but he that trusteth in the Lord, mercy shall compass him about.
Ps. 32:10

Deliver me from the deceitful and unjust man.
Ps. 43:1

The wicked are estranged from the womb: they go astray as soon as they be born, speaking lies.
Ps. 58:3

Deliver me from the workers of iniquity, and save me from bloody men.
Ps. 59:2

The workers of iniquity shall be scattered.
Ps. 92:9

Ye fools, when will ye be wise?
Ps. 94:8

The way of the wicked is as darkness: they know not at what they stumble.
Prov. 4:19

The wicked shall fall by his own wickedness.
Prov. 11:5

The wicked shall not be unpunished.
Prov. 11:21

The way of the wicked is an abomination unto the Lord.
Prov. 15:9

The seed of evildoers shall never be renowned.
Isa. 14:20

There is no peace, saith the Lord, unto the wicked.
Isa. 48:22
See also Ps. 57:21

Thou hast polluted the land with thy whoredoms and with thy wickedness.
Jer. 3:2

He will give them that are wicked to the sword, saith the Lord.
Jer. 25:31

The whirlwind of the Lord goeth forth with fury, a continuing whirlwind: it shall fall with pain upon the head of the wicked.
Jer. 30:23

If thou warn the wicked, and he turn not from his wickedness, nor from his wicked

way, he shall die in his iniquity; but thou
hast delivered thy soul.
Ezek. 3:19, 21

I have no pleasure in the death of the
wicked.
Ezek. 33:11

If the wicked turn from his wickedness, and
do that which is lawful and right, he shall
live.
Ezek. 33:19
See also Ezek. 18:21

Ye serpents, ye generation of vipers, how
can ye escape the damnation of hell?
Jesus
Matt. 23:33

What city is like unto this great city!
(city: Babylon)
Rev. 18:18

[*See also* Corruption, Decadence, Depravity, Evil, Good and Evil, Immorality, Justice, Lawlessness, Punishment, Righteousness, Sin, Sinners]

WIDOWS AND ORPHANS

If thou afflict them in any wise, and they
cry at all unto Me, I will surely hear their
cry.
Ex. 22:23

A father of the fatherless, and a judge of
the widows, is God in His holy habitation.
Ps. 68:5

Defend the poor and fatherless: do justice
to the afflicted and needy.
Ps. 82:3

Plead for the widow.
Isa. 1:17

Leave thy fatherless children, I will preserve them alive; and let thy widows trust
in Me.
Jer. 49:11

In Thee the fatherless findeth mercy.
Hos. 14:3
See also Ps. 10:14

Oppress not the widow, nor the fatherless,
the stranger, nor the poor.
Zech. 7:10

Honour widows that are widows indeed.
1 Tim. 5:3

Visit the fatherless and widows in their
affliction.
James 1:27

[*See also* Compassion, Underprivileged]

WILL POWER

See Temptation.

WINE

See Drunkenness, Liquor.

WISDOM

In the hearts of all that are wise hearted I
have put wisdom.
Ex. 31:6

Give therefore Thy servant an understanding heart to judge Thy people, that I may
discern between good and bad.
Solomon
1 Kings 3:9

Divide the living child in two, and give half
to the one, and half to the other.
1 Kings 3:25

Give her the living child, and in no wise
slay it: she is the mother thereof.
1 Kings 3:27

The wisdom of God was in him.
(him: Solomon)
1 Kings 3:28

Give me now wisdom and knowledge.
Solomon to God
2 Chron. 1:10

Behold, the one half of the greatness of thy
wisdom was not told me.
2 Chron. 9:6
See also 1 Kings 10:7

King Solomon passed all the kings of the
earth in riches and wisdom.
2 Chron. 9:22

No doubt but ye are the people, and wis-
dom shall die with you.
Job to his friends
Job 12:2

It cannot be gotten for gold, neither shall silver be weighed for the price thereof.
Job 28:15

The price of wisdom is above rubies.
Job 28:18

God understandeth the way thereof.
Job 28:23

Days should speak, and multitude of years should teach wisdom.
Job 32:7

Great men are not always wise: neither do the aged understand judgment.
Job 32:9

Hold thy peace, and I shall teach thee wisdom.
Job 33:33

Teach us to number our days, that we may apply our hearts unto wisdom.
Ps. 90:12

Whoso is wise, and will observe these things, even they shall understand the lovingkindness of the Lord.
Ps. 107:43

The fear of the Lord is the beginning of wisdom.
Ps. 111:10, Prov. 9:10
See also Job 28:28

Wisdom crieth without; she uttereth her voice in the streets.
Prov. 1:20

The Lord giveth wisdom: out of His mouth cometh knowledge and understanding.
Prov. 2:6

Discretion shall preserve thee, understanding shall keep thee.
Prov. 2:11

Happy is the man that findeth wisdom, and the man that getteth understanding.
Prov. 3:13

All the things thou canst desire are not to be compared unto her.
Prov. 3:15

Length of days is in her right hand; and in her left hand riches and honour.
Prov. 3:16

Her ways are ways of pleasantness, and all her paths are peace.
Prov. 3:17

She is a tree of life to them that lay hold upon her.
Prov. 3:18

Forsake her not, and she shall preserve thee: love her, and she shall keep thee.
Prov. 4:6

Wisdom is the principal thing; therefore get wisdom: and with all thy getting get understanding.
Prov. 4:7

She shall bring thee to honour, when thou dost embrace her.
Prov. 4:8

Say unto wisdom, Thou art my sister; and call understanding thy kinswoman.
Prov. 7:4

Wisdom is better than rubies.
Prov. 8:11

By me kings reign, and princes decree justice. By me princes rule, and nobles, even all the judges of the earth.
(me: wisdom)
Prov. 8:15–16

I love them that love me.
Prov. 8:17

Those that seek me early shall find me.
Prov. 8:17

Whoso findeth me findeth life, and shall obtain favour of the Lord.
Prov. 8:35

He that sinneth against me wrongeth his own soul.
Prov. 8:36

All they that hate me love death.
Prov. 8:36

Wisdom hath builded her house, she hath hewn out her seven pillars.
Prov. 9:1

A wise son maketh a glad father: but a foolish son is the heaviness of his mother.
Prov. 10:1

The mouth of the just bringeth forth wisdom.
Prov. 10:31

A man shall be commended according to his wisdom.
Prov. 12:8

How much better is it to get wisdom than gold!
Prov. 16:16

Even a fool, when he holdeth his peace, is counted wise.
Prov. 17:28

Through wisdom is an house builded; and by understanding it is established.
Prov. 24:3

A wise man is strong.
Prov. 24:5

My son, eat thou honey, because it is good; and the honeycomb, which is sweet to thy taste: So shall the knowledge of wisdom be unto thy soul.
Prov. 24:13–14

The sluggard is wiser in his own conceit than seven men that can render a reason.
Prov. 26:16

In much wisdom is much grief.
Eccl. 1:18

Wisdom excelleth folly, as far as light excelleth darkness.
Eccl. 2:13

The wise man's eyes are in his head; but the fool walketh in darkness.
Eccl. 2:14

How dieth the wise man? as the fool.
Eccl. 2:16

Better is a poor and a wise child than an old and foolish king, who will no more be admonished.
Eccl. 4:13

What hath the wise more than the fool?
Eccl. 6:8

The heart of the wise is in the house of mourning; but the heart of fools is in the house of mirth.
Eccl. 7:4

Wisdom is good with an inheritance.
Eccl. 7:11

Wisdom giveth life to them that have it.
Eccl. 7:12

Wisdom strengtheneth the wise more than ten mighty men which are in the city.
Eccl. 7:19

I said, I will be wise; but it was far from me.
Eccl. 7:23

A man's wisdom maketh his face to shine.
Eccl. 8:1

A wise man's heart discerneth both time and judgment.
Eccl. 8:5

Wisdom is better than strength.
Eccl. 9:16

Wisdom is better than weapons of war.
Eccl. 9:18

The words of the wise are as goads.
Eccl. 12:11

The wisdom of their wise men shall perish, and the understanding of their prudent men shall be hid.
Isa. 29:14

They are wise to do evil, but to do good they have no knowledge.
Jer. 4:22

Is counsel perished from the prudent? is their wisdom vanished?
Jer. 49:7

By thy great wisdom and by thy traffick hast thou increased thy riches.
Ezek. 28:5

Wisdom and might are His.
Dan. 2:20

He giveth wisdom unto the wise, and knowledge to them that know understanding.
Dan. 2:21

A wise man, which built his house upon a rock.
Jesus
Matt. 7:24

Neither do men put new wine into old bottles: else the bottles break, and the wine runneth out.
Jesus
Matt. 9:17
See also Mark 2:22, Luke 5:37

Wisdom is justified of her children.
Jesus
Matt. 11:19
See also Luke 7:35

Behold, a greater than Solomon is here.
Jesus
Matt. 12:42, Luke 11:31

Ye can discern the face of the sky and of the earth; but how is it that ye do not discern this time?
Jesus
Luke 12:56
See also Matt. 16:3

I will destroy the wisdom of the wise, and will bring to nothing the understanding of the prudent.
1 Cor. 1:19

The foolishness of God is wiser than men.
1 Cor. 1:25

Let him become a fool, that he may be wise.
1 Cor. 3:18

The wisdom of this world is foolishness with God.
1 Cor. 3:19
See also 1 Cor. 1:20

If any of you lack wisdom, let him ask of God.
James 1:5

[*See also* Education, Experience, Folly, Fools, Ignorance, Knowledge, Understanding]

WITCHCRAFT

Thou shalt not suffer a witch to live.
Ex. 22:18

Regard not them that have familiar spirits, neither seek after wizards, to be defiled by them.
Lev. 19:31

All that do these things are an abomination unto the Lord.
Deut. 18:12

I will be a swift witness against the sorcerers.
Mal. 3:5

Thou child of the devil, thou enemy of all righteousness.
Acts 13:10

WITNESS

See Perjury, Testimony.

WOMEN

It is not good that the man should be alone; I will make him an help meet for him.
Gen. 2:18

The rib, which the Lord God had taken from man, made He a woman.
Gen. 2:22

This is now bone of my bones, and flesh of my flesh.
Adam, about Eve
Gen. 2:23

She shall be called Woman, because she was taken out of man.
Gen. 2:23

Thy desire shall be to thy husband, and he shall rule over thee.
God to Eve
Gen. 3:16

Why should the name of our father be done away from among his family, because he hath no son?
Num. 27:4

If a man die, and have no son, then ye shall cause his inheritance to pass unto his daughter.
Num. 27:8

The Lord commanded Moses to give us an inheritance among our brethren.
(us: Zelophehad's daughters)
Josh. 17:4

The Lord shall sell Sisera into the hand of a woman.
Judg. 4:9

The lips of a strange woman drop as an honeycomb, and her mouth is smoother than oil.
Prov. 5:3

Every wise woman buildeth her house: but the foolish plucketh it down with her hands.
Prov. 14:1

Give not thy strength unto women, nor thy ways to that which destroyeth kings.
Prov. 31:3

Who can find a virtuous woman? for her price is far above rubies.
Prov. 31:10

Favour is deceitful, and beauty is vain: but a woman that feareth the Lord, she shall be praised.
Prov. 31:30

As is the mother, so is her daughter.
Ezek. 16:44

Keep the doors of thy mouth from her that lieth in thy bosom.
Mic. 7:5

If a woman have long hair, it is a glory to her.
1 Cor. 11:15

Let your women keep silence in the churches: for it is not permitted unto them to speak.
1 Cor. 14:34

If they will learn any thing, let them ask their husbands at home.
1 Cor. 14:35

It is a shame for women to speak in the church.
1 Cor. 14:35

Let the woman learn in silence with all subjection.
1 Tim. 2:11

[*See also* Beauty, Family, Man and Woman, Mankind, Marriage, Nagging]

WONDERS

What hath God wrought!
Num. 23:23

We have seen this day that God doth talk with man, and he liveth.
Deut. 5:24

The sun stood still, and the moon stayed, until the people had avenged themselves upon their enemies.
Josh. 10:13

And there was no day like that before it or after it.
Josh. 10:14

Many, O Lord my God, are Thy wonderful works.
Ps. 40:5

This is the Lord's doing; it is marvellous in our eyes.
Ps. 118:23
See also, e.g., Matt. 21:42

The way of an eagle in the air; the way of a serpent upon a rock; the way of a ship in the midst of the sea; and the way of a man with a maid.
Prov. 30:19

I will work a work in your days, which ye will not believe, though it be told you.
Hab. 1:5
See also Acts 13:41

Ye shall see heaven open, and the angels of God ascending and descending upon the Son of man.
Jesus
John 1:51

Eye hath not seen, nor ear heard, neither have entered into the heart of man, the things which God hath prepared for them that love Him.
1 Cor. 2:9
See also Isa. 64:4

[*See also* Awe, Miracles, Nature]

WORK

In the sweat of thy face shalt thou eat bread, till thou return unto the ground.
Gen. 3:19

The Lord God sent him forth from the garden of Eden, to till the ground from whence he was taken. So He drove out the man.
Gen. 3:23–24

Because thou art my brother, shouldest thou therefore serve me for nought? tell me, what shall thy wages be?
Laban to Jacob
Gen. 29:15

Six days shalt thou labour, and do all thy work: But the seventh day is the sabbath of the Lord thy God: in it thou shalt not do any work.
Ex. 20:9–10
See also Ex. 35:2, Deut. 5:13–14

Six days thou shalt do thy work, and on the seventh day thou shalt rest.
Ex. 23:12
See also Ex. 34:21, Ex. 35:2

Thou shalt rejoice before the Lord thy God in all that thou puttest thine hands unto.
Deut. 12:18

Let them be hewers of wood and drawers of water.
Josh. 9:21

Go to the ant, thou sluggard; consider her ways, and be wise.
Prov. 6:6

He becometh poor that dealeth with a slack hand: but the hand of the diligent maketh rich.
Prov. 10:4

He that gathereth by labour shall increase.
Prov. 13:11

In all labour there is profit: but the talk of the lips tendeth only to penury.
Prov. 14:23

Commit thy works unto the Lord, and thy thoughts shall be established.
Prov. 16:3

Seest thou a man diligent in his business? he shall stand before kings.
Prov. 22:29

What profit hath a man of all his labour which he taketh under the sun?
Eccl. 1:3

What hath man of all his labour, and of the vexation of his heart, wherein he hath laboured under the sun?
Eccl. 2:22

What profit hath he that worketh in that wherein he laboureth?
Eccl. 3:9

Every man should eat and drink, and enjoy the good of all his labour, it is the gift of God.
Eccl. 3:13
See also Eccl. 5:18

The sleep of a labouring man is sweet.
Eccl. 5:12

Whatsoever thy hand findeth to do, do it with thy might.
Eccl. 9:10

Come unto me, all ye that labour and are heavy laden, and I will give you rest.
Jesus
Matt. 11:28

The labourer is worthy of his hire.
Jesus
Luke 10:7
See also Matt. 10:10

One soweth, and another reapeth.
Jesus
John 4:37

We are labourers together with God.
1 Cor. 3:9

Let every man abide in the same calling wherein he was called.
1 Cor. 7:20

Do all to the glory of God.
1 Cor. 10:31

He which soweth sparingly shall reap also sparingly.
2 Cor. 9:6

Whatsoever a man soweth, that shall he also reap.
Gal. 6:7

Of the Lord ye shall receive the reward of the inheritance.
Col. 3:24

Ye serve the Lord Christ.
Col. 3:24

If any would not work, neither should he eat.
2 Thess. 3:10

The labourer is worthy of his reward.
1 Tim. 5:18

The husbandman that laboureth must be first partaker of the fruits.
2 Tim. 2:6

Study to show thyself approved unto God, a workman that needeth not to be ashamed.
2 Tim. 2:15

The cries of them which have reaped are entered into the ears of the Lord.
James 5:4

Servants, be subject to your masters with all fear; not only to the good and gentle.
1 Pet. 2:18
See also Eph. 6:5

[*See also* Business, Cooperation, Dili-gence, Effort, Employees, Laziness]

[*See also* Conformity, Materialism, Self-Denial, Spirituality]

WORLDLINESS

Thou savourest not the things that be of God, but those that be of men.
>Jesus
>*Matt. 16:23*
>See also Mark 8:33

The children of this world are in their generation wiser than the children of light.
>Jesus
>*Luke 16:8*

Ye are from beneath; I am from above: ye are of this world; I am not of this world.
>Jesus
>*John 8:23*

Be not conformed to this world.
>*Rom. 12:2*

I would have you wise unto that which is good, and simple concerning evil.
>*Rom. 16:19*

Hath not God made foolish the wisdom of this world?
>*1 Cor. 1:20*

The wisdom of this world is foolishness with God.
>*1 Cor. 3:19*

For though we walk in the flesh, we do not war after the flesh.
>*2 Cor. 10:3*

Set your affection on things above, not on things on the earth.
>*Col. 3:2*

Whosoever therefore will be a friend of the world is the enemy of God.
>*James 4:4*

Love not the world, neither the things that are in the world.
>*1 John 2:15*

If any man love the world, the love of the Father is not in him.
>*1 John 2:15*

They are of the world: therefore speak they of the world.
>*1 John 4:5*

WORRY

Why tarry the wheels of his chariots?
>*Judg. 5:28*

Cast thy burden upon the Lord, and He shall sustain thee.
>*Ps. 55:22*

Pour out your heart before Him: God is a refuge for us.
>*Ps. 62:8*

Better is an handful with quietness, than both the hands full with travail and vexa-tion of spirit.
>*Eccl. 4:6*

The abundance of the rich will not suffer him to sleep.
>*Eccl. 5:12*

The misery of man is great upon him.
>*Eccl. 8:6*

Which of you by taking thought can add one cubit unto his stature?
>Jesus
>*Matt. 6:27*
>See also Luke 12:25

Take therefore no thought for the morrow: for the morrow shall take thought for the things of itself.
>Jesus
>*Matt. 6:34*

The care of this world, and the deceitful-ness of riches, choke the word.
>Jesus
>*Matt. 13:22*
>See also Mark 4:19

Take no thought for your life, what ye shall eat; neither for the body, what ye shall put on.
>Jesus
>*Luke 12:22*
>See also Matt. 6:25

Let not your heart be troubled, neither let it be afraid.
>Jesus
>*John 14:27*
>See also John 14:1

[*See also* Burdens]

WORSHIP

He is my God, and I will prepare Him an habitation; my father's God, and I will exalt Him.
> *Ex. 15:2*

Ye shall serve the Lord your God.
> *Ex. 23:25*

Let them make Me a sanctuary; that I may dwell among them.
> *Ex. 25:8*

Thou shalt love the Lord thy God with all thine heart, and with all thy soul, and with all thy might.
> *Deut. 6:5*
> *See also, e.g., Matt. 22:37*

Serve Him with all your heart and with all your soul.
> *Deut. 11:13*

Offer not thy burnt offerings in every place that thou seest.
> *Deut. 12:13*

Turn ye not aside: for then should ye go after vain things, which cannot profit nor deliver.
> *1 Sam. 12:21*

I have surely built Thee an house to dwell in, a settled place for Thee to abide in for ever.
> Solomon to God
> *1 Kings 8:13*

Him shall ye fear, and Him shall ye worship, and to Him shall ye do sacrifice.
> *2 Kings 17:36*

The glory of the Lord had filled the house of God.
> *2 Chron. 5:14*

Who shall ascend into the hill of the Lord? or who shall stand in His holy place? He that hath clean hands, and a pure heart; who hath not lifted up his soul unto vanity, nor sworn deceitfully.
> *Ps. 24:3–4*

When Thou saidst, Seek ye My face; my heart said unto Thee, Thy face, Lord, will I seek.
> *Ps. 27:8*

Give unto the Lord, O ye mighty, give unto the Lord glory and strength.
> *Ps. 29:1*

Come, let us worship and bow down: let us kneel before the Lord our maker.
> *Ps. 95:6*

Give unto the Lord the glory due unto His name.
> *Ps. 96:8, 1 Chron. 16:29*

Worship the Lord in the beauty of holiness.
> *Ps. 96:9, 1 Chron. 16:29*

Seek the Lord, and His strength: seek His face evermore.
> *Ps. 105:4*
> *See also 1 Chron. 16:11*

Keep thy foot when thou goest to the house of God, and be more ready to hear, than to give the sacrifice of fools.
> *Eccl. 5:1*

Come ye, and let us go up to the mountain of the Lord.
> *Isa. 2:3*

With my soul have I desired Thee in the night; yea, with my spirit within me will I seek Thee early.
> *Isa. 26:9*

Unto Me every knee shall bow, every tongue shall swear.
> *Isa. 45:23*
> *See also Rom. 14:11*

Come, and let us go up to the mountain of the Lord, and to the house of the God of Jacob.
> *Mic. 4:2*

Thou shalt worship the Lord thy God, and Him only shalt thou serve.
> Jesus
> *Matt. 4:10*
> *See also Deut. 6:13*

In vain they do worship me, teaching for doctrines the commandments of men.
> Jesus
> *Matt. 15:9, Mark 7:7*
> *See also Isa. 29:13*

Ye worship ye know not what.
> Jesus
> *John 4:22*

They that worship Him must worship Him in spirit and in truth.
> Jesus
> *John 4:24*

Whom therefore ye ignorantly worship, Him declare I unto you.
> *Acts 17:23*

After the way which they call heresy, so worship I the God of my fathers.
> Paul
> *Acts 24:14*

When they knew God, they glorified Him not as God.
> *Rom 1:21*

Worship God: for the testimony of Jesus is the spirit of prophecy.
> *Rev. 19:10*

[*See also* Churches, Devotion, False Gods, God's Temple, Godlessness, Idolatry, Idols, Prayer, Rituals]

WORTHINESS

If the house be worthy, let your peace come upon it: but if it be not worthy, let your peace return to you.
> Jesus
> *Matt. 10:13*

He that loveth father or mother more than me is not worthy of me: and he that loveth son or daughter more than me is not worthy of me.
> Jesus to disciples
> *Matt. 10:37*

He that taketh not his cross, and followeth after me, is not worthy of me.
> Jesus
> *Matt. 10:38*
> *See also Luke 14:27*

The labourer is worthy of his hire.
> Jesus
> *Luke 10:7*
> *See also Matt. 10:10, 1 Tim. 5:18*

Walk worthy of the Lord.
> *Col. 1:10*
> *See also 1 Thess. 2:12*

Who is worthy to open the book, and to loose the seals thereof?
> *Rev. 5:2*

Worthy is the Lamb that was slain.
> *Rev. 5:12*

[*See also* Value]

WRATH

See Anger.

YOUTH

The flower of their age.
> *1 Sam. 2:33*

His bones are full of the sin of his youth.
> *Job 20:11*

Remember not the sins of my youth.
> *Ps. 25:7*

The young lions roar after their prey, and seek their meat from God.
> *Ps. 104:21*

I am a stranger in the earth: hide not Thy commandments from me.
> *Ps. 119:19*

The glory of young men is their strength: and the beauty of old men is the grey head.
> *Prov. 20:29*

Woe to thee, O land, when thy king is a child.
> *Eccl. 10:16*

Rejoice, O young man, in thy youth.
> *Eccl. 11:9*

Let thy heart cheer thee in the days of thy youth.
> *Eccl. 11:9*

Childhood and youth are vanity.
> *Eccl. 11:10*

Remember now thy Creator in the days of thy youth.
> *Eccl. 12:1*

Say not, I am a child: for thou shalt go to all that I shall send thee, and whatsoever I command thee thou shalt speak.
> God to Jeremiah
> *Jer. 1:7*

It is good for a man that he bear the yoke in his youth.
> *Lam. 3:27*

Your young men shall see visions, and your old men shall dream dreams.
Acts 2:17
See also Joel 2:28

Let no man despise thy youth.
1 Tim. 4:12

Every one that useth milk is unskilful in the word of righteousness: for he is a babe.
Heb. 5:13

[*See also* Age, Children, Experience]

ZEAL

I the Lord thy God am a jealous God.
E.g., Ex. 20:5

The Lord, whose name is Jealous, is a jealous God.
Ex. 34:14

The Lord thy God is a consuming fire, even a jealous God.
Deut. 4:24
See also Heb. 12:29

I have been very jealous for the Lord God of hosts.
1 Kings 19:10

Come with me, and see my zeal for the Lord.
2 Kings 10:16

God is jealous, and the Lord revengeth.
Nah. 1:2

Preach ye upon the housetops.
Jesus
Matt. 10:27
See also Luke 12:3

I persecuted them even unto strange cities.
Paul
Acts 26:11

I continue unto this day, witnessing both to small and great.
Paul
Acts 26:22

They have a zeal of God, but not according to knowledge.
Rom. 10:2

I seek not your's, but you.
2 Cor. 12:14

He which persecuted us in times past now preacheth the faith which once he destroyed.
(He: Paul)
Gal. 1:23

It is good to be zealously affected always in a good thing.
Gal. 4:18

Earnestly contend for the faith which was once delivered unto the saints.
Jude 3

[*See also* Devotion, Enthusiasm]

APPENDIX

Contents

The Ten Commandments

I am the Lord thy God, which have brought thee out of the land of Egypt, out of the house of bondage.

Thou shalt have no other gods before Me.

Thou shalt not make unto thee any graven image, or any likeness of any thing that is in heaven above, or that is in the earth beneath, or that is in the water under the earth:

Thou shalt not bow down thyself to them, nor serve them: for I the Lord thy God am a jealous God, visiting the iniquity of the fathers upon the children unto the third and fourth generation of them that hate Me;

And showing mercy unto thousands of them that love Me, and keep My commandments.

Thou shalt not take the name of the Lord thy God in vain; for the Lord will not hold him guiltless that taketh His name in vain.

Remember the sabbath day, to keep it holy.

Six days shalt thou labour, and do all thy work:

But the seventh day is the sabbath of the Lord thy God: in it thou shalt not do any work, thou, nor thy son, nor thy daughter, thy manservant, nor thy maidservant, nor thy cattle, nor thy stranger that is within thy gates:

For in six days the Lord made heaven and earth, the sea, and all that in them is, and rested the seventh day: wherefore the Lord blessed the sabbath day, and hallowed it.

Honour thy father and thy mother: that thy days may be long upon the land which the Lord thy God giveth thee.

Thou shalt not kill.

Thou shalt not commit adultery.

Thou shalt not steal.

Thou shalt not bear false witness against thy neighbour.

Thou shalt not covet thy neighbour's house, thou shalt not covet thy neighbour's wife, nor his manservant, nor his maidservant, nor his ox, nor his ass, nor any thing that is thy neighbour's.

Ex. 20:2–17
See also Deut. 5:6–21

Psalm 23

The Lord is my shepherd; I shall not want.

He maketh me to lie down in green pastures: He leadeth me beside the still waters.

He restoreth my soul: He leadeth me in the paths of righteousness for His name's sake.

Yea, though I walk through the valley of the shadow of death, I will fear no evil: for Thou art with me; Thy rod and Thy staff they comfort me.

Thou preparest a table before me in the presence of mine enemies: Thou anointest my head with oil; my cup runneth over.

Surely goodness and mercy shall follow me all the days of my life: and I will dwell in the house of the Lord for ever.

"To Every Thing There Is a Season . . ."

To every thing there is a season, and a time to every purpose under the heaven:

A time to be born, and a time to die; a time to plant, and a time to pluck up that which is planted;

A time to kill, and a time to heal; a time to break down, and a time to build up;

A time to weep, and a time to laugh; a time to mourn, and a time to dance;

A time to cast away stones, and a time to gather stones together; a time to embrace, and a time to refrain from embracing;

A time to get, and a time to lose; a time to keep, and a time to cast away;

A time to rend, and a time to sew; a time to keep silence, and a time to speak;

A time to love, and a time to hate; a time of war, and a time of peace.

Eccl. 3:1–8

The Beatitudes
from The Sermon on the Mount

Blessed are the poor in spirit: for theirs is the kingdom of heaven.
Blessed are they that mourn: for they shall be comforted.

Blessed are the meek: for they shall inherit the earth.

Blessed are they which do hunger and thirst after righteousness: for they shall be filled.

Blessed are the merciful: for they shall obtain mercy.

Blessed are the pure in heart: for they shall see God.

Blessed are the peacemakers: for they shall be called the children of God.

Blessed are they which are persecuted for righteousness' sake: for theirs is the kingdom of heaven.

Blessed are ye, when men shall revile you, and persecute you, and shall say all manner of evil against you falsely, for My sake.

Rejoice, and be exceeding glad: for great is your reward in heaven: for so persecuted they the prophets which were before you.

Matt. 5:3–12
See also Luke 6:20–24

The Lord's Prayer

Our Father which art in heaven, Hallowed be Thy name.
 Thy kingdom come. Thy will be done in earth, as it is in heaven.
 Give us this day our daily bread.
 And forgive us our debts, as we forgive our debtors.
 And lead us not into temptation, but deliver us from evil: For
Thine is the kingdom, and the power, and the glory, for ever.
Amen.

Matt. 6:9–13
See also Luke 11:2–4

On Love
from 1 Corinthians*

Though I speak with the tongues of men and of angels, and have not love, I am become as sounding brass, or a tinkling cymbal.

And though I have the gift of prophecy, and understand all mysteries, and all knowledge; and though I have all faith, so that I could remove mountains, and have not love, I am nothing.

And though I bestow all my goods to feed the poor, and though I give my body to be burned, and have not love, it profiteth me nothing.

Love suffereth long, and is kind; love envieth not; love vaunteth not itself, is not puffed up,

Doth not behave itself unseemly, seeketh not her own, is not easily provoked, thinketh no evil;

Rejoiceth not in iniquity, but rejoiceth in the truth;

Beareth all things, believeth all things, hopeth all things, endureth all things.

Love never faileth: but whether there be prophecies, they shall fail; whether there be tongues, they shall cease; whether there be knowledge, it shall vanish away.

For we know in part, and we prophesy in part.

But when that which is perfect is come, then that which is in part shall be done away.

When I was a child, I spake as a child, I understood as a child, I thought as a child: but when I became a man, I put away childish things.

For now we see through a glass, darkly; but then face to face: now I know in part; but then shall I know even as also I am known.

And now abideth faith, hope, love, these three; but the greatest of these is love.

1 Cor. 13:1–13

---

*In the King James Version of the Bible, "charity" is used as the English translation for the Latin "caritas" and the Greek "agape." Biblical scholars generally agree, however, that "love" is a more accurate translation today. For purposes of this appendix, "love" has been substituted each time the word "charity" ordinarily appears in the KJV, both for purposes of accuracy and to clearly illustrate one of the Bible's most beautiful and renowned passages on love.

KEY-WORD INDEX

Explanation

This Index gives the key words in every quotation in the book (except for "Jesus," "God," and "Lord," which appear too often to make it practical), together with a few adjacent words to provide the context. It serves two purposes.

If you remember certain words from a quotation but cannot remember the entire quotation or its citation, you can look up the word here and locate the page number on which that quotation first appears (it may be placed in other categories as well).

The Index also serves as a supplement to the categories in the book itself. For example, although there is no category titled "heart" in the main section, readers seeking quotations about that word can easily find them with this Key-Word Index.

A

abase
  a. him that is high, 328
  He is able to a., 296
abased
  exalt himself shall be a., 194
  exalteth shall be a., 11
  himself shall be a., 61
abhor
  a. him that speaketh, 75
  a. myself, and repent, 316
  a. us, for Thy name's, 151
  soul shall a. you, 180
abide
  a. day of his coming, 22
  a. in the same calling, 67
  place for Thee to a., 52
  terrible; and who can a., 222
abideth
  earth a. for ever, 105
Abiezer
  vintage of A., 283
ability
  a. which God giveth, 254
able
  a. men, such as fear, 172
  a. of these stones, 155
  a. to build Him an house, 52
  a. to deliver us, 79
  a. to kill the soul, 36
  a. to overcome, 63
  a. to save and destroy, 149
  a. to stand, 156
  a. to stand before, 370
  a. to stand before envy, 12
  believe ye that I am a., 28
  He is a. to abase, 296
  Lord is a. to give, 329
  not a. to go up, 72
  that is a. to receive, 42
  who shall be a. to stand, 151
abode
  know thy a., 153
abodest
  why a. thou among, 104
abolish
  idols He shall a., 198
abolished
  righteousness not be a., 339
abomination
  a. in the sight of, 248
  a. is he that chooseth, 198
  a. of desolation, 93
  a. to the Lord, 40
  a. to the Lord, 198
  a. unto the Lord, 367
  a. unto the Lord, 40
  false balance is a., 40

it is a., 188
lying lips are a., 233
seven are an a., 207
way of the wicked is a., 407
wicked are an a., 118
wicked is an a., 45
abominations
  all thine a., 220
  know her a., 295
  the A. of the Earth, 88
abounded
  where sin a., 140
above
  a. a beast, 193
  a. the heights, 20
  a. where Christ sitteth, 148
  affection on things a., 12
  given thee from a., 21
  I am from a., 170
  in heaven a., 158
  in heaven a., 164
  Lord is a. all gods, 152
  perfect gift is from a., 171
  shalt be a. only, 268
  that cometh from a. is a., 21
Abraham
  A. gave up the ghost, 79
  before A. was, 51
  do the works of A., 196
  God of A., 148
  if ye were A.'s children, 196
  seed of A., 219
  seed of A., 219
  up children unto A., 155
abroad
  a. the sword bereaveth, 81
Absalom
  A. O A., 176
  even with A., 59
  O A. my son, 175
absent
  a. from the Lord, 236
  a. in body, 2
  a. in the flesh, 2
  a. one from another, 2
abstain
  a. from all appearance, 27
  a. from fleshly lusts, 243
abundance
  a. of the heart, 44
  a. of the rich, 363
  a. with increase, 175
  not in the a. of, 248
  rich through the a., 70
abundant
  a. in goodness, 165
  labours more a., 282
acceptable
  a. in Thy sight, 292
  judgment is more a., 223
  patiently, this is a., 3
accepted

shalt thou not be a., 4
accepteth
  a. no man's person, 15
accomplished
  desire a., 4
according
  a. to all that she hath, 17
  a. to the greatness, 154
  a. to thy words, 9
  a. unto all his ways, 138
account
  a. of himself to God, 321
  He giveth not a. of, 60
  put that on mine a., 321
  they shall give a., 320
accursed
  a. thing from among, 69
  a. thing, lest, 66
  destroy the a., 307
  make yourselves a., 66
accuse
  a. any falsely, 69
accusers
  where are thine a., 4
accustomed
  a. to do evil, 43
acknowledge
  a. My might, 5
  a. thine iniquity, 62
  all thy ways a. Him, 5
acquaint
  a. now thyself with Him, 3
acquit
  not at all a. the wicked, 306
actions
  Him a. are weighed, 84
Adam
  A. was first formed, 22
  in A. all die, 236
  whatsoever A. called, 264
add
  a. thou not His, 344
  a. to your faith, 127
  a. unto him the plagues, 285
  a. unto the word, 343
  a. unto thy days, 59
  can a. one cubit unto, 261
  if any man shall a., 285
  shalt not a., 55
adder
  stingeth like an a., 237
adders'
  a. poison is under, 362
addeth
  a. rebellion unto, 311
administrations
  differences of a. but, 100
admonish
  a. him as a brother, 23
admonished
  who will no more be a., 7
adulterer
  a. and the adulteress, 6

adulterers
  against the a., 6
  whoremongers and a., 6
adulteress
  adulterer and the a., 6
adulteries
  out of heart proceed a.,
  261
adulterous
  a. generation, 254
adultery
  a. in his heart, 6
  a. with a woman, 6
  committeth a., 101
  divorced committeth a., 6
  do not commit a., 56
  dost thou commit a., 6
  his wife to commit a., 6
  man should not commit a.,
  6
  marry another, commit a.,
  101
  not commit a., 6
  not commit a. said also, 7
  she committeth a., 6
advantage
  a. then hath the Jew, 53
adversaries
  a. be clothed with shame,
  110
  ease Me of Mine a., 326
  lifted up upon thine a., 396
  us, or our a., 9
  vengeance on His a., 327
adversary
  a. had written a book, 4
  a. unto thine a., 10
  agree with thine a., 16
  how long shall the a., 33
  your a. the devil, 342
adversity
  brother is born for a., 143
  day of a., 142
  in the day of a., 283
  them which suffer a., 60
advice
  blessed be thy a., 7
  good a. make war, 7
  take a. and speak, 7
advocate
  a. with the Father, 209
afar
  heard even a. off, 42
  justice standeth a., 230
  not a God a. off, 158
  why standest Thou a., 18
affection
  a. on things above, 12
afflict
  if thou a. them, 408
afflicted
  a. yet he opened not, 252
  cry of the a., 292
  justice to the a., 223

more they a. them, 7
  oppress the a., 273
  smitten of God, and a., 32
affliction
  furnace of a., 155
  poor in his a., 87
afflictions
  a. of the righteous, 387
affrighted
  fear, and is not a., 70
afraid
  a. because I was naked, 121
  a. for the terror, 133
  a. nor dismayed, 108
  a. of a man, 133
  a. of the face, 220
  a. of the Lord, 192
  a. of the words, 108
  a. of thee, 50
  a. of their faces, 108
  a. of their revilings, 75
  a. of their words, 70
  a. of them, 108
  a. when one is made rich,
  112
  be a. for he beareth, 133
  be not a., 108
  be not a., 108
  be not a., 70
  be not a., 54
  be not a., 108
  be not a., 132
  be not a. only believe, 126
  dread make me a., 132
  fearful and a., 132
  neither let it be a., 54
  none shall make them a.,
  278
  not a. of them that kill, 261
  trust, and not be a., 124
  up, be not a., 63
  whom hast thou been a.,
  167
  whom shall I be a., 70
after
  before it or a., 412
again
  a. I will build, 50
  a. take root, 375
  bring him back a., 80
  brother shall rise a., 323
  cannot be gathered up a.,
  260
  except a man be born a., 37
  He shall rise a., 322
  I will come a., 346
  turn a. unto the Lord, 316
  ye must be born a., 37
against
  I, even I, am a. thee, 110
  Lord gone out a. me, 13
  not a. us is for us, 10
  not with me is a. me, 213
  who can be a. us, 63

age
  a. is as nothing, 260
  died in a good old a., 79
  even to your old a., 9
  flower of their a., 416
  good old a., 80
  good old a., 8
  he is of a., 248
  son of his old a., 132
  that are of full a., 249
  thine old a., 173
  time of old a., 8
aged
  a. understand judgment, 8
agree
  a. with thine adversary, 16
agreed
  except they be a., 69
agreement
  hell are we at a., 17
Ahab
  A. served Baal, 83
  none like unto A., 118
air
  bird of the a., 301
  birds of the a., 188
  eagle in the a., 263
  fowl of the a., 14
  fowls of the a., 35
  speak into the a., 57
alas
  a. a. that great city, 83
  a. for the day, 221
alien
  a. unto my mother's, 114
aliens
  houses to a., 64
alike
  all things come a., 81
  esteemeth every day a., 43
alive
  a. this day, 50
  art yet a., 79
  Christ shall all be made a.,
  236
  I am a. for evermore, 51
  keep a. his own soul, 260
  keep them a., 14
  kill and to make a., 181
  kill, and I make a., 156
  killeth and maketh a., 156
  living which are yet a., 235
  preserve them a., 408
  said that He was a., 12
  saved them a., 326
all
  a. are of the dust, 112
  a. are the work, 112
  a. are Thy servants, 265
  a. be made alive, 236
  a. go unto one place, 81
  a. have sinned, 245
  a. is vanity, 77
  a. is vanity, 91

slow to a., 59
slow to a., 306
slow to a. appeaseth, 12
slow to a. is, 12
sorrows in His a., 304
will not keep a., 139
angry
a. dealeth foolishly, 378
a. man stirreth, 12
a. with his brother, 12
a. with the wicked, 220
a. with us for ever, 150
friendship with a. man, 12
than with an a. woman, 246
wilt Thou be a., 139
anguish
a. her that bringeth, 31
a. is come upon, 13
a. of my spirit, 40
remembereth no more the a., 31
trouble and a., 54
anoint
a. thine eyes with, 355
arise, a. him, 231
fastest, a. thine head, 132
anointed
a. me to preach, 111
against the Lord's a., 18
face of thine a., 291
face of Thine a., 313
Lord's a., 258
though a. king, 364
touch not Mine a., 50
walk before Mine a., 329
anointest
a. my head with oil, 34
another
do we look for a., 102
feignest to be a., 83
for he hath not a., 68
love one a., 27
love one to a., 51
one as well as a., 77
one day above a., 43
answer
a. a fool, 138
a. not a fool, 138
a. turneth away wrath, 12
a. you, I will declare, 40
Almighty would a., 4
and they shall a., 304
any that will a., 18
called, ye did not a., 99
I will a. him, 292
I will a. thee, 293
know how ye ought to a., 70
right hand, and a. me, 87
timber shall a., 4
what shall I a., 67
answered
called you, but ye a., 273
have not a., 100

He a. them not, 86
Lord a. him not, 1
nor any that a., 129
answereth
God a. me no more, 1
God that a. by fire, 298
money a. all things, 77
rich a. roughly, 70
ant
go to the a., 95
antichrist
a. shall come, 14
is a. that denieth, 14
antichrists
are there many a., 14
ants
a. are a people, 95
anything
is a. too hard for, 157
Apollos
planted, A. watered, 76
who is A., 233
apostles
rejoice ye holy a., 327
apparel
silver, or gold, or a., 209
appeal
a. unto Caesar, 21
appear
a. in His glory, 211
a. not unto men to fast, 132
a. righteous unto men, 15
a. the second time, 346
a. unto men to fast, 195
a. with Him in glory, 323
when Christ shall a., 323
appearance
according to the a., 15
from all a. of evil, 27
outward a., 209
appeared
a. for this purpose, 256
appeareth
a. for a little time, 261
stand when he a., 22
appeaseth
anger a. strife, 12
appetite
a. is not filled, 11
man given to a., 147
apple
a. of his eye, 50
a. of the eye, 160
apples
comfort me with a., 238
like a. of gold, 106
appoint
who will a. Me the time, 21
appointed
a. a day, 222
a. times, 99
a. to die, 59
a. us to wrath, 221
at the time a., 15

that which is a. you, 175
approach
causest to a., 179
approveth
cause, the Lord a. not, 30
arise
a. and be baptized, 24
a. and go into Damascus, 256
a. and let us flee, 113
a. and make thy bed, 182
a. go to Nineveh, 255
a. with healing, 22
His light a., 158
let them a. if they, 198
men a. speaking perverse, 31
to the dumb stone, a., 197
when I fall, I shall a., 36
ariseth
sun also a., 67
ark
a. of God, 192
a. of God dwelleth, 52
bring into the a., 14
hand to hold the a., 309
arm
a. be broken, 206
a. fall from my shoulder, 206
a. like God, 370
a. of flesh, 370
a. of the Lord, 161
a. of the wicked, 304
flesh his a., 314
seal upon thine a., 239
with an outstretched a., 86
Armageddon
A., 93
armies
compassed with a., 109
defy the a. of God, 20
armour
a. of God, 161
a. of light, 170
whole a. of God, 342
army
a. of heaven, 157
array
a. himself with the land, 396
arrayed
not a. like the lilies, 15
arrogancy
a. come out, 16
a. of the proud, 17
arrow
a. shall go forth, 161
a. that flieth, 133
shoot an a., 86
arrows
a. drunk with blood, 326
a. of the Almighty, 13
a. shall be as of a, 4

as a. are in the hand, 348
spare no a., 327
art
graven by a. and man's, 166
as
a. for us, the Lord, 128
ascend
a. above the heights, 20
a. into the hill, 186
if I a. up into heaven, 113
ascending
angels a. and descending, 151
ashamed
a. of me and of my words, 171
a. of the testimony, 215
a. seven days, 303
forsake Thee shall be a., 23
hope maketh not a., 190
I am not a., 63
let him not be a., 51
let me not be a., 110
let me not be a., 124
man make thee a., 343
never be a., 314
not a. of the gospel, 171
not a. that wait for Me, 96
on Him shall not be a., 29
people being a., 72
prophets shall be a., 130
refusedst to be a., 353
shall be greatly a., 197
Son of man be a., 171
that needeth not be a., 96
ways, and be a., 312
were not a., 199
ashes
remembrances like a., 7
repent in dust and a., 316
wallow thyself in a., 262
aside
turn not a., 344
ask
a. and it shall be given, 293
a. and ye shall receive, 180
a. any thing in my name, 214
a. in my name, 152
a. in prayer, believing, 28
a. of me, I will give, 298
a. of me, seeing, 18
a. on, my mother, 275
a. the Father in my name, 214
a. their husbands, 412
a. what I shall give, 146
because ye a. amiss, 261
because ye a. not, 294
generations: a. thy father, 122
he is of age; a., 248
I will not a., 298

know not what ye a., 264
lack wisdom, let him a., 411
need of, before ye a., 153
of him they will a., 122
son a. bread, 225
to them that a. Him, 146
whatsoever we a. we, 294
ye a. and receive not, 261
young children a., 131
asked
a. not for Me, 68
He a. water, 83
which thou hast not a., 329
Askelon
not in the streets of A., 175
asketh
every one that a., 293
give to him that a., 37
asps
poison of a., 181
ass
a. his master's crib, 21
bridle for the a., 98
jawbone of an a., 370
riding upon an a., 193
wild a. bray, 60
assembly
a. of the saints, 133
a. of the wicked, 280
asses
ride on white a., 290
astonished
mark me, and be a., 350
astonishment
a. and an hissing, 86
become an a., 303
drink water with a., 131
astray
a. as soon as born, 25
a. in her paths, 6
a. like a lost sheep, 67
caused them to go a., 23
one of them be gone a., 283
seeketh that which is a., 283
sheep have gone a., 23
astrologers
let now the a., 19
asunder
let not man put a., 101
athirst
let him that is a. come, 116
unto him that is a., 89
atonement
a. for the soul, 35
attend
a. to my words, 177
attentive
ear now be a., 291
attire
bride her a. yet My, 23
audience

fear God, give a., 184
author
a. of confusion, 44
Jesus the a. and, 215
authority
a. over the man, 22
righteous are in a., 173
avenge
a. Me of Mine enemies, 326
a. not yourselves, 327
the Lord a., 322
avenged
God hath a. you on her, 327
people had a. themselves, 162
soul be a., 167
avenger
a. of blood, 341
avengeth
God that a. me, 326
avenging
a. of Israel, 174
avoid
a. foolish questions, 68
a. it, pass not by it, 118
awake
a. a. put on strength, 161
a. a. stand up, 397
a. a. utter, 363
a. and sing, 190
a. as in the ancient, 161
a. put on thy strength, 315
a. to righteousness, 27
of the earth shall a., 108
saith to the wood, a., 197
surely now He would a., 32
time to a., 340
awaked
sleeps, and must be a., 198
awaketh
drinketh; but he a., 96
eateth; but he a., 96
away
a. from the Lord, 65
a. when they flee, 72
anger not turned a., 150
if I go not a., 187
Lord hath taken a., 3
not cast thee a., 155
not taken a., 197
put a. his wife, 6
that which was driven a., 181
turn a. your heart, 210
awe
heart standeth in a., 7

B

Baal
Ahab served B., 83
but if B. then follow, 49

babblings
profane and vain b., 137
babe
for he is a b., 200
Babel
B. because the Lord, 57
babes
as newborn b., 165
out of the mouth of b., 48
Babylon
away beyond B., 121
B. be thrown down, 168
B. came in remembrance, 306
B. shall become heaps, 86
B. the great is fallen, 83
B. the Great, the Mother, 88
flee out of B., 114
king of B., 3
king of B. shall not, 8
palace of king of B., 192
rivers of B., 188
that great city B., 83
back
and look not b., 396
b. from the sword, 70
can I bring him b., 80
degrees, or go b., 272
drew not his hand b., 92
I will not go b. neither, 94
if any man draw b., 23
keep nothing b., 40
looking b. is fit, 95
plowed upon my b., 13
rod for the fool's b., 98
rod is for the b., 98
turned their b., 197
turned unto Me the b., 23
who shall turn it b., 150
wife looked b., 65
backs
Israel turneth their b., 72
backsliding
b. daughter, 23
backward
shadow return b., 272
bad
between good and b., 96
Balak
B. would give me, 268
balance
false b. is, 40
small dust of the b., 173
weighed in an even b., 63
balances
b. of deceit, 40
weighed in the b., 382
ye shall have just b., 40
bald
go up, thou b. head, 257
baldness
heads shall be b., 262
balm

b. in Gilead, 54
bands
b. of Orion, 288
b. of wickedness, 132
banner
b. over me was love, 238
baptism
b. of repentance, 24
one b., 24
Baptist
John B.'s head, 327
baptize
b. you with the Holy, 24
Christ sent me not to b., 117
baptized
arise, and be b., 24
arose, and was b., 68
b. you with water, 24
believeth and is b., 24
hinder me to be b., 24
repent, and be b., 24
baptizing
b. them in the name, 117
Barabbas
not this man, but B., 49
barbarian
B. Scythian, bond nor, 113
speaketh a b., 58
barbarians
Greeks, and to the B., 185
bare
naked and b., 122
barley
cockle instead of b., 206
handfuls of b., 130
barren
b. and bearest not, 135
b. woman to keep house, 135
grave; and the b. womb, 81
sing, O b., 47
bars
cut in sunder the b., 271
earth with her b., 87
battle
b. is not your's, 10
b. is the Lord's, 63
b. to the strong, 43
day of b., 396
flee in b., 72
forefront of the b., 30
Lord mighty in b., 156
none goeth to the b., 310
prepare himself to the b., 24
rusheth into the b., 203
bay
green b. tree, 118
beam
b. out of the timber, 4
cast out the b., 75
the b. in thine own eye, 32
bear

b. a son, 135
b. his sin, 33
b. no tidings, 59
b. robbed of her whelps, 79
b. robbed of her whelps, 12
b. the yoke, 276
b. with this evil, 276
downward, and b. fruit, 375
goat shall b. upon, 343
greater than I can b., 302
ninety years old, b., 135
paw of the b., 63
they b. witness of me, 5
to b. my name, 117
wounded spirit who can b., 89
beard
b. cut off, 262
head and of my b., 13
beards
b. be grown, 353
bearest
barren, and b. not, 135
bearing
b. His cross, 3
b. precious seed, 76
bears
roar all like b., 13
two she b., 304
beast
b. for b., 321
blains upon b., 284
both man and b., 135
every b. of the field, 363
killeth a b., 321
killeth a b., 302
lieth with a b., 363
life of his b., 14
manner of b., 363
preeminence above a b., 193
subtil than any b., 363
the number of the b., 119
worship the b. and his, 198
beasts
b. of the earth, 305
b. of the field, 35
of men befalleth b., 81
beat
b. him with the rod, 47
b. their swords, 278
b. them as small, 14
b. your plowshares, 401
beaten
mighty ones are b. down, 396
synagogues ye shall be b., 281
beatest
b. him with the rod, 47
beautiful
appear b. outward, 15
b. are the feet, 172

b. garments, 315
b. upon the mountains, 267
beauty
b. is departed, 212
b. is vain, 25
b. of holiness, 415
b. of old men, 122
lust not after her b., 6
perfection of b., 212
trust in thine own b., 25
because
b. the Lord loved Israel, 232
b. the Lord loved you, 50
b. ye have forsaken, 114
become
b. an astonishment, 303
bed
arise, and make thy b., 182
b. in the darkness, 91
make I my b. to swim, 362
make my b. in hell, 113
rise, take up thy b., 182
slumberings upon the b., 103
beds
evil upon their b., 74
been
hath already b., 207
that which hath b., 207
that which hath b. is, 207
Beersheba
even to B., 100
befall
evil will b., 386
things that shall b. me, 104
befallen
all this b. us, 102
befalleth
b. the sons of men, 81
of men b. beasts, 81
before
b. Abraham was, 51
b. faith came, 57
b. God, I lie not, 389
b. I formed thee, 31
b. the sun, 192
b. thou camest out, 31
day like that b., 412
do b. all Israel, 192
gone out b. thee, 63
He is b. all things, 25
stand b. this holy Lord, 156
walk b. Me, as David, 189
begetteth
he that b. a fool, 275
beggar
lifteth up the b., 86
begin
when I b., 25
beginning
b. of knowledge, 134
b. of my strength, 135
b. of strife is, 371

b. of the world, 145
b. of wisdom, 134
b. was the Word, 25
been with me from the b., 117
every man at the b., 191
heard from the b., 240
I am the b. and the end, 25
in the b. God created, 25
more than his b., 87
sinneth from the b., 342
than at the b., 224
than the b., 109
told you from the b., 152
true from the b., 344
begotten
b. the drops of dew, 309
b. through the gospel, 172
gave His only b., 115
have I b. them, 231
name of the only b., 28
only b. Son into the, 215
beguiled
serpent b. me, 32
wherefore have ye b., 83
behaviour
be in b. as becometh, 28
beheaded
the souls of them b., 247
behind
get thee b. me, Satan, 136
look not b., 378
turn thee b., 359
behold
b. the man, 4
b. thy mother, 218
woman, b. thy son, 134
being
move, and have our b., 235
while I have my b., 363
Belial
children of B., 407
daughter of B., 407
sons of B., 118
believe
all men will b., 247
b. His prophets, 124
b. in God b. also in me, 29
b. in the Lord, 124
b. in thine heart, 217
b. not every spirit, 29
b. not his writings, 77
b. not me, b. the works, 29
b. not that I am He, 251
b. not, yet He abideth, 29
b. on the Lord Jesus, 29
b. on the name of His, 57
b. that Jesus Christ is, 29
b. that Thou art Christ, 216
b. that ye receive, 126
b. to the saving of the, 78
b. ye that I am able, 28
be not afraid, only b., 126
cometh to God must b., 29

devils also b., 134
earthly things and ye b., 28
ere they b. Me, 124
except I see I will not b., 102
for them that b. not, 299
how shall they b., 29
how shall ye b., 28
how shall ye b. my words, 77
if ye will not b., 28
little ones that b., 48
Lord, I b., 29
not b. though it be told, 361
not to them that b., 385
repent ye, and b., 171
sent, Him ye b. not, 251
slow of heart to b., 299
that b. are justified, 29
wonders, ye will not b., 28
work of God, that ye b., 104
ye b. me not, 361
believed
all that b. were, 392
as thou hast b. so be, 125
b. not their words, 318
b. on in the world, 215
great number b., 68
had ye b. Moses, 29
know whom I have b., 63
ministers by whom ye b., 233
nearer than when we b., 340
not b. in the name, 28
not seen and yet have b., 29
some b. the things, 284
spoken, and some b. not, 284
ye would have b. me, 29
believeth
and b. on Him that sent, 29
b. all things, 240
b. in Him shall receive, 140
b. in Him should not, 340
b. in Him should not perish, 82
b. not is condemned, 28
b. not on me, but on Him, 29
b. on me shall never, 92
b. shall not make haste, 28
he that b. in me, 29
he that b. on me, 29
husband that b. not, 29
liveth and b. in me, 29
possible to him that b., 2
that b. and is baptized, 24
that b. not God, 29
that b. not the Son, 28

to every one that b., 171
who b. that Jesus is, 251
whomsoever b. on Him, 29
with the heart man b., 29
world, that whosoever b.,
  111
believing
  ask in prayer, b., 28
  faithless, but b., 102
belly
  b. of hell, 293
  b. shall swell, 6
  came out of the b., 90
  fill his b. with wind, 394
  formed thee in the b., 31
  make thy b. bitter, 32
  upon thy b. shalt, 76
belong
  b. the issues from death, 87
  b. unto the Lord, 226
  b. unto us, 226
beloved
  b. come into his garden,
    239
  b. is mine, 57
  b. of the Lord, 337
  b. which was not b., 155
  given the dearly b., 1
  I am my b.'s and his, 57
  I am my b.'s and my, 57
  Lord, my dearly b., 96
  this is My b. Son, 212
  this is My b. Son, 251
  voice of my b., 103
bemoan
  waste: who will b. her, 90
bend
  b. their tongues, 99
  ye that b. the bow, 327
beneath
  in earth b., 158
  not be b., 268
  ye are from b., 170
benevolence
  unto the wife due b., 246
bereaved
  b. of my children, 47
bereaveth
  sword b., 81
berries
  fig tree bear olive b., 66
beseech
  b. Thee, o Lord, 67
  love's sake I b., 233
  obey, I b., 270
  remember, I b. Thee, 142
beseiged
  remaineth and is b., 14
beside
  any God b., 152
  b. Me is no saviour, 164
  b. Me there is no God, 164
  none else b. me, 61
best

b. of them is as a brier, 69
even the b. of, 258
every man at his b., 142
Bethlehem
  well of B., 382
betray
  eateth with me shall b., 31
  one of you shall b., 31
betrayed
  b. into the hands, 31
  Son of man is b., 31
betrayest
  b. thou the Son of man, 31
betrayeth
  b. me is at hand, 31
  hand of him that b., 31
better
  b. for me to die, 92
  b. for thee to enter, 182
  b. if the will of God be, 3
  b. is a dinner of herbs, 238
  b. is a dry morsel, 352
  b. is a little with, 98
  b. is a neighbour, 19
  b. is a poor, 7
  b. is an handful, 11
  b. is it to get wisdom, 404
  b. is little with, 66
  b. is the end, 109
  b. is the poor, 44
  b. is the sight of, 89
  b. is thy love, 239
  b. than a liar, 98
  b. than laughter, 229
  b. than strength, 371
  b. than the mighty, 12
  b. than the proud, 276
  b. than the vintage, 283
  b. than weapons, 401
  b. that a millstone, 48
  b. thing under the sun, 77
  b. to be of an humble, 193
  b. to dwell in a corner, 246
  b. to dwell in the, 246
  b. to enter halt into, 78
  b. to go to the house, 81
  b. to hear the rebuke, 74
  b. to marry than to burn,
    42
  b. to thee than ten, 47
  b. to trust, 172
  b. to trust in the, 313
  blessed of the b., 22
  good name is b. than, 318
  heart is made b., 229
  living dog is b., 190
  love is b., 238
  lovingkindness is b., 153
  not in marriage doeth b.,
    42
  obey b. than sacrifice, 269
  open rebuke is b., 40
  there is nothing b., 4
  two are b. than one, 67

between
  b. me and thee, 322
  b. us and you there is a,
    184
  Lord be witness b., 9
beware
  b. lest any man spoil, 84
  b. lest thou forget, 128
  b. of covetousness, 175
  b. of false prophets, 84
  b. of the scribes, 196
  b. ye of the leaven, 196
bewitched
  who hath b., 84
bid
  if prophet had b., 7
bidden
  Lord hath b. him, 3
bind
  b. on earth shall be, 289
  b. the sweet influences, 288
  b. them about thy neck, 44
  b. up that which was, 181
  smitten, and He will b., 157
  they b. heavy burdens, 196
bindeth
  b. up their wounds, 364
  cry not when He b., 3
  sore, and b. up, 156
bird
  b. hasteth to the snare, 379
  b. of the air, 301
birds
  b. of the air, 188
  cage is full of b., 74
  singing of b., 345
birth
  come to the b., 403
  shall I bring to the b., 298
  than day of one's b., 4
birthright
  profit shall this b., 90
  sold his b., 204
bishop
  b. must be blameless, 233
  office of a b., 12
bits
  b. in the horses', 271
bitter
  b. for sweet, 233
  b. in soul, 13
  b. thing is sweet, 89
  clusters are b., 32
  evil thing and b., 23
  make thy belly b., 32
  sweet for b., 233
  sweet water and b., 66
  wives, and be not b., 246
bitterly
  curse ye b., 104
  dealt very b., 13
bitterness
  b. in the latter, 32
  b. of death, 255

b. of my soul, 40
b. to her that bare, 48
filled me with b., 32
gall of b., 112
knoweth his own b., 13
black
b. but comely, 25
one hair white or b., 267
blackness
heavens with b., 267
blade
fall from my shoulder b., 206
first the b., 176
blameless
b. than the Philistines, 205
blaspheme
shall the enemy b., 33
blasphemed
b. among the Gentiles, 196
every day is b., 33
blasphemeth
that b. against the Holy, 33
blasphemies
out of heart proceed b., 261
blasphemy
all manner of sin and b., 33
b. against the Holy Ghost, 33
of rebuke, and b., 90
put off all these; b., 27
bleating
meaneth then this b., 83
bleatings
b. of the flocks, 104
blemish
no b. in him, 24
bless
b. and curse not, 77
b. His holy name, 290
b. the Lord, 26
b. them that b. thee, 159
b. them that curse, 77
b. them which persecute, 77
b. Thy name for ever, 290
b. with their mouth, 195
b. ye the Lord, 290
being reviled, we b., 3
except thou b. me, 34
fear the Lord, b. the, 290
Lord b. thee, 161
Lord b. thee, 34
merciful unto us, and b., 34
will b. thee, 53
blessed
and b. them, 72
and call her b., 275
b. and holy is he that, 82
b. are all, 387
b. are the dead which, 82
b. are the meek, 194
b. are the merciful, 250

b. are the peacemakers, 278
b. are the persecuted, 226
b. are the poor, 193
b. are the pure in heart, 307
b. are they called, 180
b. are they that do, 235
b. are they that have not, 29
b. are they that hear, 171
b. are they that mourn, 54
b. are they that wait, 125
b. are they which hunger, 333
b. are they whose, 140
b. are ye that sow, 106
b. are ye that weep, 229
b. are ye, when men, 66
b. art thou among women, 217
b. be God, 148
b. be he that b. thee, 33
b. be he that cometh, 253
b. be the Lord, 290
b. be the Lord, 174
b. be the Lord, 148
b. be the Lord, 371
b. be the Lord, 174
b. be the name, 148
b. be the name, 3
b. be the name of, 34
b. be thou, which, 7
b. be thy advice, 7
b. be Thy glorious, 290
b. be ye, 59
b. he that keepeth, 271
b. is every one that, 134
b. is he that blesseth, 50
b. is He that cometh, 251
b. is he that considereth, 45
b. is he that readeth, 300
b. is he that waiteth, 276
b. is he that watcheth, 346
b. is he whose transgression, 139
b. is man that feareth, 134
b. is man that walketh, 58
b. is that man that, 179
b. is that trusteth, 180
b. is the man, 140
b. is the man that, 380
b. is the man whom, 179
b. is the man whose, 124
b. is the nation, 154
b. shalt thou be, 34
b. the latter end, 87
earth be b., 33
earth be b., 49
families be b., 131
God b. the seventh day, 335
less is b., 22
more b. to give, 11
mother bare me be b., 31

of the just is b., 318
thou shalt be b., 42
blesseth
blessed is he that b., 50
He b. the habitation, 34
blessing
b. and a curse, 34
b. and cursing, 235
b. be upon the head of, 40
b. if ye obey, 34
b. of the Lord, 45
delighted not in b., 223
exalted above all b., 290
hast thou but one b., 13
reserved a b., 13
same mouth proceedeth b., 35
blessings
I will curse your b., 77
blew
b. a trumpet, 24
blind
b. but My servant, 372
b. guides which strain, 196
b. lead the b., 35
b. see, 179
b. to wander, 35
b. ye should have no sin, 206
bring the b. by a way, 111
eyes of the b., 35
eyes of the b., 35
eyes of the b., 5
eyes to the b., 10
gift doth b., 38
I was b. now I see, 122
look, ye b., 372
perfect, and b., 199
poor and b. and naked, 248
stumblingblock before b., 179
the lame, the b., 42
who is b., 199
who maketh the b., 72
blood
arrows drunk with b., 326
avenger of b., 341
b. be on us, 320
b. be upon thy head, 178
b. of bulls, 141
b. of him that shed, 262
b. of Jesus, 35
b. of Naboth, 41
b. of the new testament, 35
b. of these men, 297
b. shall be poured, 325
b. shall be upon him, 178
b. shall be upon him, 32
b. shall pursue, 77
b. that is shed, 262
b. that maketh an atonement, 35
b. upon your own heads, 178

brother's b. crieth, 122
buildeth a town with b., 173
but by water and b., 24
by the b. of the Lamb, 337
drink His b., 58
drinketh my b., 115
drinketh my b., 214
drunk with their b., 41
filled with b., 324
flesh and b., 226
flesh and b. hath not, 216
flesh is the b. thereof, 35
from coming to shed b., 7
given them b. to drink, 247
hands are full of b., 178
innocent b., 32
innocent b., 262
innocent of the b., 33
is not this the b., 70
keepeth sword from b., 95
moon into b., 109
new testament in my b., 58
nigh by the b. of Christ, 51
not against flesh and b., 110
polluted with b., 197
precious shall their b. be, 390
prepare thee unto b., 77
purchased with His own b., 104
redemption through His b., 141
shall dogs lick thy b., 41
shall his b. be shed, 222
shed innocent b., 207
shed much b. upon, 304
shed the b. of saints, 247
sheddeth man's b., 222
Spirit, water, and b., 382
swift to shed b., 119
wash his feet in the b., 326
waters turned to b., 284
without shedding of b., 35
bloody
full of b. crimes, 230
save me from b. men, 230
woe to the b. city, 74
blossom
b. as the rose, 321
blot
b. out of My book, 302
blotted
b. out of the book, 110
sin be b. out, 326
sins may be b. out, 68
blow
b. the trumpet, 24
b. the trumpet, 161
bloweth
b. where it listeth, 263
blown
b. the trumpet, 310

boast
b. not thyself of to, 36
harness b. himself, 35
if thou b. thou bearest, 36
boasteth
way, then he b., 40
bodies
b. are the members of, 36
dead b., 305
bodily
b. exercise profiteth, 168
fulness of the Godhead b., 101
body
absent in b., 2
against his own b., 141
b. is of Christ, 20
b. is the temple, 36
b. not for fornication, 36
b. of this death, 13
b. shall be full of, 44
b. what ye shall put on, 137
b. without the spirit, 82
bear in my b. the marks, 282
defileth the whole b., 367
glorify God in your b., 36
head of the b., 22
home in the b., 236
kill the b. and after, 261
kill the b. but are not, 36
light of the b., 36
members of His b., 215
my b. to be burned, 46
nor care for your b., 248
one b. in Christ, 52
one bread, and one b., 134
take, eat; this is my b., 58
the b. than raiment, 248
this is my b. which is, 58
whole b. should be cast, 78
worms destroy this b., 80
ye are the b. of Christ, 51
yourselves in the b., 60
boil
b. breaking forth, 284
b. like a pot, 156
bond
b. nor free: but Christ, 113
b. of iniquity, 112
b. of perfectness, 240
neither b. nor free, 113
bondage
house of b., 142
same is he brought in b., 143
bondman
b. in Egypt, 58
b. in Egypt, 390
bonds
ambassador in b., 202
remember my b., 202
remember them in b., 60
bondwoman

children of the b., 185
bone
b. of my bones, 411
be broken from the b., 206
break a b., 252
tongue breaketh the b., 16
bones
b. are full of the sin, 406
bone of my b., 411
can these b. live, 322
dry bones, hear the word, 322
health to the b., 366
keepeth all his b., 252
members of His b., 215
move his b., 319
spirit drieth the b., 89
book
adversary had written b., 4
b. of the law, 268
b. of this prophecy, 300
blot out of My b., 302
blotted out of the b., 110
note it in a b., 186
out of the b., 300
plagues in this b., 285
printed in a b., 36
prophecy of this b., 271
seek ye out of the b., 344
seest, write in a b., 37
the b. of life, 78
words of this b., 99
worthy to open the b., 263
written in this b., 197
books
b. that should be written, 37
of making many b., 37
born
astray as soon as b., 25
b. for adversity, 143
b. in the land, 112
b. of God overcometh, 169
b. of God sinneth not, 360
b. of the flesh is, 31
b. of the Spirit is, 31
b. unto trouble, 244
clean that is b., 244
cursed be day I was b., 31
end was I b., 217
except a man be b., 24
except a man be b. again, 37
first man that was b.?, 8
had not been b., 31
I was free b., 142
man b. of a woman, 234
nation be b., 276
righteousness is b. of, 334
shall a child b., 135
that loveth is b. of God, 240
the Christ is b. of God, 251
time to be b., 25

unto us a child is b., 252
unto you is b. this day, 51
wherein I was b., 90
who is b. of God doth, 37
ye must be b. again, 37
borrow
from him that would b., 37
shalt not b., 37
borrower
b. is servant, 37
so with the b., 37
borroweth
wicked b. and payeth, 37
bosom
b. of fools, 12
carry them in thy b., 231
fire in his b., 6
lieth in thy b., 30
bottles
b. break, and the wine, 410
must be put into new b., 25
new wine into old b., 410
bottomless
b. pit, 184
bought
b. with a price, 143
father that hath b., 204
bound
b. in heaven, 289
b. in the spirit, 104
b. unto a wife, 101
b. with chains, 142
b. with this chain, 202
ready not to be b. only, 95
to them that are b., 202
word of God is not b., 172
bountifully
soweth b. shall reap, 96
bow
b. for lies, 99
bend the b., 327
every knee should b., 188
knee shall b., 9
My b. in the cloud, 71
trust in my b., 371
worship and b. down, 415
bowed
all those that be b., 162
b. His head, 75
where he b., 18
bowl
b. be broken, 96
boys
b. and girls playing, 300
bramble
b. bush gather, 65
branch
B. shall grow, 252
righteous B., 252
branches
holy, so are the b., 185
vine, ye are the b., 21
brass
b. and iron, 373

b. as rotten wood, 370
become as sounding b., 107
brow b., 373
flesh of b., 90
gates of b., 271
brawling
b. woman in a wide house, 246
bray
b. a fool in a mortar, 138
wild ass b., 60
bread
b. eaten in secret, 99
b. he shall live forever, 38
b. of God is He, 37
b. of idleness, 246
b. of tears, 176
b. shall be given, 333
b. that I will give, 312
b. to the hungry, 59
b. to the wise, 43
brought to a piece of b., 301
by b. only, 247
cast thy b., 10
day our daily b., 137
eat b. by weight, 131
eat thy b. with joy, 137
every one a loaf of b., 42
for which is not b., 393
give him b., 110
he that eateth b., 31
hired for b., 195
I am the b. of life, 38
I am the living b., 38
morsel of b., 191
neither will I eat b., 66
not a famine of b., 131
not live by b. alone, 171
one b. and one body, 134
partakers of that one b., 134
pieces of b., 130
plenty of b., 95
shalt thou eat b., 302
son ask b., 225
stones be made b., 43
take the children's b., 354
young children ask b., 131
breadth
perceived b. of the earth, 17
break
b. a bone, 252
b. me in pieces, 120
b. mine heart, 378
b. not Thy covenant, 71
b. Thou the arm, 304
bottles b. and wine, 410
built will I b., 93
I will b. in pieces, 271
time to b. down, 181
breaketh
b. me with a tempest, 374

no man b. it, 131
soft tongue b., 16
breast
draw out the b., 47
breastplate
b. of faith, 27
breasts
b. are like two young, 25
b. to clusters of grapes, 36
womb and dry b., 77
breath
b. goeth forth, 11
b. is corrupt, 80
b. of God, 345
b. of life, 72
b. of the Almighty, 234
every thing that hath b., 291
takest away their b., 14
to all life, and b., 149
breathed
b. into his nostrils, 72
brethren
b. go to war, 320
b. to dwell together, 38
daughters of thy b., 210
enemies with your b., 353
fight against your b., 277
fight for your b., 24
following their b., 277
inheritance among our b., 112
least of these my b., 46
love as b., 28
men, b. and fathers, 224
mother and my b. are, 131
of thy b., 252
our lives for the b., 336
perils among false b., 107
sell your b., 175
soweth discord among b., 17
stranger unto my b., 114
strengthen thy b., 108
ye are b. why do ye, 16
bribery
tabernacles of b., 38
bricks
b. are fallen down, 17
straw to make b., 273
bride
b. her attire, yet My, 23
voice of the b., 86
bridegroom
voice of the b., 86
bridle
b. for the ass, 98
b. in thy lips, 192
brier
best of them is as a b., 69
bright
the b. and morning star, 216
brightness

b. but we walk in, 96
reason of thy b., 61
brimstone
lake of fire and b., 306
bring
b. forth your reasons, 16
b. me up Samuel, 367
can I b. him back, 80
bringeth
b. down to the g., 156
b. low, and lifteth, 156
broad
b. is the way, 78
b. ways I will seek, 89
broken
b. and a contrite heart, 67
b. spirit drieth the, 89
b. the yokes, 41
bind that which was b., 181
body, which is b., 58
city that is b., 348
cord is not quickly b., 68
golden bowl be b., 96
healeth the b. in heart, 364
images shall be b., 93
like a b. tooth, 30
like a b. vessel, 91
mine arm be b., 206
of a b. heart, 176
one of them is b., 252
spirit is b., 364
brokenhearted
heal the b., 87
brooks
after the water b., 241
brother
a b. offended is, 139
admonish him as a b., 23
and hateth his b., 169
angry with his b., 12
b. and our flesh, 249
b. beloved, 135
b. goeth to law with b., 229
b. is born for adversity, 143
b. shall rise again, 323
b. to dragons, 91
b. trespass, 75
because thou art my b., 39
closer than a b., 143
every man against his b., 30
every man to his b., 59
every one against his b., 44
evil against his b., 38
from thy poor b., 45
hand of my b., 132
hateth his b., 38
have thy b.'s wife, 6
hunt every man his b., 262
loveth God love his b., 39
loveth his b., 240
loveth not his b., 39
man and his b., 219
mote out of thy b.'s eye, 75

mote that is in thy b.'s, 32
my b.'s keeper, 38
not Esau Jacob's b., 239
reconciled to thy b., 45
than a b. far off, 19
that loveth not his b., 39
the same is my b., 131
unto his b., 279
unto thy b., 138
usury to thy b., 392
voice of thy b.'s blood, 122
who hateth his b. is a, 181
wide unto thy b., 45
withdraw from every b., 58
younger b. shall be, 135
brotherly
b. love continue, 38
brought
b. me forth of the womb, 90
b. me home again, 79
b. you forth out, 210
gone and b. low, 223
lives they b. it, 334
brow
b. brass, 373
bruised
b. for our iniquities, 252
brutish
b. in his knowledge, 199
b. man knoweth not, 199
b. person perish, 260
hateth reproof is b., 74
bucket
drop of a b., 173
buckler
He is a b., 159
shield and b., 160
build
again I will b., 50
b. but I will throw down, 145
b. him a sure house, 329
b. Him an house, 52
b. houses, but not, 144
b. Me an house, 163
b. my church, 371
b. up the wall, 211
b. up Zion, 211
b. with hewn stones, 17
except the Lord b., 4
house which I b., 152
if I b. again, 178
intending to b. a tower, 285
labour in vain that b., 4
let us b. with you, 84
not b. an house unto, 304
time to b. up, 181
what house will ye b., 52
builded
every house is b. by, 5
he who hath b., 5
wisdom b. her house, 409
wisdom is an house b., 4

builders
stone which the b., 274
stone which the b., 328
buildeth
b. a town with blood, 173
b. her house, 188
riseth up and b., 77
woe unto him that b., 69
building
b. you an altar, 259
the b. decayeth, 39
built
b. his house on a rock, 285
b. his house on the sand, 285
b. houses of hewn stone, 96
b. O virgin of Israel, 50
b. Thee an house, 52
but He that b. all, 5
house which I have b., 52
that which I have b., 93
without a foundation b., 8
bullock
chastised, as a b., 98
eat straw like the b., 38
bulls
blood of b., 141
burden
b. upon the Lord, 162
bear his own b., 321
layest the b., 231
burdens
b. grievous to be borne, 39
bear ye one another's b., 39
bind heavy b., 196
touch not the b. with, 39
undo the heavy b., 132
buried
b. in a good age, 8
there will I be b., 79
burn
b. as an oven, 222
b. that none can quench, 150
better to marry than b., 42
fire shall b., 8
gods shall ye b., 198
jealousy b. like fire, 139
offended, and I b., 107
burned
b. in their lust, 188
bush b. with fire, 158
clothes not be b., 6
feet not be b., 6
give my body to be b., 46
thou shalt not be b., 54
burneth
wickedness b. as the, 118
burning
b. and a shining light, 207
b. fiery furnace, 79
b. for b., 222
burnt

b. with fire, 303
more than b. offerings, 334
still sacrificed and b., 197
bury
b. me not, 39
dead b. their dead, 320
field, to b. strangers, 39
none to b. her, 353
bush
b. burned with fire, 158
b. was not consumed, 158
bramble b., 65
bushel
put it under a b., 302
business
about my Father's b., 104
b. in great waters, 272
diligent in his b., 2
do your own b., 27
utter not this our b., 266
utter this our b., 9
butter
b. and honey, 97
smoother than b., 106
buy
b. of me gold tried, 127
b. the truth, 388
come ye, b. and eat, 89
buyer
as with the b., 37
let not the b. rejoice, 102
naught, saith the b., 40
buyeth
no man b. their, 13
byword
b. among all people, 313
proverb, and a b., 303

C

Caesar
appeal unto C., 21
art not C.'s friend, 383
C.'s judgment seat, 52
nor yet against C., 206
render therefore unto C., 51
things which are C.'s, 51
we have no king but C., 242
cage
c. is full, 74
Cain
C. went out, 274
gone in the way of C., 168
set a mark upon C., 159
slayeth C. vengeance, 159
calamity
c. is at hand, 303
c. of his father, 48
day of my c., 109
calf
c. and the young lion, 14
hither the fatted c., 42

call
all them that c., 19
c. any man common, 319
c. for Samson, 255
c. His name Emmanuel, 218
c. His name Jesus, 217
c. His name Jesus, 217
c. me Mara, 13
c. my sin, 46
c. no man your father, 149
c. not on Thy name, 167
c. not thou common, 307
c. now, if there be, 18
c. on My name and I, 19
c. on the Lord, 86
c. on the name of, 19
c. them My people, 155
c. unto Me and I will, 293
c. upon Him in truth, 19
c. upon His name, 174
c. upon His name, 116
c. upon Me in the day, 18
c. ye on the name, 43
c. ye upon Him while, 273
hear when I c., 292
I will c. upon God, 18
in all that they c., 291
rich unto all that c., 149
shall c. upon Me, 292
therefore will I c. upon, 292
trouble I will c., 292
whosoever shall c. on, 87
why c. ye me Lord, 85
called
as the Lord hath c., 67
c. by name of Lord, 50
c. thee by thy name, 155
c. unto them but, 100
c. upon Thy name, 92
c. us unto uncleanness, 186
c. ye did not answer, 99
c. you friends, 143
c. you unto His kingdom, 148
c. you, but ye answered, 273
he that is c., 142
in my distress I c., 291
many are c., 238
that is c. in the Lord, 30
they with Him are c., 128
Thy people are c. by, 139
vocation ye are c., 51
wherein he was c., 67
callest
why c. thou me good, 170
calleth
faithful is He that c., 149
calling
abide in the same c., 67
c. of God, 35
prize of the high c., 60

calm
sea may be c., 32
came
c. from God, 214
c. I out of my mother's, 3
c. not to judge, 221
c. unto His own, 16
lo, it c. to little, 96
wherefore c. I forth, 91
camel
easier for a c. to go, 225
sheep, c. and ass, 14
swallow a c., 196
camels
c. drink also, 224
c. were without number, 203
c. were without number, 2
Canaan
give the land of C., 71
land of C., 210
land of C. which, 210
candle
c. of the wicked, 205
c. of the wicked, 230
light of a c. shall, 86
men light a c., 302
candlestick
bushel, but on a c., 302
cankerworm
c. hath left, 93
hath the c. eaten, 93
cannot
c. go back, 297
captives
c. whose c. they were, 142
deliverance to the c., 87
liberty to the c., 202
captivity
are for c. to c., 92
gone into c., 121
shall go into c., 224
that leadeth into c., 224
turn back your c., 131
carcase
c. of Jezebel, 39
c. shall not come unto, 304
wheresoever the c., 42
carcases
c. shall fall, 79
care
by weight, and with c., 131
c. of the church, 52
c. of the world, 171
take c. of him, 171
carefully
sought it c. with, 312
careth
c. for things of world, 95
c. not for the sheep, 95
God c. for, 210
he that is unmarried c., 95
carnal
c. mind is enmity, 41

spiritual: but I am c., 41
carnally
  c. minded is death, 19
carpenter
  this the c.'s son, 213
carried
  c. from the womb, 350
carry
  c. them in thy bosom, 231
  c. you beyond Babylon, 121
  certain we can c., 82
  dieth he shall c., 112
cart
  sin with a c. rope, 360
cast
  be thou c. into the sea, 126
  body c. into hell, 78
  c. a stone, 92
  c. away a perfect man, 1
  c. away His people, 219
  c. his mantle, 232
  c. into hell fire, 182
  c. it from thee, 32
  c. it to dogs, 354
  c. me down, 369
  c. me not off, 8
  c. not away your, 63
  c. off the works, 170
  c. out devils, 182
  c. out devils, 122
  c. out the beam, 75
  c. out the mote, 75
  c. out the scorner, 371
  c. thee off for ever, 23
  c. them away, 198
  c. thy bread, 10
  c. thy burden upon, 162
  c. ye your pearls, 393
  cut it off, and c., 32
  dost Thou c. me off, 162
  feet to be c. into hell, 78
  let him first c. a stone, 4
  not c. off His people, 242
  pluck it out, and c., 78
  poor widow hath c. more, 146
  power to c. into hell, 78
  Satan c. out Satan, 122
  time to c. away, 84
  to c. down, 156
caterpillar
  hath the c. eaten, 93
cattle
  and over the c., 14
  c. of Egypt died, 284
  cursed above all c., 363
  grow for the c., 76
cause
  angry without a c., 12
  but for this c., 256
  c. came I into the world, 217
  c. His face to shine, 34
  c. My fury to rest, 150

c. of the fatherless, 205
c. of the poor, 288
c. of the poor, 223
c. that is too hard, 231
c. them to know, 157
c. Thy face to shine, 153
c. thy flesh to sin, 356
c. was of God, 156
c. which I knew not, 10
debate thy c. with, 16
hate me without a c., 110
judge not the c., 205
judge Thou my c., 223
man in his c., 30
neighbour without c., 189
not c. to bring forth, 298
opened my c., 110
persecuted me without c., 7
poor in his c., 201
poor man in his c., 201
produce your c., 16
revealed my c., 327
strive not without c., 16
to God commit my c., 18
wounds without c., 374
caused
  c. them to go astray, 23
causeth
  c. his wife to commit, 6
  c. the grass to grow, 76
  c. the vapours, 309
cease
  and reproach shall c., 371
  c. from anger, 12
  c. from strife, 16
  c. from troubling, 80
  c. to do evil, 316
  c. to pervert, 130
  night shall not c., 345
  of the proud to c., 17
  poor shall never c., 287
  remembrance to c., 14
ceased
  c. not from their own, 372
ceasing
  c. to pray, 291
  pray without c., 294
cedar
  c. in Lebanon, 176
  house of c., 52
celebrate
  death cannot c., 81
chafed
  c. in their minds, 12
chaff
  as c. that is driven, 112
  c. before the wind, 110
  c. that the storm, 406
  c. to the wheat, 20
chain
  bound with this c., 202
  compasseth them as a c., 296
chains

bound with c., 142
Chaldees
  servants of the C., 3
chambers
  c. by wrong, 69
  hills from His c., 309
chance
  c. happeneth to them all, 43
change
  am the Lord, I c. not, 149
  c. his skin, 43
  that are given to c., 259
charge
  c. of the Lord, 269
  laid to my c., 206
  sin to their c., 140
chariot
  c. of fire, 147
chariots
  c. be as a whirlwind, 325
  some trust in c., 314
  wheels of his c., 79
charity
  above all things have c., 240
  angels, and have not c., 107
  be sound in faith, in c., 28
  burned, and have not c., 46
  c. edifieth, 62
  c. envieth not, 240
  c. never faileth, 240
  c. out of a pure heart, 240
  c. shall cover the, 240
  c. suffereth long, 240
  c. vaunteth not, 240
  faith, hope, and c., 126
  greatest of these is c., 126
  lusts: but follow c., 28
  not c. I am nothing, 126
  put on c., 240
  things be done with c., 240
  with a kiss of c., 135
chase
  angel of the Lord c., 110
  c. a thousand, 370
  c. your enemies, 109
  one c. a thousand, 1
  shall c. them, 72
chasten
  c. thy son while, 47
  I love, I rebuke and c., 98
  neither c. me in Thy hot, 46
chasteneth
  c. his son, 97
  father c. not, 48
  God c. thee, 97
  loveth him c., 47
  the Lord loveth he c., 46
chastening
  despise not the c., 46
  no c. for the present, 75
  the c. of the Lord, 3

chastise
c. you with scorpions, 273
chastised
c. as a bullock, 98
c. you with whips, 273
cheek
on thy right c. turn, 139
smiteth thee on the one c., 140
cheer
be of good c., 108
be of good c., 54
be of good c., 54
c. thee in the days, 416
cheereth
c. God and man, 11
cheerful
heart maketh a c., 180
loveth a c. giver, 19
young men c., 300
cheese
curdled me like c., 72
chickens
a hen gathereth her c., 232
chide
will not always c., 139
chief
father made him the c., 132
whosoever will be c., 194
child
beareth the sucking c., 231
begetteth a wise c., 48
but a little c., 193
c. be born, 135
c. I spake as a c., 48
c. in two, 222
c. left to himself, 47
c. of the devil, 119
c. shall lead them, 48
city, the c. shall die, 77
correction from the c., 47
delivered of the c., 31
even a c. is known by, 44
for this c. I prayed, 31
forth her first c., 31
give her the living c., 59
give her the living c., 222
heart of a c., 47
king is a c., 232
kingdom as a little c., 48
poor and a wise c. than, 7
receive one little c., 48
say not, I am a c., 103
sucking c., 59
thought as a c., 48
tongue of the sucking c., 382
train up a c., 47
travail with c., 47
understood as a c., 48
unto us a c. is born, 252
virgin shall be with c., 217
childhood
c. and youth are, 416

childish
put away c. things, 321
childless
c. among women, 311
made women c., 311
children
alien unto my mother's c., 114
all the c. of God, 113
angels and are the c. of, 12
become as little c., 68
bereaved of my c., 47
blood be on our c., 320
c. are an heritage, 48
c. are come to the birth, 403
c. arise up, and call, 275
c. ask bread, 131
c. be fatherless, 77
c. be multiplied, 406
c. despised me, 343
c. die for the fathers, 304
c. for ever, 226
c. in understanding, 248
c. keep yourselves from, 198
c. let no man deceive, 334
c. obey your parents, 48
c. obey your parents, 271
c. of Belial, 407
c. of disobedience, 100
c. of light, 51
c. of the bondwoman, 185
c. of the day, 51
c. of the desolate, 48
c. of the Lord, 48
c. of the married, 48
c. of this world are, 414
c. ought not to lay, 276
c. shall be taught, 105
c. that will not hear, 99
c. walk in truth, 48
c.'s c. are the crown, 173
c.'s teeth are set, 32
called the c. of God, 278
die for the c., 304
diligently unto thy c., 55
eye shall not spare c., 14
eyes of his c., 30
father pitieth his c., 59
give me c., 47
given to the c., 183
good gifts unto your c., 146
hearts of all the c., 153
henceforth be no more c., 101
if ye were Abraham's c., 196
inheritance to c.'s c., 173
iniquity upon the c., 303
justified of her c., 410
leave thy fatherless c., 408
love the c. of God, 241
lying c., 99

malice be ye c., 119
of c. or of strangers, 377
of God, as dear c., 27
parents for the c., 276
peace of thy c., 105
provoke not your c., 13
provoke not your c., 47
resembled the c., 24
same unto us their c., 171
so are c. of the youth, 348
sorrow bring forth c., 31
stones to raise up c., 155
suffer the little c., 48
take the c.'s bread, 354
tare forty and two c., 304
than all his c., 47
than the c. of light, 414
the c. of Ammon, 309
to love their c., 247
walk as c. of light, 27
we are c. of God, 48
weep for your c., 176
woe to the rebellious c., 23
wonderful works to c., 290
you, and to your c., 187
children of Isr
against c. shall not a dog, 159
among the c. a goodlier, 257
c. did evil, 201
c. did evil again, 23
c. died not one, 284
c. for a possession, 210
c. have not hearkened, 231
c. out of Egypt, 193
c. remembered, 23
c. walked, 113
c. walked forty years, 121
from the day that the c., 88
number of the c., 50
chimney
smoke out of the c., 112
choke
c. the word, 171
choose
c. life, that, 49
c. none of his ways, 390
c. out of all the tribes, 211
c. thee one, 49
c. to us judgment, 84
c. you this day, 49
evil, and c. the good, 97
Lord doth c., 231
nor c. you because, 50
shall yet c. Jerusalem, 87
choosest
c. the tongue, 366
man whom Thou c., 179
chooseth
abomination is he that c., 198
chosen
but I have c. you, 49

c. Jacob unto Himself, 50
c. Me to put My name, 211
c. than great riches, 318
c. the foolish things, 137
c. the weak things, 403
c. thee in the furnace, 155
c. vessel unto me, 117
c. you the Lord, 49
c. you twelve, 31
fast that I have c., 132
few are c., 238
God hath c. thee, 50
have c. Jerusalem, 211
Lord hath c. Zion, 211
servant; I have c., 155
they with Him are c., 128
which ye have c., 129
witnesses c. before of, 298
ye have not c. me, 49

Christ
ambassadors for C., 254
as C. also hath loved, 27
as C. loved the church, 240
as ye have received C., 27
being free, is C.'s, 142
believe on C., 29
belong to C., 54
blood of C., 51
blood of C. cleanseth, 35
body is of C., 20
bring us unto C., 57
by faith in C., 113
C. also received, 134
C. being raised, 51
C. came into the world, 215
C. died for our sins, 76
C. died for the ungodly, 75
C. died for us, 75
C. hath made us free, 143
C. hath redeemed, 56
C. is all, 215
C. is dead in vain, 56
C. is God's, 30
C. is the head of the, 246
C. is the Son of God, 29
C. liveth in me, 215
C. maketh thee whole, 182
C. pleased not Himself, 11
C. sent me not to, 117
C. sitteth on the right, 148
C. the same yesterday, 44
C. the Saviour of the, 28
C. the Son of the living,
   218
C. to come out of her, 122
C. we shall be saved, 340
C. who is our life, 323
C.'s sake hath forgiven, 140
calling of God in C., 60
church subject unto C., 246
confess that C. is Lord, 5
counted loss for C., 217
crucified with C., 76
dead in C. shall, 51

denieth that Jesus is C., 234
do all things through C., 2
even as C. forgave, 141
fools for C.'s sake, 254
good soldier of C., 282
gospel of C., 171
grace that is in C., 141
head of C. is God, 21
head of every man is C., 21
hope in C., 323
if any man be in C., 37
if C. be not raised, 126
in C. I have begotten, 172
in C. neither circumcision,
   53
in C. shall all be alive, 236
in the name of Jesus C.,
   182
instructors in C., 37
is C. divided, 392
judgment seat of C., 113
judgment seat of C., 222
life is hid with C., 217
live godly in C., 168
love of C., 95
members of C., 36
name of C. happy are ye,
   282
not be the servant of C., 16
not ourselves, but C., 295
partakers of C.'s, 346
peace be with you in C., 35
preach C. crucified, 75
preach unto you, is C., 251
rejoice in C., 30
revelation of C., 172
Saviour, which is C., 218
saying, I am C., 130
sweet savour of C., 51
that Jesus is the C., 251
the man C., 164
Thou art the C., 216
to live is C., 236
truth C. is preached, 148
truth came by Jesus C., 56
will of God in C., 174
word of C., 165
ye are all one in C., 30
ye are C.'s, 30
ye are the body of C., 51
Christian
man suffer as a C., 51
persuadest me to be a C.,
   107
Christians
disciples were called C., 51
Christs
false C., 184
church
build my c., 371
c. is subject unto, 246
care of the c., 52
Christ also loved the c., 240
edifieth the c., 57

feed the c. of God, 104
head of the body, the c., 22
is the head of the c., 246
speak in the c., 52
churches
silence in the c., 52
Spirit saith unto c., 184
unto the seven c., 37
circumcise
c. the flesh, 52
c. the foreskin, 53
c. yourselves to the, 9
circumcision
c. availeth any thing, 53
c. is nothing, 53
c. is that of the heart, 53
c. nor uncircumcision, 113
c. which is outward, 15
profit is there of c., 53
we are the c., 30
cistern
out of thine own c., 6
cities
even unto strange c., 281
like c. not inhabited, 90
city
c. against c., 44
c. and Thy people, 139
c. Babylon be thrown, 168
c. become an harlot, 200
c. famine and pestilence, 93
c. had no need of, 152
c. is full of violence, 230
c. of David, 211
c. of Jericho, 77
c. of righteousness, 211
c. of the great King, 211
c. of the great king, 267
c. rejoiceth, 180
c. set on an hill, 232
c. set on an hill, 131
c. sit solitary, 86
c. that is broken, 348
c. which I have chosen, 211
come into this c., 86
comest nigh unto a c., 401
cry, O c., 102
cursed in the c., 303
defend this c., 160
destroy all the c., 61
entrance into the c., 249
evil in a c. and the, 93
face against this c., 169
faithful c., 211
feet enter into the c., 77
given you the c., 24
in the c. and blessed, 34
is this the c. that, 212
Jerusalem, the c., 211
like unto this great c., 408
make thee a desolate c., 90
perils in the c., 79
streets of the c., 300
that great c. Babylon, 83

the Lord keep the c., 348
what c. is like unto, 408
woe to the bloody c., 74
won than a strong c., 139
words upon this c., 102
clay
c. is in the potter's, 92
made me as the c., 142
potter power over the c.,
289
shall c. say to him, 20
we are the c., 73
clean
be ye c. that bear, 307
c. and to the unclean, 235
c. hands, and a pure, 189
c. in his own eyes, 350
c. thing out, 69
c. through the word, 186
canst make me c., 125
create in me a c. heart, 368
crib is c., 106
heads; I am c., 178
how can he be c., 244
ye are not all c., 31
cleanse
c. the lepers, 284
c. your hands, 307
cleansed
c. of the blood, 262
lepers are c., 179
what God hath c., 307
cleanseth
c. us from all sin, 35
clear
c. as the sun, 25
cleave
c. nought of the cursed, 175
c. to the roof, 9
c. to which is good, 27
c. unto the Lord, 128
Him shalt thou c., 9
cleaveth
c. to the roof, 382
climb
c. up to heaven, 114
cloak
let him have thy c., 146
no c. for their sin, 121
closed
eyes have they c., 200
closer
c. than a brother, 143
closet
enter into thy c., 293
closets
spoken in the ear in c., 123
cloth
menstruous c., 198
clothe
c. the heavens, 267
c. themselves with, 380
drowsiness shall c., 230
clothed

c. with humility, 194
c. with shame, 110
c. with shame, 109
naked, and ye c. me, 60
clothes
c. not be burned, 6
c. waxed not old, 162
rend your c., 261
clothing
c. be thou our ruler, 232
love to go in long c., 196
to you in sheep's c., 84
cloud
be as the morning c., 112
c. out of the sea, 287
coming in a c., 346
is as a morning c., 170
My bow in the c., 71
pillar of a c., 159
clouds
c. are the dust of His, 157
c. be full of rain, 309
c. they are without, 45
heights of the c., 20
regardeth the c., 230
shall come up as c., 325
truth unto the c., 153
wells without water, c., 45
clusters
c. are bitter, 32
coals
c. thereof c. of fire, 211
go upon hot c., 6
heap c. of fire upon, 353
coat
c. of many colours, 132
take away thy c., 146
coats
he that hath two c., 354
cock
before the c. crow, 88
immediately the c. crew, 88
cockatrice
shall come forth a c., 102
cockle
c. instead of barley, 206
cold
as c. waters to a, 266
c. and heat, 345
neither c. nor hot, 57
stand before His c., 157
would thou wert c. or, 111
colours
coat of many c., 132
come
antichrist shall c., 14
behold, I c. quickly, 346
c. again with rejoicing, 76
c. alike to all, 81
c. and let us join, 28
c. before His presence, 352
c. down unto me, 367
c. forth a rod, 252
c. from God, 101

c. in my Father's name, 21
c. not among, 166
c. now, and let us, 57
c. on me what will, 40
c. on thee as a thief, 346
c. to give peace, 278
c. to pass, 297
c. unto me now, 272
c. unto me, all ye, 39
c. unto you with a rod, 21
c. ye to the waters, 89
c. ye, buy, and eat, 89
Comforter will not c., 187
comfortless: I will c., 2
day of the Lord will c., 346
days to c., 279
Elias is c. already, 5
evil to c., 81
for the time to c., 186
him c. unto me, 9
hold fast till I c., 142
hour is c., 151
hour is not yet c., 384
how to go out or c., 193
I c. to Thee, 82
I will c. again, 346
in the world to c., 187
it will surely c., 224
kingdom of God is c., 225
know what hour I will c.,
346
Lazarus, c. forth, 323
lest a worse thing c., 357
let my cry c., 292
little children to c., 48
neither shall it c. to, 108
no man can c. to me, 29
no man can c. unto me, 173
not c. into this city, 86
not c. to destroy, 144
remember what is c., 286
repent or else I will c., 318
shall not c. nigh, 79
Son of man is c., 213
tarry till I c., 21
that day shall not c., 346
that is athirst c., 116
the door, I will c. in, 217
thirst, let him c. unto, 89
thither ye cannot c., 345
thou He that should c., 102
Thy kingdom c., 149
time is c., 102
time is c., 200
time is c. for Thee to, 249
was and is and is to c., 116
when I c. again, I will, 171
whosoever will c. after, 10
wrath to c., 114
ye cannot c., 18
comely
black, but c., 25
good and c. for one, 137
comest

which we cannot c., 152
comprehended
   darkness c. it not, 111
conceal
   publish, and c., 267
concealeth
   faithful spirit c., 143
   prudent man c., 35
conceit
   wise in his own c., 138
   wise in his own c., 61
   wise in your own c., 61
   wiser in his own c., 61
conceive
   c. in thy womb, 217
   sin did my mother c., 31
   thou shalt c., 135
   virgin shall c., 252
conceived
   c. all this people, 231
   lust hath c., 89
condemn
   c. Him that is most just, 60
   c. not and ye, 75
   c. the wicked, 72
   judges shall c., 321
   neither do I c. thee, 46
   to c. the world, 213
   wilt thou c. Me, 350
condemned
   believeth not is c., 28
   words thou shalt be c., 221
   ye shall not be c., 75
condemnest
   another, thou c. thyself, 75
condemneth
   thine own mouth c., 178
condemning
   fulfilled them in c., 253
confess
   c. also before my Father, 28
   c. me before men, 28
   c. that Jesus is Son of, 169
   c. with thy mouth, 217
   c. your faults, 62
   every tongue should c., 5
   if we c. our sins, 62
   shall c. me before men, 5
   Son of man also c., 5
confession
   c. unto the Lord, 316
   make c. unto Him, 316
confidence
   c. in an unfaithful, 30
   cast not away your c., 63
   dwell with c., 338
   quietness and in c., 125
   than put c. in man, 313
   than put c. in princes, 172
confident
   fool rageth, and is c., 118
confirm
   c. the feeble knees, 108

conformed
   c. to this world, 64
confound
   c. the language, 57
   c. the mighty, 403
   c. their language, 57
   to c. the wise, 137
confusion
   author of c., 44
   c. and every evil work, 64
   wind and c., 198
   with their own c., 110
congregation
   all the c., 66
   evil c., 276
conscience
   c. void of offence, 65
   charity of a good c., 240
   lived in all good c., 65
   mind and c. is defiled, 19
   trust we have a good c., 65
consent
   c. thou not, 58
consider
   c. and behold, 286
   c. her ways, 95
   c. not in their hearts, 74
   c. the things of old, 315
   c. the wondrous, 265
   c. the years, 122
   c. their latter end, 90
   c. your ways, 27
   latter days ye shall c., 391
   people doth not c., 21
considereth
   c. the poor, 45
consisteth
   c. not in the abundance, 248
consolation
   also of the c., 375
   received your c., 405
consume
   c. the tabernacles, 38
   drought and heat c., 80
   famine shall c., 131
consumed
   c. them as stubble, 310
   let sinners be c., 305
   prophets be c., 129
   the Lord shall be c., 23
   ye shall be c., 402
consumeth
   fire that c., 6
consuming
   as a c. fire, 92
   God is a c. fire, 151
contain
   heavens cannot c., 52
   heavens cannot c. Him, 52
   world could not c., 37
contempt
   some to everlasting c., 108
contend

c. with horses, 60
   earnestly c. for the, 127
content
   c. and dwelt, 66
   c. with such things as, 67
   c. with your wages, 399
   let us be c., 175
   therewith to be c., 12
contention
   c. shall go out, 371
   leave off c., 371
contentment
   godliness with c., 67
continual
   c. dropping in a, 263
   merry heart hath a c., 180
continually
   seek His face c., 162
continue
   c. in my word, 97
   c. unto this day, 381
   kingdom shall not c., 304
continued
   name shall be c., 130
contradiction
   without all c., 22
contrary
   c. to the law, 123
contrite
   be of a c. spirit, 176
   broken and a c. heart, 67
convenient
   c. for thee to go, 142
   c. season, 384
   feed me with food c., 404
converted
   except ye be c., 68
   repent, and be c., 68
   when thou art c., 108
converteth
   c. the sinner from the, 313
converts
   c. with righteousness, 212
cord
   c. be loosed, 96
   threefold c. is not, 68
   tongue with a c., 244
cords
   c. of vanity, 360
corn
   c. in the ear, 176
   c. shall make the young, 300
   treadeth out the c., 107
   withholdeth c., 40
corner
   done in a c., 347
   dwell in a c., 246
   head of the c., 328
   head stone of the c., 274
   stone for a c., 14
corners
   c. of the streets, 195
cornerstone

laid the c., 72

corpses
  were all dead c., 41

correct
  c. me, but with judgment, 177

correcteth
  Lord loveth He c., 46
  man whom God c., 46

correction
  c. is grievous, 23
  rod of c., 47
  weary of His c., 46
  withhold not c., 47

corrupt
  breath is c., 80
  c. tree bringeth forth, 44
  c. your seed, 192
  evil communications c., 45
  moth and rust doth c., 248
  moth nor rust doth c., 368

corrupted
  c. thy wisdom, 61

corrupters
  iron; they are all c., 373

corruptible
  obtain a c. crown, 60

corruption
  c. Thou art my father, 80
  Holy One to see c., 114
  of the flesh reap c., 243
  sown in c., 36
  up my life from c., 87

cost
  counteth the c., 285

couch
  my c. with my tears, 362

counsel
  c. of the heathen, 144
  c. of the Lord, 279
  c. of the ungodly, 58
  darkeneth c. by words, 199
  forsook the c., 7
  hear c. and receive, 7
  hearkeneth unto c., 7
  hide their c. from, 98
  if this c. be of men, 85
  is c. perished, 8
  nation void of c., 50
  spirit of c., 252
  that take c. but not, 23
  where no c. is, 177
  wise c. make war, 400

counsellor
  be called Wonderful, C., 218
  who hath been His c., 228

counsellors
  multitude of c., 7
  to the c. of peace, 277

counsels
  c. of old, 128
  c. of the wicked, 7
  fall by their own c., 109

multitude of thy c., 8

count
  c. all my steps, 153
  c. him not as an enemy, 23
  c. not thine handmaid, 407
  c. number of the beast, 119
  c. the dust, 2

counted
  c. as sheep, 79
  c. as the small dust, 173
  c. loss for Christ, 217
  fool is c. wise, 138

countenance
  c. of his friend, 44
  c. sad, seeing, 88
  lift up His c., 34
  maketh a cheerful c., 180
  sadness of the c., 229
  show of their c., 178

counteth
  c. me for His enemy, 280
  c. the cost, 285

countries
  disperse thee in the c., 121
  midst of the c., 90
  remember Me in far c., 121

country
  honour in his own c., 318
  news from a far c., 266
  nor see his native c., 121
  save in his own c., 299
  throughout all the c., 130

courage
  be of good c., 70
  be of good c., 63
  be of good c., 108
  strong and of a good c., 108
  strong, and of good c., 63

courageous
  be strong and c., 108
  c. among the mighty, 86

course
  finished my c., 5
  turned to his c., 203

courses
  stars in their c., 18

courteous
  brethren, be c., 28

covenant
  break not Thy c., 71
  c. had been faultless, 71
  c. is with thee, 71
  c. of salt, 71
  c. of thy fathers, 1
  c. that I have made, 71
  c. with death, 17
  c. with our fathers, 50
  He saith, a new c., 71
  keep My c., 268
  mediator of the new c., 249
  mindful always of His c., 128
  mindful of His c., 71

such as keep His c., 166
  token of a c., 71
  token of the c., 52
  words of this c., 71

covenants
  c. of promise, 92

cover
  worms shall c., 80

covered
  sins are c., 140
  there is nothing c., 347

covereth
  c. the faces of judges, 205

covering
  destruction hath no c., 156
  sackcloth their c., 267

covet
  c. thy neighbor's wife, 6
  not c. thy neighbor's, 112
  thou shalt not c., 112

coveted
  c. no man's silver, 209

covetousness
  beware of c., 175
  given to c., 69
  goeth after their c., 195
  truth, hating c., 172

crackling
  c. of thorns, 229

craftiness
  cunning c., 101
  in their own c., 74

crafty
  devices of the c., 156
  tongue of the c., 366

crane
  turtle and the c., 99

create
  c. in me a clean heart, 368
  c. new heavens, 73
  peace, and c. evil, 169

created
  by Him all things c., 73
  c. He him, 244
  c. He them, 72
  c. He them, 244
  c. him for My glory, 73
  c. it not in vain, 73
  c. the waster, 93
  commanded and were c., 265
  God c. man, 244
  God c. man, 244
  God c. the heaven, 25
  hath not one God c., 38
  man c. for the woman, 243
  work which God c., 335

Creator
  creature more than the C., 198
  remember now thy C., 148

creature
  c. of God is good, 137
  c. that was the name, 264

he is a new c., 37
served the c. more, 198
creeping
over every c. thing, 14
crib
ass his master's c., 21
c. is clean, 106
cried
belly of hell c. I, 293
c. and I would not hear, 293
c. but there was none, 86
c. out, saying, crucify, 75
c. to Me, 86
c. unto the Lord, 292
depths have I c., 91
He c. and they would, 293
cries
c. of them which have, 413
crieth
brother's blood c., 122
c. out against me, 30
needy when he c., 292
voice of him that c., 116
wisdom c. without, 409
crimes
full of bloody c., 230
crooked
c. generation, 310
c. shall be made, 272
c. things straight, 111
that which is c., 3
which He hath made c., 3
cross
bear His c., 39
bearing His c., 3
come down from the c., 251
enemies of c. of Christ, 168
glory, save in the c., 36
take up his c., 10
take up the c., 10
that taketh not his c., 9
crow
before the cock c., 88
crown
a c. of life, 116
c. is fallen, 328
c. of his head, 24
c. of old men, 173
c. of righteousness, 331
c. of thorns, 343
c. to her husband, 245
head is a c. of glory, 8
obtain a corruptible c., 60
receive a c. of glory, 331
stones of a c., 155
crowned
c. him with glory, 244
crownedst
c. him with glory, 245
crucified
c. with Christ, 76
preach Christ c., 75

would not have c., 76
crucify
saying, c. Him, c., 75
take ye Him, and c., 256
cruel
c. and have no mercy, 64
c. troubleth his own, 76
jealousy is c., 211
wicked are c., 76
wrath is c., 12
crumbs
dogs eat of the c., 354
cry
but behold a c., 96
c. and the Lord heareth, 292
c. at all unto Me, 408
c. come unto Thee, 292
c. did enter, 291
c. in Mine ears, 139
c. in the daytime, 91
c. is come unto Me, 154
c. not when He bindeth, 3
c. O city, 102
c. of the afflicted, 292
c. of the humble, 292
c. of the poor, 45
c. unto the gods, 129
c. unto the Lord, 87
ears open unto their c., 160
He shall c. yea roar, 157
hear their c., 408
how long shall I c., 201
I c. aloud, 91
I c. unto Thee, 91
not hear their c., 132
shall c. himself, but, 45
singing, and c. aloud, 47
sound of the c. of, 93
stone shall c., 4
they c. unto the Lord, 87
though they c. unto Me, 313
crying
neither sorrow, nor c., 82
soul spare for his c., 47
voice of one crying, 219
voice of one c. in the, 70
cubit
can add one c., 261
cunning
c. craftiness, 101
forget her c., 1
hands of a c. workman, 25
cup
c. is the new testament, 58
c. of water, 54
c. pass from me, 374
c. runneth over, 2
c. which my Father, 3
cannot drink the c. of, 10
drink of the c., 305
Lord, and the c. of devils, 10

curdled
c. me like cheese, 72
cured
shalt not be c., 102
curse
bless them that c., 77
bless, and c. not, 77
blessing and a c., 34
but they c. inwardly, 195
c. among her people, 6
c. God, and die, 44
c. him that c. thee, 159
c. if ye will not, 34
c. of the Lord is, 34
c. the deaf, 179
c. Thee to Thy face, 43
c. ye bitterly, 104
hear thy servant c., 74
I will c. your blessings, 77
let him c., 3
people shall c., 40
redeemed us from the c., 56
shall have many a c., 45
shall I c., 77
unto him, c. David, 144
upon me be thy c., 32
cursed
c. above all cattle, 363
c. be every one, 33
c. be he that doeth, 104
c. be he that keepeth, 95
c. be he that lieth, 202
c. be he that lieth, 363
c. be he that lieth, 202
c. be he that maketh, 35
c. be he that removeth, 299
c. be he that taketh, 18
c. be that trusteth, 314
c. be the day, 31
c. be the deceiver, 84
c. be the man, 71
c. be the man, 77
c. is he that curseth, 50
c. shalt thou be, 303
c. thing to thine hand, 175
hath not c., 77
curses
c. that are written, 197
curseth
c. his father, 275
cursed is he that c., 50
that c. thee, 33
whosoever c. his God, 33
cursing
as he loved c., 223
blessing and c., 35
blessing and c., 235
curtains
dwelleth within c., 52
custom
c. of women, 249
c. to whom c., 133
take c. or tribute, 377

ut
c. down like the grass, 406
c. in sunder, 271
c. it off, 32
c. off in their place, 267
c. off my life, 92
every beard c. off, 262
flower, and is c., 260
foot offend thee, c., 78
in the evening it is c., 244
wicked be c. off, 406

cymbal
become a tinkling c., 107

cymbals
upon the loud c., 263

D

daily
day our d. bread, 137
exhort one another d., 108
reproacheth Thee d., 74
your d. tasks, 273

dainties
eat of their d., 360

Damascus
arise, and go into D., 256
looketh toward D., 36

damnation
escape the d. of hell, 78
resist shall receive d., 311
resurrection of d., 78

damned
believeth not shall be d., 78

damsel
d. is not dead, 236

Dan
D. even to Beersheba, 100

dance
name in the d., 78
time to d., 180
with the timbrel and d., 263

danced
ye have not d., 78

dances
timbrels and with d., 205

danger
d. of the judgment, 12

Daniel
three men, Noah, D., 93

dare
would even d. to die, 82

dark
let their way be d., 77

darkeneth
d. counsel by words, 199

darkly
see through a glass, d., 53

darkness
abide in d., 111
bed in the d., 91
d. comprehended it not,
111
d. for light, light d., 233

d. hideth not from Thee,
113
d. is past, 111
d. was upon the face, 44
d. which may be felt, 236
days of d., 81
fool walketh in d., 138
full of d., 44
in Him is no d., 149
is in d., 38
land of d., 80
light be not d., 45
light excelleth d., 137
light shineth in d., 111
light, lest d. come, 227
light, there came d., 13
lighten my d., 111
make d. light, 111
men loved d., 119
rulers of the d., 110
shall not walk in d., 29
that sit in d., 111
the d. He called night, 267
there is no d., 74
thick d. in all Egypt, 267
turn them from d., 117
turned into d., 109
walk in d., 96
walked in d. have seen, 111
walketh in d., 200
way of the wicked as d.,
271
when I sit in d., 125
works of d., 170
ye were sometimes d., 217

darts
d. of the wicked, 127

daughter
backsliding d., 23
d. came out to meet, 205
d. of Belial, 407
d. of Jerusalem, 343
d. of Zion, 343
from the d. of Zion, 212
inheritance unto his d., 204
loveth d. more than me,
131
mother against the d., 131
mother, so is her d., 185
prostitute thy d., 48

daughters
d. have done virtuously,
246
d. of Jerusalem, 25
d. of thy brethren, 210
d. to pass through fire, 197
d. unto their sons, 210
horseleach hath two d., 175
love among the d., 25
saw the d. of men, 24
teach d. wailing, 176

David
as D. thy father walked,
189

ascribed unto D., 211
Christ of the seed of D.,
323
city of D., 211
D. had done displeased,
118
D. his ten thousands, 130
D. prevailed over, 395
D. thy father's sake, 250
hand of D., 124
Nathan said to D., 4
raise unto D., 252
Saul eyed D., 211
servants as D., 242
soul of D., 143
sure mercies of D., 34
the offspring of D., 216
unto him, curse D., 144

David's
servant D. sake, 160

day
alas for the d., 221
alive this d., 50
all the d. long, 134
appointed a d., 222
before them by d., 159
call upon me in d. of, 18
called the light d., 267
children of the d., 51
choose you this d., 49
continue unto this d., 381
cursed be the d., 31
d. and hour knoweth, 345
d. and night, 345
d. cometh that shall burn,
222
d. draweth near, 200
d. He shall rise again, 75
d. his thoughts perish, 11
d. I am going, 79
d. in which the Lord, 389
d. is a d. of trouble, 90
d. is holy, 186
d. is Thine, 267
d. is this scripture, 253
d. is with the Lord as, 277
d. of adversity, 142
d. of adversity consider,
283
d. of battle, 396
d. of death than the, 4
d. of his coming, 22
d. of his transgression, 23
d. of His wrath is come,
151
d. of my calamity, 109
d. of my death, 8
d. of my trouble I will, 292
d. of salvation, 340
d. of the Lord, 102
d. of the Lord at hand, 92
d. of the Lord cometh, 222
d. of the Lord is, 221
d. of the Lord is great, 222

d. of the Lord is near, 167
d. of the Lord will come, 346
d. of the Lord's anger, 93
d. of their calamity, 303
d. of trouble, 102
d. of trouble, 161
d. of visitation, 305
d. of wrath, 404
d. of your fast, 132
d. shall come to die, 276
d. shall not come, 346
d. that God doth talk, 158
d. that I knew you, 99
d. that I rise, 276
d. that Moses sent, 141
d. the Lord hath made, 42
d. their fathers came, 120
d. thou shalt bear, 59
d. when I am in trouble, 387
d. when I visit, 197
d. wherein my mother, 31
deliver them in the d., 150
deliver us only this d., 285
desire the d. of the, 222
do they unto this d., 197
done unto this d., 128
down while it was yet d., 176
dreadful d. of the Lord, 253
Egypt unto this d., 88
esteemeth every d. alike, 43
even unto this d., 62
every d. is blasphemed, 33
fear d. and night, 78
give us this d., 137
hear you in that d., 303
hid in the d., 249
him up at the last d., 115
hope in d. of evil, 190
in d. of prosperity, 283
in the d. of judgment, 320
is born this d., 51
kept me this d., 7
killed all the d., 247
knowest not what a d., 36
known this d., 152
let the d. perish, 90
light to rule the d., 20
meditate d. and night, 332
meditate d. and night, 343
more people that d., 400
more unto the perfect d., 332
naked in that d., 86
nigh unto the Lord d., 291
night shineth as the d., 113
no d. like that, 412
no rest d. nor night, 198
not be shut by d., 183
notable d. of the Lord, 109

of decision: for the d., 220
one day above another, 43
plagues come in one d., 285
raised up the third d., 298
regardeth the d., 188
remember the sabbath d., 335
remember this d., 142
renewed d. by d., 141
rise the third d., 322
seven times in a d., 140
seventh d. He rested, 72
seventh d. is the sabbath, 335
seventh d. thou shalt rest, 335
smite thee by d., 161
Sodom in d. of judgment, 202
stand at the latter d., 124
strong this d. as, 141
sufficient unto the d., 145
than d. of one's birth, 4
the first d., 267
the seventh d., 335
third d. He shall rise, 322
this d. weak, 364
this d. will the Lord, 63
this is the d. whereof, 299
thousand years as one d., 277
trouble thee this d., 73
us, who are of the d., 27
very rainy d. and a, 263
victory that d., 176
wall night and d., 348
weep d. and night, 377
while it is d., 104
wicked for d. of evil, 72
with the wicked every d., 220
withstand in the evil d., 161
days
a work in your d., 361
add unto thy d., 59
ancient d., 161
and see good d., 119
are not my d. few, 260
ashamed seven d., 303
d. are a shadow, 260
d. are as a shadow, 235
d. are as grass, 244
d. are extinct, 80
d. are fulfilled, 102
d. are like a shadow, 88
d. are sorrows, 91
d. are swifter, 90
d. as of old, 315
d. be prolonged, 168
d. may be prolonged, 275
d. not be prolonged, 93
d. of a tree, 155
d. of darkness, 81
d. of his life, 231

d. of Methuselah, 8
d. of my life, 34
d. of My people, 155
d. of my vanity, 9
d. of old, 122
d. of our years are, 234
d. of the years, 258
d. of thy life, 76
d. of thy youth, 148
d. of thy youth, 122
d. of vengeance, 222
d. shall men seek death, 82
d. should speak, 122
d. so shall thy strength, 34
d. that I shall deal, 376
d. to come, 279
earth in those d., 360
evil in his d., 67
fear prolongeth d., 134
few d. and full, 234
find it after many d., 10
forty d. and forty nights, 136
full of d., 80
have forgotten Me d., 23
in his son's d. will I, 67
in six d. the Lord, 72
in six d. the Lord, 72
in the latter d., 386
in the latter d. ye, 391
in thy d. I will not, 250
length of d. is in, 409
length of d. understanding, 8
length of thy d., 148
let his d. be few, 305
measure of my d., 260
midst of his d., 99
midst of my d., 235
number our d., 234
pain all his d., 374
precious in those d., 399
seemed but a few d., 238
shall be for many d., 145
six d. shalt thou labour, 335
six d. thou shalt do, 335
spend d. in prosperity, 300
truth be in my d., 277
with the Lord forty d., 380
daytime
cry in the d., 91
dead
better than a d., 190
blessed are the d. which, 82
Christ is d. in vain, 56
d. and the living, 209
d. and your life is hid, 217
d. are raised, 179
d. bodies shall be for, 305
d. bury their d., 320
d. dog, 120
d. in Christ shall, 51
d. is freed from sin, 82
d. know not any thing, 235

d. man out of mind, 91
d. praise not the Lord, 81
d. to the law, 56
d. which are already d., 235
d. which he slew, 4
d. while she liveth, 201
d. yet shall he live, 29
damsel is not d., 236
dealt with the d., 34
faith without works d., 82
fell down d., 18
hell delivered up the d., 222
I praised the d., 235
if we be d. with Him, 215
king's son is d., 59
living among the d., 323
not the God of the d., 149
now he is d., 3
raise the d., 182
raise the d., 323
raised from the d., 51
raised from the d., 323
raised Him from the d., 323
raised Him from the d., 217
rose from the d., 284
saw the d. small and, 222
that liveth and was d., 323
were all d. corpses, 41
without the spirit is d., 82
without works is d., 85
deadly
    full of d. poison, 367
deaf
    curse the d., 179
    d. as My messenger, 372
    d. hear, 179
    d. to hear, 179
    ears of the d., 35
    hear, ye d., 372
    maketh dumb, or d., 72
deal
    d. gently for my sake, 59
    d. very treacherously, 205
    Lord d. kindly with, 34
    neither d. falsely, 25
dealeth
    every one d. falsely, 69
dealt
    d. very bitterly, 13
dearly
    given the d. beloved, 1
death
    abideth in d., 39
    adulterer put to d., 6
    as the shadow of d., 74
    be put to d., 41
    beast be put to d., 363
    belong the issues from d., 87
    between me and d., 78
    bitterness of d., 255
    body of this d., 13
    carnally minded is d., 19

covenant with d., 17
curseth be put to d., 275
d. and hell delivered up, 222
D. and Hell followed, 15
d. and hell were cast, 82
d. cannot celebrate, 81
d. for his own sin, 178
d. is swallowed up in, 82
d. mourning and famine, 285
d. of His saints, 247
d. of the righteous, 79
d. of the testator, 82
d. part thee and me, 143
d. shall feed, 80
d. shall flee from them, 82
d. there is no remembrance, 80
d. they were not divided, 80
d. where is thy sting, 82
d. with the sword, 80
day of d. than the, 4
day of my d., 8
delivereth from d., 81
doors of shadow of d., 17
enemy destroyed is d., 82
faithful unto d., 116
gates of d., 17
good, and d. and evil, 26
guide even unto d., 116
guilty of d., 41
hate me love d., 409
home there is as d., 81
in d. or life, 242
killeth be put to d., 41
life and d. blessing, 235
love is strong as d., 239
messengers of d., 12
murderer put to d., 222
no pleasure in the d., 81
nor shadow of d., 74
not taste of d. till, 81
of the shadow of d., 380
pleasure in the d. of, 81
pursueth it to his own d., 74
put to d., 335
put to d., 302
put to d., 41
put to d., 188
save a soul from d., 313
second d. hath no power, 82
shadow of d., 63
shadow of d., 339
shadow of d., 80
shall be no more d., 82
shall men seek d., 82
shall never see d., 82
shall not see d., 80
sickness is not unto d., 151
sin bringeth forth d., 82

sleep of d., 18
slew at his d., 4
sorrowful, even unto d., 13
sting of d. is sin, 82
such as are for d. to d., 305
surely be put to d., 41
surely put me to d., 8
swallow up d., 81
this is the second d., 82
vexed unto d., 263
wages of sin is d., 115
way of d., 236
ways of d., 285
worthy of d., 206
worthy of d., 41
deaths
    in d. oft, 282
debate
    d. thy cause with, 16
debtor
    d. both to the Greeks, 185
debtors
    forgive our d., 140
debts
    forgive us our d., 140
decayeth
    building d., 39
deceit
    balances of d., 40
    d. is in the heart, 98
    d. shall not dwell, 98
    houses full of d., 74
    philosophy and vain d., 84
    wicked are d., 7
deceitful
    deliver me from the d., 160
    favour is d., 25
    from a d. tongue, 362
    heart is d., 118
    kisses of enemy are d., 74
    tongue is d., 233
deceitfully
    sharp razor, working d., 67
    vanity, nor sworn d., 186
    work of the Lord d., 104
deceitfulness
    d. of riches, 171
deceive
    children, let no man d., 334
    d. not with thy lips, 189
    d. not yourselves, 349
    d. you with vain words, 84
    diviners d. you, 84
    heed that no man d., 130
    let no man d., 62
    let no man d., 346
    lie in wait to d., 101
    no sin, we d. ourselves, 206
    whom thou trustest d., 33
deceived
    be not d., 126
    heart be not d., 129
    heed that ye be not d., 84
    let not him that is d., 314

of thine heart hath d., 61
terribleness hath d., 61
were all nations d., 84
deceiver
cursed be the d., 84
deceiveth
nothing, he d. himself, 62
decently
all things be done d., 27
decision
valley of d., 220
deckest
d. thee with ornaments, 25
declare
answer you, I will d., 40
d. His doings, 116
d. his generation, 287
d. His generation, 185
d. His glory, 116
d. His righteousness, 151
d. if thou knowest, 17
d. it in the isles, 116
d. My glory among, 116
d. the works of the Lord, 94
d. their sin, 353
d. unto us the riddle, 30
d. what he seeth, 397
Him d. I unto you, 200
if I d. it unto, 8
seen and heard d. we, 186
declared
be d. in the grave, 235
decline
d. to her ways, 6
decrease
but I must d., 258
decree
d. unrighteous d.s, 173
princes d. justice, 259
deed
d. dwell with men, 163
love in d. and in truth, 85
no such d. done, 88
ye do in word or d., 85
deeds
according to their d., 305
d. may be made manifest, 85
d. were evil, 119
make known his d., 116
partaker of his evil d., 69
without d. of the law, 85
deep
d. to boil, 156
face of the d., 44
well is d., 264
when d. sleep falleth, 103
wonders in the d., 272
defence
d. of the gospel, 172
fathers, hear ye my d., 224
God is my d., 160
He is my d., 63

Lord is our d., 348
defend
d. the poor, 223
d. this city, 160
defer
d. not to pay, 298
d. not, for Thine own, 139
deferred
hope d., 190
defied
Lord hath not d., 77
defile
d. not the land, 73
d. the temple of God, 337
d. yourselves with their, 167
within, and d. the man, 357
defiled
and conscience is d., 19
d. by them, 367
unto them that are d., 19
defileth
d. not a man, 307
d. the whole body, 367
every one that d. it, 335
into the mouth d. a man, 137
out of mouth d., 137
defraud
d. not, 56
defy
d. the armies, 20
how shall I d., 77
degree
men of high d., 44
men of low d., 44
degrees
forward ten d., 272
return backward ten d., 272
delicacies
abundance of her d., 70
delicately
they that did feed d., 192
delight
commandments are my d., 54
d. himself with God, 33
d. in burnt offerings, 269
d. is in the law, 332
d. to do honour, 61
just weight is His d., 40
law is my d., 55
Lord d. in us, 64
people that d. in war, 401
scorners d. in their, 137
soul d., 368
upright is His d., 45
delighted
d. not in blessing, 223
delighteth
d. to honour, 188
He d. in his way, 26
He d. in mercy, 139
deliver

am with thee to d., 108
bear, He will d., 63
cannot profit nor d., 415
continually, He will d., 63
d. but their own souls, 93
d. every man his soul, 114
d. him in time of trouble, 45
d. his soul, 114
d. it into the hand, 399
d. me because of mine, 87
d. me from every evil, 338
d. me from mine enemies, 110
d. me from the body, 13
d. me from the deceitful, 160
d. me from the oppression, 273
d. me from the workers, 230
d. me in Thy righteousness, 87
d. me not over, 280
d. me out of, 386
d. me, I pray, 132
d. my soul, 362
d. out of My hand, 156
d. the godly out of, 87
d. the needy, 292
d. the slayer, 209
d. thee into mine hand, 63
d. thee into the hand, 86
d. them in the day, 150
d. them into, 108
d. them into the hand, 1
d. them into thine hand, 162
d. thine enemy, 162
d. us from evil, 119
d. us from the burning, 79
d. us from the heathen, 87
d. us only, 285
d. us out, 352
d. you no more, 120
d. you out of my hands, 33
d. you out of the hand, 86
I will d. thee, 18
let them d. you, 129
not d. him in the day, 23
of foot shall not d., 114
shall the mighty d., 63
upright shall d., 87
will surely d. thee, 161
deliverance
preach d., 87
delivered
all things are d., 5
all things are d. unto, 209
d. by much strength, 124
d. for our offences, 323
d. Him up unto thee, 4
d. me from all my fears, 87
d. me out of the paw, 63

d. me to the ungodly, 7
d. of the child, 31
d. out of the mouth, 87
d. Sisera into, 389
d. the land, 64
d. them into thine hand, 109
d. them into thine hand, 395
d. you out, 86
envy they had d., 112
gods of the nations d., 17
Lord d. me into, 174
shall be d., 87
shall not be d., 114
that d. me unto thee, 178
thou hast d. thy soul, 295

deliverer
fortress, and my d., 160
help and my d., 162
the D., 218
tower, and my d., 161

deliverest
d. the poor from, 152

delivereth
d. and rescueth, 87
d. from death, 81
d. him out of them all, 387
d. the poor, 87
true witness d. souls, 189

den
d. of thieves, 52

denied
d. before the angels, 167

denieth
d. the Father and the, 14
liar but he that d., 234
that d. me before men, 167
whosoever d. the Son, 88

deny
d. before my Father, 88
d. me thrice, 88
He cannot d. Himself, 29
He will also d. us, 65
if we d. Him, 65
in works they d. Him, 85
let him d. himself, 10
whosoever shall d. me, 88
yet will I not d., 43

depart
d. away from him, 154
d. from evil, 118
d. from evil, 118
d. from evil, 26
d. from evil, 134
d. from Judah, 231
d. from me, 62
d. from me, all ye, 58
d. out of thy mouth, 268
d. to the right, 48
evil shall not d., 169
foolishness d., 138
kindness shall not d., 154
let him d., 167

mountains shall d., 154
old, he will not d., 47
return and d., 132
sword shall never d., 77
unbelieving d., 167

departed
beauty is d., 212
glory d. from Israel, 192
God is d., 1
Lord d. from Saul, 313
Lord is d., 18

departeth
d. from evil, 118
whose heart d., 314

departing
after my d. shall, 372

depths
out of the d., 91

derision
have me in d., 8

descending
d. like a dove, 187
d. upon the Son of man, 151
I saw the Spirit d., 187

desert
d. like the garden, 210
d. shall rejoice, 321
render to them their d., 223
straight in the d., 252

deserts
according to their d., 223

deserve
than our iniquities d., 250

desire
all things thou canst d., 409
d. accomplished, 4
d. is toward me, 57
d. is, that the Almighty, 4
d. not the night, 267
d. of the righteous, 122
d. of the wicked, 11
d. shall be to thy husband, 20
d. to be first, 11
d. to return, 121
d. when ye pray, 126
though I d. to glory, 36
upon earth that I d., 18
wandering of the d., 89
when the d. cometh, 190
woe unto you that d., 222

desired
d. it for His habitation, 211
d. mercy and not, 334
more to be d., 55
soul have I d., 94

desires
d. of the wicked, 292

desireth
His soul d., 156
straightway d. new, 207
what thy soul d., 143

desirous

d. of vain glory, 12

desolate
altars shall be d., 93
children of the d., 48
countries that are d., 90
d. for ever, 14
d. in the streets, 192
I will make thee d., 90
land that was d., 321
make thee a d. city, 90
shall be d. in the midst, 90

desolation
abomination of d., 93
d. thereof is nigh, 109
d. which shall come, 305

desolations
behold our d., 293

despair
perplexed, but not in d., 7

despise
d. not prophesyings, 299
d. not the chastening, 46
d. not thou the, 3
d. not thy mother, 8
d. the other, 242
do not d. a thief, 73
fools d. wisdom, 105
he will d. the wisdom, 7
honoured her d. her, 69
let no man d., 417
they that d. Me, 311
Thou wilt not d., 67
upon all those that d., 338

despised
and d. among men, 305
children d. me, 343
d. and rejected, 252
d. and we esteemed not, 192
d. of the people, 274
d. the commandment, 6
daughter of Zion hath d., 343
for we are d., 285
heart shall be d., 88
I am small and d., 128
wisdom is d., 8

despiseth
d. his neighbour, 257
d. his own soul, 98
d. His ways shall, 55
d. me d. Him that sent, 97
d. not His prisoners, 288
d. not man but God, 100
d. the word, 269
d. you d. me, 97
fool d., 48
foolish man d., 48
that d. his neighbour, 181

despitefully
d. use you, 59

destitute
d. of wisdom, 136
leave not my soul d., 190

time to d., 25
to d. is gain, 236
to morrow we shall d., 42
which d. in the Lord, 82
why shouldest thou d., 235
wicked shall d. in his, 295
wisdom shall d., 257
wise men d., 260
worthy to d., 104
would even dare to d., 82

died
cattle of Egypt d., 284
Christ d. for our sins, 76
Christ d. for the ungodly, 75
d. in a good old, 79
d. in a good old age, 80
d. unto sin once, 75
He d. for all, 76
in that He d., 75
why d. I not, 90
would God I had d., 175
would God we had d., 90
yet sinners, Christ d., 336

diest
where thou d., 79

dieth
d. he shall carry, 112
d. no more, 51
death of him that d., 81
how d. the wise man, 81
man d. and wasteth, 80
no man d. to himself, 82
worm d. not, 184

difference
no d. between the Jew, 113
teach My people the d., 53

differences
d. of administrations, 100

differeth
one star d., 183

dig
though they d. into hell, 114

diggeth
d. a pit shall fall, 118
whoso d. a pit, 343

dignity
excellency of d., 44

diligent
d. in his business, 2
d. maketh rich, 230

diligently
let it be d. done, 163
teach them d., 55

dim
gold become d., 13

diminish
d. ought from it, 343
nor d. from, 55

dinner
better is d. of herbs, 238

direct
Lord d. his steps, 26

man to d. his steps, 314

dirt
cast up mire and d., 406

disappointeth
He d. the devices, 156

discern
d. between good and bad, 96
d. between the righteous, 169
d. the face of the sky, 402
d. the signs of the, 97
hypocrites, ye can d., 97
not d. this time, 402

discerneth
wise man's heart d., 97

disciple
cannot be my d., 95
d. is not above his, 97
enough for the d., 11

disciples
d. called Christians, 51
know that ye are my d., 51
then are ye my d., 97

discord
soweth d. among brethren, 17

discouraged
anger, lest they be d., 47
fail nor be d., 223
neither be d., 107

discover
d. not a secret, 30

discretion
d. shall preserve, 378
fair woman without d., 24
heavens by His d., 73

disdained
fathers I would have d., 8

disease
d. he sought not, 136

disfigure
they d. their faces, 195

disgrace
d. the throne, 151

dish
man wipeth a d., 92

dismayed
afraid nor d., 108
be not d., 190
d. at their looks, 133
d. by reason, 108
dread not, nor be d., 63
heathen are d., 19
neither be d., 108
neither be thou d., 132
not d. at the signs, 19

disobedience
children of d., 100
one man's d., 140

disobedient
for the lawless and d., 229

disorderly
brother that walketh d., 58

disperse
d. thee in the countries, 121

displeased
David d. the Lord, 118

displeasure
do them a d., 205
hot d., 46

disposing
d. thereof is of the, 43

disputations
doubtful d., 68

disputings
without murmuring and d., 3

disquieted
why hast thou d. me, 367

dissimulation
love be without d., 239

dissolved
whole Palestina, art d., 102

distil
d. as the dew, 106
d. as the dew, 101

distress
d. I cried unto the Lord, 292
in my d. I called, 291
out of their d., 87
tribulation, or d., 95
when ye are in d., 272

distributeth
d. sorrows in His anger, 304

ditch
both fall into the d., 35
whore is a deep d., 301

divers
bag d. weights, 39
d. measures, 40
d. weights and, 40

diversities
d. of gifts, 2

divide
d. the living child, 222
d. the spoil, 353
d. the spoil, 193
d. thou it by lot, 210
nor thine, but d. it, 350

divided
d. against himself, 341
d. against itself, 173
d. against itself, 372
d. the sea, 148
father d. against the, 131
is Christ d., 392
were not d., 80

divideth
d. his sheep, 49

diviners
d. nor to your dreamers, 8
prophets and your d., 84

division
nay; but rather d., 278

divorced
  marry her that is d., 6
do
  and d. not the things, 85
  as she hath done, d., 311
  courage, and d. it, 108
  d. all that is in, 108
  d. all things through, 2
  d. all without murmurings, 3
  d. and thou shalt live, 239
  d. as I have done, 27
  d. it for thee, 143
  d. it with thy might, 106
  d. not thou this folly, 202
  d. so to him as he hath, 326
  d. that I would not, 33
  d. that which is right, 26
  d. them, that ye, 55
  d. to him as, 162
  d. to me according, 2
  d. to you, d. ye also to, 27
  d. unto him, as, 279
  d. unto thee, 174
  d. unto them, 327
  d. unto us, 174
  d. what seemeth good, 84
  d. what seemeth Him good, 2
  d. with them what seemeth, 61
  d. ye even so to them, 27
  doest, d. quickly, 31
  fear what man shall d., 64
  go, and d. thou likewise, 171
  God d. so and more, 123
  know not what they d., 140
  let Him d. to me, 387
  Lord d. so to me, 143
  Lord, and d. good, 26
  men should d. to you, 27
  my name, I will d. it, 214
  no more I that d. it, 321
  no more I that d. it, 33
  not d. this, 107
  observe to d. it, 55
  shall He not d. it, 128
  speaketh, that I must d., 268
  spoken we will d., 268
  that will I d. for, 111
  they say, and d. not, 196
  what thou oughtest to d., 262
  will I d. for you, 174
  will ye d. in the day of, 305
  ye d. d. it heartily, 106
doctrine
  become sound d., 101
  d. is not mine, 101
  d. shall drop, 101
  every wind of d., 101
  longsuffering and d., 277

teaching for d., 184
to exhortation, to d., 101
doer
  rewardeth the proud d., 128
doers
  d. of the law, 85
  d. of the word, 85
  hand of the d., 399
doest
  that thou d. do quickly, 31
doeth
  desireth, that He d., 156
  none that d. good, 69
  sayings of mine, and d., 84
  sayings of mine, and d., 100
  that heareth, and d. not, 8
  whatsoever God d., 279
  when God d. this, 79
  wherefore d. the Lord, 264
dog
  am I a d., 66
  am I a d.'s head, 208
  as a d. returneth to his, 138
  d. is turned to his own, 23
  dead d., 120
  living d. is better, 190
  not a d. move his tongue, 159
  price of a d., 45
  servant a d., 44
dogs
  cast it to d., 354
  d. eat of the crumbs, 354
  d. licked the blood, 41
  d. of my flock, 8
  d. shall eat Jezebel, 41
  d. shall eat Jezebel, 353
  holy unto the d., 393
  without are d. and, 83
doing
  suffer for well d., 3
  this is the Lord's d., 373
doings
  d. among the people, 116
  evil of your d., 316
  from your evil d., 119
  known by his d., 44
  their own d. nor, 372
dominion
  d. over the fish, 14
  glory and d. forever, 157
  glory and d. forever, 216
  sin shall not have d., 173
done
  all that she hath d., 17
  as I have d., 222
  as thou hast d., 327
  as Thou hast d. unto, 327
  believed, so be it d., 125
  d. according to the law, 55
  d. excellent things, 364
  d. unto his brother, 279

d. very foolishly, 67
d. wonderful things, 291
daughters have d., 246
do as I have d., 27
hast d. right, 67
have d. perversely, 62
have d. wickedly, 67
how I have d. it, 145
it shall be d. unto, 327
no such deed d., 88
not d. in a corner, 347
not have d. it, 7
seen what I have d., 254
sheep, what have they d., 320
spake, and it was d., 72
Thy will be d., 149
to him as he hath d., 326
what hath he d., 206
what have I d., 205
what I have d., 5
what shall be d., 188
wherefore hast thou d., 144
door
  before thee an open d., 273
  d. of my lips, 309
  entereth in by the d., 232
  I am the d., 218
  sin lieth at the d., 123
  standeth before the d., 200
  voice, and open the d., 217
doorkeeper
  rather be a d., 193
doors
  d. of my house, 309
  d. of shadow of death, 17
  d. to the traveller, 191
  keep the d. of thy mouth, 30
double
  d. heart do they speak, 98
  d. minded man is, 203
  d. portion of thy spirit, 185
  d. unto her d. her works, 120
doubt
  no d. but ye are the, 257
  wherefore didst thou d., 102
doubtful
  d. disputations, 68
doubting
  without wrath and d., 294
dove
  descending like a d., 187
  from heaven like a d., 187
  wings, like a d., 113
doves
  harmless as d., 363
  harmless as d., 79
  sore like d., 13
down
  bring d. like lambs, 93
  bring them d., 16

but I will throw d., 145
cast d. his altar, 129
cast me d., 369
come d. from the cross, 251
d. but not destroyed, 7
d. to the grave, 192
d. to the grave, 156
d. to the grave, 80
evening it is cut d., 244
gods are come d., 255
going d. of the same, 290
I will bring thee d., 114
let us go d., 57
maketh me to lie d., 54
man shall be brought d.,
   192
putteth d. one, 373
sat d. and wept, 364
those that be bowed d., 162
to cast d., 156
when thou liest d., 55
will I bring thee d., 296
will I bring them d., 114
dragons
brother to d., 91
dwellingplace for d., 86
draw
d. out Thine anger, 150
d. thy sword, 192
drawers
d. of water, 303
draweth
d. nigh unto the grave, 8
day d. near, 200
dread
d. make me afraid, 132
d. not, neither, 108
d. not, nor be dismayed, 63
let Him be your d., 133
dreadful
d. day of the Lord, 253
dream
let him tell a d., 103
old men shall d., 103
old men shall d. dreams,
   417
prophet that hath a d., 103
show me the d., 103
dreamer
d. of dreams, 129
this d. cometh, 256
dreamers
diviners, nor to your d., 8
dreameth
hungry man d., 96
thirsty man d., 96
dreams
dreamer of d., 129
hated him for his d., 103
old men shall dream d., 103
old men shall dream d., 417
prophets, nor by d., 1
scarest me with d., 103
drieth

broken spirit d., 89
drink
and ye gave me d., 60
and ye gave me no d., 76
camels d. also, 224
cannot d. the cup of the, 10
come unto me, and d., 89
d. and enjoy the, 137
d. and I will give, 224
d. but ye are not, 106
d. His blood, 58
d. in my name, 54
d. it, in remembrance, 58
d. of the water, 382
d. of the wrath, 150
d. the blood, 297
d. the sweet, 42
d. thy wine, 137
d. water by measure, 131
d. water in this place, 66
d. waters out of thine, 6
d. wine with a song, 364
eat, and to d., 77
give him water to d., 110
give strong d., 237
given them blood to d., 247
giveth his neighbour d., 103
if he thirst give him d., 140
let him d. and forget, 91
let us eat and d., 42
man should eat and d., 286
may follow strong d., 103
not d. wine of them, 96
not meat and d., 187
not to d. of the cup, 305
shall I not d. it, 3
strong d. is raging, 237
vinegar to d., 76
vineyards, but not d., 144
what ye shall d., 248
wine nor strong d., 90
drinketh
d. but he awaketh, 96
d. my blood, 115
d. my blood, 214
d. of this water, 115
d. up my spirit, 13
d. up scorning, 350
drive
d. out from before, 64
drop
d. as an honeycomb, 6
d. as the rain, 101
d. of a bucket, 173
dropping
continual d. in a, 263
drops
begotten the d. of dew, 309
dross
silver is become d., 201
take away the d., 393
drought
d. and heat consume, 80

drown
neither can floods d., 239
drowsiness
d. shall clothe, 230
drunk
arrows d. with blood, 326
d. neither wine nor, 90
d. of the wine of wrath, 70
d. old wine, 207
d. with their blood, 41
not d. with wine, 103
drunkard
d. and the glutton, 103
drunken
d. but not with wine, 103
d. man staggereth, 103
d. with wormwood, 32
have assuredly d., 305
long wilt thou be d., 4
they that be d. are d., 168
dry
better is a d. morsel, 352
d. bones, hear the word,
   322
d. land springs, 403
walked upon d. land, 113
walketh through d., 119
womb and d. breasts, 77
due
glory d. unto His name,
   174
glory d. unto His name,
   290
good to whom it is d., 174
slide in d. time, 276
spoken in d. season, 7
dull
d. of hearing, 200
dumb
d. before His shearer, 249
d. to speak, 179
maketh the d., 72
to the d. stone, Arise, 197
tongue of the d., 181
dung
d. upon the face, 39
d. upon your faces, 192
flesh as the d., 325
dungeon
life in the d., 92
out of the low d., 92
dunghill
beggar from the d., 86
needy out of the d., 59
dunghills
in scarlet embrace d., 192
dust
alike in the d., 80
all are of the d., 112
all turn to d., 112
clouds are the d. of His,
   157
d. of Jacob, 2
d. of the balance, 173

d. of the earth, 2
d. of the earth, 47
d. of the land, 284
d. shalt thou eat, 76
d. thou art, 36
dwell in d., 190
formed man of the d., 72
hide thee in the d., 113
lick the d., 192
lick the d., 192
number the d., 2
out of the d., 86
out of the d., 156
poor out of the d., 59
poured out as d., 325
remembereth we are d., 59
repent in d., 316
return to their d., 14
sleep in the d. of, 108
small as the d., 14
unto d. shalt thou, 36

duty
whole d. of man, 103

dwell
but ye shall not d. in, 96
d. in a corner, 246
d. in an house of cedar, 52
d. in dust, 190
d. in house of the Lord, 34
d. in safety, 337
d. in the land, 339
d. in the tents, 193
d. in the wilderness, 246
d. in their place, 50
d. together in unity, 38
d. with confidence, 338
d. with the lamb, 14
deceit shall not d., 98
He will d. with them, 163
here will I d., 211
house to d. in, 52
I may d. among them, 52
I will d. in the midst, 159
they that d. therein, 105
will God d. with men, 163
word of Christ d., 165

dwellest
d. in the midst of, 58

dwelleth
commandments d. in Him, 271
d. in love d. in God, 240
d. no good thing, 41
d. not in temples, 52
drinketh my blood, d., 214
God d. in him and he in, 169
God d. in us, 240
Him d. all the fulness, 101
Lord d. in Zion, 212
sin that d., 321
sin that d., 33
Spirit of God d. in, 187

dwelling

d. place of the wicked, 109
heaven Thy d. place, 138

dwellingplace
d. for dragons, 86

dwellings
more than all the d., 211

dwelt
d. in silence, 18
d. on the other side, 66
flesh, and d. among us, 213

E

eagle
fly as the e., 367
fly away as an e., 112
high as the e., 114
way of an e., 263

eagles
e. be gathered, 42
swifter than e., 70
swifter than the e., 367
with wings as e., 29

ear
because He inclined His e., 292
blade, then the e., 176
e. filled with hearing, 11
e. now be attentive, 291
e. of the wise, 227
e. to your reasons, 276
e. trieth words, 388
full corn in the e., 176
give e. o ye heavens, 366
give e. O ye princes, 363
give ye e., 295
he that hath an e., 184
He that planted the e., 158
hide not Thine e., 293
incline Thine e., 87
incline thine e., 177
incline Thine e., 19
incline Thine e., 293
man have an e. let him, 300
nor e. heard, 35
nor inclined their e., 183
spoken in the e., 123

early
and as the e. dew it, 170
cloud, and as the e. dew, 112
return and depart e., 132
rise up e., 103
seek me e., 409
will I seek Thee e., 94

earnestly
e. contend for the faith, 127

ears
cry did enter into His e., 291
cry in Mine e., 139
e. are dull, 200
e. but they hear not, 198

e. hear ye not, 373
e. of a fool, 7
e. of every one, 380
e. of the deaf, 35
e. of the Lord, 60
e. shall tingle, 324
fulfilled in your e., 253
hearing of his e., 123
His e. are open, 160
His e. are open unto, 161
openeth the e. of men, 103
opening the e., 167
sheep in mine e., 83
that hath e. to hear, 208
the e. of the Lord, 413
uncircumcised in e., 167
up into Mine e., 17
who hath e. to hear, 184
whoso stoppeth his e., 45

earth
Abominations of the E., 88
and in the e. is Thine, 183
and that are in e., 73
beasts of the e., 305
before Him, all the e., 133
between Me and the e., 71
bind on e. shall be, 289
blood upon the e., 304
breadth of the e., 17
called the dry land e., 104
cast out into the e., 275
come to give peace on e., 278
consumed out of the e., 30?
cut off from the e., 406
days upon e., 260
dust of the e., 108
dust of the e., 2
dust of the e., 47
dust of the e., 14
dust of the e., 2
e. abideth for ever, 105
e. also is Thine, 183
e. beneath, 164
e. e. e. hear the word, 91
e. full of the goodness, 105
e. given to the wicked, 205
e. hath He given, 183
e. is full of His, 151
e. is full of Thy riches, 265
e. is Mine, 104
e. is My footstool, 158
e. is My footstool, 52
e. is the Lord's, 105
e. is the Lord's, 265
e. it is His footstool, 267
e. keep silence before, 163
e. make a loud noise, 42
e. shall be devoured, 93
e. shall be filled, 151
e. shall be full, 128
e. shall pass away, 50
e. that is not filled, 81
e. was of one language, 39

e. was without form, 44
e. were passed away, 183
e. with her bars, 87
empty themselves upon e.,
  309
end of the e., 364
ends of the e., 309
ends of the e., 68
ends of the e., 220
exalted in the e., 151
face of the e., 104
face of the e., 131
fall to the e., 337
families of the e., 33
families of the e., 131
father upon the e., 149
fill heaven and e., 113
flood to destroy the e., 71
flowers appear on the e.,
  345
forsaken the e., 121
foundations of the e., 20
giants in the e., 360
hangeth the e. upon, 72
harvest of the e. is, 249
He hath made the e., 73
hear, O e. the words, 366
heaven and e. praise, 290
heaven and e. to pass, 56
heaven and the e., 25
heaven or in e., 152
heaven, and thou upon e.,
  193
high above all the e., 120
high above the e., 154
house upon the e., 8
in e. beneath, 158
inhabitant of the e., 91
inhabitants of the e., 157
inhabiters of the e., 342
inherit the e., 124
inherit the e., 194
is taken from the e., 185
joy of the whole e., 211
joy of the whole e., 212
Judge of all the e., 154
judges of the e., 172
judgment in the e., 223
judgments in all the e., 158
just man on e., 279
King of all the e., 290
kingdoms of the e., 87
kingdoms of the e., 363
kings of the e., 404
kings of the e., 377
latter day upon the e., 124
let the e. be glad, 42
let the e. hear, 295
let the e. rejoice, 156
like Me in all the e., 163
like worms of the e., 192
Lord of heaven and e., 52
made heaven and e., 19
made heaven and e., 72

made heaven and e., 72
made heaven, and e., 73
made man on the e., 72
made the e. by His, 73
meek of the e., 95
meek shall inherit the e.,
  249
men on the e., 163
nations of the e., 49
new e. and the former, 73
none like him in the e., 257
none upon e. I desire, 18
of the kings of the e., 218
on e. peace, good will, 38
or on e. beneath, 164
over all the e., 14
people of the e., 131
people of the e., 154
perish from the e., 130
perished out of the e., 167
pillars of the e., 104
power on e. to forgive, 140
praise in the e., 212
profit of the e., 69
rain was upon the e., 136
replenish the e., 20
replenish the e., 47
returneth to his e., 11
salt of the e., 44
saw a new e., 183
send peace on e., 401
sing all the e., 363
sky and of the e., 402
speak to the e., 156
stranger in the e., 226
swear not by the e., 209
that bear witness in e., 382
things on the e., 12
thou be in the e., 76
throughout the whole e.,
  158
Thy will be done in e., 149
treasures upon e., 248
vessels of e., 100
way of all the e., 79
way of all the e., 80
while the e. remaineth, 345
whole e. rejoiceth, 90
worketh wonders in e., 87
earthly
  if I told you e., 28
earthquakes
  great e. shall be, 15
easier
  e. for a camel to go, 225
  e. for heaven and earth, 56
east
  belly with the e. wind, 394
  cometh out of the e., 345
  e. wind brought, 284
  from the e. nor, 373
  on the e. of Eden, 274
  star in the e., 188
easy

e. to be understood, 57
  knowledge is e., 227
eat
  bread to e., 110
  come ye, buy, and e., 89
  comely for one to e., 137
  dogs e. of the crumbs, 354
  dogs shall e., 41
  dogs shall e. Jezebel, 353
  dust shalt thou e., 76
  e. and be satisfied, 249
  e. at thy table, 174
  e. bread by weight, 131
  e. bread nor drink, 66
  e. but not be satisfied, 77
  e. but ye have not, 106
  e. his pleasant fruits, 239
  e. of the hidden manna,
    331
  e. of their dainties, 360
  e. that thou mayest have,
    137
  e. the fat, 2
  e. the fat, 42
  e. the flesh of the Son, 58
  e. the good of the land, 270
  e. the labour of, 106
  e. the sons, 44
  e. them like wool, 93
  e. thou honey, 136
  e. thy bread with joy, 137
  e. with unwashen hands,
    307
  e. ye that which is good,
    368
  enemies shall e. it, 144
  evil, thou shalt not e., 169
  fruit thereof, and did e., 99
  hasteth to e., 367
  hear, nor e., 198
  honey shall he e., 97
  let us e. and drink, 42
  lion shall e. straw, 38
  man e. of this bread, 38
  man should e. and drink,
    286
  mayest freely e. but, 169
  me, and I did e., 32
  meat to e. that ye know,
    368
  moth shall e., 93
  neither should he e., 195
  poor of thy people may e.,
    76
  rise Peter; kill and e., 137
  shall not e. of it, 226
  shalt not e. thereof, 298
  shalt thou e. bread, 302
  sighing before I e., 13
  sons shall e. fathers, 44
  sun, than to e., 77
  take, e. this is my body, 58
  tree, and I did e., 32
  what ye shall e., 248

esteemeth
e. every day alike, 43
e. iron as straw, 370
estranged
e. from the womb, 25
eternal
blood, hath e. life, 115
e. God is thy refuge, 337
e. life through Jesus, 115
fruit unto life e., 115
given to us e. life, 116
keep it unto life e., 235
lay hold on e. life, 115
no murderer hath e. life, 263
perish, but have e. life, 82
things not seen are e., 248
Ethiopian
E. change his skin, 43
eunuchs
e. in the palace, 192
Eve
first formed, then E., 22
even
e. I only, am left, 90
e. I, am the Lord, 164
e. thou shalt say, 385
I. e. I, am He, 54
in an e. balance, 63
would God it were e., 385
evening
e. it is cut down, 244
e. withhold not thine, 95
the e. and the morning, 267
event
e. to the righteous, 235
ever
See also "Forever"
everlasting
awake, some to e. life, 108
e. king, 149
e. strength, 371
endureth unto e. life, 37
hath e. life, 29
have e. life, 340
mercy is e., 154
mercy is e., 166
mighty God, the e., 218
reap life e., 115
some to e. contempt, 108
unto thee an e. light, 177
unworthy of e. life, 49
evermore
time forth and for e., 148
every
e. man his righteousness, 329
e. one That prepareth, 139
e. purpose under, 265
not e. one that saith, 226
Thou canst do e. thing, 156
to e. thing there is a, 265
everyone
e. against his brother, 44

e. against his neighbour, 44
evidence
e. of things not seen, 127
evil
abhor that which is e., 27
accustomed to do e., 43
against them for e., 85
against them that do e., 119
all appearance of e., 27
all this great e. upon, 157
and from your e. doings, 119
bear witness of the e., 4
being e. speak good, 73
bringeth forth e. fruit, 44
bringeth forth e. things, 45
cease to do e., 316
concerning me, but e., 7
confusion and every e., 64
day is the e. thereof, 145
death and e., 26
deeds were e., 119
deliver us from e., 119
depart from e., 118
depart from e., 118
depart from e., 26
depart from e., 134
departeth from e., 118
did e. in the sight, 385
do e. in His sight, 6
do that which is e., 133
doeth e. hath not seen, 169
done e. in the sight, 121
done that which was e., 120
e. again in the sight, 201
e. against his brother, 38
e. against thee, 310
e. against thy neighbour, 30
e. against you falsely, 66
e. and adulterous, 254
e. and not for good, 169
e. and the good, 158
e. came unto, 13
e. come from within, 357
e. communications, 45
e. congregation, 276
e. entreated this people, 102
e. from his youth, 118
e. in the sight, 99
e. in your hearts, 119
e. in your hearts, 119
e. is come upon us, yet, 202
e. is in mine hand, 206
e. man out of e., 45
e. pursueth sinners, 118
e. shall hunt, 398
e. shall not depart, 169
e. shall slay the wicked, 223
e. thing and bitter, 23
e. upon their beds, 74
e. upon this place, 324
e. we will obey, 3

e. which I would not, 209
e. will befall, 386
eschew e. and do good, 49
every one that doeth e., 119
eyes than to behold e., 307
eyes upon them for e., 306
face against you for e., 305
feareth God, and
escheweth e., 257
few and e., 258
follow not which is e., 49
forseeth the e., 301
from his e. way, 316
from the e. to come, 81
God repented of the e., 139
God, and eschewed e., 332
good works but to the e., 173
good, and not e., 49
hate the e., 26
he that pursueth e., 74
heart full of e., 118
heart proceed e., 261
help the e. doers, 1
his tongue form e., 119
hope in day of e., 190
I will bring e., 14
I will fear no e., 63
I would do this e., 73
if I have spoken e., 4
if thine eye be e., 44
if ye, being e. know, 146
is thine eye e., 112
is to hate e., 118
Israel did e. again, 23
it is an e. time, 301
keep me from e., 118
keep thee from e. woman, 242
keep you from e., 128
know good and e., 169
know to refuse the e., 97
knowing good and e., 111
knowledge of good and e., 169
love the Lord, hate e., 118
man from his e., 316
me from every e. work, 338
multitude to do e., 58
not bring e. in his days, 67
not lust after e., 89
not receive e., 3
overcome e. with good, 170
partaker of his e. deeds, 69
peace, and create e., 169
preserve thee from all e., 338
proceedeth not e., 169
punish the world for e., 118
put away the e., 316
put the e. away, 118
render e. for e., 327
repent Me of the e., 139

repentest Thee of the e., 59
reward doer of e., 304
reward to the e., 230
rewarded e. for good, 4
rewarded me e. for good, 169
rewarded thee e., 67
rewardeth e. for good, 169
rise on the e. and the, 169
root of all e., 119
see all the e., 59
shall there be e. in a, 93
simple concerning e., 170
speak e. of no man, 362
speak e. of the ruler, 173
suffer for e. doing, 3
tempted with e., 380
that call e. good, 169
the e. that shall come, 13
them that imagine e., 98
they that have done e., 78
this is an e. generation, 119
though sinner do e., 168
to no man e. for e., 327
tongue from e., 189
turn from your e. ways, 119
turn ye from your e., 81
turn ye from your e., 26
unruly e. full of, 367
upon this city for e., 102
watch over them for e., 150
way of e. men, 26
wicked and the e., 304
wicked for day of e., 72
will I bring the e., 67
wise to do e., 169
withstand in the e. day, 161
wrath upon him that doeth e., 173
evildoers
seed of e., 48
evils
e. that ye have, 312
exact
e. no more than, 175
exalt
e. him that is low, 328
I will e. Thee, 291
whosoever shall e. himself, 194
will e. Him, 163
exalted
e. above all blessing, 290
e. among the heathen, 151
e. as head above all, 365
e. be the God, 290
e. far above all gods, 120
e. for a little, 223
e. in the earth, 151
e. thee out of the dust, 156
e. with His right, 214
himself shall be e., 194
himself shall be e., 11
himself shall be e., 61

name is e., 116
exalteth
e. by His power, 208
e. himself shall be, 11
that e. himself shall be, 61
examine
e. yourselves, 128
excel
shalt not e., 44
excellence
e. of dignity, 44
excellent
done e. things, 364
e. speech, 106
excellest
e. them all, 246
excelleth
light e. darkness, 137
wisdom e. folly, 137
except
e. the Lord build, 4
e. the Lord keep, 348
excess
same e. of riot, 64
wine, wherein is e., 103
exchange
in e. for his soul, 209
execute
e. great vengeance, 150
e. the judgment of, 224
e. true judgment, 27
e. vengeance, 326
e. vengeance in anger, 150
I will e. judgment, 198
revenger to e. wrath, 173
executed
e. judgments upon, 338
judgment that I have e., 151
exercise
e. profiteth little, 168
herein do I e., 65
exhort
e. one another daily, 108
e. with longsuffering, 277
expectation
e. of the poor, 190
e. of the wicked, 122
expedient
all things are not e., 27
experience
and e. hope, 190
and patience, e., 190
expert
mighty e. man, 4
extinct
days are e., 80
eye
apple of his e., 50
apple of the e., 160
beam that is in thine e., 32
e. affecteth mine heart, 354
e. for e., 324
e. hath not seen, 35

e. is not satisfied with, 11
e. of a needle, 225
e. of the Lord, 160
e. offend thee, pluck, 32
e. poureth out tears, 124
e. runneth down, 54
e. shall not pity, 262
e. shall not spare, 14
e. shall not spare, 250
ghost, and no e., 90
He that formed the e., 158
if thine e. be evil, 44
is thine e. evil, 112
kingdom with one e., 182
let not your e., 94
light of body is the e., 36
mine e. spared, 249
mote in thy brother's e., 32
mote of thy brother's e., 75
out of thine own e., 75
right e. offend thee, 78
see e. to e., 9
twinkling of an e., 367
eyed
Saul e. David, 211
eyelids
slumber to mine e., 52
take thee with her e., 6
eyes
anoint thine e. with, 355
art of purer e., 307
captivity before your e., 131
clean in his own e., 350
devil open the e., 5
e. a fountain, 377
e. are upon the haughty, 16
e. are upon the ways, 153
e. are upon Thee, 387
e. fail with looking, 91
e. had seen it, 318
e. have seen, 25
e. have seen, 254
e. have seen the King, 22
e. have they, 198
e. have they closed, 200
e. like the fishpools, 36
e. of all wait, 190
e. of flesh, 120
e. of his children, 30
e. of man are never, 11
e. of the blind, 35
e. of the blind, 35
e. of the Lord, 158
e. of the Lord, 153
e. of the Lord, 158
e. of the Lord, 161
e. of the Lord, 210
e. of the Lord are, 160
e. of the wicked, 304
e. of the wise, 38
e. of them both, 226
e. see ye not, 373
e. shall be opened, 111

e. shall not see all, 59
e. to behold the sun, 234
e. to the blind, 10
e. upon them for evil, 306
fell from his e., 68
from before Mine e., 316
he that hideth his e., 45
hide Mine e., 1
instead of e., 122
known in the e. of, 228
lift up mine e. unto, 19
lift up your e., 273
lighten mine e., 18
marvellous in our e., 373
mine e. and mine heart,
   158
mine e. have seen Thy, 251
open his e., 111
open their e., 111
open Thine e., 19
open Thine e., 293
plucked out your own e.,
   95
right in his own e., 7
right in his own e., 261
righteous in his own e., 206
rock before their e., 124
see it with thine e., 298
sight of his e., 123
sight of the e. than, 89
sleep to mine e., 52
smoke to the e., 230
tears from their e., 378
Thine e. open, 291
two e. to be cast into, 182
waters run down mine e.,
   99
wise in their own e., 61
wise man's e. are in, 138
with thine e., 96
eyesalve
   thine eyes with e., 355

F

fables
   old wives' f., 263
face
   another in the f., 43
   back, and not the f., 23
   before f. of the Lord, 293
   but then f. to f., 53
   cause His f. to shine, 34
   curse Thee to Thy f., 43
   discern f. of the sky, 402
   discern the f. of sky, 97
   down before thy f., 92
   f. of all people, 251
   f. of Israel, 159
   f. of man, 220
   f. of the deep, 44
   f. of the earth, 104
   f. of the earth, 131
   f. of the field, 39

f. of the Lord, 119
f. of the waters, 158
f. of thine anointed, 291
f. of Thine anointed, 313
f. to shine, 153
f. to shine, 410
hid His f., 293
hid I My f. from them, 311
hid not my f., 280
hide not Thy f., 18
hide not Thy f., 387
hide Thy f., 1
hidest Thou Thy f., 1
hideth His f., 158
His f. shine, 34
honour the f., 8
Me, and not their f., 197
messenger before Thy f.,
   253
not see my f., 121
repay him to his f., 129
seek His f. continually, 162
seek His f. evermore, 94
seek ye My f., 124
seen God f. to f., 22
seen thy f., 79
set My f. against, 169
set My f. against, 305
set My f. against, 228
spit in her f., 303
sweat of thy f., 302
Thy f. Lord, will I seek,
   124
thy f. with painting, 25
truth before Thy f., 223
turn away His f., 154
upon thy f., 108
wash thy f., 132
faces
   afraid of their f., 108
   disfigure their f., 195
   f. harder than a rock, 202
   f. of the judges, 205
   spread dung upon your f.,
      192
fade
   f. as a leaf, 142
fadeth
   glory that f. not, 331
fail
   children shall f., 30
   eyes of wicked shall f., 304
   f. nor be discouraged, 223
   f. with looking, 91
   He will not f. thee, 161
   man's heart f., 70
   tittle of the law to f., 56
failed
   kinsfolk have f., 237
   might hath f., 72
   not f. one word, 71
   one thing hath f., 297
faileth
   charity never f., 240

their tongue f., 131
when my strength f., 8
faint
   behold, he is f., 96
   heart is f., 374
   if thou f. in the day, 142
   power to the f., 162
fainted
   when my soul f., 70
fainthearted
   fear not, neither be f., 108
fair
   f. as the moon, 25
   f. one, and come, 335
   so is a f. woman, 24
   that they were f., 24
   vain make thyself f., 25
faith
   according to your f., 125
   add to your f. virtue, 127
   all men have not f., 127
   ask in f., 127
   be sound in f., 28
   before f. came, 57
   breastplate of f., 27
   but by the f. of Jesus, 56
   by f. ye stand, 126
   by works was f. made, 85
   children of God by f., 113
   contend for the f., 127
   f. as a grain of mustard,
      125
   f. cometh by hearing, 126
   f. hath made thee whole,
      125
   f. hath saved, 126
   f. hope, charity, 126
   f. in God, 126
   f. is the substance of, 127
   f. is vain, 126
   f. of God without effect,
      161
   f. of the saints, 4
   f. should not stand, 126
   f. to be healed, 182
   f. which worketh by love,
      53
   f. without works, 85
   finisher of our f., 215
   follow after f., 148
   follow righteousness, f., 28
   fruit of the Spirit is f., 187
   good fight of f., 127
   great is thy f., 125
   hast thou f.?, 126
   I have kept the f., 5
   increase our f., 126
   justified by f., 85
   justified by f., 57
   live by f., 126
   live by his f. by his, 125
   not by f. only, 85
   not found so great f., 125
   not of f. is sin, 126

now preacheth the f., 43
O thou of little f., 102
O ye of little f., 125
of f. unfeigned, 240
one f., 24
prayer of f., 182
profession of our f., 127
righteousness of f., 126
saved through f., 127
shield of f., 127
so f. without works is, 82
stand fast in the f., 94
though I have all f., 126
void the law through f., 56
walk by f., 27
weak in the f., 68
whether ye be in the f., 128
without f. it is, 127
ye of little f., 102
faithful
but the Lord is f., 242
f. also in much, 65
f. ambassador, 107
f. are the wounds of a, 74
f. city, 211
f. city become an harlot, 200
f. in that which is least, 65
f. is He that calleth, 149
f. man who can find, 242
f. spirit concealeth, 143
f. unto death, 116
f. witness, 218
God is f., 166
good and f. servant, 16
He is f. and just, 62
preserveth the f., 128
that sat was called F., 128
they with Him are f., 128
up a f. priest, 53
who is so f., 242
yet he abideth f., 29
faithfully
f. judgeth the poor, 259
speak My word f., 103
faithfulness
f. and truth, 128
f. in destruction, 235
righteousness and his f., 329
faithless
f. and perverse generation, 167
f. but believing, 102
fall
both f. into the ditch, 35
diggeth a pit shall f., 343
diggeth a pit shall f., 118
f. by the sword, 223
f. by the sword, 324
f. by the sword, 14
f. by their own counsels, 109
f. from my shoulder, 206

f. into the hand, 90
f. into the mouth of, 161
f. into the pit, 102
f. into the pit, 114
f. into their own nets, 324
f. to the earth, 337
f. with pain, 150
hair f. to the earth, 222
heed lest he f., 63
let me f. into the hand, 250
let me not f. into, 76
lightning f. from heaven, 341
not understand shall f., 199
people f., 177
proud shall f., 17
riches shall f., 123
sons together shall f., 271
spirit before a f., 123
thousand shall f., 79
through their f., 219
thy multitude to f., 400
transgressors shall f., 26
upholdeth all that f., 162
when I f. I shall arise, 36
wicked shall f. by, 223
fallen
Babylon the great is f., 83
bricks are f., 17
crown is f., 328
f. in the street, 230
f. unto me in pleasant, 185
from whence thou art f., 23
how art thou f., 86
Judah is f., 33
mighty f., 228
mighty f. and, 85
falleth
alone when he f., 68
dew f. on the ground, 64
f. before wicked, 206
tongue f. into mischief, 98
falling
a f. away first, 346
fallow
break up your f. ground, 316
false
against f. swearers, 6
beware of f. prophets, 84
do not bear f. witness, 56
f. balance is, 40
f. Christs, 184
f. prophets, 184
f. teachers among you, 185
f. witness that speaketh, 17
f. witness will utter, 44
f. witnesses are risen, 280
f. witnesses did rise up, 206
far from a f. matter, 189
love no f. oath, 279
not bear f. witness, 279
perils among f. brethren, 107

thefts, f. witness, 261
falsehood
f. have we hid, 98
falsely
accuse any f., 69
every one dealeth f., 69
neither deal f., 25
prophesy f. in My name, 130
fame
f. was noised, 130
families
all f. of the earth, 33
f. of the earth, 131
f. that call not on Thy, 167
family
among his f., 185
famine
and the f. within, 79
are for the f. to the f., 92
by sword and f., 129
death, mourning, and f., 285
die by the f., 14
f. or nakedness, 95
f. shall consume, 131
f. shall devour him, 93
f. was over all, 131
not a f. of bread, 131
send a f. in the land, 131
famines
and f. and pestilences, 15
far
and those that be f., 192
be not f. from, 13
be not f. from me, 18
comforter is f. from me, 54
f. be it from God, 118
f. from me, 410
f. from me, O Lord, 349
f. from the wicked, 339
f. from the wicked, 162
f. from Thee shall perish, 23
f. off shall die, 14
God be not f. from, 1
good news from a f., 266
hear, ye that are f., 5
heart is f., 10
keep thee f., 189
let it be f. from him, 223
Lord be not f. from, 18
not f. from every one, 159
put it f. away, 26
remember Me in f., 121
than a brother f., 19
they are gone f. from Me, 114
ye who sometimes were f., 51
farthings
sparrows sold for two f., 153
fashion

as your f. did, so do, 281
covenant of thy f., 1
covenant with our f., 50
die for the f., 304
f. and sons together, 271
f. found in Me, 114
f. have destroyed, 17
f. have eaten sour, 32
f. have not hearkened, 99
f. provoke not your, 47
f. shall eat the sons, 44
f. shall not die, 304
f. told us of, 102
f. where are they, 261
God of his f., 23
God of your f., 144
God of your f., 316
gods which your f., 197
have ye not many f., 37
inheritance of the f., 205
iniquity of the f., 303
Lord sware unto your f., 204
me in derision, whose f., 8
promise made unto the f., 171
sepulchre of thy f., 304
since the day their f., 120
sinned with our f., 62
sinned, we and our f., 62
sons shall eat their f., 44
statutes of your f., 167
stiffnecked, as your f., 372
sware unto their f., 303
way which their f., 23
which thy f. have set, 299
wickedness of your f., 186
your f. persecuted, 281

fatness
art covered with f., 83
delight itself in f., 368
made fat with f., 324

fatted
hither the f. calf, 42

fault
a f. among you, 229
I find no f., 256
without f. before the, 206

faultless
covenant had been f., 71

faults
buffeted for your f., 75
confess your f., 62

favorest
know that Thou f., 153

favour
f. is as dew, 12
f. is deceitful, 25
f. of the Lord, 409
f. of the Lord, 245
f. to men of skill, 367
find f. in thy sight, 174
found f., 350
good man showeth f., 146

king's f., 12
My f. have I had mercy, 59
not found f., 231
seek the ruler's f., 223

fear
be strong, f. not, 108
better is little with f., 66
by the f. of the Lord, 134
delivered me from my f., 87
f. and the pit, 91
f. before Him, 133
f. day and night, 78
f. every man his mother, 275
f. God, 173
f. God for nought, 207
f. God, and give glory, 222
f. God, and keep, 103
f. God, give audience, 184
f. Him, which hath power, 78
f. in the night, 133
f. is on every side, 79
f. no evil, 63
f. none of these things, 70
f. not, 107
f. not, little flock, 225
f. not neither be, 108
f. not them which kill, 36
f. not to be servants, 3
f. not, but let your, 70
f. not, for I, 53
f. not, neither, 108
f. not: for I have, 155
f. not: for they that, 162
f. of God, 172
f. of the Lord, 220
f. of the Lord, 133
f. of the Lord, 134
f. of the Lord, 134
f. of the Lord all the, 134
f. of the Lord is, 134
f. of the Lord is, 134
f. of the Lord is to, 118
f. other gods, 198
f. the Lord, 26
f. the Lord, 133
f. the Lord, 62
f. the Lord, 269
f. the Lord, 94
f. the Lord, bless, 290
f. them not, 395
f. them not, neither, 133
f. thou not, 190
f. thou the Lord and, 259
f. to whom f., 133
f. toward Me is taught, 195
f. what flesh can do, 133
f. what man shall do, 64
f. ye not, 54
f. ye not, 107
f. ye not Me, 22
f. ye not the reproach, 75

f. ye the people, 107
fleeth from the f., 114
for f. of the Lord, 113
God ye shall f., 319
heart from Thy f., 356
Him shall ye f., 148
I say unto you, f. Him, 78
I will not f., 63
let Him be your f., 133
love casteth out f., 133
meat unto them that f., 137
mercy is on them that f., 134
mocketh at f., 70
noise of the f., 102
not f. them, 109
of the f. of the Lord, 252
others also may f., 46
pitieth them that f., 59
pleasure in them that f., 328
roared, who will not f., 270
salvation with f. and, 340
serve the Lord with f., 193
spirit of f., 63
such as f. God, 172
that they may f. Me, 308
they would f. Me, 133
to f. Him, 55
to me; f. not, 18
toward them that f. Him, 154
unto thee; f. not, 53
unto you that f. My, 22
upon them that f. Him, 160
well with them that f., 168
who shall not f. Thee, 291
whom shall I f., 132
with them that f. Him, 133
ye that f. the Lord, 134
your masters with all f., 3

feared
as they f. Moses, 231
f. above all gods, 134
f. God, and eschewed, 332
f. him, as, 231
f. that thou hast lied, 167
f. the people, 302
f. the people, 121
God greatly to be f., 133

feareth
but a woman that f., 25
f. an oath, 113
f. the commandment, 269
f. the Lord, 134
one that f. God, 257
that f. the Lord, 134
whosoever among you f., 134
wise man f., 118

fearful
f. and afraid, 132
f. in praises, 22
f. O ye of little faith, 125

f. thing to fall, 151
fearfully
  f. and wonderfully made, 72
feast
  hath a continual f., 180
  makest a f. call the, 42
feasting
  house of f., 81
feasts
  uppermost rooms at f., 196
fed
  as f. horses, 204
  f. you with milk, 105
feeble
  confirm the f. knees, 108
  hands shall be f., 403
  lift up the f. knees, 64
feebleminded
  comfort the f., 60
feed
  death shall f., 80
  enemy hunger, f., 140
  f. among the lilies, 25
  f. me with food, 404
  f. My flock, 161
  f. my lambs, 253
  f. the church, 104
  f. the flock of God, 233
  f. the flocks, 69
  f. the poor, 46
  f. them with judgment, 220
  lamb shall f., 38
  Lamb shall f. them, 163
  righteous f. many, 7
  shepherds that do f., 69
  they that did f., 192
  worm shall f. sweetly, 80
feedest
  f. them with the bread, 176
feet
  between his f., 231
  dust of His f., 157
  enemies under His f., 365
  f. are swift, 119
  f. did not slip, 337
  f. have they but, 198
  f. in the blood, 326
  f. not be burned, 6
  f. of him that bringeth, 267
  f. of them that preach, 172
  f. shall tread, 210
  f. swelled, 162
  f. that be swift, 207
  f. to be cast into hell, 78
  f. was I to the lame, 10
  fool cutteth off the f., 266
  hasteth with his f., 309
  lamp unto my f., 111
  net for his f., 136
  path of thy f., 285
  paths for your f., 28
  pierced my f., 280
  shoes off thy f., 186

trample under their f., 204
  when thy f. enter, 77
feignest
  why f. thou thyself, 83
fell
  f. down dead, 18
  f. from his eyes, 68
fellowcitizens
  f. with the saints, 51
fellowship
  f. is with the Father, 135
  f. one with another, 28
felt
  darkness which may be f., 236
female
  male and f. created He, 72
  male and f. created He, 244
  neither male nor f., 113
Festus
  mad, most noble F., 243
fetch
  come themselves and f., 70
few
  are not my days f., 260
  f. and evil, 258
  f. are chosen, 238
  f. there be that find it, 27
  labourers are f., 117
  left but a f. of many, 376
  left f. in number, 121
  left f. in number, 303
  let his days be f., 305
  let thy words be f., 193
  save by many or by f., 63
  seemed but a f. days, 238
  woman is of f. days, 234
fewest
  f. of all people, 50
field
  beast of the f., 363
  beast of the f., 363
  beasts of the f., 35
  blessed in the f., 34
  cursed in the f., 303
  face of the f., 39
  flower of the f., 244
  forth into the f., 79
  in the f. shall die, 93
  lilies of the f., 15
  potter's f., 39
  served by the f., 69
  smell of a f., 47
  treasure hid in a f., 226
  tree of the f., 264
  trees of the f., 268
fields
  look on the f., 273
  take your f., 258
fierce
  away from His f. anger, 139
fierceness
  f. of His wrath, 139
  in the f. of His anger, 150

fiery
  burning f. furnace, 79
  f. flying serpent, 102
  quench all the f. darts, 127
fig
  and under his f. tree, 278
  f. tree bear olive, 66
  holds shall be like f., 161
fight
  a city to f. against it, 401
  against whom ye f., 85
  f. against your brethren, 277
  f. and war yet ye, 294
  f. every one against, 44
  f. for you, 108
  f. for you, 109
  f. for your brethren, 24
  f. the good f., 127
  f. with this Philistine, 70
  f. ye not against, 144
  fingers to f., 371
  fought a good f., 5
  God shall f. for us, 63
  Lord shall f. for you, 10
  may f. together, 43
  neither f., 161
  not f. against God, 3
  they shall f. against, 110
fighteth
  f. for you, 162
  Lord f. for them, 159
figs
  men do not gather f., 65
  with the firstripe f., 161
fill
  do not I f. heaven and, 113
filled
  appetite is not f., 11
  drink, but ye are not f., 106
  earth that is not f., 81
  f. me with bitterness, 32
  f. the house of God, 415
  f. with the glory, 151
  f. with the Spirit, 103
  for they shall be f., 333
  valley shall be f., 253
filleth
  f. the hungry soul, 89
filthy
  f. communication, 27
  f. lucre, 259
  not for f. lucre, 261
find
  by searching f. out God, 17
  f. a virtuous woman, 246
  f. favour in thy sight, 174
  f. it after many days, 10
  f. out all Thine enemies, 110
  f. rest for your souls, 385
  f. rest unto your souls, 54
  f. such a one as this, 230
  f. those that hate, 110

few there be f. it, 27
for my sake shall f. it, 114
life for my sake shall f., 236
seek death, and not f., 82
seek me and shall not f.,
345
seek me early shall f., 409
seek Me, and f., 94
seek, and ye shall f., 95
shall not f. her paths, 271
shall not f. it, 145
shalt f. Him, 28
that we shall not f. Him,
264
them that f. knowledge, 53
until I f. a place for, 52
findeth
f. occasions against, 280
fatherless f. mercy, 408
he that seeketh f., 11
man that f. wisdom, 180
seeking rest and f. none,
119
whatsoever thy hand f., 106
whoso f. a wife f., 245
whoso f. me f. life, 409
finding
ways past f. out, 153
fine
than much f. gold, 55
finer
vessel for the f., 393
finger
f. into the print, 102
f. of God, 284
f. of God, 380
f. shall be thicker, 352
fingers
burdens with your f., 39
f. have made, 197
f. to fight, 371
with one of their f., 196
finish
f. His work, 256
sufficient to f. it, 285
finished
f. my course, 5
it is f., 82
sin, when it is f., 82
finisher
f. of our faith, 215
fire
another f. shall devour, 114
answereth by f., 298
burn with f., 198
burned with f., 158
burneth as the f., 118
burnt with f., 303
can a man take f. in, 6
cast into hell f., 182
cast into the lake of f., 78
chariot of f., 147
coals of f., 211
consuming f., 165

consuming f., 92
f. and by His sword, 220
f. and the wood, 264
f. goeth out, 172
f. is not quenched, 184
f. mingled with the hail,
284
f. never quenched, 184
f. of my jealousy, 93
f. shall burn, 8
f. shall consume, 38
f. taking vengeance, 327
f. that consumeth, 6
f. that saith not, 81
fury come like f., 150
God is a consuming f., 151
gold tried in the f., 127
heap coals of f., 353
in a pillar of f., 159
into the lake of f., 82
jealousy burn like f., 139
lake of f. and brimstone,
306
little f. kindleth, 25
melteth before the f., 304
midst of the f., 22
out from one f., 114
pass through the f., 197
poured out like f., 150
setteth on f., 367
spark of his f., 223
tongue is a f., 119
walkest through the f., 54
went through f., 79
words in thy mouth f., 106
firmament
called the f. heaven, 68
f. sheweth His handywork,
151
first
Adam was f. formed, 22
dead shall rise f., 51
f. and great commandment,
56
f. and the f. last, 113
f. be reconciled, 45
f. cast out, 75
f. child, 31
f. heaven and the f., 183
f. man that was born, 8
f. the blade, 176
He hath made the f. old, 71
I am He; I am the f., 164
I am the f., 164
I am the f. and the last, 25
if that f. covenant had, 71
last shall be f., 190
last shall be f., 113
last; and the last f., 115
man desire to be f., 11
many that are f., 115
must f. come to pass, 15
seek ye f. the kingdom, 147
the f. day, 267

the f. resurrection, 82
firstborn
Esau thy f., 83
f. are Mine, 135
f. of thy sons, 65
Israel My f., 49
my f. my might, 135
smite all the f., 135
unto Me all the f., 65
was not the f., yet, 132
firstfruits
f. of all thine increase, 384
fish
dominion over the f., 14
fishers
f. of men, 97
fishes
f. of the sea, 156
five loaves, and two f., 102
fit
f. for the kingdom of, 95
five
lack f. of the fifty, 61
fixed
great gulf f., 184
flag
f. grow without water, 176
flagons
stay me with f., 238
flame
hath a most vehement f.,
211
tormented in this f., 184
flattereth
a man that f., 136
f. with his lips, 136
flattering
f. mouth worketh, 7
with f. lips, 98
flattery
f. of the tongue, 242
f. to his friends, 30
flea
dead dog, after a f., 120
seek a f., 120
fled
every island f. away, 93
f. apace, and look not, 396
men of war f., 86
they have f. from Me, 23
flee
devil will f., 342
f. also youthful lusts, 28
f. away naked, 86
f. before Thee, 109
f. fornication, 141
f. from idolatry, 198
f. from the face, 159
f. in battle, 72
f. out of the midst, 114
f. when none pursueth, 132
let not the swift f., 396
let us f., 113
look upon thee shall f., 90

man as I f., 70
one thousand shall f., 133
shall not f. away, 114
to whom will ye f., 113
warned you to f., 114
wicked f. when no, 133
fleeth
    f. of them shall not, 114
    hireling f., 95
    that f. from the fear, 114
    who f. from the noise, 102
flesh
    absent in the f., 2
    arm of f., 370
    born of the f. is f., 31
    bread is my f., 312
    brother and our f., 249
    cause thy f. to sin, 356
    eat the f. of the Son, 58
    eateth his own f., 230
    eyes of f., 120
    f. and blood, 226
    f. and blood hath not, 216
    f. as the dung, 325
    f. is as grass, 147
    f. is weak, 141
    f. lusteth against the, 192
    f. of brass, 90
    f. of my f., 411
    f. of your foreskin, 52
    f. profiteth nothing, 187
    f. shall I see God, 80
    f. the law of sin, 41
    fear what f. can do, 133
    give thy f. unto fowls, 35
    God of all f., 157
    good piece of f., 42
    hair of my f., 132
    heart of f., 315
    heart out of their f., 315
    in my f. dwelleth no, 41
    life of all f., 35
    live after the f., 41
    living thing of all f., 14
    lust of the f., 27
    maketh f. his arm, 314
    manifest in the f., 215
    members of His f., 215
    no f. be justified, 56
    occasion to the f., 143
    of f. reap corruption, 243
    outward in the f., 15
    perfect by the f., 23
    plead with all f., 220
    provision for the f., 349
    shall be one f., 245
    soweth to his f. shall, 243
    Spirit against the f., 192
    suffered in the f., 358
    sword shall devour f., 326
    that are after the f. do, 41
    that eateth my f., 214
    that they were but f., 139
    they that are in the f., 41

things of the f., 41
thorn in the f., 342
trouble in the f., 246
troubleth his own f., 76
twain shall be one f., 246
walk in the f., 64
war after the f., 64
weariness of the f., 105
whoso eateth my f., 115
Word was made f., 213
wrestle not against f., 110
ye are not in the f., 126
ye judge after the f., 15
fleshy
    f. tables of the heart, 280
flies
    swarm of f., 284
flieth
    arrow that f., 133
flight
    f. shall perish from the, 367
    go by f., 142
    ten thousand to f., 1
flint
    harder than f., 282
flock
    and to all the f., 397
    dogs of my f., 8
    f. was scattered, 104
    fear not, little f., 225
    feed the f. of God, 233
    not sparing the f., 372
    shepherd doth his f., 50
    ye My f. the f., 155
flocks
    bleatings of the f., 104
    shepherds feed the f., 69
flood
    f. to destroy the earth, 71
    other side of the f., 197
floods
    neither can the f., 239
floor
    out of the f., 112
flourish
    of iniquity do f., 230
    righteous shall f., 176
flourisheth
    field, so he f., 244
    morning it f., 244
flower
    a f. and is cut down, 260
    f. falleth away, 165
    f. of the field, 244
    f. of their age, 416
    glory of man as the f., 147
flowers
    f. appear on the earth, 345
flowing
    land f. with milk, 210
fly
    f. as the eagle, 367
    f. away as an eagle, 112
    f. away, and be at rest, 113

f. upon the wings, 367
flying
    fiery f. serpent, 102
foes
    f. Thy footstool, 120
    man's f. shall be they, 372
fold
    not of this f., 117
    there shall be one f., 51
folding
    f. of the hands, 288
follow
    but if Baal, then f., 49
    come and f. me, 46
    cross, and f., 10
    f. after her lovers but, 144
    f. after me, 231
    f. his steps, 215
    f. me, 97
    f. me, 232
    f. me all the days, 34
    f. me, and I will make, 97
    f. not that which is, 49
    f. peace with all men, 16
    f. that which is good, 334
    f. their own spirit, 130
    God, f. Him, 49
    not f. a multitude, 58
    the cross, and f. me, 10
    them, and they f. me, 10
    thing f. not, 129
followers
    be ye f. of me, 27
    f. of God, 27
followeth
    f. after me is not, 9
    f. me shall not walk, 29
following
    f. the Lord, 94
    f. their brethren, 277
    from f. Me, 209
folly
    do not thou this f., 202
    f. is joy to him that, 136
    fool according to his f., 138
    fool in his f., 79
    fool returneth to his f., 138
    fools is f., 136
    instruction of fools is f.,
        391
    spirit exalteth f., 136
    wisdom excelleth f., 137
food
    feed me with f., 404
    having f. and raiment, 175
fool
    a f. according to his, 138
    as a f. receive me, 15
    become a f. that he may,
        194
    begetteth a f., 275
    bray a f. in a mortar, 138
    by the hand of a f., 266
    die, likewise the f., 260

doth a f. understand, 199
ears of a f., 7
even a f. when he, 138
f. despiseth father's, 48
f. foldeth his hands, 230
f. hath said, 19
f. in his folly, 79
f. rageth, and is, 118
f. returneth to his folly, 138
f. uttereth all his mind, 301
f. walketh in darkness, 138
f. will be meddling, 138
f.'s mouth is his, 138
f.'s voice is known by, 138
f.'s wrath, 208
father of a f., 138
I shall not be a f., 36
laughter of the f., 229
more hope of a f., 61
more hope of a f., 309
no man think me a f., 15
own heart is a f., 61
played the f., 67
rod for the f.'s back, 98
seemly for a f., 138
slander, is a f., 40
speech becometh not a f., 106
stripes into a f., 74
way of a f., 7
wise man or a f., 205
wise man? as the f., 81
wise more than of the f., 315
wise more than the f., 283
foolish
avoid f. questions, 68
envious at the f., 112
f. man despiseth, 48
f. man reproacheth, 74
f. man, which built, 285
f. people and unwise, 204
f. plucketh it down, 188
f. questions avoid, 68
f. son is a grief, 48
f. son is the calamity, 48
f. son is the heaviness, 48
f. the wisdom of the, 414
f. things of the world, 137
forsake the f. and, 58
ignorance of f. men, 85
neither be thou f., 26
people is f., 137
than an old and f. king, 7
woe unto the f., 130
wrath killeth the f., 12
foolishly
angry dealeth f., 378
done very f., 67
foolishness
f. is bound, 47
f. of fools, 136
f. of God is wiser, 411
f. of man perverteth, 11

fools proclaimeth f., 35
unto the Greeks f., 75
will not his f. depart, 138
world is f. with God, 411
fools
bosom of f., 12
circumspectly, not as f., 27
companion of f., 58
f. and slow of heart, 299
f. despise wisdom, 105
f. die for want, 199
f. for Christ's sake, 254
f. hate knowledge, 137
f. make a mock, 356
f. when will ye be wise, 199
foolishness of f., 136
heart of f., 35
heart of f., 138
instruction of f. is, 391
no pleasure in f., 138
promotion of f., 147
sacrifice of f., 415
song of f., 74
suffer f. gladly, 138
wise, they became f., 61
ye f. be ye of an, 391
foot
broken tooth, and a f., 30
f. for f., 324
f. shall slide, 276
if thy f. offend, 78
keep thy f. when thou, 415
my f. slippeth, 162
shoe off thy f., 318
sole of his f., 24
swift of f. shall not, 114
withdraw thy f., 191
footmen
run with the f., 60
footstool
earth is My f., 158
earth is My f., 52
earth; for it is His f., 267
enemies thy f., 160
foes Thy f., 120
for
if God be f. us, 63
or f. our adversaries, 9
forbear
f. thee from meddling, 162
f. to vow, 297
forbeareth, let him f., 183
price; and if not, f., 266
forbeareth
f. let him forebear, 183
forbid
away His people? God f., 219
come unto me, and f., 48
f. that I should sin, 291
f. that we forsake, 128
f. that we should rebel, 310
faith? God f., 56
God f. that I should, 36

man f. water, 24
forbidden
f. to be done, 55
force
not strengthen his f., 63
forces
f. of strength, 370
forcible
f. are right words, 189
forefront
f. of the battle, 30
forehead
have I made thy f., 282
whore's f., 353
foreigners
no more strangers and f., 51
foreskin
f. of your heart, 53
flesh of your f., 52
foreskins
f. of your heart, 316
forest
lion in the f., 30
lion roar in the f., 261
foretold
f. you all things, 299
forever
abide with you f., 54
angry with us f., 150
before Mine anointed f., 329
blaspheme Thy name f., 33
bless Thy name f., 290
blessed be God f., 34
bread, he shall live f., 38
cast thee off f., 23
Christ the same f., 44
counsel of the Lord f., 279
desolate f., 14
do they live f., 261
earth abideth f., 105
Father be glory f., 291
forget us f., 1
glory and dominion f., 157
glory both now and f., 215
God doeth, it shall be f., 279
God f. and ever, 116
God f. and ever, 26
God of Israel f., 290
hide Thyself f., 1
house of the Lord f., 34
keep His anger f., 139
Lord endureth f., 388
Lord shall endure f., 148
Lord shalt endure f., 116
may fear Me f., 308
mercy endureth f., 290
mercy endureth f., 170
mercy endureth f., 154
my portion f., 141
name be f., 211
name shall endure f., 130

not His anger f., 139
not keep anger f., 139
not perish f., 190
o Lord? f. how long, 1
power, and the glory, f.,
116
reign f. and e., 116
remainest f., 116
riches are not f., 279
salvation shall be f., 339
shall be destroyed f., 230
stablish his throne f., 163
sword devour f., 326
thanks unto Thee f., 174
this is My rest f., 211
throne be established f.,
259
Thy throne is f., 51
to abide in f., 52
trust ye in the Lord f., 371
will of God abideth f., 89
wilt Thou be angry f., 139
forgave
even as Christ f., 141
forgers
f. of lies, 53
forget
covenant ye shall not f., 71
drink and f. his poverty, 91
f. her cunning, 1
f. her ornaments, 23
f. her sucking child, 59
f. not the humble, 160
f. not the Lord, 315
f. the covenant, 1
f. the Lord, 128
f. the things, 25
f. thee, O Jerusalem, 1
f. Thy precepts, 128
how long wilt Thou f., 1
nations that f. God, 166
they may f., 128
Thou f. us for ever, 1
understanding: f. it not, 227
yet will I not f., 128
forgetful
be not f. to, 12
forgettest
f. the Lord thy maker, 129
forgetteth
f. not the cry, 292
forgive
f. and ye shall be, 140
f. I pray thee, 316
f. men their trespasses, 140
f. O Lord, hearken, 139
f. our debtors, 140
f. us our debts, 140
f. us our sins, 140
f. us our sins, 62
f. you your trespasses, 177
f. your transgressions, 165
f. your trespasses, 177

Father will also f., 140
Father, f. them, 140
if he repent, f., 75
if ye do not f. neither, 177
power on earth to f., 140
repent; thou shalt f., 140
stand praying, f., 177
when Thou hearest, f., 138
will f. their iniquity, 139
forgiven
and ye shall be f., 140
blasphemy shall be f., 33
cheer; thy sins be f., 108
Christ's sake hath f., 140
Ghost it shall not f., 33
iniquities are f., 140
it shall be f. him: but, 33
it shall not be f., 187
not be f. unto men, 33
sins are f., 141
thine heart may be f., 317
to whom little is f., 140
transgression is f., 139
forgiveness
belong mercies and f., 166
f. of sins, 141
preached unto you the f.,
140
forgotten
always be f., 190
f. as a dead man, 91
f. the wickedness, 186
familiar friends have f., 237
My people have f. Me, 23
not one of them is f., 153
to come shall all be f., 279
why hast Thou f., 1
form
without f. and void, 44
formed
Adam was first f., 22
f. it to be inhabited, 73
f. man of the dust, 72
f. thee in the belly, 31
glory, I have f., 73
He that f. the eye, 158
times that I have f. it, 145
former
f. shall not be, 73
f. things passed away, 82
remember not the f., 315
fornication
body is not for f., 36
except it be for f., 101
flee f., 141
he that committeth f., 141
saving for cause of f., 6
to avoid f., 141
wrath of her f., 70
fornications
out of heart proceed f., 261
forsake
all that f. Thee, 23
all them that f., 23

anger, and f. wrath, 12
f. her not, 409
f. Him, He will cast, 23
f. His inheritance, 242
f. His people, 1
f. me not when my
strength, 8
f. me not, O Lord, 1
f. my sweetness, 11
f. the foolish and, 58
f. the Lord, 22
f. the remnant, 1
f. their own mercy, 129
f. us so long time, 1
father and my mother f., 1
father's friend, f., 143
forbid that we should f.,
128
God, f. me not, 8
He will f. you, 1
if ye f. Him, 1
Israel will not f., 131
leave us, nor f., 1
mercy and truth f., 44
never leave thee, nor f., 2
nor f. thee, 161
not f. thee, 1
that f. the Lord, 23
will not f., 390
forsaken
as ye have f. Me, 121
because ye have f., 114
f. Mine house, 1
f. the Lord, 32
hast f. the Lord, 23
have f. Me, 120
have not f. Him, 128
He hath also f., 114
Lord hath f. the earth, 121
moment have I f., 1
persecuted, but not f., 7
seen the righteous f., 1
we have f. the Lord, 355
why hast Thou f., 1
why hast Thou f., 13
Ye have f. Me, 1
forsaketh
f. not all that he hath, 95
f. not His saints, 128
to him that f. the way, 23
forseeth
f. the evil, 301
forsook
because they f. the Lord,
304
f. the counsel, 7
f. the Lord, 23
fortress
f. among My people, 299
goodness, and my f., 161
refuge and my f., 162
rock, and my f., 160
forty
f. days and f. nights, 136

f. days and f. nights, 380
f. years, 121
f. years suffered He, 219
walked f. years, 121
forward
   shadow go f., 272
fought
   f. a good fight, 5
   f. for Israel, 162
   f. from heaven, 18
   stars f. against Sisera, 18
found
   comforters, but I f. none,
      54
   f. him not, 91
   f. Him, of whom Moses,
      253
   f. in the way, 8
   f. my sheep, 180
   f. of them that sought, 68
   f. out my riddle, 30
   good things f. in, 139
   hast thou f. me, 223
   have your fathers f., 114
   He will be f., 94
   He will be f., 94
   iniquity was not f., 189
   mountains were not f., 93
   never be f., 14
   thousand have I f. but, 243
   while He may be f., 273
   wisdom is f., 391
foundation
   f. of God standeth sure,
      149
   that without a f. built, 8
foundations
   f. be destroyed, 230
   f. of the earth, 20
   let the f., 39
   stone for f., 14
founded
   Lord hath f. Zion, 212
fountain
   athirst of the f. of, 89
   doth a f. send forth, 66
   eyes a f., 377
   f. of life, 134
   f. of living waters, 149
fountains
   living f. of waters, 163
four
   f. things say not, 81
fowl
   f. of the air, 14
fowls
   flesh unto the f., 35
   meat unto the f., 305
foxes
   f. have holes, 188
   the f. the little f., 92
fragments
   gather up the f., 403
frame

knoweth our f., 59
frankincense
   f. and myrrh, 146
free
   bond nor f. but Christ, 113
   bondwoman, but of the f.,
      185
   called, being f., 142
   Christ hath made us f., 143
   f. from all men, 254
   f. from his master, 80
   I was f. born, 142
   let the oppressed go f., 132
   neither bond nor f., 113
   Son shall make you f., 142
   truth shall make you f., 142
   ye shall be f. indeed, 142
freed
   f. from sin, 82
freely
   f. ye have received, 146
   received, f. give, 146
freeman
   the Lord's f., 30
fret
   f. not thyself, 211
friend
   art not Caesar's f., 383
   countenance of his f., 44
   every man is a f. to, 143
   f. loveth at all times, 143
   f. of the world is the, 241
   f. sticketh closer, 143
   kindness to thy f., 9
   thine own f. and, 143
   thy father's f. forsake, 143
   wounds of a f., 74
friends
   called you f., 143
   f. dealt treacherously, 30
   f. have forgotten me, 237
   f. scorn me, 124
   flattery to his f., 30
   hatest thy f., 143
   have pity upon me my f.,
      59
   life for his f., 143
   rich hath many f., 143
   separateth chief f., 172
   separateth very f., 176
   wealth maketh many f., 143
friendship
   f. of the world is, 64
   f. with an angry man, 12
frogs
   f. came up, 284
frost
   God f. is given, 345
fruit
   bring forth f., 117
   bringeth forth evil f., 44
   bringeth forth good f., 44
   downward, and bear f., 375
   f. of righteousness, 69

f. of righteousness is, 278
f. of the righteous, 330
f. of the Spirit is, 187
f. of the tree, 384
f. of the wicked, 65
f. of the womb, 48
f. of the womb, 14
f. shall be a fiery, 102
f. unto life eternal, 115
forth his f., 373
known by his own f., 85
my good f., 11
peaceable f., 98
took of the f. thereof, 99
tree is known by his f., 44
trees whose f. withereth, 45
yield their f., 268
fruitful
   be f. and multiply, 47
   f. and multiply, 47
fruits
   bring forth therefore f., 85
   by their f. ye shall, 4
   eat his pleasant f., 239
   f. that thy soul lusted, 12
   gather in the f., 76
   partaker of the f., 331
fugitive
   f. and a vagabond, 76
fulfil
   becometh us to f., 103
   destroy, but to f., 144
   f. your works, 273
   not f. the lust of, 27
fulfilled
   f. the law, 56
   f. them in condemning, 253
   fathers, God hath f., 171
   law is f. in one word, 57
   our days are f., 102
   prophets might be f., 253
   scripture f. in your, 253
   scripture should be f., 253
   written may be f., 222
full
   destruction are never f.,
      184
   earth shall be f., 128
   f. of blood, 178
   f. of bloody crimes, 230
   f. of lies and, 74
   f. of sap, 265
   f. of the goodness, 105
   f. of Thy riches, 265
   f. of trouble, 234
   f. of violence, 230
   f. with travail, 11
   God f. of compassion, 154
   house f. of sacrifices, 352
   quiver f. of them, 48
   sea is not f., 41
   they that were f., 195
   was f. of people, 86
   went out f., 79

fulness
  and the f. thereof, 265
  dwelleth all the f., 101
  f. thereof, 156
  f. thereof; the world, 105
  roar, and the f., 42
furious
  f. rebukes, 150
furnace
  burning fiery f., 79
  f. of affliction, 155
furrows
  long their f., 13
fury
  f. to rest, 150
  f. upon the heathen, 150
  goeth forth with f., 150
  His f. is poured, 150
  lest my f. come forth, 150
  pour out Thy f., 167

G

gain
  contentment is great g., 67
  g. the whole world, 209
  to die is g., 236
  what things were g., 217
gained
  though he hath g., 195
Galilee
  art thou also of G., 257
gall
  g. of bitterness, 112
  grapes of g., 32
  turned judgment into g., 69
gallows
  hanged Haman on the g.,
    223
garden
  become like the g. of, 321
  beloved come into his g.,
    239
  cast into his g., 176
  from the g. of Eden, 274
  g. of Eden, 275
  g. of herbs, 112
  g. of the Lord, 210
  soul as a watered g., 180
  tree of the g., 169
garment
  covereth them as a g., 296
  eat them like a g., 93
  man put on a woman's g.,
    386
  putteth on his g., 396
  rent my g., 13
  touch His g., 125
garments
  beautiful g., 315
  heart, and not your g., 317
  keepeth his g. lest he, 346
gate
  afflicted in the g., 273

howl, O g., 102
judgment in the g., 26
rebuketh in the g., 75
strait is the g., 27
wide is the g., 78
gates
  g. of brass, 271
  g. of death, 17
  g. of hell, 371
  g. shall not be shut, 183
  loveth the g. of Zion, 211
  peace in your g., 224
Gath
  tell it not in G., 175
gather
  g. him, and keep, 50
  g. in the fruits, 76
  g. the clusters, 221
  g. they grapes, 65
  g. up the fragments, 403
  knoweth not who shall g.,
    205
  mercies will I g., 1
  thorns men do not g., 65
gathered
  cannot be g. again, 260
  eagles be g., 42
  g. into thy grave, 80
  g. together in my name,
    134
  he that g. little, 123
  he that g. much, 123
gathereth
  as a hen g. her chickens,
    232
  he that g. by labour, 404
gathering
  g. together of the waters,
    104
gave
  g. Himself for me, 215
  g. His only begotten Son,
    115
  Lord g. Job twice, 282
  Lord g. the word, 295
  return unto God who g., 81
  the Lord g., 3
gavest
  g. thou the goodly, 17
generation
  another g. cometh, 105
  arose another g., 166
  crooked g., 310
  declare his g., 287
  declare His g., 185
  evil and adulterous g., 254
  faithless and perverse g.,
    167
  fear Him from g. to g., 134
  fourth g., 303
  g. of vipers, 119
  g. of vipers, 78
  g. passeth away, 105
  g. seek after a sign, 298

g. that set not their, 99
g. wiser than the children,
  414
rebellious g., 99
this is an evil g., 119
throne from g. to g., 116
until all the g., 121
untoward g., 69
generations
  anger to all g., 150
  in the g. of old, 161
  throughout your g., 335
  truth endureth to all g., 388
  years of many g., 122
Gentiles
  blasphemed among the G.,
    196
  glory among the G., 116
  I will go unto the G., 120
  is He not also of the G.,
    149
  light of the G., 68
  light to the G., 177
  name shall the G. trust,
    213
  preached unto the G., 215
  salvation come unto G.,
    219
  sent unto the G., 117
  we turn to the G., 49
  which the G. sacrifice, 167
gentle
  g. unto all men, 225
  to the good and g., 3
gentleness
  fruit of the Spirit is g., 187
gently
  g. for my sake, 59
ghost
  Abraham gave up the g.,
    79
  gave up the g., 75
  give up the g., 90
  give up the g., 3
  given up the g., 90
  giveth up the g., 80
  See also "Holy Ghost"
giants
  g. in the earth, 360
Gideon
  came upon G., 24
  Lord, and of G., 24
gift
  come and offer thy g., 45
  g. destroyeth the heart, 38
  g. doth blind, 38
  g. in secret, 12
  g. of God, 173
  g. of God is, 115
  g. of God may be, 46
  g. that is in thee, 2
  good g. is from above, 171
  labour, it is the g. of, 286
  man hath his proper g., 203

perfect g. is from, 171
take a g., 38
unspeakable g., 174
gifts
  diversities of g., 2
  g. and calling of God, 35
  g. to all thy lovers, 197
  g. to all whores, 197
  g. unto your children, 146
  no more with your g., 33
  presented unto Him g., 146
  that giveth g., 143
Gilead
  balm in G, 54
gird
  g. thee with sackcloth, 262
  g. up now thy loins, 320
  g. up the loins, 310
  g. you with sackcloth, 262
  g. you with sackcloth, 261
girded
  like a virgin g. with, 86
girdeth
  that g. on his harness, 35
girls
  boys and g. playing, 300
give
  and I will g. you rest, 39
  ask of me, I will g., 298
  bread that I will g., 312
  daughters, crying, g. g., 175
  g. and it shall be given, 10
  g. as he is able, 45
  g. for his life, 349
  g. for the life of the, 312
  g. forth his water, 124
  g. good gifts, 146
  g. good things to them, 146
  g. him a stone, 225
  g. him bread, 110
  g. him the morning star, 331
  g. I pray, 290
  g. me a man, 43
  g. me drink, 382
  g. me half thine house, 66
  g. me here John, 327
  g. me my price, 266
  g. me neither poverty, 404
  g. me now wisdom, 147
  g. me thy vineyard, 112
  g. not thy strength, 242
  g. not which is holy, 393
  g. not your daughters, 210
  g. rain upon Thy land, 300
  g. strong drink, 237
  g. thanks unto the Lord, 174
  g. thanks unto Thee, 174
  g. thanks unto Thee, 290
  g. the land of Canaan, 71
  g. the sacrifice, 415
  g. Thee thanks, 80

g. them a miscarrying, 77
g. them after the work, 223
g. them one heart, 308
g. them to his servants, 258
g. therefore Thy servant, 96
g. thy flesh unto, 35
g. to him that asketh, 37
g. to the poor, 115
g. unto Me, 65
g. unto the children, 210
g. unto the Lord, 290
g. unto the Lord, 174
g. unto the Lord, 290
g. unto thee the keys, 226
g. unto them for me, 377
g. unto your servants, 107
g. up the ghost, 90
g. up the ghost, 3
g. us an inheritance, 112
g. us this day, 137
g. you another Comforter, 54
glory will I not g., 151
God doth g. us, 210
have, and g. alms, 46
heart, so let him g., 46
in every thing g. thanks, 174
is not mine to g., 21
Lord is able to g., 329
may g. thanks, 87
more blessed to g., 11
my name, He will g., 214
new commandment I g., 56
peace I g. unto you, 54
received, freely g., 146
such as I have g. I, 46
what I shall g., 146
what shall a man g. in, 209
what wilt Thou g., 77
given
  ask, and it shall be g., 293
  be g. him from heaven, 147
  bread shall be g., 333
  cup my Father hath g., 3
  g. me life, 234
  g. me my petition, 31
  g. meat unto, 137
  g. rest unto His people, 174
  g. thee that which, 329
  g. up the ghost, 90
  g. you a land, 210
  g. you the city, 24
  g. you the land, 210
  give, and it shall be g., 10
  much is g. of him, 271
  that which he hath g., 10
  to him shall be g., 238
  wherefore is light g., 13
giver
  loveth a cheerful g., 19
giveth
  friend to him that g., 143

g. his life, 95
g. his neighbour drink, 103
g. life unto the world, 37
g. unto the poor, 45
God g. to a man, 34
He g. thee power, 403
he that g. do it with, 46
showeth mercy and g., 37
to the sinner He g., 176
glad
  g. in the Lord, 179
  g. that Thou hast done, 147
  heart be g. when he, 146
  Jerusalem, and be g., 212
  let the earth be g., 42
  maketh a g. father, 48
  maketh a g. father, 48
  rejoice and be g., 42
  wine that maketh g., 237
gladly
  suffer fools g., 138
gladness
  g. for the upright, 179
  serve the Lord with g., 352
glass
  through a g. darkly, 53
glean
  g. even among the sheaves, 146
gleaning
  g. of the grapes, 283
glorieth
  g. let him glory, 36
glorified
  Father may be g., 152
  g. Him not as God, 167
  God is g. in Him, 151
  I will be g., 52
  she hath g. herself, 36
  Son of man g., 151
  Son of man should be g., 151
glorify
  and thou shalt g. Me, 18
  Father, g. Thy name, 151
  g. God in your body, 36
  g. Thy Son, 152
  shall not g. Thy name, 291
  Thy Son also may g., 152
glorious
  become g. in power, 370
  blessed be Thy g., 290
  g. in holiness, 22
glory
  all to the g. of God, 5
  another star in g., 183
  appear in His g., 211
  appear with Him in g., 323
  come short of the g., 245
  created him for My g., 73
  crowned him with g., 244
  crownedst him with g., 245
  death, but for the g., 151
  declare His g., 116

declare my g. among, 116
declareth g. of God, 151
desirous of vain g., 12
fear God, and give g., 222
forbid that I should g., 36
full of His g., 151
g. among the heathen, 151
g. and dominion forever,
216
g. due unto His name, 174
g. due unto His name, 290
g. honour, and peace, 85
g. in his might, 36
g. in his riches, 36
g. in his wisdom, 36
g. in the highest, 151
g. is departed, 192
g. is in their shame, 168
g. of God did lighten it,
152
g. of man, 147
g. of the Lord, 415
g. of the Lord, 151
g. of this, and, 342
g. of young men is, 122
g. that fadeth not, 331
g. to God in the highest,
291
g. to the Lord, 290
g. ye in His holy name, 179
great is the g., 151
He is the King of g., 165
head is a crown of g., 8
His g. shall be revealed,
346
image and g. of God, 243
leave your g., 113
let him g. in the Lord, 36
let him that g. in, 125
Lord g. and strength, 290
my g. and the lifter, 53
My g. into shame, 120
My g. will I not give, 151
nor of men sought we g.,
289
own g. is not g., 36
people see His g., 151
power and great g., 346
power, and the g., 152
power, and the g., 116
received up into g., 215
received us to the g., 134
salvation and my g., 147
sanctified by My g., 65
search their own g., 36
seeketh his own g., 36
Solomon in all his g., 15
this King of g., 156
though I desire to g., 36
throne of Thy g., 151
to Him be g., 215
to Him g. and dominion,
157

unto His kingdom and g.,
148
unto our Father be g., 291
unto Thy name give g., 147
what g. is it, 75
when g. is increased, 112
wise shall inherit g., 147
woman is the g. of, 243
ye are our g., 147
glutton
g. shall come to poverty,
103
gnashing
weeping and g. of teeth, 13
weeping and g. of teeth,
312
gnat
strain at a g., 196
go
all g. unto one place, 81
cannot g. back, 297
g. and cry, 129
g. and do thou likewise,
171
g. in peace, 34
g. not forth, 79
g. not in the way, 26
g. not up, 399
g. not up, 161
g. out or come in, 193
g. out with haste, 142
g. over this Jordan, 96
g. the way of all, 80
g. thou and preach, 104
g. to all that I shall, 295
g. up in peace, 250
g. up to the mountain, 188
g. up to the mountain, 95
g. up; for I will deliver, 162
g. whence I shall not, 80
g. with him twain, 69
g. ye into all the world, 97
g. your way, 42
I shall g. to him, 80
I will g. forth, 129
let her not g., 105
let him g. up, 399
let Israel g., 16
let Israel g., 166
Let My people g., 142
let my people g., 16
Lord g. before you, 142
nor g. by flight, 142
not g. empty, 142
not g. in to them, 210
not g. thither, 96
not g. up, nor fight, 277
not let the people g., 76
not let thee g., 34
then I will g., 384
to g. a mile, 69
to g. as he came, 145
way he should g., 47
whither I g. ye know, 182

whither will He g., 264
who will g. for us, 255
wilt g. with me, 384
goads
wise are as g., 177
goat
g. shall bear upon, 343
goats
and I punished the g., 32
blood of bulls and g., 141
rams with he g., 93
sheep from the g., 49
goblet
like a round g., 25
god
g. is their belly, 168
if he be a g., 129
know no g. but Me, 260
no g. with Me, 156
sacrificeth unto any g., 188
Godhead
fulness of the G., 101
G. is like unto gold, 166
godliness
follow after g., 148
g. is profitable, 297
g. with contentment, 67
mystery of g., 168
godly
all that will live g., 168
deliver the g., 87
gods
after their g., 210
all the g. are idols, 129
be as g. knowing, 111
cry unto the g., 129
exalted far above all g., 120
fear other g., 198
fear other g., 71
feared above all g., 134
g. are come down, 255
g. are g. of the hills, 86
g. of Egypt, 198
g. of gold, 198
g. of silver, 198
g. shall be a snare, 109
g. which your fathers, 197
God above all g., 152
God of g., 165
greater than all g., 152
have the g. delivered, 17
images, Ye are our g., 197
let the g. do to me, 267
Lord is above all g., 152
molten g., 198
name of other g., 197
name of your g., 43
no g. but the work of, 198
O Lord, among the g., 22
other g. before Me, 197
other g. to serve, 23
serve other g., 209
serve other g., 128
serve strange g., 22

of a g. conscience, 240
of g. courage, 63
overcome evil with g., 170
peace, but no g., 122
proceedeth not evil and g.,
169
remember for g., 329
rewarded evil for g., 4
rewarded me evil for g.,
169
rewarded me g., 67
rewardeth evil for g., 169
righteous is only g., 122
see your g. works, 84
seek g. and not evil, 49
set forth g. wine, 191
so is g. news from a far,
266
speak that which is g., 7
steps of a g. man, 26
strong and of a g., 108
teach them the g., 105
terror to g. works, 173
that call evil g., 169
that doeth g. is of God, 169
that knoweth to do g., 170
then may ye also do g., 43
they that have done g., 78
thing is not g., 104
to a man that is g., 34
to do g. they have no, 169
what seemeth g., 61
what seemeth Him g., 2
whatsoever are of g. re-
port, 66
whatsoever seemeth g., 285
whether it be g. or, 3
wisdom is g. with an, 410
wise to that which is g., 170
withhold not g. from, 174
work together for g., 126
goodlier
g. person than, 257
goodly
g. are thy tents, 24
g. heritage, 185
g. wings unto, 17
goodman
g. of the house, 43
goodness
abundant in g., 165
for Thy g.' sake, 139
fruit of the Spirit is g., 187
full of g. of Lord, 105
g. and mercy shall follow,
34
g. and my fortress, 161
g. is as a morning cloud,
170
g. of God leadeth, 171
g. the Lord shall do, 174
hungry soul with g., 89
Lord for His g., 290
goods

all my g. to feed the, 46
gospel
begotten through the g.,
172
believe the g., 171
but to preach the g., 117
defence of the g., 172
g. must be published, 117
g. should live of the g., 27
g. which was preached, 172
hope of the g., 172
if our g. be hid, 167
my sake and the g.'s, 171
not ashamed of the g., 171
obey not the g., 327
poor the g. is preached, 179
preach any other g., 185
preach not the g., 53
preach the g., 97
preach the g., 111
preach the g., 172
unto us was the g., 155
government
increase of his g., 252
grace
but g. and truth came, 56
by g. are ye saved, 127
by the g. of God, 45
g. and peace be multiplied,
228
g. be to you, 338
g. be with them that, 35
g. be with you, 35
g. did much more abound,
140
g. in Thy sight, 177
g. is no more g., 173
g. of Christ be with you, 35
g. of Christ be with you,
386
g. of the Lord, 340
g. unto the humble, 194
g. which was bestowed, 45
giveth g. to the humble,
194
grow in g., 228
if by g. then, 173
speech be alway with g., 70
strong in the g., 141
under g., 173
word of His g., 35
gracious
be g. unto us, 250
g. and full of, 59
g. God, and merciful, 59
g. unto thee, 34)
God g., 154
God is g., 154
God, merciful and g., 165
He is g. and merciful, 166
merciful and g., 59
grain
faith as a g. of mustard,
125

g. of mustard seed, 176
grape
eateth the sour g., 320
grapes
bring forth g., 96
brought forth wild g., 96
bush gather they g., 65
clusters of g., 36
g. are fully ripe, 221
g. are g. of gall, 32
g. of Ephraim, 283
have eaten sour g., 32
treader of g., 300
vines have tender g., 92
grass
bray when he hath g., 60
causeth g. to grow, 76
cut down like the g., 406
days are as g., 244
dew upon the g., 12
flesh is as g., 147
g. withereth, 165
like g. which groweth, 244
man as the flower of g., 147
shall be made as g., 133
showers upon the g., 106
wicked spring as the g., 230
withered like g., 88
grasshoppers
g. for multitude, 203
sight as g., 132
grave
be declared in the g., 235
be sober, g., 28
brought down to the g., 192
cruel as the g., 211
down to the g., 156
down to the g., 326
draweth nigh unto the g., 8
g. cannot praise, 81
g. is mine house, 91
g. where is thy victory, 82
gathered into thy g., 80
I will make thy g., 93
in the g. who shall, 80
it is enough: the g., 81
laid in the g., 80
so doth the g. those, 80
to the g. shall come up, 80
womb to the g., 350
graven
any g. image, 197
g. by art, 166
g. image, 198
g. images, 197
g. images, 198
g. upon the table, 280
maker thereof hath g., 199
profiteth the g. image, 199
graves
g. are ready, 80
that are in the g. shall, 200
gray
man of g. hairs, 92

old men is the g. head, 122
great
and of g. mercy, 59
as a g. lion, 50
as well as the g., 201
Babylon the G., 88
both small and g., 100
both to small and g., 381
brought all this g. evil, 157
by thy g. wisdom, 95
city of the g. King, 211
day of the Lord is g., 222
done to me g. things, 34
every g. matter, 231
exceeding g. reward, 159
first and g. commandment,
  56
found so g. faith, 125
g. a God as our, 152
g. and dreadful day, 253
g. are His mercies, 250
g. house there are not, 100
g. in power, 306
g. is His mercy, 154
g. is our God, 152
g. is our Lord, 152
g. is the Lord, 152
g. is the mystery, 168
g. is the wrath, 99
g. is thy faith, 125
g. is your reward, 247
g. men not always wise, 8
g. mercies, 1
g. name's sake, 1
g. nation, 50
g. offences, 301
g. prophet is risen, 22
g. revenues, 98
g. shall be the peace, 105
g. shepherd of the sheep,
  218
g. strength lieth, 207
g. things doeth He, 152
g. things for thyself, 11
g. treasure and trouble, 66
g. was the company, 295
God is g., 152
house I build is g., 152
how g. a matter a little, 25
is of g. understanding, 276
like unto this g. city, 408
Lord g. and terrible, 24
make thee a g. nation, 49
mercy is g., 153
misery of man is g., 414
name shall be g. among,
  116
same shall be called g., 56
same shall be g., 175
seen a g. light, 111
small and g. are there, 80
the dead, small and g., 222
thee do some g. thing, 7
Thou art g. O Lord, 152

two g. lights, 20
was g. among the, 64
whosoever will be g., 10
works of the Lord are g.,
  265
greater
brother be g., 135
g. he that prophesieth, 57
g. is He that is in you, 215
g. light to rule, 20
g. love hath no man, 143
g. than all gods, 152
g. than he that sent, 113
g. than Solomon is here,
  213
God g. than man, 175
God is g. than our heart,
  153
hath the g. sin, 178
My Father is g., 21
no g. joy than to, 48
punishment is g., 302
servant is not g., 113
greatest
even unto the g., 69
g. of these is charity, 126
he that is g. among you,
  232
least of them to the g., 228
least to the g., 5
greatly
g. to be praised, 152
God g. to be feared, 133
greatness
ascribe ye g. unto, 116
g. and the power, 152
g. of Thy mercy, 154
g. of Thy power, 59
g. of thy wisdom, 318
Greek
neither G. nor Jew, 113
neither Jew nor G., 113
the Jew and the G., 113
Greeks
debtor both to the G., 185
G. seek after wisdom, 298
unto the G. foolishness, 75
green
g. bay tree, 118
g. pastures, 54
wither as the g. herb, 406
greet
g. with an holy kiss, 338
g. ye one another with, 135
grew
g. and waxed a great, 176
multiplied and g., 7
word of God g., 117
greyheaded
old and g., 8
grief
acquainted with g., 252
and his travail g., 91
g. to his father, 48

g. to my sorrow, 350
though He cause g., 250
wisdom is much g., 410
griefs
borne our g., 32
grieve
that it may not g., 118
grievous
burdens g. to be borne, 39
correction is g., 23
g. to be borne, 196
gross
heart is waxed g., 200
ground
dew falleth on the g., 64
down to the g., 249
dust of the g., 72
fallow g., 316
parched g., 300
return unto the g., 302
spilt on the g., 260
standest is holy g., 186
to till the g., 274
unto Me from the g., 122
grow
field, how they g., 15
g. in grace, 228
g. instead of wheat, 206
g. like a cedar, 176
g. out of his roots, 252
g. up without mire, 176
g. without water, 176
grass to g., 76
word, that ye may g., 165
groweth
flourisheth, and g. up, 244
like grass which g., 244
grown
art g. thick, 83
beards be g., 353
g. up unto the heavens, 353
till they were g., 245
grudging
hospitality without g., 191
guide
except some man g. me,
  105
g. even unto death, 116
meek will He g., 177
upright shall g. them, 208
guides
blind g. which strain, 196
guile
lips from speaking g., 189
mouth was found no g., 206
guiltless
anointed, and be g., 18
g. before the Lord, 206
hold him not g., 326
not hold him g., 33
guilty
g. of death, 41
he is g. of all, 100
yet is he g., 55

gulf
  great g. fixed, 184

H

habitation
  desired it for His h., 211
  h. of His throne, 332
  h. of the just, 34
  h. of the strong, 327
  h. of Thy throne, 223
  holy h., 408
  prepare Him an h., 163
  the h. of devils, 83
habitations
  h. of the wilderness, 265
hail
  fire mingled with the h.,
    284
  h. shall come down, 284
  there was h., 284
  treasures of the h., 122
hair
  at an h. breadth, 4
  h. of my flesh, 132
  h. of thy son, 337
  man have long h., 15
  not an h. of him fall, 222
  one h. white or black, 267
  plucked off the h., 13
  woman have long h., 15
hairs
  h. of mine head, 2
  h. of mine head, 110
  hoar h., 9
  man of gray h., 92
  the very h. of your head,
    153
half
  give h. to the one, 222
  h. of my kingdom, 298
  h. of the greatness, 318
  h. thine house, 66
  h. was not told, 136
hallow
  h. My sabbaths, 335
hallowed
  h. be Thy name, 149
halt
  enter h. into life, 78
  h. ye between, 42
Haman
  hanged H. on the gallows,
    223
hand
  am I a God at h., 158
  betrayeth me is at h., 31
  by the h. of a fool, 266
  calamity is at h., 303
  day of the Lord at h., 92
  day of the Lord is at h.,
    221
  dealeth with a slack h., 230
  deceit are in his h., 40

deliver out of My h., 156
deliver thee into the h., 86
deliver thee to mine h., 63
deliver them to thine h.,
  162
delivered them to thine h.,
  109
drew not his h., 92
end is at h., 15
evil is in mine h., 206
fall into the h. of man, 76
for it is nigh at h., 22
h. be upon him, 249
h. for h., 324
h. I commit my spirit, 162
h. into His side, 102
h. is stretched out, 384
h. is stretched out, 150
h. is stretched out, 150
h. of a mediator, 57
h. of a mighty man, 348
h. of a woman, 395
h. of all your enemies, 86
h. of David, 124
h. of God, 3
h. of God hath touched, 59
h. of her enemies, 1
h. of him that betrayeth, 31
h. of him that slayeth, 17
h. of Joab, 68
h. of my brother, 132
h. of our enemies, 352
h. of our God, 160
h. of the diligent, 230
h. of the doers of, 399
h. of the Lord, 250
h. of the Lord, 85
h. of the Lord, 13
h. of the Lord shall be, 330
h. of the Lord was, 207
h. of the Lord was with, 68
h. of the mighty, 160
h. of the Philistines, 32
h. of the uncircumcised, 90
h. of the wicked, 205
h. of their enemies, 1
h. of this Philistine, 63
h. riches and honour, 409
h. shall be lifted, 396
h. shall find out all, 110
h. shall not be upon, 322
h. to the plough, 95
h. waxed short, 73
h. will be against, 109
h. with the wicked, 58
hour is at h., 31
I am in your h., 41
iniquity be in thine h., 26
into thine h., 395
is in her right h., 409
kingdom of God is at h.,
  339
know Mine h., 157
know what thy right h., 46

land into his h., 64
let not mine h., 32
let not thy left h., 46
lift up Thine h., 160
lifted up his h., 99
like a man's h., 287
Lord is at h., 159
man's h. against him, 109
mine h. shall not be, 73
Mine h. take them, 114
My h. made all these, 73
not put forth mine h., 258
of heaven is at h., 226
of heaven is at h., 339
on the right h. of God, 247
open thine h. wide, 45
out of h., 350
out of their h., 86
potter's h., 92
power of thine h., 174
put forth mine h., 208
put not forth thine h., 43
reach hither thy h., 102
rend it out of the h., 250
right h. forget, 1
right h. offend, 32
right h. shall find, 110
right h. shall save, 161
sat on the right h., 18
save with Thy right h., 87
sheep of His h., 154
shut thine h., 45
Sisera into thine h., 389
sit thou at My right h., 160
sit Thou on my right h.,
  120
slack not thy h., 10
slayer up into his h., 209
so are ye in Mine h., 92
stay now thine h., 250
stretch forth his h., 18
stretch out My h., 284
Thine h. is power, 156
thousand at thy right h., 79
thy h. findeth to do, do,
  106
Thy right h. O Lord, 370
time is at h., 200
time is at h., 200
to sit on my right h., 21
twoedged sword in h., 326
Uzza put forth his h., 309
with the right h., 163
withhold not thine h., 95
work of Thy h., 73
handful
  better is an h., 11
handfuls
  h. of barley, 130
handmaid
  count not thine h., 407
  lie unto thine h., 135
  remember thine h., 174
hands

can thine h. be strong, 376
cleanse your h., 307
deliver you out of my h., 33
down with her h., 188
eat with unwashen h., 307
fear not but let your h., 70
folding of the h., 288
fool foldeth his h., 230
h. are full of blood, 178
h. are the h., 83
h. be weak, 106
h. cannot perform, 156
h. full with travail, 11
h. I commend my spirit, 3
h. make whole, 156
h. of sinners, 31
h. of the living God, 151
h. of the wicked, 7
h. on the sick, 182
h. shall be feeble, 403
h. that shed innocent, 207
h. to war, 371
he that hath clean h., 189
labour of thine h., 106
laid His h. on, 182
lift up the h. which, 64
lifting up holy h., 294
over the works of Thy h., 245
pierced my h., 280
puttest thine h. unto, 413
recompence of a man's h., 399
reward of his h., 305
see in His h., 102
spread forth your h., 1
strengthen my h., 141
strengthen ye the weak h., 108
temples made with h., 52
the h. of Esau, 83
water, and washed his h., 320
which are made with h., 199
with works of your h., 301
with works of your h., 150
work of His h., 112
work of men's h., 198
work of men's h., 198
work of men's h., 198
work of the h., 25
work of their h., 223
work of their h., 155
work of their own h., 197
working with his h., 74
works of His h. are, 166
handywork
    showeth His h., 151
hang
    hands which h. down, 64
hanged

h. Haman on the gallows, 223
he that is h., 79
millstone h. about his, 48
hangeth
    h. the earth, 72
Hannah
    Elkanah knew H., 135
happy
    h. are thy men, 231
    h. are thy servants, 231
    h. are ye if ye do, 180
    h. is he that hath, 124
    h. is that people, 168
    h. is the man, 46
    h. is the man that, 48
    h. is the man that, 180
    law, h. is he, 55
    mercy on the poor, h., 59
    of Christ, h. are ye, 282
    sake, h. are ye, 334
    them h. which endure, 180
    trusteth in the Lord, h., 180
    wherefore are they h., 205
hard
    any thing too h., 157
    h. for the Lord, 123
    how h. is it, 115
    too h. for you, 231
    transgressors is h., 360
harden
    h. his heart, 76
    h. not your heart, 28
    h. not your hearts, 202
    h. thine heart, 45
hardened
    h. our heart, 356
    h. their necks, 372
harder
    h. than a rock, 202
    h. than flint, 282
    h. to be won, 139
harlot
    city become an h., 200
    played the h., 23
    sister as with an h., 325
harlots
    Babylon Mother of H., 88
harm
    amends for the h., 321
    do My prophets no h., 50
    do thyself no h., 321
    done thee no h., 16
harmless
    h. as doves, 363
    h. as doves, 79
harness
    girdeth on his h., 35
harp
    praise the Lord with h., 263
    psaltery and h., 263
    with the timbrel and h., 78
hart

as the h. panteth, 241
leap as an h., 181
harts
    princes are like h., 212
harvest
    h. is past, 91
    h. of the earth is ripe, 249
    h. truly is plenteous, 117
    rain in h., 138
    seedtime and h., 345
    sleepeth in h., 230
    white already to h., 273
haste
    go out with h., 142
    h. to be rich, 11
    h. unto me, O God, 18
    make h. to help, 18
    said in my h., 233
    shall not make h., 28
    upon them make h., 303
hasteth
    eagle that h., 367
    h. to the snare, 379
    h. with his feet, 309
hasty
    h. of spirit, 136
    heart be h. to utter, 309
    man that is h., 309
hate
    do good to them that h., 27
    dost but h. me, 83
    either he will h., 242
    find out those that h., 110
    h. him that rebuketh, 75
    h. me without a cause, 110
    h. the evil, 26
    h. thee shall be clothed, 109
    I h. him; for he doth, 7
    if the world h., 181
    if the world h. you, 282
    is to h. evil, 118
    lest he h. thee, 74
    love the Lord, h. evil, 118
    love them that h., 10
    reward them that h., 220
    that h. Me, 303
    that h. me love death, 409
    them that h. Thee, 109
    they that h. you, 65
    things doth the Lord h., 207
    time to h., 181
    weary of thee, and so h., 191
    what I h. that do I, 348
hated
    and h. him not, 209
    h. him yet the more, 103
    h. me before it h. you, 181
    h. of all men for my, 32
    hatred wherewith he h., 180
    poor is h., 143

therefore have I h., 30
therefore I h. life, 89
hatest
  h. thy friends, 143
  of them whom thou h., 86
hateth
  and h. his brother, 38
  and h. his brother, 169
  evil h. the light, 119
  h. his brother is a, 181
  h. his life, 235
  h. his own soul, 74
  h. his son, 47
  h. me h. my Father, 110
  h. reproof is brutish, 74
  h. reproof shall die, 74
  righteous man h., 233
  that h. Him, 129
  violence His soul h., 398
hating
  truth, h. covetousness, 172
hatred
  h. for my love, 169
  h. stirreth strifes, 16
  h. wherewith he hated, 180
  hideth h., 40
  stalled ox and h., 238
haughtiness
  lay low the h., 17
haughty
  eyes are upon the h., 16
  h. spirit before a fall, 123
head
  anointest my h., 34
  art exalted as h., 365
  blood upon thy h., 178
  bowed His h., 75
  crown of his h., 24
  dog's h., 208
  eyes are in his h., 138
  fallen from our h., 328
  fastest, anoint thine h., 132
  fire upon his h., 353
  go up, thou bald h., 257
  h. and not the tail, 268
  h. of all principality, 22
  h. of Christ is God, 21
  h. of every man is, 21
  h. of him that selleth, 40
  h. of the body, 22
  h. of the church, 246
  h. of the corner, 328
  h. of the wicked, 150
  h. stone of the corner, 274
  h. were waters, 377
  hair of my h., 13
  hairs of mine h., 2
  hairs of mine h., 110
  hairs of your h. are all, 153
  hoar h. go down, 326
  hoary h. is a crown, 8
  increased over our h., 353
  John Baptist's h., 327
  lifter up of mine h., 53

old men is the grey h., 122
return upon his own h., 65
return upon thine own h.,
  224
swear by thy h., 267
upon their own h., 326
upon thine own h., 324
where to lay His h., 188
heads
  blood upon your own h.,
  178
  h. shall be baldness, 262
heal
  behold, I will h., 291
  h. me, O Lord, 181
  h. the brokenhearted, 87
  h. the sick, 284
  physician, h. thyself, 75
  time to h., 181
  torn, and He will h., 157
  wound, and I h., 156
healed
  every one of them and h.,
  182
  faith to be h., 182
  h. every one, 182
  h. wist not who it was, 11
  his stripes we are h., 181
  I shall be h., 181
  pray that ye may be h., 294
  servant shall be h., 125
healeth
  h. the broken in heart, 364
healing
  h. in his wings, 22
health
  faithful ambassador is h.,
  107
  h. to the bones, 366
  time of h., 122
heap
  h. coals of fire, 353
heapeth
  h. up riches, 205
heaps
  ass, h. upon h., 370
  Babylon shall become h.,
  86
hear
  and they would not h., 293
  as I h. I judge, 221
  before it h. him, 4
  blessed are they that h.,
  171
  cried and I would not h.,
  293
  cry, and Thou wilt not h.,
  201
  deaf h., 179
  deaf to h., 179
  dost not h. me, 91
  ears to h. let him h., 184
  ears to h. let him h., 208
  ears, but they h. not, 198

ears, h. ye not, 373
fathers, h. ye my defence,
  224
graves shall h. His, 200
greater joy than to h., 48
h. a rumour, 86
h. and understand, 184
h. any more the voice, 8
h. counsel, and receive, 7
h. instruction, and be, 7
h. me, O Lord, h. me, 298
h. my prayer, 292
h. my speech, 295
h. my voice, 295
h. now, ye rebels, 298
h. O earth, 366
h. o Israel, 259
h. O Lord, forgive, 139
h. O our God, 285
h. O ye kings, 363
h. of wars and, 15
h. open Thine eyes, 19
h. the bleatings, 104
h. the rebuke, 74
h. the small, 201
h. the song of fools, 74
h. the word of the, 116
h. the word of the, 322
h. the word of the, 183
h. the word of the Lord, 91
h. their cry, 408
h. them speak, 385
h. Thou in heaven, 138
h. thy servant curse, 74
h. thy words but, 100
h. what the Spirit, 184
h. without a preacher, 105
h. ye deaf, 372
h. ye indeed, 372
h. ye that are far, 5
h. ye the word, 295
h. ye the word, 402
h. ye the word, 299
h. you in that day, 303
have an ear, let him h., 300
He did h. my voice, 291
heareth, let him h., 183
hearing they h. not, 199
Him shall ye h. in all, 21
I the Lord will h., 131
I will h. it, 231
I will not h., 183
if any man h. my voice, 217
if they h. not Moses, 284
if ye will h. His voice, 28
lest they should h., 100
let the earth h., 295
Lord will h. when, 292
man be swift to h., 13
more ready to h. than, 415
name, and I will h., 19
neither see, nor h., 198
not h. the law, 99
not h. their cry, 132

one would h. me, 206
people h. the voice, 22
pleased; h. ye Him, 251
report that I h., 266
shall He not h., 158
shall Pharaoh h. me, 231
sheep h. my voice, 10
spake, ye did not h., 99
that h. the words of, 300
that He will not h., 293
Thine ear, and h., 293
we will h., 22
which h. the word, 131
wise man will h., 183
would not h., 372
yet will I not h., 139

heard
all things I have h., 325
but they have not h., 100
h. even afar off, 42
h. for much speaking, 293
h. me, and delivered, 87
h. my voice: hide not, 293
h. not the voice, 399
h. the secret, 61
h. these words, 364
h. thy prayer, 291
h. thy prayer, 59
hast h. and live?, 22
have ye not h., 152
He h. me, 292
He hath h. the voice, 174
message that ye h., 240
nor ear h., 35
not h. long ago, 145
seen and h. declare we, 186
shall be h. no more, 86
shall not be h., 45
such as they have not h.,
    150
they that have not h., 117
things seen and h., 381
which I have h. of Him,
    325
whom they have not h., 29
words are not h., 8
words which thou hast h.,
    108

hearers
doers, and not h., 85
not the h. of the law, 85

hearest
h. the sound thereof, 263
Thou h. not, 91
when Thou h. forgive, 138

heareth
but he h. not, 167
cry, and the Lord h., 292
every one that h., 380
h. the prayer of the, 162
He h. the cry, 292
he that h. my word, 29
Lord h. the poor, 288
of God h. God's words, 20

scorner h. not rebuke, 74
that h. and doeth not, 8
that h. let him hear, 183
that h. these sayings, 100
Thy servant h., 183
truth h. my voice, 389
whosoever h. of it, 324
whosoever h. these, 84
wise son h., 74

hearing
dull of h., 200
faith cometh by h., 126
famine of h. the words, 131
filled with h., 11
h. by the word of, 126
h. of his ears, 123
h. they hear not, 199

hearken
forgive; O Lord, h., 139
h. and hear my speech, 295
h. not to your prophets, 8
h. than fat of rams, 269
h. thou unto the voice, 269
h. unto the words, 129
h. unto their judges, 129
h. unto their voice, 3
h. unto them, 291
h. unto thy father, 275
h. unto you more, 65
him ye shall h., 252
not h. unto them, 313

hearkened
h. not, nor inclined, 183
h. to My commandments,
    270
h. unto the words, 99

heart
abundance of the h., 44
according to thy h., 9
adultery in his h., 6
all that is in thine h., 108
all thine h., 241
all thy h., 28
all thy h., 44
all thy h., 57
all your h., 268
believe in thine h., 217
bound in the h., 47
break mine h., 378
broken and a contrite h., 67
brother in your h., 38
but in h. he layeth, 195
but their h. is far, 10
can thine h. endure, 376
charity out of a pure h.,
    240
circumcision is of the h., 53
comfort thine h., 191
create in me a clean h., 368
deceit is in the h., 98
destroyeth the h., 38
entered into the h., 35
eye affecteth mine h., 354
fleshy tables of the h., 280

fool said in his h., 19
foreskin of your h., 53
foreskins of your h., 316
give them one h., 308
glad the h. of man, 237
God greater than our h.,
    153
h. be not deceived, 129
h. be perfect, 269
h. be troubled, 54
h. cheer thee, 416
h. decline to her ways, 6
h. deviseth his way, 26
h. envy sinners, 211
h. full of evil, 118
h. goeth after, 195
h. hath continual feast, 180
h. is deceitful, 118
h. is faint, 374
h. is made better, 229
h. is not right, 19
h. is not with, 195
h. is privy, 64
h. is sorrowful, 229
h. knoweth his own, 13
h. man believeth, 29
h. of flesh, 315
h. of fools, 35
h. of fools, 138
h. of him that hath, 227
h. of kings, 259
h. of the righteous, 99
h. of the wicked, 189
h. of the wise, 106
h. of the wise, 138
h. of this people, 200
h. rejoiceth, 179
h. said unto Thee, 124
h. shall not reproach, 64
h. standeth in awe, 7
h. taketh not rest, 91
h. that deviseth, 207
h. waketh, 103
h. was not perfect, 23
hands, and a pure h., 189
harden his h., 76
harden not your h., 28
harden thine h., 45
hardened our h., 356
healeth the broken in h.,
    364
her beauty in thine h., 6
high look and a proud h.,
    17
hypocrites in h. heap, 3
imagination of man's h.,
    118
in integrity of h., 189
lay it to his h., 81
let h. of them rejoice, 179
let not thine h. be glad, 146
looketh on the h., 209
madness is in their h., 118
make you a new h., 236

maketh the h. sick, 190
meditation of my h., 292
meek and lowly in h., 54
merry h. doeth good, 89
merry h. maketh, 180
mine eyes and mine h., 158
no man's h. fail, 70
not thine h. be hasty, 309
of a broken h., 176
out of the h. proceed, 261
perverse h., 88
pour out thine h., 293
pour out your h., 124
prepareth his h., 139
pride of thine h., 61
pride of thine h. hath, 61
pure in h., 307
purposeth in his h., 46
removed their h., 195
rend your h., 317
said in thine h., 61
seal upon thine h., 239
set not their h. aright, 99
set not your h., 404
set Thine h. upon him, 244
set your h. and soul, 94
slow of h. to believe, 299
sorrow of the h., 364
stony h., 315
strength of my h., 141
strengthen your h., 63
such an h. in them, 133
table of their h., 280
take away the h., 237
there will your h. be, 242
thought of thine h., 317
treasure of the h., 45
trusteth in his own h., 61
truth in his h., 338
turn away your h., 210
turned their h. back, 298
uncircumcised in h., 167
understanding h., 391
understanding h., 96
upright in h., 179
upright in h., 179
uprightness of thine h., 395
vexation of his h., 77
vision of their own h., 130
war was in his h., 106
was in thine h., 209
wash thine h., 316
whose h. departeth from, 314
whose h. Thou knowest, 138
wine with a merry h., 137
wise man's h., 97
with a double h., 98
with a perfect h., 128
with a perfect h., 94
with all his h., 257
with all thine h., 388
with all thy h., 95

with all your h., 94
with all your h., 94
with all your h., 129
word hid in mine h., 55
word in thy h., 55
words in thine h., 55
hearted
merry h. do sigh, 364
that are wise h., 408
hearts
apply our h. unto, 234
consider not in their h., 74
evil in your h., 119
evil in your h., 119
h. as an adamant stone, 100
h. of all that are wise, 408
h. of all the children, 153
h. of the people, 72
harden not your h., 202
knoweth the h., 68
knoweth your h., 153
laws into their h., 57
Lord pondereth the h., 261
Lord searcheth all h., 153
mischief is in their h., 84
prepare your h., 94
purify your h., 307
rule in your h., 278
sanctify Lord in your h., 95
searcheth the h., 153
searcheth the h., 216
that be of heavy h., 237
written in our h., 381
heat
cold and h., 345
drought and h. consume, 80
on them, nor any h., 67
then they have h., 38
heathen
among the h., 121
among the h., 290
counsel of the h., 144
deliver us from the h., 87
exalted among the h., 151
fury upon the h., 167
fury upon the h., 150
glory among the h., 116
glory among the h., 151
great among the h., 116
h. are dismayed, 19
h. shall see My judgment, 151
near upon all the h., 167
polluted before the h., 151
repetitions, as the h., 293
say among the h., 116
scatter thee among the h., 121
small among the h., 305
vengeance upon the h., 326
way of the h., 26
wherefore should the h., 343
wherefore should the h., 1

heaven
army of h., 157
as an eagle toward h., 112
bound in h., 289
by the God of h., 163
called the firmament h., 68
came down from h., 214
came down from h., 38
climb up to h., 114
cometh down from h., 37
created, that are in h., 73
do not I fill h. and, 113
eagles of the h., 367
earth, as it is in h., 149
easier for h. and earth, 56
fallen from h., 86
Father which art in h., 149
Father which is in h., 279
Father which is in h., 45
Father which is in h., 131
Father which is in h., 216
Father which is in h., 177
Father which is in h., 177
Father which is in h., 146
Father which is in h., 28
Father, which is in h., 149
first h. and the first, 183
fought from h., 18
fowls of the h., 305
from h. like a dove, 187
gave us rain from h., 309
given him from h., 147
God created the h., 25
God in h. above, 164
God in h. above, 158
God in h. that revealeth, 103
God is in h., 193
God of h., 373
h. and earth praise, 290
h. and earth shall pass, 50
h. and in the earth, 183
h. even the heavens, 183
h. is high above, 154
h. is My throne, 158
h. is My throne, 52
h. of h. cannot contain, 52
h. of h. cannot contain, 52
h. or in earth, 152
hast made h., 73
hear Thou in h., 138
height of h., 152
if I ascend up into h., 113
in h. above, 164
joy shall be in h., 203
lightning fall from h., 341
Lord of h., 52
made h. and earth, 19
made h. and earth, 72
made h. and earth, 72
Master in h., 107
names are written in h., 180
not the angels of h., 345

hewn
  built houses of h., 96
  h. out her seven pillars, 409
  will build with h., 17
hid
  falsehood have we h., 98
  h. His face, 293
  h. I My face from them,
    311
  h. in the day, 249
  h. not my face, 280
  h. that not be known, 347
  h. that shall not be, 347
  hill cannot be h., 232
  hill cannot be h., 131
  if our gospel be h., 167
  life is h. with Christ, 217
  prudent men shall be h.,
    305
  sins are not h., 62
  treasure h. in a field, 226
  word h. in mine heart, 55
hidden
  eat of the h. manna, 331
hide
  h. himself in secret, 113
  h. me under the shadow,
    160
  h. Mine eyes, 1
  h. not Thine ear, 293
  h. not Thy commandments,
    226
  h. not Thy face, 18
  h. not Thy face, 387
  h. thee in the dust, 113
  h. their counsel from, 98
  h. Thyself for ever, 1
  how long wilt Thou h., 1
  of iniquity may h., 74
  Sodom, they h. it not, 353
hidest
  h. Thou Thy face, 1
  why h. Thou Thyself, 18
hideth
  evil, and h., 301
  h. hatred, 40
  h. His face, 158
  h. not from Thee, 113
  he that h. his eyes, 45
high
  abase him that is h., 328
  h. above all the earth, 120
  h. above the earth, 154
  h. as the eagle, 114
  h. places were not taken,
    197
  like the most H., 20
  Lord on h. is, 156
  maketh men h. priests, 70
  men of h. degree, 44
  Most H., 165
  mouth of the most H., 169
  my h. tower, and my, 161
  peace in His h. places, 277

record is on h., 162
set me up on h., 193
Son of the most h., 341
that hath an h. look, 17
though the Lord be h., 59
higher
  rock that is h., 337
highest
  glory in the h., 151
  glory to God in the h., 291
highway
  desert a h., 252
hill
  ascend into the h., 186
  city set on an h., 232
  city set on an h., 131
  h. is not enough, 64
  h. shall be brought low, 253
hills
  eyes unto the h., 19
  gods of the h., 86
  h. be removed, 154
  hoped for from the h., 145
  little h. like lambs, 22
  made before the h., 8
  watereth the h., 309
himself
  only upon h., 43
hinder
  who can h. Him, 156
hip
  smote them h. and thigh,
    398
hire
  h. of a whore, 45
  worthy of his h., 413
hired
  h. out themselves, 195
  oppress an h. servant, 39
hireling
  because he is an h., 95
  h. fleeth, 95
  oppress the h. in wages,
    411
hissing
  astonishment, and an h., 86
hoar
  h. hairs, 9
  h. head go down, 326
hoary
  h. head is a crown, 8
hold
  h. fast to that, 171
  h. him not guiltless, 326
  not h. My peace, 212
holdest
  wherefore h. Thy tongue,
    205
holes
  foxes have h., 188
  move out of their h., 192
holier
  h. than thou, 350
holiness

beauty of h., 415
behaviour as becometh h.,
  28
glorious in h., 22
h. unto the Lord, 186
h. without which no man,
  16
uncleanness, but unto h.,
  186
holy
  against the H. one, 17
  an h. God, 165
  be ye h., 25
  between the h. and, 53
  bless His h. name, 290
  but for Mine h. name's, 151
  day is h. unto, 186
  for they are h., 296
  glory ye in His h. name,
    179
  God that is h., 333
  greet with an h. kiss, 338
  h. h. h. is the Lord, 186
  h. h. h. Lord God, 116
  h. habitation, 408
  h. in all His works, 166
  h. is he that hath part, 82
  h. is His name, 34
  h. mountain, 330
  H. One and the Just, 218
  h. people, 50
  h. to the Lord, 136
  h. unto the dogs, 393
  h. unto the Lord, 186
  h. unto the Lord, 53
  if the root be h., 185
  is h. so be ye h., 186
  is in His h. temple, 163
  lifting up h. hands, 294
  none h. as the Lord, 186
  pollute ye My h., 33
  rejoice ye h. apostles, 327
  sabbath, keep it h., 335
  saith the H. One, 129
  shall be h., 231
  stand before this h., 156
  stand in His h. place, 186
  standest is h., 318
  standest is h. ground, 186
  suffer Thine H. One, 114
  temple of God is h., 30
  thanks to Thy name, 87
  Thou only art h., 186
  with an h. kiss, 144
  ye shall be h., 186
  your God am h., 186
Holy Ghost
  baptize you with the H., 24
  baptizing in name of H.,
    117
  blasphemeth against the
    H., 33
  blasphemy against the H.,
    33

Comforter which is the H.,
187
communion of the H., 386
Father, Word, and H., 386
giving them the H., 68
joy in the H., 187
receive ye the H., 34
resist the H., 167
speaketh against the H.,
187
temple of the H., 36
well spake the H., 299
home
h. again empty, 79
h. in the body, 236
h. there is death, 81
tarry at h., 342
homeborn
him that is h., 112
honest
whatsoever things are h.,
66
honestly
walk h. toward, 319
willing to live h., 65
honey
butter and h., 97
eat thou h. because, 136
in thy mouth sweet as h.,
32
milk and h., 210
sweeter also than h., 55
sweeter than h., 208
sweeter than h., 331
taste a little h., 121
honeycomb
drop as an h., 6
h. which is sweet, 136
honey and the h., 55
words are as an h., 366
honour
and give h. to Him, 180
before h. is humility, 193
bring thee to h., 409
crowned him with h., 244
delight to do h., 61
delighteth to h., 188
for thine h., 147
full of h., 80
glory, h. and peace, 85
h. all men, 319
h. come of Thee, 130
h. for a man to cease, 16
h. is not seemly, 138
h. is nothing, 289
h. of kings is, 259
h. person of the mighty,
132
h. the face, 8
h. the king, 173
h. the Lord with, 384
h. thy father, 275
h. thy father, 275

h. thy father and mother,
56
h. to whom h., 133
h. unto the wife, 247
h. widows that are, 408
him will my Father h., 97
him with glory and h., 245
I will h., 311
if I h. myself, 289
king's h., 172
left hand riches and h., 409
more h. than the house, 5
prophet hath no h. in, 318
prophet is not without h.,
299
receive not h. from men, 16
riches, and h., 329
sing forth the h., 363
that h. Me, 311
where is Mine h., 275
with their lips do h., 195
worthy of double h., 53
honoured
that h. her despise her, 69
honoureth
a son h. his father, 275
Father that h. me, 289
h. Him hath mercy, 59
h. me with their lips, 10
h. not the Son h. not, 5
hook
h. in thy nose, 192
leviathan with a h., 244
hope
and experience, h., 190
ashamed of my h., 124
faith, h. charity, 126
h. and quietly wait, 276
h. deferred, 190
h. for Thy truth, 81
h. hath He removed, 91
h. in His mercy, 328
h. in the day of evil, 190
h. in the Lord, 63
h. is in the Lord, 124
h. maketh not ashamed,
190
h. of Israel, 202
h. of salvation, 27
h. of the gospel, 172
h. of the hypocrite, 195
h. shall perish, 129
h. that is seen is not h., 190
h. the Lord is, 180
h. to the end, 282
His word do I h., 164
judged for the h., 281
life only we have h., 323
more h. of a fool, 309
more h. of a fool than, 61
of whom ye h. to receive,
10
poor hath h., 190
prisoners of h., 190

promise, having no h., 92
saved by h., 190
spent without h., 90
Thou art my h., 190
where is now my h., 91
while there is h., 47
hoped
in vain is salvation h., 145
substance of things h., 127
hopeth
h. all things, 240
horn
h. of my salvation, 159
hornet
sent the h., 18
horse
as the h. rusheth, 203
be not as the h., 14
behold a pale h., 15
behold a white h., 128
h. and his rider, 289
h. is prepared against, 396
he that rideth the h., 114
whip for the h., 98
horseleach
h. hath two daughters, 175
horses
as fed h., 204
bits in the h.' mouths, 271
contend with h., 60
my h. as thy h., 10
some in h., 314
Hosanna
H., 289
hospitality
h. without grudging, 191
host
destroy ye her h., 14
multitude of an h., 259
hosts
except the Lord of h., 376
God of h., 417
h. is His name, 165
h. is His name, 87
holy, is the Lord of h., 186
King, the Lord of h., 22
Lord God of h., 17
Lord of h., 165
Lord of h. hath sent, 255
Lord of h. is His name, 148
messenger of Lord of h.,
296
name of the Lord of h., 124
saith the Lord of h., 404
saith the Lord of h., 371
saith the Lord of h., 116
hot
anger be h., 150
anger of my Lord wax h.,
321
go upon h. coals, 6
h. displeasure, 46
neither cold nor h., 57
thou wert cold or h., 111

hour
 behold, the h. cometh, 200
 came I unto this h., 256
 cometh at an h. when, 310
 h. is at hand, 31
 h. is come, 151
 h. is coming, 200
 h. is not yet come, 384
 h. knoweth no man, 345
 h. of His judgment is, 222
 h. the thief would come, 43
 h. your Lord doth come, 345
 in jeopardy every h., 282
 know what h. I will come, 346
 one h. is thy judgment, 83
 the space of half an h., 22
 watch with me one h., 96
house
 an h. of merchandise, 337
 barren woman to keep h., 135
 begin at the h. of God, 221
 build him a sure h., 329
 build Him an h., 52
 build Me an h., 163
 builded the h. hath more, 5
 buildeth her h., 188
 built Thee an h., 52
 called a h. of prayer, 52
 come into thine h., 135
 depart from thine h., 77
 doors of my h., 309
 dwell in the h., 34
 dwell within my h., 98
 escape in the king's h., 280
 every h. is builded by, 5
 every man to his h., 322
 evil depart from his h., 169
 forsaken Mine h., 1
 from thy neighbour's h., 191
 glory of his h., 112
 goest to the h. of God, 415
 goodman of the h., 43
 grave is mine h., 91
 h. be divided, 372
 h. by unrighteousness, 69
 h. cannot stand, 372
 h. full of sacrifices, 352
 h. full of silver, 268
 h. is the h. of prayer, 52
 h. is the way to hell, 6
 h. of bondage, 142
 h. of cedar, 52
 h. of God, 415
 h. of Israel, 92
 h. of Judah, 375
 h. of mirth, 138
 h. of mourning, 138
 h. of mourning than to, 81
 h. of my pilgrimage, 54
 h. of Pharaoh, 284

 h. of the God, 163
 h. of the God of Jacob, 95
 h. of the Lord, 45
 h. of the Lord, 163
 h. of the righteous, 333
 h. of the wicked, 34
 h. unto My name, 304
 h. upon a rock, 285
 h. upon the earth, 8
 h. upon the sand, 285
 h. which I build, 152
 h. which I have built, 52
 half thine h., 66
 hedge about his h., 160
 how to rule his own h., 52
 if the h. be worthy, 34
 in a great h. there are, 100
 in his own h., 299
 in my Father's h. are, 54
 is the h. of Israel, 50
 like that rebellious h., 311
 Lord build the h., 4
 lost sheep of the h., 219
 make not my Father's h., 337
 master of the h. cometh, 108
 me and my h. we, 49
 midst of a rebellious h., 58
 Mine h. shall be called, 52
 more honour than the h., 5
 not covet thy neighbor's h. (112
 out of thine own h., 310
 peace to thine h., 250
 poor to thy h., 59
 rebellious h., 133
 sakes, O h. of Israel, 151
 set thine h. in order, 80
 sittest in thine h., 55
 than to h. of feasting, 81
 to thine own h., 77
 troubleth his own h., 131
 turn to his own h., 121
 watchman unto the h., 320
 what h. will ye build, 52
 what is my h., 193
 wisdom builded her h., 409
 wisdom is an h. builded, 4
 woman in a wide h., 246
household
 of his own h., 372
 ways of her h., 246
houses
 build h. but not, 144
 h. and riches are the, 205
 h. full of deceit, 74
 h. of hewn stone, 96
 h. to aliens, 64
housetops
 corner of the h. than, 246
 preach ye upon the h., 295
 proclaimed upon the h., 123

how
 h. are the mighty, 228
 h. are the mighty, 85
 h. long halt ye, 42
 h. long shall, 277
 h. long wilt thou mourn, 175
 h. shall this be, 102
 h. to go out, 193
howl
 h. O gate, 102
 h. ye; for the day, 92
 I will wail and h., 176
 lament and h., 262
 rich men, weep and h., 405
humble
 better of an h. spirit, 193
 cry of the h., 292
 forget not the h., 160
 giveth grace to the h., 194
 grace unto the h., 194
 h. yourselves in the, 194
 he that shall h. himself, 194
 refuse to h. thyself, 16
 save the h. person, 193
humbled
 h. my soul with fasting, 132
 h. themselves; therefore, 139
 mighty man shall be h., 192
humbleth
 because he h. himself, 67
 h. himself shall be, 11
 h. himself shall be, 61
humbly
 walk h. with thy God, 193
humility
 before honour is h., 193
 clothed with h., 194
 h. of mind, 194
hundred
 against eight h., 370
 do evil an h. times, 168
 h. stripes into a fool, 74
 his number is Six h., 119
 if a man have h. sheep, 283
hunger
 blessed are they which h., 333
 h. no more, 67
 idle soul shall suffer h., 230
 if thine enemy h., 140
 slain with h., 81
 to me shall never h., 92
hungred
 h. and ye gave me meat, 60
 h. and ye gave me no, 76
hungry
 bread to the h., 59
 enemy be h., 110
 filled the h., 60
 h. man dreameth, 96
 h. soul with goodness, 89
 steal when he is h., 73

to the h. soul every, 89

hunt
evil shall h., 398
h. a partridge, 120
h. every man his brother, 262
h. our steps, 102

huntest
h. my soul, 280

hurt
meddle to thy h., 401
people, but the h., 40
set on thee to h., 338
turn and do you h., 22
will do you no h., 301

husband
crown to her h., 245
desire shall be to thy h., 20
entice thy h., 30
h. is the head of the, 246
h. put away his wife, 101
h. render unto the wife, 246
h. that believeth not, 29
lament for the h., 86
please her h., 95
put away her h., 6
sanctified by the h., 29
unbelieving h., 29
woman have her own h., 141

husbands
ask their h. at home, 412
h. love your wives, 246
may be your h., 13
subjection to your h., 247
submit unto your h., 246
to love their h., 247
wives be to their own h., 246

hypocrisy
Pharisees, which is h., 196
within ye are full of h., 15

hypocrite
h. with his mouth, 362
h.'s hope shall perish, 129
hope of the h., 195
joy of the h., 118

hypocrites
and Pharisees, h., 196
as the h. do, 46
h. in heart heap, 3
h. ye can discern, 97
tempt ye me, ye h., 379

Ile
every i. word that men, 320
i. soul shall suffer, 230

Ileness
bread of i., 246

Iolaters
without are dogs, and i., 83

idolatry
flee from i., 198
iniquity and i., 372

idols
defile yourselves with i., 167
gifts, and with your i., 33
gods of the people are i., 129
i. are silver and gold, 198
i. He shall abolish, 198
keep yourselves from i., 198
slain men before your i., 93
turn ye not unto i., 198

if
i. the Lord be with us, 102
i. ye seek Him, 94

ignorance
i. of foolish men, 85
through i. ye did, 75

ignorant
i. of his devices, 342

ignorantly
i. worship, 200

ill
love worketh no i., 239
shall be i. with him, 305

image
any graven i., 197
graven i., 198
i. and glory of God, 243
in the i. of God, 244
man in His own i., 244
profiteth the graven i., 199
the beast and his i., 198

images
graven i., 197
graven i., 198
i. shall be broken, 93
molten i., 198
say to molten i., 197

imagination
i. of man's heart, 118

imaginations
deviseth wicked i., 207

imagine
i. evil against, 38
i. evil in your hearts, 119
them that i. evil, 98

imagined
devices they have i., 223
they have i. to do, 11

Immanuel
shall call his name I., 252

impossible
i. to please Him, 127
nothing shall be i., 2
nothing shall be i., 157
with men it is i., 245

impute
Lord will not i. sin, 140

imputed
sin is not i., 229

incense
sacrificed and burnt i., 197

incline
i. Thine ear, 87
i. thine ear, 177
i. Thine ear, 19

inclined
because He i. His ear, 292
hearkened not, nor i., 183

incorruptible
crown; but we an i., 60

incorruption
raised in i., 36

increase
but God gave the i., 76
firstfruits of thine i., 384
he must i. but I, 258
i. is by the strength, 106
i. of his government, 252
i. our faith, 126
if riches i. set not, 404
labour shall i., 404
land shall yield her i., 268
loveth abundance with i., 175
thy victuals for i., 392
will i. learning, 183

increased
glory of his house is i., 112
not i. the joy, 176
our iniquities are i., 353
traffick hast thou i., 95

increaseth
against Thee i., 166
i. knowledge i. sorrow, 77
i. strength, 162
woe to him that i., 74

incredible
thought a thing i., 323

indignation
i. toward His enemies, 330
stand before His i., 150

infant
woman, i. and suckling, 14

infinite
understanding is i., 152

infirmities
bear the i. of the weak, 45

infirmity
priests which have i., 70

influences
i. of Pleiades, 288

inhabit
houses, but not i., 144
which ye shall i., 73

inhabitant
hissing, without an i., 86
i. of the earth, 91

inhabitants
curse ye bitterly the i., 104
i. of the earth, 157
i. of the land, 22
unto all the i., 142
upon the i., 324

inhabited
cities that are not i., 90
formed it to be i., 73
inhabiters
i. of the earth and, 342
inherit
i. My holy mountain, 330
i. the earth, 124
i. the kingdom, 226
i. the wind, 131
meek shall i., 249
overcometh shall i., 127
righteous shall i., 329
shall i. the earth, 194
unrighteous shall not i., 225
wise shall i. glory, 147
inheritance
forsake His i., 242
I am their i., 296
i. among our brethren, 112
i. is turned to, 64
i. of fathers, 205
i. to pass, 204
Israelites for an i., 210
leaveth an i., 173
Lord is their i., 53
Lord is their i., 296
lot of your i., 71
portion of mine i., 204
remnant of Mine i., 1
reward of the i., 331
swallow up the i., 92
take of the people's i., 390
to be Thine i., 154
wisdom good with i., 410
iniquities
all their i., 343
bruised for our i., 252
hath remembered her i., 168
i. are forgiven, 140
i. are increased over, 353
i. by showing mercy, 26
less than our i., 250
pine away for your i., 176
shouldest mark i., 220
iniquity
acknowledge thine i., 62
be in me i., 205
bond of i., 112
committeth i., 23
devise i. and work evil, 74
die for his own i., 320
draw i. with cords, 360
father bear the i. of, 356
forgive their i., 139
from the workers of i., 230
full of hypocrisy and i., 15
i. be in thine hand, 26
i. do flourish, 230
i. have your fathers, 114
i. is marked before, 178
i. not be your ruin, 317
i. of the father, 356

i. of the fathers, 303
i. was not found, 189
laid on him the i., 247
mine i., 205
of i. shall be scattered, 407
reaped i., 223
shall die in his i., 295
stubbornness is as i., 372
stumblingblock of i., 404
take away the i., 67
truth and without i., 165
upon me let this i., 320
uttereth thine i., 178
we have committed i., 62
wicked for their i., 118
workers of i., 84
workers of i., 92
workers of i., 58
workers of i. may hide, 74
world of i., 119
inn
room for them in the i., 217
innocent
i. blood, 262
i. of the blood, 33
lay not upon us i., 32
rich shall not be i., 11
shed i. blood, 207
slay an i. person, 18
inspiration
Scripture is given by i., 344
instant
i. in season, 310
instead
i. of a mouth, 366
i. of eyes, 122
i. of God, 366
instruct
that he may i. Him, 153
instruction
counsel, and receive i., 7
despise wisdom and i., 105
despiseth father's i., 48
he that refuseth i., 98
heareth his father's i., 74
i. and be wise, 7
i. of fools is, 391
i. to a wise man, 7
my i. and not silver, 105
sealeth their i., 103
whoso loveth i., 74
instructors
ten thousand i. in Christ, 37
instrument
i. of ten strings, 263
instruments
stringed i., 263
integrity
i. of heart, 189
i. of the upright, 208
know mine i., 63
remove mine i., 206

retain thine i., 44
walk in mine i., 208
walketh in his i., 189
intendest
i. thou to kill, 383
intercession
i. for the transgressors, 252
now make i., 20
interpretation
dream, and the i., 103
of any private i., 299
interpretations
i. belong to God, 103
intreat
i. me not, 94
who shall i. for him, 220
intreaties
poor useth i., 70
inward
i. man is renewed, 141
iron
brass and i., 373
i. as straw, 370
i. sharpeneth i., 44
i. sinew, 373
pen of i., 280
sunder the bars of i., 271
yokes of i., 41
Isaac
God of I., 148
island
i. fled away, 93
isles
declare it in the i., 116
Israel
avenging of I., 174
but I. doth not know, 21
departed from I., 192
do before all I., 192
face of I., 159
faith not in I., 125
fought for I., 162
fourth part of I., 2
God of I., 165
He that keepeth I., 50
He that scattered I., 50
he that troubleth I., 32
hear, o I., 259
Holy One of I., 17
hope of I., 202
house of I., 92
house of I., 320
I. for His treasure, 50
I. have deeply revolted, 3
I. is My son, 49
I. loved Joseph, 47
I. shall be a proverb, 313
I. stoned him, 311
I. thou hast destroyed, 16
I. turneth their backs, 72
I. will not forsake, 390
I. will not forsake, 131
into the land of I., 210
is the house of I., 50

king over I., 351
let I. go, 16
let I. go, 166
Lord loved I., 232
master of I., 199
may prove I., 382
meet thy God, O I., 310
My people I., 71
prince over My people I.,
156
sakes, O house of I., 151
See also "Children of Israel"
sheep of the house of I.,
219
shepherds of I., 69
Solomon king of I., 210
Strength of I., 233
tabernacles, o I., 24
Thou art God in I., 152
tribes of I., 211
unto His people I., 174
virgin of I., 50
Israelite
I also am an I., 219
Israelites
I. for an inheritance, 210
I. so am I, 219
issues
belong the i. from death,
87
ivory
tower of i., 36

J

Jacob
birthright unto J., 204
dust of J., 2
dwellings of J., 211
God of J., 148
God of J. for his help, 124
house of the God of J., 95
J. said unto his father, 83
J. served seven years, 238
Lord hath chosen J., 50
not Esau J.'s brother, 239
Star out of J., 252
tents, o J., 24
voice is J.'s, 83
yet I loved J., 239
jaw
j. of an ass, 370
jawbone
j. of an ass, 370
jealous
a j. God, 165
am a j. God, 303
God is j., 327
is a j. God, 165
j. for the Lord, 417
j. God, 165
j. God, 165
whose name is J., 165

jealousy
fire of My j., 93
j. burn like fire, 139
j. is cruel, 211
j. is the rage, 211
provoked Him to j., 150
Jehovah
J. is everlasting strength,
371
J. is my strength, 371
name alone is J., 165
Jehu
J. shall serve, 83
jeopardy
j. of their lives, 334
j. of their lives, 70
lives in j., 297
stand we in j., 282
Jericho
city of J., 77
tarry at J., 353
Jerusalem
cause J. to know, 295
daughters of J., 25
die at J. for, 95
forget thee, O J., 1
garments, O J., 315
have chosen J., 211
J. a praise in the, 212
J. compassed with armies,
109
J. for it is the city, 267
J. is ruined, 33
J. J. thou that killest, 212
J. shall My name, 211
J. the city, 211
J. the city which the Lord,
211
J.'s sake I will not, 212
joy of J., 42
king unto J., 283
out of J., 375
rejoice ye with J., 212
round about J., 154
shall yet choose J., 87
spirit unto J., 104
stand up, O J., 397
testified of me in J., 70
wall of J., 211
wipe J. as a man wipeth, 92
word of the Lord from J.,
56
word of the Lord from J.,
212
Jesse
out of the stem of J., 252
Jew
advantage hath the J., 53
between the J. and the, 113
he is not a J., 15
neither Greek nor J., 113
neither J. nor Greek, 113
jewel
as a j. of gold in, 24

jewels
thighs are like j., 25
Jews
I might gain the J., 5
is He the God of the J.,
149
J. a stumblingblock, 75
J. have I done no wrong,
52
J. I became as a Jew, 5
J. require a sign, 298
King of the J., 213
King of the J., 218
more than all the J., 280
salvation is of the J., 340
Jezebel
carcase of J., 39
dogs shall eat J., 41
dogs shall eat J., 353
not say, this is J., 39
Jezreel
wall of J., 41
Joab
hand of J., 68
Job
considered my servant J.,
257
J. fear God, 207
J. twice as much, 282
latter end of J., 87
man is like J., 350
men, Noah, Daniel, and J.,
93
patience of J., 277
words of J. are ended, 109
John
J. Baptist's head, 327
prophets were until J., 225
join
come, and let us j., 28
joined
God hath j. together, 101
joint
foot out of j., 30
joints
j. of thy thighs, 25
Jonas
sign of the prophet J., 254
Jonathan
J. loved him, 143
shalt surely die, J., 123
soul of J., 143
though it be in J., 201
Jordan
not go over J., 2
other side J., 66
over this J., 96
swelling of J., 327
Joseph
I am J., 275
Israel loved J., 47
Jesus, the son of J., 343
Joshua
J. drew not his hand, 92

journey
    j. that thou takest, 147
joy
    eat thy bread with j., 137
    folly is j. to him that, 136
    fool hath no j., 138
    glad with exceeding j., 346
    good tidings of great j., 180
    j. cometh in the morning,
    179
    j. in the God, 180
    j. in the Holy Ghost, 187
    j. in the presence of, 203
    j. may be full, 180
    j. of Jerusalem, 42
    j. of the hypocrite, 118
    j. of the Lord, 370
    j. of the whole earth, 211
    j. of the whole earth, 212
    j. shall be in heaven, 203
    j. shall ye draw, 339
    j. to heaviness, 229
    knowledge, and j., 34
    no greater j. than to, 48
    not increased the j., 176
    over thee with j., 339
    peace is j., 277
    reap in j., 76
    shout for j., 179
    shout for j., 179
    songs and everlasting j.,
    142
    Spirit is love, j., 187
    turned into j., 190
    wise child shall have j., 48
    ye are our glory and j., 147
joyful
    j. mother of children, 135
    j. noise to the rock, 363
    j. noise unto God, 363
    make a j. noise, 290
    prosperity be j., 283
joyous
    no chastening be j., 75
Judah
    depart from J., 231
    house of J., 375
    J. is fallen, 33
Judas
    J. Iscariot, 30
judge
    adulterers God will j., 6
    as I hear, I j., 221
    came not to j., 221
    deserts will I j., 223
    doth j. and make war, 221
    God is the j., 373
    he shall not j., 123
    I j. no man, 15
    j. Him according to, 320
    j. him that eateth, 385
    j. His people, 220
    j. me after the law, 123
    j. my judgment is true, 221

j. not according to, 15
j. not and ye shall not, 75
j. not for man, 220
j. not that ye be not, 32
j. not the cause, 205
J. of all, 154
j. of the widows, 408
j. righteous judgment, 15
j. righteously, 223
j. righteously, 219
j. shall j. him, 220
j. standeth before the, 200
j. the fatherless, 59
j. the world, 220
j. the world, 220
j. the world, 221
j. thee according, 220
j. Thou my cause, 223
j. thy neighbor, 219
j. Thy people, 96
j. you every one, 203
j. yourselves unworthy, 49
king to j., 112
law j. any man before, 4
Lord is our j., 148
Lord shall j., 220
Lord, the righteous j., 331
matter they shall j., 231
more than unto God, j., 65
no j. of such matters, 52
prince and a j., 231
righteousness shall he j.,
    252
saints shall j., 30
shall j. the righteous, 220
the Lord j. between, 322
we shall j. angels, 12
with what judgment ye j.,
    75
ye j. after the flesh, 15
judged
    j. by the law, 221
    j. every man according, 222
    j. for the hope, 281
    judge, ye shall be j., 75
    that ye be not j., 32
    where I ought to be j., 52
    ye shall not be j., 75
judges
    faces of the j., 205
    hearken unto their j., 129
    j. of the earth, 172
    j. shall condemn, 321
judgest
    j. another man's servant,
    17
    wherein thou j. another, 75
    who art thou that j., 75
judgeth
    Father j. no man, 21
    j. the poor, 259
    j. the righteous, 220
    that j. me is the Lord, 21
    the Lord God who j., 306

judgment
    aged understand j., 8
    Almighty pervert j., 118
    bring every work into j., 84
    choose to us j., 84
    committed all j. unto, 21
    correct me, but with j., 177
    danger of the j., 12
    day of j. than for thee, 202
    enter not into j., 220
    establish j. in the gate, 26
    execute j. upon all, 306
    execute true j., 27
    feed them with j., 220
    God of j., 166
    guide in j., 177
    have done j. and justice, 1
    hour of His j. is come, 222
    I stand at Caesar's j., 52
    I will execute j., 198
    if I judge my j. is true, 221
    in the day of j., 167
    in the day of j., 320
    j. in the earth, 223
    j. into gall, 69
    j. is before Him, 220
    j. is God's, 220
    j. is turned away, 230
    j. is with the Lord, 125
    j. must begin at, 221
    j. of this world, 221
    j. of truth, 224
    j. run down as waters, 223
    j. seat of Christ, 113
    j. seat of Christ, 222
    j. that I have executed, 151
    j. was not to drink, 305
    j. without mercy, 76
    judge righteous j., 15
    justice and j., 223
    keep mercy and j., 125
    keep ye j., 26
    looked for j., 96
    Lord love j., 223
    Lord loveth j., 128
    man's j. cometh from, 223
    my j. is just, 221
    not wrest the j., 201
    one hour is thy j. come, 83
    people know not the j., 99
    persons in j., 201
    redeemed with j., 212
    righteousness and j., 332
    sit in j., 290
    there is no j., 91
    time and j., 97
    to do justice and j., 223
    unrighteousness in j., 39
    verity and j., 166
    with what j. ye judge, 75
judgments
    executed j. upon, 338
    His j. are in all, 158
    keep My j., 270

observe their j., 167
righteous are His j., 221
righteous are Thy j., 306
unsearchable are His j., 153
just
  give that which is j., 107
  habitation of the j., 34
  Him that is most j., 60
  Holy One and the J., 218
  j. and having salvation, 193
  j. and right is He, 165
  j. and true are Thy ways,
    334
  j. be delivered, 87
  j. before God, 85
  j. he shall surely live, 333
  j. man walketh in, 189
  j. shall live by faith, 126
  j. shall live by his, 125
  j. shall walk, 26
  j. upright man, 257
  j. weight, 40
  j. with God, 62
  memory of the j., 318
  mortal man be more j., 26
  mouth of the j., 333
  must be j. ruling, 172
  my judgment is j., 221
  ninety nine j. persons, 203
  not a j. man on earth, 279
  path of the j., 332
  resurrection of the j., 11
  sendeth rain on the j., 169
  shall have j. balances, 40
  teach a j. man, 7
  tongue of the j., 189
  way of the j., 333
  whatsoever things are j., 66
justice
  done judgment and j., 1
  j. and judgment, 223
  j. standeth afar, 230
  j. to the afflicted, 223
  judgment, and do j., 26
  princes decree j., 259
  to do j. and judgment, 223
justification
  raised again for our j., 323
justified
  all that believe are j., 29
  doers shall be j., 85
  j. by faith, 85
  j. by faith, 57
  j. by the law, 56
  j. in the name, 224
  j. in the Spirit, 215
  no man living be j., 220
  not j. by the works, 56
  shall no flesh be j., 56
  wisdom is j., 410
  words thou shalt be j., 221
  works a man is j., 85
justifieth
  it is God that j., 224

justify
  j. the righteous, 72
  not j. the wicked, 118
justly
  do j., 224

K

keep
  bless thee and k. thee, 161
  except the Lord k., 348
  if ye love me, k. my, 214
  k. all My statutes, 317
  k. her; she is thy life, 105
  k. His commandments, 55
  k. His saying, 88
  k. my commandments, 270
  k. My commandments, 99
  k. My commandments, 268
  k. My covenant, 268
  k. My judgments, 270
  k. my words, 217
  k. the charge, 269
  k. the commandments, 56
  k. the commandments, 55
  k. the doors, 30
  k. therefore and do, 55
  k. you from evil, 128
  k. ye judgment, 26
  k. your own tradition, 196
keeper
  Lord is thy k., 161
  my brother's k., 38
keepeth
  He that k. Israel, 50
  k. all his bones, 252
  k. not His commandments,
    100
  k. not my sayings, 100
  k. thee will not slumber,
    161
kept
  k. me this day, 7
keys
  k. of the kingdom, 339
kick
  k. ye at My sacrifice, 69
kid
  lie down with the k., 14
kill
  adultery, do not k., 56
  afraid of them that k., 261
  do not k., 7
  fear not them which k., 36
  intendest thou to k., 383
  k. and I make alive, 156
  k. and to make alive, 181
  k. Him: and the third, 75
  k. me, I pray, 350
  k. the soul, 36
  rise, Peter; k. and eat, 137
  shalt not k., 262
  some bade me k., 249
  time to k., 181

to steal, and to k., 74
killed
  after that He is k., 322
  for Thy sake are we k., 247
  hast thou k., 46
  k. hath power to cast, 78
  k. with the sword, 325
killedst
  k. me not, 174
  k. the Egyptian, 383
killest
  k. the prophets, 212
killeth
  k. a beast, 321
  k. a beast, 302
  k. a man, 41
  k. a man, 302
  k. and maketh alive, 156
  k. you will think, 281
  letter k., 56
  that k. with the sword, 325
  wrath k. the foolish, 12
kind
  k. one to another, 27
  suffereth long and is k., 240
kindled
  k. against the shepherds, 32
  k. against Uzza, 150
  that is k. against, 99
  wrath shall be k., 197
kindleth
  little fire k., 25
kindly
  Lord deal k., 34
kindness
  anger, and of great k., 166
  anger, and of great k., 59
  is this thy k., 9
  it shall be a k., 3
  k. shall not depart, 154
  showed more k., 224
king
  against the k.'s son, 208
  anointed k., 364
  children of a k., 24
  city of the great K., 211
  city of the great K., 267
  escape in k.'s house, 280
  everlasting k., 149
  eyes have seen the K., 22
  from being k., 65
  God save the k., 259
  He is K. of k., 119
  He is the K. of glory, 165
  honour the k., 173
  k. delight to do honour, 61
  k. delighteth to honour,
    188
  k. himself is served, 69
  k. is a child, 232
  K. of all the earth, 290
  k. of Babylon, 3
  k. of Babylon shall not, 8
  k. of Israel, 120

K. of K. and Lord of, 218
K. of the Jews, 213
K. of the Jews, 218
k. over Israel, 351
k. saved by the multitude, 259
K. shall reign, 252
K. Solomon passed all, 404
k. that faithfully, 259
k. unto Jerusalem, 283
k.'s favour, 12
k.'s honour, 172
k.'s son in law, 258
k.'s son is dead, 59
k.'s wrath is as, 12
keep k.'s commandment, 259
Lord and the k., 259
Lord is our k., 148
made He thee k., 232
make them a k., 3
make us a k. to judge, 112
my lord the k. be, 242
no k. but Caesar, 242
old and foolish k., 7
palace of k. of Babylon, 192
rare thing that the k., 286
Saul to be k., 312
Solomon k. of Israel, 210
truth preserve the k., 259
unto thee, O k., 83
was there no k. before, 257
we will have a k., 255
who is this K. of glory, 156
wicked from before k., 259
wise k. scattereth, 230
word of a k., 21
wrath of a k., 12
kingdom
and k. against k., 15
called you unto His k., 148
comest into Thy k., 67
half of my k., 298
His heavenly k., 338
how shall then his k., 341
k. against k., 44
k. are guiltless, 206
k. be divided, 173
k. cannot stand, 173
k. is not of this world, 21
k. is the Lord's, 172
k. shall be the Lord's, 365
k. shall not continue, 304
k. that will not serve, 212
k. there shall be no end, 51
more but the k., 11
pleasure to give the k., 225
sceptre of Thy k., 334
Son coming in His k., 81
Thine is the k., 365
thine is the k. and the, 116
Thy k. come, 149
kingdom of God

cannot enter into the k., 24
cannot see the k., 37
enter into the k., 115
enter into the k., 225
fit for the k., 95
inherit the k., 226
k. cometh not with, 225
k. is at hand, 339
k. is come nigh, 225
k. is not in word, 225
k. is not meat, 187
k. is preached, 225
k. is within you, 225
k. with one eye, 182
not inherit the k., 225
preach the k., 104
receive the k., 48
rich man to enter k., 225
seek first the k., 147
seek ye the k., 225
such is the k., 48
kingdom of heaven
enter into the k., 226
enter into the k., 226
for their's is the k., 226
great in the k., 56
k. is at hand, 226
k. is at hand, 339
k. like unto a merchant, 40
k. like unto treasure, 226
keys of the k., 339
not enter into the k., 68
their's is the k., 193
kingdoms
k. of the earth, 363
k. thy shame, 192
that all k. of the earth, 87
kings
before rulers and k., 281
by me k. reign, 259
hear, O ye k., 363
heart of k., 259
honour of k. is, 259
k. of the earth, 377
k. out of thy loins, 34
passed all the k., 404
prince of the k. of, 218
reproved k. for their, 50
salvation unto k., 259
stand before k., 2
that which destroyeth k., 242
with k. are they on, 332
kinsfolk
k. have failed, 237
kinswoman
call understanding thy k., 409
kiss
greet with an holy k., 338
k. me with the k., 238
k. that same is He, 31
Son of man with a k., 31
with a k. of charity, 135

with an holy k., 144
kisses
k. of an enemy, 74
knee
every k. shall bow, 9
every k. should bow, 188
kneel
k. before the Lord, 415
knees
confirm the feeble k., 108
k. shall be weak, 403
lift up the feeble k., 64
knew
and I k. it not, 158
and they k. him not, 5
because it k. Him not, 51
cause which I k. not, 10
day that I k. you, 99
in the belly I k. thee, 31
k. Hannah his wife, 135
k. not any thing, 206
k. not the Lord, 166
k. that they were naked, 226
things that I k. not, 206
way that they k. not, 111
when they k. God, 167
world k. Him not, 16
knife
k. to thy throat, 147
knit
k. with the soul, 143
knock
k. and it shall be, 293
k. and it shall be, 273
knocketh
k. it shall be opened, 106
my beloved that k., 103
know
all shall k. Me, 5
and k. what he doeth, 4
and ye shall k. that the, 255
as he ought to k., 227
but because ye k. it, 8
but Israel doth not k., 21
cause me to k. the way, 177
cause them to k., 157
dead k. not any, 235
father and mother we k., 343
for you to k. the times, 145
fruits ye shall k. them, 4
heathen that k. Thee, 167
I k. the things that, 153
if I k. not the meaning, 58
if ye k. these things, 180
Jesus I k., 21
k. among ourselves, 84
k. God but in works, 85
k. good and evil, 169
k. her abominations, 295
k. Him for I am from Him, 228
k. Him not, 228

■ 492 ■

k. Him, and keep His, 88
k. how to give good, 146
k. I the Father, 228
k. Me, from the least, 228
k. mine integrity, 63
k. no god but Me, 260
k. not a man, 102
k. not at what they, 271
k. not Him that sent, 228
k. not how to go, 193
k. not how to rule, 52
k. not the day, 8
k. not the judgment, 99
k. not the Lord, 166
k. not this man, 88
k. not what hour, 345
k. not what shall be, 145
k. not what they do, 140
k. not what ye ask, 264
k. not when the master, 108
k. not when the time, 294
k. nothing by myself, 194
k. that I am God, 228
k. that I am the Lord, 220
k. that I am the Lord, 228
k. that I am the Lord, 210
k. that I am the Lord, 21
k. that I am the Lord, 15
k. that I am the Lord, 228
k. that My name, 157
k. that they shall die, 235
k. that this is the, 28
k. that Thou art Lord, 87
k. that Thou art Lord, 298
k. that Thou canst do, 156
k. the number, 42
k. them which labour, 53
k. thou the God, 228
k. thou, that we k., 17
k. thy abode, 153
k. thy works, 111
k. to refuse the evil, 97
k. what hour I will come, 346
k. whether ye love, 129
k. ye are my disciples, 51
k. ye that the Lord, 165
let no man k. of these, 347
let not thy left hand k., 46
live; and ye shall k., 234
make me to k. mine end, 260
may k. Thee, 177
meat to eat that ye k., 368
not k. from whence, 305
on them that k. not God, 327
one thing I k., 122
Paul I k., 21
people shall k. My name, 319
people that do k. their, 125
say, I k. Him not, 88

see that no man k., 258
shall not He k., 153
sinner or no, I k. not, 122
that saith, I k. Him, 100
that ye may k. that I, 335
the way ye k., 182
to k. my transgression, 206
we k. in part, 200
whither I go ye k., 182
whom ye k. not, 149
wicked regardeth not to k., 288
wicked: who can k. it, 118
worship ye k. not what, 199
ye k. not the truth, 8
ye shall k. the truth, 142
knowest
if thou k. it all, 17
k. all the wickedness, 64
k. not that thou art, 248
k. not what a day may, 36
k. the commandments, 56
k. the hearts, 153
k. the people, 118
k. thou not, 32
k. thou not yet, 40
k. what thou oughtest, 262
Thou k. it altogether, 153
whose heart Thou k., 138
knoweth
as the Father k. me, 228
born of God, and k. God, 240
brutish man k. not, 199
day and hour k., 345
Father k. what things ye, 153
God k. all things, 153
k. any man the Father, 228
k. her appointed times, 99
k. his own bitterness, 13
k. not it is his life, 379
k. not the price, 391
k. not these things, 199
k. not whither he goeth, 200
k. not who shall gather, 205
k. nothing yet as he, 227
k. our frame, 59
k. the hearts, 68
k. them that are His, 30
k. them that trust, 19
k. what is the mind, 153
k. your hearts, 153
Lord k. how to deliver, 87
Lord k. the thoughts of, 153
Lord k. the thoughts of, 145
loveth not k. not God, 181
man think that he k., 227
no man k. the Son, 228
ox k. his owner, 21
that k. to do good and, 170

things of God k. no man, 149
understandeth and k. Me, 125
unjust k. no shame, 353
who k. whether he shall, 205
world k. us not, 51
knowing
k. good and evil, 111
unto Jerusalem, not k., 104
knowledge
and to virtue k., 127
because have no k., 121
beginning of k., 134
brutish in his k., 199
do good they have no k., 169
fools hate k., 137
full of the k., 128
give me now k., 147
God of k., 84
grow in the k. of our, 228
he that increaseth k., 77
He that teacheth man k., 153
k. is easy, 227
k. it hath perverted, 61
k. of God more than, 334
k. puffeth up, 62
k. rather than gold, 105
k. spareth his words, 395
law is k. of sin, 56
lips should keep k., 53
loveth k., 74
man concealeth k., 35
not according to k., 200
of His mouth cometh k., 409
right that find k., 53
so shall k. of wisdom, 410
speech, yet not in k., 107
spirit of k., 252
takest k. of him, 245
teach God k., 193
thou hast rejected k., 227
through k. shall the just, 87
through the k. of God, 228
tree of k., 169
understanding seeketh k., 227
utter vain k., 394
wisdom, and k., 34
wise men lay up k., 227
wise seeketh k., 227
wise, and k. to them, 149
words without k., 199
words without k., 199
known
child is k. by, 44
fool's voice is k. by, 138
had they k. it, 76
have not k. Me, 137
have ye not k., 152

hid that shall not be k., 347
hid that shall not be k., 347
I have made k. unto you, 325
if ye had k. me, ye, 214
k. by his fruit, 44
k. by his own fruit, 85
k. in the eyes of, 228
k. lust, except the law, 112
k. my Father also, 214
k. sin, but by the law, 56
k. the mind of the Lord, 228
k. the mind of the Lord, 153
k. toward His servants, 330
k. unto God, 145
k. what hour the thief, 43
k. what is spoken, 57
let it be k. this day, 152
make k. His deeds, 116
mighty power to be k., 87
paths they have not k., 111
peace have they not k., 191
people I have not k., 20
seen Him, neither k. Him, 215
wrath is presently k., 208
your requests be made k., 294

L

labour
according to his own l., 107
all ye that l., 39
good of all his l., 286
good of all his l., 137
he that gathereth by l., 404
know them which l., 53
l. and have no rest, 274
l. in vain that build, 4
l. not for the meat, 37
l. not to be rich, 11
l. of man is for, 11
l. of the righteous, 65
l. of thine hands, 106
l. there is profit, 297
let him l. working, 74
man of all his l., 145
man of all his l., 77
nothing of his l., 145
reward for their l., 67
six days shalt thou l., 335
strength l. and sorrow, 234
why l. I in vain, 90
womb to see l. and, 91
ye did not l., 210
laboured
l. for the wind, 77
l. under the sun, 77
labourer
l. is worthy, 413
l. is worthy, 123

labourers
but the l. are few, 117
l. together with God, 254
laboureth
husbandman that l., 331
in that wherein he l., 297
labouring
sleep of a l. man, 363
labours
l. more abundant, 282
lack
little had no l., 123
to the poor shall not l., 45
laden
labour and are heavy l., 39
laid
be strongly l., 39
l. His hands, 182
l. on him the iniquity, 247
lake
cast into the l. of fire, 78
into the l. of fire, 82
l. of fire and brimstone, 306
lama
Eli, Eli, l. sabachthani, 13
lamb
blood of the L., 337
dwell with the l., 14
L. are the temple of it, 163
l. for a burnt offering, 264
L. is the light, 152
L. of God, 213
L. shall overcome them, 119
l. to the slaughter, 81
L. which is in the midst, 163
like a l. dumb before, 249
marriage of the L. is, 16
marriage supper of the L., 180
wolf and the l. shall, 38
worthy is the L. that was slain, 76
lambs
feed my l., 253
l. to the slaughter, 93
little hills like l., 22
send you forth as l., 79
lame
feet was I to the l., 10
l. be turned out, 28
l. man leap, 181
l. walk, 179
maimed, the l., 42
lament
l. and howl, 262
l. like a virgin, 86
weep and l., 75
lamentation
neighbour l., 176
wilderness a l., 265
lamented
ye have not l., 78

lamp
commandment is a l., 177
l. of the wicked, 305
l. unto my feet, 111
Thou art my l., 124
land
a strange l., 138
all the l., 142
all the l. is before, 142
as a thirsty l., 241
born in the l., 112
bring into this l., 64
bring you into the l., 210
called the dry l., 104
consume the l., 131
defile not the l., 73
delivered the l., 64
dry l. springs, 403
dwelt in the l. of Nod, 274
ensign upon His l., 155
famine in the l., 131
fat of the l., 2
frogs covered the l., 284
given you a l., 210
given you the l., 210
gods in your l., 121
good of the l., 270
heard in our l., 345
inhabitants of the l., 22
l. became lice, 284
l. before thee, 147
l. before thee, 96
l. cannot be cleansed, 262
l. fall to whoredom, 48
l. flowing with milk, 210
l. is full of bloody, 230
l. is Mine, 299
l. of Canaan, 71
l. of Canaan which, 210
l. of darkness, 80
l. of the living, 380
l. of the shadow, 339
l. rested from war, 277
l. shall be emptied, 89
l. shall not be sold, 299
l. shall yield her increase, 268
l. that is not yours, 121
l. that was desolate, 321
l. the Lord careth for, 210
l. to be possessed, 8
l. was polluted, 197
l. whereunto they desire, 121
l. which I sware, 303
nakedness of the l., 4
pollute the l., 73
polluted the l., 201
possess the l., 330
possess the l., 204
possess their l., 64
rain upon Thy l., 300
return to his own l., 86
righteous inherit the l., 329

sound of a shaken l., 72
Leah
    like Rachel and like L., 135
leap
    lame man l., 181
leaped
    l. and walked, 182
learn
    if they will l. anything, 412
    l. not the way, 26
    l. of me; for I am, 216
    l. to do well, 26
    l. war any more, 400
    that I may l. Thy, 55
    woman l. in silence, 105
learned
    l. He obedience by, 215
    l. to be content, 12
learning
    increase in l., 7
    l. doth make thee mad, 105
    l. to his lips, 106
    will increase l., 183
least
    from the l. of them, 69
    in that which is l., 65
    know Me, from the l., 228
    l. to the greatest, 5
    that is l. among you all, 175
    unjust in the l., 66
    unto one of the l., 46
leave
    I will not l., 94
    l. me not to mine, 1
    l. my soul in hell, 114
    l. my wine, 11
    l. not my soul destitute, 190
    l. off contention, 371
    l. the ninety and nine, 283
    l. their wealth, 260
    l. you comfortless, 2
    let her not l. him, 29
    let Him not l., 1
    never l. thee, nor, 2
    not to l. thee, 94
    ye l. your glory, 113
leaven
    beware ye of the l., 196
    little l. leaveneth, 66
Lebanon
    grow like a cedar in L., 176
    tower of L., 36
led
    l. by the Spirit, 187
left
    even I only, am l., 90
    hand or to the l., 344
    hand, and on my l., 21
    l. but a few of many, 376
    l. hand know what thy, 46
    l. hand riches, 409
    l. Mine heritage, 1
    or to the l., 268
    remnant that are l., 291

right hand or to the l., 55
take the l. hand, 48
therefore have I also l., 1
Legion
    my name is L., 119
legs
    l. are as pillars, 36
lend
    if ye l. to them of whom,
        10
    l. him thy victuals, 392
    l. unto many nations, 37
    l. upon usury, 138
    not l. upon usury, 392
    sinners also l., 350
lender
    as with the l., 37
    servant to the l., 37
lendeth
    l. unto the Lord, 10
    showeth favour, and l., 146
length
    l. of days is in, 409
    l. of days understanding, 8
lent
    l. him to the Lord, 296
leopard
    l. his spots, 43
    l. shall lie down, 14
lepers
    cleanse the l., 284
    l. are cleansed, 179
less
    do l. or more, 268
    hast punished us l., 250
    how much l. man, 244
    l. is blessed, 22
    l. this house, 52
letter
    l. killeth, 56
    oldness of the l., 19
    spirit, and not the l., 53
leviathan
    draw out l., 244
liar
    better than a l., 98
    brother he is a l., 169
    commandments, is a l., 100
    God hath made Him a l.,
        29
    he is a l., 233
    l. but he that denieth, 234
    l. like unto you, 88
    true, but every man a l.,
        389
    we make Him a l., 196
liars
    all men are l., 233
liberty
    l. for an occasion to, 143
    l. to the captives, 202
    Lord is, there is l., 143
    proclaim l., 142
lice

land became l., 284
lick
    l. the dust, 192
    l. the dust, 192
    shall dogs l., 41
licked
    l. the blood, 41
lie
    before God, I l. not, 389
    cause them to l. down, 161
    high degree are a l., 44
    if two l. together, 38
    Israel will not l., 233
    l. down in green, 54
    l. down in the dust, 80
    l. down with the kid, 14
    l. is of the truth, 234
    l. not one to another, 190
    l. one to another, 25
    l. unto thine handmaid, 135
    l. with thy wives, 192
    loveth and maketh a l., 83
    not l. with mankind, 188
    that He should l., 165
lied
    l. and not remembered Me,
        167
    not l. unto men but unto,
        99
lies
    be born, speaking l., 25
    bow for l., 99
    forgers of l., 53
    full of l. and, 74
    l. our refuge, 98
    l. shall perish, 98
    should thy l. make men, 60
    speakest l. in the name, 130
    telleth l. shall not, 98
    will utter l., 44
    with l. ye have made, 99
    witness that speaketh l., 17
liest
    l. thou thus upon, 108
lieth
    from her that l. in thy, 30
    l. with a beast, 363
    l. with any beast, 363
    l. with his father's, 202
    l. with his sister, 202
life
    all the days of my l., 34
    Almighty given me l., 234
    and my l. is preserved, 22
    assurance of thy l., 78
    better than l., 153
    blood, hath eternal l., 115
    breath of l., 72
    but have eternal l., 82
    choose l. that, 49
    Christ, who is our l., 323
    cut off my l., 92
    days of his l., 231
    days of thy l., 76

desire tree of l., 190
enter halt into l., 78
findeth me findeth l., 409
for she is thy l., 105
for the l. of the world, 312
fountain of l., 134
fruit unto l. eternal, 115
gift of God is eternal l., 115
give for his l., 349
give l. for l., 222
give thee a crown of l., 116
given to us eternal l., 116
giveth his l., 95
giveth to all l., 149
hateth his l., 235
hath everlasting l., 29
hath the Son hath l., 217
have everlasting l., 340
He is thy l., 148
he that will love l., 119
His l. a ransom for many, 10
His l. is taken from, 185
I am the bread of l., 38
in death or l., 242
in Him was l., 213
it is your l., 55
keep it unto l. eternal, 235
keepeth his l., 301
l. and death, 235
l. and good, 26
l. consisteth not, 248
l. draweth nigh, 8
l. I will give thee, 113
l. is hid, 217
l. is in His Son, 116
l. is yet whole, 13
l. more than meat, 248
l. of a murderer, 41
l. of all flesh, 35
l. of his beast, 14
l. only we have hope, 323
l. unto the bitter, 13
l. unto the world, 37
l. was the light of men, 213
laid down His l. for us, 336
lay hold on eternal l., 115
leadeth unto l., 27
lose his l. for my, 171
lose his l. for my sake, 236
loseth his l. for my, 114
man lay down his l., 143
murderer hath eternal l., 263
my l. from corruption, 87
of everlasting l., 49
of the Spirit reap l., 115
our l. for your's, 266
out of book of l., 300
prolong my l., 90
restorer of thy l., 173
resurrection of l., 78
resurrection, and the l., 115
right to the tree of l., 235

righteous tendeth to l., 65
save his l. shall lose, 236
save his l. shall lose, 114
save not thy l., 402
seek my l., 90
seeketh my l., 264
seeketh my l. seeketh, 78
seeketh thy l., 78
shall lose his l. shall, 114
she is a tree of l., 409
slew in his l., 4
snare for my l., 83
some to everlasting l., 108
Son shall not see l., 28
spirit giveth l., 56
spiritually minded is l., 19
strength of my l., 70
that it is for his l., 379
that loveth his l., 235
the book of l., 78
therefore I hated l., 89
thou wilt enter into l., 56
thought for your l., 248
thought for your l., 137
thy l. shall be many, 7
to preserve l., 308
tree is man's l., 264
tree of l., 330
unto everlasting l., 37
water of l. freely, 89
water of l. freely, 116
way of l., 236
way, truth, and the l., 214
weary of my l., 88
wellspring of l., 391
what is your l., 261
wisdom giveth l., 410
ye have no l. in you, 58
years of my l., 258
lift
  He shall l. you up, 194
  l. up his spear, 370
  l. up mine eyes, 19
  l. up my soul, 292
  l. up the hands, 64
  l. up Thine hand, 160
  l. up thy prayer, 291
  l. up thy voice, 63
  l. up thy voice, 46
lifted
  l. me up, 369
  l. up his soul, 186
lifteth
  l. the needy, 59
  l. up the beggar, 86
  l. up the meek, 249
light
  abideth in the l., 240
  and there was l., 72
  armour of l., 170
  as He is in the l., 28
  bear witness of that L., 219
  burning and a shining l., 207

but now are ye l., 217
called the l. day, 267
children of l., 51
darkness for l. and l., 233
darkness rather than l., 119
darkness to l., 117
everlasting l., 177
evil hateth the l., 119
fire, to give them l., 159
God is l., 149
God saw the l., 16
greater l. to rule, 20
have seen a great l., 111
he was not that L., 219
His l. arise, 158
is as the shining l., 332
l. a candle, 302
l. excelleth darkness, 137
l. into the world, 111
l. is sown, 179
l. of candle shall shine, 86
l. of the body, 36
l. of the Gentiles, 68
l. of the wicked, 223
l. of the world, 232
l. of the world, 177
l. of the world, 214
l. shineth in darkness, 111
l. thing to be, 258
l. to the Gentiles, 177
l. to them that sit, 111
l. unto my path, 111
l. upon him, 64
l. which is in thee, 45
Lamb is the l., 152
law is l., 177
lesser l. to rule, 20
let there be l., 72
let your l. so shine, 84
life was the l. of men, 213
Lord is my l., 132
Lord shall be a l., 125
make darkness l., 111
manifest by the l., 123
rebel against the l., 74
rejoice in his l., 207
saith he is in the l., 38
send out Thy l., 177
sun l. on them, nor, 67
than the children of l., 414
Thou prepared the l., 267
Thy l. shall we see l., 147
till the morning l., 297
true l. now shineth, 111
truth cometh to the l., 85
upon them hath the l., 339
wait for l., 96
waited for l., 13
walk as children of l., 27
walk in the l., 26
walk in the l., 28
walk while ye have l., 227
wherefore is l. given, 13
lighten

l. mine eyes, 18
l. my darkness, 111
lightly
be l. esteemed, 311
lightning
as the l. cometh out, 345
beheld Satan as l., 341
go forth as the l., 161
lightnings
maketh l. with rain, 309
lights
made two great l., 20
like
l. unto him, 257
l. unto Thee, 22
none l. Me, 163
who is l. unto Thee, 152
who is l. unto Thee, 164
liken
to whom then will ye l., 164
whom then will ye l. Me, 129
likeness
l. of God, 244
l. of men, 255
l. will ye compare, 164
lilies
feed among the l., 25
l. of the field, 15
lily
l. among thorns, 25
l. of the valleys, 25
line
l. upon l., 105
lines
l. are fallen unto me, 185
lion
as a great l., 50
better than a dead l., 190
calf and the young l., 14
come up like a l., 327
devil as a roaring l., 342
heritage is as a l., 30
l. hath roared, who, 270
l. shall eat straw, 38
lay down as a l., 50
mouth of the l., 87
paw of the l., 63
roaring of a l., 12
stronger than a l., 331
there is a l. without, 121
will a l. roar in the, 261
lions
roar like young l., 9
shut the l.' mouths, 87
stronger than l., 70
young l. roar, 9
lips
bridle in thy l., 192
deceive not with thy l., 189
flattereth with his l., 136
found in his l., 189
hatred with lying l., 40

honoureth with their l., 10
keep the door of my l., 309
l. are the snare, 138
l. do honour Me, 195
l. from speaking guile, 189
l. of a strange woman, 6
l. of him that hath, 391
l. of the righteous, 7
l. of the wise, 106
learning to his l., 106
lying l. are abomination, 233
much less do lying l., 106
my soul from lying l., 362
open Thou my l., 290
openeth wide his l., 301
own l. testify against, 178
poison is under their l., 362
poison under their l., 181
priest's l. should keep, 53
refraineth his l., 355
swords are in their l., 362
talk of the l., 230
transgression of his l., 233
with flattering l., 98
liquor
wanteth not l., 25
little
am but a l. child, 193
become as l. children, 68
better is l. with, 66
exalted for a l., 223
fearful, O ye of l. faith, 125
gathered l. had no lack, 123
here a l. there, 105
l. child shall lead, 48
l. children, let no man, 334
l. cloud out, 287
l. finger be thicker, 352
l. fire kindleth, 25
l. folding of the hands, 288
l. foxes, 92
l. leaven leaveneth, 66
l. one shall become, 176
l. ones that believe, 48
l. that a righteous, 112
l. with righteousness, 98
lo, it came to l., 96
O thou of l. faith, 102
of God as a l. child, 48
receive one such l., 48
served Baal a l., 83
sleep, a l. slumber, 288
sown much, and bring l., 106
suffer the l. children, 48
take comfort a l., 260
taste a l. honey, 121
the same loveth l., 140
to whom l. is forgiven, 140
ye of l. faith, 102
yet a l. sleep, 288
yet a l. while, 82
live

and I shall l., 234
as I l. saith, 20
because I l., 235
can these bones l., 322
dead, yet shall he l., 29
die than to l., 92
die, and not l., 80
do, and thou shalt l., 239
doth my father yet l., 275
even he shall l. by me, 58
evil, that ye may l., 49
foolish, and l., 58
God; as I l., 267
hath done he shall l., 139
he shall l. for ever, 38
if we l. in the Spirit, 27
in Him we l., 235
just shall l. by faith, 126
just shall l. by his, 125
just, he shall surely l., 333
king of Babylon, and l., 3
l. after the flesh, 41
l. and ye shall know, 234
l. by bread alone, 171
l. by bread only, 247
l. godly in Christ, 168
l. of the gospel, 27
let my soul l., 234
long as I l., 292
long have I to l., 283
Lord will, we shall l., 43
Lord, and ye shall l., 234
might l. unto God, 56
nevertheless I l., 76
now we l., 127
prophets, do they l., 261
reproach me long as I l., 64
right, he shall l., 408
see Me, and l., 158
seed may l., 49
shall also l. with Him, 215
shall he l. again, 80
shall not die, but l., 94
sing as long as I l., 363
suffer a witch to l., 411
that I may l., 59
that ye may l., 55
that ye may l., 26
to l. is Christ, 236
turn yourselves, and l., 317
we might l. through Him, 215
whether we l. or die, we, 236
while I l. will I praise, 291
who shall l. when God, 79
wicked l. become old, 205
wicked shall surely l., 317
willing to l. honestly, 65
ye shall l. also, 235
lived
and l. deliciously, 36
l. in good conscience, 65
lives

save that which was l., 213
save that which was l., 213
seek that which was l., 181
sheep which was l., 180
that nothing be l., 403
lot
  divide thou it by l., 210
  l. for the scapegoat, 342
  l. is cast, 43
  l. of your inheritance, 71
  one l. for the Lord, 342
  remember L.'s wife, 100
lothe
  l. yourselves in your, 312
loud
  l. cymbals, 263
  make a l. noise, 42
  with a l. voice, 139
love
  abide in my l., 270
  all ye that l. her, 212
  and l. one another, 57
  and peace, and l., 35
  banner over me was l., 238
  better is thy l., 239
  better than secret l., 40
  breastplate of l., 27
  brotherly l. continue, 38
  but to l. one another, 239
  dinner of herbs where l.,
    238
  faith which worketh by l.,
    53
  Father, ye would l. me, 214
  few days, for the l., 238
  follow after l., 148
  for them that l. Him, 35
  God is l., 181
  good to them that l., 126
  grace with them that l., 35
  greater than the l., 180
  hate the one, and l., 242
  hatred for my l., 169
  he that will l. life, 119
  His l. upon you, 50
  how can he l. God, 39
  husbands, l. your wives,
    240
  husbands, l. your wives,
    246
  if a man l. me, 217
  if a man say, I l. God, 169
  if we l. one another, 240
  if ye l. me, keep my, 214
  if ye l. them which l., 110
  in l. dwelleth in God, 240
  in the l. of God, 28
  l. among the daughters, 25
  l. as brethren, 28
  l. casteth out fear, 133
  l. covereth all, 16
  l. for their work's sake, 53
  l. hath no man, 143
  l. her, and she shall, 409

l. Him, 241
l. him as thyself, 138
l. Him, because He first,
  149
l. is better than wine, 238
l. is of God, 240
l. is strong as death, 239
l. mercy, 59
l. no false oath, 279
l. not sleep, 230
l. not the Lord, 77
l. not the world, 64
l. of God, 386
l. of God perfected, 271
l. of money is, 119
l. of the Father is not, 241
l. one another, 27
l. one another, 56
l. one to another, 51
l. salutations, 196
l. serve one another, 11
l. the children of God, 241
l. the good, 26
l. the Lord, 241
l. the Lord, 241
l. the Lord, 26
l. the Lord with all, 56
l. the Lord, hate evil, 118
l. the truth, 278
l. their husbands, 247
l. them that hate, 10
l. them that l. me, 409
l. thy neighbour, 38
l. thy neighbour as, 57
l. to me was wonderful, 143
l. to pray standing, 195
l. worketh no ill, 239
l. ye the stranger, 38
l. your enemies, 110
l.'s sake I beseech, 233
let l. be without, 239
let them that l., 147
let us l. one another, 240
Lord l. judgment, 223
man l. the world, 241
many as I l. I rebuke, 98
mouth they show much l.,
  195
not l. in word, 85
ought to l. one another, 76
passing the l. of women,
  143
power, and of l., 63
preserveth all that l., 305
prosper that l. thee, 211
rise up, my l., 335
say I l. thee, 195
separate us from the l., 95
sick of l., 238
Spirit is l., 187
that l. Me, 303
they which l. Thy law, 55
time to l., 181
to l. their children, 247

walk in l., 27
waters cannot quench l.,
  239
we should l. one another,
  240
when we l. God, 241
whether l. the Lord, 129
wise man, and he will l., 74
with a rod, or in l., 21
loved
  as Christ also hath l., 27
  as Christ l. the church, 240
  as he l. cursing, 223
  as he l. his own soul, 143
  as I have l. you, 56
  because He first l. us, 149
  because the Lord l. you, 50
  God so l. the world, 115
  he l. him, 143
  I have l. you saith, 204
  if God so l. us, 76
  Israel l. Joseph, 47
  Jonathan l. him as his, 143
  l. are turned against, 30
  l. darkness rather than, 119
  l. the praise of men, 61
  Lord l. Israel, 232
  loveth me shall be l., 134
  Son of God, who l. me, 215
  wherein hast Thou l., 204
  yet I l. Jacob, 239
lovely
  whatsoever things are l., 66
lovers
  among all her l. she, 1
  follow after her l. but, 144
  gifts to all thy l., 197
  harlot with many l., 23
  l. of pleasures, 286
  more than l. of God, 286
lovest
  l. me not, 83
  l. thine enemies, 143
loveth
  he that l. another, 56
  he that l. pleasure, 286
  him that l. violence, 398
  l. a cheerful giver, 19
  l. abundance, 175
  l. at all times, 143
  l. father more than me, 131
  l. God l. his brother, 39
  l. him chasteneth, 47
  l. his brother, 240
  l. his wife l. himself, 240
  l. knowledge, 74
  l. me not keepeth not, 100
  l. me shall be loved, 134
  l. not his brother, 39
  l. not knoweth not God,
    181
  l. silver, 175
  l. son more than me, 131
  l. the gates of Zion, 211

double minded m. is, 203
duty of m., 103
end of that m. is peace, 257
every m. a liar, 389
every m. at his best, 142
every m. be put to death, 178
every m. is a friend to, 143
every m. is brutish, 199
every m. shall bear, 321
every m. shall die, 304
every m. shall give, 45
every m. the truth, 189
every m. to his brother, 59
every way of a m., 261
evil m. out of evil, 45
eyes of m. are never, 11
eyes upon ways of m., 153
face of m., 220
face of the old m., 8
faithful m. who can find, 242
fall into the hand of m., 76
Father judgeth no m., 21
fear every m. his mother, 275
field is m.'s life, 264
firstborn, both m. and, 135
foolish m. despiseth, 48
foolish m. reproacheth, 74
foolish m. which built, 285
for a good m. some would, 82
for a righteous m., 82
for I am a sinful m., 62
friendship with angry m., 12
from m. made He a woman, 411
give me a m., 43
glad the heart of m., 237
glory of m., 147
glory of the m., 243
God created m., 244
God created m., 244
God doth talk with m., 158
God formed m., 72
God greater than m., 175
God is not a m., 165
good for a m. that, 276
good m. is perished, 167
good m. leaveth, 173
good m. out of the good, 45
good thing any m. doeth, 171
gospel is not after m., 172
greater love hath no m., 143
hand of a mighty m., 348
happy is the m. that, 48
happy is the m. that, 180
He drove out the m., 274
He had made m., 72

He shall reward every m., 84
He that teacheth m., 153
head of every m. is, 21
head of the woman is m., 21
heed that no m. deceive, 130
herb for service of m., 76
hour knoweth no m., 345
how long shall this m., 40
how much less m., 244
hungry m. dreameth, 96
hunt every m. his, 262
hunt the violent m., 398
I am God, and not m., 250
I have coveted no m.'s, 209
I judge no m., 15
I know not this m., 88
I myself also am a m., 194
if a m. die, 204
if a m. die, 80
if a m. keep my saying, 82
if a m. think himself to, 62
if any m. draw back, 23
if any m. serve, 97
if any m. thirst, 89
if m. can number, 2
is builded by some m., 5
is my complaint to m., 60
judge not for m., 220
just m. walketh in, 189
killeth a m., 41
killeth a m., 302
killeth the foolish m., 12
know not a m., 102
labour of m. is for, 11
lame m. leap, 181
let another m. praise, 258
let no m. deceive, 62
let no m. deceive, 346
let no m. deceive, 334
let no m. deceive you, 84
let no m. know of, 347
let no m. trouble me, 282
let this m. go, 383
like a m.'s hand, 287
like unto a merchant m., 40
loins like a m., 320
m. against his brother, 30
m. among a thousand, 243
m. and his brother, 219
m. and no God, 17
m. as I flee, 70
m. be born again, 37
m. be born of water, 24
m. be just with God, 62
m. be made as grass, 133
m. be more just, 26
m. be more pure, 26
m. be profitable, 244
m. born of a woman, 234
m. can do these miracles, 163

m. can receive nothing, 147
m. can serve two masters, 242
m. chasteneth his son, 97
m. common or unclean, 319
m. created for the woman, 243
m. desire the office, 12
m. desire to be first, 11
m. dieth, and wasteth, 80
m. diligent in his, 2
m. do not so vile, 61
m. eat of this bread, 38
m. find his enemy, 109
m. forbid water, 24
m. from his evil way, 316
m. given to appetite, 147
m. glory in his might, 36
m. glory in his riches, 36
m. glory in wisdom, 36
m. hath been able, 370
m. hath his proper gift, 203
m. hath his sword, 133
m. hath no better, 77
m. hath no preeminence, 193
m. hath will he give, 349
m. have an hundred, 283
m. have his own wife, 141
m. have long hair, 15
m. having put his hand, 95
m. his days are as grass, 244
m. in whom the Spirit, 230
m. is become as one, 169
m. is born, 244
m. is brought to bread, 301
m. is justified by, 85
m. is like Job, 350
m. is like vanity, 235
m. is not delivered, 124
m. is not justified by, 56
m. is not of the woman, 73
m. is preached, 140
m. know not how to rule, 52
m. knoweth not the price, 391
m. looketh on outward, 209
m. love not Christ, 77
m. make thee ashamed, 343
m. mocketh another, 84
m. of God, 135
m. of gray hairs, 92
m. of sin be revealed, 346
m. of sorrows, 252
m. of them stand, 64
m. of understanding, 391
m. of understanding, 257
m. of war, 165
m. perverteth his way, 11
m. pleadeth, 91
m. prevail against Thee, 162

m. shall be commended, 289
m. shall be humbled, 192
m. shall be satisfied, 342
m. shall not live by, 171
m. should be alone, 237
m. should both hope, 276
m. should eat and drink, 286
m. should rejoice in his, 4
m. showeth favour, 146
m. sin against another, 220
m. sin against the Lord, 220
m. spareth his own son, 250
m. that eateth, 320
m. that feareth, 134
m. that flattereth, 136
m. that hath done, 349
m. that is a sinner, 45
m. that is an heretick, 68
m. that shall die, 133
m. that trusteth, 180
m. that walketh, 314
m. to cease from strife, 16
m. under his vine, 278
m. which is a worm, 244
m. who art thou that, 20
m. whom God correcteth, 46
m. whom the Lord, 231
m. whom Thou choosest, 179
m. whose strength, 124
m. will sue, 146
m. wipeth a dish, 92
m. wise in his own, 61
m. would swallow me up, 250
m.'s foes shall be they, 372
m.'s hand against him, 109
m.'s heart deviseth, 26
m.'s heart is evil, 118
m.'s judgment cometh, 223
m.'s life consisteth, 248
m.'s pride shall bring, 296
m.'s wisdom is despised, 8
m.'s wisdom maketh, 410
made for a righteous m., 229
made m.'s mouth, 72
make you fishers of m., 97
maketh a wise m. mad, 243
manner of m., 193
manner of m. is this, 22
mark the perfect m., 257
mean m. shall be, 192
merciful m. doeth good, 76
mercy before the m., 34
mighty expert m., 4
misery of m., 414
mouth defileth a m., 137
naked, the m. and, 199

name of a righteous m., 191
neither knoweth any m., 228
neither the son of m., 165
no m. breaketh it, 131
no m. can come to me, 29
no m. can come unto me, 173
no m. can shut it, 273
no m. cometh unto the, 178
no m. is justified by, 56
no m. knoweth the Son, 228
no m. living be justified, 220
no m. move his bones, 319
no m. shall see the, 16
no m. shall set on thee, 338
no m. that hath power, 81
no m. that sinneth not, 244
nor the mighty m. escape, 396
not a just m. on earth, 279
not a m. that He, 42
not as m. seeth, 15
not fear what m. shall, 64
not m. for the sabbath, 336
not this m. but, 49
of God knoweth no m., 149
of whom a m. is overcome, 143
one m. shall chase, 370
one m. sin, 66
oppression of m., 273
or the son of m., 245
outward m. perish, 141
owe no m. any thing, 239
peace, to every m., 85
perfect and an upright m., 257
pertaineth unto a m., 386
play the mad m., 120
plead for a m., 91
poor m. in his cause, 201
poor m. is better, 98
prayer of a righteous m., 294
profit a m., 209
profit hath a m., 145
profiteth a m. nothing, 33
prophesy, O son of m., 46
prudent m. concealeth, 35
prudent m. covereth, 208
prudent m. forseeth, 301
put on the new m., 312
rage of a m., 211
rebuke a wise m., 74
received it of m., 172
receiveth a righteous m., 191
rejoice, O young m., 416
render to every m., 329
render unto every m., 138

renderest to every m., 223
return every m., 322
reward to the evil m., 230
rich m. shall hardly, 226
rich m. to enter into, 225
righteous m. hateth lying, 233
righteous m. hath is better, 112
righteous m. regardeth, 14
sabbath was made for m., 336
See also "Son of Man"
see that no m. know, 258
seemeth right unto a m., 285
seest thou a m., 309
seest Thou as m., 120
shall be a poor m., 286
shall no m. prevail, 370
sheddeth m.'s blood, 222
should a wise m. utter, 394
show thyself a m., 44
slay both m. and woman, 14
sleep of a labouring m., 363
slothful m. saith, 121
smiteth a m., 41
so a m. sharpeneth, 44
spirit gone out of a m., 119
steps of a good m., 26
strive not with a m., 16
subvert a m., 30
suffered no m. to do, 160
taken out of m., 411
teach a just m., 7
tempteth He any m., 380
than confidence in m., 313
than for m. to hear, 74
thirsty m. dreameth, 96
this m. seeketh not, 40
thou art a m. and not, 17
thou art the m., 4
thoughts of m. are, 145
to a m. that is good, 34
to every ordinance of m., 229
together, let not m. put, 101
trust in the son of m., 314
trusteth in m., 314
unfaithful m., 30
upright m. is laughed, 257
upright m. Thou wilt, 166
vain is the help of m., 18
violence to no m., 69
way of a m. with a, 263
way of m. is not in, 314
ways of a m., 350
ways of m. are before, 153
were judged every m., 222
what can m. do unto, 63
what hath m. of all his, 77
what is m., 244

save me from bloody m.,
230
saw the daughters of m., 24
sent me to the m., 302
shall deny me before m., 88
silver shall m. call, 308
slain a thousand m., 370
sleep falleth upon m., 103
sons of m. how long, 120
spare not her young m., 14
speaketh not unto m., 57
ten mighty m., 371
than seven m. that can, 61
the witness of m., 73
those that be of m., 394
though these three m., 93
to be seen of m., 196
tongues of m. and angels,
107
voice of singing m., 8
walketh with wise m., 58
way of evil m., 26
when m. shall revile, 66
wisdom of their wise m.,
305
wise m. die, 260
wise m. turn away wrath,
12
work of m.'s hands, 198
work of m.'s hands, 198
work of m.'s hands, 198
young m. cheerful, 300
young m. shall see, 417
your alms before m., 45
Mene
M. M. Tekel, Upharsin, 263
menstruous
m. cloth, 198
merchandise
an house of m., 337
no man buyeth their m., 13
merchant
he is a m., 40
of heaven is like a m., 40
merchants
m. of the earth are, 70
m. shall weep, 13
mercies
but for Thy great m., 193
Father of m., 55
great are His m., 250
redeem us for Thy m.', 312
save me for Thy m.', 338
save me for Thy m.', 18
tender m. come unto, 59
tender m. of the wicked, 76
the sure m. of David, 34
to the Lord belong m., 166
with great m. will I, 1
merciful
be m. unto us, 34
be ye therefore m., 250
blessed are the m., 250
Father also is m., 250

God, m. and gracious, 165
gracious and m., 154
gracious God, and m., 59
He is gracious and m., 166
I am m. saith the Lord, 139
Lord is m., 59
m. God, 165
m. man doeth good, 76
m. Thou wilt show, 166
m. to me a sinner, 67
m. unto me, O God, 250
show Thyself m., 166
mercy
according to Thy m., 139
according to Thy m., 19
anger, and of great m., 59
cruel, and have no m., 64
fatherless findeth m., 408
for they shall obtain m.,
250
forsake their own m., 129
God that showeth m., 250
great is His m., 154
greatness of Thy m., 154
have m. upon, 142
He delighteth in m., 139
He will have m., 316
hope in His m., 328
I had m. on thee, 59
judgment without m., 76
keep m. and judgment, 125
let not m. and truth, 44
love m., 59
m. and not sacrifice, 334
m. and truth preserve, 259
m. before the man, 34
m. endureth for ever, 170
m. endureth for ever, 154
m. endureth forever, 290
m. He saved us, 85
m. is everlasting, 154
m. is everlasting, 166
m. is on them that fear, 134
m. O Lord, held me up,
162
m. of Lord Jesus, 28
m. on the poor, 59
m. on the poor, 59
m. on whom I have m., 154
m. shall follow me, 34
m. shall not depart, 154
m. shall the throne, 259
m. to the poor, 26
m. unto you, 35
paths of the Lord are m.,
166
plenteous in m., 154
plenteous in m., 59
reap in m., 26
righteous showeth m., 37
show m. and compassions,
59
show thee m., 249

showing m. unto thousands,
303
spare, nor have m., 93
that hath showed no m., 76
throne: m. and truth, 223
Thy m. is great, 153
with Lord there is m., 154
with you, m. and peace, 35
wrath remember m., 12
merry
drink, and to be m., 77
m. heart doeth good, 89
m. heart hath continual,
180
m. heart maketh, 180
m. hearted do sigh, 364
wine with a m., 137
message
a m. by the hand of, 266
m. from God, 18
this is the m. that, 240
messenger
deaf, as My m., 372
king is as m. of death, 12
m. of Satan, 342
m. of the Lord of hosts,
296
send My m. and he, 253
send my m. before Thy,
253
wicked m., 107
Messiah
the M., 218
Methuselah
days of M., 8
midst
dwell in the m. of thee, 159
God is in the m., 211
m. of his days, 99
m. of my days, 235
there am I in the m., 134
might
acknowledge My m., 5
all thy m., 241
do it with thy m., 106
goeth forth in his m., 147
m. hath failed, 72
man glory in his m., 36
Mine hand and My m., 157
my firstborn, my m., 135
not by m. nor by, 371
power and m., 156
power of His m., 70
spirit of counsel and m.,
252
that have no m., 162
wisdom and m. are His,
371
mightier
cometh after me is m., 175
m. than I cometh, 219
m. than the noise, 156
mighty
better than the m., 12

Counsellor, the m., 218
hand of a m. man, 348
hand of the m., 160
he that is m., 34
Lord m. in battle, 156
Lord strong and m., 156
m. expert man, 4
m. fallen, 228
m. fallen, 85
m. God, 158
m. in power, 205
m. in the war, 324
m. man glory, 36
m. man is not delivered, 124
m. man shall be humbled, 192
m. ones are beaten down, 396
m. power to be known, 87
m. shall flee away, 86
m. waves of the sea, 156
midst of thee is m., 339
more than ten m., 371
neither shall the m., 63
nor m. man escape, 396
person of the m., 132
righteousness as a m., 223
rushing of m. waters, 267
swords of the m., 400
things which are m., 403
with a m. hand, 86
ye m. give unto the Lord, 290

mile
compel thee to go a m., 69

milk
every one that useth m., 200
fed you with m., 105
gave him m., 83
m. and honey, 210
m. of the word, 165
poured me out as m., 72

millstone
m. were hanged, 48

mind
be not soon shaken in m., 63
carnal m. is enmity, 41
come into your m., 153
dead man out of m., 91
fool uttereth all his m., 301
humility of m., 194
knoweth what is the m., 153
known the m. of the Lord, 228
loins of your m., 310
love, and of a sound m., 63
m. and conscience is, 19
m. I myself serve, 41
m. of the Lord, 153
m. the same thing, 69

nor come into m., 73
spirit of your m., 19
with a willing m., 94
with all thy m., 95

minded
carnally m. is death, 19
double m. man is, 203
spiritually m. is life, 19

mindful
art m. of him, 244
ever m. of His covenant, 71
m. always of His covenant, 128
man, that Thou art m., 203

minds
chafed in their m., 12
m. will I write, 57
speak your m., 7

mine
all souls are M., 149

minister
if any man m., 254
let him be your m., 10
m. and to give His life, 10
m. of God, a revenger, 173
m. unto Him, 352
to make thee a m., 256

ministered
came not to be m., 10

ministers
m. by whom ye believed, 233
they are God's m., 21

miracles
man can do these m., 163
sinner do such m., 45
where be all His m., 102

mire
m. of the street, 14
rush grow up without m., 176
waters cast up m., 406

mirth
house of m., 138
m. what doeth it, 229

miscarrying
give them a m., 77

mischief
except they have done m., 406
falleth into m., 107
in running to m., 17
m. is in their hearts, 84
m. shall return, 65
m. will come upon, 297
seeketh m., 387
set on m., 118
tongue deviseth m., 30
tongue falleth into m., 98

miserable
m. and poor and blind, 248
m. comforters, 53
of all men most m., 323

miseries

howl for your m., 405

misery
m. are in their ways, 191
m. of man is great, 414
remember his m., 91
that is in m., 13

miss
hair breadth, and not m., 4

mistress
so with her m., 113

mock
do ye so m. Him, 84
far from thee, shall m., 192
fools make a m., 356
I have spoken, m. on, 257
m. Him and shall scourge, 75

mocked
God is not m., 257

mocker
wine is a m., 237

mockers
be ye not m., 257

mockest
when thou m., 343

mocketh
m. at fear, 70
man m. another, 84
whoso m. the poor, 33

molten
m. gods, 198
m. images, 198
say to m. images, 197

moment
anger endureth but a m., 150
for a small m., 1
hypocrite but for a m., 118
tongue is but for a m., 233

money
he that hath no m., 89
love of m. is, 119
m. answereth all, 77
m. perish with thee, 46
m. upon usury, 392
purchased with m., 46
spend m. for that which, 393
time to receive m., 175
usury of m., 392

monsters
sea m. draw out, 47

moon
fair as the m., 25
m. into blood, 109
m. stayed, until, 162
no need of the m., 152
nor the m. by night, 161

Mordecai
prepared for M., 223

more
be moved no m., 50
deliver you no m., 120
devoured m. people, 400

do so and m., 123
exact no m. than, 175
give thee much m., 329
gods do to me, and m., 267
hear any m. the voice, 8
m. are the children, 48
m. in number, 50
m. just than God, 26
m. pure than his maker, 26
m. shall your Father, 146
m. sons in my womb, 13
m. than all the Jews, 280
m. than his beginning, 87
m. than me is not worthy, 131
m. than ten mighty, 371
m. than the hairs, 2
m. they afflicted, 7
m. they multiplied, 7
m. to be desired are, 55
no m. a reproach, 211
were m. than, 4
what can he have m., 11
wise m. than the fool, 283
with us are m., 162
morning
be as the m. cloud, 112
early in the m., 41
early in the m., 103
fed horses in the m., 204
give him the m. star, 331
goodness as a m. cloud, 170
joy cometh in the m., 179
m. cometh, 67
m. is to them, 74
m. it flourisheth, 244
m. sow thy seed, 95
m. thou shalt say, 385
m. were the first day, 267
son of the m., 86
tarry till the m., 297
the bright and m. star, 216
watch for the m., 190
when it was m., 284
would God it were m., 385
morrow
m. shall take thought, 145
shall be on the m., 145
thought for the m., 145
morsel
better is a dry m., 352
m. of bread, 191
mortal
m. man be more just, 26
mortar
fool in a m., 138
Moses
as He was with M., 34
as I was with M., 9
as they feared M., 231
day that M. sent, 141
had ye believed M., 29
hear not M., 284
Him, of whom M., 253

law was given by M., 56
Lord commanded M., 241
Lord commanded M., 112
M. lifted up, 99
remember the law of M., 56
spoken only by M., 112
most
be like the m. High, 20
Son of the m. high, 341
mote
m. in thy brother's eye, 32
m. out of thy brother's, 75
moth
m. and rust doth corrupt, 248
m. nor rust doth corrupt, 368
m. shall eat, 93
mother
alien unto my m.'s children, 114
as is the m., 185
ask on, my m., 275
Babylon M. of Harlots, 88
be a joyful m., 135
behold thy m., 218
bringeth his m. shame, 47
brother, sister, and m., 131
curseth his m., 275
day my m. bare me, 31
despise not thy m., 8
despiseth his m., 48
father and m. we know, 343
father and my m. forsake, 1
father and thy m., 275
father nor my m., 347
fear every man his m., 275
forth of his m.'s womb, 81
heaviness of his m., 48
honour thy father and m., 56
honour thy m., 275
loveth father or m., 131
m. against the daughter, 131
m. and my brethren are, 131
m. be childless, 311
m. comforteth, 54
nakedness of thy m., 202
out of my m.'s womb, 3
she is the m., 222
sin did my m. conceive, 31
that smiteth his m., 41
worm, Thou art my m., 80
mount
earth, is m. Zion, 211
m. up with wings, 29
shall be as m. Zion, 29
mountain
filled, and every m., 253
holy m., 330

m. of the Lord, 188
say unto this m., 125
say unto this m., 126
the m. of the Lord, 95
mountains
as the m. are round, 154
beautiful upon the m., 267
for m. will I take up, 265
into the m. and seeketh, 283
m. shall depart, 154
m. skipped like rams, 22
m. were not found, 93
multitude of m., 145
partridge in the m., 120
pursued us upon the m., 110
shadow of the m., 132
that I could remove m., 126
mourn
blessed are they that m., 54
for ye shall m., 229
m. not, nor weep, 186
m. one toward another, 176
m. sore like doves, 13
merchants shall m., 13
nor the seller m., 102
rule, the people m., 173
time to m., 180
wilt thou m. for Saul, 175
with sackcloth, and m., 261
mourned
m. unto you, 78
mourneth
new wine m., 364
mourning
death, m. and famine, 285
house of m., 138
house of m. than to, 81
laughter be turned to m., 229
m. as for an only son, 262
victory turned into m., 176
mouth
a watch before my m., 309
bless with their m., 195
confess with thy m., 217
cut off from their m., 388
deceitful in their m., 233
depart out of thy m., 268
doors of thy m., 30
fall into the m. of, 161
flattering m. worketh, 7
fool's m. is his, 138
God be in their m., 326
he that keepeth his m., 301
hear the words of my m., 366
heart the m. speaketh, 44
honey to my m., 208
hypocrite with his m., 362
I will be with thy m., 106
in thy m. sweet as honey, 32

instead of a m., 366
into the m. defileth, 137
kisses of his m., 238
law of Thy m., 393
Lord hath put in my m., 189
m. and yet the appetite, 11
m. but in heart, 195
m. goeth a sharp sword, 187
m. is enlarged, 395
m. is smoother than oil, 6
m. like a sharp sword, 75
m. of all his prophets, 370
m. of one witness, 41
m. of the just, 333
m. of the Lord, 372
m. of the Lord, 247
m. of the most High, 169
m. of two witnesses, 41
m. proceedeth blessing, 35
m. shall show forth, 290
m. tasteth meat, 388
m. they show much love, 195
m. was found no guile, 206
made man's m., 72
near Me with their m., 195
not out of the m. of, 130
not thine own m., 258
open thy m., 223
opened He not His m., 249
opened her m., 81
opened my m., 297
opened not his m., 252
or opened the m., 64
out of His m. cometh, 409
out of the m. defileth, 137
out of the m. of babes, 48
out of the m. of lion, 87
out of your m., 16
out of your m., 27
proceeded out of thy m., 2
putteth in my m., 207
rash with thy m., 301
roof of his m., 382
roof of my m., 9
spue thee out of my m., 57
suffer not thy m., 356
sword, from their m., 160
teacheth his m., 106
thine own m. condemneth, 178
thy m. uttereth thine, 178
truth was in his m., 189
where is now thy m., 35
whoso keepeth his m., 301
wipeth her m. and saith, 6
word in thy m., 55
words in thy m. fire, 106
words of his m., 106
words of my m., 292
mouths
    bits in the horses' m., 271

m. but they speak not, 198
shut the lions' m., 87
move
    in Him we live, and m., 235
    m. his bones, 319
    m. out of their holes, 192
    not m. them with one, 196
moved
    be m. no more, 50
    I shall not be m., 63
    m. for thee to meet, 81
    shall not be m., 211
moveth
    and every thing that m., 290
moving
    m. thing that liveth, 14
much
    faithful also in m., 65
    gathered m. had nothing, 123
    him shall be m. required, 271
    looked for m. and lo, 96
    m. is given, of him, 271
    m. wisdom is m. grief, 410
    men have committed m., 122
    unjust also in m., 66
    ye have sown m. and, 106
mule
    be ye not as m., 14
multiplied
    children be m., 406
    grace and peace be m., 228
    m. and grew, 7
    m. the nation, 176
    word of God grew and m., 117
multiplieth
    m. my wounds, 374
    m. words without, 199
multiply
    fruitful and m., 47
    fruitful and m., 47
    m. thy seed, 71
    m. thy seed, 53
multitude
    by the sea side for m., 2
    cause thy m. to fall, 400
    grasshoppers for m., 203
    heaven for m., 303
    king saved by the m., 259
    m. of counsellors, 7
    m. of many people, 256
    m. of mountains, 145
    m. of people, 172
    m. of thy counsels, 8
    m. of words, 366
    m. of years, 122
    m. of your sacrifices, 334
    not follow a m., 58
    reason of this great m., 108

sea for m., 308
voice is known by m., 138
voice of a great m., 111
wrath is upon all the m., 102
multitudes
    m. m. in the valley of, 220
murderer
    life of a m., 41
    m. hath eternal life, 263
    m. shall surely be, 222
    who hateth is a m., 181
murderers
    without are dogs, and m., 83
murders
    evil thoughts, m., 261
murmur
    m. against Me, 276
    neither m. ye, 61
murmurers
    m. complainers, walking, 61
murmurings
    do all without m., 3
    m. are not against, 72
must
    so m. we do, 232
    things m. needs be, 15
    told thee what thou m., 104
mustard
    grain of m. seed, 125
    grain of m. seed, 176
muzzle
    m. the ox, 107
myrrh
    frankincense, and m., 146
mystery
    m. of godliness, 168

N

Naboth
    blood of N., 41
nails
    print of the n., 102
naked
    afraid because I was n., 121
    flee away n., 86
    go stripped and n., 176
    Hell is n., 156
    knew that they were n., 226
    n. and bare, 122
    n. and ye clothed me, 60
    n. came I out, 3
    n. shall he return, 81
    n. shall I return, 3
    poor and blind and n., 248
    that thou wast n., 178
    walk n. and they see, 346
    were both n., 199
nakedness
    famine, or n. or peril, 95
    n. of thy father, 202

n. of thy mother, 202
n. shall be uncovered, 192
nations thy n., 192
see the n. of the land, 4
seen her n., 69
thine own n., 202
name
abhor us, for Thy n.'s, 151
all in the n. of the, 85
as his n. is, 44
ask any thing in my n., 214
ask in my n., 152
ask the Father in my n.,
214
baptizing them in the n.,
117
be preached in His n., 117
believe on the n. of His, 57
bless His holy n., 290
bless Thy n., 290
blessed be the n. of, 34
call His n. Emmanuel, 218
call his n. Immanuel, 252
call His n. Jesus, 217
call not on Thy n., 167
call on My n. and I, 19
call on the n. of, 19
call on the n. of the, 87
call upon His n., 174
call upon His n., 116
called by thy n., 91
called by Thy n., 139
called thee by thy n., 155
called upon Thy n., 92
chosen Me to put My n.,
211
come in my Father's n., 21
come to thee in the n., 124
cometh in n. of Lord, 253
cometh in the n. of the, 251
command thee in the n.,
122
die for the n. of, 95
do in my Father's n., 5
drink in my n., 54
enemy blaspheme Thy n.,
33
falsely in My n., 130
Father, glorify Thy n., 151
for His n.'s sake, 332
for Mine holy n.'s sake, 151
forgiven for His n.'s, 141
gathered in my n., 134
glory due unto His n., 174
glory due unto His n., 290
glory ye in His holy n., 179
good n. is better, 318
good n. is to be chosen,
318
great n.'s sake, 1
hallowed be Thy n., 149
hated for my n.'s sake, 32
help is in the n. of, 10
His n. shall be called, 218

holy is His n., 34
honour of His n., 363
hosts is His n., 148
hosts is His n., 165
hosts is His n., 87
house unto My n., 304
I will make you a n., 131
in the n. of Jesus, 24
Jerusalem, that My n., 211
justified in the n., 224
lies in the n. of, 130
little child in my n., 48
Lord is His n., 157
Lord is His n., 165
many shall come in my n.,
130
may praise Thy n., 87
My n. shall be great, 116
my n. shall they cast, 122
n. alone is Jehovah, 165
n. be forever, 211
n. in remembrance, 228
n. in the dance, 78
n. in vain, 33
n. is blasphemed, 33
n. is exalted, 116
n. is Legion, 119
n. is The Lord, 157
n. is to be praised, 290
n. of a prophet, 191
n. of a righteous man, 191
n. of God in vain, 33
n. of God is blasphemed,
196
n. of God with a song, 174
n. of Jesus every knee, 188
n. of other gods, 197
n. of our father, 185
n. of the Lord, 148
n. of the Lord, 290
n. of the Lord, 161
n. of the Lord, 129
n. of the Lord, 50
n. of the Lord, 43
n. of the Lord, 3
n. of the wicked, 318
n. of your gods, 43
n. shall be continued, 130
n. shall endure for ever,
130
n. shall the Gentiles trust,
213
n. was called Jesus, 217
no n. in the street, 130
not believed in the n., 28
not glorify Thy n., 291
people shall know My n.,
319
pollute ye My holy n., 33
power, or by what n., 21
praise the n. of the, 265
praise Thy n., 291
publish n. of the Lord, 116
put His n. there, 211

remember the n. of the
Lord, 314
reproached for the n. of,
282
saved for His n.'s sake, 87
shalt call His n. Jesus, 217
sing praises unto His n.,
364
sing praises unto Thy n.,
290
swear by His n., 9
thanks to Thy holy n., 87
that fear My n., 22
that is My n., 151
Thy glorious n., 290
to bear my n., 117
true in the n. of, 7
unto Thy n. give glory, 147
unto us through Thy n.,
341
was the n. thereof, 264
whose n. is Jealous, 165
wrought for My n.'s sake,
151
named
which hath been is n., 207
names
n. are written in heaven,
180
them all by their n., 183
narrow
n. is the way, 27
Nathan
N. said to David, 4
nation
a great n., 49
avenged on such a n., 167
blessed is the n., 154
exalteth a n., 172
great n., 50
lift up sword against n., 400
multiplied the n., 176
n. and a company of n., 34
n. shall not lift, 400
n. shall rise against n., 15
n. that obeyeth not, 99
n. that will not serve, 212
n. void of counsel, 50
shall a n. be born, 276
small one a strong n., 176
nations
among all n., 303
among these n., 166
eyes of many n., 228
father of many n., 71
full end of all n., 155
gods of the n. delivered, 17
great among the n., 64
He should smite the n., 187
lend unto many n., 37
like all the n., 112
n. and declare it, 116
n. are as a drop, 173
n. before Him are as, 173

n. have drunk of the, 70
n. of the earth, 49
n. that forget God, 166
n. thy nakedness, 192
name among all n., 117
prepare the n., 24
published among all n., 117
reign over many n., 203
scatter among the n., 121
sight of the n., 55
teach all n., 117
the Lord, all ye n., 290
trumpet among the n., 24
were all n. deceived, 84
wickedness of these n., 395
works among all n., 116

native
nor see his n. country, 121

natural
n. use of the woman, 188
women did change the n., 188

nature
course of n., 367
that which is against n., 188

naught
n. saith the buyer, 40

navel
n. is like a round, 25

nay
not say thee n., 275

Nazareth
good thing come out of N., 77
Jesus Christ of N., 182
Jesus of N., 218

near
come not n., 161
day draweth n., 200
day of the Lord is n., 102
day of the Lord is n., 220
day of trouble is n., 102
end is n., 102
n. to come, 93
n. upon all the heathen, 167
neighbour that is n., 19
that is n. shall fall, 14
this people draw n., 195
those that be n. and, 192
trouble is n., 13
while He is n., 273
ye that are n., 5

neck
bind them about thy n., 44
hanged about his n., 48
n. is an iron, 373
n. is as a tower, 36

necks
hardened their n., 372
n. are under persecution, 274

need
and have n. of nothing, 248

n. not a physician, 19
n. of mad men, 120
no n. of the sun, 152
things ye have n. of, 153

needle
eye of a n., 225

needs
must n. die, 260
things must n. be, 15

needy
afflicted and n., 223
cause of the poor and n., 223
deliver the n., 292
I am poor and n., 18
lifteth the n., 59
n. shall not always, 190
poor and n., 39
poor and n. yet, 288
to thy n., 45
when the poor and n., 131

neglect
n. not the g., 2

neighbour
better is a n. that is, 19
cause with thy n., 16
covet thy n.'s wife, 6
despiseth his n., 257
despiseth his n., 181
destroyeth his n., 362
double unto his n., 321
even of his own n., 143
every one against his n., 44
evil against thy n., 30
flattereth his n., 136
from thy n.'s house, 191
giveth his n. drink, 103
hearts against his n., 119
judge thy n., 219
love thy n., 38
love thy n. as thyself, 57
n.'s landmark, 299
neighed after his n.'s, 204
not covet thy n.'s, 112
peace to their n., 84
peaceably to his n., 195
pleadeth for his n., 91
separated from his n., 143
smote his n., 209
teach every one her n., 176
truth to his n., 189
truth with his n., 135
witness against thy n., 189
worketh no ill to his n., 239

neighed
n. after his neighbour's, 204

neither
n. mine nor thine, 350

nest
n. among the stars, 296
n. as high as the, 114

nests
birds have n., 188

net

brother with a n., 262
fall into their own n., 324
n. for his feet, 136
spread My n., 386

never
destruction are n. full, 184
evildoers shall n., 48
eyes of man are n., 11
n. a woman among, 210
n. be ashamed, 314
n. be found again, 14
that are n. satisfied, 81

new
all things are become n., 43
full of n. wine, 343
he is a n. creature, 37
He saith, a n. covenant, 71
heart and a n. spirit, 236
make all things n., 316
make you a n. heart, 236
mediator of n. covenant, 249
n. commandment I give, 56
n. earth, 73
n. heavens and, 73
n. testament in my blood, 58
n. thing under the sun, 207
n. wine into old bottles, 410
n. wine mourneth, 364
n. wine must be put, 25
n. wine the maids, 300
of the n. testament, 35
put on the n. man, 312
saw a n. earth, 183
saw a n. heaven, 183
straightway desireth n., 207
wine and n. wine, 237
wine must be put into n., 25
write no n. commandment, 57

newborn
as n. babes, 165

newness
n. of spirit, 19

news
so is good n., 266

next
n. unto thee, 351

nigh
but not n., 252
come n. Me, 186
desolation thereof is n., 109
draw n. to God, 127
for it is n. at hand, 22
kingdom of God is come n., 225
Lord is n. unto, 176
Lord is n. unto all, 19
n. by the blood, 51
n. unto the grave, 8
n. unto the Lord, 291

n. unto thee, 55
shall not come n., 79
word is n., 171
night
all the n. make I, 362
by n. in a pillar, 159
cometh, and also the n., 67
darkness He called n., 267
day and n., 343
desire not the n., 267
desired Thee in the n., 94
drunken in the n., 168
Egypt this n., 135
endure for a n., 179
fear day and n., 78
fear in the n., 133
fled by n., 86
in the n. season, 91
meditate day and n., 332
might weep day and n., 377
n. also is Thine, 267
n. cometh, 109
n. shall not cease, 345
n. shineth as the day, 113
n. to be much observed,
142
no rest day nor n., 198
nor the moon by n., 161
not rest in the n., 91
rule the n., 20
shall be no n., 183
sleep in the n., 168
terror by n., 133
thief in the n., 346
thief in the n., 355
unto the Lord day and n.,
291
wall n. and day, 348
what of the n., 263
nights
forty days and forty n., 136
forty days and forty n., 380
nine
n. hundred sixty and n., 8
ninety
leave the n. and nine, 283
n. and nine just persons,
203
Nineveh
arise, go to N., 255
N. is laid waste, 90
nitre
wash thee with n., 178
no
n. man that sinneth not,
244
Noah
three men, N., Daniel, 93
nobles
princes rule, and n., 172
Nod
dwelt in the land of N., 274
noise
fleeth from the n., 102

joyful n. unto God, 363
make a joyful n., 363
make a joyful n., 290
make a loud n., 42
n. of many waters, 156
n. of thy viols, 192
noised
fame was n., 130
none
comforters, but I found n.,
54
n. beside Thee, 259
n. can keep alive, 260
n. else beside me, 61
n. escaped, 93
n. goeth to the battle, 310
n. holy as the Lord, 186
n. like him in the earth,
257
n. like Me, 163
n. like Me, 164
n. like Thee, 152
n. like unto Ahab, 118
n. of them is lost, 219
n. shall help, 390
n. shall open, 21
n. shall return, 4
n. shall shut, 21
n. that doeth good, 69
n. that moved, 64
n. to comfort, 1
n. to help, 13
n. to save them, 86
n. upon earth I desire, 18
n. upright among men, 167
n. were of silver, 308
people there was n., 10
pity, but there was n., 54
shall be n. to bury, 353
there is n. else, 164
there is n. else, 259
there is n. righteous, 245
there shall be n., 93
to him that hath n., 354
north
cometh out of the n., 93
stretcheth out the n., 72
nose
hook in thy n., 192
n. is as the tower, 36
noses
n. have they but, 198
nostrils
n. the breath of life, 72
note
n. it in a book, 186
nothing
age is as n., 260
and have seen n., 130
before Him are as n., 173
carry n. away, 112
carry n. out, 82
charity, I am n., 126
circumcision is n., 53

good for n., 136
had n. over, 123
hangeth earth upon n., 72
is it n. to you, all, 376
keep n. back, 40
knoweth n. yet as he, 227
left n. undone, 241
let n. be done through, 12
man can receive n., 147
n. against the truth, 389
n. among my treasures, 255
n. and yet possessing, 127
n. but which is true, 7
n. into this world, 82
n. shall be impossible, 2
n. shall be impossible, 157
n. will be restrained, 11
of mine own self do n., 2
profiteth a man n., 33
profiteth me n., 46
rich, yet hath n., 368
shall be as n., 110
something, when he is n.,
62
Son can do n. of Himself, 2
take n. of his labour, 145
there is n. better than, 4
there is n. covered, 347
whom n. is prepared, 45
wickedness profit n., 73
will bring to n. the, 62
without me ye can do n., 5
works are n., 198
ye are of n., 198
nought
counsel of heathen to n.,
144
fear God for n., 207
men, it will come to n., 85
serve me for n., 39
wicked shall come to n.,
109
work of n., 198
nourisher
n. of thine old age, 173
now
come unto me n., 272
even n. already is it, 14
glory n. and for ever, 215
hath been is n., 207
n. is the accepted time, 340
n. is the day, 340
that which n. is, 279
number
camels were without n., 203
camels were without n., 2
days without n., 23
great n. believed, 68
his n. is Six hundred, 119
left few in n., 121
left few in n., 303
man can n. the dust, 2
more in n., 50
n. of His years, 228

n. of the children, 50
n. of the fourth, 2
n. of the people, 42
n. of the stars, 183
n. ye the people, 42
teach us to n., 234
the n. of the beast, 119
numbered
head are all n., 153
not be measured nor n., 50
seed also be n., 2
wanting cannot be n., 3
nursing
bosom, as a n. father, 231

O

oath
feareth an o., 113
love no false o., 279
quit of thine o., 9
swear not by any other o.,
209
obedience
learned He o., 215
o. of one, 140
obedient
servants, be o., 362
willing and o., 270
obey
evil, we will o., 3
if they o. and serve, 300
if ye o. My voice, 268
not o. the truth, 84
o. better than sacrifice, 269
o. God rather than men, 21
o. His voice, 16
o. His voice, 269
o. I beseech, 270
o. my voice, 155
o. my voice, 32
o. not the gospel, 327
o. the commandments, 34
o. the voice, 270
o. your parents, 48
o. your parents in all, 271
that they may o. us, 271
voice will we o., 269
winds and the sea o., 22
obeyed
not o. His voice, 121
o. My voice, 49
o. not His voice, 100
o. their voice, 121
obeyeth
o. not the voice, 99
o. not the words, 71
obeying
o. the voice of the Lord,
269
oblations
bring no more vain o., 334
obscurity
behold o., 96

observation
cometh not with o., 225
observe
crane and the swallow o.,
99
o. lying vanities, 129
o. their judgments, 167
o. to do according, 344
o. to do it, 55
wise, and will o., 153
observed
night to be much o., 142
observest
but thou o. not, 167
observeth
he that o. the wind, 230
obstinate
o. and thy neck, 373
obtain
run, that ye may o., 60
occasion
liberty for an o., 143
occasions
findeth o. against, 280
offence
conscience void of o., 65
give none o., 70
man by whom the o. come,
208
Satan: thou art an o., 136
offences
delivered for our o., 323
pacifieth great o., 301
offend
eye o. thee, pluck, 32
if thy foot o., 78
o. one of these little, 48
right eye o. thee, 78
right hand o., 32
yet o. in one point, 100
offended
a brother o. is, 139
o. any thing at all, 206
who is o. and I burn, 107
offender
if I be an o., 206
offer
o. a burnt offering, 174
o. it unto the Lord, 174
o. not thy burnt, 415
o. thee three things, 49
offering
at Mine o., 69
lamb for a burnt o., 264
offer a burnt o., 174
offerings
delight in burnt o., 269
God more than burnt o.,
334
offer not thy burnt o., 415
tithes and o., 45
office
another take his o., 305
man desire the o., 12

offspring
root and the o. of David,
216
oft
how o. is the candle, 205
o. cometh their destruction,
205
oil
anointest my head with o.,
34
loveth wine and o., 286
mouth smoother than o., 6
softer than o., 106
ointment
better than precious o., 318
smell of thine o., 239
old
beauty of o. men, 122
clothes waxed not o., 162
counsel which the o. men,
7
counsels of o., 128
crown of o. men, 173
days as of o., 315
days of o., 122
died in a good o., 79
drunk o. wine, 207
even to your o. age, 9
face of the o. man, 8
good o. age, 80
good o. age, 8
hath made the first o., 71
hundred years o., 135
I am o., 8
in the generations of o.,
161
mother when she is o., 8
nourisher of o. age, 173
o. and foolish king, 7
o. and stricken, 8
o. men shall dream, 103
o. men shall dream, 417
o. paths, 385
o. things are passed, 43
o. wives' fables, 263
put new wine into o., 410
son of his o. age, 132
things of o., 315
time of o. age, 8
when he is o., 47
when I am o. and, 8
wicked live, become o., 205
young, and now am o., 1
oldness
o. of the letter, 19
olive
fig tree bear o. berries, 66
oliveyards
vineyards, and your o., 258
Omega
I am Alpha and O., 25
omnipotent
the Lord o. reigneth, 291
once

died unto sin o., 75
only this o., 291
sin only this o., 316
speak but this o., 150
one
add o. cubit unto his, 261
all go unto o. place, 81
and watereth are o., 69
are all of o., 186
being many are o., 134
but o. blessing, my father, 13
but o. receiveth prize, 60
called every o., 67
can o. be warm alone, 38
choose thee o., 49
doeth good, no, not o., 69
every o. that asketh, 293
flee at the rebuke of o., 133
God is o., 164
God is o. Lord, 259
hath not o. God created, 38
have o. ordinance, 112
have we not all o., 38
I and my Father are o., 101
mediator of o., 249
members o. of another, 135
none good but o., 170
not failed o. word, 71
not o. hair, 337
not o. is forgotten, 153
o. as well as, 77
o. baptism, 24
o. become a thousand, 176
o. body in Christ, 52
o. bread, and o. body, 134
o. chase a thousand, 1
o. event to righteous, 235
o. fold, and o. shepherd, 51
o. generation passeth, 105
o. half of the greatness, 318
o. heart, and o. way, 308
o. hour is thy judgment, 83
o. law shall be to him, 112
o. Lord o. faith, 24
o. lot for the Lord, 342
o. man among a thousand, 243
o. man esteemeth, 43
o. man shall chase, 370
o. man sin, 66
o. man sin, 220
o. manner of law, 222
o. man's disobedience, 140
o. mediator between God, 164
o. of them be gone astray, 283
o. of you shall betray, 31
o. sinner destroyeth, 69
o. sinner that repenteth, 203
o. such little child, 48
o. thing hath failed, 297

obedience of o., 140
offend in o. point, 100
pardon every o., 139
shall be o. flesh, 245
slew at o. time, 370
that o. should perish, 78
there is but o. God, 164
there is o. God, 164
there is o. lawgiver, 149
these three are o., 386
twain shall be o., 246
two are better than o., 67
voice of o. crying, 70
watch with me o. hour, 96
ye are all o. in, 30
only
even Thou o. knowest, 153
gave His o. begotten Son, 115
o. begotten Son into, 215
o. this once, 291
open
before thee an o. door, 273
devil o. the eyes, 5
he shall o. and none, 21
His ears are o., 160
none shall o., 21
o. his eyes, 111
o. rebuke is better, 40
o. their eyes, 111
o. Thine eyes, 19
o. Thine eyes, 293
o. Thou my lips, 290
o. thy mouth, 223
throat an o. sepulchre, 362
voice, and o. the door, 217
ye shall see heaven o., 151
opened
blind shall be o., 35
but I o. my doors, 191
Ephphatha, that is, be o., 182
eyes shall be o., 111
gates of death been o., 17
have I o. my cause, 110
knock and it shall be o., 293
knock and it shall be o., 273
knocketh it shall be o., 106
o. He not His mouth, 249
o. her mouth, 81
o. my mouth, 297
o. not his mouth, 252
o. the seventh seal, 22
or o. the mouth, 64
see the heavens o., 247
were o. and they knew, 226
openeth
o. the ears of men, 103
o. the eyes of the blind, 35
o. the womb, 136
o. wide his lips, 301
opening

o. of the prison, 202
o. the ears, 167
openly
reward thee o., 159
opinions
between two o., 42
opportunity
as we have therefore o., 11
oppress
let not the proud o., 17
loveth to o., 40
o. an hired servant, 39
o. not the widow, 59
o. the afflicted, 273
stranger, nor o. him, 138
that o. the hireling, 6
oppressed
I am o., 91
let the o. go free, 132
o. and he was afflicted, 252
refuge for the o., 337
relieve the o., 273
oppresseth
that o. the poor, 273
oppression
but behold o., 96
inheritance by o., 390
o. maketh a wise man mad, 243
o. of man, 273
oppressors
because of the o., 87
envy thou not the o., 390
leave me not to mine o., 1
oracles
committed the o. of God, 219
speak as the o., 296
ordain
o. a place, 71
ordained
o. by angels, 57
powers that be are o., 21
order
done decently and in o., 27
set thine house in o., 80
ordered
steps of good man are o., 26
ordinance
have one o., 112
kept His o., 33
resisteth the o. of, 311
submit to every o., 229
organs
praise Him with o., 263
Orion
loose the bands of O., 288
ornaments
deckest thee with o., 25
forget her o., 23
ought
o. but death part, 143
o. to say, If the Lord, 43

oughtest
  what thou o. to do, 262
ourselves
  not we o., 72
out
  Lord gone o. before, 63
  o. of the eater, 331
  o. of the man, 122
  o. of your mouth, 16
  they went o. from us, 242
outrageous
  anger is o., 12
outstretched
  with an o. arm, 86
outward
  appear beautiful o., 15
  circumcision which is o., 15
  looketh on the o., 209
  o. man perish, 141
outwardly
  Jew, which is one o., 15
  o. appear righteous, 15
oven
  burn as an o., 222
overcame
  o. him by the blood, 337
overcome
  able to o., 63
  Lamb shall o. them, 119
  o. the world, 54
  of whom a man is o., 143
overcometh
  him that o. will I make, 331
  o. shall inherit, 127
  o. the world, 169
  to him that o., 331
overflow
  shall not o. thee, 54
overtake
  but she shall not o., 144
  plowman shall o., 300
overthrow
  be of God, ye cannot o., 85
  violent man to o., 398
overthrown
  o. them that rose up, 310
owe
  o. no man any thing, 239
oweth
  or o. thee ought, 321
owls
  companion to o., 91
own
  came unto His o., 16
owner
  ox knoweth his o., 21
ox
  as an o. goeth to the, 6
  muzzle the o., 107
  nor his o., 112
  o. knoweth his owner, 21
  slay o. and sheep, 14
  stalled o. and hatred, 238
  strength of the o., 106

thine enemy's o., 189
oxen
  for the o. stumbled, 309
  where no o. are, 106

P

pacifieth
  gift in secret p., 12
  p. great offences, 301
pain
  be any more p., 82
  fall with p., 150
  in p. as a woman, 380
  p. all his days, 374
  put themselves to p., 144
painting
  thy face with p., 25
pair
  p. of shoes, 69
palace
  eunuchs in the p., 192
pale
  behold a p. horse, 15
Palestina
  whole P. art dissolved, 102
palm
  flourish like the p., 176
  like to a p., 36
pangs
  p. and sorrows, 380
panteth
  p. after the water, 241
  p. my soul after Thee, 241
paradise
  be with me in p., 34
parched
  p. ground shall, 300
pardon
  God ready to p., 154
  good Lord p., 139
  p. them whom I reserve, 139
parents
  but p. for the children, 276
  children, obey your p., 48
  children, obey your p., 271
  lay up for the p., 276
part
  know in p., 200
  ought but death p., 143
  prophesy in p., 200
partaker
  p. of her sins, 66
  p. of his evil deeds, 69
partner
  count me therefore a p., 144
  p. with a thief, 74
partridge
  hunt a p., 120
pass
  all ye that p. by, 376
  bring it to p., 42

come to p., 299
come to p., 297
let this cup p., 374
must first come to p., 15
p. from hence to you, 184
p. not by it, 118
p. through the land, 135
p. through the waters, 54
shall it come to p., 108
so shall it come to p., 144
turn from it, and p., 118
passed
  Elijah p. by him, 232
  old things are p., 43
passeth
  fashion of this world p., 43
  one generation p., 105
  wind that p. away, 139
  world p. away, 89
past
  darkness is p., 111
  death is p., 255
  harvest is p., 91
  winter is p., 345
  yesterday when it is p., 283
pastors
  p. that destroy, 232
pasture
  flock of My p., 155
  harts that find no p., 212
  people of His p., 154
  sheep of My p., 232
pastures
  green p., 54
path
  light unto my p., 111
  p. of the just, 332
  p. of the wicked, 26
  p. of thy feet, 285
paths
  astray in her p., 6
  her p. are peace, 409
  lead them in p., 111
  make His p. straight, 310
  not find her p., 271
  old p., 385
  p. for your feet, 28
  p. of righteousness, 332
  p. of the Lord, 166
  teach me Thy p., 177
  walk in His p., 26
patience
  and p. experience, 190
  follow after p., 148
  need of p., 277
  p. and the faith of, 4
  p. of Job, 277
  p. of the saints, 277
  run with p., 57
  sound in charity, in p., 28
  tribulation worketh p., 190
patient
  apt to teach, p., 225
  p. in spirit, 276

p. toward all men, 277
patiently
  ye shall take it p., 75
Paul
  P. I know, 21
  P. thou art beside, 105
  who then is P., 233
paw
  p. of the lion, 63
pay
  defer not to p., 298
  let him p. double, 321
  not slack to p., 297
  p. ye tribute, 21
  shall p. double unto, 321
  vow and not p., 37
  will He p. him again, 10
payeth
  wicked borroweth, and p., 37
peace
  and p. be multiplied, 228
  be at p. among, 278
  be at p. thereby good, 3
  came not to send p., 401
  come to give p., 278
  come to send p. on earth, 401
  confusion, but of p., 44
  counsellors of p., 277
  earth p. good will, 38
  end of that man is p., 257
  even enemies to be at p., 26
  Father, the Prince of P., 218
  glory, honour, and p., 85
  go in p., 34
  go up in p., 250
  God of p. be with you, 35
  gospel of p., 172
  grave in p., 326
  great p. have they, 55
  he is our p., 215
  her paths are p., 409
  hold not Thy p., 18
  hold not thy p., 108
  hold thy p., 183
  hold your p., 10
  holdeth his p., 138
  holdeth his p., 257
  I am for p., 401
  in the p. thereof, 300
  iniquity, which speak p., 84
  into thy grave in p., 80
  let the p. of God, 278
  looked for p. but, 122
  Lord give thee p., 34
  love the truth and p., 278
  lusts: but follow p., 28
  men hold their p., 60
  mercy unto you, and p., 35
  no p. unto the world, 113
  not hold My p., 212

p. and create evil, 169
p. and joy in the Holy, 187
p. and there was no p., 401
p. and truth be, 277
p. be to thine helpers, 34
p. be unto thee, 34
p. be unto thee, 53
p. be with you in Christ, 35
p. been as a river, 270
p. from God our Father, 338
p. have they not known, 191
p. I give unto, 54
p. I leave with you, 54
p. in heaven and, 151
p. in His high places, 277
p. in your gates, 224
p. of God, which passeth, 67
p. of thy children, 105
p. one with another, 134
p. return to you, 34
p. there shall be no end, 252
p. with all men, 16
p. with God through, 214
proclaim p., 401
return at all in p., 101
return in p., 309
righteousness shall be p., 333
saying P. and there was, 401
saying, p. p., 84
seek p. and pursue, 277
shall seek p. and, 93
sown in p. of them that, 278
Spirit is love, joy, p., 187
spiritually minded is p., 19
that publisheth p., 267
thereof shall ye have p., 300
thou to do with p., 359
time of p., 401
when there is no p., 84
with you, mercy, and p., 35
worthy, let your p. come, 34
peaceable
  p. fruit, 98
peaceably
  one speaketh p., 195
peacemakers
  blessed are the p., 278
peacocks
  wings unto the p., 17
pearls
  p. before swine, 393
  seeking goodly p., 40
peculiar
  p. treasure unto Me, 49
peeped

opened the mouth or p., 64
pen
  p. of iron, 280
  tongue is the p., 366
penury
  tendeth only to p., 230
people
  against the p., 72
  all the p., 100
  among all my p., 210
  ants are a p., 95
  art a stiffnecked p., 372
  as with the p., 113
  authority, the p. rejoice, 173
  be My p., 49
  be to Me a p., 155
  bid the p. return, 277
  burden of all this p., 231
  byword among all p., 313
  call them My p., 155
  cast away His p., 219
  cast off His p., 242
  city and Thy p., 139
  comfort ye My p., 54
  conceived all this p., 231
  days of My p., 155
  despised of the p., 274
  devoured more p., 400
  do unto this p., 90
  doings among the p., 116
  evil entreated this p., 102
  evil upon this p., 157
  face of all p., 251
  fear ye the p., 107
  feared the p., 302
  feared the p., 121
  fewest of all p., 50
  fire, and this p. wood, 106
  foolish p. and unwise, 204
  forsake His p., 1
  fortress among My p., 299
  full of p., 86
  give the p. straw, 273
  given rest unto His p., 174
  given to Thy p., 300
  happy is that p., 168
  hearts of the p., 72
  His deeds among the p., 116
  holy p., 50
  in the multitude of p., 172
  it is My p., 5
  judge His p., 220
  knowest the p., 118
  Let My p. go, 142
  let my p. go, 16
  looked upon My p., 154
  make you His p., 50
  Me above all p., 49
  me, and for the p., 177
  men for our p., 70
  multitude of many p., 256
  my p. are wicked, 178

my p. as thy p., 68
my p. as thy p., 10
no counsel is, p. fall, 177
no doubt ye are the p., 257
not let the p. go, 76
not take of the p.'s, 390
not to all the p. but, 298
number of the p., 42
number ye the p., 42
of all His p., 399
of all the p. able men, 172
of the p. there was, 10
p. are cut off, 267
p. being ashamed, 72
p. doth not consider, 21
p. draw near Me, 195
p. hath been lost, 23
p. have forgotten Me, 23
p. hear the voice, 22
p. honoureth me, 10
p. I have not known, 20
p. into captivity, 121
p. is foolish, 137
p. know not the judgment, 99
p. of His pasture, 154
p. of the earth, 154
p. provoke Me, 120
p. see His glory, 151
p. shall curse, 40
p. shall know My name, 319
p. still sacrificed, 197
p. that delight in war, 401
p. that do know their, 125
p. that is with thee, 120
p. that walked in, 111
p. their transgression, 46
p. were prophets, 351
p. with His truth, 220
place for My p., 71
pleasure in His p., 155
pollute Me among My p., 130
poor of His p., 212
poor of thy p., 76
portion is His p., 50
praise among all p., 131
praise Him, all ye p., 290
prayer for all p., 52
prince over My p., 156
rebellious p., 99
reproach to any p., 172
round about His p., 154
rule, the p. mourn, 173
save His p. from, 212
save Thy p., 291
say among the p., 192
seduced My p., 401
shall be My p., 9
shall be My p. and I, 71
shall be My p. and I, 95
sow them among the p., 121

spare Thy p., 139
special p. unto Himself, 50
teach My p. the, 53
that this p. may know, 298
the p. that doth not, 199
they shall be My p., 155
thy p. shall be my p., 68
thy p. with pestilence, 284
to judge Thy p., 96
to Me for a p., 49
understanding p., 50
vision, the p. perish, 177
want of p., 172
welfare of this p., 40
which were not My p., 155
ye are not My p., 313
ye shall be My p., 155
ye shall be My p., 9
perceive
see ye indeed, but p., 372
perceived
p. the breadth of, 17
perdition
draw back unto p., 78
revealed the son of p., 346
son of p., 219
perfect
be thou p., 62
be ye therefore p., 279
blind as he that is p., 199
cast away a p. man, 1
destroyeth the p., 80
every one that is p., 2
found thy works p., 85
heart was not p., 23
His way is p., 148
if thou wilt be p., 46
in heaven is p., 279
let your heart be p., 269
made p. by the flesh, 23
maketh my way p., 141
mark the p. man, 257
more unto the p. day, 332
p. and an upright man, 257
p. gift is from above, 171
p. heart and with, 94
p. love casteth out fear, 133
p. with the Lord, 62
strength is made p. in, 194
with a p. heart, 128
work is p., 148
works was faith made p., 85
perfected
love of God p., 271
Thou hast p. praise, 48
perfection
p. of beauty, 212
perfectly
made p. whole, 125
perfectness
bond of p., 240
perform
hands cannot p., 156

p. His word, 156
peril
nakedness, or p. or, 95
perils
p. in the city, 79
p. in the sea, 79
p. in the wilderness, 79
perish
believeth should not p., 82
believeth should not p., 340
brutish person p., 260
day his thoughts p., 11
desire shall p., 11
far from Thee shall p., 23
flight shall p. from, 367
hypocrite's hope shall p., 129
let the day p., 90
let the wicked p., 304
lies shall p., 98
money p. with thee, 46
not p. for ever, 190
not serve thee shall p., 212
outward man p., 141
p. but Thou remainest, 51
p. without law, 56
ready to p., 237
remembrance shall p., 130
shall all likewise p., 82
take the sword shall p., 398
that one should p., 78
they shall p., 183
ungodly shall p., 166
vision, the people p., 177
visitation they shall p., 198
when the wicked p., 81
wise men shall p., 305
perished
good man is p., 167
is counsel p. from, 8
memorial is p., 14
truth is p., 388
weapons of war p., 85
perisheth
meat which p., 37
pernicious
follow their p. ways, 130
perpetual
sleep a p. sleep, 81
perpetually
shall be there p., 158
perplexed
p. but not in despair, 7
persecute
bless them which p., 77
p. the poor, 280
revile you, and p., 66
they will also p. you, 281
use you, and p. you, 59
persecuted
being p. we suffer, 3
blessed are the p., 226
have not your fathers p., 281

if they have p. me, 281
p. but not forsaken, 7
p. them even unto strange, 281
p. us in times past, 43
princes have p., 7
persecutest
Jesus whom thou p., 281
Saul, why p., 281
persecution
necks are under p., 274
p. or famine, 95
shall suffer p., 168
persecutors
p. are swifter, 367
person
accepteth no man's p., 15
blood of this just p., 33
brutish p. perish, 260
goodlier p. than, 257
p. of the mighty, 132
p. of the poor, 132
save the humble p., 193
slay an innocent p., 18
persons
ninety and nine just p., 203
not respect p., 38
p. in judgment, 201
respect of p. with God, 132
respect to p., 70
respecter of p., 201
persuaded
p. in his own mind, 43
p. though one rose from, 284
persuadest
p. me to be a Christian, 107
perverse
p. and crooked, 310
p. generation, 167
p. heart, 88
p. in his ways, 44
p. tongue falleth, 98
speaking p. things, 31
perversely
have done p., 62
pervert
Almighty p. judgment, 118
cease to p., 130
perverted
knowledge, it hath p., 61
perverteth
man p. his way, 11
pestilence
die of the p., 14
famines, and p., 15
p. and the famine, 79
p. shall devour him, 93
thy people with p., 284
pestle
wheat with a p., 138
Peter
P. and upon this rock, 51

rise, P; kill, and eat, 137
petition
given me my p., 31
Pharisee
I am a P., 185
son of a P., 185
Pharisees
leaven of the P., 196
scribes and P., 196
Pharaoh
He showeth unto P., 103
house of P., 284
I should go unto P., 193
shall P. hear me, 231
Philistine
fight with this P., 70
hand of this P., 63
prevailed over the P., 395
uncircumcised P., 20
Philistines
blameless than the P., 205
die with the P., 79
hand of the P., 32
P. be upon thee, 78
P. be upon thee, 30
the uncircumcised P., 210
philosophy
man spoil you through p., 84
physician
Gilead? is there no p., 54
need not a p., 19
p. heal thyself, 75
physicians
but to the p., 136
p. of no value, 53
pictures
p. of silver, 106
piece
brought to a p. of bread, 301
p. of flesh, 42
pieces
break me in p., 120
dashed in p., 370
pierced
p. my hands, 280
pilgrimage
house of my p., 54
pillar
a p. in the temple, 331
p. of a cloud, 159
p. of fire, 159
p. of salt, 65
pillars
hewn out her seven p., 409
p. of marble, 36
p. of the earth, 104
pilots
cry of thy p., 93
pine
p. away for your, 176
piped
we have p. unto you, 78

pit
bottomless p., 184
diggeth a p., 118
down into the p., 81
fall into the p., 102
fall into the p., 114
fear, and the p., 91
midst of the p., 102
up out of the p., 114
whoso diggeth a p., 343
woman is a narrow p., 301
pitieth
father p. his children, 59
p. them that fear, 59
pitiful
brethren, be p., 28
pity
eye shall not p., 262
have p. upon me, 59
I will not p., 93
neither have ye p., 94
neither will I have p., 250
p. upon the poor, 10
shall have no p., 14
some to take p., 54
place
all go unto one p., 81
bring evil upon this p., 324
drink water in this p., 66
dwell in their p., 50
dwelling p. of wicked, 109
find a p. for the Lord, 52
heaven Thy dwelling p., 138
I go to prepare a p., 115
Lord are in every p., 158
Lord is in this p., 158
no p. of repentance, 312
ordain a p. for My people, 71
over the empty p., 72
p. where dogs licked, 41
p. whereon the soles, 210
p. whereon thou standest, 186
p. whereon thou standest, 318
settled p. for Thee, 52
stand in His holy p., 186
unto the p. from whence, 67
what p. my lord, 242
places
high p. not taken, 197
peace in His high p., 277
prey in all p., 113
secret p., 113
unto me in pleasant p., 185
walketh through dry p., 119
plague
p. was stayed, 209
plagues
add unto him the p., 285
p. come in one day, 285

receive not of her p., 120

plain
make it p., 53
they are p. to him that, 53

plant
p. vineyards, but not, 144
time to p., 25

planted
He that p. the ear, 158
I have p., 76
p. by the rivers, 373
p. pleasant vineyards, 96
p. shall it prosper, 176
that which I have p., 93
that which is p., 25

planteth
p. and he that watereth, 69

play
p. the mad man, 120
p. the men, 70

played
p. the fool, 67
p. the harlot, 23

playing
boys and girls p., 300

plead
Lord p. with all flesh, 220
p. for a man, 91
p. for himself, 129
p. for the widow, 408
p. the cause, 223
wherefore will ye p., 20

pleadeth
p. for his neighbour, 91

pleasant
eaten in secret is p., 99
for it is p., 364
good and how p., 38
p. fruits, 239
p. thing it is, 234
p. words are, 366
planted p. vineyards, 96
unto me in p. places, 185

pleasantness
ways of p., 409

please
flesh cannot p., 41
how he may p. his wife, 95
how he may p. the Lord, 95
impossible to p. Him, 127
may p. her husband, 95
when a man's ways p., 26

pleased
Christ p. not Himself, 11
hast done as it p. Thee, 32
if I yet p. men, 16
in whom I am well p., 212
in whom I am well p., 251
p. the Lord, 50
sacrifices God is p., 85
whatsoever He hath p., 157

pleaseth
she p. me well, 89

pleasure
do His p., 316
Father's good p., 225
he that loveth p., 286
no p. in fools, 138
no p. in the death of, 81
no p. in the death of, 81
p. in His people, 155
p. in them that fear, 328
p. in wickedness, 170
p. to the Almighty, 17
she that liveth in p., 201
soul shall have no p., 23
your fast ye find p., 132

pleasures
lovers of p., 286
years in p., 300

Pleiades
sweet influences of P., 288

plenteous
harvest truly is p., 117
p. in mercy, 59
p. in mercy and, 154

plenty
p. of bread, 95

plough
hand to the p., 95

plowed
p. wickedness, 223
p. with my heifer, 30
plowers p. upon my back, 13

plowers
p. plowed upon my back, 13

plowman
p. shall overtake, 300

plowshares
beat your p. into, 401
their swords into p., 278

pluck
p. it out, 78
p. it out and cast, 32
planted I will p., 93
time to p., 25

plucked
p. off the hair, 13
p. out your own eyes, 95

point
offend in one p., 100
p. of a diamond, 280
p. to die, 90

poison
full of deadly p., 367
p. is under their lips, 362
p. of asps, 181
p. whereof drinketh, 13

pollute
p. Me among My people, 130
p. the land, 73
p. ye My holy name, 33

polluted
p. before the heathen, 151

p. the land with thy, 201
p. with blood, 197

pomp
p. is brought down, 192

ponder
p. the path of thy feet, 285

pondereth
He p. all his goings, 153

pool
ground shall become a p., 300
p. of Siloam, 182
wilderness a p., 403

poor
at the cry of the p., 45
because he is p., 273
better is a p. and, 7
better is the p., 44
blessed are p. in spirit, 193
cause of the p., 288
cause of the p., 223
considereth the p., 45
countenance a p. man, 201
crieth; the p. also, 292
defend the p., 223
deliverest the p., 152
delivereth the p., 87
destruction of the p., 288
expectation of the p., 190
feast, call the p., 42
feed the p., 46
friends; but the p., 143
give to the p., 115
giveth unto the p., 45
gospel to the p., 111
he becometh p. that, 230
I am p. and needy, 288
I am p. and needy, 18
judge the p., 252
judgeth the p., 259
Lord heareth the p., 288
maketh himself p., 368
maketh p. and maketh rich, 156
mercy on the p., 59
mercy on the p., 59
mercy to the p., 26
mocketh the p., 33
p. always with you, 288
p. and blind and naked, 248
p. and needy, 39
p. and sorrowful, 193
p. brother, 45
p. for a pair of shoes, 69
p. from the sword, 160
p. hath hope, 190
p. is hated, 143
p. man is better, 98
p. man's wisdom, 8
p. of His people, 212
p. of thy people, 76
p. out of the dust, 59
p. out of the dust, 86
p. shall never cease, 287

p. that are cast out, 59
p. useth intreaties, 70
p. widow hath cast more, 146
p. with you always, 390
persecute the p., 280
person of the p., 132
pity upon the p., 10
pleasure shall be a p., 286
remember the p., 46
rich and p. meet, 112
rob not the p., 273
stranger, nor the p., 59
that oppresseth the p., 273
the judgment of thy p., 201
to the p. the gospel is, 179
to thy p., 45
when the p. and needy, 131
your sakes He became p., 215

portion
double p. of thy spirit, 185
my p. for ever, 141
p. is His people, 50
p. of mine inheritance, 204

portions
send p. unto them, 45

possess
go up and p., 147
p. the land, 330
p. the land, 204
p. their land, 395
the land to p. it, 210
them will we p., 64

possessed
land to be p., 8

possesseth
things which he p., 248

possessing
p. all things, 127

possession
also taken p., 46
Israel for a p., 210

possible
all things are p., 28
all things are p., 2
all things are p., 157
not p. that the blood of, 141
seduce, if it were p., 184

posterity
take away thy p., 14

pot
boil like a p., 156
thorns under a p., 229

potter
clay, and Thou our p., 73
p. power over the clay, 289
p.'s field, 39
p.'s hand, 92

pour
p. out my wrath, 150
p. out thine heart, 293
p. out Thy fury, 167

p. out your heart, 124

poured
blood shall be p., 325
p. me out as milk, 72
p. out like fire, 150
p. out like the waters, 13
p. out my soul, 90

poverty
forget his p., 91
glutton shall come to p., 103
His p. might be rich, 215
lest thou come to p., 230
p. nor riches, 404
poor is their p., 288
so shall thy p. come, 288

power
all principality and p., 22
become glorious in p., 370
but in the p. of God, 126
by what p. or by what, 21
couldest have no p., 21
earth by His p., 73
exalteth by His p., 208
gave He p. to become, 28
great in p., 306
greatness of Thy p., 59
greatness, and the p., 152
hath is in thy p., 43
king is, there is p., 21
kingdom, and the p., 116
made the earth by His p., 73
mighty in p., 205
no man that hath p., 81
nor by might, nor by p., 371
not in word, but in p., 225
of great p., 152
on the right hand of p., 120
p. and His wrath, 23
p. belongeth unto God, 288
p. but of God, 21
p. of God unto salvation, 171
p. of His might, 70
p. of Satan, 117
p. of thine hand, 174
p. over the clay, 289
p. to be known, 87
p. to cast into hell, 78
p. to get wealth, 403
p. to help, 156
p. to the faint, 162
p. to weep, 175
resisteth the p., 311
second death hath no p., 82
Son of man hath p., 140
spirit of fear; but of p., 63
strength and p., 141
Thine hand is p., 156
thunder of His p., 156
with p. and great glory, 346

powerful

word of God is p., 43

powers
p. that be are ordained, 21
subject unto higher p., 21
wrestle against p., 110

praise
above all blessing and p., 290
dead p. not the Lord, 81
grave cannot p., 81
hath breath p. the Lord, 291
He is thy p., 148
heaven and earth p., 290
His p. from the end, 364
if there be any p., 66
Jerusalem a p., 212
let another man p., 258
live will I p., 291
loved the p. of men, 61
men more than the p. of, 61
oh that men would p., 290
p. among all people, 131
p. Him in the heights, 291
p. Him upon the high, 263
p. Him upon the loud, 263
p. Him with stringed, 263
p. Him with the psaltery, 263
p. Him with the sound, 263
p. Him with the timbrel, 263
p. Him, all ye people, 290
p. Him, O ye servants, 290
p. His name in the dance, 78
p. is not of men, 53
p. the Lord, 290
p. the Lord that, 249
p. the Lord with harp, 263
p. the Lord, all ye, 290
p. the Lord, call, 116
p. the name of God, 174
p. the name of the Lord, 265
p. Thee; for I am, 72
p. Thy name, 291
p. ye the Lord, 290
p. ye the Lord, 364
p. ye the Lord, 174
p. ye the Lord from, 291
p. ye the name of the, 290
p. ye, and say, 291
prison, that I may p., 87
rejoice, and sing p., 42
show forth Thy p., 290
sing p. to my God, 363
song will I p., 363
soul shall p. Thee, 234
Thou hast perfected p., 48

praised
greatly to be p., 152
I p. the dead, 235

name is to be p., 290
she shall be p., 25
worthy to be p., 86
praises
  fearful in p., 22
  good to sing p., 291
  let the high p., 326
  let them sing p., 78
  p. unto His name, 364
  sing p., 290
  sing p. unto the Lord, 363
  sing ye p. with, 290
pray
  ceasing to p., 291
  forgive, I p. thee, 316
  heed, watch and p., 294
  I p. thee, glory, 290
  if we p. unto Him, 20
  kill me, I p., 350
  love to p. standing, 195
  men ought always to p.,
   294
  p. every where, 294
  p. for them which, 59
  p. God, if perhaps the, 317
  p. in an unknown tongue,
   294
  p. one for another, 294
  p. without ceasing, 294
  watch and p., 379
  watch ye and p. always, 294
  when ye p. believe that,
   126
prayed
  for this child I p., 31
prayer
  hear my p., 292
  heard thy p., 59
  heart thy p., 291
  house of p., 52
  house of p. but ye have, 52
  let p. become sin, 110
  lift up thy p., 291
  open unto their p., 161
  p. and supplication, 294
  p. of a righteous man, 294
  p. of faith, 182
  p. of the righteous, 162
  p. of the upright, 45
  watch unto p., 15
  whatsoever ye ask in p., 28
  yet made we not our p.,
   202
prayest
  p. enter into thy closet, 293
prayeth
  spirit p. but my, 294
praying
  stand p. forgive, 177
preach
  anointed me to p., 111
  but to p. the gospel, 117
  feet of them that p., 172
  go thou and p., 104

p. any other gospel, 185
p. Christ crucified, 75
p. deliverance, 87
p. not the gospel, 53
p. the gospel, 97
p. the gospel should, 27
p. the word, 172
p. ye upon the housetops,
 295
we p. not ourselves but,
 295
whom I p. unto you, 251
preached
  be p. in His name among,
   117
  Christ is p., 148
  gospel which was p., 172
  kingdom of God is p., 225
  p. unto the Gentiles, 215
  poor the gospel is p., 179
  through this man is p., 140
  to us was the gospel p., 155
preacher
  hear without a p., 105
  saith the p., 91
preacheth
  now p. the faith which, 43
precept
  p. must be upon p., 105
  taught by the p. of men,
   195
precepts
  because I keep Thy p., 122
  forget Thy p., 128
  way of Thy p., 208
precious
  bearing p. seed, 76
  better than p. ointment,
   318
  p. in the sight of, 247
  p. shall their blood, 390
  word p. in those days, 399
preeminence
  p. above a beast, 193
prepare
  p. a place for you, 115
  p. Him an habitation, 163
  p. himself to the battle, 24
  p. the nations against, 24
  p. the way, 271
  p. the way before Me, 253
  p. thee unto blood, 77
  p. Thy way before Thee,
   253
  p. to meet thy God, 310
  p. ye the way, 252
  p. ye the way of the Lord,
   310
  p. your hearts, 94
  yet they p. their meat, 95
prepared
  be thou p., 310
  gallows that he had p., 223
  horse is p., 396

nothing is p., 45
p. before the face, 251
p. of my Father, 21
things which God hath p.,
 35
Thou p. the light, 267
preparest
  p. a table before, 34
prepareth
  p. his heart, 139
presence
  come before His p., 352
  p. of mine enemies, 34
  p. of the angels, 203
  p. of the Lord, 274
  tremble at My p., 22
  wicked perish at the p., 304
present
  no chastening for the p., 75
  p. help in trouble, 141
  p. in spirit, 2
preserve
  discretion shall p., 378
  greatness of Thy power p.,
   59
  lose his life shall p., 114
  p. the king, 259
  p. thee from all evil, 338
  p. thee: love her, 409
  p. them alive, 408
  p. thy soul, 338
  to p. life, 308
  wise shall p., 106
preserveth
  Lord p. the faithful, 128
  p. all them that love, 305
  p. the simple, 162
press
  p. toward the mark, 60
pretence
  in p. or in truth, 148
prevail
  hell shall not p., 371
  p. against His enemies, 157
  p. against Thee, 162
  shall no man p., 370
  they shall not p., 110
prevented
  p. me in the day, 109
prey
  hold of the p., 9
  p. and a spoil, 192
  p. in all places, 113
  rise up to the p., 276
  roar after their p., 9
  spoil, and all that p., 327
  when he hath no p., 261
  will I give for a p., 327
price
  bought with a p., 143
  give me my p., 266
  knoweth not the p., 391
  p. is far above rubies, 246
  p. of a dog, 45

p. of wisdom, 409
weighed for the p., 409
pride
man's p. shall bring, 296
p. before destruction, 123
p. compasseth them about, 296
p. of thine heart, 61
p. of thine heart hath, 61
those that walk in p., 296
when p. cometh, 296
wicked in his p., 280
priest
a faithful p., 53
even unto the p., 69
p.'s lips should keep, 53
so with the p., 113
priesthood
p. of the Lord, 296
seek ye the p., 11
priests
law maketh men high p., 70
prince
Father, the P. of Peace, 218
lying lips a p., 106
p. of the kings of, 218
p. of this world, 221
p. over My people, 156
p. shall not take, 390
right hand to be a P., 214
who made thee a p., 231
princes
and p. decree justice, 259
destruction of the p., 172
give ear, O ye p., 363
p. are become like harts, 212
p. have persecuted, 7
p. rule, and nobles, 172
than confidence in p., 172
trust in p., 314
princess
p. among the provinces, 64
principal
wisdom is the p., 391
principalities
wrestle against p., 110
principality
head of all p., 22
print
p. of the nails, 102
printed
p. in a book, 36
prison
I was in p. and ye came, 60
opening of the p., 202
put in p. are standing, 114
shall cast some into p., 7
shut up in p., 67
soul out of p., 87
prisoner
sighing of the p., 202
prisoners
despiseth not His p., 288

looseth the p., 202
p. of hope, 190
prisons
p. more frequent, 282
private
of any p. interpretation, 299
privy
heart is p., 64
prize
one receiveth the p., 60
p. of the high calling, 60
proceed
heart p. evil, 261
proceeded
p. out of thy mouth, 2
proceedeth
p. not evil and good, 169
proclaim
p. liberty, 142
p. liberty, 202
p. peace unto it, 401
proclaimed
p. upon the housetops, 123
profane
holy and p., 53
p. and old wives', 263
p. and vain babblings, 137
profaned
sake, which ye have p., 151
profess
p. that they know God, 85
professing
p. themselves to be wise, 61
profession
p. of our faith, 127
profit
cannot p. nor deliver, 415
labour there is p., 297
p. is of circumcision, 53
p. of the earth, 69
p. shall this birthright, 90
pain, but shall not p., 144
riches p. not, 404
what p. hath a man, 145
what p. hath he that, 297
what p. hath he that, 77
what p. is it, 33
what p. should we have, 20
what shall it p. a man, 209
wickedness p. nothing, 73
words to no p., 16
profitable
godliness is p., 297
p. for thee that one, 78
p. unto God, 244
wise may be p., 244
profiteth
bodily exercise p., 168
flesh p. nothing, 187
p. a man nothing, 33
p. me nothing, 46

what p. the graven image, 199
prognosticators
monthly p., 19
prolong
p. my life, 90
prolonged
days be p., 168
days may be p., 275
days shall not be p., 93
promise
covenants of p., 92
hope of the p., 281
of all His good p., 71
p. is unto you, 187
p. which was made, 171
receive the p., 277
slack concerning His p., 298
wait for the p., 187
promised
as God hath p., 64
good that I have p., 157
promoted
p. over the trees, 11
promotion
p. cometh neither from, 373
p. of fools, 147
proper
man hath his p. gift, 203
prophecy
book of this p., 300
p. of the Scripture, 299
the sayings of the p., 271
the spirit of p., 416
words of this p., 300
prophesied
prophets which p., 8
to them, yet they p., 130
prophesieth
greater is he that p., 57
p. edifieth the church, 57
prophesy
not p. good, 7
p. against them, p., 46
p. falsely in My name, 130
p. in part, 200
spoken, who can but p., 270
prophesying
p. serveth not, 299
prophesyings
despise not p., 299
prophet
by Esaias the p., 299
Elijah the p., 253
if the p. had bid, 7
name of a prophet, 191
p. also as thou art, 83
p. even unto the priest, 69
P. from the midst, 252
p. hath no honour in, 318

p. is not without honour, 299
p. is risen up among, 22
p. that hath a dream, 103
receive a p.'s reward, 191
receiveth a p., 191
sign of the p. Jonas, 254
speaketh the p., 253
that Thou art a p., 5
truth this is the P., 253
when a p. speaketh, 129
words of that p., 129

prophets
and the p. did write, 253
believe all that the p., 299
believe His p., 124
beware of false p., 84
blood of saints and p., 247
do My p. no harm, 50
false p., 184
give all the p. witness, 381
hearken not to your p., 8
I am against the p., 130
if they be p., 20
killest the p., 212
let not your p., 84
mouth of all his p., 370
neither by p., 1
not Moses and the p., 284
not sent these p. yet, 130
p. be consumed, 129
p. do they live forever, 261
p. have not your fathers, 281
p. shall be ashamed, 130
people were p., 351
scriptures of the p., 253
the p. were until John, 225
where are now your p., 8
woe unto the foolish p., 130
ye holy apostles and p., 327

prosper
fatherless, yet they p., 205
He will p. us, 373
made him to p., 373
p. in all that ye do, 55
p. that love thee, 211
p. whithersoever thou, 55
planted, shall it p., 176
reign and p., 252
shall not p., 144
so shall ye p., 124
way of the wicked p., 205

prospered
p. whithersoever he went, 300

prospereth
because of him who p., 211

prosperity
day of p. be joyful, 283
days in p., 300
p. of the wicked, 112
spake in thy p., 183

prostitute
p. thy daughter, 48

proud
arrogancy of the p., 17
be not p., 296
God resisteth the p., 194
God resisteth the p., 194
high look and a p. heart, 17
let not the p. oppress, 17
O thou most p., 17
oven; and all the p., 222
p. against the Lord, 17
p. look, a lying tongue, 207
p. shall stumble, 17
rewardeth the p. doer, 128
spoil with the p., 193
than p. in spirit, 276

prove
p. all things, 298
through them I may p., 382

proverb
Israel shall be a p., 313
p. and a byword, 303
shall use this p., 308

proverbs
every one that useth p., 308

proveth
God p. you, 129

provide
p. out of all people, 172

provinces
princess among the p., 64

provision
p. for the flesh, 349

provoke
p. Me not to anger, 301
p. Me unto wrath, 150
p. not your children, 13
p. not your children, 47
people p. Me, 120

provoked
p. Him to jealousy, 150
p. Me to anger, 120
them that p. Me, 303

prudent
p. man concealeth, 35
p. man covereth, 208
p. man forseeth, 301
p. men shall be hid, 305
p. shall keep silence, 301
p. wife is from the Lord, 205
perished from the p., 8
understanding of the p., 62
wisdom of the p., 301

pruninghooks
p. into spears, 401
spears into p., 278

psalms
sing p. unto Him, 363

psaltery
praise Him with the p., 263

sing with the p., 263

publicans
do not even the p., 110
with p. and sinners, 117

publish
p. and conceal, 267
p. and set up a, 267
p. it not, 175
p. the name of the Lord, 116
p. ye, praise ye, 291

published
company of those that p., 295
gospel must first be p., 117

publisheth
p. peace, 267

puffed
charity is not p. up, 240

puffeth
knowledge p. up, 62

punish
p. the world, 118

punished
and I p. the goats, 32
p. us less than, 250
pass on, and are p., 301
when scorner is p., 105

punishment
my p. is greater, 302

purchased
p. with His own blood, 104
p. with money, 46

pure
blessed are the p., 307
charity out of a p., 240
hands, and a p. heart, 189
if thou wert p. and, 32
is nothing p., 19
keep thyself p., 69
man be more p., 26
p. all things are p., 19
stars are not p., 244
whatsoever things are p., 66

purer
p. eyes than to behold, 307

purify
p. your hearts, 307

purpose
appeared for this p., 256
p. is the multitude, 334
p. under the heaven, 265

purposed
as I have p., 144

purposeth
as he p. in his heart, 46

pursue
after whom dost thou p., 120
blood shall p., 77
p. after your enemies, 400
seek peace, and p., 277

pursued

p. us upon the mountains, 110

pursueth
flee when no man p., 133
none p. you, 132

put
as he that p. it off, 35
body what ye shall p. on, 137

Q

quench
burn that none can q., 150
q. all the fiery darts, 127
q. not the Spirit, 127
waters cannot q., 239

quenched
fire is not q., 184
fire never q., 184
wrath shall not be q., 197

questions
avoid foolish q., 68
foolish and unlearned q., 68

quick
word of God is q., 43

quickeneth
Spirit that q., 187

quickly
behold, I come q., 346
come up to us q., 10
cord is not q., 68
doest, do q., 31
with thine adversary q., 16

quiet
ere thou be q., 201
study to be q., 27

quietness
handful with q., 11
morsel, and q., 352
q. and in confidence, 125

quit
q. of thine oath, 9

quiver
q. full of them, 48

R

race
r. is not to the swift, 43
which run in a r., 60
with patience the r., 57

Rachel
like R. and like Leah, 135
serve with thee for R., 9
seven years for R., 238

rage
jealousy is the r., 211
r. against Me, 153
r. against Me, 17

rageth
but the fool r., 118

raging

strong drink is r., 237

rags
clothe a man with r., 230

raiment
and the body than r., 248
having food and r., 175
take ye thought for r., 15
white r. that thou be, 127

rain
clouds be full of r., 309
drop as the r., 101
good, and gave us r., 309
lightnings with r., 309
r. a father, 309
r. in due season, 268
r. in harvest, 138
r. is over, 345
r. on the just and the, 169
r. upon Thy land, 300
r. was upon the earth, 136
small r. upon, 106

rainy
very r. day and a, 263

raise
none shall r. him up, 17
r. him up at the last day, 115
r. Me up, 53
r. the dead, 182
r. unto David, 252
stones to r. up children, 155
that God should r., 323
three days I will r., 93

raised
Christ be not r., 126
dead are r., 179
r. again for our, 323
r. from the dead, 51
r. Him from the dead, 323
r. Him from the dead, 217
r. up the third day, 298

raiseth
all that fall, and r., 162
He r. up the poor, 59
r. the stormy wind, 265
r. up the poor, 86

rams
fat of r., 269
r. with he goats, 93
skipped like r., 22

ran
prophets, yet they r., 130

ransom
give His life a r., 10

ransomed
r. of the Lord, 142

rare
it is a r. thing that, 286

rash
r. with thy mouth, 301

rather
r. be a doorkeeper, 193

razor

like a sharp r., 30

read
book of the Lord, and r., 344
r. of all men, 381

readest
understand what thou r., 105

readeth
blessed is he that r., 300

reading
give attendance to r., 101

ready
be ye also r., 345
be ye therefore r., 310
God r. to pardon, 154
graves are r., 80
more r. to hear, 415
pen of a r. writer, 366
r. not to be bound only, 95
r. to perish, 237
r. to stone me, 90
to make all r., 310

reap
but thou shalt not r., 106
clouds shall not r., 230
due season we shall r., 277
in Thy sickle, and r., 221
of flesh r. corruption, 243
r. also bountifully, 96
r. also sparingly, 106
r. in joy, 76
r. in mercy, 26
r. life everlasting, 115
r. the whirlwind, 106
r. thorns, 144
sow ye, and r., 106
soweth, that shall he r., 106
time for Thee to r., 249

reaped
r. iniquity, 223
them which have r., 413

reaper
overtake the r., 300

reapeth
r. receiveth wages, 115
soweth, and another r., 69

reason
by r. of thy brightness, 61
dismayed by r., 108
if by r. of strength, 234
let us r. together, 57
men that can render a r., 61
r. with you, 283

reasons
ear to your r., 276
strong r., 16

rebel
if ye refuse and r., 372
r. against the light, 74
r. against the Lord, 310
r. against us, 259
r. not against, 259

r. not ye against, 107
rebelled
  though we have r., 166
rebellest
  r. against me, 17
rebellion
  r. is as the sin, 310
  r. unto his sin, 311
  taught r., 184
rebellious
  midst of a r., 58
  r. against the Lord, 99
  r. children, 23
  r. generation, 99
  r. like that r. house, 311
  r. people, 99
  they be a r. house, 133
rebels
  hear now, ye r., 298
rebuke
  flee at the r., 133
  many as I love, I r., 98
  of r. and blasphemy, 90
  r. a wise man, 74
  r. is better, 40
  r. me not, 46
  r. not an elder, 9
  r. of the wise, 74
  reprove, r. exhort with, 277
  scorner heareth not r., 74
  them that sin r., 46
  trespass against thee r., 75
rebukes
  furious r., 150
rebuketh
  hate him that r., 75
receive
  able to r., 42
  ask, and r. not because, 261
  ask, and ye shall r., 180
  believe that ye r. them, 126
  believing, ye shall r., 28
  counsel, and r., 7
  let him r., 42
  man can r. nothing, 147
  name, and ye r. me not, 21
  not r. evil, 3
  of whom ye hope to r., 10
  r. a prophet's reward, 191
  r. a thousand shekels, 208
  r. as much again, 350
  r. good at the hand, 3
  r. him as myself, 144
  r. my instruction, 105
  r. my sayings, 7
  r. my spirit, 247
  r. not honour from men, 16
  r. one such little child, 48
  r. the kingdom of God, 48
  r. the promise, 277
  r. the reward, 331
  r. ye one another, 134
  right, that shall ye r., 123

same shall he r., 171
that thou didst not r., 374
time to r. money, 175
to give than to r., 11
whatsoever we ask, we r., 294
whosoever shall r. me, 188
received
  as many as r. Him, 28
  as ye have r. Christ, 27
  freely ye have r., 146
  His own r. Him not, 16
  r. up into glory, 215
  r. up into heaven, 18
  r. with thanksgiving, 137
  r. your consolation, 405
receiveth
  but one r. the prize, 60
  every one that asketh r., 293
  he that r. me r. Him, 216
  in my name r. me, 48
  r. a prophet, 191
  r. a righteous man, 191
  r. not me but Him, 188
  r. who I send r. me, 117
reapeth r. wages, 115
recompence
  r. of a man's hands, 399
  r. of reward, 63
recompense
  for they cannot r. thee, 42
  I will r. saith the Lord, 327
  r. thee for all, 220
  r. thy ways, 250
  r. to no man evil, 327
  silence, but will r., 325
  vengeance, and r., 326
recompensed
  r. at the resurrection, 11
reconciled
  r. to thy brother, 45
record
  his r. is true, 186
  I saw, and bare r., 100
  our r. is true, 190
  r. is on high, 162
  saw it bare r., 186
  three that bear r., 386
recover
  sick, and they shall r., 182
red
  wine when it is r., 237
redeem
  r. us for Thy mercies', 312
redeemed
  for I have r., 155
  God r. thee, 58
  r. of the Lord shall, 155
  r. us from the curse, 56
  Zion shall be r., 212
redeemer
  my strength, and my r., 292
  R. is strong, 87

r. liveth, 124
thy Saviour and thy R., 148
redemption
  r. through His blood, 141
refrain
  r. thy voice, 330
refraineth
  r. his lips, 355
refuge
  eternal God is thy r., 337
  God is a r., 124
  God is our r., 141
  lies our r., 98
  r. and my fortress, 162
  r. for the oppressed, 337
  r. from the avenger, 341
  r. in times of trouble, 337
  rock of my r., 337
  tower, and my r., 159
  will I make my r., 337
refuse
  be wise, and r. it not, 7
  if ye r. and rebel, 372
  r. not to die, 206
  r. profane and old wives', 263
  r. the evil, 97
  r. to humble thyself, 16
  r. ye to keep, 99
refused
  nothing to be r., 137
  stone which builders r., 274
refuseth
  he that r. instruction, 98
  r. reproof erreth, 74
regardest
  Thou r. me not, 91
regardeth
  r. it unto the Lord, 188
  that r. the day, 188
reign
  by me kings r., 259
  He must r., 365
  Lord shall r. for ever, 116
  not r. over, 231
  r. and prosper, 252
  r. over many nations, 203
  r. over thee, 203
  r. over you, 65
  we shall also r., 375
reigneth
  that the Lord r., 116
  the Lord omnipotent r., 291
  the Lord r., 156
reins
  searcheth the r. and, 216
reject
  knowledge, I will also r., 227
  r. the commandment, 196
  second admonition r., 68
rejected
  because thou hast r., 227

because thou r. the word, 65
have r. Me, 231
Lord hath r., 308
not r. thee, 231
r. of men, 252
r. the word, 313
r. thee from being king, 65
seeing I have r., 175
which the builders r., 328

rejoice
and I therein do r., 148
authority, the people r., 173
but world shall r., 75
desert shall r., 321
enemies wrongfully r., 110
heart of them r., 179
let not the buyer r., 102
let the earth r., 156
let the heavens r., 42
let us be glad and r., 180
make a loud noise, and r., 42
man should r. in his own, 4
r. and be glad, 42
r. as partakers of, 346
r. because your names, 180
r. before the Lord, 413
r. evermore, 42
r. in Christ, 30
r. in his light, 207
r. in the Lord, 180
r. in the Lord, 180
r. in the Lord alway, 42
r. in Thy salvation, 395
r. not against me, 36
r. not when thine enemy, 146
r. not, that the spirits, 180
r. O young man, 416
r. over her thou heaven, 327
r. over thee with joy, 339
r. with me, 180
r. with the wife of, 245
r. with them that do r., 107
r. with trembling, 193
r. ye with Jerusalem, 212
righteous shall r., 326
trust in Thee r., 179

rejoiceth
city r., 180
heart r., 179
whole earth r., 90

rejoicing
come again with r., 76

relieve
r. my soul is far, 54
r. the oppressed, 273

rely
r. on the Lord, 109

remain
fragments that r., 403

remained
none escaped nor r., 93

remainest
perish; but Thou r., 51
r. for ever, 116

remaineth
r. and is besieged, 14
spirit r. among, 54

remember
if I do not r., 9
mercy r. Thou me, 139
r. all their wickedness, 74
r. break not, 71
r. from whence thou art, 23
r. his misery, 91
r. how short my time, 260
r. I beseech Thee, 142
r. Lot's wife, 100
r. Me in far countries, 121
r. me when Thou comest, 67
r. me, I pray, 291
r. me, o my God, 329
r. my bonds, 202
r. not the sins, 139
r. now how I have walked, 128
r. now thy Creator, 148
r. that thou wast, 58
r. that thou wast, 390
r. the days of darkness, 81
r. the days of old, 122
r. the Lord, 403
r. the Lord, 24
r. the name of the Lord, 314
r. the poor, 46
r. the words of, 171
r. their sin no more, 139
r. them in bonds, 60
r. thine handmaid, 174
r. this day, 142
r. thy ways and be, 312
r. what is come, 286
r. ye not the former, 315
r. ye the law of, 56
wrath r. mercy, 12

remembered
be no more r., 80
former shall not be r., 73
hast not r. Me, 167
hath r. her iniquities, 168
Lord r. her, 135
not r. the days of thy, 122
r. not the Lord, 23
r. they were but flesh, 139
thou mayest be r., 130
wept, when we r., 188
within me I r. the, 70

remembereth
r. no more the anguish, 31
r. that we are dust, 59

remembrance
death there is no r., 80

drink it, in r. of me, 58
name in r., 228
no r. of the wise, 315
r. of them to cease, 14
r. shall perish, 130
sin to r., 46
this do in r. of me, 58

remembrances
r. are like unto ashes, 7

remission
for the r. of sins, 35
of blood is no r., 35
r. of sins, 140
repentance and r. of, 117

remnant
Jerusalem go forth a r., 375
r. of Mine inheritance, 1
r. that are left, 291
r. that is escaped, 375
very small r., 376

remove
and it shall r., 125
mountain, r. hence to, 125
r. mine integrity, 206
r. not the ancient, 299

removed
cannot be r., 29
hills be r., 154
hope hath He r., 91
mountain, be thou r., 126
r. their heart, 195

rend
r. your clothes, 261
r. your heart, 317
time to r., 92
turn again and r. you, 204

render
r. therefore unto Caesar, 51
r. to every man, 329
r. to them their desert, 223
r. unto every man, 138

renderest
r. to every man, 223

renew
r. a right spirit, 368
r. our days as of, 315
r. their strength, 315

renewed
be r. in the spirit, 19
inward man is r., 141

renowned
shall never be r., 48

rent
r. my garment, 13

repay
accordingly He will r., 305
come again, I will r., 171
is Mine; I will r., 327
r. him to his face, 129

repeateth
he that r. a matter, 176

repent
except ye r. ye shall, 82
God will turn and r., 139

r. unto Him, 154
r. unto Me and I will r., 317
r. unto the ground, 302
r. unto the Lord, 316
r. ye now every man, 316
r. ye now every one, 316
reward shall r. upon, 224
same shall he r., 86
shall not r. to me, 80
shall they not r., 121
spirit shall r., 81
thither they r., 67
when I r., 309
whence I shall not r., 80
yet r. again to Me, 23
returned
  r. unto the Shepherd, 168
reveal
  Son will r. Him, 228
revealed
  blood hath not r. it, 216
  His glory shall be r., 346
  man of sin be r., 346
  r. from heaven, 168
  r. my cause, 327
  that shall not be r., 347
  things which are r., 226
revealeth
  heaven that r. secrets, 103
revelation
  taught it, but by the r., 172
revenger
  r. to execute wrath, 173
revengeth
  jealous, and the Lord r., 327
revenues
  r. of the wicked, 333
  r. without right, 98
revile
  men shall r., 66
reviled
  being r. we bless, 3
revive
  Thou wilt r. me, 79
revived
  commandment came, sin r., 56
revolted
  deeply r., 316
reward
  a righteous man's r., 191
  exceeding great r., 159
  fruit of womb is His r., 48
  great is your r., 247
  love you, what r. have, 110
  not lose his r., 54
  r. every man according, 84
  r. for the righteous, 329
  r. for their labour, 67
  r. her even as she r., 120
  r. him according to, 306
  r. of his hands, 305

r. of reward, 63
r. of your Father, 45
r. shall return upon, 224
r. the doer of evil, 304
r. thee openly, 159
r. them that hate, 220
r. to the evil man, 230
receive a prophet's r., 191
receive his own r., 107
receive the r., 331
shall be a sure r., 333
taketh r. to slay, 18
they have their r., 195
worthy of his r., 123
rewarded
  commandment shall be r., 269
  r. evil for good, 4
  r. me evil for good, 169
  r. me good, 67
  r. thee evil, 67
  work shall be r., 329
  work shall be r., 330
rewarder
  He is a r. of them that, 29
rewardeth
  r. evil for good, 169
  r. the proud doer, 128
rib
  r. taken from man, 411
rich
  abundance of the r., 363
  diligent maketh r., 230
  haste to be r., 11
  labour not to be r., 11
  merchants are waxed r., 70
  not the r. man glory, 36
  poor, and maketh r., 156
  poverty might be r., 215
  r. and poor meet, 112
  r. answereth roughly, 70
  r. fall into temptation, 12
  r. hath many friends, 143
  r. He hath sent empty, 60
  r. in good works, 85
  r. man shall hardly enter, 226
  r. man to enter kingdom, 225
  r. men, weep and howl, 405
  r. unto all that call, 149
  r. yet hath nothing, 368
  shall not be r., 286
  that thou mayest be r., 127
  thou sayest, I am r., 248
  though He was r., 215
  ways, though he be r., 44
  when one is made r., 112
  woe unto you that are r., 405
riches
  better than the r. of, 112
  both r. and honour, 329
  chosen than great r., 318

deceitfulness of r., 171
full of days, r., 80
full of Thy r., 265
glory in his r., 36
He esteem thy r., 370
heapeth up r., 205
houses and r. are the, 205
if r. increase, set not, 404
in r. and wisdom, 404
increased thy r., 95
left hand r., 409
nor yet r. to men of, 367
poverty nor r., 404
r. and not by right, 99
r. are not for ever, 279
r. come of Thee, 130
r. make themselves wings, 112
r. profit not, 404
trust in r. to enter, 115
trusteth in his r., 123
yet hath great r., 368
riddle
  declare unto us the r., 30
  found out my r., 30
ride
  r. on white asses, 290
rider
  r. hath He thrown, 289
rideth
  neither shall he that r., 114
riding
  r. upon an ass, 193
right
  Christ sitteth on the r., 148
  days is in her r., 409
  depart to the r., 48
  do that which is r., 26
  do that which is r., 317
  earth do r., 154
  exalted with His r., 214
  forcible are r. words, 189
  go to the r., 48
  hand or the left, 268
  hast done r., 67
  heart is not r., 19
  if thy r. hand offend, 32
  just and r. is He, 165
  know what thy r. hand, 46
  on the r. hand of God, 247
  on thy r. cheek, turn, 139
  r. eye offend thee, 78
  r. hand forget, 1
  r. hand of righteousness, 163
  r. hand or to the left, 55
  r. hand shall find, 110
  r. hand shall save, 161
  r. hand, and on my left, 21
  r. in his own eyes, 7
  r. in his own eyes, 261
  r. in the sight of, 65
  r. in the sight of, 269
  r. to the tree of life, 235

r. to them that find, 53
renew a r. spirit, 368
revenues without r., 98
riches, and not by r., 99
righteous are r., 7
sat on the r. hand, 18
save with Thy r. hand, 87
sit on the r. hand, 120
sit thou at My r. hand, 160
sit Thou on my r., 120
the r. ways of the Lord, 130
thousand at thy r. hand, 79
Thy r. hand, O Lord, 370
to the r. hand, 344
turned not to the r., 94
way which seemeth r., 285
ways of the Lord are r., 26
whatsoever is r., 123
righteous
a r. man's reward, 191
afflictions of the r., 387
art more r., 67
come to call the r., 295
death of the r., 79
desire of the r., 122
destroy the r., 92
discern between the r., 169
doeth righteousness is r., 334
fervent prayer of a r., 294
five of the fifty r., 61
fruit of the r., 330
God shall judge the r., 220
heart of the r., 99
house of the r., 333
in the name of a r., 191
judge r. judgment, 15
judgeth the r., 220
justify the r., 72
let the r. smite, 3
light is sown for the r., 179
lips of the r., 7
little that r. man hath, 112
Lord are over the r., 161
Lord are upon the r., 160
Lord is r., 166
Lord, the r. judge, 331
loveth the r., 153
man that is more r., 205
many be made r., 140
not made for a r. man, 229
one event to the r., 235
outwardly appear r., 15
pervert the words of r., 38
prayer of the r., 162
r. are His judgments, 221
r. are in authority, 173
r. are Thy judgments, 306
r. Branch, 252
r. considereth the cause, 288
r. cry, 292
r. in all His ways, 166

r. in all His works, 149
r. in his own eyes, 206
r. is taken away, 81
r. man hateth lying, 233
r. man regardeth, 14
r. over much, 61
r. runneth into it, 161
r. scarcely be saved, 168
r. shall flourish, 176
r. shall inherit, 329
r. shall rejoice, 326
r. showeth mercy, 37
r. tendeth to life, 65
receiveth a r. man, 191
reward for the r., 329
righteousness of the r., 23
salvation of the r., 332
scarcely for a r., 82
seen the r. forsaken, 1
sold the r. for silver, 69
that thou art r., 17
that thou mayest be r., 350
the Lord is r., 178
there is none r., 245
thoughts of the r., 7
trieth the r., 398
way of the r., 153
well with the r., 180
what can the r. do, 230
when the r. turneth, 23
wicked watcheth the r., 78
written with the r., 110
righteously
judge r., 223
judge r. between, 219
righteousness
awake to r., 27
before Thee for our r., 193
believeth unto r., 29
break off thy sins by r., 26
but follow r., 28
city of r., 211
converts with r., 212
crown of r., 331
deliver me in Thy r., 87
enemy of all r., 119
established in r., 259
every one that doeth r., 334
follow after r., 148
found in the way of r., 8
fruit of r., 69
fruit of r. is sown, 278
fulfil all r., 103
God, and His r., 147
hand of My r., 163
he that doeth r. is, 334
heavens declare His r., 151
if r. come by the law, 56
in r. He doth judge, 221
in r. shalt thou be, 333
judge the world in r., 221
judge the world with r., 220
little with r., 98

man worketh not the r., 13
not by works of r., 85
not for thy r., 395
not meat and drink but r., 187
own souls by their r., 93
paths of r., 332
peaceable fruit of r., 98
persecuted for r.' sake, 226
r. and judgment, 332
r. as a mighty stream, 223
r. as the waves, 270
r. belongeth unto Thee, 333
r. but behold a cry, 96
r. delivereth, 81
r. exalteth a nation, 172
r. I hold fast, 64
r. not be abolished, 339
r. of faith, 126
r. of the righteous, 23
r. of the upright, 87
r. shall be sure reward, 333
r. shall He judge, 220
r. shalt thou judge, 219
r. that he hath done, 139
sanctified in r., 333
sceptre of r., 334
seek r., 249
showeth forth r., 189
sow in r. reap in mercy, 26
suffer for r.' sake, 334
Sun of r., 22
thirst after r., 333
to every man his r., 329
turneth from his r., 23
with r. shall he judge, 252
word of r., 200
work of r., 333
worketh r., 338
riot
same excess of r., 64
riotous
companion of r. men, 58
with r. living, 83
ripe
grapes are fully r., 221
harvest is r., 249
rise
brother shall r. again, 323
day that I r., 276
dead shall r. first, 51
false prophets shall r., 184
false witnesses did r., 206
r. Peter; kill, and eat, 137
r. take up thy bed, 182
r. the third day, 322
r. up against Thee, 166
r. up and walk, 182
r. up early, 103
sun to r. on the evil, 169
third day He shall r., 322
third day He shall r., 75
risen
false witnesses are r., 280

great prophet is r., 22
He is r., 322
risest
  down and when thou r. up,
    55
riseth
  from whence it r., 305
rising
  from r. of the sun, 290
river
  peace been as a r., 270
  r. were turned to blood,
    284
rivers
  all the r. run, 41
  by the r. of Babylon, 188
  place from whence the r.,
    67
  r. of water, 373
  r. of waters run down, 99
  through the r., 54
roar
  let the sea r., 42
  r. all like bears, 13
  r. and lay hold of, 9
  r. He shall prevail, 157
  r. like the sea, 64
  r. like young lions, 9
  will a lion r., 261
  young lions r., 9
roared
  lion hath r. who, 270
  waves r., 148
roaring
  wrath is as the r., 12
roarings
  r. are poured out, 13
rob
  r. not the poor, 273
  will a man r. God, 45
robbed
  bear r. of her whelps, 12
  r. of her whelps, 79
  wherein have we r. Thee,
    45
  yet ye have r. Me, 45
robbery
  full of lies and r., 74
rock
  enter into the r., 113
  except their R. had sold, 1
  God my r. why hast Thou,
    1
  harder than a r., 202
  He is the R., 148
  He only is my r., 63
  house upon a r., 285
  Lord is my r., 160
  out of this r., 298
  r. of my refuge, 337
  r. of my salvation, 148
  r. of my salvation, 290
  r. of our salvation, 363
  r. that is higher, 337

serpent upon a r., 263
smote the r., 99
smote the r. twice, 254
speak unto the r., 124
upon this r. I will, 371
rod
  beat him with the r., 47
  beatest him with the r., 47
  come forth a r., 252
  r. and Thy staff, 54
  r. for the fool's back, 98
  r. he smote, 99
  r. is for the back, 98
  r. of correction, 47
  spareth his r., 47
  with a r. or in love, 21
roes
  like two young r., 25
Roman
  man is a R., 224
  man that is a R., 224
Rome
  bear witness also at R., 70
roof
  cleaveth to the r., 382
  r. of my mouth, 9
room
  no r. in the inn, 217
rooms
  uppermost r. at feasts, 196
root
  bearest not the r., 36
  but the r. thee, 36
  if the r. be holy, 185
  no r. they withered, 28
  out of the serpent's r., 102
  r. and the offspring of, 216
  r. of all evil, 119
  take r. downward, 375
roots
  out of his r., 252
rope
  sin with a cart r., 360
rose
  blossom as the r., 321
  r. from the dead, 284
  r. of Sharon, 25
rot
  thigh shall r., 6
  wicked shall r., 318
rotten
  brass as r. wood, 370
rough
  r. ways shall be made, 272
roughly
  rich answereth r., 70
round
  mountains are r., 154
  navel is like a r., 25
  r. about His people, 154
rubies
  price is far above r., 246
  wisdom is above r., 409

wisdom is better than r.,
  409
rude
  r. in speech, 107
ruin
  mouth worketh r., 7
  shall not be your r., 317
ruined
  Jerusalem is r., 33
rule
  by me princes r., 172
  let the elders that r., 53
  light to r. the day, 20
  light to r. the night, 20
  Lord shall r., 172
  man know not how to r.,
    52
  peace of God r., 278
  r. over his own spirit, 348
  r. over you, 172
  shall r. over thee, 20
  son r. over, 172
  walk by the same r., 69
  when wicked beareth r.,
    173
ruler
  clothing, be thou our r.,
    232
  many seek the r.'s, 223
  speak evil of the r., 173
rulers
  brought before r., 281
  r. are not a terror, 173
  r. of the darkness, 110
ruleth
  r. over men, 172
ruling
  r. in the fear, 172
rumour
  hear a r., 86
run
  judgment r. down as, 223
  r. and not be weary, 29
  r. in a race r. all, 60
  r. that ye may obtain, 60
  r. to and fro, 158
  r. to and fro to seek, 145
  r. with patience, 57
  r. with the footmen, 60
  strange that ye r. not, 64
runneth
  break, and wine r. out, 410
  cup r. over, 2
  nor of him that r., 250
  r. down with water, 54
  righteous r. into it, 161
running
  r. to mischief, 207
  r. waters out of thine, 6
rush
  r. grow up without mire,
    176
rusheth
  r. into the battle, 203

rushing
  r. like the r., 267
rust
  r. doth corrupt, 248
  r. doth corrupt, 368

S

sabachthani
  Eli, Eli, lama s., 13
sabbath
  do well on the s., 336
  keep the s., 335
  Lord even of the s., 336
  not man for the s., 336
  remember the s. day, 335
  s. was made for man, 336
  seventh day is the s., 335
sabbaths
  hallow My s., 335
  s. ye shall keep, 335
sackcloth
  gird thee with s., 262
  gird you with s., 262
  gird you with s., 261
  s. their covering, 267
  virgin girded with s., 86
sacrifice
  Gentiles s., 167
  Him shall ye do s., 148
  kick ye at My s., 69
  mercy, and not s., 334
  more acceptable than s.,
    223
  obey better than s., 269
  s. of fools, 415
  s. of the wicked, 45
  s. to devils, 167
  s. to the Lord, 370
sacrificed
  s. and burnt, 197
sacrifices
  burnt offerings and s., 269
  house full of s., 352
  multitude of your s., 334
  s. God is well pleased, 85
sacrificeth
  s. unto any god, 188
sad
  countenance s. seeing, 88
  heart of righteous s., 99
sadness
  s. of the countenance, 229
safe
  and I shall be s., 338
  in the Lord shall be s., 124
  into it, and is s., 161
safety
  counsellors there is s., 7
  dwell in s., 337
  s. is of the Lord, 396
said
  as thou hast s., 232
  hath He s. and not, 128

saints
  and the faith of the s., 4
  assembly of the s., 133
  death of His s., 247
  delivered unto the s., 127
  fellowcitizens with s., 51
  forsaketh not His s., 128
  patience of the s., 277
  s. did I shut up, 67
  s. shall judge the world, 30
  shed the blood of s., 247
  ten thousands of His s., 306
  ways, Thou King of s., 334
saith
  not every one that s., 226
  s. the Lord, 20
  s. the Lord, 164
  that s. I know Him, 100
  things the law s. it s. to, 21
  what the Lord s., 208
  ye say, the Lord s., 84
sake
  fools for Christ's s., 254
  for His name's s., 332
  for Mine holy name's s.,
    151
  for Mine own s., 160
  for my s., 112
  for Thy goodness' s., 139
  for Thy mercies' s., 338
  for Thy name's s., 151
  for Thy s. are we killed,
    247
  gently for my s., 59
  great name's s., 1
  hated for my name's s., 32
  Jerusalem's s., 212
  kings for my s., 281
  lose his life for my s., 171
  lose his life for my s., 236
  loseth life for my s., 114
  love for their work's s., 53
  love's s. I beseech, 233
  me for Thy mercies' s., 18
  My servant David's s., 160
  not, for Thine own s., 139
  redeem for Thy mercies' s.,
    312
  saved for His name's s., 87
  submit for the Lord's s.,
    229
  wrought for My name's s.,
    151
  Zion's s. will I not, 212
sakes
  do not this for your s., 151
  kings for their s., 50
  not for your s., 250
  your s. He became poor,
    215
salt
  covenant of s., 71
  eaten without s., 136
  pillar of s., 65

  s. have lost his savour, 136
  s. in yourselves, 134
  s. of the earth, 44
  seasoned with s., 70
salutations
  s. in the marketplace, 196
salute
  s. one another, 144
salvation
  become my s., 371
  cometh my s., 338
  eyes have seen Thy s., 251
  for s. unto the ends, 68
  God is my s., 147
  God is my s., 124
  God of my s., 125
  God of my s., 180
  He is become my s., 338
  He only is my s., 63
  hope of s., 27
  horn of my s., 159
  is become my s., 371
  just, and having s., 193
  my light and my s., 132
  now is the day of s., 340
  power of God unto s., 171
  rejoice in Thy s., 395
  rock of my s., 148
  rock of my s., 290
  rock of our s., 363
  s. belongeth unto, 338
  s. come unto Gentiles, 219
  s. is far from wicked, 339
  s. is of the Jews, 340
  s. is of the Lord, 339
  s. nearer than when, 340
  s. of God is sent, 117
  s. of the Lord, 107
  s. of the righteous, 332
  s. shall be for ever, 339
  s. unto kings, 259
  sorrowful: let Thy s., 193
  suffering of Lord is s., 277
  vain is s. hoped, 145
  wait for the s., 276
  waited for Thy s., 338
  wells of s., 339
  word of this s., 134
  work out your own s., 340
  wrath, but to obtain s., 221
same
  Christ the s. yesterday, 44
  s. Lord over all is, 149
  s. shall he return, 86
  Thou art the s., 116
Samson
  call for S., 255
  Philistines upon thee, S., 78
  Philistines upon thee, S., 30
  S. said, let me die, 79
Samuel
  bring me up S., 367
sanctified
  out of the womb I s., 31

ye s. that I am, 43
sayest
all that thou s., 269
Thou s. it, 258
saying
if a man keep my s., 82
keep His s., 88
this is a faithful s., 308
sayings
ear unto my s., 177
heareth these s., 84
heareth these s., 100
keepeth not my s., 100
receive my s., 7
the s. of the prophecy, 271
scales
eyes as it had been s., 68
scapegoat
lot for the s., 342
s. into the wilderness, 342
scarest
s. me with dreams, 103
scarlet
brought up in s., 192
sins be as s., 139
scatter
s. the sheep, 232
s. thee among the heathen,
121
s. Thou the people, 401
s. you among the nations,
121
scattered
flock was s., 104
He that s. Israel, 50
iniquity shall be s., 407
sheep shall be s., 232
whither I have s. you, 155
sceptre
s. of righteousness, 334
s. of Thy kingdom, 334
s. shall not depart, 231
S. shall rise, 252
schoolmaster
law was our s., 57
scorn
friends s. me, 124
laughed thee to s., 343
laughed to s., 257
scorner
cast out the s., 371
reprove not a s., 74
s. heareth not rebuke, 74
s. loveth not one, 74
when s. is punished, 105
scorners
s. delight in their, 137
scornful
seat of the s., 58
scorning
delight in their s., 137
drinketh up s., 350
scorpions
chastise you with s., 273

scourge
lawful for you to s., 224
s. Him, and shall spit, 75
scribes
beware of the s., 196
woe unto you, s., 196
scripture
all S. is given by, 344
prophecy of the S., 299
s. fulfilled, 253
s. should be fulfilled, 253
scriptures
s. of the prophets, 253
search the s., 253
sea
am I a s. or a whale, 120
and earth, and the s., 73
as the sand of the s., 50
cast into the s., 126
cast into the s., 48
cloud out of the s., 287
divided the s., 148
dry land in the s., 113
earth, the s. and, 72
fish of the s., 14
fishes of the s., 156
go down to the s., 272
let the s. roar, 42
midst of the s., 263
mighty waves of the s., 156
of the earth and the s., 342
perils in the s., 79
roareth like the s., 64
run into the s., 41
s. is not full, 41
s. may be calm, 32
s. monsters draw out, 47
sand by the s. side, 2
sand that is by the s., 308
thrown into the s., 289
troubled s., 406
walking on the s., 254
waters cover the s., 128
wave of the s., 103
waves of the s., 270
winds and the s., 22
sea shore
upon the s., 71
seal
opened the seventh s., 22
s. upon thine arm, 239
set me as a s., 239
sealeth
s. their instruction, 103
seals
worthy to loose the s., 263
search
earth, and none did s., 104
s. and try our ways, 317
s. for Me, 94
s. out a matter, 259
s. the scriptures, 253
s. their own glory, 36
searched

His years be s. out, 228
knew not I s. out, 10
s. out what to say, 276
searcheth
Lord s. all hearts, 153
s. the hearts, 153
s. the reins and hearts, 216
Spirit s. all things, 187
searching
canst thou by s., 17
seas
earth praise Him, the s.,
290
waters called He s., 104
season
convenient s., 384
fruit in his s., 373
in due s. we shall reap, 277
in the night s., 91
instant in s. out of s., 310
rain in due s., 268
rest yet for a little s., 277
spoken in due s., 7
there is a s., 265
willing for a s. to, 207
seasoned
s. with salt, 70
seasons
times or the s., 145
seat
at Caesar's judgment s., 52
judgment s. of Christ, 113
judgment s. of Christ, 222
sitteth in the s., 58
seats
s. in the synagogues, 196
second
appear the s. time, 346
s. death hath no power, 82
sought for the s., 71
this is the s. death, 82
secret
better than s. love, 40
bread eaten in s., 99
discover not a s., 30
gift in s., 12
hide himself in s., 113
nothing is s., 347
s. errand unto thee, 83
s. of God, 61
s. of the Lord, 133
s. things belong, 226
seeth in s., 159
secretly
didst it s., 192
secrets
talebearer revealeth s., 172
that revealeth s., 103
seduce
wonders to s. the elect, 184
seduced
s. My people, 401
see
blind s., 179

blind, now I s., 122
blind, that ye may s., 372
but they s. not, 198
cannot s. the kingdom, 37
come, let us s., 43
eyes, s. ye not, 373
for they shall s. God, 307
let him not s., 121
my flesh shall I s. God, 80
neither s. nor hear, 198
no man s. Me, 158
no man shall s. the Lord,
16
not He s. my ways, 153
not s. my wretchedness,
350
not s. the land, 303
open Thine eyes and s., 19
places that I not s., 113
s. all the evil, 59
s. eye to eye, 9
s. His glory, 151
s. in His hands, 102
s. my zeal, 417
s. now that I, 164
s. the land before, 96
s. through a glass, 53
s. Thy vengeance, 327
s. wherein his g., 207
s. ye indeed but, 372
s. your good works, 84
say, who shall s., 74
seeing s. not, 199
shall He not s., 158
shall s. him, but, 252
spoken of, they shall s., 117
that he may s., 111
that thou mayest s., 355
the heathen shall s. My,
151
young men shall s., 417
seed
bearing precious s., 76
corrupt your s., 192
grain of mustard s., 125
grain of mustard s., 176
him that soweth s., 300
multiply thy s., 53
s. also be numbered, 2
s. as the dust, 2
s. may live, 49
s. of Abraham, 219
s. of Abraham, 219
s. of evildoers, 48
s. of the land, 384
s. shall all the families, 131
s. shall all the nations, 49
s. shall be as dust, 47
seed as the s., 71
sow thy s., 95
sow your s., 144
seedtime
s. and harvest, 345
seeing

deaf, or the s., 72
s. many things, 167
s. see not, 199
satisfied with s., 11
seek
broad ways I will s., 89
for good that s. Him, 160
if thou s. Him, 94
if ye s. Him, 94
let no man s. his own, 11
Lord that s. Him, 249
many s. the ruler's, 223
needy s. water, 131
none did search or s., 104
rejoice that s. the Lord,
179
run to and fro to s., 145
s. a flea, 120
s. a sign, 119
s. after a sign, 298
s. after wisdom, 298
s. and ye shall find, 95
s. deep to hide, 98
s. good, and not evil, 49
s. Him with all, 28
s. His face continually, 162
s. His face evermore, 94
s. me and shall not find,
345
s. me early shall find, 409
s. Me, and find, 94
s. meekness, 249
s. my life, 90
s. not mine own will, 147
s. not to be loosed, 101
s. not your's, but you, 57
s. peace, and pursue, 277
s. righteousness, 249
s. that which was lost, 181
s. the Lord, 94
s. the Lord and ye, 234
s. their meat, 9
s. those things, 148
s. thou great things, 11
s. Thy servant, 67
s. ye first the kingdom, 147
s. ye My face, 124
s. ye the kingdom of God,
225
s. ye the living among, 323
s. ye the Lord, 95
s. ye the Lord while, 273
s. ye the priesthood, 11
s. you out of the book, 344
shall men s. death, 82
shall s. peace, and, 93
Son of man is come to s.,
213
soul to s. the Lord, 94
them that diligently s., 29
they s. not Thy statutes,
339

Thy face, Lord, will I s.,
124
thyself? s. them not, 11
time to s. the Lord, 317
we s. your God, 84
whom s. ye, 206
will I s. Thee early, 94
seeketh
he that s. findeth, 11
s. after a sign, 254
s. his own glory, 36
s. mischief, 387
s. my life, 264
s. my life s. thy, 78
s. not the welfare, 40
s. that which is astray, 283
s. to slay him, 78
soul that s. Him, 9
understanding s. knowl-
edge, 227
wise s. knowledge, 227
seeking
s. goodly pearls, 40
s. rest and findeth none,
119
seemeth
do what s. good, 84
s. good unto Thee, 285
what s. good unto, 61
what s. Him good, 2
seen
all things have I s., 9
and have s. nothing, 130
brother whom he hath s.,
39
deed done nor s., 88
evidence of things not s.,
127
evil hath not s. God, 169
eye hath not s., 35
eyes have s., 25
for to be s. of men, 196
God whom he hath not s.,
39
hast thou s. the doors, 17
have s. God, 22
hope that is s., 190
may be s. of men, 195
no eye had s. me, 90
not s. and yet believed, 29
s. a great light, 111
s. and heard declare we,
186
s. God face to face, 22
s. her nakedness, 69
s. His star, 188
s. me hath s. the Father,
101
s. my wrong, 223
s. of angels, 215
s. strange things, 254
s. the King, 22
s. the righteous, 1
s. this day that, 158

of God, and s. tables, 253
other gods to s., 23
s. God and mammon, 61
s. Him, 268
s. Him in sincerity, 189
s. Him in truth, 94
s. Him only, 94
s. Him with a perfect, 352
s. Him, and obey, 269
s. in newness of spirit, 19
s. Lord with gladness, 352
s. me for nought?, 39
s. other gods, 209
s. other gods, 128
s. strange gods, 22
s. strangers, 121
s. the Egyptians, 132
s. the king of Babylon, 3
s. the Lord, 139
s. the Lord, 415
s. the Lord, 44
s. the Lord, 94
s. the Lord, 49
s. the Lord Christ, 413
s. the Lord with fear, 193
s. two masters, 242
s. with thee for Rachel, 9
s. ye the Lord, 352
shall s. me, 20
that we should s. Him, 20
whom ye will s., 49
will s. Thee, 352
served
Jacob s. seven years, 238
king himself is s., 69
s. Baal a little, 83
s. on the other side, 197
s. other gods, 120
s. strange gods, 121
s. the creature more, 198
servest
God whom thou s., 63
serveth
among you as He that s., 194
and him that s. Him not, 169
between him that s., 169
own son that s., 250
service
herb for the s. of man, 76
think he doeth God s., 281
serving
s. the Lord, 194
set
s. before you the way, 236
s. My face against, 305
seven
hewn out her s. pillars, 409
s. are an abomination, 207
s. times in a day, 140
than s. men that can, 61
sevenfold
taken on him s., 159

seventh
blessed the s. day, 335
opened the s. seal, 22
s. day He rested, 72
s. day is the sabbath, 335
s. day thou shalt rest, 335
s. year let it rest, 76
seventy
until s. times seven, 140
sew
time to s., 92
shadow
as the s. of death, 74
darkness and the s., 80
darkness nor s. of death, 74
days are as a s., 235
days are like a s., 88
days upon earth are a s., 260
doors of the s. of death, 17
of the s. of death, 380
s. go forward, 272
s. of death, 63
s. of death, 339
s. of the mountains, 132
s. of Thy wings, 160
s. of Thy wings, 337
s. return backward, 272
shake
s. at the sound, 93
shaken
if they be s., 161
shame
awake, some to s., 108
bringeth his mother s., 47
cause my s. to go, 202
clothed with s., 110
clothed with s., 109
cometh to s., 406
him that causeth s., 12
kingdoms thy s., 192
man covereth s., 208
my face from s., 280
naked and see his s., 346
pride, then cometh s., 296
s. shall be seen, 192
s. shall be the promotion, 147
son that causeth s., 230
unjust knoweth no s., 353
shameth
s. his father, 58
Sharon
rose of S., 25
sharp
like a s. razor, 30
mouth like a s. sword, 75
s. as a twoedged sword, 79
sharpened
s. their tongues, 362
sharpeneth
iron s. iron, 44
s. the countenance, 44
sharper

s. than a thorn, 69
s. than twoedged sword, 354
shaven
s. then my strength, 263
shearer
dumb before His s., 249
sheaves
bringing his s., 76
even among the s., 146
shed
blood be s., 222
blood of him that s., 262
blood that is s., 262
blood which is s., 35
from coming to s. blood, 7
s. innocent blood, 207
s. the blood of saints, 247
sheddeth
s. man's blood, 222
shedding
without s. of blood, 35
sheep
as for these s., 206
astray like a lost s., 67
bleating of the s., 83
careth not for the s., 95
come to you in s.'s, 84
feed my s., 253
great shepherd of the s., 218
hath been lost s., 23
keeping the s., 348
life for the s., 95
like s. they are laid, 80
lost s., 219
man have an hundred s., 283
other s. I have, 117
s. for the slaughter, 79
s. going astray, 168
s. have gone astray, 23
s. hear my voice, 10
s. in midst of wolves, 79
s. not having a shepherd, 232
s. of His hand, 154
s. of My pasture, 232
s. shall be scattered, 232
s. what have they done, 320
s. which was lost, 180
shepherd divideth his s., 49
shepherd of the s., 232
slay ox and s., 14
sheepfolds
among the s., 104
shekels
s. of silver, 208
shepherd
as a s. doth his flock, 50
as a s. putteth, 396
chief S. shall appear, 331
fold, and one s., 51
good s., 218

seek a s., 119
seek after a s., 298
seeketh after a s., 254
tongues are for a s., 385
signs
except ye see s., 28
s. of heaven, 19
s. of the times, 97
s. which I have showed, 124
shall show s. and, 184
sights and great s., 15
worketh s. and wonders, 87
silence
dwelt in s., 18
keep not s., 212
keep not Thou s., 18
keep s. before Him, 163
let your women keep s., 52
Lord keep not s., 18
prudent shall keep s., 301
time to keep s., 40
to s. the ignorance of, 85
was s. in heaven, 22
will not keep s., 325
woman learn in s., 105
woman to be in s., 22
silent
am not s., 91
silly
envy slayeth the s., 12
Siloam
pool of S., 182
silver
coveted no man's s., 209
dross from the s., 393
gods of s., 198
gold in pictures of s., 106
idols are s. and gold, 198
instruction and not s., 105
like unto gold, or s., 166
loveth s., 175
neither their s. nor, 150
none were of s., 308
reprobate s., 308
righteous for s., 69
s. and gold, 268
s. and gold have I none, 46
s. be weighed, 409
s. cord be loosed, 96
s. is become dross, 201
s. is Mine, 404
satisfied with s., 175
shekels of s., 208
thirty pieces of s., 31
thousands of gold and s., 393
tongue is as choice s., 189
vessels of gold and s., 100
simple
but the s. pass on, 301
making wise the s., 55
preserveth the s., 162
s. concerning evil, 170

s. is made wise, 105
s. understand wisdom, 391
simplicity
do it with s., 46
went in their s., 206
sin
all manner of s. and, 33
bare the s. of many, 252
bear his s., 33
blind ye have no s., 206
but s. that dwelleth, 33
by one man s., 203
came, s. revived, 56
cause thy flesh to s., 356
ceased from s., 358
cleanseth us from all s., 35
cloak for their s., 121
death for his own s., 178
declare their s., 353
did not Solomon s. by, 210
die for his own s., 304
died unto s. once, 75
flesh the law of s., 41
fools mock at s., 356
forbid that I should s., 291
freed from s., 82
fruit of the wicked to s., 65
go, and s. no more, 357
God doth not commit s., 37
hath the greater s., 178
he that is without s., 4
His steps: Who did no s., 215
I do it, but s., 321
I had not known s., 56
if a soul s., 55
if any man s., 209
in Him is no s., 215
in s. did my mother, 31
knowledge of s., 56
lay not this s. to, 140
Lord will not impute s., 140
lust bringeth forth s., 89
make me to know my s., 206
man of s. be revealed, 346
my s. only this once, 316
no s. in thee, 297
not of faith is s., 126
not s. against Thee, 55
one man s., 66
one man s., 220
prayer become s., 110
rebellion unto his s., 311
remember their s., 139
righteousness, and s., 27
s. against innocent, 262
s. against the Lord, 220
s. be blotted out, 326
s. bringeth forth death, 82
s. is a reproach, 172
s. is ever before me, 62
s. is not imputed, 229
s. is of the devil, 342

s. is the transgression, 358
s. lieth at the door, 123
s. no more, 357
s. of his youth, 406
s. of witchcraft, 310
s. rebuke before all, 46
s. shall not have dominion, 173
s. to remembrance, 46
s. upon them, 197
s. will find you, 346
say that we have no s., 206
servant of s., 357
sting of death is s., 82
strength of s. is, 82
taketh away the s., 213
they are all under s., 245
to persons, ye commit s., 70
unrighteousness is s., 334
vanity, and s., 360
wages of s., 115
wanteth not s., 366
what is my s., 264
where s. abounded, 140
whosoever committeth s., 357
whosoever committeth s., 358
sincerity
love Christ in s., 35
s. and in truth, 189
sinew
iron s., 373
sinful
for I am a s. man, 62
sing
awake and s., 190
good to s. praises, 291
how shall we s., 121
rejoice, and s., 42
s. forth the honour, 363
s. many songs, 130
s. O barren, 47
s. praise to my God, 363
s. praises, 290
s. praises to His name, 364
s. praises unto Him, 78
s. praises unto the Lord, 363
s. psalms unto Him, 363
s. unto God, ye kingdoms, 363
s. unto Him, 363
s. unto Him with the, 263
s. unto the Lord, 363
s. unto the Lord, 363
s. unto the Lord, 364
s. unto the Lord, 364
s. unto the Lord, 364
s. unto the Lord, 289
s. unto the Lord, 363
s. unto the Lord as long, 363

ox goeth to the s., 6
sheep for the s., 79
slay
  evil shall s. the wicked, 223
  in no wise s. it, 59
  in no wise s. it, 222
  not s. you, 326
  s. an innocent person, 18
  s. both man and woman, 14
  s. me thyself, 205
  s. me, yet will I trust, 124
  seeketh to s. him, 78
  sword, and s. me, 192
slayer
  deliver the s., 209
slayeth
  before him that s. thee, 17
  envy s. the silly, 12
  hand of him that s., 17
  s. Cain, vengeance, 159
sleep
  awake out of s., 340
  let us not s., 397
  love not s., 230
  neither slumber nor s., 50
  not give s. to mine, 52
  not suffer him to s., 363
  of the hands to s., 288
  s. a perpetual s., 81
  s. but my heart, 103
  s. falleth upon men, 103
  s. in the dust, 108
  s. of a labouring man, 363
  s. the s. of death, 18
  they s. not, except, 406
  they that s. s. in the, 168
  yet a little s., 288
sleepeth
  is not dead, but s., 236
  s. and must be awaked, 198
  s. in harvest, 230
sleight
  s. of men, 101
slew
  dead which he s., 4
  s. at one time, 370
  s. in his life, 4
  when He s. them, 133
  woman s. him, 192
slide
  s. in due time, 276
sling
  could s. stones, 4
  s. and with a stone, 395
  s. out, 109
slippery
  way be dark and s., 77
slippeth
  my foot s., 162
slothful
  s. man saith, 121
slothfulness
  s. the building decayeth, 39
slow

Lord is s. to anger, 306
merciful, s. to anger, 166
of a s. tongue, 106
s. of heart to believe, 299
s. of speech, 106
s. to anger, 59
s. to anger, 59
s. to anger, 12
s. to anger, 12
s. to anger, 59
s. to speak, 13
s. to wrath, 276
s. to wrath, 13
sluggard
  go to the ant, thou s., 95
  s. is wiser, 61
  s. to them that send, 230
slumber
  keepeth thee will not s.,
    161
  neither s. nor sleep, 50
  s. to mine eyelids, 52
  sleep, a little s., 288
slumberings
  s. upon the bed, 103
small
  both s. and great, 100
  every s. matter, 231
  for a s. moment, 1
  hear the s., 201
  I am s. and despised, 128
  is it a s. thing for you, 120
  left unto us a very s., 376
  s. among the heathen, 305
  s. and great are there, 80
  s. as the dust, 14
  s. dust of the balance, 173
  s. one a strong nation, 176
  s. rain upon, 106
  strength is s., 142
  the dead, s. and great, 222
  witnessing both to s., 381
smell
  but they s. not, 198
  eat, nor s., 198
  s. of a field, 47
  s. of my son, 47
  s. of thine ointments, 239
smite
  I may s. thee, 284
  let the righteous s., 3
  Lord shall s., 42
  s. all the firstborn, 135
  s. the shepherd and the,
    232
  s. thee by day, 161
  s. thee on thy right, 139
smiteth
  s. his father, 41
  s. thee on the one cheek,
    140
  that s. a man, 41
smitten

commandest me to be s.,
  123
s. and He will bind, 157
s. five or six times, 111
stricken, s. of God, 32
smoke
  s. out of the chimney, 112
  s. to the eyes, 230
smooth
  ways shall be made s., 272
smoother
  mouth is s., 6
  s. than butter, 106
smote
  in My wrath I s., 59
  s. his neighbour, 209
  s. them hip and thigh, 398
  Uzza, and he s. him, 150
snare
  bird hasteth to the s., 379
  gods shall be a s., 109
  pit, and the s., 91
  s. for my life, 83
  s. of his soul, 138
  s. unto us, 40
  taken in My s., 386
  taken in the s., 102
  taken in the s., 114
snared
  s. by the transgression, 233
snout
  gold in a swine's s., 24
snow
  consume the s. waters, 80
  s. in summer, 138
  treasures of the s., 122
  white as s., 139
  whiter than s., 307
soap
  take thee much s., 178
sober
  be s. be vigilant, 342
  be s. grave, 28
  let us watch and be s., 397
  of the day, be s., 27
  s. and watch unto prayer,
    15
  young women to be s., 247
soberly
  think s., 194
soberness
  words of truth and s., 243
sockets
  s. of fine gold, 36
Sodom
  land of S. than for thee,
    202
  more tolerable for S., 167
  S. and Gomorrah, 83
  should have been as S., 376
  sin as S., 353
soft
  s. answer turneth away, 12
  s. tongue breaketh, 16

softer
  s. than oil, 106
sojourners
  s. with Me, 299
sold
  except their Rock had s., 1
  land shall not be s., 299
  s. his birthright, 204
  s. the righteous for, 69
soldier
  good s. of Christ, 282
sole
  s. of his foot, 24
soles
  s. of your feet, 210
solitary
  city sit s., 86
Solomon
  did not S. king of, 210
  greater than S., 213
  King S. passed all, 404
  S. in all his glory, 15
something
  s. when he is nothing, 62
son
  Absalom, my s. my s., 175
  Absalom, my s. my s., 176
  against the king's s., 208
  and bear a s., 252
  and the s. of man that, 244
  as for an only s., 262
  bear a s., 135
  because he hath no s., 185
  believeth not the S., 28
  blood of Christ His S., 35
  bring forth a s., 217
  bring forth a s., 217
  bring forth a s. and, 217
  but in his s.'s days, 67
  chasten thy s. while, 47
  chasteneth his s., 97
  Christ is the S. of God, 29
  Christ, the S., 218
  Christ, the S. of God, 216
  Father sent the S., 216
  Father, and of the S., 117
  Father, save the S., 228
  fellowship is with His S.,
    135
  foolish s. heaviness of, 48
  foolish s. is a grief, 48
  foolish s. is calamity, 48
  glorified in the S., 152
  glorify Thy S., 152
  hair of thy s., 337
  hand of thy s., 250
  hateth his s., 47
  have no s., 204
  His only begotten S., 115
  honoureth not the S., 5
  if his s. ask bread, 225
  if thou be the S. of God, 43
  if Thou be the S. of God,
    251

is a wise s., 269
Israel is My s., 49
Jesus, the s. of Joseph, 343
Jonathan my s., 201
judgment unto the S., 21
king's s. is dead, 59
life is in His S., 116
loveth s. more than me,
  131
neither the s. of man, 165
no man knoweth the S.,
  228
no more servant but a s.,
  51
no s. to keep my name, 228
O my s. Absalom, 176
on the name of His S., 57
only begotten S., 28
only begotten S. into, 215
or the s. of man, 245
s. against the father, 131
S. also may glorify, 152
S. can do nothing of, 2
s. eat thou honey, 410
s. heareth his father's, 74
s. honoureth his father, 275
s. maketh a glad, 48
s. of a Pharisee, 185
S. of God who loved me,
  215
s. of her womb, 59
s. of his old age, 132
s. of perdition, 219
s. of the morning, 86
S. of the most high, 341
s. rule over, 172
S. shall make you free, 142
s. shall not bear, 356
s. that causeth shame, 230
S. will reveal Him, 228
sent not His S. into, 213
shall be My s., 162
smell of my s., 47
spareth his own s., 250
that acknowledgeth the S.,
  217
that denieth the S., 14
that hath the S. hath, 217
that Jesus is the S., 169
the iniquity of the s., 356
the s. of perdition, 346
this is My beloved S., 212
this is My beloved S., 251
this is the S. of God, 100
this the carpenter's s., 213
though He were a S., 215
thy curse, my s., 32
truly this was the S., 5
trust in the s. of man, 314
truth Thou art the S., 100
turn away thy s., 209
unto us a s. is given, 252
what s. is he whom, 48

whosoever denieth the S.,
  88
wise s. maketh a glad, 48
woman, behold thy s., 134
worm? and the s., 244
son in law
  king's s., 258
son of man
  a word against the S., 33
  betrayest thou the S., 31
  coming of the S., 345
  flesh of the S., 58
  now is the S. glorified, 151
  S. also confess before, 5
  S. came not to be, 10
  S. cometh at an hour, 310
  S. coming in a cloud, 346
  S. hath not where to lay,
    188
  S. hath power, 140
  S. is betrayed, 31
  S. is betrayed, 31
  S. is come, 213
  S. is come to seek, 213
  S. is Lord of sabbath, 336
  S. is not come, 251
  S. should be glorified, 151
  S. sit on the right, 120
  S. standing on the right,
    247
  s. that Thou visitest, 203
  see the S. coming in, 81
  shall the S. be ashamed,
    171
  the S., 218
song
  drink wine with a s., 364
  Lord is my strength and s.,
    338
  Lord my strength and s.,
    371
  Lord's s. in a strange, 121
  name of God with a s., 174
  new s. and His praise, 364
  s. will I praise, 363
  strength and my s., 371
  the s. of fools, 74
  utter a s., 363
songs
  s. and everlasting joy, 142
  sing many s., 130
  statutes have been my s.,
    54
sons
  are the s. of God, 187
  befalleth the s. of men, 81
  daughters unto their s., 210
  fathers and the s., 271
  fathers shall eat the s., 44
  fight for your s., 24
  firstborn of thy s., 65
  s. be with me, 80
  s. in my womb, 13
  s. of Belial, 118

■ **542** ■

him that s. seed, 300
s. and another reapeth, 69
s. bountifully, 96
s. discord among brethren, 17
s. sparingly shall, 106
s. to the Spirit shall, 115
that s. to his flesh, 243
to him that s., 333
whatsoever a man s., 106
sown
light is s., 179
s. in corruption, 36
s. in peace, 278
s. the wind, 106
s. wheat but, 144
ye have s. much and, 106
spake
s. ye did not hear, 99
they s. against me, 343
well s. the Holy Ghost, 299
spare
back, neither will I s., 94
eye shall not s., 14
eye shall not s., 250
let not your eye s., 94
s. me according, 154
s. no arrows, 327
s. them, as a man s., 250
s. Thy people, 139
s. ye not her young, 14
spared
mine eye s., 249
s. not the angels, 12
spareth
s. his rod, 47
sparing
not s. the flock, 372
sparingly
soweth s. shall reap, 106
spark
s. of his fire, 223
sparrows
are not five s. sold for, 153
more value than many s., 203
speak
alone, that I may s., 40
be not afraid, but s., 108
command thou shalt s., 295
days should s., 122
double heart do they s., 98
dumb to s., 179
evil, s. good things, 73
from me to s. unto, 17
heavens, and I will s., 366
heed to s. that which, 189
I s. they are for war, 401
I s. to the world, 325
I will s. and the word, 299
if any man s., 296
it is not ye that s. but, 207
let not God s., 22

mouths, but they s. not, 198
neither s. they through, 198
s. a vision, 130
s. a word against the, 33
s. as the oracles, 296
s. but this once, 150
s. every man truth, 135
s. evil of no man, 362
s. evil of the ruler, 173
s. forth the words, 243
s. I pray, 347
s. in our tongues, 385
s. in the anguish, 40
s. in the church, 52
s. into the air, 57
s. Lord; for Thy, 183
s. My word faithfully, 103
s. not in the ears of a, 7
s. that which is good, 7
s. the word only, 125
s. they of the world, 130
s. thou the things, 101
s. thou with us, 22
s. to the earth, 156
s. ye that ride, 290
s. ye the truth, 189
s. ye unto the rock, 124
s. your minds, 7
shall I s., 207
slow to s., 13
that s. unto thee am He, 251
that will I s., 208
though I s. with the, 107
time to s., 40
we cannot but s. the, 381
when s. well of you, 136
word that I shall s., 299
word that men shall s., 320
speakest
s. lies in the name of, 130
speaketh
abhor him that s., 75
all the Lord s., 268
false witness that s., 17
Father which s. in you, 207
heart the mouth s., 44
of whom s. the prophet, 253
one s. peaceably, 195
s. against the Holy, 187
s. in an unknown tongue, 57
s. lies shall perish, 98
s. not unto men, 57
s. of himself seeketh, 36
s. shall be a barbarian, 58
s. the truth, 338
s. the words of God, 20
s. truth, 189
s. with tongues, 57
when a prophet s., 129
speaking

be born, s. lies, 25
God s., 22
heard for their much s., 293
lips from s. guile, 189
s. perverse things, 31
spear
comest with a s., 124
lift up his s., 370
stretched out the s., 92
sword and s., 124
spears
pruninghooks into s., 401
s. into pruninghooks, 278
special
s. people unto Himself, 50
speech
excellent s. becometh, 106
hear my s., 295
of one s., 392
rude in s., 107
s. be alway with grace, 70
s. shall distil, 106
s. shall distil, 101
slow of s., 106
understand one another's s., 57
speed
biddeth him God s. is, 69
spend
s. our years, 234
wherefore do ye s., 393
spendest
s. more, when I come, 171
spent
s. without hope, 90
spices
ointments than all s., 239
spies
ye are s., 4
spilt
as water s., 260
spin
neither do they s., 15
spirit
a wounded s. who, 89
also walk in the S., 27
and vexation of s., 11
anguish of my s., 40
be of a contrite s., 176
begun in the S., 23
believe not every s., 29
better of an humble s., 193
body without the s., 82
body, and in your s., 36
born of the S. is s., 31
bound in the s., 104
but the same S., 2
commend my s., 3
commit my s., 162
drinketh up my s., 13
faithful s. concealeth, 143
filled with the S., 103
flesh, but in the S., 126
follow their own s., 130

fruit of the S. is, 187
hasty of s., 136
hear what the S. saith, 184
heart and a new s., 236
heed to your s., 246
His s. upon them, 351
I saw the S. descending, 187
if a s. hath spoken, 3
if we live in the s., 27
justified in the S., 215
led by the S., 187
lusteth against the s., 192
lying s. in the mouth, 370
man, thou unclean s., 122
mind of the S., 153
My s. remaineth among, 54
newness of s., 19
of the S. reap life, 115
patient in s., 276
poor in s., 193
portion of thy s., 185
power over the s., 81
power, but by My s., 371
present in s., 2
quench not the S., 127
receive my s., 247
renew a right s., 368
rule over his own s., 348
S. against the flesh, 192
s. and not the letter, 53
s. before a fall, 123
s. drieth the bones, 89
S. gave them utterance, 385
s. giveth life, 56
s. indeed is willing, 141
s. is broken, 364
S. is truth, 187
s. of counsel, 252
S. of God, 158
S. of God descending, 187
S. of God dwelleth, 187
s. of God hath made, 234
S. of God is, 230
S. of our God, 224
S. of the Lord, 143
S. of the Lord, 24
S. of the Lord, 207
S. of the Lord, 313
S. of the Lord, 207
s. of the Lord shall, 252
S. of the Lord upon me, 187
s. of wisdom, 252
S. of your Father, 207
s. of your mind, 19
s. prayeth but my, 294
S. searcheth all things, 187
s. shall return unto, 81
S. that beareth witness, 187
S. that quickeneth, 187
S. the water and blood, 382
s. to retain the s., 81
s. was not stedfast, 99

soweth to the S. shall, 115
than proud in s., 276
that are after the S., 41
the s. of fear, 63
the s. of knowledge, 252
the s. of prophecy, 416
things of the S., 41
vexation of s., 77
walk in the S., 27
water and of the S., 24
when the unclean s., 119
which way went the S., 17
with my s. within, 94
with you in the s., 2
woman of a sorrowful s., 47
worship God in the s., 30
worship Him in s., 359
spirits
    have familiar s., 367
    Lord weigheth the s., 350
    rejoice not, that the s., 180
spiritual
    law is s., 41
spiritually
    s. minded is life, 19
spit
    s. in her face, 303
    s. upon Him, and shall, 75
spitting
    from shame and s., 280
spoil
    s. of your enemies, 353
    s. the vines, 92
    s. thee shall be a s., 327
    s. to all their enemies, 192
    s. with the proud, 193
    s. you through philosophy, 84
spoiled
    emptied, and utterly s., 89
spoken
    albeit I have not s., 84
    angel hath s., 3
    day whereof I have s., 299
    for I have s., 21
    for the Lord hath s., 89
    hath He s., 128
    I have s. it, 42
    I have s. mock on, 257
    I the Lord have s., 42
    if I have s. evil, 4
    known what is s., 57
    Lord hath not s., 129
    Lord hath not s., 101
    Lord hath s. who can but, 270
    not s. of myself, 21
    of the Lord hath s., 372
    ran: I have not s., 130
    s. in due season, 7
    s. in the ear, 123
    s. only by Moses, 112
    s. unto them but they, 100
    that the Lord hath s., 268

that the prophets have s., 299
to whom He was not s. of, 117
which thou hast s., 164
word fitly s., 106
word which I have s., 186
words that are s., 74
sport
    may make us s., 255
spots
    leopard his s., 43
spread
    s. dung upon your faces, 192
    s. forth your hands, 1
    s. My net, 386
spreading
    s. himself like a green, 118
spring
    s. as the grass, 230
springs
    s. of water, 403
    springs of w., 300
staff
    rod and Thy s., 54
stagger
    s. but not with drink, 103
staggereth
    drunken man s., 103
stalled
    s. ox and hatred, 238
stamp
    s. them as the mire, 14
stand
    able to s. before, 156
    able to s. before envy, 12
    awake, s. up, 397
    by faith ye s., 126
    faith should not s., 126
    house cannot s., 372
    it shall not s., 108
    kingdom cannot s., 173
    not hear me, I s. up, 91
    s. and am judged, 281
    s. at the latter day, 124
    s. before kings, 2
    s. before the judgment, 113
    s. before thee, 64
    s. before thine enemies, 69
    s. before you, 370
    s. before you whole, 182
    s. fast in the faith, 94
    s. fast in the Lord, 96
    s. fast in the Lord, 127
    s. fast, and hold, 102
    s. in His holy place, 186
    s. praying, forgive, 177
    s. still, and consider, 265
    s. still, and see, 107
    s. still, that, 283
    s. thou still, 325
    s. up and bless, 26
    s. up, and save, 19

s. up; I myself, 194
s. we in jeopardy, 282
shall then his kingdom s., 341
shepherd that will s., 21
so shall it s., 144
the dead, s. before God, 222
who can s. before His, 157
who can s. before His, 150
who shall be able to s., 151
who shall s., 220
who shall s. when, 22
standard
s. toward Zion, 338
set up a s., 267
set ye up a s., 24
standest
place whereon thou s., 318
s. is holy ground, 186
why s. Thou afar, 18
standeth
counsel of the Lord s., 279
foundation of God s., 149
heart s. in awe, 7
s. in way of sinners, 58
thinketh he s. take heed, 63
standing
s. in the synagogues, 195
s. in the temple, 114
Son of man s., 247
there be some s. here, 81
star
bright and morning s., 216
give him the morning s., 331
one s. differeth from, 183
S. out of Jacob, 252
seen His s., 188
stargazers
astrologers, the s., 19
stars
nest among the s., 296
number of the s., 183
s. are not pure, 244
s. in their courses, 18
s. of heaven, 303
s. of the heaven, 71
state
man at his best s., 142
stature
one cubit unto his s., 261
s. is like to a palm, 36
statutes
commandments and My s., 26
keep all My s., 317
keep my s., 268
s. have been my songs, 54
s. of your fathers, 167
seek not Thy s., 339
testimonies and His s., 269
walk in My s., 270
walk in My s., 268

way of Thy s., 55
staves
comest to me with s., 66
thief with swords and s., 20
stay
Lord was my s., 109
none can s. His hand, 157
s. me with flagons, 238
s. now thine hand, 250
steadfast
be ye s., 95
steal
ashamed s. away, 72
break through and s., 248
but for to s., 74
kill, do not s., 56
s. to satisfy his soul, 73
shall not s., 25
shalt not s., 73
that stole s. no more, 74
where thieves do not s., 368
stem
rod out of the s., 252
step
s. between me and death, 78
Stephen
stoned S., 256
steps
count all my s., 153
direct his s., 314
directeth his s., 26
enlarged my s., 337
follow his s., 215
hunt our s., 102
s. of a good man, 26
steward
blameless, as the s., 233
stiffnecked
art a s. people, 372
be no more s., 53
be ye not s., 372
s. and uncircumcised, 167
still
be s. and know, 228
beside the s. waters, 54
stand s. that, 283
stand thou s., 325
strength is to sit s., 230
sting
death, where is thy s., 82
s. of death is sin, 82
stingeth
s. like an adder, 237
stir
s. him up, 50
stolen
s. waters are sweet, 99
stomach
wine for thy s.'s, 237
stone
cast a s., 92
first cast a s., 4

give him a s., 225
hands, wood and s., 198
head s. of the corner, 274
hearts as an adamant s., 100
houses of hewn s., 96
not take of thee a s., 14
ready to s. me, 90
s. for foundations, 14
s. graven by art, 166
s. shall be a witness, 315
s. shall cry, 4
s. which the builders, 274
s. which the builders, 328
sling and with a s., 395
tables of s., 280
tables of s., 380
to the dumb s. Arise, 197
wood and s., 198
works do ye s. me, 5
stoned
s. him with stones, 311
s. Stephen, 256
should have been s., 302
stones
able of these s., 155
build with hewn s., 17
by these s., 315
command that these s., 43
could sling s., 4
s. of a crown, 155
strength of s., 90
waters wear the s., 94
stonest
the prophets, and s., 212
stony
s. heart, 315
stood
s. between the dead, 209
stoppeth
s. his ears, 45
stork
s. in the heaven, 99
storm
chaff that the s., 406
whirlwind and in the s., 157
stormy
raiseth the s. wind, 265
straight
cannot be made s., 3
crooked shall be made s., 272
crooked things s., 111
make His paths s., 310
make s. in the desert, 252
s. paths for your feet, 28
s. the way of the Lord, 219
who can make that s., 3
straightway
goeth after her s., 6
strain
s. at a gnat, 196
strait
s. is the gate, 27

strange
even unto s. cities, 281
lips of a s. woman, 6
s. woman is a narrow, 301
seen s. things, 254
serve s. gods, 22
served s. gods, 121
song in a s. land, 121
stranger in a s. land, 138
tongue of a s. woman, 242
stranger
both for the s., 112
law for the s., 222
love ye the s., 38
neither vex a s., 138
s. and ye took me in, 60
s. did not lodge, 191
s. in a strange, 138
s. in the earth, 226
s. nor the poor, 59
s. that is with him, 219
s. that sojourneth, 112
s. thou mayest lend, 138
s. unto my brethren, 114
surety for a s., 37
strangers
field, to bury s., 39
for ye were s., 38
inheritance turned to s., 64
of children, or of s., 377
s. from the covenants, 92
s. in the land of Egypt, 138
shall ye serve s., 121
to entertain s., 12
ye are no more s., 51
ye are s., 299
straw
as when there was s., 273
iron as s., 370
lion shall eat s., 38
s. to make brick, 273
stream
as a mighty s., 223
street
fallen in the s., 230
lodge in the s., 191
lodge not in the s., 78
mire of the s., 14
no name in the s., 130
streets
cannot go in our s., 102
corners of the s., 195
desolate in the s., 192
playing in the s., 300
s. of Askelon, 175
s. of the city shall, 300
slain in the s., 121
voice in the s., 409
strength
as my s. was then, 141
awake, put on s., 161
beginning of my s., 135
confidence shall be s., 125
delivered by much s., 124

everlasting s., 371
forces of s., 370
from s. to s., 141
give not thy s., 242
glory and s., 290
God is my s., 371
God is my s., 141
God of my s., 162
God, my s., 160
great s. lieth, 207
great s. lieth, 30
have s. when thou goest, 137
if by reason of s., 234
increaseth s., 162
Jehovah is my s., 371
Lord is my s., 160
Lord is my s., 371
Lord is my s. and song, 338
Lord is s. of my life, 70
Lord is your s., 370
man whose s., 124
my s. which teacheth, 371
not when my s. faileth, 8
put on thy s., 315
refuge and s., 141
renew their s., 315
s. and my redeemer, 292
s. in time of trouble, 332
s. is made perfect, 194
s. is small, 142
s. is to sit still, 230
s. labour and sorrow, 234
S. of Israel, 233
s. of my heart, 141
s. of sin is, 82
s. of the ox, 106
s. shall no man prevail, 370
s. the s. of stones, 90
s. to bring forth, 403
s. to the upright, 269
s. will go from, 263
seek His s., 94
so is his s., 44
so is my s. now, 141
so shall thy s., 34
voice with s., 63
wisdom is better than s., 371
young men is their s., 122
strengthen
I will s. thee, 163
s. me, I pray, 291
s. my hands, 141
s. that which was sick, 181
s. thy brethren, 108
s. ye the weak hands, 108
s. your heart, 63
strong shall not s., 63
strengtheneth
Christ which s., 2
wisdom s., 371
stretch
s. forth his hand, 18

s. out My hand, 284
stretched
hand is s., 384
hand is s. out still, 150
His hand is s., 150
s. out the heavens, 73
s. out the spear, 92
stretcheth
s. out the north, 72
stricken
esteem him s., 32
strife
anger appeaseth s., 12
be done through s. or, 12
beginning of s. is, 371
cease from s., 16
envying and s. is, 64
man stirreth up s., 12
of sacrifices with s., 352
s. and reproach cease, 371
talebearer, the s., 172
strifes
hatred stirreth s., 16
that they do gender s., 68
stringed
s. instruments, 263
strings
instrument of ten s., 263
stripe
s. for s., 222
stripes
his s. we are healed, 181
s. above measure, 282
s. into a fool, 74
stripped
go s. and naked, 176
strive
of the Lord must not s., 68
s. against Him, 60
s. not about words, 16
s. not with a man, 16
striveth
s. with his Maker, 184
strong
ants a people not s., 95
as s. this day, 141
battle to the s., 43
be s. and courageous, 108
be s. and quit, 70
be s. fear not, 108
be s. in the Lord, 70
be thou s., 44
destroy the fat and s., 220
follow s. drink, 103
from him that is too s., 152
habitation of the s., 327
hands be s., 376
know God shall be s., 125
let your hands be s., 70
Lord is a s. tower, 161
Lord s. and mighty, 156
love is s., 239
out of the s., 331
Redeemer is s., 87

s. and of a good, 108
s. and of good courage, 63
s. drink is raging, 237
s. hold in the day of, 161
s. holds shall be like, 161
s. in the grace, 141
s. is the Lord who, 306
s. meat belongeth, 249
s. men have been slain, 6
s. reasons, 16
s. shall not strengthen, 63
small one a s. nation, 176
stagger, but not with s., 103
we that are s., 45
weak say, I am s., 401
weak, then am I s., 371
wine nor s. drink, 90
wise man is s., 371
won than a s. city, 139
stronger
God is s. than men, 371
s. than a lion, 331
s. than lions, 70
s. than we, 72
they were s., 86
strongly
foundations be s., 39
stubble
consumed them as s., 310
do wickedly, shall be s., 222
s. before the wind, 406
shall be as s., 8
stubborn
s. and rebellious, 99
their s. way, 372
stubbornness
s. is as iniquity, 372
study
s. is a weariness, 105
s. to be quiet, 27
s. to show thyself, 96
stumble
know not at what they s., 271
proud shall s., 17
stumbled
ark; for the oxen s., 150
stumbleth
glad when he s., 146
stumblingblock
s. before the people, 271
s. of their iniquity, 404
take up the s., 271
unto the Jews a s., 75
subdue
earth, and s. it, 20
s. all thine enemies, 109
subject
even the devils are s., 341
s. unto higher powers, 21
spirits are s. unto, 180
subjection
silence with all s., 105

submit
s. to every ordinance, 229
s. unto the elder, 9
wives, s. yourselves, 246
substance
faith is the s. of, 127
honour with thy s., 384
wasted his s. with, 83
suburbs
s. shall shake, 93
subvert
s. a man in his cause, 30
suck
s. to their young, 47
sucking
beareth the s. child, 231
s. child, 59
tongue of the s., 382
suckling
infant and s. ox, 14
virgin, the s. also, 92
sucklings
mouth of babes and s., 48
sue
s. thee at the law, 146
suffer
being persecuted, we s., 3
how long shall I s. you, 102
if we s., 375
if ye s. for, 334
man s. as a Christian, 51
proud heart will not I s., 17
s. fools gladly, 138
s. for well doing, 3
s. not a woman to teach, 22
s. the little children, 48
s. Thine Holy One, 114
soul shall s. hunger, 230
when ye do well, and s., 3
which thou shalt s., 70
suffered
s. He their manners, 219
s. in the flesh, 358
s. no man to do, 160
things which He s., 215
suffereth
charity s., 240
sufferings
partakers of Christ's s., 346
partakers of the s., 375
sufficiency
s. is of God, 2
sufficient
s. to finish it, 285
s. unto the day, 145
summer
meat in the s., 95
s. and winter, 345
s. is ended, 91
snow in s., 138
sun
as long as the s., 130
be as the s., 147
before the s., 192

behold the s., 234
better thing under s., 77
clear as the s., 25
from rising of the s., 290
laboured under the s., 77
light and the s., 267
new thing under the s., 207
no need of the s., 152
s. also ariseth, 67
s. down upon your wrath, 13
s. is gone down, 176
s. light on them, 67
S. of righteousness, 22
s. shall be turned, 109
s. shall not smite, 161
s. stood still, 162
s. stood still, 156
s. to rise on the evil, 169
sight of this s., 192
taketh under the s., 145
supper
marriage s. of the Lamb, 180
supplication
by prayer and s., 294
s. before the Lord, 291
supplications
present our s., 193
voice of my s., 174
support
s. the weak, 390
sure
s. mercies of David, 34
surely
s. deliver thee, 161
s. put me to death, 8
shall s. be the Lord's, 309
shall s. die, 22
uprightly walketh s., 44
surety
s. for a stranger, 37
sustain
He shall s. thee, 162
swallow
crane and the s., 99
man would s. me up, 250
s. a camel, 196
s. up death, 81
s. up the inheritance, 92
swallowed
death is s. up in, 82
sware
s. unto their fathers, 303
s. unto them, 1
s. unto your fathers, 204
swear
he that s. by heaven, 267
neither s. by thy head, 267
s. by His name, 9
s. not at all, 267
s. not by heaven, 209
s. unto me, 9
tongue shall s., 9

swearers
swearers
   against false s., 6
sweareth
   every one that s., 279
   he that s. as he, 113
   s. by the throne, 267
sweat
   s. of thy face, 302
sweet
   bitter for s. and s., 233
   bitter thing is s., 89
   drink the s., 42
   how s. are Thy words, 208
   in thy mouth s. as honey,
     32
   labouring man is s., 363
   s. influences of Pleiades,
     288
   s. melody, sing many, 130
   s. savour of Christ, 51
   s. to the soul, 4
   s. to the soul, 366
   s. to thy taste, 136
   s. water and bitter, 66
   stolen waters are s., 99
sweeter
   s. also than honey, 55
   s. than honey, 208
   s. than honey, 331
sweetly
   worm shall feed s., 80
sweetness
   came forth s., 331
   forsake my s., 11
swelled
   feet s., 162
swelling
   lion from the s., 327
swift
   feet that be s., 207
   he that is s. of foot, 114
   let not s. flee away, 396
   perish from the s., 367
   race is not to the s., 43
   s. to hear, 13
   s. to shed blood, 119
   s. witness against, 411
swifter
   persecutors are s., 367
   s. than a weaver's, 90
   s. than eagles, 70
swim
   make I my bed to s., 362
swine
   gold in a s.'s snout, 24
   pearls before s., 393
sword
   are for the s. to the s., 305
   back from the s., 70
   beareth not s. in vain, 133
   by His s. will the Lord, 220
   by s. and famine, 129
   comest to me with a s., 124
   death with the s., 80

   devoured with the s., 372
   die with the s., 93
   draw thy s., 192
   every man hath his s., 133
   fall by the s., 223
   fall by the s., 324
   fall by the s., 109
   it is for the s., 406
   keepeth s. from blood, 95
   killeth with the s., 325
   lift up s. against, 400
   mouth goeth a sharp s., 187
   mouth like a sharp s., 75
   near shall fall by s., 14
   no s. in the hand, 124
   or peril, or s., 95
   perish with the s., 398
   poor from the s., 160
   s. bereaveth, 81
   s. devour forever, 326
   s. devoureth one, 77
   s. hath made women, 311
   s. in their hand, 326
   s. is without, 79
   s. of the enemy, 79
   s. of the Lord, 324
   s. of the Lord, 24
   s. of the Lord is, 324
   s. of the Lord, how long,
     201
   s. shall devour, 41
   s. shall devour flesh, 326
   s. shall never depart, 77
   s. without, and terror, 92
   saveth not with s., 124
   send peace, but a s., 401
   shall my s. save, 371
   sharp as a twoedged s., 79
   sharper than twoedged s.,
     354
   slain with the s., 81
   take the s. shall perish, 398
   than the s., 400
   wicked to the s., 305
swords
   beat their s., 278
   plowshares into s., 401
   s. are in their lips, 362
   s. of the mighty, 400
   thief with s. and staves, 20
   were they drawn s., 106
sworn
   nor s. deceitfully, 186
synagogues
   chief seats in the s., 196
   s. ye shall be beaten, 281
   standing in the s., 195
Syrian
   S. language, 347

T

tabernacle
   put off this my t., 82

   t. of God is with men, 163
   t. shall be sanctified, 65
tabernacles
   t. of bribery, 38
   thorns in their t., 306
   thy t. O Israel, 24
table
   before them in a t., 186
   eat at thy t., 174
   from their masters' t., 354
   graven upon the t., 280
   preparest a t. before, 34
   with me on the t., 31
tables
   not in t. of stone, 280
   of God, and serve t., 253
   t. of stone, 380
   t. of the heart, 280
tail
   head, and not the t., 268
take
   t. me not away, 235
taken
   from him shall be t., 238
   hath not shall be t., 238
   Lord hath t., 3
   not t. away, 197
   t. in the devices, 223
taketh
   t. away, who can hinder,
     156
   that t. not his cross, 9
tale
   t. that is told, 234
talebearer
   t. among thy people, 172
   t. revealeth secrets, 172
   where there is no t., 172
   words of a t., 172
talk
   t. of the lips, 230
   t. of Thy wondrous, 208
   t. with man, 158
   t. ye of all, 363
talketh
   it is He that t., 251
tame
   tongue can no man t., 367
tare
   t. forty and two, 304
tarry
   if we t. till, 297
   lies shall not t., 98
   t. at home, 342
   t. at Jericho, 353
   t. for them till, 245
   t. not, 367
   t. till I come, 21
   t. ye here, and watch, 54
   though it t., 224
   why t. the wheels, 79
tarrying
   Lord make no t., 162
tasks

your daily t., 273
taste
but t. a little honey, 121
not t. of death till, 81
sweet to thy t., 136
t. in the white, 136
words unto my t., 208
tasteth
mouth t. meat, 388
taught
fear toward Me is t., 195
neither t. it, but by, 172
t. of the Lord, 105
t. rebellion, 184
which ye have been t., 102
teach
dost thou t. us, 17
earth, and it shall t., 156
meek will He t., 177
men, apt to t., 225
shall do and t. them, 56
suffer not a woman to t., 22
t. a just man, 7
t. all nations, 117
t. God knowledge, 193
t. me Thy paths, 177
t. me Thy way, 26
t. me to do Thy will, 269
t. me, O Lord, the way, 55
t. My people the, 53
t. the young women, 247
t. thee what thou say, 106
t. thee wisdom, 183
t. them diligently, 55
t. them the good, 105
t. us of His ways, 26
t. us to number, 234
t. your daughters, 176
years should t. wisdom, 122
teachers
false t. among you, 185
teachest
t. thou not thyself, 8
which t. another, 8
teacheth
He that t. man, 153
heart t. his mouth, 106
t. my hands to war, 371
who t. like Him, 208
teaching
t. for doctrines, 184
tears
bread of t., 176
eye poureth out t., 124
fountain of t., 377
mind, and with many t.,
194
seen thy t., 291
seen thy t., 59
sought carefully with t., 312
sow in t., 76
thine eyes from t., 330
water my couch with t., 362
wipe away all t., 378

teeth
and gnashing of t., 13
and gnashing of t., 312
children's t. are set, 32
skin of my t., 113
t. shall be set on, 320
vinegar to the t., 230
Tekel
Mene, Mene, T. Upharsin,
263
tell
elders, and they will t., 122
not t. whence it cometh,
263
shall I t. it thee, 347
t. it not, 175
t. me nothing, 7
t. me, I pray, 30
who can t. if God, 139
temperance
fruit of Spirit is t., 187
temperate
be sober, grave, t., 28
tempest
breaketh me with a t., 374
clouds carried with a t., 45
temple
against the t., 206
body is the t., 36
defile the t. of God, 337
destroy this t., 93
is in His holy t., 163
Lord and Lamb are the t.,
163
pillar in the t., 331
saw no t. therein, 163
standing in the t., 114
t. of God is holy, 30
t. of the living God, 159
voice out of His t., 291
which t. ye are, 30
ye are the t. of God, 30
temples
dwelleth not in t., 52
temporal
things seen are t., 248
tempt
do ye t. the Lord, 20
neither will I t., 298
t. the Lord, 26
t. ye me, ye hypocrites, 379
thou shalt not t., 43
why t. ye God, 43
why t. ye me, 17
temptation
enter not into t., 379
lead us not into t., 119
rich fall into t., 12
that endureth t., 380
temptations
godly out of t., 87
tempted
t. with evil, 380
tempteth

t. He any man, 380
ten
better than t. sons, 47
instrument of t. strings, 263
tender
t. mercies come unto, 59
t. mercies of the wicked, 76
upon the t. herb, 106
vines have t., 92
tenth
t. unto Thee, 384
tents
goodly are thy t., 24
t. of wickedness, 193
terrible
great and very t., 222
haughtiness of the t., 17
Lord great and t., 24
mighty God and t., 158
terribleness
t. hath deceived, 61
terrified
commotions, be not t., 15
terrifiest
t. me through visions, 103
terror
be not a t., 190
caused my t., 380
rulers are not a t., 173
t. by night, 133
t. of the shadow, 380
t. within, shall destroy, 92
testament
blood of the new t., 35
cup is the new t., 58
where a t. is, 82
testator
death of the t., 82
testified
Lord hath t. against, 303
t. of me in Jerusalem, 70
testify
lips t. against, 178
sins t., 178
t. against any person, 41
testimonies
commandments and His t.,
269
testimony
ashamed of the t., 215
t. of Jesus is the, 416
t. of the Lord, 55
thank
good to you, what t., 27
receive, what t. have ye, 10
thanks
give t. unto the Lord, 174
give t. unto the Lord, 170
give t. unto Thee, 174
give t. unto Thee, 290
give Thee t., 80
giveth God t., 188
in every thing give t., 174
t. be to God, 115

t. be unto God, 174
t. to Thy holy name, 87
t. unto the Lord, 174
thanksgiving
magnify Him with t., 174
received with t., 137
sing with t., 364
supplication with t., 294
thefts
out of heart proceed t., 261
thick
art grown t., 83
thicker
finger shall be t., 352
thief
as a t. in the night, 346
come on thee as a t., 346
do not despise a t., 73
partner with a t., 74
t. be found, 321
t. cometh not but for, 74
t. in the night, 355
t. with swords and staves, 20
what hour the t., 43
thieves
den of t., 52
t. do not break through, 368
where t. break through, 248
thigh
smote them hip and t., 398
sword upon his t., 133
t. shall rot, 6
thighs
joints of thy t., 25
things
the t. that be of God, 394
think
an hour when ye t. not, 310
if ye t. good, give, 266
killeth you will t., 281
t. himself something, 62
t. me a fool, 15
t. not that I am come, 401
t. not with thyself, 280
t. on these things, 66
t. soberly, 194
t. that he knoweth, 227
t. they shall be heard, 293
t. upon me, 34
wherefore t. ye evil, 119
thinketh
that t. he standeth, 63
yet the Lord t. upon, 288
third
raised up the t. day, 298
rise the t. day, 322
t. day He shall rise, 322
t. day He shall rise, 75
thirst
die for t., 90
faileth for t., 131
give him shall never t., 115

I t., 218
if any man t., 89
if he t. give him drink, 140
no more, neither t., 67
nor a t. for water but, 131
shall never t., 92
t. after righteousness, 333
t. they gave me vinegar, 76
tongue cleaveth for t., 382
water shall t. again, 115
thirsteth
every one that t., 89
soul t. after Thee, 241
soul t. for Thee, 94
thirsty
as a t. land, 241
t. and ye gave me drink, 60
t. and ye gave me no, 76
t. give him water, 110
t. land springs, 300
t. man dreameth, 96
waters to a t. soul, 266
thirty
t. pieces of silver, 31
thistles
t. grow instead of wheat, 206
thorn
sharper than a t., 69
t. in the flesh, 342
thorns
crown of t., 343
lily among t., 25
of t. men do not gather, 65
reap t., 144
sow not among t., 316
t. in their tabernacles, 306
t. in your sides, 109
t. under a pot, 229
up thy way with t., 271
thought
morrow shall take t., 145
surely as I have t., 144
t. a thing incredible, 323
t. as a child, 48
t. can be withholden, 347
t. for your life, 137
t. of thine heart, 317
take no t. for the morrow, 145
take no t. for your life, 248
take ye t. for raiment, 15
which of you by taking t., 261
thoughts
day his t. perish, 11
heart proceed evil t., 261
knoweth the t. of man, 145
My t. are not your t., 26
t. of the righteous, 7
t. of the wicked, 118
t. of the wise, 153
t. shall be established, 373
vain t., 118

thousand
chase a t., 1
chase a t., 370
day is as a t. years, 277
one man among a t., 243
one shall become a t., 176
slain a t. men, 370
t. at thy right hand, 79
t. instructors in Christ, 37
t. shall fall, 79
t. shall flee at, 133
t. shekels, 208
t. years as one day, 277
t. years in Thy sight, 283
two put ten t., 1
thousands
David his ten t., 130
mercy unto t., 303
slain his t., 130
ten t. of His saints, 306
than t. of gold and, 393
unto David ten t., 211
three
offer thee t. things, 49
t. days I will raise, 93
t. that bear record, 386
t. that bear witness, 382
t. things that are never, 81
there t. are one, 386
threefold
t. cord is not quickly, 68
thrice
deny me t., 88
throat
knife to thy t., 147
speak through their t., 198
t. is an open sepulchre, 362
throne
disgrace the t., 151
fault before the t., 206
for it is God's t., 267
habitation of His t., 332
habitation of Thy t., 223
heaven is My t., 158
heaven is My t., 52
in the midst of the t., 163
kings are they on the t., 332
mercy shall the t., 259
stablish his t., 163
sweareth by the t., 267
t. from generation, 116
t. shall be established, 259
t. shall be established, 259
Thy t. is for ever, 51
through
t. them I may prove, 382
thrust
t. in Thy sickle, 221
thunder
t. of His power, 156
thunderings
voice of mighty t., 111
thyself

neighbor as t., 38

tidings
bear no t., 59
good t., 267
t. of great joy, 180
with heavy t., 266

till
to t. the ground, 274

tilleth
t. his land, 95

timber
beam out of the t., 4

timbrel
praise Him with the t., 263
with t. and dances, 205
with the t. and harp, 78

time
appear the second t., 346
appoint Me the t., 21
deliver in t. of trouble, 45
die before thy t., 235
discerneth both time, 97
for a little t. and then, 261
forsake us so long t., 1
from this t. forth, 148
high t. to awake, 340
in due t., 276
it is an evil t., 301
John: since that t., 225
know not when the t., 294
not discern this t., 402
now is the accepted t., 340
short my t. is, 260
silence in that t., 301
sinned this t., 178
slew at one t., 370
strength in t. of, 332
t. and chance happeneth, 43
t. appointed the end, 15
t. cometh, 281
t. for Thee Lord to work, 166
t. is at hand, 200
t. is at hand, 200
t. is come, 102
t. is come, 200
t. is come for Thee to, 249
t. is near to come, 93
t. is short, 273
t. of health, 122
t. of old age, 8
t. of peace, 401
t. of the end, 108
t. of the singing, 345
t. of their coming, 99
t. of their visitation, 198
t. of thy trouble, 198
t. of trouble, 30
t. of war, 401
t. to be born, 25
t. to break down, 181
t. to build up, 181
t. to cast away, 84

t. to come for ever, 186
t. to dance, 180
t. to die, 25
t. to every purpose, 265
t. to get, 3
t. to hate, 181
t. to heal, 181
t. to keep, 84
t. to keep silence, 40
t. to kill, 181
t. to laugh, 229
t. to lose, 3
t. to love, 181
t. to mourn, 180
t. to plant, 25
t. to pluck, 25
t. to receive money, 175
t. to rend, 92
t. to seek the Lord, 317
t. to sew, 92
t. to speak, 40
t. to weep, 229

times
discern signs of the t., 97
do evil an hundred t., 168
for you to know the t., 145
in t. of trouble, 18
knoweth her appointed t., 99
loveth at all t., 143
of ancient t., 145
persecuted us in t. past, 43
smitten five or six t., 111
t. of trouble, 337
trust in Him at all t., 124
until seventy t. seven, 140

tingle
ears shall t., 324
heareth it shall t., 380

tithe
t. of the land, 384

tithes
t. and offerings, 45

tittle
t. of the law to fail, 56

today
Christ the same t., 44
seen strange things t., 254
t. shalt thou be with me, 34
while it is called T., 108

together
all things work t., 126
can two walk t., 69
dwell t. in unity, 38
let us reason t., 57
lion and the fatling t., 14
shall feed t., 38

toil
t. not, neither do they, 15

token
t. of a covenant, 71
t. of the covenant, 52

told
believe, though it be t., 361

fathers t. us of, 102
half was not t., 136
not t. it my father, 347
t. me all that ever I, 213
t. you from beginning, 152
tale that is t., 234

tolerable
more t. for Sodom, 167
more t. for the land of, 202

tomorrow
against t., 307
boast not thyself of t., 36
t. I will deliver, 108
t. shalt thou, 80
t. thou shalt be slain, 402
t. we shall die, 42

tongue
a soft t. breaketh, 16
dog move his t., 159
every t. should confess, 5
flattery of the t., 242
from a deceitful t., 362
His word was in my t., 207
hold my t., 3
lying t. is but for, 233
not a word in my t., 153
of a slow t., 106
perverse t. falleth, 98
proud look, a lying t., 207
refrain his t. from evil, 119
speaketh in an unknown t., 57
t. and their doings, 33
t. can no man tame, 367
t. cleave to the roof, 9
t. deviseth mischiefs, 30
t. faileth, 131
t. from evil, 189
t. is a fire, 119
t. is deceitful, 233
t. is the pen, 366
t. keepeth his soul, 301
t. of the crafty, 366
t. of the dumb, 181
t. of the just, 189
t. of the sucking, 382
t. shall swear, 9
t. with a cord, 244
t. words easy to be, 57
unknown t., 294
wherefore holdest Thy t., 205

tongues
bend their t., 99
sharpened their t., 362
speak in our t., 385
speaketh with t., 57
t. are for a sign, 385
t. of men and of angels, 107
use their t. and say, 130

tonight
save not thy life t., 402

tooth

■ 551 ■

like a broken t., 30
t. for t., 324
torment
  t. and sorrow give her, 36
tormented
  t. in this flame, 184
torn
  t. and He will heal, 157
touch
  neither shall ye t. it, 226
  not to t. a woman, 42
  t. all that he hath, 43
  t. not Mine anointed, 50
touched
  as many as t., 125
  hand of God hath t., 59
tough
  t. His garment, 125
tower
  high t. and my deliverer, 161
  intending to build a t., 285
  Lord is a strong t., 161
  my high t., 159
  neck is as a t., 36
  nose is as the t., 36
  t. and a fortress, 299
town
  buildeth a t. with blood, 173
tradition
  hold the t. of men, 100
  keep your own t., 196
traditions
  hold the t., 102
traffick
  t. hast thou increased, 95
train
  t. up a child, 47
trample
  t. them under their feet, 204
transgressed
  all have t. against Me, 20
  because they have t., 23
  t. against the Lord, 62
transgression
  day of his t., 23
  make me to know my t., 206
  no law is, there is no t., 229
  people their t., 46
  sin is the t. of, 358
  t. of his lips, 233
  whose t. is forgiven, 139
transgressions
  added because of t., 229
  all your t. so iniquity, 317
  forgive your t., 165
  wounded for our t., 252
transgressor
  make myself a t., 178
transgressors

intercession for the t., 252
t. shall fall, 26
way of t., 360
travail
  hands full with t., 11
  sinner He giveth t., 176
  sorrows, and his t., 91
  t. with child, 47
travaileth
  wicked man t., 374
  woman that t., 380
traveller
  doors to the t., 191
treacherously
  deal not t., 246
  deal very t., 205
  friends dealt t. with, 30
  t. against the wife, 246
  upon them that deal t., 205
  why do we deal t., 30
tread
  feet shall t., 210
treader
  t. of grapes, 300
treadeth
  t. out the corn, 107
treasure
  evil man out of evil t., 45
  Israel for His t., 50
  peculiar t. unto Me, 49
  righteous is much t., 333
  t. and trouble, 66
  t. hid in a field, 226
  t. in heaven, 115
  t. of the heart, 45
  where your t. is, 242
treasures
  nothing among my t., 255
  t. in heaven, 368
  t. of the hail, 122
  t. of the snow, 122
  t. of wickedness, 73
  t. upon earth, 248
  wind out of His t., 309
tree
  and waxed a great t., 176
  corrupt t. bringeth, 44
  days of a t., 155
  desire t. of life, 190
  every good t., 44
  every t. of the garden, 169
  fig t. bear olive, 66
  fruit of the t., 384
  gave me of the t., 32
  green bay t., 118
  hope removed like a t., 91
  like the palm t., 176
  like to a palm t., 36
  of the t. of knowledge, 169
  right to the t. of life, 235
  she is a t. of life, 409
  sit under his fig t., 278
  t. is known by his fruit, 44
  t. is known by his own, 85

t. of life, 330
t. of the field, 264
t. planted by the rivers, 373
trees
  promoted over the t., 11
  t. of the field, 268
  t. of the Lord, 265
  t. whose fruit withereth, 45
  t. with the firstripe, 161
tremble
  inhabitants of the land t., 22
  will ye not t., 22
trembling
  clothe themselves with t., 380
  rejoice with t., 193
  with fear and t., 340
trespass
  brother t., 75
  t. against thee seven, 140
  t. is grown, 353
trespassed
  because they t. against, 311
trespasses
  Father forgive your t., 177
  forgive men their t., 140
  forgive your t., 177
tribes
  t. of Israel, 211
tribulation
  out of all t., 386
  t. or distress, 95
  t. worketh patience, 190
  through much t., 225
tributary
  is she become t., 64
tribute
  earth take custom or t., 377
  pay ye t., 21
  t. to whom t. is due, 377
tried
  that ye may be t., 7
trieth
  ear t. words, 388
  t. the righteous, 398
triumph
  enemy doth not t., 153
  let not mine enemies t., 110
  shall the wicked t., 69
  voice of t., 179
triumphed
  He hath t. gloriously, 289
triumphing
  t. of the wicked, 118
trodden
  t. the winepress, 10
trouble
  be with him in t., 292
  born unto t., 244
  call in day of t., 18
  day of my t. I will call, 292
  day of t., 90
  day of t., 161

t. our ways, 317
tumult
  t. is come up, 17
  t. of those that rise, 166
turn
  and I will t. unto you, 311
  cheek, t. to him other, 139
  God will t. and repent, 139
  how long will ye t., 120
  if the wicked will t., 317
  not your garments, and t.,
    317
  repent, and t., 317
  t. again and rend you, 204
  t. again to the Lord, 317
  t. again unto the Lord, 316
  t. and do you hurt, 22
  t. aside to the right, 268
  t. away from His fierce, 139
  t. away from you, 139
  t. away His face, 154
  t. away thy son, 209
  t. away your heart, 210
  t. back your captivity, 131
  t. from it, 118
  t. from these vanities, 199
  t. in to me, 18
  t. not aside, 344
  t. not aside, 94
  t. not away the face, 291
  t. not away the face, 313
  t. not from it, 55
  t. not thou away, 37
  t. thee back, 192
  t. thee behind, 359
  t. their reproach, 326
  t. thou to thy God, 125
  t. thou unto Me, 316
  t. Thou us unto Thee, 315
  t. ye from your evil, 81
  t. ye from your evil, 26
  t. ye not aside, 415
  t. ye now from, 119
  t. ye unto Him, 316
  t. ye unto Me, 311
  t. yourselves, and live, 317
  who shall t. it back, 150
turned
  anger is not t. back, 262
  loved are t. against, 30
  t. aside after lucre, 69
  t. away from the Lord, 65
  t. not to the right, 94
  t. quickly out, 23
  t. their back unto Me, 197
  t. their heart back, 298
  t. to his course, 203
  t. to the Lord, 257
  t. unto Me the back, 23
  we shall be t., 315
turneth
  t. back from the sword, 70
  t. upside down, 343
turning

wiping it, and t., 92
turtle
  times; and the t., 99
  voice of the t., 345
twain
  go with him t., 69
  t. shall be one, 246
twelve
  chosen you t., 31
twice
  t. as much, 282
twinkling
  t. of an eye, 367
twins
  young roes that are t., 25
two
  between t. opinions, 42
  can t. walk together, 69
  he that hath t. coats, 354
  if t. lie together, 38
  no man can serve t., 242
  t. are better than one, 67
  t. of every sort, 14
  t. tables of stone, 380
twoedged
  sharp as a t. sword, 79
  sharper than t. sword, 354
  t. sword in their hand, 326

U

unawares
  entertained angels u., 12
unbelief
  help Thou mine u., 102
  u. make the faith, 161
unbelievers
  before the u., 229
unbelieving
  u. depart, let him, 167
  u. husband is sanctified, 29
uncertain
  trumpet give an u. sound,
    24
uncircumcised
  hand of the u., 90
  stiffnecked and u., 167
  the u. Philistines, 210
  u. Philistine, 20
uncircumcision
  circumcision nor u., 113
  nor u. but faith, 53
  u. is nothing, 53
unclean
  any man common or u.,
    319
  clean out of an u., 69
  clean, and to the u., 235
  man, thou u. spirit, 122
  nothing u. of itself, 19
  to be u. to him it is u., 19
  u. spirit is gone, 119
uncleanness
  called us unto u., 186

uncover
  shalt thou not u., 202
uncovered
  nakedness shall be u., 192
under
  put it u. a bushel, 302
understand
  aged u. judgment, 8
  doth a fool u., 199
  have not heard shall u., 117
  hear ye indeed, but u., 372
  hear, and u., 184
  His power who can u., 156
  make me to u., 208
  neither do they u., 199
  not u. one another's, 57
  people that doth not u.,
    199
  simple, u. wisdom, 391
  u. his way, 301
  u. more than ancients, 122
  u. the lovingkindness, 153
understandest
  u. thou, which is not, 17
  u. what thou readest, 105
understandeth
  easy unto him that u., 227
  for no man u., 57
  God u. the way, 409
  plain to him that u., 53
  u. and knoweth Me, 125
understanding
  any u. in them, 50
  be ye of u. heart, 391
  children in u., 248
  depart from evil is u., 118
  get u. forget, 227
  getting get u., 391
  give me u., 269
  give me u., 55
  give me u., 234
  him that hath u., 119
  is of great u., 276
  knowledge and u., 409
  length of days u., 8
  man of u., 391
  man of u. holdeth, 257
  man that getteth u., 180
  men of u., 367
  mule, which have no u., 14
  passeth all u., 67
  sing ye praises with u., 290
  to them that know u., 149
  u. be men, 119
  u. heart, 96
  u. is a wellspring, 391
  u. is infinite, 152
  u. is unfruitful, 294
  u. it is established, 4
  u. of the prudent, 62
  u. of their prudent, 305
  u. people, 50
  u. seeketh knowledge, 227
  u. shall keep thee, 378

u. thy kinswoman, 409
u. wisdom is found, 391
void of u., 98
wisdom and u., 252
with a woman lacketh u., 6
your wisdom and u., 55
understood
u. as a child, 48
wise, that they u., 90
words easy to be u., 57
undone
for I am u., 133
left nothing u., 241
unequal
are not your ways u., 123
unfaithful
confidence in an u., 30
unfruitful
understanding is u., 294
ungodliness
increase unto more u., 137
ungodly
Christ died for the u., 75
counsel of the u., 58
delivered me to the u., 7
help the u., 10
u. and for sinners, 229
way of the u., 166
where shall the u., 168
unity
dwell together in u., 38
unjust
deceitful and u. man, 160
on the just and the u., 169
u. also in much, 66
u. in the least, 66
u. knoweth no shame, 353
unknown
speaketh in an u. tongue,
57
unmarried
u. careth for the things, 95
unpunished
wicked shall not be u., 407
unrighteous
be an u. witness, 58
decree u. decrees, 173
u. shall not inherit, 225
unrighteously
all that do u. are, 40
unrighteousness
all u. is sin, 334
house by u., 69
no u. in judgment, 39
unsavoury
u. be eaten, 136
unsearchable
kings is u., 259
u. are His judgments, 153
unseemly
working that which is u.,
189
unspeakable
u. gift, 174

unstable
double minded man is u.,
203
u. as water, 44
until
u. seventy times seven, 140
untoward
u. generation, 69
unwise
foolish people and u., 204
wise, and to the u., 185
unwittingly
smote his neighbour u., 209
unworthy
u. of everlasting life, 49
up
down one, and setteth u.,
373
get thee u., 108
grave, and bringeth u., 156
hold Thou me u., 338
Lord held me u., 162
low, and lifteth u., 156
raise Me u., 53
u. no more, 80
u. to the mountain, 188
Upharsin
Mene, Mene, Tekel, U.,
263
uphold
u. thee with the right, 163
upholdeth
u. all that fall, 162
uppermost
u. rooms at feasts, 196
upright
behold the u., 257
gladness for the u., 179
integrity of the u., 208
just u. man, 257
none u. among men, 167
perfect and an u. man, 257
prayer of the u., 45
pure and u., 32
righteousness of the u., 87
strength to the u., 269
u. in heart, 179
u. is sharper, 69
u. man Thou wilt show, 166
wilt show Thyself u., 166
uprightly
he that walketh u., 44
him that speaketh u., 75
him that walketh u., 54
that walk u., 329
that walketh u., 338
uprightness
integrity, and in u., 189
walketh in his u., 44
way of the just is u., 333
upside
turneth u. down, 343
upward
fail with looking u., 91

Uriah
U. in the forefront, 30
use
change the natural u., 188
despitefully u. you, 59
u. not vain repetitions, 293
usurp
nor to u. authority over, 22
usury
as with taker of u., 93
giver of u., 93
lend upon u., 138
thy money upon u., 392
u. of money, 392
u. of victuals, 392
u. to thy brother, 392
utter
u. a song, 363
u. not this, 266
u. this our business, 9
utterance
Spirit gave them u., 385
Uzza
kindled against U., 150
U. put forth his hand, 309

V

vagabond
fugitive and a v., 76
vain
beauty is v., 25
bring no more v., 334
Christ is dead in v., 56
comfort in v., 199
created it not in v., 73
deceive with v. words, 84
desirous of v. glory, 12
faith is v., 126
go after v. things, 415
grace bestowed not in v.,
45
His name in v., 33
in v. is salvation, 145
labour I in v., 90
labour in v. that, 4
made all men in v., 260
name of God in v., 33
none shall return in v., 4
not said in v., 73
not the sword in v., 133
profane and v. babblings,
137
sow your seed in v., 144
use not v. repetitions, 293
utter v. knowledge, 394
v. is the help of man, 18
v. make thyself fair, 25
v. shalt thou use, 102
v. they do worship, 184
v. thing for you, 55
v. thoughts, 118
v. to serve God, 33
watchman waketh in v., 348

wise, that they are v., 153
vainglory
    through strife or v., 12
valley
    lily of the v., 25
    multitudes in the v. of, 220
    v. of the shadow, 63
    v. shall be filled, 253
value
    physicians of no v., 53
    v. than many sparrows, 203
vanished
    wisdom v., 8
vanisheth
    and then v. away, 261
vanities
    observe lying v., 129
    turn from these v., 199
    vanity of v., 77
vanity
    all is v., 77
    all is v., 77
    all is v., 91
    all that cometh is v., 91
    are v. and the work, 198
    beast: for all is v., 193
    cords of v., 360
    days of my v., 9
    low degree are v., 44
    man is like v., 235
    state is altogether v., 142
    that they are v., 145
    this also is v., 91
    trust in v., 314
    up his soul unto v., 186
    v. of v., 91
    v. of vanities, 77
    v. shall be recompence, 314
    youth are v., 416
vapour
    v. that appeareth, 261
vapours
    causeth v. to ascend, 309
vehement
    a most v. flame, 211
vengeance
    days of v., 222
    execute great v., 150
    execute v. in anger, 150
    flaming fire taking v., 327
    God will come with v., 108
    Me belongeth v., 326
    see Thy v., 327
    see Thy v. on them, 110
    seeth the v., 326
    slayeth Cain, v., 159
    take v., 311
    to whom v. belongeth, 326
    v. belongeth unto Me, 327
    v. is Mine, 327
    v. on His adversaries, 327
    v. to Mine enemies, 220
    v. upon the heathen, 326
verity

of His hands are v., 166
vessel
    as unto the weaker v., 247
    he is a chosen v., 117
    I am like a broken v., 91
    v. for the finer, 393
vessels
    bear the v., 307
vex
    neither v. a stranger, 138
    v. my soul, 120
vexation
    and v. of spirit, 11
    v. of his heart, 77
    vanity and v., 77
vexed
    v. unto death, 263
vials
    the v. of the wrath of, 151
victory
    giveth us v. through, 115
    glory, and the v., 152
    grave, where is thy v., 82
    swallow up death in v., 81
    swallowed up in v., 82
    v. that day turned, 176
victuals
    lend him thy v., 392
vigilant
    be sober, be v., 342
vile
    behold, I am v., 67
    for thou art v., 93
    so v. a thing, 61
vine
    every man under his v., 278
    I am the true v., 20
    I am the v., 21
    the clusters of the v., 221
    v. languisheth, 364
vinegar
    thirst they gave me v., 76
    v. to the teeth, 230
vines
    spoil the v., 92
    v. have tender grapes, 92
vineyard
    give me thy v., 112
    v. of the Lord, 50
vineyards
    fields, and your v., 258
    plant v. but not, 144
    planted pleasant v. but, 96
vintage
    v. of Abiezer, 283
violence
    city is full of v., 230
    him that loveth v., 398
    v. covereth them, 296
    v. to no man, 69
    with v. shall that city, 168
violent
    hunt the v. man, 398
violently

took v. away, 321
viols
    noise of thy v., 192
vipers
    generation of v., 119
    generation of v., 78
virgin
    lament like a v., 86
    v. of Israel, 50
    v. shall be with child, 217
    v. shall conceive, 252
    young man and the v., 92
virtue
    add to your faith v., 127
    if there be any v., 66
    to v. knowledge, 127
virtuous
    find a v. woman, 246
    v. woman is a crown, 245
virtuously
    daughters have done v.,
    246
vision
    ashamed of his v., 130
    end shall be the v., 108
    shut thou up the v., 145
    v. of angels, 12
    v. of their own heart, 130
    where there is no v., 177
    write the v. and, 53
visions
    terrifiest me through v., 103
    young men shall see v., 417
    young men shall see v., 103
visit
    day when I v., 197
    v. the fatherless, 408
    v. their sin, 197
visitation
    day of v., 305
    time of their v., 198
visited
    sick, and ye v. me, 60
visitest
    son of man, that Thou v.,
    203
    that Thou v. him, 244
vocation
    walk worthy of the v., 51
voice
    carry the v., 301
    fool's v. is known by, 138
    graves shall hear His v.,
    200
    He did hear my v., 291
    hear my v., 295
    heard my v. hide, 293
    heard not the v., 399
    heardest my v., 293
    hearken thou unto the v.,
    269
    hearken unto their v., 3
    her v. in the streets, 409
    if ye obey My v., 268

if ye will hear His v., 28
lift up thy v., 63
lift up thy v., 46
meaning of the v., 58
my v. and open the door, 217
not obeyed His v., 121
obey His v., 16
obey His v., 269
obey my v., 155
obey my v., 32
obey the v., 270
obey the v. of, 3
obey the v. of the, 270
obeyed My v., 49
obeyed not His v., 100
obeyed their v., 121
obeying the v. of the Lord, 269
sheep hear my v., 10
the v. of God, 22
there was no v., 129
truth heareth my v., 389
v. from weeping, 330
v. is Jacob's v., 83
v. of a great multitude, 111
v. of him that crieth, 116
v. of many waters, 111
v. of my beloved, 103
v. of my supplications, 174
v. of one crying, 70
v. of one crying, 219
v. of singing men and, 8
v. of the bridegroom, 86
v. of the Lord, 158
v. of the Lord, 99
v. of the turtle, 345
v. of thy brother's, 122
v. of triumph, 179
v. roareth, 64
v. will we obey, 269
with a loud v., 139

void
have made v. Thy law, 166
he that is v. of wisdom, 257
nation v. of counsel, 50
v. of understanding, 98
v. the law through faith, 56
without form and v., 44

vomit
dog returneth to his v., 138
staggereth in his v., 103
turned to his own v., 23

vow
forbear to v., 297
shouldest not v. than, 37
v. a v. unto the Lord, 297
v. and not pay, 37
when thou v. a v. unto God, 298

W

wages

content with your w., 399
oppress hireling in w., 411
reapeth receiveth w., 115
w. of sin is death, 115
what shall thy w. be, 39

wail
I will w. and howl, 176

wailing
daughters w., 176
weeping and w., 265

wait
all they that w., 125
ashamed that w. for Me, 96
eyes of all w., 190
good unto them that w., 9
I w. for the Lord, 190
I will w. for the God, 125
if I w. the grave, 91
laid w. for us in the, 110
layeth in w., 195
lie in w. to deceive, 101
soul doth w., 190
that w. upon the Lord, 124
that w. upon the Lord, 315
though it tarry, w., 224
w. for light, 96
w. for the promise, 187
w. for the salvation, 276
w. on the Lord, 276
w. on thy God, 125
w. ye upon Me, 276

waited
have w. for Thee, 250
w. for Him, 276
w. for light, 13
w. for Thy salvation, 338

waiteth
blessed is he that w., 276
soul w. for the Lord, 190
soul w. upon God, 338
w. for the Lord, 276

waketh
but my heart w., 103
watchman w. but in vain, 348

walk
also w. in the Spirit, 27
and w. by the way, 290
but they w. not, 198
can two w. together, 69
children w. in truth, 48
every one, so let him w., 67
good way, and w., 385
just shall w., 26
lame w., 179
mark them which w., 258
rise up and w., 182
shall not w. in darkness, 29
take up thy bed, and w., 182
those that w. in pride, 296
to w. therein, 382
w. after the Lord, 128

w. after the Lord, 269
w. among you, 49
w. as children of light, 27
w. before Me, 62
w. before Me, as David, 189
w. before Mine anointed, 329
w. by faith, 27
w. by the same rule, 69
w. by the way, 79
w. circumspectly, 27
w. honestly toward, 319
w. humbly with thy God, 193
w. in all His ways, 26
w. in all His ways, 269
w. in all the ways, 26
w. in darkness, 96
w. in His paths, 26
w. in His ways, 55
w. in His ways, 269
w. in love, 27
w. in midst of trouble, 79
w. in mine integrity, 208
w. in My statutes, 270
w. in My statutes, 268
w. in the flesh, 64
w. in the light, 26
w. in the light, 28
w. in the Spirit, 27
w. in Thy truth, 26
w. in wisdom, 381
w. not in the statutes, 167
w. through the valley, 63
w. while ye have light, 227
w. with me in white, 307
w. worthy of God, 148
w. worthy of the Lord, 27
w. worthy of the vocation, 51
w. ye in Him, 27
way wherein I should w., 177
way, w. ye in it, 26
wherein they must w., 231
wherein they should w., 105
withhold from them that w., 329

walked
and w. in the way of, 385
David thy father w., 189
leaped and w., 182
that w. darkness, 111
w. before Thee, 128
w. forty years, 121
w. in all the sins, 48
w. not in his ways, 69
w. not in the way, 23
w. upon dry land, 113
way their fathers w., 23

walkest
w. by the way, 55
w. through the fire, 54

walketh
fool w. in darkness, 138
good to him that w., 54
poor that w., 44
that w. disorderly, 58
that w. uprightly, 338
w. in darkness, 200
w. in his integrity, 189
w. in His ways, 134
w. not in the counsel, 58
w. through dry places, 119
w. to direct his steps, 314
w. uprightly surely, 44
w. with wise men, 58
walking
w. on the sea, 254
wall
cry out of the w., 4
sit upon the w., 302
thorns, and make a w., 271
w. of Jerusalem, 211
w. of Jezreel, 41
w. unto us, 348
waters were a w., 113
wallow
w. thyself in ashes, 262
wander
w. in the wilderness, 121
w. out of the way, 35
wandering
w. of the desire, 89
want
I shall not w., 160
w. of wisdom, 199
wanting
art found w., 382
that which is w., 3
wants
let all thy w., 78
war
all the men of w. fled, 86
brethren go to w., 320
counsel make thy w., 400
fight and w. yet ye, 294
good advice make w., 7
hands to w., 371
hear of w. and, 15
judge and make w., 221
learn w. any more, 400
man of w., 165
man of w., 15
mighty in the w., 324
people that delight in w., 401
rested from w., 277
speak, they are for w., 401
they that w. against, 110
time of w., 401
w. after the flesh, 64
w. against me, 401
w. against the soul, 243
w. was in his heart, 106
weapons of w., 401
weapons of w., 85

warm
how can one be w., 38
warn
w. the wicked, 295
warned
w. you to flee, 114
warning
he that taketh w., 114
wash
w. away thy sins, 24
w. his feet in the blood, 326
w. in the pool of, 182
w. me, and I be whiter, 307
w. thee with nitre, 178
w. thine heart from, 316
w. thy face, 132
washed
water, and w. his hands, 320
waste
Nineveh is laid w., 90
wasted
w. his substance with, 83
waster
w. to destroy, 93
wasteth
dieth, and w. away, 80
watch
heed, w. and pray, 294
let us w. and be, 397
Lord w. between me, 2
set a w. before, 309
settest a w. over, 120
tarry ye here, and w., 54
w. and pray, 379
w. for the morning, 190
w. over them for evil, 150
w. therefore: for ye, 345
w. with me one hour, 96
w. ye therefore, 108
w. ye therefore and pray, 294
watched
come, he would have w., 43
watcheth
blessed is he that w., 346
wicked w. the righteous, 78
watchman
go, set a w., 397
set thee a w., 320
w. waketh but in vain, 348
w. what of the night, 263
water
as w. spilt, 260
baptized you with w., 24
but by w. and blood, 24
clouds without w., 45
drawers of w., 303
drink w. in this place, 66
drinketh of this w., 115
dry land springs of w., 403
filled with w., 81

fire and through w., 79
flag grow without w., 176
give forth his w., 124
give him w., 110
He asked w., 83
here is w., 24
land springs of w., 300
letteth out w., 371
like w. before the face, 293
living w., 115
man be born of w., 24
man forbid w., 24
melted, and became as w., 72
needy seek w., 131
not by w. only, 24
panteth after the w., 241
pool of w., 403
rivers of w., 373
runneth down with w., 54
scorning like w., 350
Spirit, w. and blood, 382
sweet w. and bitter, 66
take w. of life freely, 116
thirst for w. but, 131
unstable as w., 44
w. and washed his hands, 320
w. by measure, 131
w. came out, 254
w. my couch, 362
w. of life freely, 89
w. of the well, 382
w. out of the wells, 339
w. out of this rock, 298
w. that I shall give, 115
w. to drink in my name, 54
weak as w., 403
wells without w., 45
wine mixed with w., 201
wrath upon them like w., 150
watered
planted, Apollos w., 76
soul as a w. garden, 180
watereth shall be w., 146
watereth
He w. the hills, 309
planteth and he that w., 69
w. shall be watered, 146
waters
as cold w. to a, 266
beside the still w., 54
bread upon the w., 10
business in great w., 272
come ye to the w., 89
consume the snow w., 80
face of the w., 158
fountain of living w., 149
head were w., 377
judgment run down as w., 223
living fountains of w., 163
Lord is upon the w., 158

■ 558 ■

noise of many w., 156
passest through the w., 54
poured out like the w., 13
rivers of w. run down, 99
running w. out of, 6
rushing of mighty w., 267
sitteth upon many w., 88
sow beside all w., 106
stolen w. are sweet, 99
voice of many w., 111
w. are come unto my soul, 18
w. called He Seas, 104
w. cannot quench love, 239
w. cast up mire, 406
w. cover the sea, 128
w. out of thine own, 6
w. shall be sure, 333
w. turned to blood, 284
w. wear the stones, 94
w. were a wall, 113

wavereth
w. is like a wave, 103

wavering
ask in faith, nothing w., 127
faith without w., 127

waves
lifteth up the w., 265
sea, whose w. roared, 148
w. of the sea, 156
w. of the sea, 270
w. of the sea, 103

wax
as w. melteth before the, 304

waxed
clothes w. not old, 162
hand w. short, 73

waxen
art w. fat, 83

way
be turned out of the w., 28
broad is the w., 78
commit thy w. unto, 387
delighteth in his w., 26
error of his w., 360
every w. of a man, 261
forsaketh the w., 23
from his evil w., 316
from his wicked w., 295
go thy w., 182
go your w., 191
go your w., 42
goest on thy w., 137
good w. and walk, 385
heart deviseth his w., 26
heart, and one w., 308
hedge up thy w. with, 271
His w. in the whirlwind, 157
His w. is perfect, 148
house is the w. to hell, 6
I am the w., 214

in the w. of Cain, 168
let their w. be dark, 77
make straight the w., 219
maketh my w. perfect, 141
man from his evil w., 316
man perverteth his w., 11
narrow is the w., 27
nor walk by the w., 79
not My w. equal, 123
prepare the w., 253
prepare the w., 271
prepare Thy w. before, 253
prepare ye the w., 252
prepare ye the w. of the, 310
quickly out of the w., 23
stubborn w., 372
teach His w., 177
teach me Thy w., 26
the good w., 105
the w. ye know, 182
this is the w. walk, 26
turn thee back by the w., 192
understand his w., 301
understandeth the w., 409
w. he should go, 47
w. of a fool, 7
w. of a man, 263
w. of a serpent, 263
w. of a ship, 263
w. of all the earth, 79
w. of all the earth, 80
w. of an eagle, 263
w. of death, 236
w. of evil men, 26
w. of his father, 385
w. of life, 236
w. of Lord is strength, 269
w. of man is not in, 314
w. of righteousness, 8
w. of the heathen, 26
w. of the just, 333
w. of the Lord, 23
w. of the Lord, 382
w. of the righteous, 153
w. of the ungodly, 166
w. of the wicked, 343
w. of the wicked, 205
w. of the wicked is, 407
w. of the wicked is as, 271
w. of Thy precepts, 208
w. of Thy statutes, 55
w. of transgressors, 360
w. that he came, 86
w. that they knew not, 111
w. they call heresy, 184
w. wherein I should walk, 177
w. wherein they must, 231
w. which seemeth right, 285
walk by the w., 290
walkest by the w., 55
wander out of the w., 35

which w. went the Spirit, 17

ways
according to all his w., 138
according to thy w., 220
all thy w. acknowledge, 5
amend your w., 270
broad w. I will seek, 89
choose none of his w., 390
consider her w., 95
consider your w., 27
despiseth His w. shall, 55
equal? are not your w., 123
err from Thy w., 356
every one after his w., 203
eyes upon w. of man, 153
from your evil w., 81
heart decline to her w., 6
just and true are Thy w., 334
misery are in their w., 191
neither are your w. My w., 26
not He see my w., 153
perverse in his w., 44
pervert the right w. of, 130
recompense thy w., 250
remember thy w. and be, 312
righteous in all His w., 166
rough w. made smooth, 272
show me Thy w., 177
teach us of His w., 26
their pernicious w., 130
try our w., 317
turn from your evil w., 119
unstable in all his w., 203
w. are w. of pleasantness, 409
w. of a man, 350
w. of death, 285
w. of her household, 246
w. of man are before, 153
w. of the Lord are right, 26
w. past finding out, 153
w. to that which destroy, 242
walk in all His w., 269
walk in all the w., 26
walk in His w., 269
walked not in his w., 69
walketh in His w., 134
when a man's w. please, 26
your evil w., 26

weak
flesh is w., 141
for I am w., 142
gain the w., 5
hands be w., 106
infirmities of the w., 45
knees shall be w., 403
let the w. say, I am, 401
strengthen ye the w., 108
support the w., 390

this day w., 364
w. became I as w., 5
w. in the faith, 68
w. then am I strong, 371
w. things of the world, 403
who is w. and I am not,
  107
weaker
  as unto the w. vessel, 247
weakness
  made perfect in w., 194
  w. of God is stronger, 371
wealth
  every man another's w., 11
  leave their w. to, 260
  power to get w., 403
  w. maketh many friends,
    143
weapons
  better than w., 401
  w. of war, 85
wear
  surely w. away, 120
  woman shall not w., 386
wearied
  footmen and they have w.,
    60
  w. in the multitude, 8
  w. the Lord with your, 120
weariness
  w. of the flesh, 105
weary
  for you to w. men, 120
  lest he be w. of thee, 191
  run, and not be w., 29
  w. be at rest, 80
  w. in well doing, 277
  w. in well doing, 334
  w. my God also, 120
  w. of His correction, 46
  w. of my life, 88
  w. with repenting, 120
weaver
  w.'s shuttle, 90
weep
  blessed are ye that w., 229
  merchants shall w., 13
  mourn not, nor w., 186
  power to w., 175
  time to w., 229
  w. and lament, 75
  w. day and night, 377
  w. not for me, but w., 176
  w. sore for him, 121
  w. with them that w., 107
  what mean ye to w., 378
  ye rich men, w., 405
  ye shall mourn and w., 229
weepest
  woman, why w., 54
weepeth
  goeth forth and w., 76
weeping
  take up w., 265

voice from w., 330
w. and gnashing of teeth,
  13
w. and gnashing of teeth,
  312
w. may endure, 179
weighed
  actions are w., 84
  w. for the price, 409
  w. in an even balance, 63
  w. in the balances, 382
weigheth
  Lord w. the spirits, 350
weight
  eat bread by w., 131
  in meteyard, in w., 39
  just w., 40
weights
  bag divers w., 39
  divers w. and, 40
welfare
  seeketh not the w., 40
well
  know that it shall be w.,
    168
  lawful to do w., 336
  learn to do w., 26
  out of thine own w., 6
  suffer for w. doing, 3
  thou didst w., 209
  w. done, thou good, 16
  w. is deep, 264
  w. of Bethlehem, 382
  w. with the righteous, 180
  weary in w. doing, 334
  when ye do w. and suffer, 3
wells
  w. without water, 45
  water out of the w., 339
went
  w. to God, 101
  whithersoever they w., 85
wept
  Jesus w., 376
  that I sat down and w., 364
  w. in the ears, 60
  w. when we remembered,
    188
west
  east, nor from the w., 373
  shineth even unto the w.,
    345
whale
  am I a sea or a w., 120
what
  w. doest Thou, 156
  w. doest thou Elijah, 104
  w. have I to do with, 341
  w. is mine iniquity, 205
  w. is my house, 193
wheat
  chaff to the w., 20
  grow instead of w., 206
  sown w. but, 144

w. with a pestle, 138
wheels
  w. of his chariots, 79
whelps
  bear robbed of her w., 79
  bear robbed of her w., 12
when
  w. thy feet enter, 77
whence
  w. shall I help, 18
where
  w. and who is He, 90
  w. is now their God, 1
  w. is their God, 343
  w. is their God, 192
  w. thou lodgest, 94
  w. to lay His head, 188
  w. wast thou when, 20
while
  for a little w., 223
whip
  w. for the horse, 98
whips
  chastised you with w., 273
whirlwind
  chariots be as a w., 325
  driven with the w., 112
  fury, a continuing w., 150
  His way in the w., 157
  reap the w., 106
  w. of the Lord, 150
whisperer
  w. separateth friends, 172
white
  behold a w. horse, 128
  not make one hair w., 267
  ride on w. asses, 290
  w. already to harvest, 273
  w. as snow, 139
  w. of an egg, 136
  w. raiment, that thou be,
    127
  walk with me in w., 307
whited
  w. sepulchres, 15
whiter
  w. than snow, 307
whither
  w. I go ye know, 182
  w. I go, ye cannot, 18
  w. thou goest, 94
who
  say, w. shall see, 74
  w. am I, O Lord, 193
  w. art Thou, Lord, 200
  w. is God, 164
  w. is like Me, 21
  w. is on the Lord's, 9
  w. is so faithful, 242
  w. is that God, 33
  w. is the Lord, 16
  w. is there among, 399
  w. will appoint, 21
  where and w. is He, 90

whole
Christ maketh thee w., 182
faith hath made thee w.,
125
garment, I shall be w., 125
His hands make w., 156
joy of the w. earth, 211
life is yet w., 13
made perfectly w., 125
stand here before you w.,
182
they that be w., 19
under the w. heaven, 156
w. body should be cast, 78
w. duty of man, 103
w. earth is full, 151
w. earth rejoiceth, 90
whomsoever
w. the Lord, 64
whore
great w. that sitteth, 88
hire of a w., 45
to be a w., 48
w. is a deep ditch, 301
w.'s forehead, 353
whoredom
land fall to w., 48
land with thy w., 201
w. and wine, 237
whoremongers
w. and adulterers, 6
without are dogs, and w.,
83
whores
gifts to all w., 197
whoring
hast gone a w., 23
w. after other gods, 129
whorish
by means of a w., 301
why
Lord be with us, w., 102
w. are ye come, 272
wicked
angry with the w., 220
arm of the w., 304
blood of the w., 326
candle of the w., 205
candle of the w., 230
casteth the w., 249
condemn the w., 72
counsels of the w., 7
death of the w., 81
desire of the w., 11
desires of the w., 292
desperately w., 118
deviseth w. imaginations,
207
dwelling place of the w.,
109
evil shall slay the w., 223
expectation of the w., 122
eyes of the w., 304
falleth before w., 206

far from the w., 162
fiery darts of the w., 127
from his w. way, 295
fruit of the w., 65
give them that are w., 305
hand of the w., 205
hand with the w., 58
hands of the w., 7
head of the w., 150
heart of the w., 189
how long shall the w., 69
if I be w. why then, 90
if I be w. woe, 3
if the w. turn from, 408
if the w. will turn, 317
in the house of the w., 34
lamp of the w., 305
let the w. fall, 324
light of the w., 223
mercies of the w., 76
my people are w., 178
name of the w., 318
no peace unto the w., 113
not acquit the w., 306
not justify the w., 118
not over much w., 26
path of the w., 26
perfect and the w., 80
proceedeth from the w., 73
prosperity of the w., 112
revenues of the w., 333
riches of many w., 112
righteous and the w., 220
righteous and the w., 169
righteous with the w., 92
righteous, and to the w.,
235
sacrifice of the w., 45
salvation far from w., 339
scattereth the w., 230
so let the w. perish, 304
sorrows be to the w., 124
take away the w., 259
thoughts of the w., 118
triumphing of the w., 118
w. and him that loveth, 398
w. are estranged, 25
w. are like the troubled,
406
w. be no more, 305
w. borroweth, and payeth,
37
w. cease from troubling, 80
w. devoureth the man, 205
w. flee when no, 133
w. for the day of evil, 72
w. for their iniquity, 118
w. have inclosed, 280
w. He turneth upside, 343
w. in his pride, 280
w. is snared, 233
w. live, become old, 205
w. man is loathsome, 406
w. man travaileth, 374

w. messenger, 107
w. not be unpunished, 407
w. regardeth not to know,
288
w. shall be cut off, 406
w. shall be turned, 166
w. shall fall by, 223
w. spring as the grass, 230
w. watcheth righteous, 78
w. will He destroy, 305
warn the w., 295
way of the w. is, 407
way of the w. is as, 271
way of the w. prosper, 205
when the w. perish, 81
when w. beareth rule, 173
woe unto the w., 305
years of the w., 134
wickedly
all that do w., 222
God will not do w., 118
have dealt w., 62
have done w., 320
have done w., 67
sinned, we have done w.,
62
still do w., 402
we have done w., 62
wickedness
bands of w., 132
fall by his own w., 223
forgotten the w., 186
have committed w., 62
heart from w., 316
I have done no w., 6
land become full of w., 48
pleasure in w., 170
plowed w., 223
remember all their w., 74
return thy w., 324
reward his w., 304
tents of w., 193
that He should do w., 118
to work w., 118
treasures of w., 73
turn from his w., 408
turn from their w., 183
turn not from his w., 295
w. burneth as the fire, 118
w. of these nations, 395
w. proceedeth, 73
w. which thine heart, 64
whole world lieth in w., 170
whoredoms and thy w., 201
wide
open thine hand w., 45
w. is the gate, 78
widow
city become as a w., 86
oppress not the w., 59
plead for the w., 408
poor w. hath cast more,
146
wife a w., 77

made me in the w., 38
mother's w., 3
mother's w. naked, 81
of the w. to see, 91
openeth the w., 136
out of the w., 90
out of the w. I, 31
shut up her w., 47
son of her w., 59
sons in my w., 13
them a miscarrying w., 77
w. to the grave, 350
women
  became as w., 72
  blessed art thou among w., 217
  childless among w., 311
  custom of w., 249
  love of w., 143
  shall become as w., 192
  shame for w. to speak, 52
  singing w., 8
  strength unto w., 242
  w. childless, 311
  w. did change natural, 188
  w. keep silence, 52
  w. to be sober, 247
won
  harder to be w., 139
wonderful
  hast done w. things, 291
  love to me was w., 143
  many are Thy w. works, 290
  name shall be called W., 218
  w. works of God, 385
  w. works to the children, 290
wonderfully
  fearfully and w. made, 72
wonders
  except ye see signs and w., 28
  praises, doing w., 22
  signs and w. to seduce, 184
  w. in heaven and in, 87
  w. in the deep, 272
wondrous
  all His w. works, 363
  talk of Thy w. works, 208
  w. works of God, 265
wood
  bears out of the w., 304
  brass as rotten w., 370
  fire and the w., 264
  fire, and this people w., 106
  hands, w. and stone, 198
  hewers of w., 303
  saith to the w. Awake, 197
  silver, but also of w., 100
  w. and stone, 198
  w. devoured, 400
  where no w. is, 172

yokes of w., 41
wool
  eat them like w., 93
word
  beginning was the W., 25
  beheaded for the w. of, 247
  but by every w. of God, 171
  by the w. of the Lord, 72
  choke the w., 171
  clean through the w., 186
  continue in my w., 97
  despiseth the w., 269
  doers of the w., 85
  dry bones, hear the w., 322
  every idle w. that men, 320
  every w. that proceedeth, 247
  good is the w., 164
  hath spoken this w., 89
  he that heareth my w., 29
  hear the w. of the, 116
  hear the w. of the, 183
  hear the w. of the Lord, 91
  hear ye the w., 295
  hear ye the w., 402
  hearing by the w. of, 126
  His w. do I hope, 164
  His w. was in my tongue, 207
  if the w. of the Lord, 20
  in awe of Thy w., 7
  in w. of deed, do, 85
  law fulfilled in one w., 57
  leave the w. of God, 253
  let the w. of Christ, 165
  Lord gave the w., 295
  not a w. in my tongue, 153
  not add unto the w., 343
  not failed one w., 71
  not in w. but in power, 225
  not love in w., 85
  perform His w., 156
  preach the w., 172
  rejected w. of the Lord, 65
  show the w. of God, 325
  sincere milk of the w., 165
  sower soweth the w., 117
  speak the w. only, 125
  that hear the w. and, 171
  the Father, the W. and, 386
  Thy w. have I hid, 55
  to seek the w. of the, 145
  unskilful in the w., 200
  w. against the Son of, 33
  w. fitly spoken, 106
  w. is a lamp, 111
  w. is nigh, 171
  w. is true, 344
  w. is truth, 165
  w. is very nigh, 55
  w. let him speak My w., 103
  W. of God, 218

w. of God grew, 117
w. of God is not bound, 172
w. of God is quick, 43
w. of His grace, 35
w. of the Lord, 56
w. of the Lord, 268
w. of the Lord, 399
w. of the Lord, 313
w. of the Lord, 83
w. of the Lord, 299
w. of the Lord endureth, 165
w. of the Lord from, 212
w. of this salvation, 134
w. spoken in due season, 7
w. that God putteth, 207
w. that I shall speak, 299
W. was God, 25
W. was made flesh, 213
W. was with God, 25
where w. of a king is, 21
which hear the w., 131
whoso keepeth His w., 271
words
  according to thy w., 9
  add not unto His w., 344
  afraid of their w., 70
  ashamed of me and my w., 171
  attend to my w., 177
  believed not their w., 318
  break me in pieces with w., 120
  by thy words thou shalt be, 221
  deceive you with vain w., 84
  do not My w. do good, 54
  ear trieth w., 388
  famine of hearing the w., 131
  for his w., 103
  forcible are right w., 189
  from the w. of the book, 300
  hasty in his w., 309
  hear thy w. but, 100
  heard these w., 364
  heareth God's w., 20
  hearkened unto the w., 99
  heed unto all w., 74
  keep my w., 217
  know of these w., 347
  known by multitude of w., 138
  let the w. of my mouth, 292
  let these my w., 291
  let thy w. be few, 193
  make an end of w., 201
  multitude of w., 366
  My w. upon this city, 102
  not afraid of the w., 108
  not the w. of him that, 243

obeyeth not the w., 71
pleasant w. are, 366
remember the w. of, 171
shall ye believe my w., 77
spareth his w., 395
speaketh the w. of God, 20
strive not about w., 16
sweet are Thy w., 208
that my w. were written, 36
trust not in lying w., 99
w. are not heard, 8
w. easy to be understood,
   57
w. in thine heart, 55
w. of a talebearer, 172
w. of Job are ended, 109
w. of my mouth, 366
w. of that prophet, 129
w. of the Lord, 269
w. of the righteous, 38
w. of the wise, 177
w. of this prophecy, 300
w. of truth, 243
w. shall not pass away, 50
w. shalt be condemned, 221
w. smoother than butter,
   106
w. were softer than oil, 106
w. without knowledge, 199
w. without knowledge, 199
wearied the Lord with w.,
   120
will make My w. fire, 106
wisdom of thy w., 7
work
   according to his w., 223
   and do all thy w., 335
   are not ye my w. in the, 30
   bring every w. into, 84
   desireth a good w., 12
   devise iniquity, and w., 74
   do thy w., 335
   doers of the w., 399
   doeth the w. deceitfully,
      104
   finish His w., 256
   if any would not w., 195
   in the w. of the Lord, 95
   love for their w.'s sake, 53
   my w. with my God, 125
   no man can w., 109
   rested from all His w., 335
   shalt not do any w., 335
   this w. be of men, 85
   time for Thee Lord to w.,
      166
   w. a w. in your days, 361
   w. is perfect, 148
   w. of errors, 198
   w. of God that ye believe,
      104
   w. of His hands, 112
   w. of men's hands, 198
   w. of men's hands, 198

w. of men's hands, 198
w. of nought, 198
w. of righteousness, 333
w. of the hands, 25
w. of their hands, 223
w. of their hands, 155
w. of Thy hand, 73
w. out your salvation, 340
w. say of him that made, 88
w. shall be rewarded, 329
w. shall be rewarded, 330
w. that they must do, 231
w. the works of Him, 104
w. together for good, 126
w. wickedness, 118
worship the w., 197
workers
   from the w. of iniquity, 230
   w. of iniquity, 84
   w. of iniquity, 92
   w. of iniquity, 58
   w. of iniquity do, 230
   w. of iniquity shall be, 407
   where w. of iniquity, 74
worketh
   man that w. good, 85
   profit hath he that w., 297
   that w. deceit shall not, 98
   w. righteousness, 338
   w. signs and wonders, 87
   wrath of man w. not, 13
working
   razor, w. deceitfully, 30
   w. with his hands, 74
workman
   hands of a cunning w., 25
   w. is worthy of his meat,
      107
   w. made it therefore, 199
   w. that needeth not be, 96
works
   according to his w., 84
   according to his w., 306
   according to their w., 222
   according to Thy w., 152
   all His wondrous w., 363
   all their w. they do, 196
   be rich in good w., 85
   believe the w., 29
   by w. was faith made, 85
   commit thy w. unto, 373
   declare the w. of, 94
   do not ye after their w.,
      196
   do the w. of Abraham, 196
   double according her w.,
      120
   faith without w., 85
   found thy w. perfect, 85
   fulfil your w., 273
   holy in all His w., 166
   how manifold are Thy w.,
      265
   I know thy w., 111

known are all His w., 145
many are Thy wonderful
   w., 290
marvellous are Thy w., 152
men may see your good w.
   84
no more of w., 173
not by w. of, 85
rejoice in his own w., 4
righteous in all His w., 149
see the w. of the Lord, 272
set him over the w., 245
so faith without w. is, 82
talk of Thy wondrous w.,
   208
terror to good w., 173
their w. are nothing, 198
w. a man is justified, 85
w. among all nations, 116
w. do ye stone me, 5
w. of darkness, 170
w. of Him that sent, 104
w. of His hands are, 166
w. of the law, 56
w. of the Lord are, 265
w. that I do in my, 5
w. they deny Him, 85
w. to the children, 290
with w. of your hands, 301
with w. of your hands, 150
wonderful w. of God, 385
wondrous w. of God, 265
world
   already is it in the w., 14
   beginning of the w., 145
   begotten Son into the w.,
      215
   believed on in the w., 215
   but w. shall rejoice, 75
   came I into the w., 217
   care of the w., 171
   children of this w., 414
   conformed to this w., 64
   established the w., 73
   established the w., 73
   fashion of this w., 43
   foolish things of the w., 13
   friend of the w. is the, 241
   friendship of the w. is, 64
   gain the whole w., 209
   giveth life unto the w., 37
   go ye into all the w., 97
   God so loved the w., 115
   He was in the w., 16
   I am not of this w., 170
   I speak to the w., 325
   if the w. hate you, 181
   if the w. hate you, 282
   into the w. to save, 215
   judge the w., 220
   judge the w., 220
   judge the w., 221
   judgment of this w., 221
   kingdom not of this w., 21

life in this w., 235
life of the w., 312
light into the w., 111
light of the w., 232
light of the w., 177
light of the w., 214
long as I am in the w., 214
love not the w., 64
made the w., 52
man love the w., 241
neither in the w. to come, 187
neither in this w., 187
not to j. the world, 221
nothing into this w., 82
of God overcometh the w., 169
overcome the w., 54
prince of this w., 221
punish the w., 118
saints shall judge the w., 30
save the w., 221
Saviour of the w., 28
Saviour of the w., 216
set the w. upon, 104
sin entered into the w., 203
sin of the w., 213
Son into the w., 213
speak they of the w., 130
than he that is in the w., 215
that the w. through Him, 213
they are of the w., 130
things of the w., 95
things that are in the w., 64
to condemn the w. but, 213
unto the end of the w., 50
w. and all things, 295
w. and they that dwell, 105
w. is Mine, 156
w. itself could not, 37
w. knew Him not, 16
w. knoweth us not, 51
w. lieth in wickedness, 170
w. of iniquity, 119
w. passeth away, 89
w. seeth me no more, 82
w. was made by Him, 16
weak things of the w., 403
wisdom of this w., 414
wisdom of this w. is, 411
without God in the w., 92
ye are of this w., 170
worm
I am a w. and no man, 274
man, that is a w., 244
man, which is a w., 244
w. dieth not, 184
w. is spread under, 81
w. shall eat, 93
w. shall feed sweetly, 80
w. Thou art my mother, 80
worms

like w. of the earth, 192
w. cover thee, 81
w. destroy this body, 80
w. shall cover, 80
wormwood
drunken with w., 32
worse
lest a w. thing come, 357
worship
are come to w. Him, 188
heresy, so w. I the, 184
Him shall ye w., 148
ignorantly w., 200
vain they do w., 184
w. and bow down, 415
w. God in the spirit, 30
w. God: for the, 416
w. Him must w. Him in, 359
w. Him, all ye gods, 188
w. the beast and his, 198
w. the Lord, 260
w. the Lord in beauty, 415
w. the work, 197
w. ye know not what, 199
worth
wicked is little w., 189
worthy
fruits w. of repentance, 85
house be w., 34
if it be not w., 34
in white: for they are w., 307
labourer is w., 413
may be accounted w., 15
not w. of me, 131
not w. of me, 9
not w. to unloose, 219
shoes I am not w., 175
show himself a w. man, 222
w. is the Lamb that was slain, 76
w. of all acceptation, 308
w. of death, 206
w. of death, 41
w. of double honour, 53
w. of his meat, 107
w. of his reward, 123
w. to be praised, 86
w. to die, 104
w. to open the book, 263
walk w. of God, 148
walk w. of the Lord, 27
walk w. of the vocation, 51
wound
w. and I heal, 156
w. for w., 222
wounded
a w. spirit who, 89
cast down many w., 6
He was w. for our, 252
woundeth
He w. and His hands, 156
wounds

bindeth up their w., 364
faithful are the w., 74
multiplieth my w., 374
talebearer are as w., 172
wrath
anger, and forsake w., 12
appointed us to w., 221
children to w., 13
day of His w. is come, 151
day of the Lord's w., 150
day of w., 404
fierceness of His w., 139
flee from the w., 114
fool's w., 208
hypocrites heap up w., 3
in My w. I smote, 59
king's w. is as, 12
pour out my w. upon, 150
provoke Me unto w., 150
put off all these; w., 27
revenger to execute w., 173
sentest forth Thy w., 310
slow to w., 276
slow to w., 13
sun go down upon your w., 13
the vials of the w. of, 151
turneth away w., 12
w. for His enemies, 150
w. is against, 12
w. is against all, 23
w. is cruel, 12
w. is upon all, 102
w. killeth the foolish, 12
w. of a king, 12
w. of God abideth, 28
w. of God cometh, 100
w. of her fornication, 70
w. of man worketh, 13
w. of the Almighty, 150
w. of the Lord, 99
w. remember mercy, 12
w. shall be kindled, 197
wicked is w., 122
winepress of the w. of, 151
wise men turn away w., 12
without w. and doubting, 294
wrestle
w. not against flesh, 110
wretched
knowest that thou art w., 248
w. man that I am, 13
wretchedness
not see my w., 350
write
minds will I w., 57
prophets, did w., 253
seest, w. in a book, 37
w. it before them, 186
w. no new commandment, 57
w. the things thou hast, 207

w. the vision and, 53
writer
pen of a ready w., 366
writings
believe not his w., 77
written
adversary had w., 4
all that is w. therein, 344
books that should be w., 37
he of whom it is w., 253
if they should be w., 37
not w. unto you because, 8
plagues that are w. in, 285
w. in heaven, 180
w. in our hearts, 381
w. in the book of life, 78
w. in this book, 197
w. may be fulfilled, 222
w. with a pen, 280
w. with the finger, 380
w. with the righteous, 110
what I have w. I have w.,
43
words were now w., 36
wrong
chambers by w., 69
doest me w., 401
Jews have I done no w., 52
seen my w., 223
to do them w., 160
w. one to another, 16
wronged
if he hath w., 321
wrongeth
w. his own soul, 409
wrongfully
enemies w. rejoice, 110
wrote
for he w. of me, 29
wroth
w. with all, 66
wrought
hath God w., 22
w. for My name's sake, 151

Y

yea
let your y. be y., 209
year
seventh y. let it rest, 76

years
day is as a thousand y., 277
days of our y. are, 234
days of the y., 258
forty y., 121
hundred y. old, 135
Jacob served seven y., 238
ninety y. old, 135
number of His y., 228
restore to you the y., 139
six y. thou shalt sow, 76
spend our y., 234
stricken in y., 8
threescore y. and ten, 234
unto thy days fifteen y., 59
walked forty y., 121
y. in pleasure, 300
y. in Thy sight, 283
y. of many generations, 122
y. of the wicked, 134
y. of thy life, 7
y. shall have no end, 116
y. should teach wisdom,
122
yesterday
are but as y. when, 283
Christ the same y., 44
yield
land shall y. her increase,
268
y. yourselves unto God,
379
yielding
y. pacifieth, 301
yoke
bear the y., 276
take my y. upon you, 216
unaccustomed to a y., 98
yokes
broken the y., 41
make them y. of iron, 41
young
breasts are like two y., 25
calf and the y. lion, 14
gently with the y. man, 59
glory of y. men is, 122
roar like y. lions, 9
spare ye not her y., 14
suck to their y., 47
y. and now am old, 1
y. children ask bread, 131
y. children despised me,
343

y. lions roar, 9
y. man and the virgin, 92
y. man, in thy youth, 416
y. men cheerful, 300
y. men shall see, 417
y. men shall see visions,
103
y. women to be sober, 247
younger
elder serve the y., 135
they that are y., 8
y. brother shall be, 135
youth
childhood and y. are, 416
children of the y., 348
days of thy y., 148
days of thy y., 122
evil from his y., 118
husband of her y., 86
man despise thy y., 417
not but a y., 15
rejoice in thy y., 416
sin of his y., 406
sins of my y., 139
trust from my y., 190
wife of his y., 246
wife of thy y., 245
y. even unto this day, 62
yoke in his y., 276
youthful
flee also y. lusts, 28

Z

zeal
z. for the Lord, 417
z. of God but not, 200
zealously
good to be z., 417
Zion
build up Z., 211
comfort Z., 212
daughter of Z., 343
daughter of Z., 212
earth, is mount Z., 211
law go forth of Z., 212
Lord dwelleth in Z., 212
Lord hath chosen Z., 211
Lord hath founded Z., 212
loveth the gates of Z., 211
not the Lord in Z., 91